Once in a Lifetime:

City-building after Disaster in Christchurch

Books published by Freerange Press

Analogue Architecture: Between Imagination and Memory
Christchurch: The Transitional City Pt IV
Chur Chur: Stories from the Christchurch Earthquake
Congress Book V1.0
Crowd-share Innovation: Intensive, Creative Collaborations
Infostructures: A Transport Research Project
Practicing: U.Lab Handbook of Design
Tsunami Box
Youtopia: A Passion for the Dark

Journals

Freerange Vol. 1: The Self and the City
Freerange Vol. 2: Gardening and Violence
Freerange Vol. 3: The Trickster
Freerange Vol. 4: Almost Home
Freerange Vol. 5: Dangerous and Wrong
Freerange Vol. 6: The Untitled Issue
Freerange Vol. 7: The Commons
Freerange Vol. 8: Humanimal 3.0

Once in a Lifetime:

Ōtautahi tū ki te rua o te mate;
Ōtautahi whakaarahia ake anō

City-building after Disaster in Christchurch

Edited by
Barnaby Bennett
James Dann
Emma Johnson
Ryan Reynolds

Freerange Press   2014

Once in a Lifetime: City-building after Disaster in Christchurch
ISBN 978-0-473-28940-9

A catalogue record for this book is available from the National Library of New Zealand.

Freerange Press
Christchurch
New Zealand
www.projectfreerange.com

Designed and typeset by Cameron Ralston

Cover by Matthew Galloway

Printed and bound by Printlink Ltd
Wellington, New Zealand

Typefaces: Frutiger & Plantin
Paperstock: Sumo Offset 100gsm, Kaskad Canary Yellow 80gsm,
Crescendo 1 sided board 300gsm (cover)

This edition was made possible with the support of:

We would like to also acknowledge funding support of the Royal Society's Marsden Fund.

Foreword

Helen Clark

Helen Clark is the Administrator for the United Nations Development Programme.

The lives lost and the damage inflicted as a result of the 2011 Christchurch earthquake were a sad reminder that our country is highly vulnerable to the hazards of nature. The process of recovery from this tragedy, however, presents opportunities to *build back better*. For this reason, I welcome the release of *Once in a Lifetime: City-building after Disaster in Christchurch*, for its contribution to dialogue about recovery, both in New Zealand and around the world where other communities face similar challenges.

In the immediate aftermath of the major earthquake, emergency systems functioned, with support coming from throughout New Zealand and beyond. This in itself is a significant achievement. As Administrator of the United Nations Development Programme (UNDP), I have become well aware that capacity to respond effectively to such disasters is far from universal.

The road to longer-term recovery is never clear-cut, and it involves far more than finding the money for reconstruction. There are many reasons why some countries recover faster than others, and equally as many why some are stuck in a cycle of disasters and relief, with recovery forever elusive. Government priorities, capacities, and resources; population's expectations; donor commitments and international partner support, in the case of developing countries, are variously at play.

Too often, recovery is seen as mostly a physical 'bricks and mortar' process. Governments, and their international partners where present, may, in their haste to return to normality, place near exclusive emphasis on physical reconstruction, without taking the time to assess and plan for a resilient recovery, which identifies and addresses the latent weaknesses that exist.

Yet recovery can be an opportunity for change, and that opportunity should be seized. Common sense tells us that if weak construction was partially to blame for a building collapse during an earthquake, then building codes should be strengthened before reconstruction begins, along with the capacity to implement them. When economic systems have shut down, however, and vital infrastructure has been lost, returning quickly to the status quo ante is often the first priority for governments and peoples.

Resource constraints may also impact on planning for far-sighted recovery, and limit ambition for mainstreaming risk reduction. Yet building more resilient communities means integrating risk-related concerns into the very fabric of societies. That takes time, resources, and public and political will, which may be in short supply after a disaster.

In an ideal scenario, a post-disaster risk assessment will highlight the weaknesses and the actions that need to be taken to address them. Then, laws, policies and institutions need to be adapted.

All this requires capacity, and commitment to the long-term process of recovery, which in many cases can take at least five to seven years, and maybe longer. Recovery spans many sectors, and initiatives need to be coordinated and prioritised. That requires leadership from the top.

Where these capacities and commitments are not present, the aftermath of a disaster in a developing country will lead to increased poverty; migration from rural to urban areas – and probably the fast growth of informal settlements; a lack of health services, especially for maternal health and patients with HIV/AIDS; a drop in school attendance, especially for girls; and the overall redirection of aid towards reconstruction and away from socio-economic development. These factors and more have long-term consequences on countries and communities that will linger far beyond the emergency response phase.

It is important therefore to take a long-term view, and see disaster recovery as needing to be resilient recovery, and an opportunity to build back better.

This publication, *Once in a Lifetime: City-building after Disaster in Christchurch,* brings together the reflections of a wide range of experts. It looks at multiple stages of the recovery process, from the initial assessments and planning, to taking these plans to the public, through to the first sods being turned on the sites in the city.

Many of the world's poorest countries are experiencing rapid and unmanaged urbanisation, resulting in precarious housing, overpopulation, a lack of social services and unfulfilled basic needs. Much more analysis is needed therefore of disaster risk in urban settings. This constructive critique of the recovery process in Christchurch gives insights from an urban setting, and is very useful to those who now, or in the future, must respond to disasters in cities.

Development and disasters are inextricably linked. Development can alleviate risks through effective disaster risk reduction. Under-development exacerbates risks, and invites future high levels of loss from disasters. Development is also about rebuilding sustainable and resilient communities – a future that we all hope for Christchurch and for other communities badly affected by natural disasters now and in the future.

Helen Clark
Administrator, UNDP

Acknowledgments

The editors would like to thank:

Irene Boles, Eugenio Boidi, Denise Mill and the team that produced
    Christchurch: The Transitional City, Pt. IV
Coralie Winn, Hannah Mulrine, Jesse Newman
Kaila Colbin, Jessica Halliday
Toby Manhire, Russell Brown, Rebecca Macfie, Philip Matthews,
    Anake Goodall
Rachael King and the WORD Christchurch Writers and Readers Festival
Melanie Oliver and the Physics Room
Brick Farm and the Moore Family
Ana Pearson and the Pearson family
The Commons, Ministry of Awesome, University of Canterbury School of
    Fine Arts, Susan Stewart, Jacquie Kasunic and UTS Sydney
Cameron Ralston, Luke Wood, Matthew Galloway, Tony de Lautour,
    Holly Best, Jamie Hanton
Sam Elworthy at AUP, Scorpio Books
The *Press*, *Listener* and *New Zealand Herald*
Wellington City Council, Rosabel Tan and The Pantograph Punch,
    Renee Tanner
Helen Clark and her office at UNDP
Monique Devereux
Nazy Karimi, David Byrne and Talking Heads
Vanessa Coxhead, Phil Heath, Douglas Horrell, Greta Bond, Stefanie Lash,
    Lauri Dann, Lindsay Macbeth
Jason Mill, Sabin Holloway, Chris Keen, Scott McKenzie, Gerard Smyth,
    Sylvia Smyth, George Shaw, Shannon Shaw, Reuben Woods, Erica
    Austin, Liv Worsnop, Richard Sewell, Ian Lochhead, Juliet Arnott,
    Ben Cannon, Marcia Butterfield, Sam Johnson, Rhys Taylor, Sarah
    Mankelow, Hippathy Valentine, Danny Squires, Clayton Prest, Liz
    Phelan, Jo Mair, Joe Wylie, Lyndon Hood
Hugh Nicholson and Laura Taylor at CCC, Annemarie Mora and Hannah
    Seeley at SCIRT
Jessie Moss, Mara TK, Jeanette King, Te Marino Lenihan, Craig Pauling
Win Bennett, Ben Doherty, Federico Monsalve, Jenny Bennett, Mark
    Newton, Anthony Rohan, Camia Young
Samurai Bowl for costing less than Denny's
Suzanne Vallance and Royal Society of NZ (Marsden), Chris Boyle at GIB,
    Karen Warman at Resene, Tracey Berry at Kiwibank, Barry Dacombe
    and the Warren Architects' Education Charitable Trust, Jill Rawnsley at
    Creative NZ, Stephannie Liechti at Spicers
All the authors and contributors who have supported this book and anyone
    else we may have forgotten.

Authors would like to acknowledge:
Suzanne Vallance would like to thank Dr Hamish Rennie for his feedback
Steven Judd wishes to like to credit Ian Dalziel for coining the 'Enervation
    Precinct' pun
Jon King would like to thank Michael Hromek and Professor Steve Harfield

Glossary

An Accessible City
The Government's transport plan – an addendum to the Christchurch Central Recovery Plan – which was made public fifteen months after the CCRP's release.

Anchor Projects
The large government-mandated projects that were located on sites as part of the Blueprint.

Blueprint
The Government's spatial plan for the central city recovery. It was developed in 100 days and details the placement of the anchor projects and precincts.

Canterbury Earthquake Recovery Authority (CERA)
The Government organisation created to oversee the rebuild process.

Canterbury Earthquake Recovery Act (CER Act 2011)
Legislation passed by Parliament to enable a coordinated response to the destruction in Christchurch.

CBD
Central business district, also called the central city.

Central city red zone
The area of the central city cordoned off to the public and monitored by the New Zealand Defence Force. The exclusion area was reduced over time, but the final cordon was not removed until 30 June 2013 – 859 days after the earthquake. For residential red zone see Land Zones.

Christchurch Central Development Unit (CCDU)
A special unit within CERA, created by the Minister in April 2012. It developed, and is now in charge of implementing, the 100-day Blueprint.

Christchurch Central Recovery Plan (CCRP)
Government's recovery plan for central Christchurch. It was developed over the course of 100 days and released on 30 July 2012. It was based on, but made significant changes to, the Council's draft Central City Plan (CCP).

Christchurch City Council (CCC)
Local government authority.

Draft Central City Plan (CCP)
Christchurch City Council's initial recovery plan. Council, in conjunction with Gehl Architects, conducted the Share an Idea consultation campaign to involve the residents of Christchurch in developing this plan.

Earthquake Commission (EQC)
The government body providing natural disaster insurance for residential properties.

Environment Canterbury (ECan)
The regional council that manages Canterbury's air, water and land. The Government dismissed the fourteen elected councillors following a review and replaced them with seven appointed commissioners.

Historic Places Act (1993)
Legislation established to record, mark and preserve places of historic interest in New Zealand.

Land Use Recovery Plan (LURP)
Document that defines land-use policies and regulations across the Canterbury region post-quake.

Land Zones
CERA's colour-coded categorisation of Christchurch land to indicate the degree of land damage: red – infrastructure and land classed as too damaged for timely and cost efficient repairs; orange – requires further assessment; green – no significant damage so building can occur (which is subdivided into three technical categories); white – yet to be categorised.

New Zealand government
The NZ head of state is the Queen of England. The country is governed by a single chamber of parliament of 120 MPs that is elected every three years via a mixed-member proportional system.

Ōtautahi
The modern Māori name of Christchurch, based on the name of a significant Ngāi Tahu ancestor, Tautahi.

Resource Management Act 1991 (RMA)
Key piece of legislation for environmental management in New Zealand, which promotes sustainable management of natural and physical resources.

Recovery Strategy for Greater Christchurch
CERA's guiding document in terms of strategy to coordinate the many and varied recovery activities.

Share an Idea campaign
City-wide consultation campaign that gathered over 106,000 ideas for Christchurch from the public. The data from this was used to develop Council's Draft Central City Plan.

Stronger Christchurch Infrastructure Rebuild Team (SCIRT)
Public-private alliance of five companies and three government entities, responsible for rebuilding Christchurch's horizontal infrastructure.

The Black Map
Edward Jollie's 1850 original survey of Christchurch.

Treaty of Waitangi
The treaty was first signed on 6 February 1840 between representatives of the British Crown and Māori chiefs. While it is generally recognised as the founding document of NZ as a nation, there were significant differences in the Māori and English versions of the treaty. This has led to ongoing debate and negotiation.

Commonly used Māori terms

hapū
sub-tribe

iwi
tribe

kaimoana
seafood

kāinga
settlement

mana whenua
local people with authority

marae
communal facilities

mātauranga
Māori knowledge

pā
hill fort

Papatipu Rūnanga
sub-tribe authorities

rūnanga
tribal authority

tangata whenua
local people

whare
house

Ngāi Tahu
central Christchurch mana whenua

Ngāi Tūahuriri
mana whenua north of Christchurch

Timeline

Major earthquakes

4 September 2010 4:37am – magnitude 7.1
'the September quake'

26 December 2010 10:30am – magnitude 4.9
'the Boxing Day quake'

22 February 2011 12:51pm – magnitude 6.3
'the February quake'

13 June 2011 1:00pm – magnitude 5.9

13 June 2011 2:20pm – magnitude 6.4

23 December 2011 3:18pm – magnitude 6.2

Political actions

1 May 2010 – Environment Canterbury (regional council) elected councillors are replaced by government-appointed commissioners.

14 September 2010 – The Canterbury Earthquake Response and Recovery Act 2010 is passed.

23 February 2011 – A National State of Emergency is declared.

29 March 2011 – The Canterbury Earthquake Recovery Authority (CERA) is created.

18 April 2011 – The Canterbury Earthquake Recovery Act 2011 is passed.

10 May 2011 – The National State of Emergency ends.

26 November 2011 – A nationwide election is held. The National Party receives the largest proportion of the vote and forms a government with support from ACT, United Future and the Māori Party.

18 April 2012 – The Christchurch Central Development Unit (CCDU) is established. Warwick Isaacs (formerly in charge of the CERA demolition programme) is appointed as Director.

27 June 2013 – The major cost-sharing agreement between the Crown and local government is announced.

12 October 2013 – A local body election is held. Lianne Dalziel is elected mayor; only four out of thirteen councillors are re-elected.

Planning decisions

18 April 2011 – The CER Act is passed, requiring CCC to produce a central city recovery plan for ministerial approval.

14 May 2011 – The six-week Share an Idea consultation begins with a two-day expo.

11 August 2011 – The Christchurch City Council draft Draft Central City Plan is released for consultation.

21 December 2011 – The revised CCC Draft City Plan is presented to Minister Brownlee.

18 April 2012 – Minister Brownlee announces the 100-day blueprint design process.

30 July 2012 – The Christchurch Central Recovery Plan (including the Blueprint spatial plan) is launched by Prime Minister John Key.

31 July 2012 – The Christchurch Central Recovery Plan comes into law.

30 October 2013 – CERA's An Accessible City transport plan is released.

Other events

19 November 2010 – Two explosions at Pike River Mine on the West Coast kill 29 men.

25 November 2010 – First-ever Gap Filler project on Colombo Street opens.

22 Feb 2011 – The central city red zone cordon is established.

18 March 2011 – A national earthquake memorial service is held in Hagley Park with Prince William in attendance.

9 September 2011 – The Rugby World Cup 2011 opens in Auckland. Christchurch was scheduled to have five group games and two quarter finals, which were moved to venues in other cities due to damage to the stadium.

20-28 October 2012 – The inaugural Festival of Transitional Architecture (FESTA) takes place.

23 October 2012 – Lonely Planet names Christchurch one of the top ten cities to visit in 2013.

16 November 2012 – Prince Charles and Duchess Camilla visit Christchurch.

30 June 2013 – The central city red zone cordon is removed, 859 days after it was created.

8 July 2013 – A government Crown Manager is appointed to manage the CCC's building consent crisis.

4 December 2013 – Christchurch is selected as one of 33 cities worldwide to join the Rockefeller Foundation's 100 Resilient Cities Network.

10 January 2014 – The New York Times features Christchurch as a 'place to go' in 2014.

14 April 2014 – Prince William, Kate Middleton and Prince George visit Christchurch.

Contents

Introduction

What a day it was

It all began with a sharp jolt at 4:37 a.m. on 4 September 2010. Radio New Zealand shifted to their emergency broadcast (which unfortunately was the Beach Boys' song *Good Vibrations*) and a collective thought emerged from New Zealanders that would be repeated endlessly over the next few years: 'Christchurch isn't supposed to have big earthquakes.'

When dawn rose and the dust settled after this first quake in September, it felt like a bullet had been dodged. The damage was significant; buildings were evacuated; there was talk of widespread demolition. Yet somehow, almost magically, no one was killed.

The quake altered the political landscape, and the previously unpopular mayor Bob Parker surged to a second term in the November local body elections. Local MP and Minister Gerry Brownlee was given the new role of Minister for Canterbury Earthquake Recovery (CER), and Parliament passed the first version of the CER legislation to enable a coordinated response to the destruction. Little did these leaders or the people of Christchurch know what was still to come.

At 12:51 p.m. on 22 February 2011, a violent aftershock centred in Lyttelton shook the city, causing extensive damage to buildings and land across the region. The city's power, water, sewerage, roading and governance systems were overwhelmed. The next day the New Zealand government declared the second-ever national state of emergency. It would emerge that 185 people from seventeen different countries died as a result of the quake. The majority of these deaths were due to the collapse of two relatively modern central city buildings: the Canterbury Television and Pyne Gould Corporation buildings. The heroism in the hours and days after the quake was extraordinary – involving thousands of volunteers, police, fire service, armed forces and urban search and rescue teams from around the world. This book looks at what happened next, as the people of Christchurch were forced to recreate their broken city.

It was immediately evident that the post-quake demolition and planning processes were going to be long and complex. Shortly after the February quake, the Government reconfigured its portfolio and Minister Brownlee continued to lead the official response as Minister for Canterbury Earthquake Recovery, alongside the mayor, Civil Defence and other officials. At the end of March a new government organisation, the Canterbury Earthquake Recovery Authority (CERA), was created to oversee the reconstruction processes. A few weeks later a major piece of legislation was passed that gave the Minister extraordinary powers to bypass most other New Zealand laws to accomplish the reconstruction.

That legislation obliged the Christchurch City Council to undertake a process to determine the planning of the central city, and present it for ministerial approval or revision. Pre-quake, the city council had already sought recommendations to improve the liveability of the city, engaging internationally recognised urban research and design consultancy Gehl Architects. Gehl Architects were utilised again post-quake, and helped facilitate the large city-wide consultation campaign that became known as Share an Idea. Through digital media, snail mail and in-person workshops, more than 100,000 ideas for Christchurch were garnered from a population that was still reeling from the impact of the February quake just three months prior, and experiencing regular and often violent aftershocks. In total, Christchurch has suffered more than 13,000 aftershocks, including two more large and damaging shakes on 13 June and 23 December 2011.

The abundant ideas were recorded by Council and analysed for commonalities and patterns. This led to the development of five overarching themes: a green city; an accessible city; a stronger built identity; a compact central business district; 'a place to live, work, play, learn and visit'. These themes in turn informed the urban design in the Council's draft Central City Plan (CCP), which was revealed to the public and opened for feedback in August 2011, less than six months after the fateful day.

In November 2011 a nationwide general election was held, and the National Party – including Minister Brownlee – was re-elected to government for a further three years.

The next month, as per the legislation, the Christchurch City Council presented a revised CCP to the Minister for his approval, having digested public feedback on the August draft. The Minister opened the opportunity for further submissions to be made regarding the Council's plan.

After what had felt like the rapid development of the Council's plan, it took the Minister four months to announce that, while the principles of the plan were solid, the spatial layout was not well enough defined and the rules that underpinned the plan were too restrictive. On 18 April 2012 the Minister announced the establishment of a new unit within CERA, called the Christchurch Central Development Unit (CCDU), and appointed former Timaru District Council Chief Executive Warwick Isaacs to lead it. His most recent experience had been coordinating the building demolitions programme for CERA. The first task of the CCDU was to pull together a team of designers and come back with a more developed design – a blueprint for the city – within 100 days.

New Zealand-based planning and design consultants Boffa Miskell led a consortium of designers and architects from firms in Christchurch and Sydney: Woods Bagot, Populous, Sheppard and Rout, RCP, and Warren and Mahoney.

The designers and consultants were pulled together to substantially revise the spatial framework of the Council's CCP and largely rewrite the regulatory framework: the zonings, consent obligations and other foundational rules.

The group's major task was to find sites for the series of anchor projects that the Government had decided would comprise their recovery plan.

On 30 July 2012, almost a year since the Council's first draft plan and seventeen months since the worst quake, Prime Minister John Key joined Minister Brownlee and Mayor Bob Parker to launch the national Government's new Christchurch Central Recovery Plan (CCRP) and Blueprint at the Council's Civic Offices. While the city's politicians, businessmen and leaders applauded the occasion, people outside could be seen protesting the slow progress of repairs and lack of attention to housing.

Christchurch now had the controversial plan that was to become the primary document in the reimagining of the central city.

The new Blueprint placed a series of major buildings and precincts across the city. Most of these were carried over – in a slightly different form or scale – from the Council's draft plan, such as a Metro Sports Facility, the re-design of the Avon River and surroundings, a large children's playground, a convention centre and a new central library.

A handful of significant new projects emerged in the Blueprint: the Performing Arts Precinct, Justice and Emergency Services Precinct, Innovation Precinct and a new stadium in the city. The most notable change was the formalisation and extension of the desire, expressed in the Council's plan, to have greenways along the edges of a more compact central city. The new Blueprint entailed the purchase of large areas of the central city to develop a massive green edge called The Frame, encompassing around twelve entire city blocks. The goals of The Frame were to create a government-owned land bank to protect property prices in the city, to create an edge to prevent the central city from bleeding into the light industrial areas to the east and south and to provide future opportunity for inner-city residential development.

The integrated public approach, seen in the earlier Council plans, was now gone. The Council's CCP had proposed large publicly-funded projects, but also included incentives and regulations, with frameworks for how to incorporate education, housing, public art, high-quality streetscapes, character, identity and heritage. The Government CCRP removed environmental standards for buildings in the city, directives to investigate light-rail for the city, and any strategic approach to how to manage the city's diverse and important heritage stock. It progressed from a framework that encapsulated a wide range of community ideals to a minister-led masterplan.

The differences between the Council plan and the new Blueprint are evident in the process as well. The Council draft plan was developed from a city-wide consultation exercise. They sought feedback on the draft plan, with a travelling roadshow that more than 6000 people visited. A further 4700 submissions were received on the draft plan, and 427 people presented in person to the Council over eight days in October 2011. The government-led Blueprint was launched on 30 July 2012 and became law the following day – with no further feedback or review process. The new government-led process does, however, continue the significant and historic relationship with Ngāi Tahu.

It soon became clear that many of the anchor projects in the ambitious Blueprint were placed where there were existing buildings that had survived the quakes. Thus, it was unstated but insinuated that the Majestic Theatre would be demolished for a proposed road to be widened; the old council offices for a new transport interchange; the Centennial Pool complex for a large family playground; the NG building of art galleries, shops and offices for the new stadium and so on. Other controversial aspects included the apparent assumption that the Christchurch Town Hall would be demolished and the inclusion of a Cricket Oval in Hagley Park.

The transport-related aspects of the plan had been excluded from the Blueprint and postponed to a separate addendum. It was to be another fifteen months before the transport plan, An Accessible City, was released and adopted into the larger planning law of the city. This long process did, however, give stakeholders and the public the opportunity to submit feedback. The main aspects of this plan were to retain the people-focused urban design of the spatial plan and to restrict travel speeds to 30 km/h in the central city. Controversially, most of the one-way streets were preserved, a decision that overturned the Council's proposal to remove the one-way system that, it claimed, encourages people to drive *through* rather than *to* the city.

The new plan required significant investment from local and central government. It led to tense negotiations between these organisations, behind closed doors, with many of the city's own elected councillors excluded. The negotiations were only publicised once a deal was signed between the two agencies – despite involving billions of dollars of public money. On 27 June 2013, a deal was announced: $4.8 billion of funding for the rebuild was to be split, with $2.9 billion coming from central government and $1.9 billion from local government.

In October 2013 Council elections were held and Lianne Dalziel – who stepped down as Member of Parliament for hardest-hit Christchurch East electorate to stand for the role – was elected mayor, along with nine new city councillors and only four incumbents. They rode a wave of public enthusiasm to clean house, to revitalise the dysfunctional bureaucracy with a stronger council that could both work with, and stand up to, central government. Changes to the local government had already transpired prior to the elections, with the CEO resigning amidst controversy around his salary and his handling of an issue that resulted in the Council being stripped of its accreditation to issue building consents.

There is considerable tension between the local and central governments, with overlapping areas of planning and governance in the central city and competing views on financial priorities. This leads to complex power relations. Central government can impose a new stadium in the city that the local government must partly pay for; Council can assert some autonomy and decide to repair the Christchurch Town Hall, which contradicts the CCDU plan for a Performing Arts Precinct. In this post-quake tangle, every issue has become thornier.

While the central government is covering a significant amount of the costs they also stand to recoup a considerable percentage of this through taxes from increased economic growth as a result of the rebuild. The local government on the other hand has large debt problems and is in danger of not being able to meet its commitments to the large projects.

By 2014 it was abundantly clear that the rebuild was going to take longer than most initial projections. The cost, complexity and scale of the whole process continue to surprise everyone. Most major projects are running behind schedule; it is likely to be at least ten years on from the first quake before all the major projects are completed. The entire earthquake recovery is estimated to cost around $40 billion, the majority of this coming from insurance companies, with central and local government contributing significant amounts, and comparatively small amounts of new private investment emerging to support the city so far.

Two years after the launch of the Blueprint, on-site work has begun on just four of the eighteen government-mandated anchor projects: the Cricket Oval, Justice and Emergency Services Precinct, Te Papa Ōtākaro / Avon River Precinct and the Bus Interchange. Many are in various stages of tendering, designing or documentation with little public discussion or presence. A number of projects such as the Arts Precinct, the Stadium and Te Puna Ahurea Cultural Centre are contested, or there has been little progress to date.

Like the land, the people of Christchurch are well-surveyed. Coming up to four years after the first quake all data still indicate that people here are suffering considerably more hardship and stress than normal. The quakes that at first united everyone and brought together communities of people from different economic and class backgrounds now risk amplifying those differences as the well-off and financially independent are able to adjust and adapt more readily.

Amid these many controversies and complexities, it is important to acknowledge that much that could have gone wrong hasn't. There has not been a collapse in land value, mass emigration, a ruined local economy, widespread fraudulence or a general lack of basic provisions. There has been significant adaptation and innovation by government institutions in health, justice and economic support. And many of the unplanned activities in the city – private developments like C1 Espresso; community groups like Addington Action and the Student Volunteer Army; cultural inventions like the new Festival of Transitional Architecture, the Ministry of Awesome and the many Gap Filler projects – have been both inspirational and influential.

In short, it's all very complicated.

There is no clear dividing line between the disaster and the subsequent plans, actions and developments. The city's character is saturated with the disaster; the earthquake remains an inescapable daily presence and topic of conversation.

Alongside the continuing trauma, this crisis has helped form profound friendships and a collective sense of purpose. In a complex web comprising multiple layers of government, local and external developers, community groups, NGOs, architects, planners and all the residents of the city, we have the daunting chance not just to rebuild, but to reimagine our city.

Once in a lifetime

The title 'Once in a lifetime' indicates both an opportunity and a threat: the unparalleled occasion to grow, develop and explore, and an imperative not to miss our collective 'only chance'. This phrase captures something of the simultaneous liberation and pressure felt in Christchurch in the past few years.

In an interview about the Talking Heads' song of the same title, songwriter David Byrne said: 'We're largely unconscious. We operate half-awake, on autopilot. And we end up with a house and family and job and we never stop and ask how did we get here.' Thus, his song actually implies that *every* moment is a once in a lifetime opportunity and burden – though people don't often think in this way.

In nearly every facet of our lives – work, relationships, home environment – humans are constantly navigating between fully investing ourselves in the choices we've already made and opening ourselves to new possibilities and ways of being. We may reveal these inner struggles to our friends and family, but it is rare that these personal considerations take collective form.

In times of crisis, many issues that were previously hidden, unknown or private become temporarily communal. Whole societies of people must suddenly debate their collective values and future. Balancing, on a city-wide scale, the inevitable sense of urgency and need for decisiveness with the sense that meaningful change may be possible is one of the most daunting tasks that individuals and societies can face.

The real once-in-a-lifetime prospect in Christchurch, then, is that these questions – of whether and how to re-assert our old values and choices or take time to flirt with rare new possibilities – are unavoidable, shared and city-wide. A few years on from the major earthquakes many key decisions and plans have been made, including the crucial final Government Blueprint for the recovery, but the consequences have not been fully reaped. The purpose of this book is to reflect on these issues while it is not too late to make informed changes.

City of dreams

In late 2013, the editors of this book felt that what had been a fairly widespread optimism about the rebuild – for both the official plans and the unofficial activities and developments – was steadily wearing away. This seemed to be the occasion to examine whether we, collectively as a city, might be missing our chance to make this new city the best representation of our shared values, to make the most of this awful situation. We put a call out, seeking contributions on a wide range of urban recovery topics from planning, economics, arts and health, to anything else people wanted to propose. The fact that most of the authors transcend their disciplinary boundaries may indicate the convolution of this unprecedented post-quake scenario: nobody is an expert and no discipline can work in isolation. This process yielded a unique collection of multidisciplinary essays by professional journalists, politicians, students, planners, academics, publicans, artists, designers, economists and much more.

Recognising the diversity of the submissions, we opted to group the essays not by topic or discipline, but by their underlying theme or consequence. The chapter sequence tells a story of the past few years, from exploring different methods and philosophies of Making Plans, to the marketing, politics and genuine consultation involved in Selling the Plan to the general public and investors. Implementing the envisioned change requires Rewriting the Rules to permit new ways of acting. During this process, we have been Considering the Common Good, asking how we might shape our city to reflect our shared values, and debating what those values might actually be. Along the way there are repeated reminders of the importance of Thinking Big, Acting Small and Meeting in the Middle, which refer not only to the scale of responses, but also to hierarchies and power relationships. This cognisance leads to many real and imagined possibilities of Building Back Better, and culminates in Reimagining Recovery, dreaming of ways in which we might yet enact deep-seated change.

Within each of these chapters there are at least two different currents, revealing perhaps the most persistent theme of the book: the relationship between the official responses of those in power and the many and varied unofficial responses. As an example, the chapter Rewriting the Rules focuses on the Government's extraordinary powers and the legislation that granted them – but also on the ways certain developers, community groups and concerned citizens have been subverting conventions to reshape some of the unwritten rules and habits of our city. Similarly, the chapter Making Plans includes pieces representing both 'sides': the tendency of the official architects' and politicians' plans to concentrate on the finished product, and the tendency of the unsanctioned approaches to emphasise who's involved and the process by which the eventual plans are made or enacted.

This leads to the next most prominent, and multifaceted, theme of the book: means and ends, or the correlation between process and product. Are closed-door decisions necessary in order to act quickly and guarantee quality outcomes? Or will exclusive processes inevitably lead to an exclusive city? Can deep and meaningful consultation occur once and inform many subsequent plans, or must consultation be a recurring and iterative process to be valid? Must every process begin with the people, buildings, resources and activities that already exist? Or does starting from scratch allow for more innovation?

There is also a third current coursing through the book: anger. Of course, anger has been present from the very first moments the quakes disrupted the lives of people in Canterbury. Like the issues that radiate from the earthquakes, anger and frustration have spread to other aspects of life in the city such as traffic problems, dealing with insurance companies and government agencies, school closures, rent increases, political decision-making and more. But it is belittling to treat this anger as simply an emotional consequence of the quakes to be mitigated by holidays and relaxation. Much of this anger is justified. It can be the motivating factor for people to clearly articulate difficult issues, and it's certainly part of the creative process that leads to new solutions.

A central motivation for this book is our shared belief that argument, debate and discussion are a necessary and important part of city-building. A disagreement doesn't always represent an obstacle in the way of progress; disagreements and controversy, if managed carefully, can lead to better, more thorough and more creative outcomes.

Living through the past few years has been difficult here, but it has also provided moments of joy, engagement and a sense of collective effort rarely experienced in the routines of normal daily life. We've tried to capture some of the liberating potential of the city through the range of visual essays throughout the book, many of which document and celebrate things – sanctioned and unsanctioned – that *have* been happening in the city. Along with the anger we hope that some of this excitement and adventure comes through the pages of *Once in a Lifetime*.

Though this is undoubtedly a book about Christchurch, there are contributing authors from around the country and the world. Partly, this is in recognition that for those who've been living in Christchurch, we editors included, it can be hard to see the wood for the trees. External eyes, voices and calm minds are more important than ever. We also draw upon parallel situations in post-disaster New Orleans and Italy, post-riot UK, and even find key similarities in 'healthy' cities in Australia and the USA. As with the multiple meanings of the phrase 'once in a lifetime', we must recognise the singularity of this state of affairs and simultaneously learn from its many precedents.

This must be the place

In addition to the themes discussed above – official versus unofficial responses, tension between means and ends, and the anger and joy beneath the surface – is one last idea that has been prominent in much of rhetoric here in the past four years: putting people first. While cities are extraordinarily complex collectives of systems, objects, infrastructures, ecosystems and other unnamed things, humans are the glue that holds them together.

Hutia te rito o te harakeke, kei whea te korimako, e kō?
Ka rere ki uta, ka rere ki tai.
Ki mai koe ki au, he aha te mea nui o te ao?
Māku e ki atu,
He tangata! He tangata! He tangata!

Pluck out the flax shoot and where will the bellbird sing?
It flies inland, it flies seawards.

Ask me, what is the most important thing in the world?
I shall reply,
It is people! It is people! It is people!

The last three lines of this whakatauāki (proverb) have been widely quoted in post-quake Christchurch. In a place where there has been such significant grief, hardship and radical change, it is easy to understand why the focus on humanity in this message has resonated.

Yet, when used post-quake, the first two lines of the whakatauāki are almost always missing, and these are important to understanding the latter half. The saying – credited to the Te Taitokerau (Northland) region – tells us that if the young flax shoots are not protected the bellbirds will leave. While the proverb is interpreted a number of ways – as all good proverbs are – all versions utilise the sophisticated mixing of human and natural metaphors. Flax grow in a radial fashion, with the need to protect the young fresh shoots at the centre, and the harvesting of the older mature leaves for production.

It is a reminder that to truly care for humans we must also care for the environment – in all its forms – that supports our wellbeing. It is clear that we all share a desire to care for people in post-quake Christchurch, but how to cultivate the wellbeing of the places, ecologies and institutions that support and care for all the humans that live here is less often discussed.

How do we use this rare and unique, this terrible, opportunity to (re)make a city that cares and provides for the things we hold important? It is a question that has many different and competing answers.

This collection of 55 essays spans arts, economics, ecology, architecture, planning, philosophy, health and much more, and introduces the complex problems and opportunities this situation has provoked. Reflecting from the midst of this entanglement is essential for the future of Christchurch and New Zealand, and what emerges should be of increasing interest to cities worldwide as the challenges of the twenty-first century confront us.

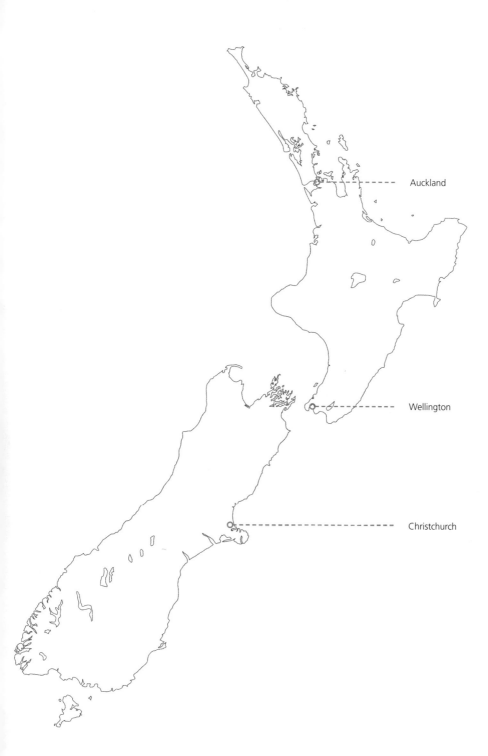

Auckland

Wellington

Christchurch

Christchurch Maps

1. Historical Growth of Christchurch
Page 29
Six maps illustrating the growth of Christchurch city until 2010 from the Christchurch City Council Final Draft City Plan in 2011
(Copyright: Christchurch City Council)

2. The Black Map
Pages 30-31
Edward Jollie's 1850 survey of Christchurch City
(Copyright: Public Domain. Archives reference: CAYN 23142 CH1031/179 273 3)

3. Maps of Christchurch City Council Draft Plan
Pages 32-33
Multiple plans illustrating the green spaces, transport, transition, and significant projects from the Christchurch City Council's Final Draft City Plan in 2011
(Copyright: Christchurch City Council)

4. CCDU Blueprint
Pages 34-35
The Blueprint as it was launched on 31 July 2012 by the Christchurch Central Development Unit
(Copyright: CERA)

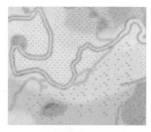

Natural Heritage

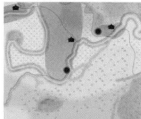

Pre-1850s

1850-1880

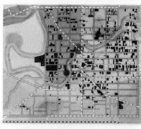

1880-1914

1914-1960

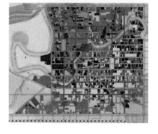

1960-2010

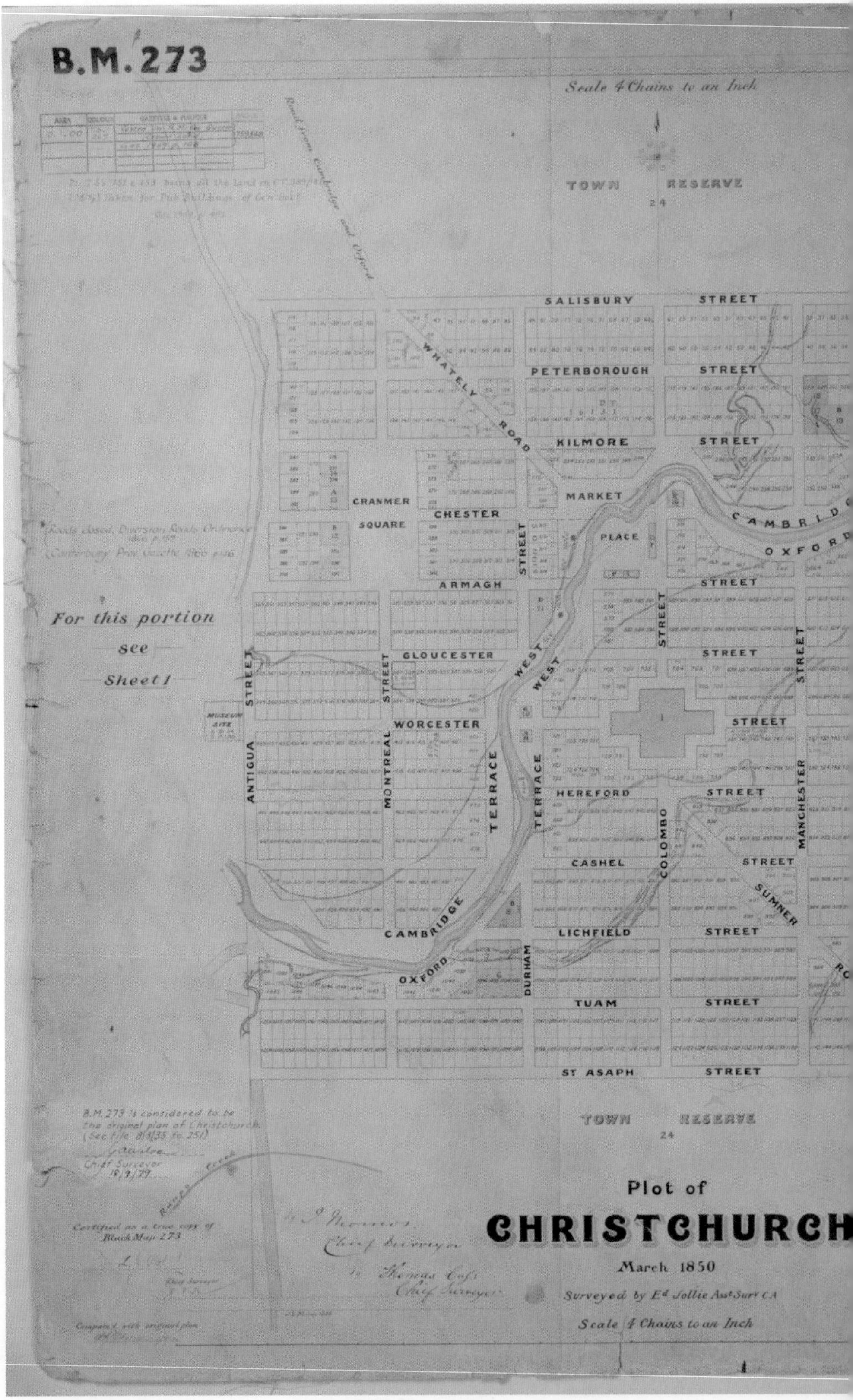

B.M. 273

Scale 4 Chains to an Inch.

TOWN RESERVE
24

SALISBURY STREET

PETERBOROUGH STREET

KILMORE STREET

CRANMER SQUARE

CHESTER STREET

MARKET PLACE

ARMAGH STREET

CAMBRIDGE

OXFORD

For this portion
see
Sheet 1

GLOUCESTER STREET

WEST

WORCESTER STREET

ANTIGUA STREET

MONTREAL STREET

TERRACE

HEREFORD STREET

MANCHESTER STREET

COLOMBO STREET

CASHEL STREET

CAMBRIDGE

LICHFIELD STREET

SUMNER

OXFORD

DURHAM

TUAM STREET

St ASAPH STREET

TOWN RESERVE
24

Plot of
CHRISTCHURCH

March 1850

Surveyed by Edᵈ Jollie Assᵗ Surᵛ CA

Scale 4 Chains to an Inch

Scale 4 Chains to an Inch.

C
20

CEMETERY   CEMETERY

BOTANICAL
21
GARDEN

N 22   O
                       23

STREET

BARBADOES

TOWN ALLOTMENT
24

Reserves

A   Parsonage and School
B   Church of England
C   Church of England Cemetery
D   Hospital
E   Association Store
F   Immigration Barracks
G   Survey Office
H   Mechanics Institute
I   Exchange
J   Town Hall
K   Police Court
L   Post Office
M   Jail
N   Cattle Market
O   Abattoir
P   Observatory

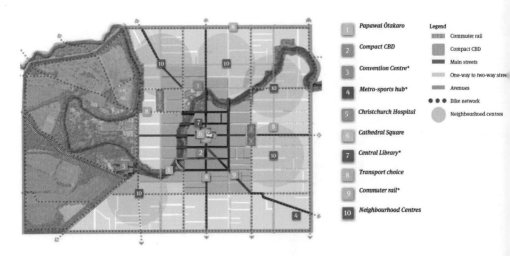

1 Papawai Ōtakaro

2 Compact CBD

3 Convention Centre*

4 Metro-sports hub*

5 Christchurch Hospital

6 Cathedral Square

7 Central Library*

8 Transport choice

9 Commuter rail*

10 Neighbourhood Centres

Legend

|||||||| Commuter rail

Compact CBD

Main streets

One-way to two-way stree

Avenues

● ● ● Bike network

Neighbourhood centres

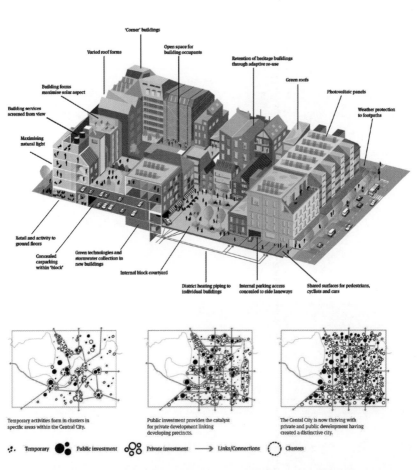

'Corner' buildings

Varied roof forms

Open space for building occupants

Retention of heritage buildings through adaptive re-use

Green roofs

Photovoltaic panels

Weather protection to footpaths

Building forms maximise solar aspect

Building services screened from view

Maximising natural light

Retail and activity to ground floors

Concealed carparking within 'block'

Green technologies and stormwater collection in new buildings

Internal block courtyard

District heating piping to individual buildings

Internal parking access concealed to side laneways

Shared surfaces for pedestrians, cyclists and cars

Temporary activities form in clusters in specific areas within the Central City.

Public investment provides the catalyst for private development linking developing precincts.

The Cental City is now thriving with private and public development having created a distinctive city.

∴· Temporary   ● Public investment   ⚬ᠻ Private investment   ⟶ Links/Connections   ◯ Clusters

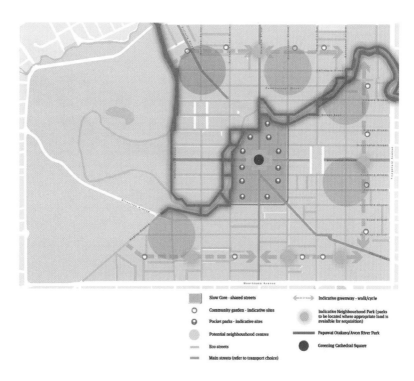

Slow Core - shared streets

○ Community garden - indicative sites

◉ Pocket parks - indicative sites

Potential neighbourhood centres

Eco streets

Main streets (refer to transport choice)

⬅⋯➡ Indicative greenway - walk/cycle

Indicative Neighbourhood Park (parks to be located where appropriate land is available for acquisition)

Papawai Otakaro/Avon River Park

⬤ Greening Cathedral Square

Legend

Slow core - shared streets

- - - - Historic tram route

Temporary interchange/Central Station

Main streets

River promenades

⬅⋯➡ Indicative greenway - walk/cycle

Cycle paths

One-way to two-way streets

Avenues (distributor/arterial)

The Blueprint Plan

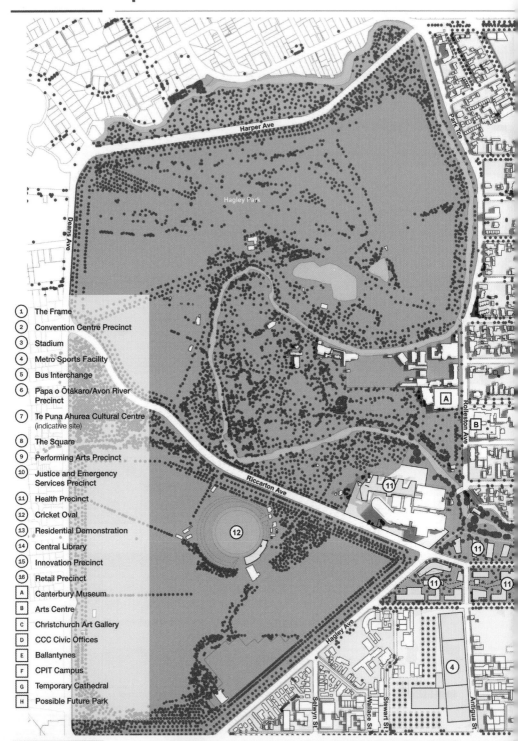

1. The Frame
2. Convention Centre Precinct
3. Stadium
4. Metro Sports Facility
5. Bus Interchange
6. Papa o Ōtākaro/Avon River Precinct
7. Te Puna Ahurea Cultural Centre (indicative site)
8. The Square
9. Performing Arts Precinct
10. Justice and Emergency Services Precinct
11. Health Precinct
12. Cricket Oval
13. Residential Demonstration
14. Central Library
15. Innovation Precinct
16. Retail Precinct
A. Canterbury Museum
B. Arts Centre
C. Christchurch Art Gallery
D. CCC Civic Offices
E. Ballantynes
F. CPIT Campus
G. Temporary Cathedral
H. Possible Future Park

CERA
Canterbury Earthquake
Recovery Authority

Christchurch Central
Development Unit

Christchurch
City Council

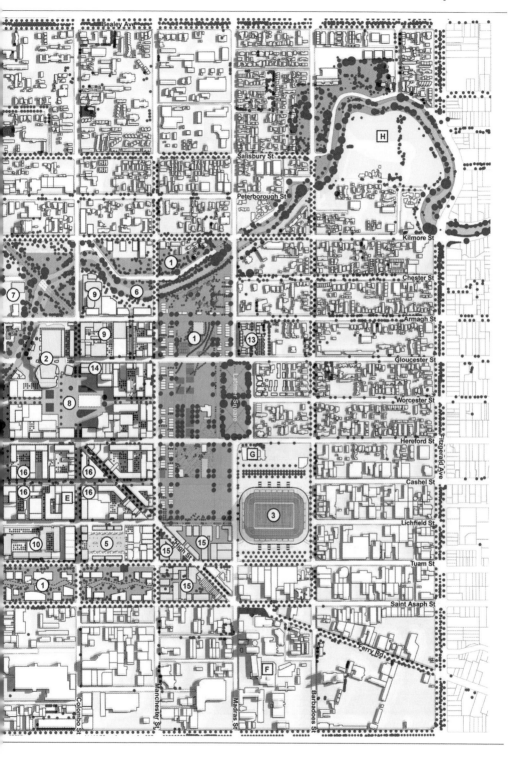

New Zealand Government

AHU

Christchurch in 2014

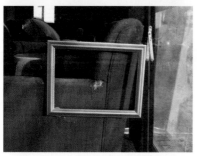

Chapter 1

Making Plans

He mahere ka whakaritea

So . . . what's the plan? As soon as the shaking slowed down, that was the question that our leaders, our media and, most importantly, the people in the street were asking. Plans. Order. Instructions. Systems. Normality. We start this chapter, and this book, by taking a step back and pondering different styles of planning. Nearly everyone agreed that a plan (or plans) was necessary – and that was about where the consensus ended. There were great differences not only in what people wanted contained within a plan, but also in the very conception of what a plan should be.

The Blueprint plan, which is the central pivot of the recovery (and of this book), was not the first plan for post-quake Christchurch. The Christchurch City Council produced a draft Central City Plan (CCP) in late 2011, which was informed by the large-scale Share an Idea community consultation campaign and set out a vision for the central city based on five themes, outlining a series of projects and wider framework for stimulating and guiding the recovery. The Government wasn't fully satisfied by this plan, or the approach it took to planning. They then commissioned their own 100-day plan – the Christchurch Central Recovery Plan (CCRP). This was a different *style* of plan that centred around a spatial blueprint. This plan placed large construction projects and precincts on the city map, giving a tangible articulation to the future built form of the city, in large part to provide certainty to potential investors.

The Government and some planners make a strong case that such prescription and detail were necessary. Others in this chapter advocate different concepts and methods of planning – or (perhaps cheekily) none at all. We encounter a strong critique of the prescriptive 'blank canvas' approach; a case for looser and more permissive incentives-based planning; and an argument that we must always conceive 'the future' as plural and changeable. Within this, we receive an important history of urban planning and the often-overlooked role that disasters have played over the centuries in evolving the content, and process, of planning.

Broken buildings

In an urban disaster buildings represent the most immediate visual signs of disorder and damage. The social and cultural damage is harder to capture in images – so here, as elsewhere, the physical damage is used as a stand-in for the entirety of the disaster. Being so heavily symbolic, the demolition or repair of old buildings and the construction of new buildings have distinct psychological effects on the residents of the city. The photos below portray some of the places and buildings lost or damaged in the past four years.

[1–6]

[7–15]

Broken buildings

[16–23]

Resisting erasure

Sally Blundell

Dr Sally Blundell is a freelance journalist and editor living in Christchurch. She writes for a number of magazines locally and internationally and, in 2007, edited *Look This Way: New Zealand Writers on New Zealand Artists* (AUP), which was short-listed for the Montana New Zealand Book Awards.

'There's a vitality about Christchurch,' enthused *Sydney Morning Herald* travel writer Sue Bennett. 'And some of the world's most creative minds are there to work on a blank canvas.'[1]

'Basically, we had a blank canvas in the CBD,' said Real Estate Institute of New Zealand regional director for Canterbury Tony McPherson, 'and we can get it right.'[2]

'The city's arts, sports, and retail facilities will be rebuilt and improved,' assured the Canterbury Earthquake Authority (CERA), 'to make the most of the blank canvas the earthquakes' devastation created.'[3]

Warwick Isaacs, head of the Christchurch Central Development Unit (CCDU), went further: 'Between these four avenues there is in excess of 1000 buildings being demolished . . . the landscape is almost back to Ground Zero.'[4]

Blank canvas? *Ground Zero?*

This is the dream of new beginnings, the promise of unfettered opportunity. Out of the trauma and devastation of the earthquakes, a new city will arise. Modern, progressive, successful.

It has always been a seductive goal. Plato, Leonardo da Vinci, Albert Durer, Thomas More, Francis Bacon, H. G. Wells – all bent their imaginations to an ideal city built on the foundations of aesthetics, ethics and functionality. In the fifteenth century Florentine sculptor and architect Antonio di Pietro Averlino (Filarete) designed Sforzinda, a utopian Renaissance city based on the talismanic powers of geometry and astrology. As a cityscape it was ordered, purposeful, rational, inhuman.

Such cities, of course, remained mere fantasies, the indulgent dreams of artists, philosophers and romanticists. As P. D. Smith writes, 'Building an invisible city in the mind is like writing a novel made up of many narrative strands – national identity, local history, trade and commerce, culture, religion and architectural traditions . . . New towns may begin as a fantasy, a vision of gleaming towers, but cities cannot survive long in the ideal realm.'[5]

According to US economist Edward Glaeser, author of the alarmingly named *Triumph of the City*, cities generally evolve organically, developing around transport routes (rivers, ports, railways) into haphazard arrangements for working, living and wayfaring, later shuffled into shape by emerging planning regulations to meet the needs of growing populations.

Planned cities – military outposts or colonial settlements – are the exception.

Malvern, England, 1847. Colonial theorist Edward Gibbon Wakefield and Irish squire John Robert Godley confer on the aspirational Canterbury plan. A year later the fledgling Canterbury Association discusses the foundation of a Church of England settlement in New Zealand. Surveyor Captain Joseph Thomas sallies forth to select one million acres of dry or easily drained land. He rejects the Wairarapa. He considers the head of Lyttelton Harbour, present-day Teddington, but the required land reclamation is too costly and the distance from the plains ill-suited to agricultural development. He regards the land on the other side of the Port Hills, land previously dismissed as 'swamp and mostly covered with water', and sees expanses of potential farmland, a navigable river and good stands of forest.

In March 1850 assistant surveyor Edward Jollie has completed his map for the new city of Christchurch. Jollie is a Benthamite. His model city gives expression to the Benthamite ideal of the greatest happiness for the greatest number. As well as specified sites for a cathedral, college, marketplace and civic buildings, he inks in parks, wide streets, avenues of trees; a town reserve to improve the environment for the working class, separate the city from the country, control city expansion and guard against – and protect – 'the natives'. Underlying this largely orthogonal streetplan is the notion of virgin land, unclaimed and uninterrupted. While roads and bridges tend to avoid the streams and springs that score the landscape, the network of seasonal settlements, travel routes and physical expressions of whakapapa (geneaology) established by three waves of Māori migration – the Waitaha, Ngāti Māmoe and Ngāi Tahu – are disregarded.

For the earliest European settlers this was fallow land, a desert waiting to be made productive as farmland and gardens. As Jane Deans, matriarch of Christchurch's pre-Adamite (settling in Christchurch before the arrival of the first four ships) pioneer family, wrote in 1887: 'All (of the Canterbury Plains) was waiting the advent of a white race of people to reclaim them and make them useful or beautiful as a garden.'[6]

As the city grew swamps were drained, springs capped, streambeds built over. The powerful force of the Waimakariri, the importance of the wetlands, the nature of a spring-fed land, the implausibility of a southern city in an English-style park were ignored. There was, writes John Cookson, 'a world of difference between Christchurch's development and the totally planned garden city being tried in England'. But the city's parks and substantial gardens gave rise to its reputation as a garden city, a distinctly English antipodean settlement. Canterbury, claimed a 1914 guidebook, 'is essentially English; but its English is English at its very best'.[7] Even as successive generations replanted native plants, restored wetlands and promoted the daylighting of streams, the true character of the plains that shaped so much of its pre- and early human history was wiped clean.

The devastation wrought by the 2010 and 2011 earthquakes brought about a rash of map-raking. Much of the city, we were reminded, was built on swampland, watery and unstable. The Pyne Gould Corporation building, where eighteen people died, was built on top of an old levee where a number of buried streams converge. Did we forget? Did we really believe we could rewrite the plains city character?

Under the 2011 Canterbury Earthquake Recovery Act, the Christchurch City Council was tasked to produce a recovery plan for the inner city. As part of its Share an Idea campaign, run in partnership with Danish urban designers Gehl Architects, over 10,000 people used Post-it notes, video clips, Lego creations, workshops and websites to pitch their suggestions for a remodelled central city.

The resulting two-volume plan, completed in eight months, presented a modest but compelling vision, a compact and radically low-rise city incorporating cycleways, riverfront parks, a performing arts venue, a region-wide light rail system, an extension of the successful laneways and a range of green initiatives all facilitated by new height regulations, more adaptive re-use of heritage buildings and a range of business incentives.

Many of these ideas were familiar. Before the earthquake the Christchurch City Council was already looking for ways to revive a flagging central city and bring more residential life into the city. A 2009 study by Gehl Architects recommended a more intimate, ecologically sound 'traffic-calmed city centre', a new urbanist vision based on small, sustainable, mixed-use human-scale neighbourhoods as articulated in Copenhagen, Dublin, Milan and Rotterdam.

In August 2011 the Minister for Canterbury Earthquake Recovery, the Honourable Gerry Brownlee, described the Council's aspirational vision of a 'city in a garden' as a 'pretty big wish list'. He directed CERA to establish a new unit, the Christchurch Central Development Unit (CCDU), to revise and implement the draft rebuild plan. The resulting Christchurch Central Recovery Plan (CCRP), compiled in a heroic 100 days by a consortium led by landscape planning and design consultancy Boffa Miskell, described seventeen anchor projects, a series of precincts and a more condensed – hence higher value – central city focusing on the Avon River and contained to the south and east by a green frame.

Some of the elements of the Share an Idea process were included (although CERA did not reanalyse or reinterpret the Share an Idea data). The commitment to a low-rise city remained, as did an Avon River park, but regulations requiring improved environmental performance from buildings were removed, financial incentives for rebuilding were dropped, the majority of transport provisions was deferred and the call for a sustainable, green city was subverted into the green frame, large chunks of which, we have been told, will be developed into medium density residential housing.

As Diane Brand and Hugh Nicholson note, the plan focused on 'national government priorities, providing a regulated vision embodied in a range of catalyst projects that involve rebuilding critical public and economic infrastructure.'[8] These include the hospital redevelopment, a new convention centre and large outdoor stadium – as Brownlee alarmingly told media in 2013, Christchurch will be the sports capital of the country.

In its rush to 'start afresh', the government Blueprint ignores existing structures. As it stands the planned Performing Arts Precinct is on the other side of the river from the current Christchurch Art Gallery and Arts Centre. The footprint of the proposed 35,000-person capacity sports stadium obliterates the historic NG building, a vital venue for arts organisations and small boutique operations in the immediate post-earthquake cityscape. To facilitate the anchor projects and new frame the CCDU has begun negotiations to buy land and buildings from existing property owners. In an inner city that has already lost approximately 1500 buildings, some of those that remain, including newly completed or repaired buildings, are now under threat. As I write this a gang of excavators is pulling apart the art deco Majestic Theatre. Completed in 1930 it was Christchurch's first fully steel framed building, promoted as 'The Show Place of Christchurch', and strategically placed close to the planned Innovation Precinct and the Christchurch Polytechnic Institute of Technology (CPIT). According to CERA the building was badly damaged. This was not backed up by an engineering report, but the building is in the way of the street-widening plans for Manchester Street as part of CERA's Accessible City transport chapter.

Other buildings, even without specific architectural or heritage merit, are nevertheless physical anchors in a city rapidly drifting away from its structural past. Our relationship with a city is based on such readings: familiar or evocative sites or structures that make up our personal maps, that lock us into a specific place far more than the shining new projects fresh from the designer's drawing table. As Simon Schama says, 'landscape is the work of the mind. Its scenery is built up as much from the strata of memory as from layers of rock'.[9]

In the path of the new Blueprint are the Oaks SmartStay building, the IRD building, the Gloucester Street carpark, the Calendar Girls building. All are critical to the story of Christchurch and the individual memories of those who live, or have lived, here. All, argues Christchurch lobbyist James Dann, 'should be spared and put to use'. Dann has instigated the Those Left Standing campaign to protect the last vestiges of a cityscape that says so much 'about who we are, and what we've been through'. Wouldn't it be quicker, he asks, 'for us to try and refurbish an existing building, which might take three or six months, than the government acquiring it, bowling it, flogging it off to a developer and then waiting for something to happen?'[10]

Demolishing over half a city, agrees engineer Kit Miyamoto of Miyamoto International, is the wrong way to go. Instead of creating a blank canvas upon which the city would quickly recreate itself, he told Christchurch journalist Rebecca Macfie, the demolition crews would leave behind a bleak canvas of empty lots that would take up to 50 years to be rebuilt. 'In a modern society like this, the taking down ratio should not exceed 10% or 20% maximum.'[11] With its pre-determined network of precincts and anchor projects, the new city Blueprint also ignores the plethora of community initiatives already succeeding in bringing new life and energy into the city – goals that, according to the CCDU plan, require a lengthy and destructive scorched-earth programme to fulfil. Since 2011 Gap Filler, Greening the Rubble, Life in Vacant Spaces and FESTA (the Festival of Transitional Architecture) have all succeeded in drawing people, activities and a much-needed sense of engagement into the inner city. Exposed walls have been painted, pocket gardens established, events planned, not on a blank and flattened cityscape but in and in relation to existing structures, features and historic uses.

The all encompassing masterplan, the realisation of an idealised vision that ignores what has gone before, is not a winning formula. Radical Swiss modernist architect Charles-Édouard Jeanneret-Gris (Le Corbusier) believed in the blank canvas. His 1925 plan for central Paris involved demolishing a swathe of the historic Right Bank and replacing it with tower blocks, expressways and parks. His plan wasn't adopted but the modernist ideology that favoured the single, purposeful masterplan emerged elsewhere in the drear functionality of the central city expressway, the mall, the gated community and marooned campus. The impact of Le Corbusier and the modernist movement on town planning is now regarded as a disaster, a model, writes Australian poet and editor Laurie Duggan, 'of totalitarian absurdity, undermining social fabric and destroying streetlife'.[12]

Consider Brasilia, Brazil's new capital, an heroic attempt to turn its back on its colonial past. In 1960 it emerged, as if fully formed, out of the scrubland. The civic buildings, mostly designed by modernist architect Oscar Niemeyer, are strong, linear, beautiful, but as a dynamic urban centre it has failed at the task. There is no streetlife, no chaos, no clutter of human complexity, no mess. Cars take precedence over people, pedestrian walkways are shadowed by tower blocks, iron-clad zoning reduces space to a single function. Today, writes Benjamin Schwartz, 'the city is quite correctly regarded as a colossally wrong turn in urban planning'.[13] According to Marshall Berman, this is the dream of modernism without urbanism, a 'highly developed, super-technological, self-contained exurban world, comprehensively planned and organized'.[14]

Over half a century earlier, in 1911, a competition for the design of a new federal capital for Australia was announced. Each competitor received a small wooden crate containing entry conditions, topographic maps, geological reports and a list of required buildings including a national art gallery, library and museum. Many of the resulting entries, wrote Duggan, ignored the topography, 'treating the brief as a licence to produce utopian diagrams, modules which could, in theory, be placed anywhere'. These included a transplanted Paris of the Belle Époque, a 'pastiche of world architectures' and an 'improbable relic of totalitarianism in the Australian bush'. While the winning entry by Walter Burley Griffin (promptly combined with elements of other designs) respected the local geography, its use of precincts, linked nodes of government, commerce and the military, serves as 'a metalanguage which makes sense only in the other-dimensional space of town planning. Its practical absurdity is demonstrated in the ideal of the "arts precinct", a space, such as the one in Melbourne, which assumes its visiting population will wish to be able to move between the art gallery, the theatre and the opera house as quickly as possible, preferably on the one day.'[15] Canberra's problems are brought about by 'visionary' town planning, says Duggan, implicit in modernity's drive to produce a 'homogeneous environment' accomplished either through 'total erasure or through the totalitarian adherence to an unvarying neoclassical paradigm'.

Canberra today functions as a 'displaced suburb' of Sydney or Melbourne. 'Politicians fly in and out from elsewhere. When the children of the administrators grow up, they leave. A city which rarely holds among its population families of more than two generations is a purely modern phenomenon.'[16]

Largely designed in its entirety, such a city remains fixed in time, purpose and population. As Smith says, 'Ideal cities are very much the product of their own ages. Designed as complete urban statements, they bear the unmistakeable imprint of their own culture and world view in every street and building . . . to be successful a city has to be open to continuous development, free to evolve and grow with the demands of the new times. Like science fiction accounts of the future, ideal cities quickly become outmoded.'[17]

Precincts date quickly or are quickly subverted. Large scale projects – convention centres, stadia, multi-purpose arts venues – support activities, writes Art History associate professor at the University of Canterbury Ian Lochhead, that usually present blank faces to the street: 'And why should activities that primarily support the needs of visitors be given the best sites?'[18]

For Gehl the priorities for a city are human interaction, inclusion and intimacy, a shift from a single heroic vision to a more iterative evolution of what cities can become. Rather than being frozen in time cities need to grow, ripen, evolve – as architect and design critic Edwin Heathcote says, the city remains stubbornly resistant to perfection.[19] In cities around the world churches become mosques or takeaway bars, petrol stations become markets, power stations become art galleries, successive waves of migration impact on the city streets, a saw-tooth tannery, as in Christchurch's The Tannery, emerging beyond the parameters of the planned map of the inner city, becomes a destination bar, cafe and retail centre.

Take London, says Deyan Sudjic, director of London's Design Museum. 'It has grown, layer on layer, for 2000 years, sustaining generation after generation of newcomers. It's a place without an apparent structure that has proved extraordinarily successful at growing and changing.'[20] The London street has 'citiness', agrees Heathcote. 'It is incoherent. Incoherent is good.'[21]

For many crucial months after the release of the Blueprint Miyamoto's prediction of the much-touted blank canvas tipping into a far less enticing bleak landscape gained credence. Projects stalled. Investors pulled out. Even today buy-in from the local population is flagging in the face of think-big planning and a lack of public engagement in the conversations around urban planning and design. There are cost-sharing wrangles between the overnment and Council and uncertainty over the anchor projects. After purchasing four of the ten properties required for the planned Performing Arts Precinct (PAP), the Crown has now pushed pause, claiming the Council's decision to spend $127.5 million restoring the Town Hall leaves a paltry $30.5 million to build a venue for the Music Centre of Christchurch, a new Court Theatre and a facility for the Christchurch Symphony Orchestra (CSO). (The Council is expected to fund the precinct, while the Crown buys the land.) Already the CSO is looking at a permanent facility at the Air Force Museum in Hornby and a report prepared for the Ministry for Culture and Heritage warns that other potential tenants have concerns over the PAP project.

While the Health and the Justice and Emergency precincts have strong clients actively involved in the planning of their respective areas, others lack a committed buy-in from key tenants. This year EPIC (the Enterprise Precinct Innovation Centre) announced it was abandoning plans for its large inner-city innovation 'village' of small tech-development businesses, an extension of its pilot Sanctuary building on the corner of Manchester and Tuam Streets, blaming design delays and escalating land prices for eroding its list of prospective tenants (since then telco giant Vodafone has announced an 8000 square metre $50 million investment in the precinct).

The CCDU's decision to force the agglomeration of commercial development in the Retail Precinct is cutting out the small businesses and landowners that typified Christchurch and gave character and social and economic energy to the city. In the push to woo investors the needs of those who live, work and play in Christchurch are at risk of being overshadowed. As Lochhead says, 'The central city has been treated as a blank canvas, its grid of streets a chessboard across which key projects have been moved until a game plan emerged. For the planners this may have seemed a winning strategy; as far as public participation is concerned, it is checkmate.'[22]

The danger, he says, is that an increasingly disillusioned public will simply ignore the central city and continue to make do with the reconfigured city that has grown up on its edges.

The 2010 and 2011 earthquakes, states the introduction to the Government's recovery plan, 'struck one of New Zealand's oldest cities, a community with deep ties to the land, the environment and each other'.[23] To date the heartbeat of this community has been sustained by local people and grassroots initiatives reclaiming the city and being involved in discussions about its future. Somewhere in the promise of a blank canvas this vital energy has been put at risk, those ties loosened. As Sudjic reasons, politicians just love cranes. 'They need solutions within the time frames of elections and cranes deliver them . . . The result is a constant cycle of demolition and reconstruction that is seen as the substitute for thinking about how to address the deeper issues of the city.'[24] This is what some critics call the 'colonial project', the opportunity presented by bare land, the enduring desire to wipe clean the slate and start again. This is not an option for Christchurch. The cities that work best, Sudjic claims, 'are those that keep their options open, that allow the possibility of change'.[25] Our most creative minds are working on such possibilities, on the opportunities presented not by an imaginary blank canvas but by an adaptive, resourceful city carrying its unique story into the future.

A blank canvas for new beginnings

Roger Sutton

Before he was appointed as CEO at CERA, Mr Sutton was the Chief Executive Officer of Orion New Zealand Limited, a position he held for eight years. He was also chairman of the Energy Efficiency Conservation Authority.

Planning and developing a new city from scratch is a daunting task by anyone's standards, but to do so off the back of a devastating and tragic natural disaster added a substantial layer of complexity.

From the very start of this process I was well aware that there would not be universal acceptance, applause or accolades. What we were planning to do, and given the time frame we planned to accomplish it, was a fast-paced exercise with seemingly little room for discussion. And let's be frank – we were allowed to work in an unorthodox and exciting way.

The ongoing criticism I hear and read two years on from the reveal of the new inner city's design definitely reflects those sentiments. But I would like to invite you to take a step back and consider our plan and its process in a dispassionate way – and perhaps, three years on from the quakes themselves, this is the time to do so.

Because I believe that what has been achieved in Christchurch since the February quake is remarkable and inspiring. What we have delivered is a strong commitment to rebuild the city better than ever, and to keep building on this new foundation.

The potted history is well known; the earthquakes necessitated the creation o a Crown agency to assist the Canterbury community to get back on its feet. This job was clearly too big for the Christchurch City Council (CCC) and Waimakariri and Selwyn District Councils to manage alone, not to mention the other agencies and community groups who were suffering in the wake of the tremors.

The special legislation created to allow this to happen circumvented normal regulatory processes, with a singular aim to get the recovery moving. Time was of the essence.

Right from the start there were two clear areas of recovery that needed immediate attention, and for purposes of simplicity I will call them the 'people' and the 'place'.

Our people – our friends, our family, our colleagues – suffered. We all know people who lost a friend, a home, a business or a way of life as a direct result o the earthquakes. And helping people first was the non-negotiable fundamenta requirement of the Canterbury Earthquake Recovery Authority (CERA).

Along with supporting the health sector in the wellbeing space, the physical zoning of the various damaged residential land areas was the best way to give the people so drastically affected an option to move on.

For those whose homes were filled with liquefied soil, or perched on perilous, crumbling hillsides, this was a good solution. Peer-reviewed geological data identified the worst land, and by that I mean land that simply was not going to be easily remediated to the point where rebuilding homes would be possible in a time frame that would be acceptable.

It wasn't a universal fiscal win – but it was never intended to be. Taking up the Crown offer for residential red zone land was an option for people to move on. The vast majority have done so and have started new lives, new communities and are well and truly on the recovery journey.

The second real priority for CERA to address was the rebuild within the central city.

I have heard the criticism time and time again that sorting the inner city and its buildings should not have shared the same level of importance as the people and their homes. But I absolutely disagree because what is a city without its heart? Why would people even be here if they don't have a place to work and play as well as live?

The creation of CERA's Christchurch Central Development Unit and its Recovery Plan (CCRP) is every bit as important as helping people in their homes. Together, the two components create our city, our home – our Christchurch.

I'd like to explain a bit more about our approach to that inner city development planning. As I have indicated, this is an area in which we hear constant debate and criticism – and that's okay. In fact it's more than okay. It is an absolutely essential part of the recovery process, as much so as the planning and delivery of the new city.

Given the massive impact of this plan and the absolute necessity for it to be the very best it could be despite the challenging time frame, it really does seem incredible to look back and realise that there were a mere 34 people involved.

That number included staff from CERA, the CCC, Environment Canterbury and those from the various groups that made up the local firm Boffa Miskell consortium that won the tender for the Blueprint design job.

We were acutely aware that their plan and its implementation would be watched by the rest of the world, not just the people who live here and were affected by the earthquakes. Right from the start we had a responsibility to deliver.

In 2014, six of the anchor projects will physically get underway in the city in one form or another. These are the large facilities and city assets that the

Crown and the Christchurch City Council have committed to building: a convention centre, a sports facility, a new library, an arts and entertainment hub, a bus interchange.

There is a perception that it has been a long and slow road to get to this point, way too slow for some people. But this city-wide redevelopment is not something that can or should be created without deliberate and informed planning.

I actually believe in some respects we may be in danger of working too quickly, simply to address that perception. As the ridiculously over-used cliché notes, Rome was not built in a day.

What I do accept is that the 100-day project that saw the new city plan designed was done at breakneck speed. This was a phenomenally challenging time frame but absolutely crucial. For a community still suffering, still shocked, and literally still shaking, there clearly needed to be a plan put in place as quickly as possible.

There could be no delay. The process itself had to be quick and not constrained by debate. Collectively, we agreed that the cost of doing nothing or allowing the redeveloped inner city to germinate in an uncoordinated way would actually be far more detrimental to our city than if we made some quick, tough choices and then got that plan rolling.

We had to ask ourselves if we really wanted to simply replace exactly what Christchurch was before? Or did we look at this as a silver lining to the disaster, a blank canvas opportunity to create a vibrant new city, where its residents want to live, work and play, and its economic and retail heart – new and old – could prosper?

Let's look at this this way: to ensure Christchurch's rebuilt and repaired homes retain their value in the future, the city itself must be reborn. There must be a genuine desire for people to live in and move to this region – jobs, businesses, attractive tertiary programmes and facilities.

Christchurch needed to have it all, and soon. And we had the perfect opportunity to make that happen. This opportunity was centred squarely with our Recovery Plan. And as daunting and difficult as this redevelopment would initially appear, we knew we had a secret weapon for success, courtesy of the groundwork already done by the CCC in its award-winning Share an Idea campaign.

We knew our city development planning had to be bold but we also knew that our city was filled with bold, innovative and inspiring people – people who had already told the CCC exactly what they wanted their new city to contain during the Share an Idea consultation project.

So with that invaluable databank of information and ideas already available, the CCDU team unashamedly tapped into the resource as it formed the Blueprint. They carefully analysed the key groupings that the council's process had highlighted, as well as calling in one of the staff who had worked on Share an Idea to provide a more detailed overview of what the community had called for.

The naysayers in the community routinely like to argue this point – but they simply are wrong. The creation of the new inner city, its smaller, greener and more accessible space, can be directly linked to the ideas and concepts put forward by the community. This may not have been a consultation process in itself, but the 106,000 individual ideas were on tap and available. I believe there will be many a resident across the city who can now look at the Blueprint for the city and say 'hey, that's sort of like what I suggested'.

Soon after we launched the Blueprint, I remember telling a reporter that I believed, in other Western countries, a recovery plan of the magnitude we were working to probably would not have been managed with any democracy at all. I think this was in response to critics who called the Blueprint an undemocratically managed exercise.

As I said then – and I stand by it today – democracy has not been regulated away here. In a nutshell, the Government was elected to run the country by the people. The work it decides to do is by mandate of the community and this recovery is part of that work. The Government has made it abundantly clear that the rebuild of Christchurch is one of its top priorities.

As I said before, Christchurch needed to be reborn and it needed to be done immediately. Democracy gave us that opportunity and we took it with both hands so that the very people who chose the government to govern would be best served.

On reflection, the initial Blueprint design has probably been the easiest part of all.

The concepts that we wanted to put in place needed a fail-safe and robust delivery mechanism surrounding them. We were redefining land and its use, and taking land from the private market to do so. This was clearly an unprecedented manoeuvre and was not exactly appreciated across the board.

But I make no apology for that. This plan, our plan, is not for Mr and Mrs Christchurch circa 2011. This is a plan for our children's children, and the generations that will follow them because what is being built is being built to last.

This is exactly what Minister for Canterbury Earthquake Recovery Gerry Brownlee meant when he said 'look to the future, be bold' in his wide-sweeping instruction to the CCDU about building a new city.

It's huge. It's brave and controversial. But we have no right to simply replace what was here. This new development is intended to be inspiring and innovative, and it's for your grandchildren.

In tandem with producing the design-focused plan, CCDU had to cocoon the vision with a delivery mechanism. It settled on the acquisition process. In comparison to the vibrant design this was seen as a very stark, hard process.

I understand that sentiment. But again, this is what we believe is the best way forward.

The Crown needed to buy the land it needs to put the anchor projects within the Blueprint in place and the ideal was of course by negotiation. While the land would inevitably become the Crown's, it was decided that there should still be an ability for current property owners to negotiate that sale, and in some cases have a future hand in the development of that site.

That plan is playing out as expected. A lot of the property being purchased is being used to deliver the Frame concept. The use of that land is changing from strictly business to recreational and high-end residential.

In other areas the property will be repackaged with titles merged to create larger land parcels, improved through the provision of new infrastructure and their future use redefined.

And yes, this is a hard line we've taken. As some property owners have asked in the past two years, why should their land be earmarked for change and that development opportunity opened to the general market without them having any say in the matter?

And again I go back to the same answer – this plan is a big picture. We have used the central city as a blank canvas and that means widespread change.

But it is not just for kicks.

Let's reflect honestly on what Christchurch was before the quakes – a sprawling city with few restrictions, doing little to provide any sense of cohesiveness and vitality in its inner city area. There was more office space in the central city than the market required, which meant there were a lot of empty spaces. And the retail sector was really not competing well against the various suburban malls that anchor the corners of the city, with their ease of access and good parking. Was the inner city – Cathedral Square, the wind-tunnel of Armagh Street – genuinely a place for you and your families to 'own' and utilise?

As per the key requirements identified in Share an Idea, the Blueprint plan is about creating a greener, more compact, more accessible and safe inner city that is easy to move around and better for living and working.

A good example of putting that concept into practice is the Retail Precinct. Through these three city blocks, we want to see north-south lanes that will make the retail developments more permeable, and buildings more accessible

We don't want people to have to walk around an entire block to get through to the other side. And we want to address the beastly easterly wind issue by emphasising a north-south axis in these lanes – they will get sunlight at lunchtime, and will be sheltered from our chilly prevailing northeasterly wind.

Other factors of the plan include safety. The East Frame, for example, will feature residential housing along each side of the central park. The park area needs to be a width that will allow passive surveillance by the people living in the houses, yet spacious enough for the residential community to feel they are not intruding on a private space.

It's ambitious but eventually we want to have some 20,000 people living in our redefined central city, inhabiting a mix of townhouses and apartments in the East and North Frame areas.

These people will have the more compact city right outside their front doors, a green space with ease of accessibility running through the Frame, a world-class playground for their children just a block or two away and everything an innovative mid-sized city can offer right at their fingertips.

We also looked carefully at how the larger city facilities could function to get best integration with the new concepts of the city design and it has been great to see that planning embraced by other agencies. Take for example the Justice and Emergency Services Precinct, which has essentially been designed around a courtyard. This really is a fantastic new way of providing the myriad of emergency services in one large precinct while harking back to the style of Christchurch's heritage buildings.

If you think about it, this courtyard concept is the same as the Arts Centre's quadrangle and the Provincial Chambers' courtyard. This is smart planning as it provides shelter from the prevailing winds as well as fully utilising the buildings' accessibility.

The heartening bit for me is knowing that CERA or CCDU did not dictate the design; it is the creative response to the Blueprint's shift in focus for the way this city can be built better. We put the wider plan out there, and it is being understood and embraced.

Our planning has not just covered the nuts and bolts of the city of course. Our sparkling jewel, the Avon River, is the centrepiece that will change the way we interact with our inner city. This waterfront space was simply not fully appreciated or utilised before the earthquakes, and there was no long term plan to do anything about that. Without the incredible opportunity to redefine our city in the way we have done, this city asset may have been ignored for another 100 years.

The work so far on the Avon River Precinct has improved the habitat for fish, including whitebait and brown trout, which have spawned successfully. The silt that ended up in the river after the earthquake is being removed, and in places the river has been narrowed so people can enjoy the rush of the water on the cobbles – a function that also serves as a natural flush for the river.

And this is all hugely successful because of good, innovative and creative planning – albeit completed under the incredibly tight 100 day time frame. That's because our initial Blueprint planning started with the river.

That team of 34 people essentially sat down and said 'Let's look at our city – what have we been missing here?'. From that it was obvious, the river was a forgotten treasure. What was even more evident was the link it provides for all other aspects of the central city and beyond.

Take a look at the Blueprint map and see just how central the river's focus is now and compare that to before the earthquakes. How often did you stroll the river bank in the central city, or sit beside it to eat your lunch?

In the very near future this crucial part of our city will be a beautiful and inviting landscape, an interactive space for families, city workers, people exercising – tourists and residents alike. The river is the key to the plan that will produce a new central city that people want to spend time in, whether it be working, shopping, cycling, playing sport or just relaxing. It will all be there for them.

The role of CERA has always been clear, as we must lead and facilitate the recovery. But the community remains at the heart of the vision and its succes ensuring Christchurch is able to sustain itself for generations to come.

The physical, tangible inner-city transformation is only just beginning to appear, but within five years, Christchurch will be a vastly different city. And because of the planning that has been done – regardless of how unorthodox and hastily completed it may seem – this new city will absolutely set an international benchmark for urban design, innovation and liveability.

And in my old age, I will look back at what we delivered here, and be incredibly proud.

Share an Idea

The public provided more than 106,000 ideas about how to rebuild Christchurch during the Share an Idea public engagement campaign. The six-week operation was launched by the Christchurch City Council three months after the February 2011 earthquake to inform the development of the Draft Central City Plan.

The Share an Idea website became a virtual noticeboard where people could upload ideas and see other people's ideas. The campaign was launched with a two-day expo attended by 10,000 people. The combination of high-tech opportunities, including video booths and Facebook, and low-tech options, such as Post-it notes, proved remarkably successful.

[1–5]

To plan or not to plan

David Sheppard

Qualified as an architect and urban designer, David has been in practice now since 1967, working in the USA, UK and New Zealand. He has been resident in Christchurch since 1975. In 1982 he formed Sheppard and Rout Architects with fellow architect Jonty Rout. In the ensuing 32 years he has carried out a diverse range of architectural and urban design projects throughout New Zealand and overseas. David is Immediate Past President of the New Zealand Institute of Architects and an adjunct Professor of the University of Auckland.

It would be fair to say that the frightening major events of 2010 and 2011 called into question the basis of the Christchurch City Plan and many other planning documents and tools in place at the time. Though it had been known for a couple of decades, from a study by respected engineers, that a large part of the city's built environment could suffer serious damage from liquefaction (land settlement) in the event of a major earthquake, very little work had been done to identify specific areas of land likely to be at risk and buildings that could suffer.

This advice was of interest and concern when it first emerged, but, like much news, it faded fairly quickly and planning and building continued almost unchanged. Even up to a year or so before the event of 4 September 2010, timetables for earthquake strengthening of older buildings, including the city's many valuable heritage buildings, gave their owners up to 30 years. Buildings to be strengthened were classified according to occupancy intensity. Those with high occupancy were to be strengthened within 10 years, medium occupancy 20 years and low occupancy 30 years.

Clearly the authors of these timetables were influenced by owner resistance to having to pay for often quite expensive repairs more than by concern about imminent risk of a damaging seismic event. As a result, a large proportion of the city's older buildings and certainly the majority of those recognised as having heritage value have been lost. It is important to say here, however, that those older buildings that did receive some strengthening in the last two decades largely survived, many virtually unscathed.

Planners and engineers, especially earthquake specialists, cannot be singled out for failing to warn the community that a major earthquake might well occur in the short term. The sciences of prediction and of probability, for all the work done by many over a long period, are still baffling to those involved and no reliable forecasting techniques have emerged.

Certainly, in the Canterbury region, there were no clear signs of previous seismic events. Studies that had identified the region as having some laterals extending onto the plains from the main alpine earthquake fault, which runs the length of the South Island, were regarded with some suspicion but not fear.

Effects of the earthquake events on planning

The earthquakes of 2010 and 2011 occurred then with no effective plans in place and certainly none at the scale required to deal with the magnitude of the events that struck the region. They necessitated a broad look at the future planning of the region and the city in particular. The weeks following the 4 September earthquake were, for most, the period of identification and emergency work helping the community, involving Student Volunteer Army, Civil Defence and Urban Search and Rescue efforts.

Out of this period emerged recognition of the need to review existing planning policies and direction. It was also seen as a time of opportunity. The city was so badly damaged at that point that many could see the very basis of its planning required total review. The events occurred at a time of increasing concern about global warming, sea level rise and tsunami risk, with low-lying Christchurch situated close to an ocean coast.

Local architects were among the first in September 2010 to see the need for and the opportunity to review the plan for the city and how it might be recast to provide direction for the 'new Christchurch'. We could see that there was very little likelihood of its returning to its previous state pre-September 2010, however nice that may have been as a place to live and work. We also knew that the city had been languishing in its condition for some decades and there were many buildings that were underutilised. A plan that could get the city back on its feet and reinvigorated was seen as a valuable and worthwhile objective.

The architects then mounted, with considerable voluntary effort, an exhibition entitled 'Christchurch Before – After'. We posed a series of questions and ran forums, seeking ideas from the community as to what sort of city it would like Christchurch to be in the future.

The initiative had a major influence on Christchurch City Council's subsequent Share an Idea forum that was held a few months later in mid-2011, at the start of the preparation of its recovery plan for the central city. By then the city had realised there was not only the need for a review of its existing plan for the city, but that it also presented a unique opportunity to bring into being a new and invigorating plan. Many ideas for how to improve and enhance the city had been put forward over the years by the Council and by the community – now was the opportunity to consider these and aim to fold the best of them into the plan for the future of the city.

In mid-2011 central government gave the city a six-month window to produce its plan for the recovery of the central city and to identify key actions that would help bring it about.

The plan that resulted and, in particular, the city's list of key actions, were generally well received by the community and many business interest groups. More detailed review of the proposed key actions, however, indicated that these were mostly 'nice to do' but would not drive the speedy recovery needed, especially the economic recovery. The architects and many others submitting their responses to the city identified this shortcoming and put forward alternative key actions.

At this stage, after the major earthquakes, central government had set up the Canterbury Earthquake Recovery Authority (CERA) via special legislation to administer the recovery of the city. A division of CERA, the Christchurch Central Development Unit (CCDU), picked up on the architects' submission and invited discussion on some of the ideas put forward in it. At these discussions, the architects identified that a missing major component in the planning was masterplanning input. We noted that there was much analytical material already in existence and a lot of broad-brush ideas, such as the provision of more green space, but there was no overall outline plan for the city where such ideas might be realised. For want of a better definition of the missing link, the architects referred to it as 'masterplanning'.

When asked a short time later by CCDU how long it might take to produce such a plan, the architects suggested this could be achieved by way of an intensive work session over a period of about three months. A short time period was seen as essential in the interests of the city's early recovery.

Preparation of the Blueprint plan

A month or so later, CERA released an advertisement inviting consultants to submit their interest in preparing a recovery blueprint for the central city in 100 days. The architects were delighted that our suggested plan of action had been picked up by the body heading the recovery. CERA's request of the selected consultants was to identify the locations of a number of key anchor projects to provide the economic impetus necessary for the central city recovery. This plan would become the definitive document for the central city and no objections or appeals against the plan were to be permitted. The plan was completed in the 100 day period specified. It was announced to the public on 31 July 2012.

Throughout the eighteen-month period from the devastating February 2011 earthquake to the production of the Blueprint, there was substantial support for the concept of masterplanning. The Blueprint that emerged was heralded as a major step forward for the recovery of the city and all sectors of the economy considered it to offer an exciting and strong new framework for the city.

What has happened since?

Since its publication in July 2012, there has been a lot of support for the Blueprint and the ideas contained in it. This support has come from many in the business community as well as from the residents of Christchurch.

Strong support has been expressed for the overall concept; the introduction of major additional new green space, especially on the east and south sides of the central city; celebration and enhancement of the Avon River as it winds through the central city; compressing and containing the central business core of the city, making it a highly walkable and lively area; focusing retail on Cashel Mall; bringing a number of key anchor projects closer in to the city centre to add to its vitality; and encouraging central city residential developments and promoting the construction of a high-quality model 'urban village' as a demonstration.

CERA stated that there would be no reviews of the Blueprint plan and there would be no right of appeal by anyone or any party that considered any part of the plan affected them. This assertion was made possible under the terms of the Canterbury Earthquake Recovery Act. It included the ability to take private land for the purpose of the plan. While this was considered draconian by many, it at least gave certainty that the plan would be implemented in the form it was proposed.

Substantial areas of privately owned land were designated for the construction of the proposed anchor projects to ensure their realisation in the locations proposed in the plan.

In the midst of general support for the plan in the months following its publication, numerous affected land owners objected strongly to their land being designated. Key amongst these were owners who had begun work on repairing their buildings and those whose buildings were new or had come through the earthquakes relatively unscathed. Some of these owners are still in negotiation with the Crown. Others are refusing to settle with the Crown until they see if their land is actually required for the purposes of the plan.

It is now almost two years since the plan was launched and much has been done in support of its implementation. To that extent, progress has been steady and reasonably speedy.

A lot has already occurred. A significant number of sites for most of the proposed anchor projects have been purchased. The design of several of the proposed anchor projects, including the Justice and Emergency Services Precinct, the Bus Interchange, the Metro Sports Facility and the Avon River Precinct is underway. A competition for the detailed design of the proposed Residential Demonstration Project has been held and the winner announced.

Projects that are experiencing delay, at least for the landowners and affected community, include the proposed Convention Centre Precinct; the Stadium; the central retail area focused around Cashel Mall; the formation and conceptual base of the proposed South Frame, whether it is open 'campus' style or more intensively developed; and new initiatives in medium density residential development. Meanwhile new greenfield sites are thriving on the outskirts of the city.

Projects that have taken a different direction, or appear to be being rethought include the Innovation Precinct and the Performing Arts Precinct. Since the launch of the plan, strong advocacy emerged to save the Town Hall, affecting the integrity of the Performing Arts Precinct indicated in the Blueprint Plan. With the decision now made to repair the Town Hall, CERA is signalling its intention to lift the designation on the land earmarked for its replacement in the plan. This is having an effect on the integrity of the planned precinct.

Private investment response to the Blueprint

Even though it can be said that the implementation of the plan is proceeding at a steady and reasonably rapid pace, some altogether unexpected results are evident.

The most spectacular of these is the construction of a substantial quantum of new commercial and retail space on the periphery of and mainly outside the boundaries of the Blueprint plan. While the planning of the central area continues and demolition continues, developers are responding to the demand for office space and related retail in areas of the city where there are fewer controls and limitations. This is strongly evident on Lincoln Road and Victoria Street, and the western side of the Avon River in the central city.

Much of the demand for office space is thus being met in these areas of the city. In the central areas where office development is being encouraged to focus, there are now fewer tenants looking for space. Even in the emergent areas outside the central city developers are now seeing a decline in the number of enquires for new office space. Some of the recently completed space is taking longer to lease.

The Blueprint foresaw a limit on the amount of floor space that the city needed in the short term and into the future and the total is coming close to being fully provided by the private market outside the area planned for this activity. Central city property owners are now beginning to wonder who their tenants might be. Those still planning larger buildings are looking with increased interest for the few government departments, banks and larger corporations in the hope that they might yet be able to entice these into the central city.

It is safe to say that some demand will continue but may be limited in the short term. As businesses reach the end of their leases in buildings on the periphery of the city, in say five to ten years, they may become interested to move back into the central area. They will, however, be almost certainly looking at higher leasing costs. Their current landlords will be reluctant to lose their tenants and will be in a good position to offer attractive lower rentals, which would suggest that fewer businesses may be inclined to move back into the central area.

There is evidence of work proceeding in numerous parts of the area covered by the Blueprint. While there are still a significant number of damaged buildings to be demolished and others that are to go to make way for the anchor projects, those who are following the rollout of the Blueprint can see the bones of it beginning to appear. Sections of the upgraded Avon River corridor are being worked on including the north end of the East Frame where the new Margaret Mahy Family Playground is planned. The large area of land set aside for the Metro Sports Facility and the new Justice Precinct are now cleared. The site for the new Bus Interchange is partially cleared.

But almost nothing, with the exception of the new food and beverage facilities that replace The Strip on the eastern side of the Avon River, is occurring within the central city. Plans for development of this area are still subject to review by the CCDU under a range of planning rules introduced to guide this particular area. In the meantime, the Re:START Mall is proving to be the saviour of activity in the central city and a necessary complement for the few remaining retail outlets, including the key anchor tenant of the area, Ballantynes. It is known that some of the landowners fronting the old Cashel Mall have been gracious in allowing the complex to remain in the short term but this has really only happened because their own plans for the land have been frustrated to a large extent by the hoops they have had to jump through to get CCDU buy-in. It has not been for want of trying to get building going that there is still so little concrete happening in the city's core.

It is interesting to note that, while there is quite a substantial quantum of building going on around the periphery, many of the broader objectives for the redevelopment of the city seem to have taken a back seat. There is also a lack of evidence for sustainability, improved energy use, studies of alternative transport modes and so on. Just recently, also, the CCC has extended the time frame for its ambitious plan to introduce a city-wide cycle network estimated to cost $67 million.

The city has been placed in overseas media on several international lists of top cities to be watched. It was seen as a place that had a unique opportunity to learn from past practices and plan the recovery of the city on state of the art principles and methods. It would be fair to say at this point that Christchurch could well fall off these lists because of the lack of commitment to these principles and methods. There is the very real danger that the city will be built back largely as it was and not become an exemplar of how to rebuild and reinvigorate a city. This is not to say that there will not be any innovation, but it may occur in specialist building areas like foundations and superstructure engineering. New community structures, local social networks and the like may be overlooked.

So, has the Blueprint approach been worthwhile?

It may be a little early to judge the success of following a masterplanning approach. There will always be critics of any approach, especially those who are seeking rapid recovery.

The alternatives to such a plan are several, ranging from the 'do nothing' approach where everyone is free to do what they want where they want, through to a fully worked out, dictatorial approach. New Zealand supports neither of these extremes and can point to schemes where the many interests of a community have been considered and resolved successfully in the interests of the individual and the group. The Blueprint is an example of this approach.

Whatever scheme is introduced, it will take time to develop and implement. Developing a plan before the work starts leads to a better outcome than the laissez-faire approach. It is also essential where major investment is needed and the money has to come from somewhere else.

In my view, the introduction of the Blueprint was the way to go. It of course required commitment to make it work and care to bring the community and business interests along with it. If there is any criticism of the process to date, it would be that those responsible for implementing it may not be keeping the community and interested groups fully informed, especially where changes are being considered. The Government committed at the outset to implementing the plan that was produced and said it would not brook any objectives and appeals to the scheme. It therefore behooves the team formed by Government to be open and transparent about any changes it may wish to make. The Government likewise has an obligation to stick to the plan. The community is likely to accept changes if it has an opportunity to debate them. It will be intolerant, as it should be, if it discovers that the plan is being changed without consultation.

At the present time, the Blueprint appears to be providing a solid basis for the recovery of the city and its eventual wellbeing. The community for the most part trusts those implementing the plan. It will accept a slower time frame for the recovery if this is found to be necessary for economic, or any other, reasons so long as it is kept fully in the picture. If it takes five to ten years to fully recover, does it really matter so long as the basic needs of the business community and the residents are being met in the meantime?

New buildings

When so much of the city's built form has been lost it is wise to question how the new city will look and what style it will be built in. After the 1931 quakes in Napier and Hastings, art deco dominated the reconstruction and now defines the city. It will take decades to rebuild the thousands of Christchurch buildings lost and demolished, but the first wave of construction is now appearing. The initial focus has been on safety, affordability and short-term functionality; so far, concrete, steel and glass dominate the new buildings.

[1–6]

[7–13]

[14–20]

On the origin of precincts

Gary Franklin

Gary is a trustee of Life in Vacant Spaces Charitable Trust, and a volunteer with New Zealand Business Mentors and Poetica, the Urban Poetry Project. He has worked as a consultant and technologist in the US, Europe and now New Zealand.

> Nothing dates faster than people's fantasies about the future. This [Brasilia] is what you get when perfectly decent, intelligent, and talented men start thinking in terms of space rather than place; and single rather than multiple meanings. It's what you get when you design for political aspirations rather than real human needs.
> – Robert Hughes on the fabricated capital of Brazil[1]

To set the scene, imagine crossing Christchurch's future health or justice precincts at night, on foot, to get to a more social area. The streets are empty, the building lights are off, and the walls of glass reflect the street lights. You are alone because there is no reason for people to walk here at night. A police car and ambulance pass by at speed. Cameras track your progress and a loudspeaker announces with a robotic voice, 'Move along, please.' You realise this is just like walking the old Cashel Mall retail gauntlet at night, or the Financial District in London, or downtown Houston, and think, 'Is this the best we could do?' This same precinct will be the scene of morning and afternoon traffic jams as the precinct workers leave multi-level car parks to travel to other precincts and beyond to the suburbs.

A potential reason that precincts are so prevalent in the Christchurch Central Recovery Plan is that they are the expected solution from well-intentioned and often highly paid consultants, both logically and psychologically. Logically, consultants proceed from a complicated starting point and reduce it to perceived essential terms, and based on the timeline given to them (not proposed by them) propose a solution that they are fairly sure is one the client wants – in this case, based on certainty, speed and cost. Psychologically, consultants are motivated towards clear solutions (such as precincts) that they can later point to and document as achievements. Unfortunately, cities that are designed with clear building blocks, such as Brasilia and Canberra, are not high on lists of quality of life and tourist appeal, except as architectural curiosities.

As a long-time consultant, I could have perhaps been employed to help work on the plan, but I chose not to, because I didn't think I could change what was going to happen. Instead, I have focused on supporting community-led projects in the empty spaces and buildings of the transitional city, hoping the community through them can influence the future city from the ground up.

The alternative to single-use precincts would be incentive-driven mixed-use zones, creating city blocks where people can work, eat, shop, sleep, create, learn and play, interspersed with green spaces and 'anchor' community, government and business buildings. Even America is coming back to this vision, with US real-estate websites no longer focusing on suburban subdivisions and instead featuring a Walkability Rating to show how easy it is to walk or ride a bicycle from a home to local amenities.

There is evidence that incentives affect mixed-use city development, even in ways not initially foreseen. In Amsterdam, the propensity of tall, narrow and deep houses is due to an historical tax on street frontage. The result is a high density of housing with a minimum of roading and transport infrastructure per person, but a side-effect was the availability of ground floors for shops and restaurants and offices, while leaving residential space above and behind. Even the most extreme example, the smallest house in Amsterdam, only 2 metres wide and 6 metres deep, has had over the years a watchmaker, optician, boutique and florist on the ground floor.[2]

Proposing a system of incentives rather than tangible precincts is risky for a consultant, because the resulting uncertainty makes it more difficult to predict the results. You must put more faith in the community that will take advantage of incentives, and it is harder to convince the client of the potential result. If the client were a farm owner, they would rather see mature trees stuck into the ground (if told that was possible), than to be told that proper soil, conditions, seeds and share-croppers left to their own means would evolve into a prosperous environment.

The arsenal of potential incentives is well stocked: tax (credits or rebates for GST, rates, income, excise); fees (reduced consent, licensing, or loan fees); grants (heritage, cultural, creative); processes (dedicated central city mixed-use consent team and processes); duty (import, export, and the opportunity for a free-trade zone); loans (reduced interest for developers and home-buyers); subsidies (on rents, building costs, strengthening etc.); and also standards (for example, a young creative signs and accepts a slightly sub-code lodging and studio in exchange for reduced rent, which is what they did informally before).

It is interesting that most incentives are not a spend out of current coffers, but a reduction in future revenue or increase in future costs, which could be offset by additional revenue from economic activity within the renovated area. Incentives to remain in the central city would have been one of the means to reduce the exodus of investment to the suburbs, along with zoning restrictions.

This is not a Right versus Left political discussion, as it could be said that defined precincts are totalitarian yet are also social engineering, and that incentives allow more liberty in action yet also represent policy engineering.

Incentives would have to be accompanied by some rules. Purely as an example, in a mixed-use zone if you build a three-story building with a shop or restaurant on the ground floor, you have to provide apartments above. If buildings either side of you have already gone for apartments above, you have the option to provide offices above instead. Incentives to sell or demolish for green space are available until the green space allotment for the area is met. Would it be easy to create this ecosystem of incentives? No, it would be challenging and fluid. However, it is a skill that our children are already developing as they play farming and civilisation games online by seeding and interacting, rather than placing finished products onto a map.

Ultimately, since the precinct plan is going ahead, it should be modified so the full needs of the community can be better met. In order to justify the $300 million Justice Precinct, a Vice Precinct is a must. This is not completely in jest – the city plan ignores (or actively disputes) the reality and opportunity to improve conditions for the (legal) prostitution industry, their inevitable clients and neighbours – even knowing they will otherwise boom in all directions in a construction gold-rush town. There is also the absence of a Slum Precinct, which would allow young creative people a place they can afford to live, make art and music, start creative or technology businesses and in the process turn it into the Hip Precinct, which would then be sold off and the creatives forced to move to a failed precinct and begin there anew. An exodus of creatives to Melbourne, Auckland and beyond has already begun, even as simultaneously a top-down drive to favour science, technology, engineering and maths (STEM) over the arts is under way nationally. A stale city could result that won't attract people with freedom to choose other places to live. Every time a creative leaves, a leaf falls from the city, revealing a bare stem.

It is easy to say that New Zealanders want their own patch of yard and shed in the suburbs and wouldn't want to own or rent in the central city. In fact, apartments were on the increase in the central city before the earthquake, but often in luxury high-rise buildings. Who would answer that they would want to live in low-rise apartment living, above shops or offices or restaurants? Ask the young, the dynamic, the educated, who could drive vibrant city life. Ask those struggling to afford rental housing or fuel for commutes, or those waiting on state housing lists, who could participate if given a supporting incentive to do so. In five years, ask those who chose to move to suburbs across the plains, lured by slogans such as 'Live where you play', who may well have learned that when they drive to work, there's hell to pay.

Robert Hughes wrote on the lesson of modernism as being one choice among many:

> The first casualty of this was the idea that architects or artists can create working Utopias. Cities are more complex than that, and the needs of those who live in them less readily quantifiable. What seems obvious now was rank heresy to the modern movement: the fact that societies cannot be architecturally "purified" without a thousand grating invasions of freedom; that the architect's moral charter, as it were, includes the duty to work with the real world and its inherited content. It is better to recycle what exists, to avoid mortgaging a recyclable past to a nonexistent Future, and to think small.[3]

In the case of Christchurch, the recyclable past in the central city was small, but therefore precious. It was communally soul wrenching when it was bulldozed along with the unsalvageable into the dust clouds of memory. Still, the recyclable past may also mean memories, in my case, of sitting on a sunny terrace and looking up at a tenant hanging laundry out on a balcony, while a Jack Russell Terrier chased a ball down Poplar Lane between the legs and shadows of people shopping. Could parts of the central city or zones within the existing defined precincts still be defined as 'freedom precincts', with incentives that could energise property owners, developers and business owners, including those stranded in the past and new ones, to create true town and village living and working?

There is an area of two square kilometres in Amsterdam that houses not only the small Red Light District that tourists seem to selectively recall for the rest of their lives, but also the University of Amsterdam, residents, lawyers, police, hotels, businesses, shops, restaurants, museums, schools, parks and waterways. It would have been impossible to design; it could only have evolved. We should have no paralysing fear that property owners, developers, architects, workers and residents could not take advantage of a time of government-incentivised prosperity to create a Golden Age for Christchurch.

A history of planning through the broken lens of disaster

Suzanne Vallance

Dr Vallance is a Lecturer in Urban Studies at Lincoln University, with particular interests in urban planning and policy for sustainability and resilience. Her research focuses on the collective ways in which we can make our cities and settlements better, safer, healthier places to live. Her research areas include the future of cities and city-regions, the meanings and practices associated with urban sustainability and resilience, co-creating knowledge for disaster risk reduction, and exploring ways in which formal and informal planning approaches diverge.

Planning has a long and colourful history with the 'art' of planning evolving alongside the transition from a nomadic life to more permanent settlement. Long before Westminster, the White House or the Beehive, people have been coming together to give their aspirations for place some kind of form and content over ever-larger scales; we could call this the *substance* of planning. The substance of planning – transport, housing, sanitation, infrastructure – has been profoundly shaped by disasters, including war, plague, floods and fire; however, the connection between catastrophe and the evolution of planning is rarely acknowledged. This first task of this chapter is to illustrate this connection more fully by documenting some of the ways in which disasters of many different kinds have shaped the history of planning. The second and more difficult task is to highlight how several more recent events – including the Canterbury earthquakes – have exposed the importance of planning *processes*. A focus on the procedural aspects of planning opens up a more critical line of enquiry, and raises intriguing questions about who plans, for whom, why and how. This chapter therefore presents a brief history of planning substance *and* process, through the broken lens of disaster. I use this lens to explore an important question facing every city after disaster, that is, 'How do we build back better?'.

Early planning

Some of the earliest forms of planning can be seen as attempts to avoid disaster, though their approach and the nature of the disaster might sound rather odd to us now. The spatial plan of the twelfth century city of Angkor in Cambodia, for example, was a means of communicating with the celestial beings above – a plea for benign sponsorship, guidance and protection.

Early Roman architect Marcus Vitruvius also adopted a god's-eye perspective of the city as seen from above, but instead favoured a radial plan (resembling the spokes on a wheel) that facilitated the movement of goods and people to, and wastes from, the city's ruling class at the centre. In the glory days of the Roman Empire, courting divine intervention through urban form was perhaps seen as less important than keeping the elites clean, well-fed and content.[1]

While the radial plan facilitated this inward-outward flow, the advent of gunpowder and the canon put the elites at the centre at risk from such long-range, straight-shooting weaponry, and this urban form fell from favour. Household or compound defensive strategies became more common, with Florence (Italy) and Seville (Spain) good examples of cities of dead-ends, blind alleys and enclaves. Many medieval towns are a labyrinth of twisting, small streets that confuse the invader (and, more recently, the tourist) and reduce the effectiveness of long-range weapons, but which are still legible and easily navigated by locals. Such cities also reflect the challenges of rapid growth and a leadership preoccupied with colonial expansion rather than convenience or sanitation.

From the fire: Technical planning

Another well-documented historical example of planning and regulation to avoid disaster was London's Building Act of 1619,[2] designed to prevent the numerous fires that often raged out of control in the city of wood and thatch. The Act specified brick exteriors and minimum wall thicknesses that would slow the spread of fire, but enforcing the Act proved difficult. In September 1666 the Great Fire of London was accidentally started by a baker in Pudding Lane. It burned for nine days and left 80 per cent of the city in ruins.

Like all places post-disaster, London was presented with the opportunity to 'build back better' and, as Ramroth noted, 'The debris from the fire was hardly cold when Christopher Wren [most famous for the design of St Paul's] stood before King Charles II on September 10, 1666, to present a masterplan for new London . . . Wren's London was rational, geometric, and grand, with a mathematician's eye for beauty – all in keeping with the Age of Reason.'[3] It was also 'completely unworkable' as it would require large-scale land acquisition and compensation, and would involve considerable delays in rebuilding.[4] Instead tax benefits were given to those who rebuilt with brick or stone facings (according to the new Building Act of 1667) with some compensation for those who gave ground to street widening. Four housing 'sorts' to guide rebuilding were introduced, as were new codes around guttering and drainage. Perhaps most importantly, *qualified* building officials were appointed to ensure compliance with new codes. Consequently, the greatest legacy of the Great Fire was that the responsibility for the performance of cities started to shift from military generals, religious leaders or no-one at all, to professional planners who began developing a distinctly modern, *technical* approach.

The unsanitary city: Progressive planning

While the seeds of planning as a technical exercise were planted in late medieval cities, and were exported with colonial expansion, this early version of modern planning lacked the progressive element that was to emerge in the wake of a creeping disaster of a rather different sort: rapid urbanisation, overcrowding and disease on the back of the Industrial Revolution. In 1712 Thomas Newcomen had used a coal-fired pump to extract water from a coal mine, giving us one of the first well-known examples of the transition from a somatic (or body-based) energy regime to the exo-somatic (fossil- and nuclear-) fuelled world we live in today. People flocked to work in the new factories, and many cities grew rapidly. As one example, in 1744 Manchester's population was 24,000, but by 1801 it had trebled to 70,000. Urbanisation ultimately brought many of the benefits (and ills) we now take for granted, but these benefits were distributed very unevenly thanks to a new ideology around the purpose of growth (and planning).

In 1776 Adam Smith, who is now widely regarded as the founding father of modern economics, had published his *Wealth of Nations*. This prompted a complete revision of the state's role in commerce where governmental interference was reconfigured as an impediment to the creation of wealth. Extreme interpretations saw any attempt at regulation as a threat, including town planning. The unbridled pursuit of wealth and the lack of any effective regulatory environment to preserve the amenities of rapidly industrialising cities had often fatal consequences for urban poor. Laurence reports that in Manchester in the 1840s, the average age at death for a male labourer was a mere seventeen years (with a rural labourer's life expectancy around 38 years).[5] Disease in these industrial cities was rife and, as just one example, London's calamitous cholera epidemic of 1848-49 killed at least 60,000 people. One in five people ended up in the asylum, the poorhouse or jail. As John Ruskin wrote in his *Letters to the Clergy on the Lord's Prayer and the Church*:

> The great cities of the earth . . . have become . . . loathsome centres of fornication and covetousness – the smoke of their sin going up into the face of heaven like the furnace of Sodom; and the pollution of it rotting and raging in the bones and souls of the peasant people round them, as if they were each a volcano whose ashes broke out in blains upon man and beast.[6]

Many cities in the United States faced similar problems with 'overcrowded and unsanitary tenement buildings (that) were little more than fetid Petri dishes for disease, causing untold misery, health problems and death'.[7] Tension began to grow between those who sought socially progressive reform through regulation and planning, and those advocating laissez-faire policies, where even the most worthy protectionist or humanitarian motives were seen as the antithesis of free trade and national prosperity.

The debate was never exactly settled, but the late 1800s saw the development of several key planning movements that were more modern in combining technical and socially progressive elements. Among the more prominent were the Garden City movement, the City Beautiful movement and the Tenement Reform movement. Ebenezer Howard's garden cities, for example, were designed to accommodate 30,000 people in towns with a concentric ring pattern, with appropriate uses – residential, commercial, recreational – assigned to each ring or zone. While only a handful of such towns were ever built, his thinking shaped our contemporary notions of suburbia and helped establish the practice of zoning. Together these three movements consolidated the progressive role for planners as advocates of basic human rights to housing, education, greenspace and employment through regulatory means.

Planning, in this context, clearly represented a form of political orientation and spoke of one's belief in the rightful activities and methods of state enterprise.

Wars, madness and reason: Rational planning

The political ferment between those who were avidly against any state intervention (which was seen as inimical to the creation of wealth), and those who believed more regulation was required in order to redress the plight of the urban poor (or, more recently, 'save the environment') would come to a head in the wake of disasters of a very different kind: World Wars I and II. Involving over 30 different countries, it is estimated that between 50 and 80 million people lost their lives in the Second World War. Many European cities were devastated by extensive bombing and lack of investment in infrastructure as funds were diverted to military purposes.

The post-war popularity of the idea of rational standards of living can be attributed, in part, to the ways in which technology, mechanisation, mass production and standardisation had helped win the war. These factors seemed to provide a winning formula that could then be usefully applied to society more broadly. On the back of a war that had demanded citizens lay down their lives for their country, state provision of minimum standards of living also served as a compromise between interventionists and those advocating a more laissez-faire approach. As A. C. Pigou claimed in 1914:

> It is the duty of a civilised state to lay down certain minimum conditions in every department of life, below which it refuses to allow any of its free citizens to fall. There must be a minimum standard of conditions in factories, a minimum standard of . . . leisure, a minimum standard of dwelling accommodation, a minimum standard of education, of medical treatment . . . and of wholesome food and clothing. The standards must all be upheld . . . and any man or family which fails to attain independently any one of them must be regarded as proper subject for State action.[8]

Scientific standards and the imposition of social order had interesting implications for town planning. The provision of masterplanned state housing tracts became widespread in countries like New Zealand and the UK where state homes were mass produced in almost formulaic fashion according to the anticipated number of residents.

Zoning to separate industrial and residential uses, regulate shading and fire danger, relieve congestion and assist with the provision of services became a standard part of planning practice. It was often combined with other rigid forms of regulation and standardisation. Wagner, a famous German planner, advocated that districts with 10,000 inhabitants should have '13 hectares of woods, 2.4 hectares of playing fields, 1.6 hectares of sports grounds, and 0.5 hectares of walkways'.[9]

Scott, in his text *Seeing Like a State*, described this version of modern planning as 'a strong, one might even say muscle-bound, version of the self-confidence about scientific and technical progress, the expansion of production, the growing satisfaction of human needs, the mastery of nature (including human nature), and above all, the rational design of social order commensurate with the scientific understanding of natural laws'.[10] There were, however, changes underway that would come to challenge this confidence in science to reveal reality and deliver progressive social outcomes.

The toxic ghost in the machine: Reflexive modernity

The Swiss-French architect Le Corbusier's 'machines for living' are often held up as an exemplar of modern town planning as a technical, progressive and rational enterprise. For instance, his tower blocks providing large-scale, standardised housing became the model upon which Pruitt Igoe (St Louis, USA) was built. Completed in 1954, Pruitt Igoe was initially promoted as a magnificent example of man's triumphant mastery over the full range of urban ills described above. Unfortunately, due to its fundamental purpose (housing for the urban poor), huge size (10,000 residents at densities of 175 people per acre), lack of maintenance and poor design, it eventually became 'the poster child for everything that is wrong about low-cost, high-rise housing projects'.[11] It was deliberately blown to bits in 1972 and its demolition not only reduced the buildings to rubble, but also challenged the viability of rational and technological approaches to planning. People, it would seem, are not machines after all.

A series of similarly monumental failures continued to shake people's faith in modern approaches to planning, and modernisation more generally. One of the most famous was the Love Canal (New York) which was originally designed to help generate DC power supply, but which was subsequently used for waste disposal. The area was eventually covered with schools and housing, generally for lower- and middle-income groups.[12]

Sadly, residents there suffered unusually high rates of miscarriages, birth defects, and other illnesses, including cancer. One study found 33 per cent of residents had suffered chromosomal damage (compared with about 1 per cent in an average population). After a long battle, in 1978 residents secured federal emergency funds that, for the first time, were applied to a *non-natural disaster*.

Previously, catastrophic events had been configured as natural events or random acts of God, but this new wave of disasters (including Bhopal in India, Chenobyl in the USSR, mad cow disease, deforestation and even climate change) were seen as having all-too-human causes. This new responsibility means we now live in a 'risk society' that reflects more carefully on the potential negative effects of modernisation.[13] This age of reflexive modernity is more uncertain about the hidden costs of technological innovation, and less trusting of the ability of experts – including planners – to deliver progressive social outcomes or serve the public good.

This distrust is pervasive: Gunder, for example, has claimed that the New Zealand planning framework and the Resource Management Act 1991 (RMA) represent a form of deliberate, if subtle, oppression.[14] This reflects international scholarship arguing that claims about rational planning should more accurately be described as 'rationalisations' deployed once a decision has been made to justify actions that serve the elite at the expense of the general public.[15] Consequently, the substance of planning – land use, infrastructure, 'pipes, roads and rubbish' – that has long been regarded as a technical and professional enterprise has become haunted by a subjective, opinionated and irrational ghost: the general public who are noisily demanding transparency, accountability and a closer examination of process.

The eye of the storm: Hurricane Katrina and the 'procedural' turn

While debates about separating the substantial 'what' of planning from the procedural 'how' are not new, it took another less-than-natural disaster to fully expose the importance of process. New Orleans was founded in 1718 on a narrow slice of high ground along the Mississippi but, with faith in an expanding network of pumps, levees and floodwalls, New Orleanians eventually drained and 'reclaimed' areas lying below the river, below sea-level and below nearby lakes Ponchartrain and Borgne. At the same time, the ability of the surrounding wetlands to act as buffers for storm surges and hurricane winds had been compromised by the building of the Mississippi River-Gulf Outlet (MR-GO) connecting the port of New Orleans to the Gulf of Mexico. Besides allowing in salt water that kills stabilising fresh water marsh vegetation, MR-GO also formed 'an expressway for storm surges'.[16] The system of levees that had been designed to protect the city was compromised by 'complex construction and maintenance arrangements between the Corps of Engineers and the multitude of levee boards [and] resulted in reductions in design standards and construction quality'.[17] This was exacerbated by an unwieldy planning framework that had enabled residential development to occur in areas not yet protected. Although New Orleans 'had a masterplan, a comprehensive zoning ordinance, subdivision regulations and a building safety department . . . charged with . . . enforcing compliance with the National Flood Insurance Program', the masterplan lacked authority to force compliance, and the land use component of the masterplan was not always consistent with the zoning.[18] The natural disaster that was Hurricane Katrina became reconfigured as a man-made disaster of monumental proportions.

Critical analyses have also starkly exposed the ways in which the devastating effects of the disaster were so unfairly distributed; although approximately 80 per cent of the city was submerged, and 1600 people lost their lives, destruction and death fell disproportionately on socio-economically disadvantaged people. Low-income groups – many of whom were African Americans – were less likely to have adequate insurance and were more likely to have to rely on public transport, which became a huge problem when mass evacuation was required. They also tended to live in the low-lying areas of low-cost housing worst affected by the storm; consequently, this human-induced disaster was interpreted by some as nothing less than ethnic cleansing.[19]

Having borne the brunt of the disaster, many affected residents wanted to have a voice in the rebuilding of New Orleans but were confounded by the confusing array of recovery programmes and strategies, conflicted leadership and massive uncertainty over the viability of levees. Importantly, without adequate engagement with those affected by the decisions, the technical

debate over whether to rebuild or retreat from the most vulnerable areas –
areas that were home to many African Americans – looked like an attempt to
'transform the racial and political power of the city'.[20] The faltering 'recovery'
of New Orleans can be attributed, at least in part, to an inability to balance
'the need for both speed and deliberation'.[21] Importantly, Katrina has
sensitised disaster scholarship and practice to the vital importance of process,
and it is within this context that the engagement processes in the aftermath of
the Canterbury quakes are likely to be evaluated.

Deliberative and inclusive participatory planning processes after disaster

There is now a growing consensus in the academic literature that, along
with formal recovery authorities, the public has a vital role to play in disaster
recovery.[22] Many have argued that participating and getting involved after
a disaster can be cathartic because taking positive action gives victims a
sense of control that, in turn, facilitates recovery. Besides promoting public
buy-in to the recovery process, other benefits of public participation include
the identification of workable solutions to problems; cost effectiveness;
better delegation of duties; and promoting sustainability in the sense that
communities do not become dependent on external sources of funding for
the recovery.

In explaining the varied nature of involvement, peacetime planning theory
draws upon a number of well-established models including Arnstein's ladder
of citizen participation, Pretty's typology, or the International Association
of Public Participation's (IAP2) spectrum, which is alluded to in CERA's
Recovery Strategy for Greater Christchurch.[23]

Each documents a continuum of participatory practices that range from
token or passive informing through consulting, involving and collaborating,

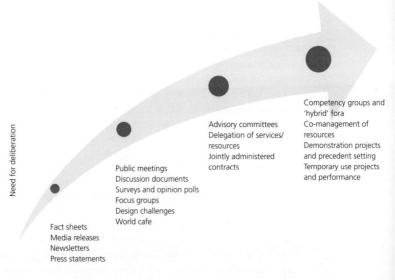

Need for deliberation

Competency groups and
'hybrid' fora
Co-management of
resources
Demonstration projects
and precedent setting
Temporary use projects
and performance

Advisory committees
Delegation of services/
resources
Jointly administered
contracts

Public meetings
Discussion documents
Surveys and opinion polls
Focus groups
Design challenges
World cafe

Fact sheets
Media releases
Newsletters
Press statements

Figure 1: The influence
of formal control
and deliberation on
participatory processes

Level of community participation in decision-making processes and problem framing to active *empowerment*. The left of figure 1 arguably speaks to what is referred to as an 'information deficit' model where the public is seen as lacking adequate knowledge of an issue. As a corollary, it is assumed that more information will lead to greater endorsement and/or compliance (presumably through 'informed consent'). Increasingly, however, the reliance on token participation-as-information-provision is seen as inadequate and ineffective,[24] particularly given the increased scepticism of experts and elite decision-makers in the risk society.

There is also less confidence that the substance of planning can, or should, be separated from the processes through which plans come to be.[25] The quest to find the technically correct solution, though seemingly neutral, is fundamentally framed by the way in which the problem is defined in the first place. Geotechnical and structural engineering assessments and Green Star ratings that specify ways of 'building back better', for example, preclude important questions about building back better *for whom*.

The procedural turn recognises that if substance and process are mutually reinforcing, public participation actually speaks to the fundamental ability to shape very concrete realities. In the post-disaster context, this right finds its parallel in shaping and defining recovery. Consequently, emphasis in both disaster and peacetime planning practice has shifted towards the right of figure 1, which draws on increasingly deliberative and inclusive participatory processes (or DIPs)[26] to develop holistic solutions that resonate more fully with people's everyday lifestyles, hopes and expectations. DIPs seek to achieve consensus or generate agreement among sometimes disparate groups, often through mediation and negotiation, and rely on tools as diverse as concerts, art programmes, traditional workshops, on-site charettes and online crowd-sourcing techniques.

Though the tools are important, more critical still are the underlying process and, particularly, the degree to which the issue or problem has already been defined. 'Consultation' can be seen as inadequate if those being consulted expect to help shape and define the problem, but are instead limited to stating their preferences for a set of predetermined options. This speaks to the extent to which the process is *deliberative*. The other underlying consideration is the extent to which the process goes beyond involving the usual suspects and invites usually marginalised or disadvantaged groups to participate in decision-making that affects them. This speaks to the extent to which the process is *inclusive*.

We've seen some examples of this in other places undergoing recovery such as the Community Congress II in New Orleans, which incorporated rap songs, poetry and art to 'engage the participants at the level of head and heart'.[27] It has been noted that although the Unified New Orleans Plan (UNOP) did not look radically dissimilar to its failed predecessors, the processes underpinning it were different in being transparent, deliberative, inclusive, and credible, and there are now signs that things are improving there.[28]

There have also been some examples here in Christchurch: the pre-quake Greater Christchurch Urban Development Strategy (which informed the post-quake Land Use Recovery Plan) bucked the trend promoted by the RMA in being both strategic and collaborative. Post-quake, the Christchurch City Council's Share an Idea campaign provided a useful *starting* point for a deliberative and inclusive participatory process; however, it is not altogether clear how this was then translated into the Christchurch Central Development Unit's Blueprint. The Breathe, New Urban Village competition generated some very innovative housing development ideas, though this initiative stalled for a time when the site was acquired by the Canterbury Earthquake Recovery Authority (CERA). An unusual initiative where responsibility is actually delegated to community groups has seen the CCC provide funding support (and only fairly loose guidelines and conditions) to grassroots community initiatives such as Gap Filler and Greening the Rubble. These charitable trusts have undertaken a range of temporary installations in the central city and the *New York Times* recently rated Christchurch the second best place in the world to visit in 2014, specifically mentioning the work of these two groups as good reasons to make the journey here.[29]

DIPs address many of the shortcomings of information deficit models, and have been used successfully in both peacetime and recovery planning, but they can be messy and have very unpredictable results. This is highly unnerving for those with a vested interest in achieving a certain outcome. DIPs are also very expensive and time-consuming, and they can seem like an impediment when urgent decisions need to be made. This tension is evident in debates over the work of the Stronger Christchurch Infrastructure Rebuild Team (SCIRT) that focuses on 'replacement' rather than 'improvement'. While residents clearly want functional infrastructure back in place as soon as possible, many are clearly frustrated that the opportunity to 'build back better' is not taken while the labour and machinery are on-site. Instead they face either the prospect of further disruption at some later date while improvements are made or, worse, no improvement. Adequately engaging with communities over the nature of possible improvements might lead to a better outcome, but only after a considerable delay. Unfortunately, at the very time that they are most necessary and most valuable, DIPs are least likely to be invoked.[30]

Where to now?

The history of planning – and planning approaches – involves a far more complex narrative than the one presented here. I have told a particular story in order to inform a discussion about where we might go from here and how we might 'build back better'. Some questions that I hope history can help us answer include:

Q: Does it take a blueprint to build back better?
A: History has shown that blueprints – from Wren's London to Bring New Orleans Back's New Orleans – rarely work out as intended.

Q: If we are to build back better, shouldn't we be reducing risk from future disasters?
A: While different disasters have profoundly shaped planning, historically planners rarely explicitly acknowledge their role in disaster risk reduction.

This is particularly true in New Zealand where disaster risk reduction is ostensibly managed by the Ministry of Civil Defence and Emergency Management (MCDEM) and regional CDEM Groups. These groups identify potential local hazards (e.g. floods, earthquakes, rockfall); calculate the probability of them occurring; and try to estimate the impact across the social, economic and built environments. Yet, this overall risk assessment does not necessarily inform or influence Regional Policy Statements and Regional Plans, or District/City Plans. Because man has recently assumed the burdens that used to be acts of God, a better alignment between 'peacetime planning' and 'disaster risk reduction' is probably overdue.

Q: What was all that stuff about *substance* and *procedure* again?
A: One of the contributions that the Canterbury earthquakes will make to both disaster scholarship and, ultimately, peacetime planning practice will likely be a better understanding of how substance (what is planned) and process (how it is planned, by whom, for whom) can be reconciled. The procedural turn has exposed the dark side of planning, illustrating the ways in which the focus on substance as a rational, technical exercise is an excellent way of excluding some people from decision-making processes that affect them.

Q: If your history can be extrapolated forward, aren't you suggesting a muddle where it is all about process, and everyone is an opinionated expert?
A: Yes. A radical swing from 'expert-technician' to 'community-led' process might be very dangerous. Canterbury has an excellent opportunity to lead the world in exploring a middle ground where knowledge and understanding is co-produced and collaboratively deployed.

So, the question is not 'How do we build back better?' but 'How do *we* build back better?'.

Why Christchurch should not plan for the future

Stuart Candy

Stuart Candy, PhD, works around the world as a strategist, educator, facilitator and producer of transmedia interventions. Currently based in Toronto, he is director of the Situation Lab and Assistant Professor of Strategic Foresight and Innovation at OCAD University. Stuart helped launch the Festival of Transitional Architecture (FESTA) in post-earthquake Christchurch, worked on the award-winning 'massively multiplayer forecasting game' *Superstruct*, and served as advisor to the Future We Want project for the United Nations Rio+20 Summit. This article is based in part on the closing presentation delivered by the author at TEDxChristchurch in October 2013, 'Whose Future Is This?'.

It is nothing new to remark on the complexity of the contemporary change environment, or its relentlessly accelerating pace.[1] And it does not take a military strategist to recognise the wisdom in the observation that 'no plan survives first contact with the enemy',[2] because these days the enemy of most large-scale human enterprises – what often brings them to grief – is not an opposing army, but rather the sheer difficulty of keeping up with what is going on both within and around them.

As Christchurch gets on with the epochal task of 'planning for the future', or reimagining and rebuilding itself, this essay offers a simple reminder in three parts: first, that what we call 'the future' is not really a singular thing, but an imaginary space of plural possibilities; second, that a city is not a product, but a process; and third, that a community shaping itself is inherently not a task for the few, but a participatory and co-creative act to be shared in by as many as possible.[3]

The upshot of these three observations – on plurality, process and participation – is that the idiom of 'planning' may not be the best fit for this situation. What is called for may be better framed as 'design for emergence'. I suggest that the need for rethinking governance through design and emergence is more urgent and far-reaching, and simultaneously more possible, than most of us seem to realise.

Plurality

My work as a futurist involves helping people map and navigate the possibility space of an unknowable future more creatively and systematically. I have done strategic foresight consulting and facilitation with many groups and agendas around the world. I think the wellbeing of communities of every sort and scale depends on how well we are able to engage with what might lie ahead.

The foresight field[4] takes as its point of departure a recognition that the future is by definition unwritten, and should therefore always be treated as plural.[5]

On this view, thinking ahead well means construing the future as a space of alternative possibilities. This allows us to exercise anticipation while also avoiding the trap of constantly trying to predict, and constantly being wrong.[6]

A key activity in this regard is crystallising, out of the fog of possibility space, a set of specific stories – 'scenarios' – to represent a range of alternative futures that could unfold, and to consider carefully what we might do in each case. Futurist and political scientist Jim Dator worked out in the 1970s that the countless possible stories we tell about the future may be boiled down to a handful of trajectories or narrative logics, which he called the 'generic images of the future'.[7] These are now widely used as a way to craft illuminating scenario sets, and there are various other ways to do the same thing.[8]

Scenarios are at this point seen as essential to doing policy, strategy and planning well in a wide variety of settings.[9] So here is an important question for the present discussion: what kinds of assumptions about the future have been embedded in planning conversation to date, and what if events were to challenge or overturn any of those assumptions? (For instance, what kinds of thinking are we doing about the potential collapse of cheap oil, which has fuelled the last century of global economic growth, including ubiquitous personal vehicles and enormous flows of people and goods?)

It is impossible to account exhaustively for all possible eventualities. But at this point, to undertake a city-scale design project without comprehensively addressing the palpable uncertainties of our planetary future would be rampant folly. As one of Kurt Vonnegut's characters says 'History is merely a list of surprises. It can only prepare us to be surprised yet again.'[10]

Process

Futurists have for decades been speaking of possible, probable and preferable futures.[11] All three of these categories are subjective, contested and in constant motion: the future is a process, not a product. The same is true of organisations, communities, cities, countries and civilisations.[12]

Among the twentieth century's key futures scholars was a Dutch sociologist named Fred Polak, who was Jewish and spent the Second World War hiding out in Nazi-occupied Netherlands. Amazingly, he emerged from that experience with a strong sense of humanity as a 'future-creating being',[13] and went on to write a seminal two-volume work called *The Image of the Future*.[14] Polak looked at how the future had been imagined in societies throughout time, and he found the following pattern: 'The rise and fall of images of the future precedes or accompanies the rise and fall of cultures. Once the image begins to decay and lose its vitality, the culture does not long survive.'[15]

In other words, our collective ability to realise a positive future depends upon our ability to imagine it.

The importance of such vision can also be seen, perhaps even more readily, on smaller scales. An organisation begins to lose staff and stock value when people lose confidence in it. A relationship is in trouble when the people in it can't imagine being happy together any longer.

What about cities, regions or even countries? It may be tempting to conclude that a well-engineered plan – an official image of the future – must be the key to success, regardless of its origins. This would be to draw the wrong lesson from Polak or, more to the point, from history. If the future imaginary is diagnostically useful or historically catalytic, it is because of what it reflects about the state of health of a culture, the ever-unfolding process that is a human community. We may wonder whether a meaningful future image can be made to order like an industrial product (as in Chairman Mao's catastrophic Great Leap Forward), and well may we doubt any approach to urbanism that assumes a country or city's future should be blueprinted in the same way that a building can be.

Long-range plans are brittle without a foresight context to make them elastic; but what's really needed is the lifeblood of a learning process circulating continually throughout. It is all too common for organisations of various sorts to assume that it should be enough to pay attention to some suitably remote round-number date, say 2030 or 2050, on a one-time basis, then to sit back and wait for some inevitable surprise to come along and blow away their best laid plans.[16] By contrast, I recently led a foresight process for the Singaporean government to identify and test assumptions underpinning their National Sustainability Blueprint for the year 2030, which was originally prepared in 2008.[17] Recognising the inherent uncertainties of change by revisiting a visionary document – as they did in this case – means admitting, in effect, 'we might be wrong'. No wonder it is uncommon.

It is critical to recognise and take account of the open-ended, constantly self-reinventing quality of community. This means seeing how the planning process is an *ongoing* part of a wider process – also ongoing – that is the city itself.

Winston Churchill observed that 'We shape our buildings, and afterwards they shape us.'[18] Casting his gaze further upstream, Marshall McLuhan is said to have made the same remark in relation to our tools.[19] And moving yet further in this direction, the point holds in regard to the visions and plans in service of which we wield those tools. We shape our imaginaries, while they shape us, and on the cycle goes.

Participation

We may speak about the role of participation in all this by borrowing an insight from the software world. Some years ago, computer programmer Eric Raymond evoked the difference between the top-down orderliness of the traditional way of making software – programmed, planned and engineered – versus the bottom-up emergence inherent in the software whose code is Open Source and thus written, edited and co-created in peer-to-peer fashion by a community. He used an architectural metaphor to contrast the two approaches, dubbing them respectively the 'cathedral' and the 'bazaar'.[20] Many organisations and governments, being themselves in a sense blueprinted edifices, have a persistent bias in favour of the cathedral. But being far-sighted doesn't mean simply planning and building things to last forever. On the contrary, the temporariness and transitionality of the bazaar are part of life, and the seeds of the better future are often planted not by 'visionary' plans, but by experiment, improvisation and accident. The will to permanence is a trap. As John Lennon is supposed to have said, 'Life is what happens while you're busy making other plans'. Wise words for city-makers to heed.

In Christchurch, Gap Filler and the Festival of Transitional Architecture (FESTA) are wonderful examples of bazaar-like structures.[21] As a member of the advisory board for the inaugural FESTA, I recall how thrilled we were when the opening for its first year (October 2012) brought crowds to the downtown core that were larger than any seen since the earthquakes.[22] This was not an official city programme and by no means was it lavishly funded. It was an ingenious, resourceful and authentically citizen-led activity: a case of a structure enabling life to go on while we were making other plans. The question arises, then, to what extent does and can the city rebuild take its cue from the cathedral, and to what extent from the bazaar? This is for others to answer, but I suggest it is worth pausing to consider.

A broader context for this conversation seems to be the question of how one can 'plan' for a bazaar. The challenge in hand involves what the hybrid artist-engineer and New York University professor Natalie Jeremijenko has called 'structures of participations'.[23]

The crowd-created Wikipedia, the world's fifth most visited website, is a striking example, consisting of 30 million articles in 287 languages (4.5 million in English) – and counting. The contents are generated by users, and enabled by the affordances and constraints of a platform maintained by the Wikimedia Foundation.[24]

For a real life illustration, consider the Burning Man festival in the Nevada desert, where for one week each year some 70,000 participants – the community has grown exponentially since the first gathering of twenty people in 1986 – co-create a temporary city on the blank canvas of an alkali dustbowl, before leaving without a trace.[25]

A third example: during my former role as a full-time foresight consultant, in 2012 I led the process design for a project called CoMConnect, which was about enlisting the public in helping to devise a Digital Strategy for the City of Melbourne.[26] The weekend-long kick-off event involved a maximum-capacity group of 150 attendees from across all sectors. Every session was proposed and run by participants, with no detailed advance agenda or training necessary.[27] The result was described by the one of the city's staff a month later as an 'epiphany'. It is not yet common practice for governments to include citizens so comprehensively and so early in a policy conversation, but this is going to have to change.[28]

Whether collecting a vast body of knowledge, enabling a temporary urban community of tens of thousands, or crafting a city's digital strategy: each of these designed structures of participation is fundamentally about governance. (We may even venture that the design of suitable structures of participation is the primary task of governance.) In any case, with organisations aspiring to cathedralesque orderliness increasingly obviously outpaced by massive complexity, exploring participatory and bazaar-like governance structures to harmonise with and harness such complexity becomes increasingly necessary.

Designing for emergence

There is evidently a tension between, on the one hand, accommodating actors' autonomy and agency while, on the other, making certain executive decisions that constitute the rules and parameters for the website, physical space, event or whatever. This trade-off is not susceptible to a one-size-fits-all solution. It requires a case-by-case consideration of what one shall attempt to fix in place by design, and what operations and opportunities shall be left to surprise and learning.

Designer Greg Van Alstyne and physicist Robert Logan have written on the relationship of design and emergence, pointing out that the former is characterised by 'the intentionality of the designer', 'top-down' structure and 'controlling' agendas, while the latter in contrast is about 'the autonomy of massively multiple agents', 'bottom-up' and 'influencing' agendas.[29] In a sense we might say that the notion of design for emergence is precisely the challenge of balancing the cathedral and the bazaar.

Van Alstyne and Logan's 'design for emergence' seems a much more suitable frame for understanding what is at stake, and is more likely to help with the challenge at hand than the common default frame of 'planning for the future'

What then should be done? Many points of intervention are available, but among the most potent and underappreciated is public imagination. (Remember: way upstream of buildings, we shape our imaginaries, and thereafter they shape us.) From my point of view as a design futurist, this has to do with enabling what Richard Slaughter called 'social foresight'[30] by co-creating, and helping others also to co-create, *experiential futures* – immersive, tangible and playable fragments of the possible worlds before us.[31] Experiential futures practice cultivates a cultural capacity for collective imagining, and thereby a basis for wiser choices.[32]

With this in mind, one of the most powerful catalysts for emergent co-creation would be to establish a participatory, plural process for public imagination.[33] It has been encouraging to see elements of the conversation in Christchurch gesture in this direction, for instance through a series of reports in the *Press* published three years to the day after the worst earthquake struck. These stories embodied alternative 'versions' of Christchurch on 22 February 2031, the disaster's twentieth anniversary.[34]

The rebuild of a city after a seismic upheaval is bound to be a fraught process, but it comes with an opportunity to respond to profound challenges increasingly evident in all quarters, not only within but also well beyond Canterbury and New Zealand. There is a chance here to approach afresh how the political process occurs. Consider the Arab Spring, Wikileaks, and the Occupy movement: three recent systemic warnings that our existing political designs are ill-equipped to accommodate the technology-enabled emergence of powerful networked movements. We should expect more profound disruptions to come. What if we saw this moment in Christchurch as a gift of history: an invitation to reimagine not just how the city looks, but the very processes through which it is made?

Among the first structures to seek to build, it seems to me, are processes properly enabling people to generate and pursue their own diverse preferred futures. Co-authoring our collective story is the challenge of our time, and from the multitude of possible worlds, the future we get is – or at least ought to be – a story we tell together.

Everywhere we look, the task at hand is about deepening people's awareness, understanding and capacity to realise genuine alternative futures.

It is not about selling them one.

Chapter 2

Selling the Plan

Kia whai hoa ai te mahere

Design and democracy
Barnaby Bennett

The Enervation Precinct
Stephen Judd

Planning documents

Great plan, but where are the investors?
John McCrone

Anchor project billboards

Valuing everyday life
Claes Caldenby

A message and a messenger
Matthew Galloway

Newspaper headlines

Telling our own tales
Gerard Smyth

Blueprint launch

Will a plumber cost me more now?: Christchurch from an
Auckland perspective
Liam Dann

Blueprint launch video

Open conversations
Nick Sargent

We live in a world in which we are constantly being sold things, sometimes without even knowing it. A city is no different. Cool Melbourne, Romantic Paris, Vibrant New York. Even before there was a plan, we were being sold – and probably *wanted* to be sold – the idea of a new city, a recovery, a brighter future. In the 50s, the future was one of flying cars and colonies in space. The fictional future in *Back to the Future* is now a date in our real past. The main lesson we can take from these 'predictions' is that the future we are sold – and the one we buy into – will differ greatly from the one that's created.

The desired result of the plan was to successfully sell Christchurch's recovery to the people of the city, the region, the country and ultimately the world. It's a tall order: for the plan and its various projects to succeed, they need widespread buy-in. This means general public approval, willing investors for specific ventures and cooperation from the future 'users' of the city – people who will utilise the buildings, parks and particular developments that comprise the plan.

When the quake happened, the eyes of the world were on Christchurch for a brief moment. The reporting soon became less frequent, until it concentrated solely around anniversaries or aftershocks. This possibly led to the assumption that the rebuild was progressing well (no news is good news), but also led to a false perception of the Christchurch situation. With a significant chunk of money for the rebuild coming from the New Zealand government, and the majority of New Zealand taxpayers living outside of Christchurch, how can the country gauge whether its investment has been a prudent one?

This chapter contains calls for more public participation and end-user involvement in the plan and its projects. It also has accolades for and analyses of the public consultation that has been conducted. Underlying this is the significant point that 'selling' is an important creative act in many aspects of human life. At the end of the day, a vibrant future Christchurch is something that we all want to believe in.

Design and democracy

Barnaby Bennett

Barnaby is an award-winning designer and has worked on community architecture projects in Christchurch, Australia, Colombo, Samoa, Vancouver and Johannesburg. Since moving to Christchurch in early 2012 Barnaby has supported a number of projects such as the Festival of Transitional Architecture and co-edited *Christchurch: The Transitional City Part IV.* He is currently completing his PhD thesis, through UTS, Sydney, which examines the relationship between the public and temporary architecture.

It might seem strange to suggest that there is an important relationship between how we are governed and how we imagine and make buildings. By drawing these two things together I am not calling for designers to enter into representative politics (although there are some notable examples of this, such as the young architect mayor who transformed Curitiba in Brazil), or, more frighteningly, for politicians to become more involved in the design of buildings and public spaces (which rarely ends well). Rather this article will suggest that there is a common glue that is frequently misunderstood – and all too often feared – by both designers and law makers that translates between design and democracy: the public. It is this misunderstanding and fear that has, I suggest, led to the need to sell the plan to the public, rather than it being something collaboratively developed with the people of Christchurch.

In the 1920s the great American philosopher John Dewey and bright young journalist Walter Lippmann engaged in an extended argument about how democracy might work in an increasingly complex and interdependent world.[1] More than ten years of discussion led them to a shared belief that the public is composed of many smaller publics that emerge (and dissolve) in response to issues and problems that relate to them. We don't need to look fa in Christchurch to see this, as groups and publics have formed in response to the many problems of EQC (Earthquake Commission), affordable housing, rock fall, red zoning, asbestos, demolitions, elections and of course the various plans developed for the central city.

While it is easy to see each of these issues as a failing of government, it is unrealistic to expect our institutions to seamlessly recover from such a vast and devastating event. After disaster publics form to supplement a government no longer able to deliver the normal services that make our cities, like roads, water, sewerage and schools.

This counter movement might explain the feeling of temporary utopia that developed after the quakes – the freedom, support and care shown for each other in the absence of the systems we normally depend upon. This mirrors a comment from Dorothy Day about people in San Francisco after the 1906 earthquake: 'While the crisis lasted, people loved each other.'[2] In these moments of localised governance, design and democracy collapse into specific and necessary actions such as removing a chimney or closing a road. Naturally there is a freedom in this response, but this also involves the separation of immediate needs from unwanted consequences (sewerage in the river is temporarily okay; personal property becomes less important than human safety; polluting fires are allowed). It's a state that can't continue and would become destructive if it did without consideration of these and other unknown consequences.

To be an effective designer or politician requires the management of unknowable consequences; a decision is made (often forced) and because we can't anticipate all the things in the world (earthquakes, storms, economic and social movements) it creates new issues and new problems, and subsequent new publics are produced. After the quakes publics in Christchurch formed in response to the issues that concerned them, and demonstrated extraordinary capacity for care, inventiveness and intelligence in regards to these issues. This reflects Dewey and Lippmann's conception of the public as not just one homogenous unit whose consent is needed to progress, but rather as a series of interested, vested and increasingly expert groups. In the Christchurch recovery, how then did the government make use of these publics and work with the extensive knowledge embedded within them when developing its plans for the recovery process?

In the months after the quake, the Christchurch City Council (CCC) was asked by Minister Brownlee to prepare a plan for the central city. They embarked on a process that started with the Share an Idea campaign, and finished later that year with the submission of the Draft Central City Plan (CCP) to the Minister. The CCP was far from perfect: there wasn't enough consultation with specific user groups; there was insufficient detail in the final document; and there wasn't enough knowledge of the financial risks and costs of the plan to see if it was feasible. It did however engage in a meaningful, respectful, and ongoing manner with the people of Christchurch, who were suffering from a continuing swarm of earthquakes with further damage to their homes and city at the time.

In early 2012 the Minister announced that he thought the Council's plans were good in principle but the specifics needed reconsidering, which led to the rapid development of the 100-day plan or Christchurch Central Recovery Plan (CCRP). Soon after the launch of this new plan I went to a public 'information session' presented by staff from Canterbury Earthquake Recovery Authority (CERA) and the designer Don Miskell. It was during a weekday so the majority of the audience was elderly. It was telling that the session was treated by the government staff as an opportunity to explain the plan, not to take any information back from the extensive knowledge of the people who had lived in and created the city for decades previously.

These sessions could easily have been reframed, and at the end of the two hours CERA could have had a series of meaningful notes giving feedback on their ideas, and the people could have felt like they were being included and listened to. Instead questions were met with defensive answers and contributions offered by citizens seemingly ignored. At the end of the session I asked two questions. Firstly, given the scale of the suggested projects, I asked if there would be any international peer review of the plan. My second question was 'Would there be any opportunities in the future for citizens of Christchurch to engage with the new Blueprint?'. The answer to both questions was no. True to their word, by mid-2014 there has been no further public consultation on the plan and no external peer review.

Given the response of the public during the major quakes, and the enthusiasm for engagement shown during CCC consultation procedures, it is odd that the government decided that they would lead the development of the central city by removing the public from an ongoing say in the issues developing and emerging from the city rebuilds. The Minister has, on a number of occasions, strongly rejected the notion that the design of the Blueprint and its implementation are the result of processes that did not and do not engage with the community. The CCC's 2011 Share an Idea campaign is cited as the consultation, and we have no good reason to question the Minister or CEO Roger Sutton when they say the principles developed from the Share an Idea campaign led the formation of the CCRP.

The question is not whether the plan is based on the needs and wishes of people in Christchurch, but whether the public is being given the opportunity to participate and engage with the city plan as it inevitably develops in response to the changing urban environment and with the emergence of new unanticipated consequences of other actions.

It's easy to misunderstand public engagement as a symbolic obligation best bypassed when urgency requires it, and certainly it is reasonable to revise the methods and modes of engagement in the unusual and unpredictable circumstances after disaster. There are many new forms of citizen engagement being created around the world at the moment: online tools such as Loomio are enabling people to converse about complex issues without needing to be in the same place; there is an international movement in citizen-led placemaking; in Auckland the large scale Unitary Plan is developing with significant involvement of citizens.

There is an obvious political temptation to 'show leadership' and to 'take control of a situation', but personally I don't see much leadership in using the extraordinary power of government to take decision-making away from the local council, and to decide not to engage with the people of the city about the plans you then develop – particularly when these plans involve using the full force of the government's power to forcefully purchase large amounts of the central city, and to bypass normal procedures to demolish scores of buildings. There is an unfortunate tendency to think that we need to choose between benevolent dictatorship and complete consensus, when there is a rich spectrum of options between these two poles.

This removal of the public from the procedures of planning and design can only be understood as being based on either a fear and distrust of what that engagement might produce, or an ignorance of how these procedures can be done meaningfully and quickly (especially with new digital technologies). Whether based on distrust or ignorance the effect is the same and I believe this removal has had negative impacts on three particularly important aspects of the rebuild: the psychology of the people post-quake, the trust in the political processes and the quality of the resulting places.

The Prime Minister's Chief Science Advisor Sir Peter Gluckman wrote a letter in May 2011, soon after the quakes. He acknowledged the very real tension between the need to show progress and the complexity of making planning decisions: 'In every disaster there is an inevitable tension between the desire for an immediate response and the need for planning (by multiple layers of authority) and risk reduction.' But he was quite clear about the psychosocial risks of excluding the people from the decision-making processes saying 'the key issue is a psychological sense of empowerment'. While council procedures like Share an Idea, campaigns like All Right? and the rare pieces of CERA-led consultation such as with the large playground are to be celebrated, they do not mitigate the very real consequences of denying the populace their say in the ongoing recreation of their city. 'It follows that, from the psychosocial perspective, those involved in directing the recovery should create governance structures that understand and actively include community participation and enhance individual and community resilience.'[3]

There are also political consequences of excluding the public that I think reveal a naivety about city governance and urban issues. The CCRP is a huge document with consequences that span decades and will cost billions of dollars. Rightly, this level of consequence was examined and approved by Cabinet with advice from Treasury and other high levels of government. Yet the inability of people and interested parties in the city to participate and comment on specific details and particular projects leads to an unproductive binary of either supporting the plan or outright rejecting it. This escalates the discussion from very specific and productive feedback on particular projects to a simplistic political narrative of either supporting or not supporting the Minister and the Government.

I am not asking for anything unusual; it's not radical to suggest that excluding people is disempowering. The Local Government Act that the CERA legislation overrules is quite clear about the obligation to consult: 'persons who will or may be affected by, or have an interest in, the decision or matter should be provided by the local authority with reasonable access to relevant information in a manner and format that is appropriate to the preferences and needs of those persons', and 'the views presented to the local authority should be received by the local authority with an open mind and should be given by the local authority, in making a decision, due consideration'.[4]

The government funds the 'Quality Planning Website', which was developed to assist quality and timely developments. It clearly states 'While early consultation is important, councils should approach consultation as an ongoing iterative process through all stages of a plan development exercise. Make sure this is not a one-off event or series of disjointed encounters, and not perceived as a token effort.'[5] It is this ongoing, iterative, and multiple-event form of consultation that has been notably lacking in the recreation of the central city.

Lastly, and perhaps most importantly for the long-term health of Christchurch and its people, the removal of public input into the designs of the city, and the anchor projects, risks having negative effects on the quality of these projects. In some cases, like the Avon-Ōtākaro project, this is quite obvious – $100 million of public money for a huge new park that spreads through the city 30 metres either side of the Avon with almost no consultation. At mid-2014 work has begun on this project and after the original British firm was removed and a redesign initiated, the public still has no idea what it is going to look like. This is quite unbelievable, and makes a joke of the Minister's claim that the CCDU is operating based on 'international best practice'.[6]

In other instances, the scale and type of projects chosen seem at odds with expert and public opinion. The light rail proposed in the CCC plan was judged by the Minister to be a luxury and dropped from the Blueprint and subsequent transport plan, yet a large inner city covered stadium costing a similar amount to the light rail was included. This isn't to say we need to poll the residents to see which project they favour, rather it is to acknowledge that the hundreds of thousands of people that live in this place probably have some thoughts on these projects that might be helpful, and that a meaningful discussion of the issues involved is only enabled when a public is able to form around the issues that concern it.

We live in a democracy based on a principle of political representation; we elect politicians to represent us. This is complicated in Christchurch because the politicians making the big decisions are elected to represent all of New Zealand and there's a risk that they make decisions that favour this constituency over the people of Christchurch, as the two things are not always synonymous. For example it might be important to push the rebuild along to keep the national economy going even if it risks making rushed decisions, or making the rebuild look like its in better shape than it is for an upcoming election. These things may or may not be happening, but they are mechanisms that are enabled by the particular political setup. The fact is a politician wouldn't be doing her job properly if she wasn't prioritising the national economy or the success of her party. It's a set up that means for a minister to do her job properly (short-term goal), she might have to make decisions that are not in the best interests of Christchurch (long-term goal). If the agencies making the large decisions in Christchurch were both more independent from central government, and had a stronger public representation, this wouldn't be a problem.

But perhaps the most dangerous risk is much more subtle than this. In any big building or urban project it is critical to identify who the project is for, the client. A client is the person or organisation paying for the project but also the people that will use it. In the case of the CCRP the client is clearly the public of Christchurch (and other organisations such as the CCC and Ngāi Tahu). If the public is the main client, who then represents the public when important design decisions are being made? In the procedures and processes that have followed the launch of the 100-day plan it really isn't clear who is representing the public. If the public is denied access to these processes, and information is blocked, then how do we know parties are not being captured by other political or economic interests? It makes it much harder for the designers to make long-term and innovative moves in favour of the public good if the public is not there to defend these interests.

A system has been setup that enables this sort of capture to happen. Allowing the public an ongoing and iterative role in the design process (as the CCC does with its projects such as the Central Library and Town Hall) not only allows for the articulation and expression of difficult issues, it also keeps the needs of the public in the foreground of the design process. The removal of the public puts designers in a difficult situation; if they don't toe the line on a particular issue they risk losing the job or not getting future projects. I think the larger grouping of architecture and design firms in Christchurch have failed to realise the collective threat of this, and rather than approaching these issues as a profession, and lobbying for more public engagement and more transparency, they have instead chosen to prioritise their own firms by keeping their heads below the parapet. This strategy is counterproductive and does little to improve the design quality of the city.

With this article I don't mean to suggest that there are groups consciously developing plans fundamentally at odds with the mood of the public, or that engagement with the public is ever a tidy or easy process. Rather I worry New Zealand has developed political and design cultures that misunderstand the powerful role that publics play in extrapolating the complex issues involved in a project and the deeper values and motives that lie underneath big decisions that are revealed through public discussion. If the quakes taught us anything surely it is that dormant within the public is an extraordinary capacity for hard work, imagination, ingenuity and care for each other. It is sad that these characteristics that were so recently expressed here in Christchurch have not been allowed to continue into the ongoing planning of the new city. Most worryingly it also suggests an erosion of the trust that is needed between the public and its representatives for democracy to function. Our cities are not going to grow into the great places we all want them to be without it.

After the quakes we saw what an extraordinary resource the public is, so it's curious that these same groups are considered of little value to the major projects developed by the government and designers in their plans. The CCDU's Blueprint required selling; a large planning document like this is pointless if it doesn't convince the many important clients, local businesses, international investors, arts groups, local councils and iwi that it is worth supporting and committing to. With the benefit of hindsight it now seems obvious that rather than facilitating a rapid recovery, the exclusion of the public from the ongoing development of the plan has hindered the recovery. Luckily cities are never finished and there is time to learn from our mistakes.

The Enervation Precinct

Stephen Judd

Stephen Judd moved to Christchurch from Wellington in 2012 to set up the Christchurch branch of a large NZ ICT company. In his spare time he plays capoeira, dabbles in politics and rides bicycles.

On 3 May 2014 the *Press* reported that EPIC (a campus-style development for local innovation-based companies) had given up on the designated Innovation Precinct in the government-planned Christchurch rebuild: 'A key tenant of the central-city innovation precinct has "given up" and pulled out of the project, saying delays and overpriced land make the project infeasible.'[1] The original EPIC Sanctuary was the right idea at the right time, and it is sad that the founders could see no way forward here.

My personal experience is in the ICT sector. In that sector, startups and small companies play a significant role. But even with mature companies, we all have some things in common: we don't meet clients at our premises much; if they're in the same city we go to them or meet in cafes, but often they're elsewhere anyway. We don't need specialised fitout in our premises. And we employ a lot of younger people, especially in startups with their greater risks.

And that means that we tend to hang about central business district fringes, in the lowest tier of rental space, and former light industrial areas, where it's cheap and young people can find the kinds of cool businesses to serve them that prosper in a low-rent environment. Look at Wellington: the bulk of startups are upstairs in the side streets of Dixon, Allen, Blair, Tory, Cuba etc., away from the Golden Mile, or in shabby suites in the least desirable buildings downtown. No doubt the next wave of high-tech in Wellington will be in Newtown.

This is why I suspect the very idea of an innovation precinct was dubious at best. In the words of Eric Raymond's famous essay on software development 'The Cathedral and the Bazaar', 'Release early. Release often. And listen to your customers.'[2] In more explicitly relevant terms, Richard Gabriel wrote that '. . . it is often undesirable to go for the right thing first. It is better to get half of the right thing available so that it spreads like a virus. Once people are hooked on it, take the time to improve it to 90 per cent of the right thing.'[3]

Cheap and cheerful premises sit nicely in a technology culture that has been taken over in the last couple of decades by 'agile' methods, rapid and repeated refinement of crude initial prototypes and a philosophy of continuous improvements that respond to feedback from users.

The Innovation Precinct concept confuses correlation with causation. High tech areas evolved in other cities where there was cheap space close to research institutions. Then, over time, those areas prospered with their inhabitants. But the shiny office parks and palatial refits that have been built by the most successful inhabitants of Silicon Valley and San Francisco are the signs of their success, not the cause of it.

What would have made more sense is applying the Re:START Mall concept to office space. Amongst the clothing stores, cafes and bars, put up prefab offices and increase the diversity of the area and the hours of the day it's busy.

Because of the earthquakes, Christchurch lost, along with everything else, the run-down premises that are the natural home for emerging businesses that don't need to impress customers with their facilities. That's what your tech startup wants (and also your small design firms, decent ethnic restaurants, grungy bars, specialist tool stockists and other animals of that part of the civic ecosystem). What's needed is an old-school, low-rent area – precisely what we cannot have in a plan where the raison d'etre is preserving high land values.

(How has that value been preserved, by the way? There are no market transactions to demonstrate it, no cash flows to justify it, no intangible amenities. If it's the prospect of a future that provides value, that future is failing.)

The rebuild has a choice. On our bulldozed earth we can try to replant and nurture a forest, with a diverse ecosystem, that will be self-sustaining and ultimately go its own way. Or we can plant a formal garden, with monotonous beds in rectangular plots, trying to make things grow that don't want to and suppressing unwanted and unstoppable pests.

The whole idea of an expensive shiny Innovation Precinct is flawed from the get-go. I expect it was someone's pet idea, and the reason the plans are so late is that everyone knows it won't work but it can't be killed. I feel this way about the precinct idea in general, but the tech sector is my turf and I know that particular part of the plan isn't going to work.

Cyril Northcote Parkinson was a naval historian who achieved fame in an unlikely way, through a satirical book *Parkinson's Law*, which described institutional pathologies that are still quite recognisable today. In the chapter 'Plans and Plants' he claims that perfectly designed premises are the sign of a moribund institution: 'It is now known that a perfection of planned layout is achieved only by institutions on the point of collapse . . . perfection of planning is a symptom of decay. During a period of exciting discovery or progress there is no time to plan the perfect headquarters. The time for that comes later, when all the important work has been done. Perfection, we know, is finality; and finality is death.'[4]

It was and still is funny stuff. I can't help thinking of it as I contemplate the shiny, purpose-built futures proposed for us in precinct plans. In extreme cases, Parkinson writes, the institution might die young before the completion of their perfect building, as in the case of the headquarters of the League of Nations.

Real plans change. You learn new things, the environment shifts and responds to what you do. External and unpredictable events take place, and you change your plan accordingly. Let's hope that's what happens now. Otherwise what we have isn't a plan, just a fantasy getting further and further away from reality.

Planning documents

It is perhaps inevitable that the people of Christchurch have had many and varied planning documents to consider since the quakes. Ranging from Council-led local masterplans to large regional resource and transport documents, these plans are sometimes carefully coordinated, sometimes sequential; some supersede others; and at times they overlap or are contradictory. Prominent amongst the planning documents are Council's Draft Central City Plan (CCP), the CCDU's Christchurch Central Recovery Plan (CCRP) and associated Blueprint spatial plan, local masterplans, the Land Use Recovery Plan (LURP), the District Plan, the Accessible City transport plan and the Christchurch City Council's latest three-year plan.

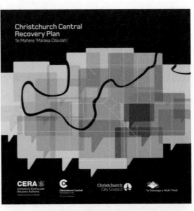

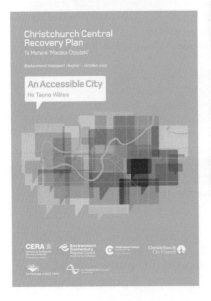

[1–6]

Great plan, but where are the investors?

John McCrone

John is a senior journalist at the *Press* in Christchurch and has written extensively about different post-quake issues including analyses of the Blueprint and the Innovation Precinct. A version of this article first appeared in the *Press* on 8 March 2014.

When feelings run high, judgments tend to be black and white. So no surprise that views on Christchurch's central city Blueprint recovery plan range from 'an utter balls up' to 'nicely on track'. Warwick Isaacs, director of the Christchurch Central Development Unit (CCDU), the government agency charged with delivering the Blueprint, spreads his latest map across the table. Look, he says. It is February 2014. About a year and a half since the Blueprint was first announced in July 2012 and there are now 118 building projects progressed at least as far as the architects' sketches and consent applications. So plenty of action happening.

Slippages in the schedule? Among the seventeen anchor projects, only the Metro Sports Facility has lost about nine months replies Isaacs.

It is the same story from landscape architect Don Miskell who led the original 100-day Blueprint design team as a hired consultant and is now the CCDU's design and planning manager. We are standing on the freshly grassed East Frame, the seven downtown blocks between Manchester and Madras Streets that the Government took to give the rebuilt central city a sharply defined margin. It was talked of as a green space land bank, a clever move to prop up post-quake property values by creating an artificial land shortage in the city core. But quicker than expected, the Government is turning around to sell it off in nine 'super lots' designated for inner city housing.

Perhaps 750 apartments in complexes of four to six storeys, says Miskell. About $300 million in investment with a 50-metre-wide ribbon of parkland and cycleway running down the centre, connecting the Avon River to the planned Innovation Precinct.

Imagine, he beams. Another whole loop out of Hagley Park and around the reborn city for the joggers and dog walkers. Another big step to achieving the goal of 20,000 people living within the four avenues – the 6 per cent of the city population that international research shows is the critical mass.

Isn't this the kind of bold future for Christchurch we talked about when the Blueprint was launched? So give it time, says Miskell. The success of the Blueprint cannot be judged right now and probably not even in five years. It will only be looking back in 20 or 30 years that we will know for sure.

The Blueprint or Christchurch Central Recovery Plan (CCRP) certainly was a bold choice. Following the February 2011 earthquake, the Government passed the Canterbury Earthquake Recovery Act (CER Act), which required Christchurch City Council (CCC) to produce a recovery plan for the devastated central business district (CBD).

After hasty public consultation, the council delivered a two-volume draft in nine months. The first volume was an aspirational vision of a 'city in a garden', the second a bumper manual of planning rules designed to enforce a look and feel on the streetscapes. These volumes then sat on Earthquake Recovery Minister Gerry Brownlee's desk for seven months until it was decided Christchurch deserved something more ambitious, more interventionist.

Miskell and a team of local and international experts were recruited to produce a rewrite in 100 days. The CBD is a blank canvas they were told. Knock up a plan that gives us a proper twenty-first century city.

Looking back reminds us how a disaster is inevitably a roller coaster of emotions. The Council was tasked to produce its masterplan while the city was still burying its dead, still experiencing the further destruction of major aftershocks in June and December 2011. Confusion ruled. Hope was tentative. The Blueprint by contrast caught the wave of optimism when it was realised the city was well insured, the local economy had not collapsed as first feared, remarkably few people had taken flight.

The Canterbury earthquakes were a huge natural disaster. The damage equated to 20 per cent of national GDP (annual gross domestic product). In comparison, Japan's 2011 tsunami was 4 per cent and the United States' 2005 Hurricane Katrina just 1 per cent.

So the Government really did need to worry that Christchurch, the second biggest city, might simply implode from the shock. Yet it didn't. And then among those in charge of the recovery, it should not be underestimated what a psychological impact the construction of a temporary rugby stadium at Addington had.

Completed in a heroic 100 days in time for the opening game of the 2012 Super Rugby season, a patriotic alliance between the government and the New Zealand construction industry – after that, there seemed every possibility of the authorities dreaming big and building back better. Thus if it is about lessons and conclusions, lesson number one of the Christchurch recovery is that plenty of feelings were always in play. Mood affected decision making.

And yet when it comes to the Blueprint, it is significant that it did not emerge looking like a complete 'back of an envelope' exercise. Which leads to lesson two. In a crisis like the Canterbury earthquakes, a vacuum is created that sucks in pre-existing 'good ideas'.

It turned out almost every element of the Blueprint was a proposal that had been kicking around in someone's mind for a long time.

The government had a national convention centre strategy. Rugby authorities had been agitating for a covered stadium. There was a view within the arts community that the Town Hall auditorium was too large, its James Hay theatre too cramped, the symphony orchestra and Christchurch School of Music could do with premises in a precinct in the heart of city.

So it continued. The QEII swimming pool was too far out as a competitive facility. The central library ought to be bigger as the single most visited public space. The Avon River had long been overshadowed by office buildings. The inner city needed cycleways, laneways, 'active' street frontages, concealed car parking.

Miskell confesses the anchor project list just about wrote itself. The team's job was to fit all the pieces on the board. The only real innovation was the adoption of a green frame to give the city core a shape and protect its property values – an idea coming from some bright spark seconded from Treasury.

Lesson two also happens to be lesson three. With a recovery, pre-existing projects pop out of the woodwork. But so can pre-existing political problems.

Historical tensions between CCC and the central city business community, and between local and national government, both quickly bubbled to the surface to affect the Blueprint.

Prior to the earthquakes, a long running struggle over the future of the city had been going on with business leaders feeling the council had become an inward looking bureaucracy, stuck in an eternal planning loop and favouring certain developers.

The bailing out of bankrupt developer Dave Henderson – the Council's purchase of five of his properties with no independent valuation for $17 million in 2008 – led to open warfare with then Mayor Bob Parker and chief executive Tony Marryatt.

However relationships had long been fraught. Harcourts' Stephen Collins, a property investor and past president of the Canterbury Employers' Chamber of Commerce, spent eight years on the Central City Mayoral Forum.

'But the only thing we managed to do was get some new tiles, some seats and another tree put into Cashel Mall,' he grumbles.

There was a distrust on both sides and so a rather arm's length approach to any dealings.

Then there was the story of the Government and CCC. The context there was the Council was plainly overwhelmed by the sheer scale of the disaster.

As one former councillor admits privately, New Zealand local government is a creature of statute. It doesn't get to make laws but instead has to follow law that have deliberately been framed to restrict executive power.

'For local government to wake up in the morning and put the jug on, just about requires you to go out and consult. So you can add six weeks to anything because the 2002 Act puts that obligation on us.'

In retrospect says the councillor, the Government should probably have come in and taken over, frozen the Council's capital spending budget and formed some collective body to work through the strategy for the recovery.

But this was too politically sensitive a step. The Government had only just removed the democratically elected regional council, Environment Canterbury, because it was not moving fast enough on water and irrigation plans.

So instead, the Government tried to wrap a government department around the council. It formed the Canterbury Earthquake Recovery Authority (CERA) and then its offspring, the CCDU. Another arm's length relationship was created that became a prime problem for the Blueprint. So the scene was set. Big ambitions coupled to fractured relationships. A plan that could be cobbled together at speed because there was already a pre-quake wish list of projects, but also an underlying political fragmentation that was never properly addressed.

The result could be predicted. And it is what those closest to the process are saying is largely the case. The Blueprint itself is great, but the implementation is where it is breaking down. Christchurch investment banker Tim Howe, co-founder of Ocean Partners, says in baldest terms, the task of the Blueprint was simple – to connect capital to a plan. And to date, the results have been dismal.

Howe, who represents potential US and European investments of around $100 million, has had project after project tip over. 'The frustrating thing is we haven't been able to spend one dollar in development so far.'

And big names have been leaving. The Triangle Centre's Michael Ogilvie-Lee who had plans for a $100 million shop and office complex in the Blueprint's Retail Precinct, abruptly sold up and pulled out, saying the going had become too hard.

Others, like Harcourts' Collins, are vocal of their unhappiness. 'If I could go back a year or eighteen months, knowing what was going to happen, I would've probably just taken my money and invested somewhere else,' he says.

Howe says despite Isaacs' bland assurances of developments charging ahead, private sector investment has stalled largely because of uncertainty over the actual detail of the public sector anchor projects.

For the first half of 2013, the Government and CCC were locked in a protracted closed door wrangle over cost-sharing – the question of who was going to pay for facilities like the arts precinct or rugby stadium.

The Council's argument was it didn't ask for the ambitious Blueprint so why should it spend a dollar more than had been set aside for its own original CBD masterplan – the one the Government so humiliatingly rejected? Not sorting out the politics at the start became a serious source of friction.

But there were other uncertainty-inducing delays too. In particular the transport chapter of the Blueprint, An Accessible City, was slow arriving. It took until October 2013 – some further fifteen months – for the CCDU to confirm even the general outline of street layouts and parking rules.

Collins says the entire Blueprint approach seemed cumbersome – guaranteed to bog down. The convention centre was put out to market as a single giant precinct project. The Government wanted to attract a bidder who would build the surrounding hotels and shops as well.

As a result, says Collins, the rest of 2014 will be taken up just in parties replying to a 400-page request for information. 'I've heard that for the two consortia still interested, it's going to cost them over $1 million each just to come up with their proposals.'

Collins says if the Government had hired an architect and got on with it, the convention centre could have been open by the end of 2014. 'If you have a centre that can seat 2000 people, the hotels will come, the shops will come. They're not stupid.'

Another cumbersome bit of process was the CCDU's decision to attempt to force the agglomeration of commercial development in the four-block Retail Precinct around Ballantynes department store.

By requiring the submission of outline development plans covering at least 7500 sqm – about a whole block – the hope was that large investors would step in with comprehensive designs.

This worked with a property owner like The Terrace's Antony Gough, who through family holdings did have control over a whole block. But it became a mess of battles on other sites where a collection of individuals wanted to determine their own destinies.

So there is a picture of a general lack of clarity says Collins. 'Everyone wasn't aboard the same bus.' The consequence of too much arm's length dealing.

There is always a damned if you do, damned if you don't, aspect to complex reality.

It has been pointed out that one of the ironies of the Blueprint is the Government tried to do commercial property owners a favour by propping up their land values through the Green Frame. Yet then the complaint became development was being paralysed by the central city's high property prices.

Likewise, the business community appears to wish the Government had used its CER Act powers for still more dramatic market interventions.

Collins reveals that early on, CERA was urged to impose a moratorium on commercial building consents outside the CBD to prevent areas like Victoria Street taking off in the way they did.

To give the Blueprint time to get into gear, it seemed obvious the Government ought to have locked down the rest of the city, despite the kicking and screaming this would have provoked.

The same with the faltering Retail Precinct. Howe says the CCDU had powers of compulsory purchase. It could have banged heads to break the ownership deadlocks. Instead – worried by already having the CER Act challenged in court – the Government hung back in the hope 'the market would decide'.

Those in charge were often on a loser no matter which choice they made. Yet it comes back to the fact that if a disaster recovery is going to strike out with bold ambition, this has to be matched by astute process. And here attention turns to the people and culture of the CCDU.

One of the stories of 2013 was a letter sent to Gerry Brownlee's office by three of the city's key influencers – Bruce Irvine, chair of council-owned Christchurch City Holdings Limited; Tony Sewell, chief executive of Ngāi Tahu Property; and business investor Humphry Rolleston.

The trio called for Isaacs and his CCDU team to be replaced by property professionals with international experience. Their argument was that a former Timaru town clerk like Isaacs, or a landscape architect like Miskell, could not have the suitable skills for the job.

The Blueprint demanded world-class procurement specialists – civil servants with an investment banking background and used to handling public-private partnerships. The ability to structure a deal and then step back to let the winning bid deliver.

It was implied the CCDU was instead staffed by risk-averse bureaucrats whose instinct was to micro-manage the detail. Whenever in doubt, stop and study the plans some more.

Howe and Collins agree it fits with what they see. Howe says the CCDU was meant to be a facilitating agency but has ended up looking like a doing agency. 'They stayed in command and control mode. They never made the transition to collaboration.'

Collins says the CCDU has become swollen with bodies in the attempt to get the Blueprint moving. Yet the people that get hired are not those with market experience – who understand how capital works.

The ease with which the Blueprint came together might have led to an underestimation of how difficult it would be to make happen.

And there were always alternatives to running the rebuild through a government department like the CCDU.

Collins says the Government could have done nothing and left it to the market – simply let CCC do the anchor projects it felt it could afford and private capital put its own buildings back up.

The speed at which office developments are shooting up outside the Blueprint – in Victoria Street and Addington – demonstrate that central Christchurch could have been half rebuilt by 2014.

Others remark on the success of the Stronger Christchurch Infrastructure Rebuild Team (SCIRT), the alliance formed between the authorities and the construction industry to fix the city's broken roads and pipes.

There, all the parties have been around the same table making decisions. There, an experienced Australian in Fulton Hogan's Duncan Gibb was flown over to be the general manager.

History played its part again. The New Zealand Transport Agency had pre-quake experience of industry alliances. The construction firms had also just proved themselves over the temporary rugby stadium. So a basis of trust existed and different choices were made.

In summary, the plan was good but the key players were left dealing with each at arm's length. The result is much of the steam has leaked out of the central city rebuild.

The talk has become of bananas and donuts. With the Blueprint at a standstill, the city's lawyers, accountants and other prime tenants have been signing long leases on new buildings outside its Green Frame perimeter.

Canterbury Employers' Chamber of Commerce chief executive Peter Townsend says the CBD is looking like it will end up a banana curve with three hubs in Victoria Street, the city and Addington.

Others more pessimistically predict a donut ring, with very little ending up back in the central city at all.

Townsend says there are calls to scrap the Blueprint, give up on its high ambitions, and let property owners go back to rebuilding on an individual commercial basis. But he believes instead the only choice is to go bigger.

The strategy for Christchurch has to be to focus on growing its population and economy to the point where it can afford its convention centres and stadiums, where there is the commercial energy to refill the central city with shops, offices and people.

Howe agrees, saying in the long run the Blueprint will happen as imagined because much of it is natural – what Christchurch would have been doing over the next few decades in any case. The earthquakes were just an opportunity to accelerate change.

But Howe says the stumbling implementation means that at least one investment cycle has been missed now. Too many potential tenants have signed five- to ten-year leases outside the Blueprint and so cannot even think of a return until the 2020s.

So as Miskell suggests, look back in 20 or 30 years' time and the Blueprint will be remembered as a brave plan. The thousand gaps will have been filled. A central city with excellent bones will have been fleshed out. But until then, there could be quite a few thin years.

Anchor project billboards

A significant amount of central city land has been purchased by government agencies to build the large anchor projects such as the Frame (including the Margaret Mahy Family Playground), the Metro Sports Facility, the Breathe Residential Demonstration Project and Convention Centre Precinct. As the sites have been cleared of buildings and earthquake damage, large billboards promoting the projects have begun to emerge across the city. The first wave of billboards concentrated on key information; the second wave has emphasised the future vibe and experience of the completed anchor projects. These billboards serve as a bridge between the various planning documents and physical spaces in the city as the latter undergo dramatic reconfiguration.

[1–6]

Valuing everyday life

Claes Caldenby

Claes Caldenby is an architect. He has been the editor of *Arkitektur*, the Swedish review of architecture, since 1977. His main interest has been in twentieth-century architecture, especially Swedish post-war developments, ranging from the social and political conditions of planning and building to an interest in the nurturing of an architectural culture. Since 1998 Caldenby has been a professor in the theory and history of architecture at Chalmers University of Technology. He has written some 70 books.

> The award goes to: Christchurch Recovery Plan by Gehl Architects, Denmark, for its plan for rebuilding the New Zealand town after the 2011 earthquake. It retains the existing city grid while limiting building heights, reducing car traffic and making the city greener, all based on a "social fabric fortified by catastrophe" and a diligent community engagement programme thus rebuilding the urban fabric and the community.

Such was the motivation of the jury for giving Christchurch City Council in conjunction with Gehl Architects one of four prizes in the competition Architecture of Necessity organised by Swedish Virserum Art Museum in 2013.[1] Architecture of Necessity was an appeal for sustainable community building that was launched internationally in 2009 and has since developed into an exhibition and triennial. It emphasises an architecture that is responsible, diligent, sustainable, just and open. This involves professional knowledge and expertise, proper long-term planning, acknowledging everybody's right to the city and remaining open to citizens' participation in it over time. The jury found these aspects well fulfilled by the Draft Central City Plan, which demonstrated sustainability not only in the technical sense of ecology but most importantly in the social and cultural senses. Among the 140 contributions to the Architecture of Necessity competition, from single buildings to planning proposals, Christchurch immediately stood out as the most inspiring planning project.

The Draft Central City Plan is a very touching and consoling example of opportunities found in a post-catastrophe situation. There is much to be learned from this for the rest of the world. Jan Gehl's simple theory 'Life first, then space, then buildings' is strongly based in another post-catastrophe situation – the 1970s aftermath of 1960s late-modern urbanism. Gehl's insistence that cities are for people is something that we need to be reminded of all the time even in Scandinavia, the origin of his ideas. In his own hometown Copenhagen the recent large-scale development of Ørestaden has been described by Danish architects not as 'life between buildings', referring to the title of Gehl's first book from 1971, but as 'death between buildings'.

Gehl Architects describe their work with the recovery plan as a learning process for all involved, both professionals and the public. They came to Christchurch with indepth experience from similar, if less dramatic, tasks. The Share an Idea campaign is in itself an example of Gehl's 'Life first' principle. People expressed the wish to go back to basics. The future Christchurch outlined in the campaign is not futuristic – it is about a city life where people can recognise themselves, according to David Sim and Simon Goddard, the architects behind this project.

The difficulty with city planning is finding the balance between the hunt for an outward identity and valuing the everyday life of its citizens. This is strange, since achieving a good everyday life would make a city attractive to visitors of all sorts, from tourists through to professionals and politicians looking for models to bring back home.

The promotion of a good everyday life for a city's citizens involves sustainability (ecological and social), urban density and subsequently, urban life. There is no contradiction between a green city and a compact centre. Research shows that cities that are both dense and have good access to parks are the most attractive. And density is also green in the sense of ecologically sustainable, with less energy use and transportation. There is also no contradiction between compactness and an identity that is low-rise. Dense-low makes sense in an earthquake-prone area; it respects the heritage buildings, fosters urban life and can give efficient floor area ratio. A mixed city is both a sustainable and an accessible city, where visitors are welcome but where the basics are about a liveable city for all stages of life. An accessible city should not only be accessible for walking, cycling and public transport, but also for everyone, irrespective of their class, gender, age or culture. That makes a just, open and thus socially sustainable city.

Acknowledging the complexity of building a city is to show responsibility and diligence. Building a city is a collective effort, as Christchurch has shown through the Share an Idea campaign and subsequent Draft Central City Plan. Nobody would wish to be forced to start anew, like Christchurch had to. But given that fate the city has seized the opportunity to build a city for the twenty-first century. The world is watching what is being done. If the rebuild is carried out in the participatory and unpretentious way in which it was started, it will become an international model.

A message and a messenger

Matthew Galloway

Matthew Galloway is a lecturer at the Otago Polytechnic School of Design. His practice is often concerned with examining visual identities and the implications of branding. In 2011 he began publishing *The Silver Bulletin* – a quarterly art and design publication based in Christchurch – for which he fulfils the role of editor and designer.

'Place branding increasingly stands as both a visual practice and a modality c governance. That is what makes it slippery. There is much more to branding than a logo or style. It is a manifestation of power.'
– Metahaven, *Uncorporate Identity*[1]

Design, certainly graphic design, is a messenger. It exists as a façade – a way in. It is the means of communicating a message, rather than the message itself. When done well, the two (the message and its means of delivery) can be hard to separate. They play off each other, and meaning is illuminated in a way only manageable through visual form. Usually this relies on a strong message – content that doesn't need dressing up, that simply needs representation in a way that is visually astute or 'in keeping', if you like. But how often does this kind of clarity exist in such a process, especially one that involves the murky world of state branding, or the identity of a city?

The hegemonic nature of stamping a trademark symbol or narrative on a place leads to questions of power: who is controlling the narrative, and to what end? From this follows a further series of interlocking questions around perception of place. Can a branding exercise ever *really* alter how a place is perceived from both inside and outside? Most likely, the success of such a process relies little on how a brand might look, or the story it is trying to tell, but more so on how wide the gap is between the perception of a place via its brand narrative and perception gained from a firsthand, on-the-ground experience of that place. In any situation where this gap is significant, the roles of the message and the messenger start to blur, as the latter attempts to fill gaps in absence of the real thing.

On the surface, the Share an Idea campaign that former Christchurch Mayor Bob Parker launched on 5 May 2011 was all about messages. A mass forum facilitated by the Christchurch City Council (CCC), it consisted of Post-it notes and comment boards filled with messages from the people of Christchurch concerning what they wanted their new city to be. The campaign was labelled as a success, attracting over 100,000 ideas. But beside a good turn out, what – if anything – did this process actually achieve?

After the earthquakes, with much of the fabric of Christchurch's inner city destroyed, and every aspect of its future shape up for negotiation, natural disaster had suddenly become the defining feature of Christchurch as a place I want to suggest that, instead of being viewed as a slick crowd-sourcing campaign, Share an Idea should be seen as a rebranding exercise, a first step towards regaining control of the brand narrative of Christchurch – how it should be perceived as a place to both live and visit. Of central importance here is the visual language of the campaign – a combination of bright colours and pictures of Christchurch residents revolving around a speech bubble motif that both illuminates and extends what could be seen as the true motivations of the campaign: to begin rebuilding a sense of place, and to promote a sense of democratised power.

A sense of place

The Share an Idea campaign was sold as a 'creation process'[2] – a canvassing of public opinion through a democratic act of participatory design – and presented through an eye-catching visual language of bright, multi-coloured speech bubbles (fig. 1). As the campaign developed, these speech bubbles began to fill with messages and suggestions from Christchurch residents – framing them as bright ideas part of a larger conversation that everyone was participating in. These speech bubbles were broadcast in real time through the Share an Idea website and, from there, out through social media platforms and eventually into print media through the Press and a tabloid style city-wide mail drop.

Figure 1: Visuals from early in the Share an Idea campaign, encouraging participation

But underneath this bright and bubbly exterior, some other incredibly critical ideas were up for grabs – chief among them being the very identity of the city. Before the 22 February 2011 earthquake, Christchurch, known as the 'Garden City', had a strong visual identity based around its English heritage buildings and gardens. These elements were brought together on the city logo: the Avon River, surrounded by greenery and sky, leading to the central motif of a stylised Christ Church Cathedral (fig. 2).

By May 2011, with the Cathedral cordoned off and crumbling, and the Avon River polluted and winding its way in and out of the central city red zone,

Figure 2: The Christchurch City Council logo remains unchanged in 2014.

a severe dissonance existed between the way the city had been known and represented and the reality on the ground. At this early stage in the recovery process, it was important for those in power to address how Christchurch ha changed, and the effect this was having on perceptions of the city as both a place to live and a place to visit. The implication of this dissonance was that the identity of the city was up for grabs, and the Share an Idea campaign was trying to shift the brand narrative of the city; it was an early chance for the CCC to convey a message of both stability and opportunity against the backdrop of a central city effectively destroyed by a natural disaster.

Given this context, Share an Idea can be seen as a sort of covert rebrand, as opposed to a simple crowd-sourcing campaign. As much as it was about pegging down grand ideas of future cities flying around in the heads of its residents, this was an exercise in brand perception. Share an Idea was asking what Christchurch looks like post-earthquake, and answering the question at the same time: a place where the people are listened to, and where new cities are designed collectively by those who will live in them.

A sense of control

> The concept of network power reveals complexities in the connection between the idea of consent and the idea of freedom . . . A standard is pushed toward universality, and its network becomes poised to merge with the population itself. It is "pushed" by the activity of people evaluating consequences and, ultimately, choosing to adopt a dominant standard because of the access it allows them to forms of cooperation with others.
> – David Singh Grewal, *Network Power*[3]

Share an Idea could also be seen as an exercise in network power, where a feeling of public consensus is gained through notions of collective responsibility; people choose to agree because of the inherent sociability this permits. By painting a picture of democratic process, the CCC was able to subtly sell a brand of governance and assert a level of control over outcomes of the campaign through obtaining consent and buy-in from its citizens. The visual language of the campaign reinforced these concepts. The speech bubbl design, which forms the central motif of the brand, overtly signifies freedom of thought and opinion. Building from this starting point the design implies vibrancy, youth and diversity through a layered, multi-coloured arrangement, giving the effect of many voices stacked upon each other, collecting together into new forms, and new conversations. As the campaign developed, and ideas were shared, this common theme of a collective voice and the power of that voice was continually reinforced and built upon. In conjunction, pictures of real people grounded these visual concepts. Christchurch residents who contributed ideas were paired with speech bubbles that hovered over their heads, each idea given a face, a name and even the suburb where it hailed from (fig. 3).

Figure 3: From inside the Council's draft recovery plan

This imagery of real people alongside their ideas for a new Christchurch was employed throughout the CCC's Draft Central City Plan, which was presented to Minister for Canterbury Earthquake Recovery Gerry Brownlee who – according to the legislation that created his ministry – was granted unprecedented powers, including the right to 'specify . . . any changes to the draft Recovery Plan as he or she thinks fit'.[4] In fact, he did set aside much of the CCC plan and public consultation, directing a new central government unit to create an implementation plan in 100 days. Through this action, the democratic process and perception of power that Share an Idea promoted was severely undermined. Despite this, the original speech bubble motif has continued to be used and expanded upon.

On the cover of the central government's 100-day plan, the Christchurch Central Recovery Plan (CCRP), numerous multi-coloured speech bubbles of different shapes and sizes overlap one another and are placed on top of the Avon River and central Christchurch streets, creating an abstract visual expression of the city regenerating through word of mouth (fig. 4). In this way, despite the actual process undertaken, the plan manages to sell both a clear brand message (something new is happening here) and a mode of governance (it's happening through democratic process).

The concept that the ideas being shared were those of actual people – and had real world implications – was continually built upon. The speech bubble motif – at first used as a flat, two-dimensional visual device with which to present content – later began to represent a kind of building block. The best example of this use of the device can be found in a promotional video released alongside the central government's CCRP. Supported by a voiceover stating that 'the people of Christchurch have spoken', multi-coloured speech bubbles emerge from the rubble of the city centre and stand upright, before further materialising into convention centres, shopping malls and sports stadiums (fig. 5). Here, the message could not be clearer: the voice of the people, as represented by bright icons of free speech, had been listened to and the shape of the new city had been directly informed by this collective voice. In other words, what was implied through this visualisation was a sense of collective power, achieved not only through ownership of process, but ownership of outcomes.

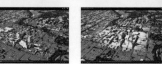

Figure 4: (left) The cover image of the Christchurch Central Recovery Plan

Figure 5: (right) Screenshots from a promotional video that supported the release of the Christchurch Central Recovery Plan

What's interesting to consider here, however, is whether any real power actually changed hands. Contextualised as an act of network power, Share an Idea was very effective in implying ownership and, as an extension, coercing a level of perceived collective responsibility for the future of the city. But beyond giving the people a positive outlet for ideas, did it actually have any real impact on the bricks and mortar reality of future developments? Any power that was granted through this process was quickly diluted as the number of participants grew and the ideas shared 'pushed toward universality'[5] – the majority of them simply reinforcing the status quo. The obviousness and conservative nature of the crowd-sourced opinions acted as stamp of approval for the preconceived ideas likely held by those in power. Of course people want more green spaces, bike lanes, cultural events and better public transport, and so of course that wasn't really the point of all this.

This begins to point toward the futility of the exercise as actual idea generation, and towards the value of Share an Idea as an attempt to soft sell concepts of change, through the veil of democratic process. To lessen the burden of having to sell a new city plan to its citizens, the CCC – through the campaign's ability to imply the idea of consent and freedom – was seemingly employing the people to sell it back to themselves.

This becomes especially dubious when coupled with the extreme executive power now wielded by the new government ministry, with Brownlee using the same visual language to represent his altered plan – perhaps an attempt to cash in on Share an Idea's use of symbolism to imply democratic design, decision-making and ultimately power. But with this process a far cry from what was originally on offer, all this has achieved is an ever-widening gap between the message and the messenger.

Newspaper headlines

The launch of the CCDU Blueprint was a carefully managed event that was curated to coincide with the 6:00 p.m. news. The next day the four major newspapers all led with news and information of the plan. The Auckland-focused *NZ Herald* said 'Christchurch rebuild plan revealed'; Wellington's *Dominion Post* led with 'Brownlee praises rebuild plan' and 'Low-rise, compact blueprint for "new" Christchurch'; Dunedin's *Otago Daily Times* wrote 'Garden city plan identifies main sites' and 'Key won't put figure on quake rebuild plan'; and the Canterbury newspaper opened with the front image below. (Image below used with permission of Fairfax Media New Zealand and the *Press*)

[1]

Telling our own tales

Gerard Smyth

Gerard Smyth began his screen career in 1969 as a cameraman for the state broadcaster NZBC. Since turning director 30 years ago, he has directed over 80 documentaries on everything from the disabled to the arts. Qantas-nominated for his 2008 feature documentary on cinematographer Alun Bollinger, Smyth was awarded 'Best Director, Documentary' at the NZ Television Awards for his 2011 *When a City Falls*, an acclaimed account of the quakes in his hometown of Christchurch.

What happens in a community after a sizeable calamity has struck and there is very little mainstream television media presence?

To get to this question I shall tell a tale.

July 2012 – a year and half after the worst of the Christchurch earthquakes. The New Zealand government, in an effort to keep up momentum, gives a chosen group a deadline to come up with a plan for a new city centre. The Christchurch Central Recovery Plan is to become known as the Blueprint.

These were extraordinary days. Eighty per cent of the centre of my home town was in the process of being demolished. At the heart of the destruction, in a central city building, teams of designers and engineers were in 'lock down', creating a new city centre. This gathering was contracted to produce a plan in 100 days. Many rumours were circulating about just how radical the plans were to be. But not a word had escaped. Media had been kept well awa

It must have been on about day 90 that I rang the Canterbury Earthquake Recovery Authority (CERA) communications team and asked if television footage had been recorded inside the lock up. The very thought was met with incredulity. 'Of course not - it's a lock up. Plans will be made public at the launch in a month's time.'

Of course CERA communications is well used to arranging media moments, as they did weeks later when the Prime Minister, in front of a selected audience and a live band, unveiled the Blueprint. 'But,' I argued, 'this is an historic time. Do you really intend that no archival footage be taken of this achievement? Won't these 100 days become significant in years to come?'

I could hear the hesitation, 'Oh – well – I'll talk to someone and we'll get back to you.'

They did, and the next day I was invited to spend half an hour inside the epicentre of our recovery. Groups of elated and exhausted engineers, designers and kindred disciplines were hunched over tables deep in conversation with each other. A sense of urgency and purpose really did mak for some memorable footage.

Extraordinarily, to my knowledge, I now own the only footage from the time of the 'lock up'. I have been asked by other broadcasting interests for the footage. It seems that this has already become the valuable footage it was always destined to be. But why was I the only one to knock on the door? Why was this 100-day event not eagerly filmed by all the major television networks in New Zealand? Obviously, the Auckland-based networks were just not interested. Surely this would be of significant interest to the 341,000 who live in the city of Christchurch? To the half a million who live in province of Canterbury?

Those thoughts beg a bigger question. The question I started with.

We in Christchurch have been blessed with a local newspaper and over the last three years their journalists have been prolific, investigative and inquisitive – and thank God for them. We are also fortunate that a nightly current affairs programme from one of the Auckland-based networks has featured countless tales from Christchurch. But of course these have to rate for the larger Auckland audience. So populist tales about the little guy being mistreated by the Goliaths – the insurance companies or the Earthquake Commission – are featured again and again. There is a local television channel that enthusiastically records daily events in Christchurch, but they are seen by only a small percentage of households, their budget is tiny and their staff ill-resourced to handle the complexities of so many stories.

In New Zealand, state-funded television is broadcast from Auckland in the North Island. A third of our 4.5 million population lives there, over 1000 kilometres from Christchurch. Increasingly over the last 25 years, the two-thirds of New Zealanders who do not live in Auckland have been largely forgotten by our national broadcasters.

In 2012 a study by Media and Communication students at the University of Canterbury analysed who told what stories on prime time New Zealand television. Over a three month period they watched and categorised all publicly funded programmes, with the exception of news and current affairs, that were broadcast on any of the six national free to air channels. Over these three months Christchurch appeared on national screens on average for 33 minutes a week. Aucklanders saw themselves for 659 minutes – twenty times Christchurch's lot. And this was after we had had an earthquake.[1]

We, in Christchurch, have long been used to watching the lives of others.

What's more, any story shot in Christchurch for network television has to be of interest to an Auckland audience. In that sense, we in Christchurch are without the ability to tell our own stories for our own needs – and that is why the lock up was not recorded. Auckland audiences were just not interested. So how were the earthquakes recorded here when the quakes hit? How well were we resourced to speak to each other via television about our traumatised lives? What vehicles did we have?

For the first weeks – months even – Christchurch was covered head to toe with television crews parachuting in from other lands. The world's media were here. And they, along with our very own squadrons from Auckland, were fascinating to observe in action.

At the time I was living in the heart of the city and recording events from the point of view of a freelance and unfunded documentary maker. With fallen buildings and unfolding stories all around I figured I didn't need the accreditation pass hung around my neck. I chose to work alone.

I was learning first hand what veteran American news anchor Ted Koppel meant when he famously explained that it is not the task of mainstream media to be investigative – that is the domain of the fringe media. That sure was true of what happened here in Christchurch in those terrible first weeks. It does not seem to matter what the network, the stories by each were so often clones of each other – competing media were bussed together to the same events, all under the prescribed direction of governmental communication advisors.

But those days are well over now. These days the community of Christchurch is focused on rebuilding our city. Again the medium of television is by far our most effective resource when it comes to informing the people.

The statistics in Christchurch remain extraordinary. Around 91 per cent of homes were damaged,[2] 17,000 houses uninhabitable,[3] thousands of residents displaced. The heart of the city has been removed. The rebuild is said to be the second largest insured loss pay-out anywhere, anytime.[4]

But in Christchurch there remains almost no vehicle on state-funded television for us to talk and debate with and for each other. We have no regular mainstream state-funded television outlet to speak specifically to local audiences.

Many would say that the New Zealand government has chosen a top-down approach to lead Christchurch's recovery. One Minister of the Crown has been given extraordinary powers by New Zealand's right-wing government to lead very much from the front. Minister Brownlee is famous for his hands on approach. CERA, his government department, likes to hang on to the notion that the Christchurch City Council's public participation scheme Share an Idea has been the underlying motivation for decisions that shape the city. But many observe that the 106,000 ideas the community supplied are able to prop up or deny any proposed direction. The city partially retaining its one-way street system would be an example. Is this what the people requested in the Council's survey?

Many residents protest that we are spectators on the sideline, unable to find a forum for public debate. How many of the people's wishes about the future of the abandoned land in the eastern suburbs are likely to be realised? What debate is being heard? A very up-market central city swimming pool complex has been planned. What voice is the public having in this far-reaching decision? What do we know of our own psychological wellbeing? Are our people facing post-traumatic stress that has not been seen in New Zealand in previous times? How are our children faring? Our old people?

In some ways the lack of strong and functional mainstream television media in Christchurch must be a godsend to those who are making decisions. Their subjects are placid and have long learned to acquiesce to being voiceless. But is this really how a vital community best functions?

I am in my sixties, old enough to remember very different times. Twenty years ago publicly funded broadcasters TVNZ and the NZBC before them had over 300 staffers based in Christchurch. Each day a team of around 40 put together a five night a week, half hour show. It was made by us, about us and for us. From the middle of the city, journalists and camera crews produced daily in-depth stories about all manner of subjects. Interestingly most of the reporters were mature, intelligent and respected storytellers. Often not trained journalists, they were a far cry from today's fresh young faces. Imagine if we had had this resource over the last three years! For on every corner in this town is a story that would make headlines for weeks in any other city.

I want to live in a city that, right now, is alive with debate. It's ideas time in Christchurch and shall be for a long time to come. For the people to personally buy into a sense of our own recovery, we need to feel involved. A half hour breakout every evening on state-funded television would help all of us enormously. Because only when we can tell our own stories in our own community will we be able to sense our own wellbeing.

That sense is foreign to so many of us here today.

Blueprint launch

On 31 July 2012 the 100-day CCDU-led Blueprint was launched in the foyer of the Christchurch City Council building. This was a major news event that featured Prime Minister John Key, Minister for Canterbury Earthquake Recovery Gerry Brownlee and Christchurch Mayor Bob Parker. This was the first time that images of the new city plan were seen by the public or media. While the announcements were being broadcast live on national television, a vocal crowd gathered on the street to protest various aspects of the post-quake response.

[1–8]

Will a plumber cost me more now?: Christchurch from an Auckland perspective

Liam Dann

Liam is Business Editor at the *New Zealand Herald*. He was born and raised in Christchurch, growing up in Beckenham and Cashmere. He has a BA in Sociology from Canterbury University.

The point of this piece is to reflect on the Christchurch rebuild from an Auckland-based, business-oriented point of view. That's my professional perspective. It is a difficult thing for me to write about though. I was born a Cantabrian and will always be one. My heart is there. I've lived in Auckland for nearly twenty years and for most of that time I have been a financial journalist.

I wouldn't be doing anyone any favours if I were to sugar-coat reality and pretend there is not a high level of fatigue for Christchurch's redevelopment story in Auckland. As focus shifts from the human tragedy to the future of the city, the story is inescapably hampered by the centrality of local government issues. Local government stories seldom play well in the media, at least outside of the community they affect. Transport, drainage and zoning are always other people's problems until they are specifically your own problem.

There is an indifferent attitude in Auckland. There is a feeling that New Zealand has spent the money on Christchurch now, something is underway and the plans, as presented two years ago, looked pretty good.

Now get on with it. We're busy getting on with the economic recovery up here. There is a sense in which the quakes can now be filed away with the Global Financial Crisis as part of a difficult period in New Zealand history.

Just transpose the collapsing of financial institutions in the economic meltdown of 2008 for collapsing buildings in the geological meltdown of 2011. Both of these epic events might now be something for the history books, if it wasn't for the inconvenient reality of life in Christchurch nearly four years on.

Of course Aucklanders do understand that the reality is complex and it is too soon to put the quakes in the past tense just yet. This year's flooding issues highlighted that.

But Auckland is booming again. There is a development buzz about the city that has been missing for the best part of a decade. Ironically it is the sort of buzz Christchurch needs but is desperately lacking.

We are building motorways and planning rail loops and skyscrapers up here. Auckland has a building boom underway as the council and central government work to increase the housing stock by 39,000 and accommodate the fast-growing population.

That this excitement is diverting the attention of Aucklanders away from anything south of the Bombay Hills seems unfair at a time when Christchurch is stuck in development limbo, up to its neck in plans and political debate about projects that still seem distant prospects.

In Auckland when we talk about Christchurch it is seldom in great detail or with great passion. While there is sympathy, we don't talk much about convention centres or stadiums or how to get business back into the central city.

The Christchurch rebuild is, along with dairy export prices, one of the most commonly cited reasons for the economic upswing of 2014. So we hear the name of the city a lot in a positive context. We talk about opportunity and the prospect of an impressive new city down south.

In this context the economic questions are about timing rather than the specifics that impact on residents. So we are asking: When is the projected peak for the rebuild? How will that affect the nation's economic capacity for construction? In other words: What will it do to the price of building a new block of flats in the Auckland suburbs of New Lynn or Onehunga? At the macro end of the economic scale, what is the GDP growth effect? How much pressure is it putting on inflation and therefore how is it distorting official cash rate projections? At the most micro-economic end of the scale: what is it doing to the cost of hiring a plumber to do up my bathroom?

I'm not immune from that myopic focus, even though I have a family connection to the city and hear the stories first hand.

I flew to Christchurch after the February 22 quake and toured with the foreign press, visiting the major sites when the disaster was still raw. I remember a howling nor'west gale, dust flying everywhere. With Iroquois helicopters buzzing overhead and army trucks on the street corners, it had an apocalyptic feel. It is hard to describe how shocking it felt to step onto the Square and see the Cathedral in ruins on the ground. It is a feeling only someone who grew up in Christchurch can understand.

Those images of disaster jar with everything that Christchurch was. My home town was not a CNN breaking-news kind of place – and hopefully won't ever be again. Almost four years later Christchurch can still shock you if you go looking. Try walking the length of the Avon River, from South Brighton to the Square. If you stick to the banks of the river you'll get a unique view of a suburban wasteland to rival the set of *The Walking Dead*. You'll arrive in the central city disheartened and with little to cheer you by way of progress on a new urban centre.

Those closer to the rebuild will point out that there is activity and positive development on the urban fringe. And the lives of my friends and family through southern and western Christchurch are far from apocalyptic. Yet they are all still dealing with it, in the background, every day. Their stories don't translate well to national media. They are the mundane frustrations of calls to insurance companies, botched repair jobs and endless life-disrupting delays. Some are minor, while some are hugely stressful and seemingly without end. The extent to which insurance companies play hardball can seem cruel and unforgiving.

My sense is that if living in Christchurch is not miserable for everyone it is almost always a bit weird. It has to be weird to live around that giant dead spot of ruins where the heart of a city used to be.

The people of Christchurch live with a collective sense of loss and hope. But the hope is tested as time drags on. The longer the rebuild takes, the longer the debates rage about how the new city should be, the more entrenched the views become. That long wait makes the politics of the rebuild more difficult as needs change and organic growth takes the city off in unplanned directions. The city has no shortage of plans including the high-level Blueprint unveiled to great acclaim in July 2012. At the time, Mayor Bob Parker said the plan was a 'bold vision' and the *New Zealand Herald* reported that 'the blueprint received rave reviews from developers and investors' at a glitzy launch at Christchurch City Council (CCC) headquarters.

But life, as John Lennon said, is what happens while you are busy making other plans.

Nearly two years since the Blueprint's launch there is plenty of organic growth in Christchurch. Some of it looks more interesting than the grand visions rendered by the long-term planners. It is important that the Blueprint remains a live document open to revision, so that it incorporates developments driven by the residents of the city. The exposed red brick façades around Lichfield, Tuam and Manchester Streets – covered with graffiti, murals and ancient advertising – make a fascinating home to new cafes and pop-up art galleries. According to the Blueprint this space is destined to be the Innovation Precinct. Let's hope the central planners understand how well this kind of bohemian environment can fit with the spaces they will need to create to attract hip young tech entrepreneurs and workers to the area.

Hopefully the environment springing up there can survive the transition. It might happen. It is workable within the scope of the Blueprint but getting it right will require a fine balance of competing needs and political forces. It must be particularly frustrating for small businesses that are starting to thrive in these areas to know they have a limited life expectancy. There will always be some casualties in a rebuild of this scale. We could abandon central planning and just let the city evolve organically. But in doing that there is a greater casualty – the lost opportunity to create something bold and new. There are no easy answers.

The time frame over which these events inevitably unfold is a nightmare for planners. The Blueprint looked good precisely because it didn't go for the quick fix. Since it was released the discovery of budget short falls has made timing issues worse. The city has to think on historic scales of twenty years or more, but it has to be liveable for residents now. It has to prioritise. But what is important to you isn't always the same as what is important to me. And the politics of each decision become laborious.

The traditional political divide breaks down. The Right traditionally says leave it to organic growth and limit government involvement. The Left traditionally favours central planning and government-led development. Yet the quake and the rebuild often have the two sides fighting in opposite directions to that old formula. Lack of debate can lead to a city that residents don't want. Endless debate leads to stasis. If ever there was a time to drop old ideological battle lines now must surely be it.

If you look at the roll that Auckland is on now it is clear that getting local and central government on the same page was crucial. The Auckland 'super city' (merger of eight regions and districts into one council) was a catalyst for the change. It was a circuit breaker that – after years of arguing about key infrastructure problems and housing development – enabled both sides to give ground. Auckland now has a thirty-year Unitary Plan with support at all levels of government. There is more debate to come as it is worked through suburb by suburb, but the broad vision is there. Some momentum, any momentum has been positive and starts to feed off itself. Momentum really everything. It drives progress. Christchurch needs some. It needs a kickstart – something exciting to re-energise its citizens and remind them that there is hope for an amazing new city in their lifetime.

My hope for Christchurch is that we see one or two big projects fast tracked – a flash new retail precinct perhaps, like Auckland's Britomart. Or a central stretch of the Avon River landscaped into a lively, family friendly urban space – the way the Wynyard Quarter has transformed Auckland's waterfront.

These distinct quarters of Auckland city have been built up at either end of the downtown waterfront. Britomart, in the space beside the central railway station, has turned a maze of disused alleys and a bus depot into an upmarket mix of fashion stores, bars and restaurants anchored by one large-scale office building. About a kilometre west, the Wynyard Quarter transformed the old fishing dock area into a family friendly promenade with a playground and cafes, drawing thousands of visitors on weekend mornings.

The highly visible success of these projects has played a big part in turning around Aucklanders' attitudes towards city development.

While issues like drainage and roads remain crucial for Christchurch, efforts to fast track a feel good urban project for the city would have disproportionate benefits for the redevelopment process.

You can't underestimate the feel good factor – especially when people have been feeling so bad for so long.

Central government and the CCC need to bite the bullet and agree on some short-term goals that have broad appeal.

It is vital to reignite optimism and do it quickly because it seems to be running dangerously low. When things start moving forward then even the political debate becomes more constructive.

As Auckland has seen, once you have a culture of progress no one wants to pull the handbrake and grind it to a halt. People may want to steer it in new directions and the political system is there to ensure it is taking the majority of the city's people with it. But Auckland needed momentum. It has it now. Christchurch now needs it more than Auckland ever did.

That's the challenge for the political powers overseeing the rebuild of my hometown. More than three years after the quake it is more pressing than ever.

Blueprint launch video

There is an unprecedented opportunity in the heart of the South Island of New Zealand. On the edge of the sweeping Canterbury Plains lies the beautiful city of Christchurch. Recently, the central heart of this city has faced incredible challenges; in the wake of the 2010 and 2011 earthquakes over 70 per cent of buildings in the centre have been, or will be, demolished. But the people of Christchurch have responded with over 106,000 ideas that have informed both the spatial blueprint and the Christchurch Central Recovery Plan. The Blueprint identifies a number of key projects that will catalyse development, provide certainty, clarity and inspire confidence. A frame of open green space will ensure a dense and vibrant core, while the Avon River will create a link between key projects.

Living spaces, parks, businesses and commerce will evolve and grow to create a prosperous and exciting central city where people of Christchurch, Canterbury, New Zealand and the world will come to live, do business and experience all that the city has to offer.

The Performing Arts Precinct will sit alongside a purpose-built state-of-the-art convention centre. Together they will form the centrepiece of an exciting cultural and entertainment area in the heart of the city. The hospital will become the focus of the new Health Precinct. The Metro Sports Facility will be a top-class facility accessible to people of all ages, abilities and sporting skill. With the Blueprint in place, the foundation is set for a whole host of successful initiatives – initiatives based around clearly identified precincts that will attract a vibrant mix of people, commerce, technology, culture and sport.

The Christchurch Central Recovery Plan isn't just a quick fix; it's a long-term vision that incorporates cutting-edge design and the latest ideas in urban planning. It's achievable, it's full of potential, and it's ready to fly. Join us in making the most of this unparalleled opportunity to create a central city that will transform Christchurch and inspire the world.

– transcript from Blueprint launch video

[1–10]

Blueprint launch video

[11–18]

Selling the Plan

Open conversations

Nick Sargent

Born and raised in Christchurch, Nick Sargent is a graduate architect and architectural educator with eight years' experience working for architectural practices and universities in New Zealand, Australia and Asia.

The effects that traumatic events have on the way people communicate were immediately obvious to a Christchurch visitor after the earthquakes. Just as the earthquakes crossed property lines they destabilised social boundaries, with strangers freely sharing both emotional stories about their experiences and hopes for the future of their city. These latter stories were the source of much excitement for a young architect accustomed to public apathy about the built environment. In them lay the hope these newly emptied spaces could be filled with a more engaged city where ordinary citizens' wishes were better expressed – a city that might dare to try and be better than the one before it for most of its people. However this optimism appears to be waning with community groups and members of the public complaining of not being given a voice in decision-making, of slow progress, tortured bureaucracies, unfair buy-outs, dull glass boxes and a return to 'business as usual'. This is a complex and multi-layered problem within which the city's authorities appear to, willfully or otherwise, be missing a unique opportunity to engage unparalleled public interest in urban development.

Following the February 2011 earthquake the Christchurch City Council (CCC) initiated a widely praised campaign – Share an Idea – that encouraged citizens to contribute ideas for rebuilding through a range of events and mediums. The CCC collected over 100,000 submissions, which they distilled into five key drivers: a green city, a stronger built identity, a more compact central business district, an accessible city and, more ambiguously, a place to 'live, work, play, learn and visit'. These drivers then (somewhat opaquely) informed a Council Draft Central City Plan (CCP). The CCP was subsequently passed onto the Government's newly established and uniquely powerful Canterbury Earthquake Recovery Authority (CERA), whose minister accepted it in principle, but heavily revised the plan's details with a group of chosen experts (the selection criteria and definition of 'expert' were kept secret) to make it 'investment ready'.[1] The outcome of this process was the Christchurch Central Recovery Plan (CCRP) that was passed into law without any public consultation.

In the space of a few months an extraordinary participatory energy had dramatically been transformed into a non-negotiable plan that prioritised the values of investors. Christchurch was now being described generically as a '$40 billion opportunity' supported by 'a unique recovery agency with the power to remove barriers and get things done,'[2] – the establishment of which would also prove remarkably unsuccessful in attracting investors.

Whilst it was always the CCC's intention to turn Share an Idea quickly into a fixed plan, the enthusiasm generated revealed an appetite for this type of public conversation about our urban environment. As celebrated as the initiative was, it also raised questions about why this successful public conversation (to which new communication technology is perfectly matched) couldn't be a part of an ongoing democratic approach to urbanism in Christchurch. In this sense the earthquakes had accidentally created an opportunity for social change within the ordinarily closed process of urban development.

Adam Kahane, a consultant and author on using narratives for social change, states that 'the type and quality of the conversations people have is the most important indicator of whether or not their change initiative will be successful'.[3] This conversation must be deep and slow, moving through similarities and differences into generating new shared purpose and change, a process that requires a patience and commitment to talking and listening that 'most of us . . . and certainly most institutions . . . have limited capacity for'.[4] The initially dynamic public conversation instigated by the disaster and encouraged by the CCC's Share an Idea quickly became a private conversation where decision-making criteria and purpose have been concealed, thus removing the ground from which meaningful debate could occur. This fits with what Kahane calls 'downloading', a form of dialogue that 'maintains the status quo, maintains the (artificial) wholeness of the system and re-enacts the patterns of the past'.[5] Downloading is 'being polite, not listening, saying what we already know, following the rules'.[6] It is the lowest of four increasingly complex stages of talking and listening that Kahane claims are necessary to have the type of generative conversation that would ensure a successful outcome with widespread public support.

But it is too easy to dismiss this shift from public conversation to private decision-making as a deliberate strategy for excluding citizens from participation in the rebuild (although it is of course probable that this is true to some degree). On Radio NZ Kim Hill put the allegation that Share an Idea had been ignored to Peter Marshall, managing director of Warren and Mahoney architects and a key expert in designing the CCRP. He explained that the key themes people asked for – a greener, more pedestrian friendly, lighter, more sustainable and safer city – were all taken into account. Marshall sounded genuinely concerned that an intention to give people what they asked for was being criticised.[7]

Story-writing educator Robert McKee states that 'If the story you're telling, is the story you're telling, you're in deep shit,' which fundamentally means that a good story is driven by its underlying arcs of change. During a story, characters change for better or worse (or not at all) through a string of causal connections that reflect our own responses to life experiences. This veiled inner structure is what stories are really about, rather than the specific characters, places or events we empathise with. These superficial details are instead the devices used by the audience to access the deeper structure.

Whilst this advice is intended for literary stories, it holds equally true for the dominant rebuilding narrative being designed and told by city authorities like Marshall. The stories told by citizens contributing to Share an Idea were not fundamentally about a greener, more pedestrian friendly, lighter, more sustainable and safer city (an absurdly generic exercise in reduction). Instead a simpler embodied story was being told about a phenomenal number of people contributing to the future of their city, in an act of empowered imagination that takes on therapeutic dimensions in a disaster scenario. In stating that the key drivers 'were all taken into account', development authorities have replaced the underlying story that was really being told (about open public participation) with a story of their own fabrication – apparently under the misapprehension that they are doing what they'd been asked to.

In a global context where Western democracy is proving relatively ineffective in responding to complex problems, the authoritarian drive in this narrative substitution is understandable. However, from the perspective of public participation in urbanism, to conceal motivations and close the public conversation is also a backward response to a situation where the opportunities to try something new and visionary are undeniable. The Christchurch earthquakes laid bare the procedural nature of urban development, mobilising individual desire at a historic moment where our prior urban assumptions are being questioned by increased global awareness and our organisational behaviours are being modified by new communication technology. The tragic disaster opened a space into which our contemporary knowledge about past urban mistakes could be used to bravely and collectively attempt something new.

To paraphrase what famous English architect Peter Cook once said to a student who had produced a technically competent but banal project: *it's like I asked you to get me socks and you went and got me socks, but really I wanted something more interesting.* Leafing through the plans and architects' illustrations of future Christchurch I feel similarly. Isn't this the architectural equivalent of ordinary socks? Peter Robb of the *Sydney Morning Herald* states that 'a larger social imagination was hard to find in play over my three days in Christchurch' and concluded that 'the future looks like being a letdown'.[8] The problem almost certainly lies where I suspect Adam Kahane and Robert McKee would locate it: in the deeper relationships and conversations – a failure whose responsibility must stop with the city's new leaders who have, possibly unwittingly (or perhaps just witlessly), thrown out the real story and taken the entire weight upon themselves. But the new rebuilding plans and the five key drivers established by the CCC are, after all, a piece of fiction, and if the stories told by authorities are unsatisfying then alternatives can be written. If any city has the potential to open up our contemporary narratives about participation in urban development it is Christchurch where natural disasters have violently, and tragically, opened a space for them.

Chapter 3

Rewriting the Rules

He ara hou ka tāraia

Societies are diverse collections of people, kept in check by norms of behaviour and explicit rules and laws. These rules are the end result of hundreds of years of trial and error, discussion, argument and sometimes even war. When disaster strikes, the displacement and upheaval in society often requires a more nimble response than councils and governments are used to providing. A rapid rewriting of the rules may be required, and is often accompanied by swift changes in people's customs and habits.

In the minutes, hours and days immediately after the February 22 earthquake, order had been replaced by chaos, and people started rewriting the rules. The usual methods of enforcing rules – police and government – were overwhelmed. In many parts of the city, basic services such as power, water and sewerage were unavailable. Many stores weren't open, and a number of the ones that were quickly ran out of essential supplies. But people are adaptable animals; ways and means were found to ensure that an absence of order didn't lead to the unravelling of society.

However, extraordinary circumstances can't go on indefinitely. The army was deployed and Government created and invoked the powers of the Canterbury Earthquake Recovery Act, which is reviewed in this chapter. These rules resulted in some of the most sweeping changes ever applied to the country in peacetime, and some people fell on the wrong side of them. The case of the Quake Outcasts showed exactly what happened when a small but significant group of property owners didn't quite fit within the new rules.

Rules that are devised and amended through electoral cycles and common law over generations can seem irrelevant in a time of crisis. The communities that came together to negotiate their local issues created their own forms and structures. This gave people a taste of a highly participatory mode of democracy – one that jarred with the controlling responses of CERA, Civil Defence and other authorities. One legacy of the disaster has been the re-awakening of the concept of people power, of people reshaping the way in which we interact and rethinking both the explicit and implicit rules of our society.

Adopting and implementing a legislative framework for recovery

Gerard Cleary

Gerard is a special counsel in Anthony Harper's property team specialising in resource management law. Since the earthquakes in Canterbury, he has advised clients on the wide ranging implications of the Canterbury Earthquake Recovery Act 2011. Gerard has also represented clients in the development of the various recovery plans prepared under this legislation.

Extraordinary times call for appropriate measures. That the task of recoverin from New Zealand's largest ever series of natural disasters would require a bespoke legislative framework was immediately recognised in the aftermat of the first significant earthquake to hit the Canterbury region on 4 September 2010.

The subsequent and significantly more devastating earthquake of 22 Februar 2011 effectively meant that the recovery of greater Christchurch had become matter of national significance, one requiring even broader legislative measure After February 2011, Parliament acted with commendable speed in firstly establishing the Canterbury Earthquake Recovery Authority (CERA) on 29 March 2011, a central government agency whose task was to 'provide strategi leadership and to coordinate activities to enable an effective, timely, and coordinated rebuilding and recovery effort in Canterbury'.[1] Shortly afterward on 12 April 2011 and with almost universal support from all political parties, the New Zealand Parliament enacted the Canterbury Earthquake Recovery Act 2011 (the CER Act). The Act received assent on 18 April 2011.

This overview briefly explores the wide-ranging powers available to the Minist for Canterbury Earthquake Recovery and CERA under the Act, and then examines the checks and balances against the misuse of these powers. Attentio is then turned to the specific powers of the Minister to direct the development of a range of planning instruments intended to guide recovery, a number of which have been developed under the CER Act process. These include the mandatory development of an overarching Recovery Strategy for Greater Christchurch and also subordinate plans such as the Christchurch Central Recovery Plan (CCRP). It is this latter document that is perhaps of greatest significance to planning for the recovery of greater Christchurch, its focus bein on the recovery of the heart of Christchurch, the central business district.

Executive powers

Central to the CER Act is the extensive range of powers conferred on the executive branch of government to make decisions so as to enable a timely, focused and expeditious recovery. These provide the Minister and CERA with ability, among other things, to:

- direct the development and implementation of a range of planning instruments, including a Recovery Strategy for Greater Christchurch and subordinate recovery plans (these planning instruments are intended to provide a foundation for implementing recovery)
- suspend, amend, or revoke the whole or any part of a policy statement or plan prepared under separate legislation,[2] including the Resource Management Act 1991 (RMA)[3] and Local Government Act 2002 (the Minister can override the provisions of any pre-existing plan or policy statement to, for example, provide additional residentially zoned land to meet the demands of residents whose land and houses were damaged beyond economic repair by the earthquakes)
- suspend or cancel, in whole or in part, any activity authorised by either resource consent, existing use rights, or a certificate of compliance
- disseminate information, commission reports and undertake investigations on any matter[4]
- carry out or commission works on or under land including the demolition of all or part of a building or structure[5] (a power that has been exercised predominantly to authorise the demolition of earthquake damaged buildings within the central city, including an extensive number of heritage buildings)
- require adjoining owners to act for the benefit of other adjoining owners[6]
- acquire or dispose of public or private property.[7]

Opportunities for affected parties to challenge the exercise of any of the above powers are severely curtailed by the Act. With very limited exceptions, there is no right of appeal against decisions made by the Minister or the Chief Executive of CERA[8] pursuant to the Act. So, for example, the holder of a resource consent that has been cancelled by the Minister under section 27(3) cannot appeal its cancellation. Likewise, the owner of land compulsorily acquired by CERA cannot appeal against acquisition, rather his or her remedy is limited to challenging the amount of compensation offered.[9] Further, the Act contains a protection from liability clause, which precludes any action being taken against the Crown or any officer or employee of a Minister of the Crown to recover any damages or loss suffered as a consequence of actions taken under the Act.[10]

Checks and balances?

This mix of wide-ranging executive powers and an absence of the usual avenues for redress in the Courts prompts the question of what constraints and safeguards, if any, apply to prevent abuses of power. In examining this question, regard must be had to the particular constraints set out in section 10 of the Act, which essentially requires the Minister and CERA to act in accordance with the purposes of the Act, and exercise or claim a power only when they consider it necessary.

The purposes of the Act that they must uphold are set out in section 3, as follows:

The purposes of this Act are—
a) to provide appropriate measures to ensure that greater Christchurch and the councils and their communities respond to, and recover from, the

impacts of the Canterbury earthquakes:

b) to enable community participation in the planning of the recovery of affected communities without impeding a focused, timely, and expedited recovery:

c) to provide for the Minister and CERA to ensure that recovery:

d) to enable a focused, timely, and expedited recovery:

e) to enable information to be gathered about any land, structure, or infrastructure affected by the Canterbury earthquakes:

f) to facilitate, co-ordinate, and direct the planning, rebuilding, and recovery of affected communities, including the repair and rebuilding of land, infrastructure, and other property:

g) to restore the social, economic, cultural, and environmental well-being of greater Christchurch communities:

h) to provide adequate statutory power for the purposes stated in paragraphs (a) to (g):

i) to repeal and replace the Canterbury Earthquake Response and Recovery Act 2010.

There is a tension: the Act confers many additional powers, but imposes (especially in sections 3 and 10 above) obligations and restrictions. One incident led to this interrelationship being considered by the New Zealand Court of Appeal in *Canterbury Regional Council v Independent Fisheries Limited* CA 438/2012 NZCA 601. The background to this case involved decisions the Minister made in October 2011 under s. 27 of the CER Act to set in place an airport noise contour protecting the use and development of the Christchurch International Airport and direct where residential development should occur within greater Christchurch over the next 35 to 40 years. He revoked an existing part (PC1) of the regional planning policy, and introduced two new chapters. An application for judicial review of these decisions followed. In *Independent Fisheries Limited v Minister for Canterbury Earthquake Recovery* [2012] NZHC 2572, the High Court found the Minister's decisions to be unlawful. The Court observed, at paragraph 103:

> rather than serving earthquake recovery purposes, the underlying purpose . . . was to resolve longstanding issues by setting long-term planning strategies. Given that the revocation of PC1 is inextricably linked to those [two additional] chapters, that decision is also tainted by the same illegality.

The High Court's decision was upheld in the Court of Appeal, albeit for different reasons. In considering whether or not the purposes of the CER Act should be interpreted broadly or restrictively, the Court of Appeal was firmly of the view that the broad approach to interpretation was to be preferred:

> we accept Mr Cooke's submission that the concept of "recovery" is not, as Mr Goddard submitted, so open ended that almost anything is covered. As the references to "recovery", "restoration", "rebuilding" and "repairing" make clear, the starting point must be to focus on the damage that was done by the earthquakes and then to determine what is needed to "respond" to that damage. But, as the purposes and definitions also make clear, the response is not limited to the earthquake damaged

areas. Recovery encompasses the restoration and enhancement of greater Christchurch in all respects. Within the confines of the Act, all action designed, directly, or indirectly to achieve that objective is contemplated.

and:

The fact that the powers are significant and must be exercised for the purposes of the Act does not mean that the purposes should be interpreted restrictively when Parliament has made it clear that they should be interpreted broadly. The Act is designed to confer adequate powers on the Executive to achieve the full social, economic, cultural and environmental recovery of greater Christchurch in the wider sense.

As to the meaning of the words 'reasonably considers it necessary' in s. 10(2), the Court of Appeal stated:

in short, two elements are involved:
a) The Minister must consider the exercise of the power "necessary", that is, it is needed or required in the circumstances, rather than merely desirable or expedient, for the purposes of the Act.
b) . . . The Minister must therefore ask and answer the question of necessity for the specific power that he intends to use. This means that where he could achieve the same result in another way, including under another power in the Act, he must take that alternative into account.

It is clear therefore from the Court of Appeal's ruling that, while the purposes of the Act are to be interpreted broadly, the powers available to the Minister and CERA must be exercised in a manner that is capable of objective justification. That is, s. 10 imports a significant degree of rigour in the decision-making process, one that includes the requirement to consider alternative means of achieving a desired goal or result and the consequences flowing from a decision.

Development and implementation of planning instruments under the Act

Subpart 3 of the CER Act contains detailed provisions setting out the respective responsibilities of the Minister and the Chief Executive of CERA for the development of a number of planning instruments.

The key planning document mandated by the Act is a Recovery Strategy for Greater Christchurch, which is to be supplemented by a recovery plan for central Christchurch and, if considered necessary, other recovery plans to deal with discrete issues. In terms of a hierarchy of importance, all recovery plans must be consistent with the Recovery Strategy,[11] with the Minister having the power to direct changes to these plans to ensure consistency. Furthermore, the provisions of existing plans and policies prepared under the RMA must not be interpreted or applied in a way that is inconsistent with the Recovery Strategy.[12]

Recovery Strategy for Greater Christchurch

Section 11 of the Act requires the Chief Executive of CERA to develop a Recovery Strategy for the approval of the Minister within nine months of the Act coming into force. The Recovery Strategy is described in s. 11(3) as 'an overarching, long-term strategy for the reconstruction, rebuilding, and recovery of greater Christchurch'.

Section 11(3) specifies that the Recovery Strategy include provisions which address, amongst others, the following issues:
- areas where rebuilding or other redevelopment may or may not occur, and the possible sequencing of rebuilding or other redevelopment
- location of existing and future infrastructure and the possible sequencing of repairs, rebuilding and reconstruction
- the nature of the recovery plans that may need to be developed and the relationship between the plans
- any additional matters to be addressed in particular recovery plans, including who should lead the development of the plans.

This Recovery Strategy for Greater Christchurch was drafted and made available for public comment in September 2011 and subsequently finalised on 31 May 2012. It can best be described as a document that is very high level in nature, one which provides more of a broad vision as to how recovery of Greater Christchurch is to be achieved as opposed to a detailed setting out of the steps to recovery.

The Recovery Strategy identifies six components of recovery with associated goals and work programmes. These are:
- leadership and integration – includes research and information, communication, funding and finance, and the governance, coordination and project management of recovery activities
- economic recovery – includes investment, businesses, labour and insurance liaison
- social recovery – includes education, health and community support services
- cultural recovery – includes the arts, culture, heritage buildings and places and sports and recreation
- built environment – includes land use, housing, buildings, transport and infrastructure
- natural environment – includes air quality, biodiversity, the coast, land, groundwater and surface water quality, and natural hazards.

While all of the above components fit within a broad interpretation of recovery, a key shortcoming of the Recovery Strategy is the almost complete absence of the matters anticipated by s. 11(3) of the Act. Specifically, the strategy contains no hard detail as to the location of redevelopment or future infrastructure necessary to support the rebuild. Such omissions are readily explained by ongoing earthquake activity throughout the strategy's development. In addition, the enormity and complexity of the task of recovery would appear to have made inclusion of all anticipated matters impossible to achieve in the time frame allocated. With the benefit of hindsight therefore, the nine month time frame within which to develop the Recovery Strategy can easily be assessed as unrealistic in the circumstances. That aside, the high level nature of the Recovery Strategy's provisions is such that they can mean all things to all people. The end result is that it is difficult to imagine a circumstance where the contents of either a subordinate recovery plan or a document prepared under the RMA could be said to be inconsistent with the Strategy.

The Recovery Strategy is currently under review by CERA and is expected to be amended to contain a much higher level of detail on the various work streams and programmes identified as necessary to achieve recovery.

Christchurch Central Recovery Plan

Section 16 of the Act provides the Minister with the discretion to direct responsible entities, including the various local authorities within greater Christchurch, to develop a recovery plan for all or part of greater Christchurch. Section 17 of the Act specifically mandates the development of a recovery plan for the central city by the Christchurch City Council (CCC). As with the Recovery Strategy, a nine month time frame for the preparation of a draft for ministerial approval is prescribed by the Act.[13] The task of preparing a draft recovery plan was ably managed by the local council. During its development, the CCC managed to achieve a high level of public participation through both formal and informal means. This included a public hearing, whereby all parties who made submissions on the Draft Central City Plan (CCP) were invited to make a presentation to Council. On a number of important matters, such as proposed height limits within the central city and the issue of existing use rights, it is clear from the final draft presented to the Minister in December 2012 that Council listened to community input.

Under the Act, the final approval of a recovery plan is entirely in the hands of the Minister. In deciding whether or not to approve a draft recovery plan prepared by a responsible entity, s. 21 of the Act provides that the Minister may:
 a) make any changes, or no changes, to the draft Recovery Plan as he or she thinks fit; or
 b) withdraw all or part of the draft CCP.

In April 2012, the Minister announced that he supported the CCC draft plan 'in the main' but was setting aside all the transport elements and the entirety of Volume 2, which contained the changes to the District Plan to realise the vision contained in Volume 1. Instead, Brownlee announced the establishment of the Christchurch Central Development Unit (CCDU), a unit within CERA whose task was to implement the recovery plan. In addition, the Minister announced that the CCDU would prepare, within 100 days, a further blueprint for the redevelopment. In contrast to the council-led stage, the development of the Blueprint was a task completed behind closed doors, with no opportunity for public comment or scrutiny of its contents.

The final, now renamed, Christchurch Central Recovery Plan (incorporating the Blueprint map of key anchor projects) was released to the public on 30

July 2012. While to some extent remaining faithful to the draft prepared by the Christchurch City Council, the ministerial version of the plan included a number of new and highly significant features, including:

- a much reduced central Core of approximately 40 hectares, to be framed on the southern and eastern boundaries by open spaces and low intensity residential and campus-style office development (by reducing the Core, the intent was to correct the historic over-provision of commercially zoned land within the central city, which had resulted in a dispersed and largely uncoordinated business district)
- identification of the location of key anchor projects including a Justice and Emergency Services Precinct, Earthquake Memorial, Performing Arts Precinct, Metro Sports Facility and the Southern and Eastern Frames (anchor projects are intended to replace and supplement existing facilities destroyed by the earthquakes and to stimulate private sector investment within the central city)
- identification of a retail precinct in the Core Zone, within which development is subject to a comprehensive outline development process
- a Central City Mixed Use Zone surrounding the Core Zone, a Zone intended to provide for activities complementary to those permitted within the Core. (Again, the purpose behind this mixed use zone is, in part, to reduce the focus of commercial activity of Christchurch. In addition, the Mixed Use Zone provides much greater opportunities for residential development in proximity to the Core.)

Use of designations to protect anchor projects

While a number of the anchor projects outlined above are currently being progressed, as the CCRP was released it was acknowledged that detailed business cases were required before the New Zealand government would commit further funding towards their development. In addition, the majority of anchor projects were proposed on private land with many landowners progressing a repair or rebuild of damaged buildings on their land. A mechanism was therefore needed to allow time to develop the necessary business cases and to ensure that private landowners would not, in the interim use or develop their land in a way that would compromise the anchor projects. The planning mechanism chosen to achieve these ends was a designation.

A designation is effectively a 'spot' zone which allows the holder of the designation (the requiring authority) to undertake any works within the scope of the designation without having regard for the provisions of any relevant RMA plans and without requiring any planning approvals. In addition, if a designation is included in a district plan no person may, without the prior written consent of the requiring authority, do anything in relation to the land that is subject to the designation that would prevent or hinder the public work or project to which the designation relates. In practice, this means that the use of land subject to a designation can be effectively frozen at the point in time at which the designation was imposed.

The use of designations as a means of providing for major infrastructure projects such as roads, railways and government buildings has been commonplace since the Town and Country Planning Act 1953. That said, the wholesale use of the designation tool within the CCRP is unprecedented in scale, affecting as it does in excess of 800 individual properties. Further, the statutory process for obtaining a designation normally involves an extremely rigorous and at times lengthy (years rather than months) process, whereby the need for, and impacts of, the designation and any available alternatives are subject to detailed scrutiny. Members of the community, including affected landowners, normally have wide rights to participate in the designation process, including an automatic right of appeal to the Environment Court. In stark contrast, the designation process for the anchor projects was completed within the 100-day period allocated by the Minister for the preparation of the Blueprint.

Perhaps surprisingly, despite this extremely limited time frame and despite the significant implications for private landowners effectively deprived of any right to participate in the Minister's decision to designate their land, there have been no legal challenges to date against the anchor project designations. Certainly there has been ongoing evidence of frustration at the time taken by the Crown to negotiate the acquisition of properties affected by these designations; the ongoing review of the necessity for some of the designated land; and the limited pace of progress with the majority of the anchor projects. These frustrations should of course be put in the context of the enormity of the task of delivering these projects; the reality, however, is that the 100-day deadline to prepare the Blueprint and impose the necessary designations was an entirely inadequate time frame to allow for a proper analysis and justification for the anchor projects.

Masterplanning large developments within the core

A key goal within the Christchurch Central Recovery Plan is that development should be well planned, coordinated and meet the highest possible standards of urban design. Public acceptance of the desirability for redevelopment of the city to conform with principles of good urban design had been a consistent theme of the CCC-managed phase of the development of the CCRP. Accordingly, all new buildings within the Core Zone are required to undergo a streamlined urban design approval process whereby proposals are assessed against a range of urban design criteria.[14] The process for obtaining urban design approval for new buildings would appear to be working efficiently.

An additional measure of interest within the Core Zone is the identification of an area referred to as the Central City Retail Precinct. For retail development to proceed within this Retail Precinct, Outline Development Plan (ODP) approval must be obtained from the Council for a contiguous area of no less than 7500 square metres.[15] There is a specified range of matters to be included within an ODP, including the location of car parking, open space provision and pedestrian connections throughout the ODP area. Development of individual sites below the 7500 sqm threshold is discouraged, making it very difficult for the majority of individual owners within the Retail Precinct to rebuild on their properties.

While well intentioned in theory, this experiment in enforced masterplanning has simply not worked in practice. Rather, what has occurred is that multiple overlapping ODPs have been approved by the local council for essentially the same areas within the Retail Precinct. For the most part, these ODPs have been controlled by larger commercial interests and have been approved with limited input from all affected landowners. Unsurprisingly, development within the approved ODPs has stalled primarily because of a lack of cooperation between landowners and the effective moratorium on the development of individual sites within the Retail Precinct. This state of inertia has been well documented in local news media, but remains unresolved.

Looking to the future

The implementation stage is well underway with numerous positive signs of recovery throughout greater Christchurch. There is no doubt this implementation stage will extend over a decade or more.

The Act itself is scheduled to expire in April 2016, although it remains to be seen whether or not it will be extended. Should an extension be contemplated, then a thorough review of the powers available to the executive must be a priority. While the extent of these powers may well have been necessary as a short term measure to ensure that the initial recovery obtained some momentum and did not get bogged down by the business-as-usual process under other legislation, objectively considered the need for these powers has receded over time. Equally, given the history of successful challenges to the exercise of powers under the Act to date, there is a strong argument that the rights of Christchurch communities to fully participate in recovery decision-making should be restored as a matter of some priority.

The executive will retain an important role in recovery for many years to come. There is a strong possibility that CERA and CCDU will remain in existence beyond April 2016, albeit perhaps with reduced roles to play. In the interest of restoring full democracy to Christchurch, it would seem desirable to transition to a state where local authorities such as the Christchurch City Council take back full control of planning for the future of greater Christchurch. As a final point, a review of the CCRP would also be timely, allowing as it would a more robust analysis of the various obstacles to recovery within the current version and the chance to account for unexpected developments since its release. Clearly, there are provisions within the CCRP that are impeding progress, including the uncertainty regarding the actual area of land required to be designated for a number of the anchor projects and the impasse created by the requirement for ODP approval for developments within the Retail Precinct. Looking to the future, a more flexible planning regime would seem desirable, particularly given that, in many ways, recovery has not proceeded as expected.

Christchurch – a state of emergency

Jane Smith

Jane Smith is a Christchurch resident with an interest in democratic processes and transparency.

'In time of crisis a democratic, constitutional government must temporarily be altered by whatever degree is necessary to overcome the peril and restore normal conditions.'
-Clinton Rossiter[1]

The recovery of Christchurch has been characterised by the most successful public engagement campaign in New Zealand's history with 106,000 ideas generated through Share an Idea, and a self-organised programme of urban activism from groups such as Gap Filler, Greening the Rubble, Ministry of Awesome and others that has been recognised internationally in the *New York Times* and by Lonely Planet.

At the same time we have seen the establishment of a government ministry that has superseded a significant part of the role of local government, unparalleled constitutional reform that has overridden a significant number of New Zealand statutes and the suspension of democratic regional council elections and extension of appointed commissioners for an additional three years (or six years in total).

How has Christchurch ended up with a level of top-down ministerial control vested with exceptional powers that have seldom been seen in New Zealand outside the world wars?

State of exception

The governance of Christchurch can be seen as a 'state of exception' that invests one person (the Minister for Canterbury Earthquake Recovery) with the power and voice of authority over others, which extends well beyond where the law has existed in the past. Giorgio Agamben traces the idea of a state of exception back to the French Revolution where the French Assembly included an article in the Constitution that allowed Emperor Napoleon to suspend the constitution in response to siege, armed revolt or disturbances that threatened the security of the state.[2]

Agamben traces the history of the state of exception in different western countries in careful detail. As part of this historical account he identifies a division between the western states that regulate the state of exception in the text of the constitution or by law and those that prefer not to regulate the problem explicitly. In the first group he identifies France and Germany while the second includes Italy, England and the United States.[3] The situation in Christchurch is akin to the second group where the state of exception has not been established through a pre-existing constitutional provision but rather through a specific act

of Parliament, the Canterbury Earthquake Recovery Act 2011 (CER Act).
The CER Act provides the Minister with the powers to override, for the
purposes of the Act, instruments prepared under the Resource Management
Act 1991, the Local Government Act 2002 (except for the Funding Impact
Statements in an Annual Plan or Long Term Plan), the Land Transport Act
2003, the Public Transport Act 2008, the Conservation Act 1987, the Reserve
Act 1977, the Wildlife Act 1953 and Council by-laws made under any Act.[4]

The CER Act also provides the Minister with the powers for the purposes
of the Act to determine where rebuilding may not occur and the possible
sequencing of rebuilding;[5] to determine the location and sequencing of future
infrastructure including repairs and reconstruction;[6] to give directions to
councils;[7] to call in duties or responsibilities of councils;[8] to require consent
for specified council contracts;[9] to acquire land compulsorily and determine
compensation;[10] to approve cadastral surveys;[11] to require information
from individuals;[12] to enter private property and take samples and remove
objects;[13] to carry out building demolitions on private and public land and
recover the costs;[14] to restrict access to private property and roads;[15] to erect
temporary buildings on private and public land;[16] to stop legal roads;[17] to
request an Order in Council providing an exemption to the provisions of 23
statutes;[18] and to prosecute people who fail to comply with directions given
under the Act.[19] The CER Act also removes most rights of appeal against the
Minister's decisions except on points of law.[20]

At first glance it seems like a huge leap to compare the CER Act, which was
passed by the New Zealand Parliament in response to the natural disaster
in Canterbury, with the emergency controls adopted in times of war or in
response to terrorist threats described by Agamben.[21] The motivation for the
state of exception may be different but the risk of the loss of legal protection
and of human rights is still relevant. The motivation for Christchurch's state
of exception seems to be what David Bromwich calls the 'paternal state'
whose duty is to prolong lives and to secure the health and prosperity of the
people. Bromwich calls paternalism a disorder with symptoms of secrecy and
suppression, and suggests that it is 'an ideology proper to a government that
treats the governed as children'.[22]

In his blog *Secrecy, Surveillance, and Public Safety*, Bromwich discusses the
trade-off between the anti-democratic secrecy and surveillance evident in
the United States and the perceived threat of terrorist actions. While the
motivation for Christchurch's state of exception is clearly different there is
a similar tendency towards secrecy and information control (although not
surveillance), despite the major risk being a political one – the loss of votes.
Arguably much of the 'secret' activity – the making of plans for the city's
recovery – is positive and would be well received by the public.

Faced with the scale of disaster in Christchurch after the series of earthquakes
in 2010 and 2011 it was quickly apparent that 'business as usual' could not
deal with the scale of the problems or the speed of response that was required.
Agamben recognises the theory of necessity as a recurrent explanation of the
state of exception although he discounts its theoretical validity on the grounds
that 'necessity is not a source of law, nor does it properly suspend the law'.[23]

However, the need for extraordinary action in Christchurch was evident to many Christchurch residents who subsequently supported a 'state of exception'. The more pressing issue is to find the most appropriate boundary between the state of exception and the ordinary law. In order to discuss this boundary it is useful to consider the benefits and disadvantages of Christchurch's state of exception so far.

Structural issues

The CER Act establishes a dual governance model for Christchurch. It establishes a minister with exceptional powers, and a new ministry, the Canterbury Earthquake Recovery Authority (CERA). However it leaves the mandate of local authorities largely unchanged, and while the Minister clearly has the final say on the matters outlined in the CER Act, neither he nor CERA have any direct line of management or control over the local councils. In effect the CER Act sets up a new organisation with a similar role to existing councils without clearly establishing a joint governance model or clearly distinguishing between their respective roles.

The difficulty of this situation is exacerbated by conflicting political paradigms within national and local government. The National Party's government was elected on a platform of national asset sales in order to reduce debt levels, while the Christchurch City Council has consistently refused to sell assets, choosing to establish a series of generally profitable council-owned companies and use these profits to reduce rates. With the rebuild of Christchurch budgeted to include billions of dollars of public funding there has been an ongoing tension about how this should be funded and by whom.

Benefits of emergency powers

The earthquakes have resulted in major changes in the classification and use of land in Christchurch. The most significant change has been the strategic retreat from the residential red zone, suburban areas where more than 7600 houses will not be rebuilt due to subsidence and land damage.[24] The decision about which areas to strategically withdraw from has been primarily based on economic factors by comparing the cost of remediating land and providing flood protection against the value of the land, infrastructure and houses.

Resolving this issue quickly and fairly in order to allow affected residents to get on with their lives has largely been achieved through the state of exception or the extraordinary powers vested in the Minister. The 'paternal state' is evident in the government's commitment to pay residents the balance of the value of the property above any current insurance claims. While one might dispute the fairness of the valuation benchmark, the appropriateness of the communication style or a small number of exceptions that do not fit the proposed methodology, in general terms an extremely difficult and complex problem has been resolved quickly and relatively cleanly with a reasonable attempt at minimising the distress and potential financial losses for individuals.

Another example of the benefits of the state of exception relates to the disposal of rubble from building demolitions. The amount of rubble generated by the destruction and demolition of buildings in the earthquakes was approximately equivalent to a 40-year landfill under ordinary circumstances. Sufficient space to sort the demolition materials and to landfill the rubble was not available. The Minister used his exceptional powers to designate sites for sorting and storing demolition materials, and enabled the use of clean-fill to extend the working area for container port in Lyttleton through an Order in Council.[25]

Although there has been criticism of the port reclamation from an environmental perspective, generally these 'exceptions' have been positive, enabling the recycling and reuse of demolition materials and deriving an economic benefit for Christchurch out of a potential problem.

Disadvantages

Professor Eva Horn, in her analysis of the logic of political secrecy, describes the relationship between secrecy and the state of exception, and the paradoxical role of secrecy in suspending the law in order to preserve it.[26] Both Horn and Bromwich see the need for secrecy as deriving from the risk of criminal, terrorist or military threats. The need for secrecy as part of the response to a past natural disaster seems more questionable.

Much of the operation of the Canterbury Earthquake Recovery Authority has been characterised by a high degree of secrecy. Minimal information has been released about the progress of key anchor projects or the future of land in the red zone. The reasons for this level of secrecy are generally supposed to be commercial or political sensitivity. While in some situations there clearly are commercial sensitivities relating to land purchases or contract negotiations, these are generally no more commercially sensitive than those handled by local authorities and government departments throughout the country under pre-existing legislative requirements.

Pelling and Dill, in their analysis of the role of natural disasters as catalysts for political change,[27] found that political leaders in both democratic and authoritarian regimes manipulate disaster recovery to enhance their popular legitimacy. Clearly earthquake recovery in Christchurch has been a political football in both the local government elections in 2013 and the national elections in 2014, with a wide range of politicians seeking to use earthquake recovery (or lack of it) to support their political campaigns.

Pelling and Dill also identify the potential risk to political parties as various political actors reposition themselves in the aftermath of disasters.[28] The level of secrecy in Christchurch seems to have been partly an attempt to minimise potential political risk and partly an attempt to control information in order to enhance popular legitimacy.

Closely related to the culture of secrecy is the control of access to parts of the city. After the February earthquake a cordon was established around the central city and manned by the New Zealand Defence Force in order to restrict public access. Access was only possible with the permission of CERA in the form of red zone passes that were issued for a limited period.

This state of exclusion was set up to limit the risk to members of the public from dangerous buildings and further earthquakes. It was also intended to prevent looting and criminal activity within earthquake damaged buildings. While these controls were appropriate in the immediate aftermath of the earthquakes and during the height of the demolition period for perhaps twelve to fifteen months after the earthquakes, the cordon was kept in place for twenty-nine months. For the latter half of this period much of the land within the cordon was vacant, the dangerous buildings had been removed and the risk from ongoing demolitions could have been effectively managed through site fences.

The central city cordon has been detrimental to the recovery of the central city. While inner city areas outside the central business district (CBD) such as Addington and Victoria Street have started to recover and flourish since the earthquakes, little reconstruction has started within the CBD with potential investors and developers dissuaded by the lack of access and uncertain future.

Anchor projects

Perhaps the greatest disadvantage has been the lack of community involvement in the recovery since the CER Act overrode the general legislative requirements to consult with the public over significant government and local authority projects. Following on from the highly successful Share an Idea campaign, the cessation of most forms of public consultation around the anchor projects from the Christchurch Central Recovery Plan (with the exception of the consultation over the new central library) is both surprising and highly evident.

This lack has been particularly palpable in the planning for the Avon River Precinct. This project received strong support from the public as part of the Share an Idea campaign, with people suggesting that the river and its surrounds were a unique part of the city's identity that could be improved. People wanted wide walkways and cycleways, with plenty of seating, green space, lighting and cafes, and felt that the project had the potential to attract locals and tourists to the central city.

In spite of the overwhelming public support for the project there has been no effective public consultation since Share an Idea. While Share an Idea formed a good basis to work from, effective consultation requires ongoing engagement with the opportunity for the public to view proposals and support them or ask for changes. Even with the best intentions it is seldom possible to 'get it right' at the first attempt, and by providing people with opportunities to be involved in a meaningful way they are more likely to have ownership of the project and support the outcomes.

'There are no ultimate institutional safeguards available for ensuring that emergency powers be used for the purpose of preserving the Constitution. Only the people's own determination to see them so used can make sure of that.'[29]

Central city red zone

For 859 days the centre of Christchurch was closed to public access and controlled by the New Zealand Defence Force. On 30 June 2013 the final portion of the city centre, including Cathedral Square, was reopened to the public. It was the Defence Force's longest domestic deployment ever, with soldiers working twelve hours a day, five days a week on two-month rotations. The original red zone covered much of the downtown area including the residential properties of around 7000 inhabitants. The cordon was gradually reduced until only a few central blocks remained closed. The closure of the central city lasted much longer than anticipated – the initial government estimate suggested the city would be open by April 2012.

[1–6]

[7–12]

The Quake Outcasts and the third source of government power

Natalie Jones

Natalie graduated from the University of Canterbury with an LLB (Hons) and a BSc in physics. She is an admitted barrister and solicitor of the High Court of New Zealand. In 2013 she co-founded the Canterbury branch of Law For Change, an organisation aiming to enable students and recent graduates to use their legal skills to benefit the community.

What can the government do, beyond what the law expressly allows it to? It's a vexed question, even at the best of times. Like individuals, the government can't act contrary to law – law contained both in statutes passed by Parliament, and in the decisions made by the courts. But when the law is silent, what then? For individuals, there is an assumption of freedom of action unless there is an express legal prohibition. But what about the government?

This question becomes especially significant in the aftermath of a major disaster. How far do the limits of executive power extend? Following the Canterbury earthquakes, the Canterbury Earthquake Recovery Act 2011 vastly expanded the limits of the government's express legal authority: it conferred wide powers and obligations on the executive branch of government to make decisions to ensure the expeditious recovery of Christchurch, including powers to purchase or compulsorily acquire land, override a range of planning documents and disseminate information and advice. But leaving that aside, the issue of what the government can do outside that Act was considered in the Quake Outcasts litigation. The answers were surprising and controversial, with potential implications for the wider recovery.

The third source of power

To answer the question posed at the beginning: New Zealand has inherited the English concept of the 'third source' of power – essentially, a residual governmental freedom to do anything that is not prohibited by law.[1] This is the same freedom that any ordinary person has to do anything that isn't illegal. It's known as the 'third' source to distinguish it from the 'first' (the authority given to the government by statutes made by Parliament) and the 'second' (the common law powers unique to the government, such as summoning Parliament or exercising the prerogative of mercy).

The government can therefore carry out everyday actions like entering into contracts and distributing written information without needing to pass a law. This is practical – it means that the government can carry out its day-to-day functions and respond quickly, flexibly and relatively unhindered with the action it considers appropriate to meet the sometimes unexpected societal needs. There would be huge logistical difficulties if all government power had to be codified.

Conversely, unchecked governmental power opens up huge potential for abuse and arbitrary decision-making. Unchecked power is also antithetical to the rule of law, that is, the idea that all government action should be subject to law, which is a foundational concept of any democracy. In short, it's a nightmare for any kind of democratic accountability or transparency, since it is through Parliament that the decisions of the government are opened up for public scrutiny.

Clearly, then, this third power – the power to do anything not prohibited by law – needs checks and balances. One established safeguard is that the government can't use this residual freedom to do anything that affects the legal rights and liberties of individuals. (Taxes or search and seizure, which can affect our private property rights, or arrest and detention, which can contravene our fundamental rights to life and liberty, must all be executed via other powers.) In addition, the third source only exists to the extent that there is no other positive law that deals with the circumstances in question.[2] There is still considerable academic debate about the third source, however.[3]

The residential red zone

How, then, does the esoteric concept of the third source relate to the Canterbury recovery? There's a story to it. In June 2011, roughly four months after the 22 February earthquake, the Minister for Canterbury Earthquake Recovery announced the division of Christchurch into four coloured 'zones': red (land and infrastructure damage meant rebuilding would likely not occur any time soon), green (no significant land damage; rebuilding could start), orange (further work required to determine if rebuilding could occur) and white (area where further damage assessment was required). Simultaneously, the Minister announced that the Government would offer to purchase insured residential properties in the red zone at 100 per cent of the 2007 government valuation, in order to create the confidence and certainty necessary to allow those affected people to move on with their lives. Due to the combined effect of the red zoning and the 100 per cent offers, most residents left the area.

However, owners of *uninsured* property or *vacant* sections of land in the red zone were left in the dark until August 2012, when the Chief Executive of the Canterbury Earthquake Recovery Authority (CERA) offered them only 50 per cent of the 2007 government valuation.

The Quake Outcasts go to the High Court

A group of 46 of this latter group, styling themselves the 'Quake Outcasts', were understandably less than happy. They were left in a very precarious position by the 50 per cent offers, because of the significant shortfall between the amount derived from the offer and the cost of acquiring a home elsewhere; in many cases they were retired, and not in a position to take on any significant debt. They felt that they had been forgotten for over a year already. In the back of their minds, too, were the warnings given to red zone owners in June 2011 that the Christchurch City Council would 'not be installing new services in the residential red zone' and 'may reach the view that it is no longer feasible or practical to continue to maintain services to the existing properties', and that CERA had the power to compulsorily acquire their property.[4]

The Quake Outcasts took their concerns to the High Court, together with the company Fowler Developments Limited, which owned uninsured residential sections. They sought a declaration that the red zoning and offers, being unlawful, could not affect their existing rights as residential property owners. They also wanted the offer decisions to be set aside and made again by the Minister and the Chief Executive in accordance with law.[5]

In the High Court, Justice Panckhurst took a broad approach to the issues, finding it necessary to look at the legality of the red zoning decision itself. The fundamental question in the case was this: from where did the government get the authority to declare the red zone and to offer to purchase properties in it?

This question was particularly interesting because there are several powers under the Act that could conceivably have been used to make these red zoning decisions.[6] For instance, the Minister has the power to suspend, amend or revoke any planning document pertaining to greater Christchurch, which effectively provides the power to change land zoning. The Chief Executive, similarly, has powers to disseminate information and acquire property. There was also a statutory obligation to create a Recovery Strategy, which contemplated this kind of zoning decision being made. But notably, the Government didn't even try to argue that it used these statutory powers; the Act confers obligations on decision-makers in addition to powers and also puts safeguards on those powers. The evidence was that the Government hadn't complied with these corresponding obligations and safeguards when making the red zone decisions.[7] For instance, in order to exercise any of the statutory powers, the Government must show that the use of the powers is objectively 'necessary' for the purposes of the Act, rather than merely desirable or expedient. This means that when the same result could be achieved in another way, that alternative must be taken into account.[8] In addition, many of the powers in the act come with consultation obligations – for example, the Recovery Strategy option would have required a public notification and comments procedure.[9] But from the Government's perspective, it wanted to act practically and quickly to secure certainty for badly affected residents, and so it was more convenient to go around the Act.

The Government argued, therefore, that the authority came from the third source of power. The decisions could be, and were, made outside of the Act – no statutory authority was needed, since all they did was publish information, rather than anything that affected legal rights. Although the Act conferred extraordinary powers upon the Minister, it did not exclude or limit powers that existed independently of the Act. On the other hand, the Quake Outcasts said that the authority should have come from the Act (and therefore should have come with obligations as above), since the Act offered sufficient power to make the decisions and the decisions affected legal rights.

The Court's decision

The Court sided with the Quake Outcasts. It said that that the red zoning and offer decisions overrode the existing residential zoning designations of the land in planning documents – the planning documents were still operative in theory, but in reality the decisions meant that over time the red zone would cease to be residential, and would become open space. This was to remove a fundamental human right by 'declaration', as the red zoning decisions arbitrarily and unlawfully interfered with the fundamental right to the use and enjoyment of one's home.[10]

This led to the conclusion that the Minister was required to use his powers under the Act to make the red zone decisions; he could not make them using the third source alone. The Government could create and define the red zone using the powers in the Act; yet the Minister had failed to use those powers. The Minister could not simply step outside the Act. Therefore, the Court declared that the decision to create the red zone was unlawful and therefore could have no legal effects on the property rights of the Quake Outcasts. As a further consequence, the 50 per cent offer was also unlawful, since it was not made in compliance with the requirements of the Act, nor with the Act's recovery purposes. It was set aside, and the Court directed that the Government reconsider and make a new offer in accordance with law and with regard to the reasons given in the judgment – in effect, to 're-do' the decision under the Act.

The Court also took the opportunity to criticise the reasons that the Government had put forward for the reduced size of the offer compared with that given to insured property owners fourteen months earlier, and in doing so laid down guidelines for an acceptable approach to decision-making under the Act. The recovery purposes of the Act demanded societally equitable decision-making; the Government had cited certainty and confidence as key reasons for the 100 per cent offers, which equally applied to these land owners. It was apparent that payments of only 50 per cent of the land value would not enable many of these owners to make a fresh start. Justice Panckhurst was satisfied that the plight of this group was not adequately considered in light of the purposes of the Act.

The Court of Appeal ups the ante

As could be imagined, the Minister and the Chief Executive were unhappy with this decision, and appealed.[11] Unfortunately for them, the Court of Appeal confirmed the High Court's ultimate conclusion that the 50 per cent offer was unlawful.

However, the Court reversed the High Court's decision about the third source of power. The Government could, in fact, declare the coloured zones using its residual freedom. This was nothing more than the distribution of information to the public about the state of the land, and a recognition of the severe damage caused by the earthquakes – it did not create that damage. Further, legal rights weren't affected: the red zone didn't prohibit building or the granting of building consents, it didn't stop residents from continuing to live in the red zone, nor did it require residents to demolish or repair their homes. Although the practical effect of the creation of the red zone and the 100 per cent offers was the exit of most residents from the area, there was in fact no legal step to change the relevant planning documents. In addition, none of the existing statutory provisions in the Act provided quite the right kind of power for the Government to achieve the same objectives. The Court found that earthquake recovery objectives necessitated this decision-making.

Significance for recovery

The Court of Appeal judgment is, to say the least, concerning. Surely, it must be stretching the third source of power to its limits, at the very least. Even if the decisions didn't affect rights, they had an extraordinary practical effect – they were certainly not the day-to-day, routine activities that the third source of power usually encompasses. Moreover, can it really be said that legal rights weren't affected? Even though no planning documents were altered, in practice the planning documents didn't matter anymore. Thousands of people moved out of the red zone. Land values of red-zoned properties dropped dramatically, even compared with neighbouring green-zoned land.[12] In July 2013, New Zealand Post announced it would no longer be delivering mail to red-zoned properties.[13] At the time of writing there are ongoing disputes about payment for maintaining essential infrastructure services in the red zone, and there is talk of compulsory acquisition of the remaining properties.[14] Even though the Government's actions were allegedly founded in the third source, they had effective control or influence over a section of the community. In 1992, Professor B. V. Harris wrote:

> an information and advice pamphlet issued to the public by the government may not directly override the legal rights of any citizens, yet it still may have a decisive influence on the decision-making of many individual people. People may feel compelled by the pamphlet to take action in a particular way because of the respect they have for government advice.[15]

Both the Government and the Court of Appeal took a pragmatic attitude: they argued that the Government took the steps it needed to 'get things done', and since this couldn't occur under express statutory authority, even with the vastly increased powers in the Act, the Government had to use the third source of power. But it is exactly in situations like this that administrative law should play its role to ensure that such decisions are made with caution. The limits of executive power exist for a reason, namely to ensure that the rights and privileges of individuals are not trod on by an overzealous executive. The third source of power to an extent defies statutory and judicial means of government accountability, and so significantly expanding its limits is not to be taken lightly, especially in the name of expediency. Although, perhaps, in a post-disaster context, the public is more likely to accept the third source of power – leading public lawyer Mai Chen says that in times of crisis, the populace looks to the government for certainty[16] – this increased acceptance by no means justifies the Government's actions.

Further implications for recovery

The third source aside, this case has other implications for recovery. It firmly reinforces that the Government must act within its powers when making decisions under the Act – which will be crucial in the wider recovery given the wide scope of power granted under the Act and the sweeping nature of the Recovery Plan. Before this case, the Government had already been pulled up by the courts once for acting outside its powers.[17] This shows a 'somewhat cavalier attitude at the highest levels of government to the exercise of executive power', which is 'at best, bad practice and at worst a dangerous disregard for the basic principles of the constitution'.[18]

Also, the Government's reaction to the court decisions has been very telling, showing a marked lack of compassion and dismissive attitude towards people facing genuine hardship. In the aftermath of the High Court judgment, Prime Minister John Key threatened to simply 'walk away' without making another offer, although he later apologised.[19] The Minister for Canterbury Earthquake Recovery, Gerry Brownlee, went further and publicly criticised Justice Panckhurst, implying that he ought not to be a judge.[20]

Where to from here?

The Court of Appeal expanded the limits of the third source of power in a significant way. In terms of the red zone decision, the same effects could have been achieved using a variety of undoubtedly lawful procedures, but the Government chose to ignore these in favour of expediency in what it saw as a state of emergency. The Court of Appeal legitimised this, in an unsettling relaxation of constitutional safeguards at precisely the moment when those safeguards are most needed. Legal academic Andrew Geddis writes that he suspects that 'if you were so inclined, you could probably rewrite this judgment to reach the exact opposite conclusion'.[21] At the time of writing, the Quake Outcasts have applied for leave to appeal to the Supreme Court, and while a substantive decision is likely still months away, it will be interesting to observe how Geddis's suspicion plays out. In the meantime, three years after the creation of the red zone, the Quake Outcasts are still waiting.

Cargo containers

The invention of the standardised cargo container in the middle of the twentieth century revolutionised international trade and was a major factor in powerful changes in labour, consumption and politics that made globalisation possible. Recently, the value of the container as an architectural device was widely recognised. They were employed in a variety of ways in post-quake Christchurch: as large walls to stop rock fall; small and temporary storage and accommodation; a temporary inner city shopping district; venues for arts and community events; and bracing for damaged buildings.

[1–6]

Beware when opportunity knocks

Johnny Moore

Johnny is the co-owner of Smash Palace and writes a regular column for the *Press*.

Pre-earthquake Christchurch was a different place. The consensus seems to be that the central city was dying a slow death of under-tenanted and out-of-date buildings. But as Sam – owner of C1 Espresso on High Street – says: 'Weeds will always grow between cracks in the cement.'

So while it may have been stagnant and downtrodden in places, pockets of revitalisation were happening. The most significant of these were around the laneways on the south side of the city where property prices were lower and the old buildings had survived the ravages of earlier development.

Enough developers had visited the hugely successful Melbourne Laneways and seen potential in the former industrial side of the city. Laneway developments SOL Square and neighbouring Poplar Lanes grew around High Street, Christchurch's home of fashion.

It wasn't much. But it was just enough. Weeds were growing in the cracks indeed.

I had a vested interest in these laneway developments. Over five years I worked in planning and constructing SOL Square. I worked in marketing the area and invested a portion of my life trying to make the south side of the city a great place.

I opened two businesses in the neighbourhood and bought my first apartment there – on 100 per cent loan. Ah the good old days – I didn't just write the hype; I believed it.

Then the global economy changed. Some developers folded and others survived. But what stayed were the laneways they had revitalised. Those lovely old buildings had been given a second life. Big collapse needn't smash small business and lots of owner-operated businesses survived and ticked along, contributing to the area's unique identity.

In 2011 I was running my bar – Goodbye Blue Monday – in Poplar Lanes. It was a great wee pub, open late with the best live music Christchurch had to offer. It wasn't the biggest and best bar in the world, but my family and I – who owned and ran the place together – loved it. It kept us employed and we were masters of our own destiny.

It would get very busy at night as people packed in to see the bands. That's why I'm glad the two major earthquakes that levelled Christchurch happened when the bar was closed.

On 22 February 2011 I was standing in the bar and avoiding doing work. When the earthquake struck, the buildings next door fell on top of ours, so while we had been earthquake strengthened, no engineer had accounted for next door in their calculations.

The building was smashed up and with it the business. Luck had smiled upon me and I was standing in exactly the right place. I walked out of the building with nothing more than mortar dust in my eyebrows. I couldn't have planned it better.

As you live through a disaster like this, it all feels like a deeply personal experience. You're writing a new chapter in your book that you hadn't planned. Do you stay or do you go? How the hell, with no income, are you going to pay a mortgage on your home that you can't live in? I lost my business, was out of my house and had to adjust to a new way of life.

Now I see that my experience wasn't particularly special. Somebody, somewhere, is going through disaster survival right now. Chances are that their life was harder than mine before any disaster as I come from a pretty affluent country where poverty doesn't exist on the scale that it does in large parts of the world.

It's not the situation, it is how you respond to the situation that's unique.

If you find yourself in a disaster, the best thing you can do is accept the help offered and use someone else's experience to help you find some semblance of normality. Hopefully somebody that has been through a similar experience will be able to offer a more informed, less emotive response. So take advice.

Here is my advice: be very careful about giving up democracy and watch out for grand plans. Somewhere in a grand plan people will be making moral decisions that they oughtn't. Moral decisions will tend to forget the dark corners of society where illicit activities take place. Perfectly planned cities forget this, which is dangerous.

As Robert Hughes so eloquently said of humans in his lovely *Shock of the New* series: 'It seems that like plants we do need the shit of others for nutriments.'

The dirty underbelly of a city is never imagined in utopias. But the goal should not be to manufacture a better city; it should be to create an environment in which a better city can emerge.

Once governments start dreaming about an imagined future it becomes apparent that utopia is a place mainly inhabited by an exclusive group. There's no crime, no traffic jams, no homeless people sleeping on park benches . . . Reality gets engineered out in grand plans and one person's paradise is another's personal hell.

Socially engineered utopias were the stuff of the twentieth century. People really believed that they could plan perfection with happy workers and cities that operated like computer programmes. Modernist architecture at its grandest was a statement about creating perfection. The modernists imagined they could build massive apartment blocks to house the masses that would allow city populations to grow. Everyone would be satisfied in these perfect, sterile environments.

This turned out to be bullshit. If you stack enough people on top of one another in soulless boxes, you're going to get nothing but trouble in the long run.

Once our city was unnecessarily bulldozed, the Government decided it needed to completely re-plan things in the centre. They'll put an Arts Precinct here, a Justice Precinct there and six lanes of traffic stampeding through the middle of the city so that imagined people can get to an imagined stadium that nobody needs.

Land was forcibly purchased so that they could define the perimeter of the central business district. This was bought at a price set by them with the intention of on-selling it to a bunch of pointy-shoed developers who would get rich fitting into the plan.

Who knows what the outcome of this plan will be? We may find that the boffins in power who believe they know exactly how to manipulate the market have gotten it wrong and even their greedy developer mates won't be able to make the figures work.

Then we will be left with empty land where buildings and businesses once were, sitting and waiting for an imaginary developer of the future.

While all this purchasing is taking place, moral decisions are being made. This sits very badly with me. In one block we have two new buildings, both built after the quakes. One's occupied by a gym and deemed acceptable enough to stay. The other's occupied by a strip-club and deemed not to be part of the utopian vision being forced down the public's throat.

This is dangerous stuff. The gym, Les Mills, is slick and modern. Not your banging-a-bag, old-school gym. More of a beautiful people leading beautiful lives sort of a gym. I'm sure their perfect vision is similar to that of the overzealous planners. I think they are an excellent business to encourage to stay in the city – but not at the expense of 'less desirable' businesses.

The strip club – Calendar Girls – is also shiny and new. Not your standard sleazy strip club, but the slick, modern type sold to us through movies and pornography. It was built at some cost and must have made plenty of money to afford the fit-out that screamed tacky and expensive at the same time.

So you've got two buildings of a relatively similar age, both safe and modern and both running successful, modern takes on old businesses. Somebody, sitting high in an office somewhere, has read a utopian masterplan and made a moral decision that exercise is more valid than vice in the new city. More specifically, Les Mills is okay and Calendar Girls isn't.

I'm not a huge fan of strip cubs. There is an air of desperation there that depresses me. But who am I to judge them? Just because I don't want to go there doesn't mean I should try and stop others doing so. Everybody there seems to be a consenting adult and I'm sure if you are wanting to restrict vice, then keeping it in the central city would be a good idea.

I thought this was what the law was for. Deciding what is legal and what is not. Surely, once something is legal then people have a right to operate a business.

I suppose what offends me is that this somebody is running a successful business in a city that was in decline. Somebody had seen fit to invest a heap of money in a new building, and is no longer welcome in the glossy new vision being thrust upon the public.

So their building gets forcibly acquired at a price set by the buyer, in an environment where the cost of building grows every day, meaning this once thriving business has little option but to close down. If you saw the hurdles they're placing in front of you to develop anywhere else in the city you wouldn't bother. Another business killed – not by the disaster but by those supposedly running the rebuild.

Like I said, I've run businesses in the city and I feel like the people being left out of the rebuild are those who were able to make it work in the old, shitty city that everybody said wasn't an attractive option. There's a bunch of fuckwits that have showed up from out of town and are telling the city how it should look and behave.

Good people – the public – sat down after the earthquakes and imagined a new city. A green city, strong and resilient and ready to thrive in the twenty-first century. At the same time, greedy people sat down and imagined how they could exploit and control the rebuild. Given the choice now, I'd say imagining a new city is fine, just make sure you put mechanisms in place to ensure that people can create the city they want. Lots of small visions are much more appealing than one, massive vision that doesn't share the city with anyone different.

I honestly don't know what the solution is. I only know what the solution is not. And that is what we were duped into in Christchurch.

Be very careful of bold visions; they have a tendency to be bullshit masquerading as a solution while somebody gets rich at the expense of those with real interests in the city. Remember the businesses that were there previously and help them up before you invite others in.

Cities are organic places that grow over hundreds and thousands of years. Good things happen in cities but so do bad things. Be careful of imagining a city where nothing bad ever happens. You might just find it's a nightmare, not a dream.

Street art

The radical reconfiguration of the built environment in central Christchurch has enabled an explosion of street art in the past four years. A need for visual signs of life, a shift in aesthetic values and the exposure of new walls and surfaces have created an extraordinary opportunity for both formal and informal street art. Local artists active before the quakes, new artists and visiting national and international artists have all made the most of this opportunity. Events such as From The Ground Up (all images on page 165) and the Oi YOU! presents RISE Festival (all images on page 166) have led to the creation of some significant and large-scale works.

[1–6]

[7–13]

Street art

[14–20]

Desire for the gap

Ryan Reynolds

Dr Ryan Reynolds received his PhD from Canterbury University for putting forward a new theory of political action via performance, and is a long-standing performer and designer with experimental troupe Free Theatre Christchurch. He co-founded and now chairs the Gap Filler Trust, a charitable initiative combining architecture, design and performance to activate vacant city sites with temporary creative projects. He is presently a researcher in the Faculty of Environment, Society and Design at Lincoln University.

For more than three years now, Christchurch has been a city completely in transition, almost without a present tense. It is a *post* city, the remains of the complicated, contradictory, post-colonial place it once was, with a centre that is 70 per cent destroyed and sparsely populated. It is also, now, a *pre* city, with three years' worth of plans, consultation, ideas and designs that exist mainly as a massive set of aspirations yet to be enacted. In between the past and future, the present tense consists mostly in still cleaning up and continuing to demolish the old; and making grand plans, lodging consent forms, battling insurance companies, and waiting for government and private developers to rebuild our city.

One of the relatively few and relatively prominent things actually happening in the present tense has been Gap Filler, an initiative started in October 2010 that has been running creative projects on vacant sites in Christchurch. We've been conceiving events and installations, building community and experimenting amidst the ruins of the nineteenth and twentieth century city. We temporarily reshape the urban environment in a quick and rough way, without waiting for the government's or developers' plans and permissions.

It was predictable that people here would take what they could into their own hands. When the normal ways of doing things are inadequate, those in power have to start revising the rulebook and reasserting control. Others inevitably start doing what they feel is necessary and lacking, and hope that the rulebooks will catch up.

This DIY approach has gained many fans, supporters and accolades along the way and given rise to an experimental creative movement in Christchurch among which we'd include Greening the Rubble, Life in Vacant Spaces, FESTA (the Festival of Transitional Architecture), The Social, Plant Gang and more. This vibrant movement is striving to reinvent the city, but it's unclear whether and how these temporary activities might have a lasting impact – which is what I want to question in this essay.

A propositional mode of development

I don't blame private developers for taking their time and being cautious, when eight- and nine-digit sums are at stake in a place rife with uncertainty.

And I don't wish to reproach governments (too much) for being slow, especially if that slowness is due to fulfilling their moral and statutory requirements to involve the community in large-scale publicly funded projects.

Broadly speaking, these two conventional modes of development generate the entire built form of a city. Nearly every structure is a private development undertaken by an individual, organisation or company as an investment, or a public creation (building, park, square, artwork, road, footpath) funded and commissioned by the government on behalf of its constituents.

Private developments are made without public consultation, or rather with an arcane form of consultation that involves trying to predict market forces and future consumer demand. Public developments are obliged (as they should be) to be consultative, though the nature of much consultation methodology entails that outcomes are almost always conservative and comfortable; there's not much room for pushing boundaries.

Another possibility, which Christchurch has been exploring, is what we've come to call a *propositional* mode of development. After the September 2010 quake, we hypothesised (quite safely) that people were suffering from a dearth of places to gather and socialise in the central city. We borrowed a patch of dirt where two buildings had been demolished and spent several hundred bucks to turn it into a kitschy public park for two weeks, with fake turf, garden furniture from the dump and beach umbrellas. We invited people to hang out and bring a picnic, and we had an open mic if anyone wanted to take it.

Figure 1: (left) The first Gap Filler project, cheaply turning unused vacant land into a public space

Figure 2: (right) Word of mouth and social media attracted hundreds back into the city for live music, poetry readings, nightly film screenings and more.

Our hypothesis seemed true: people came in greater numbers than we expected, and the camaraderie was palpable. The 'stage' was in constant use; over two weeks, more than 30 bands played, and there were poetry readings, circus performances, puppetry shows and more. People told us that, if they weren't a planner, developer or architect, they felt left out of the rebuild. Taking the stage was a way for them to feel involved.

The turnaround time and organisational lead-in were incredibly short, and we were self-funding it, so the site itself was a bricolage of readily available materials. The performances, too, were readily available, pre-existent. No performances, music or films were created especially for this project (apart from a poem or two). Rather, the content already existed and was thrown together in this new context. Human interactions were the glue that held the disparate elements together.

The public response to this small accomplishment totally exceeded our expectations. Many people confided in us their own ideas for what could or should be: the gap became a space that allowed people to project their own desires, at least some of which spoke to the much bigger picture of what Christchurch could be – less stuffy and conservative, more inclusive and collaborative, open to trying new things. People responded less to what we actually created, our kitschy garden and performance space, and more to the concept of the gap itself as a space of possibility. We've now created around 45 projects and facilitated 40 more, and have learned a great deal from our experiments – and we still carry with us this original discovery that people care less about us and what we create than about the implicit invitation to engage their own imaginations.

This propositional mode, we now believe, is well suited to generating public support for innovation. We try to perceive and identify deficiencies in the city and offer active solutions, involving enthusiasts and professionals at any stage. We create a project – an artwork, a public space, an amenity – and place it in the public realm as a temporary, small-scale, low-cost and low-risk experiment. More consultation, so to speak, comes from monitoring how the public uses, embraces, ignores or rejects the project. We have to watch, listen and reflect, then adapt it (or remove it) in response to implicit or explicit feedback. If a project 'fails', not much time and money is 'lost', and it provides useful learning for future projects. If a project 'succeeds', it can last longer, or have iterative additions. We operate, in this respect, like an agile small business – but our bottom line is the benefit to the public. It's a form of social entrepreneurship.

Figure 3: The Think Differently Book Exchange was originally intended to be there for just a couple months until the landowner was ready to rebuild; it's been there three years.

Our best bang for buck has to be the Think Differently Book Exchange, a broken old commercial refrigerator that was salvaged, placed on a vacant site and filled with books at a time when the city libraries were all closed. (The basic idea was suggested to us by a temporarily out-of-work librarian.) We placed a bench nearby, and a pathway of paving stones leading from the footpath, and left it there for anyone to use any time of day or night. All up it cost us maybe a hundred dollars.

Anything could have happened: everyone might have ignored it, or someone might have 'stolen' all the books, knocked it over or vandalised it. But people used it, and kept donating books. And the neighbours started caring for it, putting calls out over social media for more donations when it was getting empty. What was originally intended to be there a few months lasted much longer. It has subsequently been knocked over and the glass shattered, but somebody picked it up, sealed it and cleaned up the glass before we even knew about it. Now three years have passed and it's still being used regularly – and there have been a few 'copycat' exchanges created in the suburbs by others.

Fluidity of roles

We have developed into a values-based and outcome-focused organisation. We strive for social impact – engaging the community, empowering people to be involved in the tangible reimagining of the city, collectively experimenting and sharing the results of those experiments. The result is that we tend to evaluate the 'success' of our projects differently to how government or a private developer would.

A few months on from the February quake a land owner in Lyttleton, a little port town just over the hill from Christchurch, rang and offered us temporary use of her vacant site. Lyttelton had never had a town square, and with all of the bars and cafes closed there was a palpable lack of gathering spaces. We met a bunch of locals, spread the word and hosted a few working bees to transform the barren site into a social space. A bit of residual foundation was designated as the 'stage' and people set about building tables and chairs out of recycled timber and pallets, and levelling some of the ground to create a petanque pitch.

The Lyttelton Petanque Club, as it was named, was far from polished and pretty. But people used it, and seemed to feel pride in it. Every time I ventured back to the site, there were additions: someone made more furniture, someone planted herbs, someone dug out a sandpit and left toys there, and so on. This was perhaps unexpected, but we view it now as a sign of success. People felt empowered to contribute, even without our permission or involvement, and to continue to transform the space, which was perhaps more public in practice than any 'public' park we know of. By traditional 'park' criteria, the site was unkempt, unplanned and unfinished, but these very characteristics seem to have helped it be empowering, participatory and unrestricted.

With these atypical notions of 'quality' and 'success', we have developed into quite a fluid organisation. Sometimes we are the artists or creative initiators who conceive and create a project; other ideas are suggested to us and we develop and implement the idea with the originator; sometimes we develop briefs, or run competitions, and act as the producer or funder of a project. When there's a good idea that aligns with our objectives, we play whatever role or roles we must to help see it through to fruition and secure the social outcomes. This does cause confusion at times because people (and funders and sponsors) are more accustomed to defined roles: architects design buildings but don't construct them; builders follow plans but don't make them. We blur such restrictions and disciplinary boundaries – challenging some of the social conventions that operate, in practice, like rules.

Figure 4: (left) Several community working bees yielded the Lyttelton Petanque Club; whoever turned up to work (or brought baking) was involved deciding what the site became.

Figure 5: (right) Using what's there: The remnant of a concrete foundation serves as a stage for Lyttelton musician Delaney Davidson – with a power cord running from the neighbouring cafe.

Both conservative and progressive

All of our projects are in some ways based on conservative principles – restoring lost amenities; indulging some nostalgia and sentimentality; creating a 'village gathering' atmosphere, with a strong emphasis on physical presence and interactions outside of commodity culture; and often embracing 'amateur' content. But every project also has a progressive element, or perhaps those traditional distinctions no longer hold.

Figure 6: (left) Ten riders fastened their own bicycles into the specially made stands to run the Cycle-Powered Cinema.

Figure 7: (right) The films were all cycle-themed, and the project was on the site where a cycle shop used to be – projecting directly onto the adjoining bare wall.

For our fourteenth project we created the Cycle-Powered Cinema, which ran for two weeks on a city site where Christchurch's oldest cycle shop used to be. It took ten riders at a time – who connected their own bikes into the system – to power the sound and projector to screen the cycle-themed films. It was a bittersweet occasion: remembering and farewelling the old Cycle Trading Company; providing an outdoor cinema when all the central city cinemas had been destroyed; and enjoying many films that celebrated (or mourned the passing of) a 'simpler' time when cycles outnumbered cars and life was less hectic. But the form or frame for this nostalgic content – and the inherent symbolism of activating dead private space and making it public – gives it a different colour. Cycle power is both pre-modern (simple and mechanical) and absolutely contemporary in terms of sustainability and cutting-edge urbanism. We gave a tangible expression to the much-voiced possibility of Christchurch becoming a model for sustainable twenty-first century cities.

The book fridge is arguably similar. It's a token (conservative) gesture at restoring some of the city's lost services. But the layout of the site may invite new thoughts and experience. We deliberately put no sign on the footpath explaining it, and one can't tell what's inside from that far away. A big fridge on a vacant site doesn't make immediate sense, but it is obviously intentional, with a pathway leading there. It invites people to overcome social barriers, become curious and venture onto the site. The book exchange arguably becomes more than a simple book service or amenity (though it is that too): it can provide a brief experience outside of our conventional social logic.

Whether these projects ultimately support or challenge the status quo may hinge on the question of whether they are seen to 'just' fill a need until a more permanent solution can be found, or have ongoing influence inspiring new ways of thinking about the creation – and 'ownership' – of city space. At the end of a project the landowner still owns the site and will doubtless build something unaffected by our activities. If we have long-term impact, it's unlikely to be material; it will be in the immaterial realms of memories and desires.

The transitional

Gap Filler originated shortly after the September 2010 quake, when there were perhaps a couple dozen demolished buildings. We conceived of Gap Filler in both a spatial and temporal sense as trying to fill those few bare sites with activity, with no thoughts on changing the city in the longer term.

But we discovered an unexpected value in our first couple of projects and, with the far more damaging quake of February 2011, we began to view these small-scale and short-term projects as great ways to encourage experimentation and express a different mode of city-building that can evolve and possibly feed into long-term plans.

I now sometimes feel we are saddled with a name – Gap Filler – that has conservative and pejorative connotations. It implies that we're just biding time and distracting people until the 'real' rebuilding can happen, rather than (as we wish) engaging people, involving them in the city's renewal and transforming how they desire their urban environment to be shaped.

After two years as a Gap Filler project, the Lyttelton Petanque Club site has been bought by the city to be developed into the town square Lyttelton never had. We hope that, after experiencing a space where they felt able to contribute and make additions, people will demand a different sort of space from, and relationship with, the city – that residents and local government both learn something from our experiment, as we did.

We and our sibling organisations stopped referring to our various projects, and ethos, as 'temporary' and began to use the now-preferred term 'transitional'. Through using this term, we (imperfectly) try to encapsulate this aspiration to influence what comes next. Perhaps a term like 'trailblazing' would be clearer; we try to forge some alternative paths and ease the way for others to take them too.

Figure 8: The Pallet Pavilion at night – a space open to the public, with free power and wi-fi, twenty-four hours a day

Gap Filler built and operated the Pallet Pavilion, a large community event space constructed out of 3000 pallets. The Pavilion had some costly design flaws, and taught us about navigating tricky parts of the Council's consent process. Both of these things we record and make public, so that we and others can do similar projects better and faster the next time. During its 16-month lifespan, it attracted other projects to the vicinity with a similar vibe and communal outlook: collectively built micro-architecture, social enterprises and small businesses (especially food trucks). The Pavilion has been deconstructed (as planned), but the site retains the flavour the Pavilion established and is developing into The Commons, a values-based cooperative development (see page 228). One use influences the subsequent.

The site of The Commons is adjacent to one of the Government's major rebuild anchor projects, the Avon River Park. We've had a few discussions with the contractors designing that project, but it remains to be seen whether our experiments on this site will in any way influence their so-called 'permanent' plans. Certainly they don't seem to be employing anything of the inclusive process we use to conceive, develop, build and activate our projects, instead preferring to develop their designs behind closed doors and without public input or involvement. The development *process*, then, might become the political battleground of our 'transitional city' movement.

The metropolis and mental life

In some ways, Christchurch has been cast back to the turn of the twentieth century when it was an emergent city, and is experiencing the same disputes over what a city is and how it should develop. 'The Metropolis and Mental Life' is a well-known 1903 essay by Georg Simmel. Reflecting from the midst of the first period of rapid urbanisation, he regards cities as creations where the dialectic of individual and society is for the first time revealed as a root condition of human life. Cities force us to debate and determine how individuals can and should form societies – or how societies can allow room for individual choices, behaviour and absurdities.

Simmel writes of the metropolis: 'Here in buildings and in educational institutions . . . is to be found such a tremendous richness of crystallizing, depersonalized cultural accomplishments that the personality can, so to speak, scarcely maintain itself in the face of it.'[1] An opposition to this depersonalised mode would have to develop techniques to liberate space and engender fluidity.

With the massive and controlling city plan that's underway, Christchurch is in some key respects an even more rule-bound society than previously, despite the chaos and disorder. This inflexibility makes something like the 'transitional city' movement both crucial and probable – carving out spaces and times where the little people are asserting creative impulses and self-determination.

It's interesting to consider that so far these gaps, these possible spaces for self-determination, have been populated primarily by a bricolage of arguably regressive or at least pre-existent contents but that it is the frame or form – the symbolic making public of private space, the absurd twists that make these assemblages more than mere amenities – that opens a progressive potential and invites unconventional thoughts and behaviours.

I found that Simmel offers perspective on this form-content relationship as well. In a 1910 essay on sociability and conversation, he writes:

> In the serious affairs of life men talk for the sake of the content which they wish to impart or about which they want to come to an understanding – [whereas] in sociability talking is an end in itself; in purely sociable conversation the content is merely the indispensable carrier of the stimulation.'[2]

In sociable conversation, the most widely inclusive sort, the contents are largely pre-established and known. We might say the same of many of the Gap Filler projects, not that the content is a matter of indifference – it must be interesting and significant – only it is not the purpose of the projects that the contents yield objective results. Our city-wide mini-golf course is not 'about' golf or trying to 'say' anything about golf. That content is just the vessel for provoking people to explore their city and see the potential for experimentation and participation where they mightn't otherwise.

Desire for the gap

Here I return to our initial discovery that people respond not only to the specific content of Gap Filler projects, but also, or more so, to the *ideas behind* or even the *image of* Gap Filler.

The content, sometimes superficial, is often eclipsed by a *desire for the gap*. I mean this in a spatial, temporal and political sense. A gap is a void where many things are possible. But it is not a complete absence of form: there are physical characteristics, like neighbouring walls, buildings or features. There is a heightened sense of history on each individual site and, standing on a bare site in full view of mass destruction and ongoing demolitions, one is squarely within a specific recent history.

I propose that many people have a desire for the gap in this spatial sense. Unlike most built form, which forcefully determines the sort of activities and interactions that can take place within it, a gap is largely indeterminate. It's a space for self-determination that people find appealing, with just enough form to incite ideas. People find the enormous featureless sites of the East Frame, for instance, daunting and unappealing, with nothing to 'bounce off'.

This desire for the gap also takes a temporal form. Anyone can run a project without sacrificing their existing commitments if there's no need for it to endure. The temporary nature can encourage the trying out of ideas: there's less pressure to get everything 'right' and design out uncertainties as with a major 'permanent' development.

This desire for the gap also exists in the political sense as a craving for meaningful difference when it feels like all political parties are just offering us different seats to the same show. We desire an inkling of possibility for fundamentally reshaping social interactions, for spaces conducive to sociability without pressure to shop, for inclusivity and for the possibility to be truly surprised.

In the immediate aftermath of the big quakes, there was – among the shock – a widespread sense that anything was possible. These gaps, at their best, can be preservations of that brief liberating potential: little bubbles in space-time that sustain the desire and belief – and therefore possibility – that meaningful change is achievable.

Fluidity of rules

Singing the praises of gaps, I risk sounding anti-development. It's hard to know how we can rebuild major developments whilst accounting for these 'transitional city' discoveries. The last essay Simmel ever published I find highly relevant: 'Life must either produce forms or proceed through forms. But forms . . . contradict the essence of life itself, with its weaving dynamics, its temporal fates, the unceasing differentiation of its parts.'[3] So he posits a ceaseless cycle where life creates cultural forms (buildings, institutions, organisations, anything) and then immediately finds the forms too constraining and starts rebelling against them. He writes: 'Life perceives "the form as such" as something forced upon it. It would like to puncture not only this or that form but form *as such*.'[4] We have collectively established these gaps as having a high degree of freedom from form in terms of space, time and ideology – yet with enough hint of those forms to trigger creative responses.

This observation suggests that *rewriting* the rules of our society is insufficient. The closest we could come to reconciling the individual and society would be by creating a society that more or less constantly rewrites its rules – its laws and regulations as well as its social norms and habits.

One of our most popular projects has been the Dance-O-Mat. It's essentially an open space and a jukebox. We salvaged a coin-operated washing machine from a Laundromat and rigged it so that you plug in your music player or phone, drop a coin in and the speakers and lights come on for half an hour. It clearly fills multiple needs as a home for dance groups to rehearse and a venue for social events. But it also invites new social relations and interactions (where else would you find professional flamenco dancers mixing with hip-hop boys?) and is a springboard for other creative responses.

Figure 9: (left) Another formerly fallow private space that's now open all hours for anyone to use – a site for interesting chance encounters

Figure 10: (right) Prince Charles expressed an interest in learning more about the grassroots creative movement on his visit to Christchurch, where he took a spin on the Dance-O-Mat.

Dance-O-Mat is nothing more than a framed empty space, a space that suggests or invites 'music and dance here'. Dance-O-Mat doesn't contravene any rules, but it shatters certain conventions. When we first proposed the project, many people warned us that nobody in conservative Christchurch would dance in public – it was too far outside the social norms here. But people do! We made it okay for people to dance in public, not literally (through signs and text) but symbolically (through the arrangement of space).

When we removed the Dance-O-Mat from one site, we spotted a few people the following day dancing in the dirt of the site with a portable boom box. We'd transformed people's conception of that space even beyond the physical presence of the project. But why wouldn't they dance like that all over the city, and why hadn't they been doing it all along? Even as we helped to relax the conventions of one space, we may have been implicitly reinforcing the conservative conventions of the rest of the city's spaces. In addressing one need or issue, one inevitably creates others.

We try very hard to be fluid, responding to the changing context of the city and refusing to repeat ourselves. But we've also become part of the systems of the city, with ongoing support from Council, citizens, businesses and property owners. The test for us is to remain fresh and relevant. If we stagnate – or are perceived to stagnate – we need to step aside.

How else might one continuously challenge conventions to create a permanently transitional city, always creating itself anew?

Rewriting the Rules

Protest signs

The scale of the damage to Christchurch has forced many large, difficult and controversial decisions. Some people have expressed their frustration and disagreement to these through protest – and particularly through the use of graphics and signage. The issues are diverse and include problems with insurance and EQC, opposition to compulsory government land purchases and the demolition of heritage buildings. Opposition has been conventional and innovative, comic and serious, hastily and beautifully crafted.

[1–4]

[5–10]

Reimagining and rebuilding local democracy

Bronwyn Hayward

Dr Bronwyn Hayward is a senior lecturer in political science at the University of Canterbury, a trustee of the London think tank Foundation for Democracy and Sustainable Development and a Visiting Fellow for the Sustainable Lifestyles Research Group, University of Surrey. An advocate for children, youth and deliberative democracy, her book *Children, Citizenship and Environment: Nurturing a Democratic Imagination in a Changing World* (London, Earthscan / Routledge) was selected as a feature of the 'LitCam: Active Citizenship' event at the Frankfurt Book Fair 2012.

In this essay I reflect on ways we might begin to recover and rebuild our local democracy in Christchurch after the 2010 and 2011 earthquakes and the political upheavals that followed the disaster. Healthy democracies are characterised by three principles of decision-making: inclusion, participation and accountability.[1] In this discussion I offer some thoughts about ways we might ensure these principles inform the institutional 'reform', procedural 'retrofitting' and the foundational rebuild of our local democracy so that it is fit for the future.[2]

Introduction: Why democracy matters

Politics is about how we make decisions (and non-decisions) that affect the opportunities and lives of others in a 'polis' or community of citizens. What is distinctive about *democratic* politics is that the authority for political decisions and actions ultimately rests with us, the *people*, through three key principles of decision-making: inclusion, participation and accountability. Improving the way public decisions are made is one of the key challenges facing all cities in an urban century. By 2050, seven out of ten humans will live in urban areas. One hundred years ago just two out of ten people lived in urban areas.[3] The Nobel prize winning economist Amatrya Sen reminds us that in this process of rapid urbanisation we no longer have the luxury of ignoring those whose views we don't agree with. Even if we try to separate ourselves and mix only with people 'like us' – whether it is by living in gated communities, sending our children to private schools or just building high fences around our increasingly fortress-like homes – we will be confronted more and more by other people with differing values, priorities and life experiences from our own. Learning to live with that difference and tolerate it is both the challenge and the joy of urban democratic life. Cities can be vibrant places of new ideas, entertainment and innovative business, but they can also be places of stark inequality and tension. How we make decisions in cities needs careful thought and can't just be left to chance.

It is not a coincidence that the first democracies emerged from the innovative crucible of the early Greek city-states. The Greeks developed a novel idea that free men in cities should determine their lives, a thought that came to be the guiding principle of democratic government. However it took another 2000 years before this radical Greek idea of democracy was extended to women and ethnic minorities, and it is a matter of huge civic pride that universal suffrage was first won by women of New Zealand, in a campaign spearheaded by the efforts of Christchurch citizen-suffragist Kate Sheppard and her colleagues. The ideals of democracy still motivate people to give up their lives to secure o defend this right for freedom and the responsibility to govern their own lives.

But simply recognising that democracy is valuable doesn't settle how we make the principles of inclusion, participation or accountability work in decision-making for a city recovering from a major disaster. It is difficult to make collective decisions at the best of times. People often have strong, seemingly unreasonable views, while others appear to have no opinion at all. In the midst of the confusion, frustration and suffering that accompanied the earthquakes it was tempting to imagine that if we just left the decisions to a few experts, key business or political leaders for example, it would all be easier. The poor performance of local politicians, who seemed slow to grasp the strategic priorities they needed to tackle after the September 2010 earthquake, together with the demands of a plethora of deregulated insurance agencies and competing interests, made the idea of using experts or a strong leader to 'get things moving faster' even more appealing. Some began to joke that 'democracy was overrated' while others argued (more seriously) that the city had enough 'community advocates' and what it needed now were 'more strong leaders'.

Yet as democracy theorist Bonnie Honig reminds us,[4] disasters will become increasingly common in a dynamic world of climate change and associated severe weather events. We won't be able to keep suspending democracy every time we have an emergency. We need to find ways to maintain democratic values and help citizens retain their hard won freedoms and rights. Rebuilding a healthy local democracy is also essential to our community recovery. Consciously or unconsciously, as citizens we value our democratic 'agency', that is, our ability to 'imagine and effect desired change about thing that matter the most to us'. A healthy democracy isn't just a nice-to-have matter of convenience; it enables us to flourish as fulfilled citizens.[5]

In the weeks, months and years following the earthquakes, however, the loss of citizen agency has become a pressing problem as many report frustration with their lack of voice and the lack of transparency and accountability in the city rebuild process. New Zealanders often express their agency in physical terms – enjoying for example a freedom to get around, and a sense of do-it-yourself creativity and problem solving. So feeling unable to get on with our lives – in damaged homes, frustrated by traffic snarl ups, lacking access to public space or amenities, exhausted by drawn out battles with national or private insurance providers and centralised government departments – we can feel a deep grief that threatens to undermine our wellbeing, and adds significantly to high levels of reported stress in the community.[6]

In this context we urgently need to rethink the democratic problems of who should have how much say about what. Delegating responsibility for all our key decisions (in Christchurch's case to the Minister for Canterbury Earthquake Recovery) is not an effective nor a sustainable solution for a complex city rebuild. Yet how might we enhance our democratic decision processes? Few people have time for town meetings but feel frustrated when excluded from decisions that affect their lives. If petitions and pop up protest are not effective, what other forms of participation might be helpful? How much involvement can we fairly expect of citizens with busy lives? A range of ways of enhancing democracy are possible, such as more local public debate in local media, greater use of online referenda, better use of local wards to make delegated neighbourhood spending decisions, and tackling growing income inequality to ensure citizens in the poorest homes have the resources they need to exercise their capabilities for citizenship. But democratic innovation also requires us to address the problems of how our concerns are registered, new ideas trialled and decisions scrutinised so we are assured that decision-making is both innovative and transparent and that inaction or mistakes are addressed in a timely and effective manner.

The democratic philosopher Jean-Jacques Rousseau reminded us two centuries ago that we should always be wary of those who advocate significant democratic reform in a crisis; he argued you need a clear head and a calm mind to make big political changes. Had we radically reorganised the structure of local government processes in the immediate aftermath of the quakes, without a strong democratic mandate, through public discussion and an agreed process of public legitimisation (for example using referenda), it would have created greater public disquiet. Now, four years after these earthquakes began, however, it is time to think about how we might achieve democracy for our community that enables a more inclusive conversation about visions for our city that better consider the needs of Christchurch's most vulnerable citizens (the young, the elderly, the economically marginalised and new ethnic minorities), so we can support current citizens and future residents.

A political quake: Understanding how local democracy was eroded then disrupted

Christchurch citizens living in the post-quake period have experienced a significant democratic upheaval. However, a slow erosion of local democracy had preceded the disruptive political changes that followed the earthquakes of 2010 and 2011. The most serious erosion of democratic values began many years ago with the unjust acquisition of 34.5 million acres of Ngāi Tahu tribal land by the New Zealand Company and the Crown in the 1840s, and the subsequent seizure of small remaining reserves for public works' purposes, together with the exclusion of Ngāi Tahu from meaningful participation in key decisions affecting other taonga (treasured things), and failure to provide promised schools and hospitals.[7] More recent examples of the pre-quake erosion of democratic principles include the passing of the 2010 legislation that suspended elections for Environment Canterbury (ECan), the regional council responsible for natural resource management including water. Other examples include declining voter turnout for local elections (complexly tied with growing income inequality in the city) and widely reported frustration with councillors and highly paid city managers who were seen to exclude citizens from the scrutiny of key local decisions on the grounds of 'commercial sensitivity'.[8]

After the earthquakes of September 2010 and February 2011, four significant political upheavals exposed this underlying fragility in our local democratic landscape. In the first instance the introduction of the Canterbury Earthquake Recovery Act 2011 (CER Act) sidelined locally elected decision makers by overriding them with centrally appointed managers and officials. The CER Act was needed initially to secure much-needed national resources as the city struggled to cope with a national disaster. But the ongoing use of new powers now stand in the way of local democratic community recovery.[9] A centralised government department, the Canterbury Earthquake Recovery Authority (CERA), has been established, with a single minister who has far-reaching powers. The Minister is supported by a chief executive and staff who are rarely enabled to speak out. Creating a brand new central government agency with far-reaching power has arguably exacerbated already confused lines of communication as public servants report to Wellington rather than the local community. CERA's power and reach now threaten to make future reintegration with locally elected institutions more difficult.

The CER Act was followed by the extension of the Environment Canterbury (Temporary Commissioners and Improved Water Management Amendment) Act 2013, which prolonged the previous suspension of regional government (ECan) elections in Canterbury until the new date of 2016. This Act provoked a widespread public outcry and a variety of constitutional experts and professionals, academics, residents groups, members of the public and even the appointed commissioners themselves objected strongly.[10] ECan manages natural resources like water, resources that are under intense pressure from changes including the intensification of the Canterbury dairy industry in a changing climate. Suspending elections could be argued to exemplify efficient management and to enable 'co-governance' models of decision-making that give greater voice to previously excluded stakeholders, particularly Ngāi Tahu, who now have a guaranteed seat at decision-making tables when determining the future use of natural resources. However there i nothing democratic about any governance model if in the process it privilege the voices of already powerful business elites and landowners, particularly those in the dairy industry, effectively legitimising private use of a public good (water) while taxing residents. This is further highlighted by the lack of opportunity for people to hold appointed decision makers to account via regular community elections.

Post-quake, the Local Government Amendment Act 2013 also weakened local democracy by limiting the purpose and powers of local authorities. This act narrowed the purpose of local authorities as set out in the Local Government Act 2002, from fostering 'social, economic, environmental and cultural well-being of communities' (known as the four wellbeings) to a much more limited role of 'providing for good quality local infrastructure, public services and regulatory functions at the least possible cost to households and business'. Worldwide, local governments are struggling to meet the needs of their communities. Many city councils have limited access to revenue to support essential infrastructure (a particularly acute problem in Christchurch where the city has suffered from under-insurance and has experienced the flight of capital as some key businesses took insurance payments they received and left to begin again elsewhere). But narrowing the purpose of

New Zealand's local government to focus only on roads, rates and rubbish empoverishes our democratic vision. Cities require both the resources and the authority to meet the wide-ranging needs of urban populations.

Concerns about loss of citizen voice and vision in local government were also compounded in Christchurch after the earthquakes by a rushed process to close and merge a number of local schools with inadequate public consultation. Schools are a lynchpin of urban communities. So it was deeply disturbing that Ministry of Education officials, for reasons that were not always clear, began to reorganise education at a time and pace counter to humanitarian best practice for meeting children's needs post-disaster.[11] The consequent outpouring of grief, confusion and anger in the community over what was seen as unnecessarily high-handed behaviour underscored the failure of the Minister of Education and the Ministry officials to reflect on their actions and delay reform (for example by calling a moratorium on forced mergers and closures). Education officials have subsequently sought to justify their action by arguing that children will take their cue in how to respond to the education disruption from parents who, they argue, 'are often more upset than children' (as if family suffering could be somehow quantified and individualised) and that children will 'get over it eventually'. I argue this reasoning allows officials to avoid having to accept responsibility for a serious failure in their duty of care for local children at a time of a disaster by not following best practice and continuing schooling where possible post-disaster. The resulting community grief and anger at the loss of local voice in city, regional and school board decision-making spilled over into city-wide protests to 'bring back democracy' including a public protest I led on Suffrage Day in 2012.

Reforming institutions

The future for city democracies can be one of great democratic innovation as Benjamin R. Barber's provocatively titled book *If Mayors Ruled the World* reminds us.[12] His work builds on the earlier writing of urban sociologist Jane Jacobs.[13] Barber argues that cities will be the sites of some of our most significant decision-making in this century. But here in Christchurch it is still not clear how we might restore healthy local democracy. Nor is it clear that that there is any adequate planning for the end of the temporary political solutions introduced after the earthquakes. Political 'institutions' are the organisations that are established to put the will of the people and the policies of their elected representatives into practice. At present we have a temporary institutional arrangement of CERA, city and district councils, and appointed commissioners. What happens next matters a great deal. The worst-case scenario is that a vital public discussion about options for reforming these institutions will be left until close to the legislative deadlines for the end of CERA and appointed ECan commissioners, risking a manufactured governance crisis and an angry community backlash. If any institutional reform is to be legitimate, a careful process of planning with significant public consultation is needed from the earliest possible time and any recommended changes should be endorsed by public referendum. The experience of democratic reform to create a 'super-city' in Auckland also suggests merging functions of a number of local authorities may not enhance democracy.

Voting turnout has not significantly increased in Auckland since its local council mergers and in fact some communities report feeling even more alienated from decision-making in the new larger local electorates.[14]

Auckland's ambivalent democratic experience of institutional reform should give Christchurch pause for thought. Before we launch into institutional reform, we need to be clear about what the problem is. For example, why would we adopt a one size fits all institutional restructure and merge city, district and regional councils when some district councils surrounding Christchurch report positive experiences and appreciate their locally elected representatives' management of disaster recovery?[15]

Retrofitting democratic procedures

Alongside the possibility for institutional reform, there is also a potential to engage in what political theorist Mark Warren describes as 'democratic retrofitting', that is, reform to existing democratic processes (voting, public consultation and deliberation for example) to better meet our needs as a city. Retrofitting our democratic procedures may significantly help to enhance the inclusion, participation and accountability of existing decision processes. For example the Christchurch City Council (CCC) has begun to reopen decision-making to greater public scrutiny through live streaming CCC meetings. Elsewhere in New Zealand councils have experimented with other democratic procedural retrofits, including introducing seats for Māori representatives in communities (as opposed to appointing commissioners) or introducing Single Transferable Voting (STV).[16] Christchurch rejected using STV in an earlier referendum and has opted to stay with a process that allows candidates to stand for loose local parties, an approach that arguably provides the voter with some broad information about the values, alliances and orientation of local candidates. If changing the type of voting method is not an option, Christchurch citizens might at least want to consider retrofitting our democracy by supplementing existing elected decision-making with more regular ward level discussion and online public engagement processes. The large number of residents who turned out to Share an Idea in the early stages of the city plan process, for example, reminds us that people do want to be heard on issues they care about.

Supplementing postal voting with carefully trialled e-voting might be another option for retrofitting our democracy in the future, but more immediate steps could include simple measures such as using supermarkets and garages as polling booths for local elections, or for information sharing to reach a wider community. Other procedural innovations might include opening up the process of setting annual expenditure priorities to the public for comment through 'participatory budgeting'. Such experiments have merit, but each must also be accompanied with careful consideration of the risk to ensure that new democratic procedures do not simply reinforce decision-making capture by privileged interests. I suggest that alongside an institutional reform and a democratic retrofit, we also need to embark on a basic foundational rebuild our local democracy.

Rebuilding the foundations of local democracy

Beyond institutional reform and procedural reform, healthy democracies need fundamental regular 'inspection' to ensure they rest on strong foundations of shared community values, tolerance and respect for the views and opinions of others who differ from us. In 1993, Christchurch won the German Bertelsmann Foundation award for 'democracy and efficiency' as a result of high levels of resident satisfaction with its local decision processes. Christchurch has also been home to many world class democratic thinkers, including leading suffragist Kate Sheppard, the peace activist Elsie Locke and the electoral reform campaigner and Green politician, Rod Donald. Yet as a city we can't rest on our laurels. Maintaining this rich democratic vision takes constant renewal and nurturing. As the social environment of Christchurch changes, for instance with the arrival of new migrants and larger numbers of retirees, we need to think carefully about how we enable meaningful voice for indigenous Māori communities while also growing and maintaining local democracy to meet the needs of future citizens. Children and teens are citizens of this city whose voices are easily marginalised in precarious economic times. Could Christchurch lead New Zealand and follow the example of Scotland, Austria and other communities by finding ways to enable 16-year-olds to vote in local elections for example? Is it possible to create cross-generational forums for civic conversation where participants listen and try to understand each community's differing needs and cultural experiences in order to find new synergies and ways to collaborate?[17]

Building a strong democracy requires us to pay attention to the virtues of good citizenship like tolerance and active listening. Great democracies need strong foundations; we have to keep modelling democratic processes to children and in everyday life. It matters that we listen to those who differ from us with respect. To be democratic, public consultation must be elicited by inclusive discussion and not, for example, by a competition of ideas (as in the unfortunate recent experiment with local school children for an otherwise wonderful new Margaret Mahy Playground). We need to be self conscious and proactive as a city about the ways new citizens are welcomed and integrated into the community. How do people know they are a valued and valuable part of a local democracy? How do they know their energy, efforts and new perspectives are appreciated? What formal and informal means can we use to rebuild a sense of citizen solidarity?

In rebuilding the foundations of our democracy, Christchurch also has a unique opportunity to forge a new social contract or a new agreement between citizens. Today, four winters after the earthquakes first began, inequality is growing in Christchurch amongst vulnerable elderly and children.[18] This situation demands a fundamental rethinking of our mutual obligations to each other to ensure we provide for greater human security. It will take an enormous amount of democratic discipline to think of the long term and of our duties and responsibilities to others as we recreate a city that offers all citizens, young and old, whānautanga or mutual support. Our city has suffered much in the earthquakes, and it is up to us to ensure that our rich legacy of local democratic thinking and practice is not lost in political upheavals now facing Christchurch.

Chapter 4

Considering the Common Good

He hua mā te iti me te rahi

The common good is understood to include those things we share that provide mutual benefit to all of us: clean water, affordable shelter, food, air, the rule of law and many other intangible things. Some of these goods require restrictions on individuals; tax may be needed to supply clean water, or restrictions on behaviour to keep the rule of law. The idea of the common good is often held up in opposition to individual rights. It's a long-held debate that goes as far back as Plato's *Republic*.

Yet, in times of disaster it becomes clear that the ideals of the individual and the collective good are not simple opposites. The military power of the state kept people safe from dangerous buildings while at the same time individuals formed groups and supported their neighbours with food and water. It is only when the convenience of services that we use every day – such as roads and sewerage systems – is taken away that we realise how much of the common good we take for granted.

As the city starts planning its future, these reconsiderations of the common good continue to resonate. CERA and its Blueprint are an attempt to promote a consolidated approach to the city's rebuild; protect land values and investment; provide safety and confidence; and avoid the potential chaotic jumble of buildings that could result from developers having unrestricted rights in the city.

Affordable housing, heritage and public transport are areas that require public funding to produce their common good and yet have struggled, due to a lack of means, to achieve this. There have also been many small acts – what might be called public gifts – that add to the cultural amenity and collective identity of the city.

The events of the past four years have illustrated that community networks are a particularly valuable form of infrastructure, as valuable as any pipes and power lines. But like pipes, power lines and other amenities, they need to be regularly maintained if they are to continue to produce the common goods that we benefit from.

A city that loves?

Michael Gorman

Michael is the City Missioner at the City Mission in Christchurch.

Christchurch is busy rebuilding, although some say it is not enough or soon enough. Demolition, planning, new foundations, new structures, glazing and landscaping are underway to replace some of what we have lost. Unfortunately it is not so easy to replace the people we have lost or to repair those who have suffered and make them safe and whole again. At the Christchurch City Mission, we deal with those who are poor, marginalised, addicted, homeless and lonely. We did this before the quakes and we are doing it now, but with a new urgency and for more people.

We who live in Christchurch, and want to keep loving it, can easily feel defeated. Feelings of powerlessness, depression and a lack of hope are not jus the preserve of property owners but of all who call Christchurch home. Alon with many in Christchurch, we who work in the red zone were displaced and had to find temporary accommodation. With hard work and help from the community the Christchurch City Mission only had to close for four days. During that time we kept contact with as many of our people as possible and extended our services providing food, counselling, and instilling a sense of hope. Many of our clients tried to cope by reverting to methods that they ha used in the past but which were toxic and unhealthy. Alcohol and drug use appeared to increase. Now, as well as counselling for addiction, our workers are dealing with depression and more complex social problems.

In the days immediately after the earthquake we pulled together and helped each other. We were united by a common sense of shock. Some people witnessed death; for many others it felt like a death. We need a chance to mourn and to regain strength. We need time to adjust to what we have lost. We also need to believe we have a future and to have hope in it.

To help us recover, policy makers and bureaucrats could look at ways to actively avoid increasing our stress but at the Mission we have not always seen signs of this. There has been no plan to rebuild bedsits, many of which were lost in the quake. Low-cost accommodation is being left to the market to provide but, as there is little profit to be made, no one seems to be picking up the challenge. In the meantime, we are hearing stories of horrific rental increases, evictions and overcrowding. In the immediate aftermath of the quakes family and friends helped each other find shelter, but now, three years later, goodwill and relationships are being strained as many long to have safe, affordable and healthy homes of their own. Some business and trades people could treat us with more tolerance and avoid exploiting us because we are hurting, stressed, tired and depressed. Insurance companies could stop playing games with our lives by giving correct information and not looking for clauses in contracts to avoid payments and acting in ways that may be legal but are of questionable morality. Politicians could work together, stop point-scoring and actively intervene to help us.

Repair and construction will be an important part of rebuilding Christchurch and business must be encouraged and helped to re-establish and grow. People in the east need to know their needs are being heard and that they are important also. However, it will be an empty city if we do not take care of each other on a more personal level. If we feel marginalised because of poverty, if some landlords exploit us, if those in power don't look at our basic needs for safe, healthy homes, then we may have a city that has glossy buildings but we will not have a city that loves.

The rest of New Zealand has been good to us. We have been well supported. But the country will slowly forget, like a person who mourns the death of a loved one and then gradually moves on. Our tragedy will be replaced by a new tragedy somewhere else and time will cause a dimming of memory. If we in Christchurch do not forget and are unable to move on, forgive us. We are trying.

The inverse care law

Philippa Howden-Chapman, Amber L. Pearson, Rosemary Goodyear, Elinor Chisholm, Kate Amore Graciela Rivera-Muñoz & Esther Woodbury

Prof. Philippa Howden-Chapman is a public health professor and director of He Kainga Oranga Housing and Health Research Programme and the New Zealand Centre for Sustainable Cities at the University of Otago, Wellington, where Kate Amore, Elinor Chisholm, Graciela Rivera-Muñoz and Esther Woodbury are, or have been, doctoral students. Dr Amber L. Pearson is a health geographer with a focus on social justice and understanding. Dr Rosemary Goodyear is a senior analyst in housing at Statistics New Zealand and has published research on crowding and commuting patterns.

Globally, most people now live in towns and cities, and this number is rising so urban resilience is increasingly critical. Cities build resilience by investing in sustainable infrastructure, which minimises energy consumption while simultaneously improving quality of life. People in resilient cities, whether they rent or own, live in safe, warm, dry housing, which is conveniently located in supportive communities close to public transport. They can go about their daily school, work and leisure activities, without having to spend most of their income on housing and transport. Cities that are resilient are able to respond well to shocks, such as earthquakes, as well as extreme events such as droughts, flooding and other consequences of climate change.[1]

Recovery efforts after natural disasters, particularly those led by government should prioritise resilience by adopting principles of distributive justice to ensure that collective efforts are most focused on those most in need.[2] These efforts should be closely monitored. Though there is an extensive literature in New Zealand about the geophysics of the Canterbury earthquakes[3] and several reports about their effects on housing,[4] analysis of the distribution of health hazards[5] or the differential impact of the housing rebuild on health an wellbeing is less common.[6]

The Canterbury Earthquake Recovery Authority (CERA) reports on wellbeing indicate that Christchurch city residents feel that the earthquakes have had a strong negative impact on their everyday life and rate their quality of life less positively than the residents of the nearby Selwyn and Waimakarir districts. Dealing with the Earthquake Commission (EQC), other insurance issues, making decisions about house damage and repairs, and having to relocate were top of the list of negative stressors.[7]

In this chapter we look at the extent and geographic distribution of housing damage, recovery efforts as they relate to neighbourhoods' socio-economic deprivation, and residential mobility. We consider the priority given to the repair and rebuild of housing for people who are especially vulnerable: people on low incomes and people with chronic illness or disability.

The effects of the earthquakes on housing

The Canterbury earthquake sequence of 2010-2011, followed by over 13,733 aftershocks, was the largest natural hazard event in New Zealand's written history.[8] The expected cost to the Crown alone of rebuilding Canterbury is $23 billion[9] and the overall cost is estimated at $40 billion – much more than the relative impact of Hurricane Katrina on the economy of the USA or the Great Eastern Japanese Earthquake on the Japanese economy.[10]

The earthquakes not only severely damaged the city's infrastructure, but also an estimated 100,000 homes in the region.[11] Taking into account the pre-earthquake rate of building, there are about 11,000 fewer habitable dwellings in greater Christchurch than there would be had the earthquakes not occurred.[12] In the residential red zone, where the ground experienced severe liquefaction, rebuilding has been prohibited (fig. 1). This will result in the eventual loss of around 8000 dwellings. Because of historical patterns of building low-income housing on cheaper land in low-lying areas, much of the red zone is an area of higher socio-economic deprivation. Red zone demolition is partly underway and, by September 2013, an estimated 3012 dwellings in the residential red zone had been demolished.[13]

The Crown made offers to purchase these red zone houses and several thousand home-owners accepted, so many houses are empty. The 2013 Census counted 16,953 empty dwellings in greater Christchurch, an increase of 9828 (138 per cent) since the 2006 Census.[14] Most of these empty dwellings (14,556) were located in Christchurch city and mainly in the severely affected, socio-economically deprived eastern suburbs.[15] These houses not only represent personal and financial loss, but also the scale of ongoing social disruption. In some cases, people have had to move many times, repeatedly experiencing one of life's most stressful events,[16] while others have continued living in damaged houses.

While an estimated 7000-8000 people left Christchurch immediately following the February earthquake, there were further declines over time. By June 2012, the population had declined another 1.5 per cent.[17] Primary health organisation (PHO) data show distinct population flows out of the central city and eastern suburbs, which have seen the most dramatic population decline, into the growing western and northern suburbs (fig. 2).

Effects of the earthquakes on the vulnerable

The destruction of so much housing, and particularly low-income housing, has exacerbated the problem of rent affordability. According to tenancy bond data the number of rental properties fell by about 19 per cent between December 2010 and December 2012. Incoming workers have also increased the demand for rental housing. The shortage of rental properties has led to a sharp rise in rents. The 2013 Census showed that the median weekly rent paid by a one-family household in Christchurch city was $320, up 39

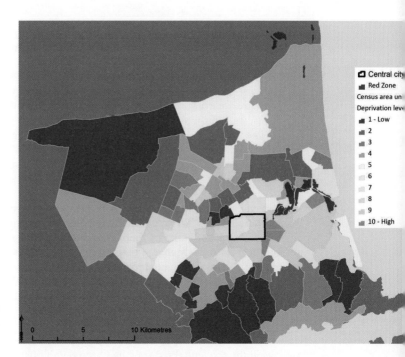

Figure 1: Map of central city, designated red zone and neighbourhood deprivation status for Christchurch city

per cent since 2006, almost double the rate of inflation (19.2 per cent) durir this period. Rent rises have made access to affordable and decent rental housing particularly challenging for people on low incomes.[18] The number o bonds lodged for low-cost rentals (less than $300 per week) fell from about 900 per month in 2010 to about 362 per month by mid-2013.[19]

The Christchurch Tenants Protection Association surveyed 365 renters in mid-2013. Survey respondents noted that rents in the private sector had markedly increased: only 5 per cent of private tenants spent less than 25 per cent of their income on rent, which is a widely used threshold for housing affordability.[20] Housing quality problems were common among the respondents: 60 per cent lived in earthquake-damaged homes and 27 per ce: reported problems with wastewater drainage. Some of those problems may have preceded the earthquakes; only 40 per cent thought their homes were insulated, another 27 per cent did not know, and 48 per cent reported moul in their homes. Renters in this survey who experienced higher rent increases reported being unable to find suitable housing; feelings of stress, worry and fear of the future; and being unable to afford food, doctors' visits, heating an electricity bills, or extras such as holidays or clothes.[21]

Government response to the recovery

A number of government agencies are involved in the recovery. The Canterbu: Earthquake Recovery Agency (CERA) was set up by the Government in 201 with extraordinary powers that override those of the Christchurch City Counc (CCC) and Environment Canterbury. In the first phases of CERA's Blueprin the central government has concentrated on high visibility public infrastructu and privately-owned commercial buildings.

Considering the Common Good

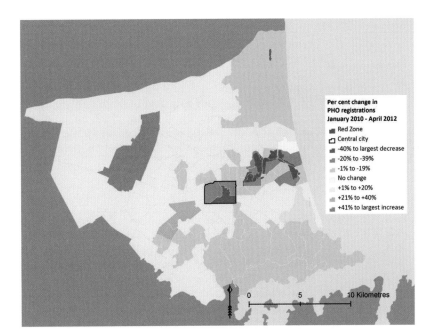

Per cent change in
PHO registrations
January 2010 - April 2012

- Red Zone
- Central city
- -40% to largest decrease
- -20% to -39%
- -1% to -19%
- No change
- +1% to +20%
- +21% to +40%
- +41% to largest increase

0   5   10 Kilometres

Figure 2: Population movement from the pre-earthquake period January 2010 to April 2012, using PHO registrations as a proxy

The arrangements for rebuilding housing involve multiple agencies and usually entail public-private partnerships. Two years after the earthquake, CERA established a Land Use Recovery Plan (LURP) designed to speed up land development. CERA used its extensive powers to ensure that 26,000 sections within the urban boundary (not necessarily additional sections) were available for residential development,[22] but in contrast to the broader aims of the previous CCC's Urban Development Strategy, this has resulted primarily in high-end greenfield housing.

The Government entered into a public-private partnership with Fletcher Construction Company, which has completed repairing or rebuilding over 51,550 houses.[23] While some repairs and rebuilds have been completed through private insurers, the situation in relation to social and affordable housing remains problematic. In recognition of the housing affordability problem, CCC and Auckland's council have now signed agreements under the Housing Accords and Special Housing Areas Act 2013.[24] This legislation was designed to enable local and central government to work together to identify and overcome barriers to housing supply and affordability. Through partnership with the private and community sectors, and direct intervention, the Government and CCC agreed to increase the proportion of new-build consents under $250,000, reduce the number of people paying more than 30 per cent of their income in housing costs by 10 per cent, and increase the number of social housing units by 700 by 2016.[25] Under the Act, if an accord with a council cannot be reached, central government can intervene by establishing special housing areas. These areas do not prioritise compact development over greenfield development.

This provision, and others that allow council plans to be disregarded when granting consents, undermines local democratic control to determine the future shape of the city.[26] Combined with the instability and high price of central city land these changes have encouraged dispersed land development in greenfield areas. Some developers have placed restrictive covenants on these developments to exclude affordable housing. The Social Housing Unit within the Ministry of Business, Innovation and Employment (MBIE) has however supported a number of community-housing developments and commissioned the Breathe competition for affordable housing on an inner city site.[27] CCC recently indicated it is considering stepping into the affordable rental housing market to help alleviate Christchurch's accommodation shortage.[28]

The inverse care law

There are implications for social inequality from the 'insurance-led' recovery and urban renewal efforts that followed after the initial emergency management phase ended. The policy frameworks are arguably drivers of the inverse care law, a term coined by the British doctor Tudor Hart to describe how health or social care is often disproportionately accessed by or allotted to the wealthy.[29] The severest effects of the earthquakes were predominantly felt in the residential areas with the highest socio-economic deprivation, whose populations had the least income and wealth to cope with the aftermath. These people were the most reliant on collective action to rebuild their houses, but have been the last focus of housing recovery efforts. While the slow start to surveying housing for structural repairs in severely affected low-income areas relates in part to the extent and severity of the land damage and ongoing earthquakes, it also relates to the lack of priority accorded to those with fewer assets and therefore less political voice.

There has been little provision of permanent, affordable housing for displaced households, particularly for those in the low-income part of the city. The decrease in social housing as a consequence of the earthquakes has also constrained housing options for the most vulnerable. CCC was the second largest provider of social housing in New Zealand, with a stock of over 2600 houses. Of these, about 440 (17 per cent) were evacuated due to earthquake damage.[30] Replacement of these units has been slow, largely due to insurance issues. The Earthquake Recovery Minister has on various occasions used exhortations and threats to try to increase the rate of building of council housing.[31]

Housing NZ lost 330 of its 5771 units in Canterbury, and estimated that 5000 units needed repair. It has committed to building a house a day, or 700 units by the end of 2015, in a policy designed to improve the housing problems of low-income social renters.[32] However, it remains unclear whether these houses are being built to be on-sold or retained as state house rentals. Although the Minister of Housing has made it clear that the Government does not consider 'large scale property development' as part of Housing NZ's core business,[33] the agency has been using its asset base and organisational capacity to encourage compact, mixed-tenure developments in Christchurch. In September 2013 three two-bedroom units were the first new dwellings to be built by Housing NZ after the earthquakes. Construction of a mixed-income development at 399 Manchester Street has begun; eleven of the houses will be Housing NZ rentals and the rest will be sold privately.[34] There is a lack of clarity about the Government's policy aims in these developments where more of the housing is on-sold than managed as social rental properties. In the context of unmonitored housing deprivation and a dire shortage of low-income rental housing, Housing NZ's dual objectives of building predominantly for sale and secondarily for rental are unlikely to have the desired equity effect of significantly reducing housing insecurity, particularly for low-income renters.

Predictably, social housing waiting lists have grown, suggesting that rental shortages are affecting the most vulnerable – another indication of the inverse care law. At the end of 2013, there were 400 people on Housing NZ's waiting list (now administered by the Ministry of Social Development), and 150 in the top priority category of CCC's social housing waiting list. For both of these agencies, this category includes people who are homeless, or have been told they need to vacate their home in the next seven days, as well as other eligibility criteria such as low income, household type, inability to access other housing, and vulnerability.[35] Numbers in the top priority waiting list category are at least three times the pre-earthquake number.[36]

The evidence of inadequate housing for those on low incomes is alarming. In 2012, MBIE estimated that there has been a rise in homelessness or 'severe housing deprivation' following the earthquakes, with people living precariously in cars, tents, camping grounds or crowding in with other households; an estimated 5510-7400 people were living in such insecure housing, up from 3750 before the earthquakes.[37] These estimates have now been confirmed by the 2013 Census, which showed an increase in households living in motor camps or mobile dwellings (1122 in greater Christchurch, a 57 per cent increase since 2006, against an increase of 6 per cent nationally), as well as an increase in households living in improvised dwellings (264 in greater Christchurch, a 35 per cent increase since 2006, against 9 per cent nationally).

There has also been an increase in households (probably including displaced households) sharing accommodation, including garages, with a 44 per cent increase in two-or-more family households in greater Christchurch since 2006 (2.5 percent versus 1.7 per cent), more than twice the national increase.[38] This is concerning for household stress levels and the potential risk of close-contact infectious diseases.[39] Overall the number of people living in crowded households in greater Christchurch increased slightly, from 24,438 to 25,572 (6.1 to 6.3 per cent of people in households), compared with a small decline nationally (from 10.4 to 10.1 per cent of people in households). Crowding increased more markedly for households in the lowest equivalised household income quintile in greater Christchurch, with a 29.3 per cent increase in this category, compared with an overall increase in crowding in greater Christchurch of 3 per cent.

A particularly vulnerable population, which we know little about in relation to the earthquakes, is people with chronic illnesses or disabilities. This population tends to have low incomes, and some also have special housing needs, making housing accessibility even more challenging. While New Zealand signed the *UN Convention on the Rights of Persons with Disabilities* in 2007, addressing the special housing needs of people with disability has not been a high priority in Christchurch. Accounts suggest that people with disabilities have coped largely with the help of family, friends and community service providers, who had to do much more for this population with budgets that were already thinly stretched.[40] The Government's focus has been less on direct provision of accessible housing and more on encouraging the private sector to utilise universal design principles in new dwellings or renovations, so that current or future occupants with disabilities can live in them easily and comfortably. There is also a commitment to universal design principles in new state houses, but we do not have information about the proportion of existing state houses or private rental housing that have accessibility features.

Insurance issues

In contrast to other natural disasters around the world, 90 per cent of the overall earthquake damage in Canterbury is covered by insurance.[41] Paradoxically this high rate of replacement insurance and the diversity of insurance contracts is one of the main reasons for the slow rate of rebuilding Christchurch's housing stock. Christchurch residents hold an array of 80 different kinds of insurance policies. This has complicated apportionment of payments between private insurers, 55,000 reinsures and the Earthquake Commission (EQC) for approximately 750,500 claims relating to land, houses and contents.[42]

EQC was a government response to the Napier Earthquake of 1931, at a time when home ownership rates in New Zealand were among the highest in the world. It is a government-owned Crown entity that provides natural disaster insurance for residential property, but only if the property is already privately insured. For many homeowners this complicated state of affairs has devolved into protracted battles with EQC, commercial insurers and reinsurers. An additional complication was a High Court ruling that EQC's coverage was renewed after each earthquake, effectively re-triggering the $100,000 cap on the amount EQC covers.

CCC and other parties have called for the establishment of an independent tribunal to make the process for resolving insurance disputes more efficient. It has also established the Build Back Smarter service to encourage people to repair or build houses that are warm, dry and energy efficient.[43] As government intervention in the recovery of Christchurch's housing sector is mainly through EQC, home-ownership has become a prerequisite for accessing assistance. This is another example of the inverse care law, as those on low incomes are more likely to be renting.

Green housing

Natural disasters such as earthquakes provide an opportunity to rebuild more sustainable housing, the design and location of which can help to mitigate climate change, as well as being better adapted to the more extreme weather events that climate change brings.[44] CERA exemptions permitting the use of temporary accommodation for displaced people do not follow the United Nations Disaster Relief best practice, which states that accelerated reconstruction of high quality, permanent housing is preferable to temporary housing.[45]

Resilient houses are energy efficient: occupants should be able to heat and cool their houses without experiencing fuel poverty (i.e. spending more than 10 per cent of household income on energy) or causing pollution.[46] In New Zealand, higher quality housing has been positively associated with higher neighbourhood resilience, even after adjusting for neighbourhood socio-economic deprivation.[47] As most injuries requiring hospitalisation occur in the home, housing should be rebuilt with fewer known housing-injury hazards,[48] and should follow universal design principles. Moreover, housing should be built to create and enhance the local community, which, like the indoor environment, has been shown to affect health and wellbeing.[49] Housing should be located near public transport, schools, parks and other amenities. The location of most new housing in the suburbs of Christchurch raises doubts about such access, but no systematic data on this are yet available.

Apart from higher standards, the rebuild provides an opportunity for new, innovative construction techniques.[50] New materials and designs should be carefully evaluated using both independent measures and pre- and post-occupancy surveys.[51] New Zealand has no equivalent of the publicly-funded Australian Housing and Urban Research Institute, which commissions systematic evaluations of innovations in construction methods for affordable housing, as well as monitoring the effects of compact, mixed-community developments.[52] In Christchurch it is not clear what proportion of new houses exceed the minimum standards set by the Building Code and what proportion of repairs have brought existing houses up to the current Building Code. Indeed, the rebuild seems to be focused on quantity rather than long-term sustainability and resilience, due to the pressure to resolve housing issues as quickly as possible.

Lessons learnt

Disasters lay bare the structure of society and can demonstrate the inverse care law. Historically, housing for low-income communities has been built on cheaper land, often in low-lying areas prone to flooding. As in New Orleans, the earthquakes have had a proportionally greater impact on low-income areas in the eastern areas of Christchurch.

The central government could have stepped in and provided, or subsidised, housing insurance – giving a priority to financing housing over so-called 'anchor projects' in the central city. It could have required developers to build a proportion of affordable houses in each new housing development and disallowed covenants that exclude rental properties.

Institutional barriers have slowed rebuilding of affordable housing, whether for ownership or rental. The speed of the residential rebuild is slow; building affordable housing is not favoured by the market as it involves lower profits, more risk and less capital gain for developers.[53] The Government's reliance on the market to rebuild affordable housing in Christchurch is likely to leave many people on low incomes living in very poor housing at the start of the fourth winter after the earthquakes. Those with chronic health problems and disabilities are likely to have been particularly affected.

The earthquakes were unavoidable, but that their impacts linger longest on low-income people is not. Low-income homeowners are the least likely to be able to rebuild, due to their relative lack of private insurance and consequent ineligibility for EQC insurance. The slow rebuild of housing has seriously affected the number of people who are homeless or living in crowded households. Rents have risen and the quality of many rental properties has declined, while the social housing waiting list has climbed due to the quick destruction and slow rebuild of social housing units.

There is some evidence of innovative green buildings, but these have had a slow start.[54] Indeed, there is an absence of evidence that the Government has prioritised compact, connected communities, or sustainable and affordable housing. So far, we have missed a major opportunity to build in physical and social resilience to environmental change, and to build houses that keep occupants – particularly the most vulnerable – safe, warm and dry. In a city where the extreme effects of climate change, such as flooding, are increasingl and painfully evident, there is a strong case for more strategic land-use planning and housing provision that addresses inequalities.

Plant Gang

Artist Liv Worsnop started Plant Gang in mid-2013. It is an initiative that reconsiders the many lots around the central city so they are not seen as demolition sites, but as spaces for potential and growth. Weeds are not seen as weeds but as participants in our environment, beneficial to animals, the air, the soil and ourselves. In taking this approach, Plant Gang opens up important conversations about the relationship between plants and people. More than fifteen sites have been carefully cleaned and reorganised by the Plant Gang crew, who follow a subtle environmental philosophy of letting what is be.

[1]

[2–6]

Considering the Common Good

[7–13]

The structures that support bad transport decisions

Simon Kingham

Simon is a professor in the Geography Department at the University of Canterbury, where he is also the director of the GeoHealth Laboratory. He researches and teaches on a range of urban issues including sustainable urban development, transport, health and air pollution.

Transport has been one of the most debated areas of the recovery and rebuild of Christchurch. Whether it be about a new bus exchange, opportunities for rail, where and how parking should be provided, or the provision of infrastructure for pedestrians and cyclists, everyone has an opinion and most people are experts. Transport infrastructure and public transport services are provided by national or local government and such investments are often seen as public goods; once provided they are available for all to use.[1] Consequently the rationale for decision-making around transport is sometimes viewed differently than for other services and infrastructure. Terminology is also important: funding for road projects is often termed 'investment', whereas public transport is deemed 'subsidised'.

Transport in Christchurch will, without a doubt, change in the coming years as the city recovers and is rebuilt. But how it will change and what the impact will be on our travel behaviour is less clear. To be able to consider and understand this, this chapter will start by examining how transport affects us, then examine how transport decisions are made, and end with some reflections on how transport in a future Christchurch might look.

Transport impacts

What are the benefits of different modes of transport, and how might this be factored into transport decision-making? There are a number of well-established ways in which transport can affect us. Some of the major considerations are examined below.

Environmental pollution

Clearly non-motorised modes (i.e. walking and cycling) produce little or no pollution and this is obviously better for the environment and health than motorised modes. Buses will generally produce more pollution than cars although when the numbers of passengers in a vehicle are factored in then public transport will nearly always result in lower per person pollution emission rates. A less obvious and understood facet of pollution in relation to transport is the concentration of pollution people are exposed to while travelling.[2] This can vary significantly between modes, with studies largely finding that people travelling by car are exposed to the worst quality of air, pedestrians and cyclists exposed to the cleanest air, and public transport users somewhere in between. The evidence for this includes research carried out in Christchurch.[3]

Physical activity

Clearly those who walk or cycle get more physical activity than those travelling by motorised modes, and gain the associated health benefits. These benefits have been shown to be significant and substantial.[4] What is less obvious are the benefits of increased physical activity for those using public transport. An increasing number of studies show significant health benefits through walking to and from public transport stops and stations,[5] including for rail and light rail.[6]

Social inequality and exclusion

There is a growing body of research that examines links between social inequality and transport. There are multiple ways that transport affects social inequality including car access being required for full participation in modern industrialised societies; lack of car access being a key factor in social exclusion; changing land use; and work and lifestyle patterns increasing car dependence and exacerbating the problem of poor access for non-car-owning households.[7] Clearly car access is a key here, and the Organisation for Economic Co-operation and Development (OECD) has concluded that communities with better active and public transport can reduce social disparities.[8]

Land use

Transport infrastructure uses space. In New Zealand it has been estimated that 25-30 per cent of land in New Zealand's towns and cities is given over to transport through roads, car parks, driveways etc. Clearly different modes have different land use needs with car travel requiring substantially more space than other modes, as seen in figure 1,[9] but perhaps more easily visualised in figure 2. Any road space used for transport cannot be used for other public activities such as parks or other uses of communal open space.

Cost

Transport comes with economic costs. These include *individual* costs, such as paying for vehicles (car or bike), maintenance, running costs (fuel, repairs etc.) or fares for public transport; and *public* costs, such as the provision of public good services (e.g. bus and rail services) and infrastructure (e.g. road building and maintenance or cycling infrastructure). In 2005, the Ministry of Transport produced the Surface Transport Costs and Charges Study

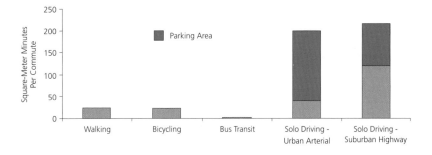

Figure 1: Space required by travel mode

Figure 2: Road space required to transport 69 people

(STCCS), which assessed the following: the costs that road and rail users were paying, the costs that they imposed on society as a whole and who pays for land transport.[10] It concluded that 'no one is overpaying and that all land transport users are underpaying to varying degrees'. Specifically, the report asserts that cars directly cover only 64 per cent of their costs, trucks 56 per cent, buses 68 per cent and rail 77 per cent. The remainder of the costs are paid out of general taxation and local rates. It should be noted that these figures do not include any health impacts associated with physical activity, which we know will be substantial. As a result it is fair to say that the figure for cars will be significantly lower than 64 per cent.

The bottom line is that the costs of all motorised modes are substantially subsidised by general taxation with cars being the most subsidised form of transport. On the other hand, investment in active transport (cycling and walking), which was not included in the STCCS, has been demonstrated in an increasing number of studies as having significant economic benefits.[11] From this we can see that there is an increasing and compelling body of evidence that strongly demonstrates that investing in active and public transport is sound economically.

How do we make transport planning decisions?

So how are transport decisions made? What are the key drivers that shape how and where transport investment is made? In Christchurch there are three main agencies involved in the provision of transport: the New Zealand Transport Agency (NZTA), who manage state highways; Christchurch City Council (CCC), who manage local roads; and Environment Canterbury (ECan), who manage public transport. In the context of post-earthquake Christchurch, the Canterbury Earthquake Recovery Authority (CERA) also needs to be included. Much of these organisations' effort is spent maintaining existing services, whether this is road repairs or public transport routes. Decisions on the provision of new transport or changing transport priorities rely on finding new funding within a funding-scarce environment. Each player has different criteria and mechanisms that decide how much they spend on different activities.

Considering the Common Good

Ultimately the body that has most power in this is the one that controls the largest pot of 'new' funding. In New Zealand this is the Ministry of Transport through the Government Policy Statement (GPS) on Land Transport Funding, which decides 'the government's outcomes and priorities for the land transport sector'.[12] The 2010 GPS unashamedly states that the aim is to realign 'transport expenditure to better support economic growth' and that the key part is 'a significant programme of improvement in key land transport infrastructure, with an intention to invest nearly $11 billion in new infrastructure for New Zealand's State highways over the 10 years from 2009 to 2019'. This allocates around 40 per cent of the budget for new state highways, 40 per cent for maintenance of existing roads, 10 per cent for public transport services and less than 1 per cent each for public transport infrastructure, and walking and cycling – a similar amount to that allocated for 'Management of the funding allocation system'. This is given effect by the NZTA-managed National Land Transport Programme (NLTP) and funds are available from the National Land Transport Fund (NLTF). State highway projects are managed by NZTA and are in essence uncontested. For local non-state highway projects (new or maintenance), local government (CCC or ECan) has to either fully fund through local taxes and/or, in the case of public transport, farebox recovery,[13] or co-fund and seek the remainder from the NLTP. To actually get the NLTP fund, CCC and ECan have to apply for funds through the Regional Land Transport Plan (RLTP) that feeds into the NLTP. There are three hurdles to non-roading projects getting funded through this process. Firstly, projects need local support to be part of the city plan; this is not always a given when in competition with other spending priorities. Secondly, they have to get national support, by fitting within the GPS targets – there is no point applying for large funds from a part of the GPS that has little budget, and unfortunately the GPS has little available for non-roading projects. Finally, there have to be no logistical hurdles to implementation (e.g. the public or businesses objecting during any consultation process).[14]

For any transport project to get into the RLTP, it has to demonstrate value for money and is compared against other projects from the whole region, from Kaikoura down to Waimate. One method of doing this is to use NZTA's Economic Evaluation Manual which allows organisations to 'evaluate the economic efficiency of their investment proposals in line with the Transport Agency's Assessment Framework'.[15] This evaluation process is based on economic efficiency and is assessed by the use of a benefit cost ratio. This is very much an economic approach, with no scope for including the public good unless a competitive economic value can be attached to it. It is possible for CCC or ECan to fund projects entirely out of local funds, but these are then not supported by any central government funds, and are in direct competition for funds with all other local non-transport projects.

In other words, there is little central government funding available for any new public transport or major walking and cycling projects.

Transport in Christchurch's recovery and rebuild

The first opportunity to develop a transport plan for Christchurch came through the hugely successful and popular Share an Idea campaign. The key transport points that came out of this can be seen in figure 3. Key features were a shift to a more walkable, cycleable city, with good public transport – including light rail or trams. The first recovery document was the CCC-produced Draft Central City Plan.[16]

The central city then became the responsibility of the newly created Christchurch Central Development Unit (CCDU), who turned this into the Christchurch Central Recovery Plan.[17] There were some key changes from the CCC Draft Central City Plan, the most notable being that there was only brief reference to transport, and detail was delayed to a later date. The transport plan came out as an addendum: An Accessible City.[18] There were two main significant changes compared to the original CCC plan. Firstly, a slow core 30 km/h centre was introduced. Secondly, plans for light rail, which were a key part of the CCC Draft Plan, were removed from the CCDU plan.

At the same time as the Accessible City report was being prepared, Christchurch City Council produced its longer-term Transport Plan 2012-2042.[19] It has four goals, which are to improve access and choice; create safe, healthy and liveable communities; support economic vitality; and create opportunities for environmental enhancements. The notion of the public good being included in transport decisions is more visible in this longer-term plan. However, towards the end of the document is a warning that the GPS 'means the funding available for public transport, cycling and walking networks as outlined in this Plan will be heavily constrained for much of the early recovery period'. Investigations into the feasibility of passenger rail or light rail are mentioned as part of a public transport network. This plan also includes reference to a connected cycle network including major cycleways and flagship projects. The latter has come to fruition with the CCC budgeting in the region of $70 million for thirteen new separated cycleways to be completed within five years.[20]

Figure 3: Key transport ideas from the Share an Idea campaign

The future

What is becoming increasingly clear worldwide is that many public good transport initiatives, which are likely to lead to a more sustainable and resilient future (specifically public transport and active transport) now stack up very competitively when assessed economically. However, under the current central framework for funding transport projects in New Zealand (largely driven by the GPS) these are unlikely to get funded. The Roads of National Significance, the current priority for the Government, are in many cases poor economic value.[21] Yet when questioned, the Government defends its spending, ironically on the grounds of the public good, and refers to this as investment.[22] Public and active transport are either seen as insignificant, or referred to as subsidies. This suggests that, in the current political climate, projects are unlikely to get funded unless they fit the roading agenda, with public and active transport investment not favoured. Yet, it is known that many active and public transport projects have stronger economic cases, and that many of the journeys we make are short and ideal for active modes.

So what is the future for Christchurch? The CCC has demonstrated its commitment to investing in active transport modes. However, the future looks less bright for more expensive transport projects such as light rail, irrespective of the medium- or long-term benefits that may be demonstrated, due to central government policies and funding mechanisms.

RAD Bikes

'Recycle A Dunger' is a community bike shed where people can fix or build a bike. It was established by Gap Filler in collaboration with ICECycles (Inner City East Cycles) with support from local businesses. Launched during FESTA (Festival of Transitional Architecture) in October 2013, RAD Bikes has been open at least four days a week ever since. The workshop has all of the tools and parts to get a bike running again, and eight amazing volunteers providing guidance to those using the space. RAD's continued use benefits from donations of old bikes, parts and tools, as well as financial koha (donations).

[1]

[2–4]

Losing our collective memory: The importance of preserving heritage architecture

Jessica Halliday

Dr Jessica Halliday is an architectural historian. She is the director of the Festival of Transitional Architecture (FESTA) and founder of the Christchurch Centre for Architecture and the City.

The position of heritage architecture in post-earthquake Christchurch has been controversial since the first Canterbury earthquake in September 2010. Politically there has been a divide between local and central government perspectives on heritage, and between the right-wing government and the opposition. The National Party's coalition government has not sufficiently understood the public and long-term benefits of heritage architecture and the historic environment, nor has it employed these benefits to support Christchurch's earthquake recovery. Since the earthquakes of 22 February 2011, the architecture of the past has been rejected (or, at best, ignored), labelled a 'roadblock' to recovery or seen as a scourge to be erased from the city. Yet from architectural heritage stem a range of benefits that touch many aspects of our lives: social, economic, environmental and cultural. While there are considerable challenges in retaining heritage buildings and streetscapes in an earthquake-damaged city, the public good of built cultural heritage is substantial and irreplaceable and should have been considered as a key pillar of recovery. Instead, the Government pilloried historic buildings from the outset, unnecessarily pitting them against other forms of good, both public and private. This has resulted in the demolition of heritage on an unprecedented scale. The alternative wasn't to retain every possible significant building, but to acknowledge the multivalent roles of historic architecture and the cultural landscape as public goods and establish plans and policies to support and facilitate their patrimony for the benefit of current and future citizens.

In the modern era, theories of cultural heritage and methodologies to identify, protect and manage the cultural significance of the architecture of the past have grown and evolved until we have arrived at a position where there are well-established, globally recognised protocols, multinational declarations and international organisations dedicated to protecting and managing built cultural heritage.[1] In New Zealand the promotion and protection of cultural heritage is legislated in the Resource Management Act 1991 (RMA) and the Historic Places Act 1993. The public benefits of retaining and protecting historic buildings in private ownership have been acknowledged over decades by the provision of public funding towards repair and strengthening programmes, research and advice. It is important to recognise that public participation in political processes that determine the fate of heritage buildings has to date been one of the few direct and effective ways the public has been able to influence the precise nature of their built environment.

Despite its protection in law and decades of public investment, the public good of heritage architecture was never seriously factored into Christchurch's earthquake recovery. Well before considered recovery strategies were formed and the Canterbury Earthquake Recovery legislation written, the Government's earliest public statements on heritage buildings set the agenda for the scope and nature of the city's earthquake recovery. One of the first things that Minister for Canterbury Earthquake Recovery Gerry Brownlee did after the 22 February earthquake was to take a flight over the city in an Iroquois helicopter. That first-hand impression of the city from a military aircraft seems to have shaped and fixed his views on what was necessary for Christchurch to recover from the effects of the earthquake: 'I'm pleased I did that because it puts it, in a very short period of time, into the sort of perspective we're going to need here. The devastation is considerable. It makes me appreciate the way in which we have to attack this.'[2]

Four days later, on 28 February, it was announced that as many as 500 buildings in the central city were unsafe and might have to be destroyed, with Prime Minister John Key saying that officials would probably want to 'clear away as many of the condemned buildings as they could at one time'.[3] The following day came the Minister's most infamous pronouncement on historic architecture, which was widely and repeatedly reported, as in this *Press* story:

> [Brownlee:] "Quite frankly people have died in this last earthquake trying to save old buildings. We're not going to do that any more. My absolutely strong position is that the old dungas [sic], no matter what their connection, are going under the hammer." The local council refused consent to allow some old buildings damaged in the first quake to be destroyed, but Brownlee said it would not have a say this time. "The previous method of doing things hasn't served us well, and we're not going to work with that any more. Old stuff, if it's got any damage at all, needs to be got down and got out, because it's dangerous and we don't need it."[4]

In the wake of the 22 February earthquake, many saw buildings as killers. One hundred and eighty-five people died as a consequence of the tremors, 44 of them due to the collapse of unreinforced masonry buildings and the majority in buildings of modern construction. The over-simplification of heritage buildings as killers was as irrational as deciding that there could be no more office buildings, no more concrete buildings or no more multi-storey buildings in Christchurch. Historic buildings became a convenient scapegoat to mask decades of government inaction on the known risks of earthquake prone buildings.[5] The public's very real fears were used as a lever to justify this extreme position, allowing the government to be seen to be acting swiftly in response to this natural and human disaster.

Yet the events in Christchurch also demonstrated that earthquake-prone buildings can be successfully strengthened to protect human life, cultural heritage and economic and social wellbeing. 'Research conducted for the

[Canterbury Earthquakes Royal Commission of inquiry] showed that buildings retrofitted to 100 per cent of new building strength performed well in the February earthquake; those strengthened to 67 per cent performed moderately well.'[6]

In times of crisis and disaster, rational, long-sighted leadership should protect the public good in all its complexity, rather than destroy it when it is expedient. The Government's perspective on the value of historic architecture and landscapes severely curtailed the capacity of heritage buildings to contribute to the city's recovery. Those very early statements were made with no public consultation, were announced without reference to best practice, existing law or multinational declarations. Other than the demolition of the buildings themselves, possibly the most damaging consequence of the Government's attitude to historic architecture is that it instantly polarised the issue. The stance has been so extreme that anyone arguing for the retention of historic buildings could be classed as a sentimental extremist who valued buildings more than human life, who were forming 'a roadblock to recovery' and obstructing private property rights rather than advocating a position that was well established and internationally recognised.

The value of built cultural heritage

Socio-cultural, economic and environmental public goods are produced by the promotion and protection of historic buildings and places. While economic and environmental goods are measurable, socio-cultural public benefits are largely intangible.

The primary 'good' or socio-cultural benefit of historic architecture is rooted in the broader belief that access to and participation in culture is a human right.[7] As a fundamental part of human culture, works of architecture and historic environments 'connect individuals to their communities and histories and [are] integral to human identity and interpretations of reality'.[8] Active and habitual encounters with architecture enrich our daily lives with the breadth and depth of direct and indirect experiences they offer us. This is achieved through patterns of behaviour and rituals held in specific spaces, a process of deepening familiarity with particular buildings, and social and multi-generational experience of streets, public spaces and inhabited environments over time. These distinctive, layered cultural landscapes allow us to feel connected with, committed to and inspired by the communities of a place.

Implicit in this view is the understanding that knowledge of the past is of immense value to society.[9] Historic buildings and urban fabric provide one of the most accessible and immediate forms of engagement with the past available to us on a regular basis. Their design and changing use over time express the patterns of life, values and priorities of previous societies.

Our past is also seen as an essential component of our sense of identity. This remains true even when perceptions of personal, community and national identity shift over time. The very fact and acknowledgment of that change becomes a part of our current sense of self, and the past allows us to recognise and integrate that change. Historic buildings shelter, contain and even shape collective memory. Paul Connerton proposes that the organisation of collective memory, via several means, is a dimension of and lever on political power.[10] Seen from this perspective, cultural heritage can serve to shape and support civil society.[11]

A historically layered city is a daily source of diverse aesthetic experience. Individual buildings and historic environments are rich and varied in their aesthetics. Spatial dynamics and the manipulation and play of light, pattern, texture, form, colour, rhythm and other qualities make architecture the everyday art. The particular spatial and material qualities and scale of architecture cannot be understood by photographs and other two-dimensional representations and instead require a fully embodied experience in the actual place.

There are five major measurable economic impacts in heritage conservation. Donovan Rypkema's research findings detail significant economic benefits for jobs and household income; centre city revitalisation; heritage tourism; property values; and small business incubation. Rypkema also highlights the need for countries and cities to address the negative long-term economic effects of cultural globalisation via the specific local qualities of built heritage:

> While economic globalization has many positive effects, cultural globalization has few if any benefits, but has significant adverse social and political consequences in the short term, and negative economic consequences in the long term. If cities are to succeed in economic globalization, they will have to be competitive worldwide. However, their success will be measured not just by their ability to foster economic globalization, but equally in their ability to mitigate cultural globalization. In both cases, a city's cultural heritage will play a central role.[12]

The environmental benefits of building conservation and adaptive reuse over new construction, even new energy-efficient buildings, are considerable. A recent study in the United States used life-cycle analysis to demonstrate that adaptive reuse and retrofitting of existing buildings provided immediate benefits for climate change, human health, ecosystem quality and resource depletion. By comparison, it can take up to 80 years for a new, more energy efficient building to overcome the environmental impacts of its construction.[13] This study's findings may not translate directly into a situation where significant material intervention is required to retain earthquake-damaged buildings. Nonetheless, it is clear that the environmental impact of demolishing 80 per cent of Christchurch's inner city and building new is substantial, especially when there have been no mechanisms put in place to ensure Christchurch's new construction meets the energy efficiencies assumed in the American study.

The fate of Christchurch's historic buildings

Within a week of the 22 February earthquake the Government had made their position clear: the public good of historic buildings was now irrelevant in Christchurch. That initial ministerial reaction set the tone and agenda for decision-making on historic buildings in the months and years that followed.

It was clear from the Minister's early statements that the Christchurch City Council would no longer be the body with the statutory power over heritage buildings. Section 38 of the CER Act 2011 gave the CEO of the Canterbury Earthquake Recovery Authority (CERA) the ability to demolish any building and gave the Minister the power to suspend, amend, or revoke the whole or any part of a number of plans including an RMA document or a council plan or policy. The Minister subsequently directed a change to the city regulations and by-laws that made the demolition of a building by CERA under s. 38 a permitted activity, irrespective of any existing rules restricting changes to a heritage listed building in the CCP.[14] These are the means by which CERA has been able to demolish at least 235 listed or registered heritage buildings in Canterbury to date without any public recourse.[15]

One of the fundamental problems with the CER legislation is its top-down approach, where 'The Minister has the ultimate responsibility for setting the vision for recovery and rebuilding, and has numerous coercive powers which may be used to trump decisions and actions of local authorities and other agencies.'[16] The approach and design of the Christchurch Central Recovery Plan (CCRP) has minimal regard for the remaining fabric of the city and instead treats the cultural landscape within the Frame as a tabula rasa, a blank slate on which to imagine and build a new city. The new plan dictated the unnecessary demolition of remaining heritage buildings and notable works of architecture within the designated precincts. These include Miller's Building by George Hart (1936), one of the earliest modernist buildings in New Zealand, demolished to make way for the new Bus Exchange; Alan Manson's Majestic Theatre (1930), the first steel-framed building in Christchurch, demolished to allow for the widening of Manchester Street by 9 metres; and Warren and Mahoney's national award-winning Christchurch Public Library (1981) which will be demolished to be replaced by a large convention centre.[17] It is revealing that in a city whose identity had been built on its notable historic buildings, not one of the Government's major recovery projects outlined in the Blueprint involves harnessing the varied benefits of reusing a historic building.

The Government's only strategic document for architectural heritage in post-earthquake Christchurch is the Heritage Buildings and Places Recovery Programme (HBPRP), released for public consultation in December 2013 and intended to 'ensure heritage buildings and places remain an important part of greater Christchurch's identity'.[18] The programme was in draft form during the writing of this book, but the very fact that the programme was released for consultation nearly three years after the 22 February earthquake and the demolition of over 200 heritage buildings is, in the words of heritage advocacy group ICONIC, 'woefully inadequate'.[19]

Lessons from Christchurch for built cultural heritage

Disasters are complex, multi-dimensional phenomena. A disaster is not simply a single, triggering event but instead is understood as a socially constructed process, an interaction of social, cultural, political and economic factors that form mutually influencing responses to external events. Christchurch's central city wasn't destroyed solely by an earthquake but by a range of social and political factors. This is a form of urbicide, 'the destruction of urban centres that are deemed undesirable ... with a view to achieving a more superior, 'modern' form and content for the city ... '.[20]

What we have lost is not just individual buildings but the gradually evolving city, characterised by the multi-layered accretion of many generations. This is what architect and theorist Aldo Rossi called 'the city as a man-made object, as a work of architecture or engineering that grows over time'.[21] Such a place provides a living, diachronic sense of the past and allows the accrual of architectural experience that is distinctly urban.

One of the dangers in removing material evidence of our past is that it restricts re-interpretation of it or, even worse, allows a few to control what and how the past is understood. Losing the material cultural remains of the past greatly impedes ongoing engagement in developing discourses on our national and provincial histories and myths.

The alternative approach would have been to develop the necessary processes and strategies to sustain cultural heritage. This would have produced a set of principles for the relevant governing authorities to manage the future of damaged Christchurch heritage buildings in an informed way. Technological tools can swiftly support complex forms of cultural urban analysis by mapping locations and analysing the feasibility of retaining important buildings, sites, areas and spaces of cultural heritage and overlaying it with crucial information about building ownership as well as structural stability, engineering evaluations and strengthening strategies by engineers with heritage qualifications and experience.

The last point can be taken for granted, but not all structural engineers are capable of assessing or designing for heritage buildings. As leading engineers Dr Stefano Pampanin and John Hare acknowledge:

> Dependable seismic assessment and retrofit, particularly of older heritage buildings, can be extremely complex, requiring experience and skills only achieved through a number of years' practice, knowledge of national and international best practice and recently developed cost-effective technologies. Sympathetic treatment of heritage buildings and fabric can add significantly to the complexity.[22]

Early in disaster management, the government should seek and accept offers of support from international organisations and bodies experienced in cultural emergencies, as their experience shows that 'if the response is well-targeted and delivered at the earliest possible stage there is much greater probability of salvaging cultural heritage'.[23]

There are significant complications to retaining heritage buildings: cost, insurance, expertise and time. The question remains: who should pay for the cost of strengthening heritage buildings? In acknowledgment of the public benefit of heritage, Historic Places Trust chief executive Bruce Chapman suggests a range of incentives could be used by central and local government to support the owners of heritage buildings: 'flexible zoning provisions, low interest loans, fee waivers, tradable development rights . . . incentive funds and rates relief'.[24]

Despite the odds, a number of strengthened and reoccupied heritage buildings are already contributing to the recovery of the central city. The former High Street Post Office houses a range of hospitality, office and cultural activities that along with the NG building will anchor the recovery of this quarter of the city. The same can be said for New Regent Street, Saint Michaels, Christ's College, the Canterbury Museum, Warren and Mahoney's former offices at 65 Cambridge Terrace, the Registry building at the Arts Centre and Bonningtons Building in High Street. When this list is joined by rest of the Arts Centre, the COCA Gallery, the façade and restored interior of the Theatre Royal and the Christchurch Town Hall, the benefit of heritage buildings to the city's recovery will be evident in myriad ways. These gains throw into sharp relief the lost potential of the demolished heritage of Christchurch.

Our values, our culture and our city

'It is self-evident that no society makes an effort to conserve what it does not value.'[25]

The widespread demolition of historic architecture since the 22 February earthquake, the inadequate Government response to plan for heritage recovery and the comparatively subdued nature of the populace in response to this demolition might suggest that the time has passed when New Zealanders value the 'sanctity and inherent meaningfulness' of our architectural heritage.[26] Or is it that the case for heritage has been swamped by the complexity of architectural conservation in a seismically active zone; by the opportunism that disaster management has provided to politicians, demolition companies and building owners alike; by the very real immediate personal pressures and burdens faced by the people and households of Christchurch after the earthquakes? Clearly what has happened to Christchurch historic architecture has implications for heritage buildings in other parts of the country. The question of inadequate wider social and cultural ties and legal protection for our past holds a warning for anyone in New Zealand who values any part of our material culture.

Heritage is entangled with the strategic agendas of political forces and commercial interests and this is magnified in times of disaster. Christchurch, like all cities unexpectedly in the middle of a disaster, its citizens dealing with trauma and chaos and focused on basic survival, required leadership that could take a calm, considered approach to decisions that would shape our long-term recovery. Instead blanket statements and knee-jerk reactions became the foundation for the situation the city finds itself in three years later: 80 per cent of its inner city demolished, its sense of place and identity shattered and on a far harder road to recovery than was necessary.

Lost heritage

Before the quakes Christchurch was recognised as a city rich with a variety of historical and heritage buildings and urban streetscapes. Of particular importance were the collections of Victorian Gothic architecture, which included the Canterbury Provincial Council Buildings, and post-war modern buildings such as the Christchurch Town Hall. At the time of writing, 1307 buildings have been demolished in the central city, including 130 heritage-listed places. A small number of prominent buildings such as those at the Arts Centre, COCA, Christ's College, Canterbury Museum and the Provincial Council Buildings are likely to be restored.

[1–5]

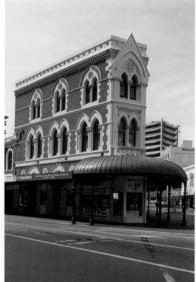

[6–12]

[13–20]

[21–25]

Considering the Common Good

Placemaking and post-quake identity – creating a unique Ōtautahi identity

Rebecca Kiddle and Amiria Kiddle

Dr Rebecca Kiddle is interested in the intersection between social processes and space. In particular, her research focuses on the role of urban design in creating place identity and the transfer of urban design ideas across cultures. Amiria is involved in the Ōtautahi Christchurch rebuild, working in the fields of architecture and art. Her interests lie in the relationship between Māori and New Zealand identity.

The form and identity of New Zealand towns and cities have been heavily influenced by both colonisation and globalisation. Both of these phenomena have resulted, for the most part, in towns and cities that have struggled to reflect Māori identity.

The recent Ōtautahi earthquakes have shaken up the English-inspired urban form of Christchurch and stimulated a conscious re-think of the 'new' city's identity. In parallel, there is concern worldwide about globalisation creating places that look and feel the same. This paper examines the Christchurch Central Recovery Plan (CCRP) through an exploration of a set of design principles that work to promote Ngāi Tahu and Ngāi Tūāhuriri identity and acknowledge Christchurch's bicultural underpinnings. It asks the questions, 'What factors might be important in creating uniquely Aotearoa New Zealand places?' and 'How can Ngāi Tahu and Ngāi Tūāhuriri kaupapa (principles) and tikanga (customs) inform place identity?'.

Ensuring that Ngāi Tahu identity is celebrated in the Christchurch rebuild is important for two key reasons. Firstly, acknowledging Ngāi Tahu identity can only but contribute to the creation of unique places given that these histories are not found elsewhere in the world. This has other spin-offs for all Cantabrians including encouraging a sense of local pride, stimulation of tourism opportunities and the local economy and, as discussed in detail below, a rebuild that recognises the needs of future generations through a sustainable response. Secondly, the CCRP states that 'a city's identity is made up of its collective memories which create a sense of place'.[1] For the most part, Christchurch's identity was recognisably colonial prior to the earthquakes. Acknowledging the collective memories of Ngāi Tūāhuriri as the manawhenua (traditional authority) signals both due diligence and the city's obligation to uphold this authority under the Treaty of Waitangi.

The CCRP states that 'there will be numerous opportunities to integrate the Ngāi Tahu narrative into the new city through planning and design of the anchor projects and precincts'.[2] This paper is speculative, exploring potentials outlined in the CCRP and additional opportunities to integrate Ngāi Tahu identity as the rebuild process moves from strategic principles to implementation.

Ngāi Tahu has had solid involvement in the development of the CCRP. This was influenced by two key factors. Firstly, Ngāi Tahu secured statutory mandate for involvement through the Canterbury Earthquake Recovery Act 2011 (CER Act) alongside local authorities. Secondly, by the time the quake hit, Ngāi Tahu had built substantial capability and experience working with the Crown due to their 1998 Treaty of Waitangi settlement and its subsequent implementation.

The involvement of Ngāi Tahu in the CCRP resulted in enhanced relationships as well as an authentic recognition of Ngāi Tahu values within the plan; however, the actualities of involvement in the detailed design and implementation of the plan are potentially more difficult. There are two potential concerns here. Cost constraints and the timing of engagement on specific projects may make it difficult to enable the inclusion of Ngāi Tahu's voice. Additionally, there remains a general lack of baseline understanding of Ngāi Tahu history and values amongst mainstream planners and designers. This places the 'burden of proof' on Ngāi Tahu to educate those tasked with realising specific designs, increasing the workload for Ngāi Tahu and creating capacity difficulties.

Ngāi Tahu is developing a set of design guidelines in response to these concerns whilst continuing to work collaboratively with Canterbury Earthquake Recovery Authority (CERA), Christchurch City Council (CCC) and designers. This paper does not seek to disrupt that process, but provides suggestions of a broad design framework that could be used by Ngāi Tahu as they develop their own hāpu- and iwi-specific design principles.

A design framework for making places

The CCRP suggests a strong 'green' element (e.g. the restoration of the Ōtākaro Avon River) aligning well with Ngāi Tahu's aspirations that include the 'protection and enhancement of waterways and the appropriate use/reuse treatment and disposal of water' and 'reduction and prevention of wastes and pollution (to air, land and water)'.[3] Heritage, both Māori and European, will be celebrated and the urban building fabric will speak of 'our sense of place, our identity, our shared cultural heritage'.[4]

The next step will be working out what this means in practice. Suggestions around inclusion of Ngāi Tahu identity in the CCRP include use of markers, Ngāi Tahu artworks, a new cultural centre and the incorporation of indigenous flora within new open spaces.[5] Whilst these are important foundations of identity, further work is needed to ensure a comprehensive consideration of Ngāi Tahu identity across the different parts of the spatial environment.

Urban commentators Duffy and Brand assert that different parts of our environment change at different rates.[6] For instance, buildings often last decades, potentially hundreds of years. The public space system (streets, roads and squares) tends to last thousands of years but the environmental infrastructure (e.g. ecosystems and habitats) is the longest lasting, thus deserving of the most intellectual 'grunt'. If we damage the longest lasting parts, they are the most difficult to rectify as they govern the spatial system.[7]

By structuring a set of design principles according to longevity, designers can consider both the parts of the environment that they can influence and the relationships between the different parts in order to design a coherent place. The parts of the environment considered here, in order of longevity, are environmental infrastructure; block/plots; buildings; and exterior details (fig. 1).

Longest lasting   Shortest lasting

ure 1: Morphological
el structure

Environmental infrastucture   Blocks/plots   Buildings   Details exterior

Overlaid on this temporal spatial structure are considerations of 'place'. Place here is used to mean spaces that hold some sense of identity for their users. Butina Watson and Bentley's book *Identity by Design*[8] outlines a place-identity framework that provides an overall structure for creating a sense of place, developed through analysis of places in a range of cultural contexts.[9]

Four key factors are identified:
1. Choice: in terms of spatial form, use and ultimately meaning as tools for opening up opportunities for all people.[10]
2. History: space rooted in its history is more likely to counter the homogeneity users experience in many urban settlements.
3. Transculturality: highlights the need to consider the fact that many contemporary societies are now multicultural, as is true in Ōtautahi. Uniquely, the Treaty of Waitangi sets up a bicultural governance structure within which recognition of this multicultural make-up is possible.
4. Nature: biophilic tendencies and cultural precedent, in the case of local Māori communities, promote a connection with nature.

Organising the temporal and placemaking frameworks outlined in a matrix form would provide the basis on which to identify specific principles with the potential to promote a strong Ngāi Tahu place identity. Examples relating to the two longest-lasting parts of the environment are considered below.

Environmental infrastructure

The CCRP focuses on the revitalisation of the environmental infrastructure through the reinvigoration of the Ōtākaro Avon River.[11] Here the plan outlines Ngāi Tahu's connection with this water source and includes the introduction of indigenous plants and mahinga kai areas (places where traditional food and other natural resources are obtained).[12] The CCRP also identifies the retention of a number of other green spaces, and the introduction of a new green frame surrounding the city centre. However, as it stands the plan is human-centric. Given the cultural and strategic importance of ecosystems and biodiversity, the value of different types of green space to both humans and wildlife should be identified. Promotion of a vital urban ecosystem requires provision of a range of spaces with differing levels of human-nature interaction. At one end of the spectrum is green space, manicured and primarily for human use, as seems to be promoted by the CCRP; at the other end is space provided for the sole use of wildlife, flor and fauna, protected from human contact.

Figure 2: Continuum of green space types

At the smaller scale, the introduction of rain gardens and planted swales in the CCRP[13] speaks to Ngāi Tahu's aspirations to protect natural resources. However, a fundamental reconsideration of indigenous topography and waterways at the larger scale would affirm this aspiration more concretely. This may include reinstating historical waterways, widening greenways and dissuading development in swamp areas (fig. 3).

Ngāi Tahu's aspiration document[14] outlines a desire to provide for cultural practices such as mahinga kai, which is also provided for in the CCRP.[15] The benefits of mahinga kai are numerous and include access to healthy food and opportunities for community building. However, for the promotion of mahinga kai to become more than just a demonstration project, there are implications for the current relatively large size of residential plots. The New Zealand dream had been to own a quarter acre plot offering outdoor private space capable of housing private gardens. However, anecdotal evidence suggests that the more private outdoor space offered the less likely people are to use public space, decreasing the level of vitality in these spaces and thus the opportunities for spontaneous community building.

In New Zealand, a reduction in the provision of private outdoor space might be contentious, but Christchurch is in a unique position to consider shifting some of its urban spatial resources into public use to support community building through mahinga kai. A number of different models could facilitate this, including locating smaller scale gardens within the centre of a city block primarily for those living in the block, as is found in Notting Hill, London, UK (fig. 4) or housing community gardens more publicly as is currently the case with the Agropolis project in Christchurch.

Public space

Opportunities for 'face-to-face' or 'kanohi-ki-te-kanohi' connections are important in Māori culture.[16] Jane Jacobs, whose seminal work *The Death and Life of Great American Cities* has informed contemporary urban design thinking worldwide, also talks of the importance of face-to-face interactions

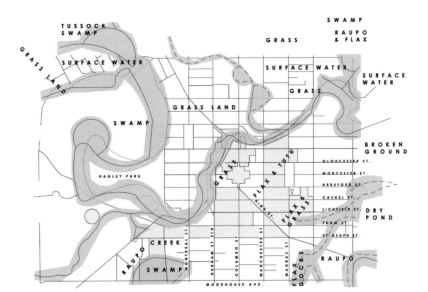

Figure 3: Historical waterways, swamp and vegetation reinstated alongside the existing street network

Figure 4: Block typology with internal communal garden

in the city, for much the same reasons that kanohi-ki-te-kanohi interactions are important for Māori: trust. She writes:

> The trust of a city street is formed over time from many, many little public sidewalk contacts. It grows out of people stopping by at the bar for a beer, getting advice from the grocer and giving advice to the newsstand man, comparing opinions with other customers at the bakery . . . Most of it is ostensibly utterly trivial but the sum is not trivial at all. The absence of this trust is a disaster to a city street.[17]

Space design cannot force people to engage in dialogue and develop trust, but if done badly, it can close down opportunities for this. How then might public space encourage opportunities for face-to-face interaction? A number of strategies are possible. Firstly, safe spaces are encouraged through the use of well-placed lighting;[18] orientation of buildings that clearly front onto streets; and public spaces creating natural surveillance and 'eyes on the street'. Images used for buildings such as the stadium[19] and the cultural centre[20] do not appear to follow this method. Secondly, a walkable public space network aids the possibility of social interaction. Currently the Accessible

City transport plan focuses primarily on cars over cyclable streets followed lastly by pedestrians. It is pedestrians who hold the key to social interactions and the development of trust as they are more likely to make eye contact, acknowledge passers-by and stop to chat.

Figure 5: Perimeter block structures with windows and doors on to the street create natural surveillance and safe places for 'trust' to be built.

Walkable and safe neighbourhoods are encouraged when the needs of pedestrians take priority over vehicular movement, city block sizes are small enough to feel walkable and streets are vital and interesting places to walk along.

The existing transitional projects in the city offer a unique forum in which to test trust-building spatial possibilities. These projects offer a 'softly, softly' approach where ideas are tested and those that do not work are discarded. It is unclear from the CCRP whether these projects are understood to be the valuable testing bed that they are, with the potential to inform more permanent projects, or just something to literally 'fill the gap' until other development happens. Transitional projects offer opportunities to explore different realisations of 'Ngāi Tahu-ness' in the city to find out which ones fit and which ones do not.

Face-to-face dialogue tends to happen more frequently when challenges and interests are shared. Numerous stories of communities rallying together after the earthquake highlight the synergistic nature of disasters. Local marae (meeting places) offered the city leadership and stability providing whanaungatanga (a sense of kinship) to those in need.[21]

Māori tikanga and kawa (protocols) offer formal ritualised processes for tangi that mean that those grieving do not have to deal with the unknown in the midst of grief. The move away from established religion has meant that many Pākehā are now unsure how to deal with the death of a loved one. The plan outlines the development of a permanent memorial but there is potential to go further, drawing on the exemplar of marae to provide for the city's ongoing unmet need. Are there opportunities for new models of urban, bicultural facilities, presided over by Ngāi Tahu, based on the utility and kaupapa of marae to meet the needs of those who do not have places to tangi their dead? Questions of tikanga and kawa will arise, however there is potential to offer a unique platform on which to build cross-cultural understanding whilst upholding the mana whenua of local iwi and hapū: a unique and fitting memorial, perhaps.

Conclusion

Creating tangible design outputs that signal Ngāi Tahu place identity is key in this next phase of the rebuild of Ōtautahi. We argue that iwi and hapū identities are integral to creating uniquely Aotearoa New Zealand places. The rationale for doing this is not only to respond to Treaty of Waitangi obligations but also because unique places stimulate social, economic and, we argue, environmental good for all communities inhabiting these places.

This paper suggests a design framework that differentiates parts of the built and natural environment according to their rate of change, arguing that it is those parts of our environment that change at the slowest rate that deserve the most intellectual and fiscal resourcing, to get these right for future generations. Alongside this sit four place identity elements identified through an analysis of unique places worldwide, which, when combined with the former, create a framework on which to consider Ngāi Tahu and Ngāi Tūāhuriri kaupapa and tikanga and their relationship to place identity.

The CCRP highlights possibilities for celebrating Ngāi Tahu identity including Ngāi Tahu art works, the Te Puna Ahurea Cultural Centre and, most importantly from our perspective, the revitalisation of the Ōtākaro Avon River. However, as this strategic plan is realised, a more fundamental consideration of Ngāi Tahu identity is possible. In particular, Ngāi Tahu's sustainability imperatives should dictate that the longest lasting parts of the spatial system are given most attention. In our view, it is this, overlaid by the detail inherent in the parts of the environment that change more quickly (building design and exterior details such as public art) that will carve out an Ōtautahi that is clearly a unique place that celebrates the history and identity of its indigenous inhabitants.

The Commons

The Commons is located on a council-owned site where the Crowne Plaza Hotel used to be and is managed by Gap Filler as an ever-evolving space for small-scale experimentation. The Pallet Pavilion (2012-2014) was located here, and the site has accommodated a variety of movable offices (Gap Filler, Life in Vacant Spaces, Volunteer Army Foundation), the Arcades Project, Makercrate, a pizza oven and many different food trucks serving delicious fare. The long-term plans for the site are unclear, but for the meantime it will continue to foster small, community-based projects, events and activities.

[1]

[2–4]

Territorial visions in post-quake Aquila Creating community and identity

Claudia Mattogno

Claudia is a Professor of Urban Planning at the Sapienza University of Rome. Her main fields of research are urban design, community spaces and gender studies. She has recently focused on the idea of the public good in post-quake L'Aquila, where she was living just before 2009.

The magnitude 5.8-6.3 earthquake that struck L'Aquila and 56 other villages on 6 April 2009 caused irreparable damage to the urban area, to its surrounding region, and to the economic and social community, which include approximately 150,000 local inhabitants as well as 14,000 university students.

L'Aquila is the capital city of the Abruzzo region in central Italy. It was founded in the mid-thirteenth century, resulting from a process of aggregation of various surrounding fiefdoms. According to tradition, the urban fabric was based on the idea of 99 units, each consisting of a palace, square, fountain, church and houses. The number 99 also reflected the number of surrounding villages and fiefdoms, which have contributed unique characteristics, family names and traditions to the city of L'Aquila.[1] The urban structure is based on two perpendicular axes, plotted in relation to the territorial topography. This layout results in a city where inhabitants are constantly aware of the mountainous landscape, which they use to orient themselves. The landscape and surrounding villages have formed a strong part of the identity of L'Aquila.

The conceptual strength of the urban system has been maintained over time, but now the city has to face the devastating consequences of another major earthquake. The community has been weakened and buildings have been destroyed, resulting in the loss of civic and cultural identity.[2] The severing of the relationship between the historical city, the outskirts and the territory has accelerated. As a result, the gap has widened between a communal vision of the territory on one hand, and its selfish and careless use on the other. The lack of an urban reconstruction plan has compelled residents to build new homes without consideration for the impact on public space. These public spaces are an elemental aspect of city and civic life in Italy.

The aftermath: The loss of public spaces and the loss of public life

The area affected by the earthquake is approximately 4500 sqkm, 476 sqkm of which belongs to the municipality of L'Aquila and its 70,000 inhabitants. The most serious damage occurred in the historic centre of the city, which is now completely abandoned.[3] In 2014, the reconstruction of the centre has barely started, with only a few dozen reconstruction sites. A large part of the urban fabric, composed of narrow streets and alleys, remains deserted.

Considering the Common Good

Category	Description	Private Buildings	Public Buildings	Total
A	Viable buildings	36,924	1181	38,105
B	Buildings temporarily unusable, to be slightly repaired	8931	467	9398
C	Buildings partially unusable	1905	73	1978
D	Buildings partially unusable: to be reviewed	567	33	600
E	Buildings uninhabitable: to be demolished	19,105	405	19,510
F	Buildings uninhabitable due to external causes	3827	66	3893
	Total buildings valuated by experts in Summer 2009	71,259	2225	73,484

	City Centre	Outskirts	Hamlets	Total
Buildings uninhabitable: to be demolished (Category E)	1567	2289	3268	7124
Buildings uninhabitable due to external causes (Category F)	288	274	678	1240

A carpet of moss covers large sections of public space and many roads are still blocked with rubble.

After 6 April 2009, the entire historical centre was declared a 'red zone'. Military forces prevented access to this public space and only residents were allowed to cross the rigid military cordon for recovery of personal items. This led to the dereliction of the historical centre and the loss of the city's identity – particularly the part connected to everyday life – as these spaces remained inaccessible to the rest of the population.

Parallel to this, political forces have chosen to focus on the construction of new temporary settlements, rather than quickly repairing the partially damaged houses. This has further contributed to the dissolution of urban identity. These new buildings have been situated randomly, without an overall vision of planning. Many empty warehouses have been converted into shopping centres or unsuitable spaces for university activities. New houses are being hurriedly built in an uncontrolled fashion and are scattered everywhere, even near riverbeds and in the middle of cultivated fields.

The sprawl of temporary settlements has impacted upon the landscape and the territory's identity. Twenty new residential emergency settlements, improperly baptised as 'new towns', are now located along the Aterno valley – suddenly introducing 15,000 people and 185 buildings to a rural area. Another 3535 smaller provisional accommodations have been built in peripheral villages. Thirty-four provisional schools, serving a total of over 6000 students, have been built around the city centre.[4] The sense of territory and land has been overlooked for expediency.

Political and administrative weaknesses, as well as a lack of accountability, have created this situation. The post-earthquake emergency response was implemented entirely by the national government and the Civil Protection Department, completely discrediting the local administration and preventing any possible public participation. All the decisions to rebuild the destroyed houses

Figures 1 & 2: L'Aquila city centre. A large part of the old town was deeply injured. Four years on many roads are still blocked with rubble.

elsewhere were made by the former head of the national government and later by a high-ranking commissioner; as a result, the assignment of responsibility for the reconstruction was not shared with the people nor the local governments.[5]

These choices, which have long-term impacts, were made using emergency logic: within a very short time, without due consideration and with a focus on areas that were immediately available. Accordingly, the chosen areas were construction-free, located on level land, and thus easier and faster to urbanise for those awarded the construction contracts. There has been no link of continuity with the existing settlements, no connection with the road infrastructure, no hypothesis to reunite with the patterns of the territory, and no connection with the structure of the landscape. The 'simple' addition of a quantity of buildings has had devastating effects.

The city of L'Aquila now extends over 20 km. One perpetually clogged road has become the principle commuter route for a population dispersed among the new dormitories, the sheds where they have relocated offices, schools and shopping centres, all of which have replaced the pedestrian streets of the old town. It is a never-ending stream of cars.

The need to rediscover a sense of community through links with the territory

In a territorial framework that has been so severely compromised, we need to tackle the challenge of rebuilding through the theme of care. Caring is a complex practice that refers to a system of activities, processes related to accountability, and a commitment to someone or something.[6] In a planning context, accountability and participation, ethical motivation, and thus the practice of care, will lay the groundwork for the future.[7]

The practice of care involves the close relationship of specific sites to the larger context of territory. The territory we inhabit, which is the subject of an

Considering the Common Good

ongoing physical transformation through the rebuild process, is an area that
has a stratified dimension: it is a geographical, political and social expression.
It is a physical space in which the communities recognise themselves. It is a
physical space where they accumulate experiences and stories, institutional
practices and emotional ties, cultural models and social customs. We can
understand this landscape as a living transformation of memory and identity.

Until a few years ago, the remains of a territorial identity could be seen in
woodlands, textures of farmland, rows of trees and old sheep trails. The
emergency relocation erased this complex equilibrium through an illogical
urban sprawl, compromising every open space available.[8] However, these
spaces are our most valuable heritage: they constitute the networks of an
ecological continuity and an expression of landscape morphology. We have
to take care of this heritage, as inhabitants and designers. Our vision of
the future must be based on the role of green spaces because they are the
generative structure of the landscape and a physical mark of an ongoing
dialogue between past and present.[9]

Creating shared visions for the future

Our habitat is a living organism that needs attention, not only because
our country is an earthquake zone, but also because agricultural activities,
which contribute to the protection of the land, have been abandoned. Many
activities need to be undertaken for the reconstruction of the city, all of which
are demanding in terms of technical and financial support. At the same time,
the chain reactions of relevant initiatives shouldn't be underestimated: small
local activities promoted by local authorities could enhance the sense of a
shared identity and political consensus. During such an economic crisis,
activities can be started on four main scales of intervention.

Figure 4: Progetto C.A.S.E. All the new residential settlements are located far from the city in the middle of nowhere without the richness of old town public spaces.

Figure 5: Parts of the city centre remain unchanged.

Urban scale

The interventions to be immediately implemented are the redevelopment of public spaces in the historic city. Public spaces and squares represent the core of the community and the place of social relationships. They have the ability to create new social life for the old town, now abandoned, and restart other activities, such as trade and services.

Heritage

Monuments represent historical and architectural values, and are also very important symbols for the entire local community. Their restoration could help inhabitants to regain their cultural and religious places, but also would be very useful in terms of social cohesion and urban identity.

Landscape

Open spaces play an important role in renewing generative structure, and the landscape expresses a concrete sign of an ongoing dialogue between past, present and future. It is therefore essential to stop the urban sprawl that has completely eroded the agricultural areas. Stopping this type of land use also involves demolishing all of the buildings that have invaded the open spaces in order to re-establish the continuity of the ecological and landscape network.

Sustainability

In light of the recent general economic crisis, it seems necessary to develop local economies that could re-establish a relationship with the roots of historical settlements, long disadvantaged by globalisation.[10] Improving proposals and projects for land reutilisation in terms of agricultural production, livestock and agroforestry, could be a useful means to combat the abandonment of the land and, at the same time, to undertake new forms of economic activity, without falling into nostalgic visions or living in the past. In this way, new working horizons could be expanded (e.g. farmers markets, slow food, urban agriculture etc.) with undeniable advantages for the reorganisation of the landscape in terms of environmental and economic sustainability.

The city of L'Aquila, including the old town, as well as its suburbs and territory, have all been devastated. The Government has focused on emergency housing, yet this type of reconstruction has destroyed the fabric of local communities and deeply altered the territory and the agricultural landscape. Five years on from the 2009 earthquake, reconstruction of the city centre has not yet begun, and the revival of the economy and public life

Considering the Common Good

is under threat. During these years, the municipality has expressed neither a vision nor a strategy for the role of the city in the near future.

We need to apply the practice of care, where expert knowledge and appropriate skills are combined with principles of continuity that allow the renewal of the bonds between spaces, things and people. This involves redeveloping squares and public spaces, restoring historical buildings and preserving the texture of the urban fabric within the context of the territory and landscape.

People's wellbeing is determined not only by their shelter, but perhaps more importantly by the intensity of their social life and their relationship with public space.[11] The links between the territory and its physical, historical and social layers must guide our work as we are faced with a dramatic, illogical urban sprawl that could irreversibly jeopardise the great heritage of open green spaces and L'Aquila's identity. This, combined with shared responsibility where inhabitants and local authorities work together, would reinforce the sense of community.

Chapter 5   Thinking Big

Whāia te iti kahurangi

We live in an age in which our collective knowledge of the world around us, and the world that has come before us, grows every day. Yet with all this information, we still seem unable to adequately respond to the critical issues of our time. We know about the limits of our environment and the rise of intergenerational inequity, but don't seem to make the link between the two: the city.

As more and more people worldwide come to live in urban environments (the UN predicts that two-thirds of the world's population will live in cities by 2050), the twenty-first century will see a redefinition of the city. This unprecedented context and its new challenges call for new responses and fresh ways of thinking. As we re-shape Christchurch after disaster, we have an opportunity to set an example as a progressive city for the world to follow. This chapter examines the environmental and economic factors involved in recovery and city-building, and the various scales inherent within this. The essays suggest that thinking big involves a combination of small acts, bold steps and paradigm shifts – a holistic approach, where the short- and long-term, the micro and macro, are interdependent.

'Thinking Big' looks to sit the recovery in a wider, slower and more global context. We encounter pieces that consider the timely and pressing ideas of how we can prepare for a century where humans constantly push against the limits of our environment; how people get around a city; and how different economic approaches could avoid leaving future generations with an unjustified debt burden.

We engage with questions of how Christchurch will present a viable – and appealing – alternative to other city centres. As we see in this chapter, big thinking can be applied to everything from pressing global issues like climate change, to the rebuilding and economics of one city, to the waste produced from a single house. These essays open up a discussion about what being a resilient and sustainable city means in the twenty-first century.

What should a garden city in the twenty-first century aim to be like?

Luke Engleback

Studio Engleback was formed in 1996 and has been involved in many projects that deal with the interface between urbanism, ecology and environmental sustainability employing a whole-system approach, termed ecourbanism. Luke Engleback, a chartered landscape architect and ecourbanist with over 30 years' experience of environmental design and planning, leads the studio.

We need to reassess what a garden city in the twenty-first century should be, since the World Bank has forecast that the same collective global area of cities in 2000 will be replicated by 2030[1] – this has huge environmental consequences for people and the planet. Accordingly, the context and drivers for city planning are now completely different from those that led to Ebenezer Howard's garden city vision in Victorian Britain.[2] A whole system approach is required, with simultaneous consideration of macro, meso and micro scales. New garden cities need to move beyond purely ornamental space to provide multifunctional environmental infrastructure that delivers a series of environmental services.

Ecourbanism is a pragmatic approach that embraces the different scales and functions of natural systems, which is particularly apposite for the new garden city. It recognises five key interlinked and interdependent issues promoting resilience: climate change adaptation and mitigation; human and ecosystem health; and the resource challenges of water, energy and food provision.

A changed context means we must reassess our approach

Since the Europeans discovered New Zealand three centuries ago, city dwellers have increased from approximately 3 per cent to over 50 per cent of the total global human population, with a trajectory to about 70 per cent by 2050. In the same period overall human population has increased by 700 per cent, and is forecast to peak at between nine and twelve times that level by mid-century,[3] with significant implications for approaches to city-region planning. Cities have always relied on their respective hinterlands to supply goods and services – today these have a global reach.

The fifth Intergovernmental Panel on Climate Change (IPCC) bulletin spells out the need to tackle some big issues now.[4] These include major reductions in greenhouse gas emissions from conventional energy use and cement manufacture, the biodiversity-loss crisis that underpins our existence, the threat to global food security and water supplies, and the potential for human conflict resulting from food, water and energy challenges.

New Zealand, a global player selling and buying goods and services worldwide, is a land of plenty where sheep and cattle vastly outnumber the human population. Yet this is a double-edged sword, for embodied in a litre of milk are 900 litres of water, 23 litres of excreted bovine urine[5] and 16 litres of belched methane.[6] The natural capital creating this wealth is being eroded and polluted, and this worrying context should be reflected in current approaches to city (re)building.

At the macro scale, global resource depletion combined with climate and demographic changes may amplify inherent risk within the global supply chain. Whilst urban living encourages innovation and efficiency, concentrations of population also make them less flexible and resilient to rapid environmental change. The various micro scale 'alternative' activities in Christchurch, challenging the current status quo, are testament to an appetite for change, and the need for pragmatism and flexibility for resilient reconstruction.

The back-story: The evolution of the garden city

The garden city idea was part of a reform movement to improve living conditions for the masses in industrialised Victorian Britain. Yet it was a sentimentalised utopian vision: it was an attempt to turn back the clock during a period of exodus from rural Britain to the new industrial cities. The garden city concept was informed by the Arts and Crafts movement and involved a model for verdant towns of limited size situated close to nature, which established a national architectural style.[7]

Model towns and villages were nothing new. In the seventeenth century Cardinal Richelieu realised his Renaissance vision of an 'ideal city' in the Indre-et-Loire region of France, which embodied social order and human dominion over nature.[8] It is a grid-planned settlement surrounded by farmland with views extending to the horizon cut through local forests. Christchurch was also based on the grid and was a garden city ahead of its time – founded several decades before Howard even published his concept. It was contemporaneous with the British Reform Movement,[9] and one of the earliest socially informed model industrial villages, Saltaire, in Yorkshire.[10]

Howard had described a new type of city in which people lived in harmony with nature, but unlike the model villages of the industrialist philanthropists (such as Titus Salt and the Cadbury brothers at Bourneville), it would be a city for all, not one tied to factory owners.[11] Howard's work lies at the mid-point in the current industrial age, the same distance in time separating the early years of the Industrial Revolution from his vision and today. The deurbanised vision was not universally accepted and was challenged 25 years later by Le Corbusier. His modernist, grid-based *Ville Radieuse* was also hugely influential on city planning, but at the opposite pole of density: while both Howard and Le Corbusier made use of zones and sought space and light in cities, Le Corbusier's landscape provided a backdrop, not functions.

Over this past century the context and drivers for a different approach to urbanism have altered radically. Le Corbusier promoted a radical rationalist view, but our current approach really began with the environmental

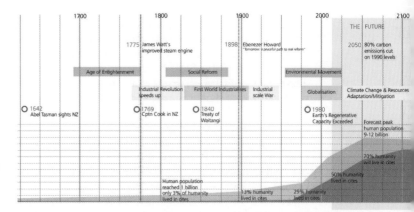

Figure 1: Placing the garden city idea in context. The total human and urban dweller populations set against key events and eras.

Within a decade three major environmental pressure groups were established commencing with the WWF (World Wildlife Fund), and the 'green' movement gathered an inexorable momentum.[13] The idea of garden cities still has currency today, and perhaps a nostalgic political expediency. It is re-emerging in the UK as the topic for the 2014 Wolfson Economics Prize; the UK Policy Exchange think-tank is calling for at least one garden city; and subsequently the UK government has aspirations to build them.[14]

It is important, however, that we do not extend a defunct garden city model that was a reaction to its own immediate problems and does not address the consequences of today's crowded world.[15] Howard's ideas led to the propagation of low-density suburban sprawl – enabled by trains and later by private transport – resulting in rush-hour congestion and air pollution. De-urbanisation also created issues of distance and inequality, as articulated in the work of American urbanist Peter Calthorpe. In the UK, this model led to an area the size of Wales becoming urbanised in the second half of the twentieth century alone,[16] and since first visiting New Zealand in the 1980s, I have witnessed the same type of rapid, low-density growth in greater Auckland. It is not a sustainable solution because land is a precious resource.

An increasingly crowded, globalised and mature industrialised society places enormous pressure on the already dwindling resources on which we rely. These are placed at further risk by pollution and human-induced climate change. Therefore any sustainable and resilient response must address the fate of our common inheritance. Failure to do so damages the ability of the earth to support a huge human population with the same amount of land, as it reaches its carrying capacity. As the first city in the Rockefeller Resilient Cities programme, Christchurch should lead by thinking differently – to quote Albert Einstein, 'No problem can be solved from the same level of consciousness that created it.'

Drivers for a changed approach

Concerns about rapid urban population growth, unlimited resource consumption and an increasingly interdependent world have been voiced since the time of Thomas Malthus in 1798.[17] Malthusianism was controversial but influential to evolutionary biologists such as Charles Darwin and the emerging science of ecology; it was revisited in the Club of Rome's 1972 seminal report *The Limits to Growth*.[18] Concurrently, the British economist E. F. Schumacher had written about natural capital in his 1973 collection of essays entitled *Small is Beautiful: Economics as if People Mattered*, in which he championed the view that 'the aim ought to be to obtain the maximum amount of well being with the minimum amount of consumption'.[19]

The idea of living within our environmental limits came about with the realisation that if everyone on earth lived as those in the Developed World, the productivity of more than three planet earths would be required to sustain us. As the earth is essentially a closed system, the concept of One Planet Living (OPL) was born. Since 1980 the regenerative capacity of the earth has been exceeded by human development and in 2014 we are living collectively 50 per cent beyond the biocapacity of the planet.[20] We are using our inherited natural capital, whilst also denying equity to a large section of humanity, both now and in the future.

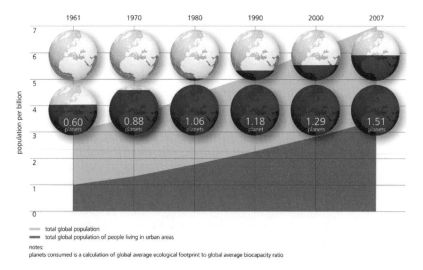

Figure 2: Planets consumed against total global population and total population in urban areas

In 1999 Hawkens and Lovins proposed that the key ideas for a new industrial future would be 'the conservation of resources through more effective manufacturing processes, the reuse of materials as found in natural systems, a change in values from quantity to quality, and investing in natural capital, or restoring and sustaining natural resources.'[21] This thinking from our own time should inform city planning and retrofitting in the twenty-first century.

Ecourbanism and the systems approach

I believe that given the challenges of today, we should take a whole system approach to city planning, starting by re-establishing the human bond with natural processes, which is termed 'biophilia' by the eminent scientist Edward O. Wilson. Establishing the primacy of an underlying and multifunctional environmental infrastructure that delivers environmental services is vital. This approach, stressing quality over quantity in interventions, should redefine the garden city in particular. We must do more with less.

Our planet is a complex system, in which a degree of uncertainty or surprise is inherent. The ecosystem approach embraces complexity[22] and is considered to be one of the most important principles in sustainable environmental management. It was adopted by the Convention on Biological Diversity (CBD) 1992,[23] an international legally binding treaty. In his paper 'The Ecosystem Approach: From Principle to Practice' Prof. E. Maltby stated:

> The ecosystem approach is a strategy for the integrated management of land, water and living resources that promotes conservation and sustainable use in an equitable way, and which recognises that people with their cultural and varied social needs, are an integral part of ecosystems.[24]

As signatories to the CBD, 193 States have effectively embraced this ecological approach.

This vision of interconnectivity informs ecourbanism,[25] which considers the whole system simultaneously at macro, meso and micro scales because the systems that make up our world are generally interdependent. Studio Engleback has been developing this way of thinking since its foundation in the late 1990s, inspired by the ecological planning pioneered by landscape architect Ian McHarg.

Resilience informed by environmental metrics

The Bruntland Commission's 1987 report stated that 'Sustainable development is development that meets the needs of the present without compromising the ability of future generations to meet their own needs.'[26] Key concepts embodied in this were needs, limitations and intergenerational equity.

Resilience is a concept that adds a useful perspective to this notion of sustainable development. It includes the ability to absorb and respond to a perturbation or disturbance by resisting damage or recovering quickly. Ecosystem resilience underpins our existence, and because human activity has adversely affected this, the socio-ecological dimension is an important component of the ecosystems approach to city planning.

In turn, environmental metrics help us to understand resilience and to take measures mitigating its damage and promoting its restoration. The cumulative force of micro scale actions affects the carrying capacity and health of a system, and thus resilience. However, decisions at the macro scale may promote or discourage those myriad small actions.

William Rees applied the concept of the ecosystem's carrying capacity to the earth system and, with Mattias Wackernagel, created a way to calculate this based on the available productive land. They called this the ecological footprint (EF) – it assesses the demands we make on natural capital and the biosphere's ability to regenerate resources and provide associated services. It is a great example of environmental metrics highlighting the impacts of micro actions on the macro scale. We see the demands we make on natural capital with land. It is a fixed resource, with only a third of it available for agriculture (one third is covered in ice, the other forest). Yet the average of productive land per person reduces every year as the human population rises.

In 2007 the world-average ecological footprint was calculated at 2.7 global hectares (gha) per capita, but there was a huge difference between average EFs for each country. The United Arab Emirates topped the EF league table with an average of 10.68 gha per person, whilst Bangladesh used just 0.62 gha per person. New Zealand had the sixth largest ecological footprint on earth.[27] The significant changes made to natural resources in New Zealand in little over 150 years demonstrate why. Changes continue apace – a million cattle have been added to New Zealand's national herd in the past six years.[28]

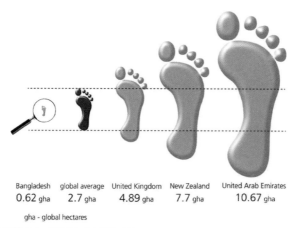

Bangladesh	global average	United Kingdom	New Zealand	United Arab Emirates
0.62 gha	2.7 gha	4.89 gha	7.7 gha	10.67 gha

gha - global hectares

Figure 3: Ecological footprints: relative use of the planet's resources

The New Zealand Resource Management Act (1991), a landmark piece of legislation, was the first to adopt the principle of sustainability. Subsequently, a sustainable development programme in New Zealand was announced in 2003, but cancelled in 2009. This needs reinstatement to guide low-impact design and management initiatives, and to address increased calls for greener growth.[29]

Sustainability must underpin all aspects of city planning and repair, and be incorporated at all scales of intervention through policy and action. Material inputs must be reduced, and there should be an increased use of recycled goods. Importantly, 'settings' that promote health and wellbeing,[30] coupled with policy and design to assist a benign change in behaviour, are imperative.

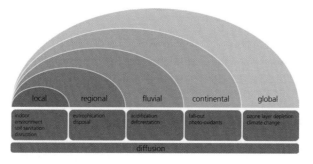

Figure 4: Scales of diffusion: micro, meso and macro scales

The old Scottish saying 'many a mickle makes a muckle' encapsulates the bottom-up approach. Assessment and evaluation can guide development at the micro scale as well – the pre-eminent tools today being the British BREEAM and the American LEED systems.[31] Both provide a rating against which the environmental performance of buildings can be measured, but to date, public realm and social considerations are less well served.[32] These environmental tests tend to be quantitative but not especially qualitative, so Einstein's maxim 'Not everything that counts can be counted, and not everything that can be counted counts' should be borne in mind.

Creating resilience involves a mesh of many ingredients. The 'precautionary principle' is a key concept when dealing with interventions and interactions between the biosphere and physical components in a complex system, because many variables are hidden or unexpected. Some scientists, like James Lovelock, believe that it is too late for sustainable development and that 'Sustainable Retreat'[33] will offer a degree of resilience. In recent years, this previously unthinkable approach has been taken up by the UK Environment Agency for some coastal areas.

Thinking differently

We live at a critical point in the collective understanding of the management of our interconnected planetary and local life support systems, and of the challenges that arise at different scales. Environmental change, rising population and an altered demographic will impact the goods and services that the Developed World has hitherto taken for granted. To increase resilience we should plan to become less dependent on other world regions. How we plan and design cities can contribute to this.

From the dawn of civilisation 10,000 years ago, living collectively has been linked to the land's capacity to supply goods and services. One of the earliest cities, Uruk in modern-day Iraq, flourished over 6000 years ago and supported a population of around 50,000 at its zenith. Unforeseen disasters, coupled with the unforeseen consequences of their way of living, led to Uruk's decline – when the river Euphrates followed a new route, over-irrigated fields became salinated and crop yields declined. Little has changed to support urban living since that time, except that the productive hinterlands are now dispersed globally. Accordingly, environmental factors elsewhere are of increasing concern for our collective wellbeing.

The IPCC's *Fifth Assessment Report* states that climate change will reduce the global grain harvest by 2 per cent each decade, whilst concurrently, demand will increase by 14 per cent. There are other fundamental limiting factors to food production, including finite phosphates reserves,[34] water resources, soil health and biodiversity. Cities in the twenty-first century must be more environmentally efficient.

Climate change adaptation and mitigation

We need adaptation to, and mitigation of, future climate change – two sides of the same coin that require wise investment in measures that will improve our collective future. Yet a balance must be struck between the two. Here lies the potential for new manufacturing, fitting and servicing opportunities in city-building and repair.

The term 'global warming' is familiar, but this appellation obscures the real problem, which is climate disruption. The exaggeration in extreme weather events seems to be increasing with economic consequences that go far beyond the boundaries of where they occur. The 2011 floods in Thailand not only devastated 20,000 square kilometres of farmland, but led to knock-on effects for the computer industry in Japan, because most of the computer hard discs manufactured in the world are made in Thailand.

The IPCC's *Fifth Assessment Report* raises the stakes with regard to addressing the increased variability of weather patterns, intensity of storms, and resulting problems ranging from droughts and flooding, to food shortages and loss of biodiversity. Adaptation makes urban environments more robust, but building this capacity can also make cities more attractive, enhancing quality of life.

Resource challenges: Water, energy and food

As a result of climate disruption and living beyond our environmental capacity, we will face critical resource challenges. Declining fresh water resources already impact global grain harvests raising the cost of staple foods. Much of the global harvest is irrigated, and many aquifers are being drawn down faster than they are being replenished.[35] As a major food exporter New Zealand faces serious concerns about water use in relation to agriculture.[36] As the nitrous oxide and methane emitted from farming are 300 and 25 times (respectively) more powerful than carbon dioxide, Dr Fredrik Hedenus of Chalmers University in Sweden states that '. . . reducing meat and dairy consumption is the key to bringing agricultural climate pollution to safe levels'.[37]

Arjen Hoekstra created the concepts of embodied water and water footprints as measures of water consumption.[38] Embodied water is the water needed to produce a product, whether it is a crop, an item like steel or conventionally generated electricity. In June 2011, the UK National Ecological Assessment calculated that 66 per cent of the total water used by the UK population is embodied water used in the production of imported goods and that 33 per cent of food and fibre consumption is supplied from overseas.[39] Due to the global reach of markets, even countries with wetter climates now source much of their embodied water from countries with challenged supplies.

Fossil energy use has fuelled modern urban living in the UK and the world. Its exponential use has been mirrored by the population rise – both having doubled in the last 50 years. Indeed, David McKay at the University of Cambridge, pointing to the problems involved with weaning ourselves off fossil fuels and the yields reaped from renewables without an overall reduction in energy consumption, has written that 'the climate problem is mostly an energy problem'.[40] By the same token we might also say it has caused excessive resource use in general.

Low carbon cities require a reduction in primary energy consumption and energy use. Renewable energy alternatives are needed, as well as construction methods that have lower embodied carbon: this includes recycling and reuse of existing urban fabric. To date, renewables comprise only a small part of the global energy supply. New Zealand is in an enviable position with some 37 per cent of electricity coming from renewable sources in 2012.[41] Despite this, the average Kiwi still has a larger carbon footprint than people in Western Europe.

We should consider passive urbanism and building design as much as gardens in a garden city, since this reduces energy demand. A Low Impact Development (LID)[42] approach to planning and design can deliver on a number of fronts, including investment in water conservation, soils and vegetation as active carbon sinks linked to low energy building.

Wholesale ecosystem changes resulted in a third of all the land area on earth being converted to agriculture to feed our cities. This contributes significantly to carbon emissions over and above natural global carbon dynamics, which is now affecting food production. Food security is a global concern where an increased burden is placed on food producer countries. Inevitably food prices will continue to rise with the decline in fresh water availability and changing weather impacting yields. This gives rise to concerns about food availability and nutritional density available to poorer sections of society.

Andre Viljoen has made the case for re-incorporating a productive landscape into cities.[43] Howard had envisaged food production within and around his garden cities with plots of about 260 sqm per residential space – the amount he calculated that was necessary to feed a family. Creating space for urban food production, development of healthy soils and water sensitive urban design should be key components of any city, especially a garden city, even in a food-producing nation.

Interconnected human and ecosystem health

There is a link between human and ecological wellbeing, because the environment is our life support system. The emerging discipline of ecotoxicology investigated the fate and effects of chemicals in ecosystems and their toxicity to humans (a topic central to Rachel Carson's book *Silent Spring*), and this is now referred to as ecosystem health.[44]

The First International Symposium on Ecosystem Health and Medicine held in Ottawa, Canada (1994), discussed the interconnections between human and environmental wellbeing. In 1998 the World Health Organisation defined 'settings' as the context within which environmental, organisational and personal factors of peoples' lives interact and affect their health and wellbeing.

Healthy cites must address social capital and social sustainability by considering a range of factors that can improve public health outcomes connected with ecotoxicology and ecosystem health, safety from injury due to crime or traffic, and raising immune system responses by lowering stress levels.[45] Careful design of a biophilic public realm can address these issues through an understanding of, and by responding to, 'place', which in turn provides opportunities for social interaction. Location-specific responses can generate a particular accent for each city.

Geoff Mulgan of Nesta (National Endowment for Science Technology and the Arts) has said 'The great challenge of the twenty-first century urban design is mastering ecological and social design.'[46] Long-term urban sustainability requires more than a garden approach – it needs to combine social, economic and environmental best practice. A twenty-first century garden city will need to densify, while still serving as a biodiverse, biophilic and productive urban landscape.

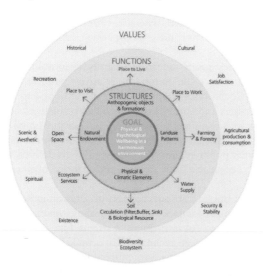

Figure 5: Landscape management with goals of psychological and physical wellbeing

Weaving the fabric of the garden city

The process of designing or repairing a city can be likened to the craft of spinning and weaving. Having sheared the sheep, the staples of fleece are teased to remove dirt, carded to align fibres, and then spun and dyed. First the tensioned warp is set up on the loom and cannot be changed – it is the basis for weaving the fabric. The weft may be varied and interface differently with the warp to provide a distinctive pattern. In a way, the warp provides the macro framework; the weft defines the detail, but is still informed by the warp. A deeper understanding of 'place' is the warp. It is an issue that informs my work, and is also championed by the landscape architect Di Lucas in New Zealand.

The imposition of a formal city grid over a braided river system in Christchurch showed a lack of understanding of natural capital, because dominating nature rather than working with it is costly. In-filled marshes and channels are prone to liquefaction during seismic activity – there is a similar problem in San Francisco where sand dunes overlaying bedrock prevents building. For the bottom-up approach to work in city-building, space is needed from the outset for environmental infrastructure and its subsequent services. These interventions should be multi-functional, which saves space and may reduce primary resource inputs and costs, thus adding value and resilience to the city. A key point in this holistic approach is that decisions taken at the macro level can affect the flexibility or cumulative impact of decisions made at meso or micro levels of intervention. For example, a policy to implement comprehensive environmental (or green) infrastructure across the city can reduce embodied-carbon in conventional engineering whilst also dealing with water run-off, and thus improve energy saving, air quality, biodiversity and human wellbeing.

Today's imperatives are to reduce carbon emissions, and energy and water use; to bolster biodiversity and to produce food. We need to adapt to a fast changing world, but in doing this we should also respect cultural heritage because once this is lost, it may be too late to rescue. This has particular resonance for Christchurch where it seems a very large number of heritage buildings have been needlessly swept away post-earthquakes.

Our urban fabric needs to foster benign behavioural change, since most habits change only if the options are relatively painless responses to new challenges. Social sustainability is a key driver here, and this is linked to shared activities and conviviality, which can be fostered by providing the framework for meeting other people. The Danish Architect Jan Gehl sets this out in his work *Life Between Buildings*, where he highlights the crucial role of a high quality public realm. More life spent outside increases the frequency with which people are likely to meet and to strike up social relationships.

Promotion of public transport reduces private traffic but requires city planning that makes routes viable financially – this means developing critical mass on key routes. An investment in streets, bike-safe junctions and facilities is required to encourage cycling, whilst a walkable city requires density, and the proximity of key destinations coupled with a sense of safety fostered through passive surveillance from overlooking dwellings – not CCTV cameras

Christchurch may benefit from a reappraisal of some land-uses, led by the pragmatics of landscape rather than real estate or political concerns. Taking bold steps is usually very challenging, but lateral thinking can yield results – an example is the conversion of the former municipal airport in the northern Spanish town of Vitoria-Gasteiz into an internationally significant wetland reserve.

Placing a monetised value on environmental or ecological services has never been the norm, so these have rarely been valued – but they should

Figures 6 & 7: Studio Engleback's vision of a multifunctioning landscape at Watercolour: a mixed-use development for 520 homes on a brownfield in Surrey, UK

be. The STRATUM system developed by the US Forest Service valued urban trees, which were costed according to the climatic zone to show a value corresponding to savings in energy, water run-off and over 100 other readouts; it became iTree. The Green Infrastructure Valuation Toolkit[47] pioneered cost-benefit assessment of landscape design interventions in the UK, in which Studio Engleback's design for Kevin McCloud's company HAB was used as an exemplar. This showed an approximate added value of NZ$850,000 for a low-cost scheme that far exceeded the cost of installation.

Cites comprise, and are part of, complex systems with interconnected and interdependent networks. A set of overarching rules can define the direction for achieving resilience, but it is the detailed application of ideas that creates a 'place'. A city that has achieved more than most in the past half century is Freiburg, Germany. About 80 per cent of its historic core had been destroyed during World War II, but that catastrophe provided an opportunity. Today the city has a charter that promotes resilient urban development.[48] Its nine key objectives fit well with how a garden city might be repaired or extended:
• conservation of identity, strengthening of neighbourhood, encouraging cultural diversity and distinctiveness
• expansion of public transport connecting existing and new communities
• wise use of public resources, minimal additional land-take, encouragement of moderate degrees of urban density
• safeguarding the interconnection of greenspaces, networks, and conserving public spaces
• assurance of social harmony and the advancement of social and functional interaction
• safeguarding jobs and creating new and innovative employment
• advancement of a culture of discourse
• creation of long-term partnerships between community, public and private sectors
• participation in life-long processes and seeing urban life in its wider context.

For the first time in several generations of 'progress' in the developed world, the younger generation may no longer see themselves advancing on the living conditions experienced by earlier generations. They can expect to work much longer before enjoying smaller pensions, and may find it harder to live in their own properties and to pay rising bills. These people are the future of any city, and they must be engaged in the process.

Are 'traditional' ways of site clearance and engineering the right ones in a post-earthquake setting? Should areas that were formerly river or marsh be made so again?[49] Can we conserve more of the cultural heritage without wanton destruction? Can we create the conditions for a more robust way of living in the twenty-first century? I do believe that we can, but this requires considerable courage, endurance and greater engagement with more people. It needs a different approach to planning and design.

There is a fantastic opportunity to create a city-specific charter for rebuilding Christchurch that takes the ecourbanism approach to create a resilient and modern garden city.

New motorway developments

Christchurch motorways are part of the major Roads of National Significance programme currently being implemented across the country. Motorways along the northern, western and southern transport corridors are undergoing significant upgrades with the goal of improving connections between the international airport, Lyttelton Port and the central city. $800 million is budgeted for these projects, with a goal of improving travel times and the safety of roads. The motorway projects are being led by the New Zealand Transport Agency in association with Christchurch City Council, Environment Canterbury regional council, Waimakariri District Council and Selwyn District Council.

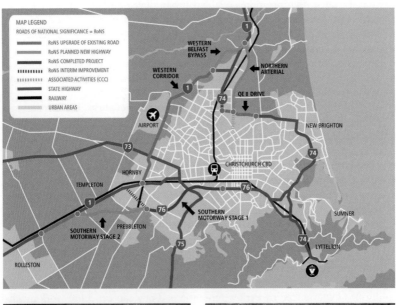

[1–3]

Next generation infrastructure

Peter Cockrem and Clayton Prest

Generation Zero is a youth-led organisation with the central purpose of providing solutions for New Zealand to cut carbon pollution through smarter transport, liveable cities and independence from fossil fuels. Peter Cockrem studied engineering, worked as a transportation engineer in Christchurch and Sydney and is part of Generation Zero's policy team. Clayton studied architecture and is Generation Zero Christchurch's external relations coordinator, while working on the WikiHouseNZ project.

'Addressing climate change is the great challenge of our age. All nations are affected so we must all play our part.'
– Hon. Tim Groser, Minister for Climate Change Issues, December 2013[1]

Post-earthquake Christchurch faces a multitude of issues that test our current resolve and question our future ambitions. Climate change may seem intangible next to the many immediate recovery issues, yet its environmental, social and economic impact will ultimately shape our city over the next 50 years. The current rebuilding of our city's land use, transport and energy infrastructure presents an opportunity to steer away from a fossil-fuel dependent pathway and avoid passing on the cost of solving these challenges to the next generation.

Two conclusive reports from the Intergovernmental Panel on Climate Change (IPCC) in early 2014 are an urgent reminder to evaluate how the Christchurch recovery is responding to climate change. This essay reviews why the recovery needs to respond to climate change, examines what is happening locally to reduce carbon emissions and addresses how we can better mitigate and adapt to its impacts. Christchurch's potential transition from recovery to carbon-zero is not only a chance to be global leaders in clean energy, but to create a more prosperous city and better lives for current and future generations of Cantabrians.

Why does the recovery need to respond to climate change?

As one of the biggest challenges facing our society in the twenty-first century, climate change will affect the way we live in Christchurch. There is global scientific consensus that increasing greenhouse gas emissions, particularly carbon dioxide from the burning of fossil fuels, is linked to changes in global climate.[2] Research shows the link to be as certain as that between smoking and lung cancer.[3] In early 2014, the IPCC released their comprehensive *Fifth Assessment Report*, which analyses the causes, impacts, adaptive measures and mitigation solutions to climate change.[4] The report has prompted calls for urgent action to curb our accelerating emissions, which have already raised the average global temperature by 0.85 degrees and sea levels by 200 mm since 1880.[5]

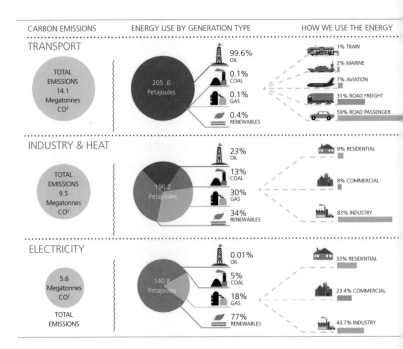

TRANSPORT

TOTAL EMISSIONS 14.1 Megatonnes CO²

205 .6 Petajoules

99.6% OIL
0.1% COAL
0.1% GAS
0.4% RENEWABLES

1% TRAIN
2% MARINE
7% AVIATION
31% ROAD FREIGHT
59% ROAD PASSENGER

INDUSTRY & HEAT

TOTAL EMISSIONS 9.5 Megatonnes CO²

190.2 Petajoules

23% OIL
13% COAL
30% GAS
34% RENEWABLES

9% RESIDENTIAL
8% COMMERCIAL
83% INDUSTRY

ELECTRICITY

5.6 Megatonnes CO²

TOTAL EMISSIONS

140.8 Petajoules

0.01% OIL
5% COAL
18% GAS
77% RENEWABLES

33% RESIDENTIAL
23.4% COMMERCIAL
43.7% INDUSTRY

Figure 1: Sources of energy that were used in New Zealand in 2013.

The consequences of inaction will affect us in New Zealand and we're not prepared. A 2013 report from the Ministry for the Environment (MFE) indicates that our agricultural industry is threatened by severe droughts that are predicted to become more frequent as the planet warms. A 0.8 metre sea level rise before the end of the century will increase our vulnerability to sever heavy rainfall events, particularly in Christchurch where land subsidence from the earthquakes has already resulted in flooding in March and April 2014.[6] New Zealand is part of an international agreement to limit global warming to a relatively tolerable two degrees, which will require large-scale transition away from our fossil-fuel dependent cities and economies.

However we are doing poorly in response to climate change compared to other countries. The 2013 Climate Change Performance Index ranked New Zealand forty-first in the world, with a 'very poor' grade for its climate policy.[7] Climate Change Issues Minister Tim Groser claims we are doing 'our fair share' to reduce emissions, yet we have the fifth-highest per-capita emissions in the OECD, emitting more per person than countries like the UK and Japan.[8] Although our electricity generation is mostly from renewabl sources, electricity makes up only 28 per cent of Christchurch's energy use, with the remainder being predominantly petrol and diesel used for transpor MFE sets unconditional targets of a 5 per cent reduction in greenhouse gas emissions from 1990 levels by 2020, and 50 per cent reduction by 2050.[10] With our carbon emissions having increased by 32 per cent since 1990, we are not on track to meet even these low targets and have few mitigation policies to transition to clean energy.[11] The Government states that this responsibility is being left to local governments, yet the Christchurch rebuild is an opportunity to collectively lead climate change mitigation and adaptation to reduce its harmful effects.[12]

What is Christchurch doing about climate change?

'People and communities actively work towards a climate smart Christchurch that reduces its greenhouse gas emissions and is resilient to the social, economic and environmental effects of climate change.'
– Christchurch City Council's Climate Smart Strategy[13]

Before the February 2011 earthquake, Christchurch's carbon dioxide emissions were rising, despite the inclusion of climate change in local government policies. In 2008, 80 per cent of the city's energy came from fossil fuels, with only 20 per cent from renewable sources including hydroelectricity, wind and wood fires.[14] Two-thirds of our total emissions came from transport, and 18 per cent from fossil fuels used to heat our homes and buildings.[15] The energy use for transport and buildings in Christchurch grew by 33 per cent per capita from 1990 to 2008.[16] In response the Christchurch City Council (CCC) released its Climate Smart Strategy in 2010, which looks at the necessary steps for mitigation and sets emissions targets of 20 per cent reduction by 2020.[17] Although a step forward, it is small compared to targets set by cities such as Copenhagen (carbon neutral by 2025).[18] In 2008 CCC was far more ambitious with a vision for 2050 where 'Christchurch's energy supplies are provided solely from renewable sources, and the city's energy systems are efficient and secure, ensuring sustainability and net zero impact on climate, local environment and public health.'[19]

Yet the reality is that emissions have only increased further since the earthquakes. Land use has changed significantly in the east and around the periphery of the city, increasing average trip distances and reducing the efficiency of public transport and attractiveness of walking and cycling.[20] The dip in overall energy use caused by the earthquakes has more than rebounded and is now 3.7 per cent higher than pre-quake levels.[21] Our current business-as-usual construction of housing and infrastructure locks in these increases for the long term, and risks leaving these assets stranded if travel behaviour is forced to change due to land use and the rising cost of oil.

The central Government's Christchurch Central Recovery Plan (CCRP) considers this in its vision for 'a greener, more attractive central Christchurch, which includes measures against climate change'.[22] The CCRP sets out a compact central city of special-use precincts, constrained by a frame of green space and residential development. The Land Use Recovery Plan affects the rest of Christchurch and Canterbury, allowing limited intensification in some areas, but also releasing large amounts of greenfield land outside the existing city. The planned central-city living has been too slow to absorb the post-earthquake housing demand, which has been displaced to greenfield sites. The District Plan is being urgently reviewed, yet its land-use policies make few changes from present. Mixed-use development is limited to existing neighbourhood centres with little expansion of their extents, though increased residential density in existing centres is a positive step.

There are several major transport plans that will determine the city's development and future emissions profile. The CCRP urgently designated land uses long before the transport chapter, An Accessible City, put in place objectives to support a mode shift away from driving with a people-orientate core that is walking and cycle friendly. Separating land-use and transport planning makes it difficult for effective and efficient urban development to occur. The CCC has allocated funding for the construction of thirteen majo cycleways, for completion in eight years. Its District Plan review aims 'to reduce dependency on private motor vehicles and promote the use of public and active transport' and 'minimise the adverse effects on the environment from the transport network', but continues to mandate the provision of car parking spaces with most developments.[23] The exclusion of neighbourhood centres from parking requirements, and the reduction from two to one space for residential units are steps in the right direction. However, mandating any parking increases the cost of development and reduces the perceived cost of owning and operating a car, thus inducing greater demand for emissions-intensive car travel.

The CCRP acknowledges that 'Greater Christchurch has an opportunity to build green, healthy and resilient buildings that have a lasting, positive legacy'. It suggests Green Star building ratings for the recognition of sustainable buildings, but makes no commitment to assessment.[24] It does lay out possible plans for a District Energy Scheme, which would increase energ efficiency and could be powered by renewable sources. The IPCC recognise that 'Building codes have been among the cost-effective instruments for emissions reduction', yet NZ building standards set no mandatory targets on energy use or embodied emissions.[25] The NZ Green Building Council, in conjunction with CCC, have developed BASE (Building a Sustainable Environment) as a simple assessment for new buildings in Christchurch to achieve 20 per cent more energy and water efficiency than the building code.[26] Sustainable energy initiatives, like trialling energy performance improvements in the repair of earthquake damaged homes and the Build Back Smarter Project, indicate a shift towards an energy efficient built environment, but this is not enough in terms of meeting climate targets.[27]

How can we better mitigate and adapt to climate change?

The recovery presents the opportunity to build a mitigation pathway toward a carbon-zero Christchurch by 2050. If Christchurch is going to even achiev its emissions targets then pre- and post-earthquake trends need to be turned around. To do so, rebuild plans need to include specific and measurable policies to address land use, transport and building energy use and emission

Land-use patterns that reduce the distances people need to travel are the key to major reductions in carbon emissions. The IPCC recommends 'co-locatin high residential with high employment densities, achieving high diversity and integration of land uses'.[28] Exemplar 'density done well' competitions such as the Breathe urban village and community-driven developments such as the Viva Project could lead the way for this in Christchurch.[29] This is important in attracting and retaining skilled and mobile young workers and entrepreneurs, who value vibrant urban life and choose to live predominantl in central areas.[30]

Transport options that provide an alternative to car travel could substantially reduce carbon emissions in Christchurch, while providing economic and social co-benefits including reduced travel costs, travel times and road deaths and injuries.[31] The Congestion Free Network plan for Auckland, developed by Generation Zero and Transport Blog, offers inspiration for the potential of a multimodal transport network to provide people with the choice of travelling without traffic congestion. In Christchurch, high-frequency public transport on key routes with priority to increase speed and reliability would make a big difference to the attractiveness of the system. The energy efficiency of public transport can be further improved by changing from diesel buses to hybrid or battery electric buses, or electric light rail, though shifting trips from private vehicles is more important for the system as a whole.[32] Commuter rail service to satellite towns on the railway lines north and south of Christchurch would reduce carbon emissions substantially compared to private car travel, though risks increasing the attractiveness of low-density lifestyle blocks dependent on car use for non-work trips.[33]

Buildings are a focus of the rebuild and could be much warmer, healthier and more efficient in the use of energy and emission of greenhouse gases. The IPCC suggests that a well-designed, insulated and passively-heated building cuts energy use by 50 to 90 per cent.[34] There are also emissions associated with producing and assembling new building materials, which is typically a quarter of the emissions over a 60-year lifetime. Constructing a new steel or concrete building releases almost half a tonne of carbon dioxide per square metre, while timber buildings are less carbon-intensive to construct.[35] However, it should not be overlooked that the buildings that require the least energy and emissions to construct are those already standing. Christchurch can retrofit existing buildings for greater performance and set the standard with new buildings tested for mandatory Green Star and Home Star assessments, including monitoring energy use and emissions. In addition to energy cost savings, mitigating emissions in buildings creates considerable co-benefits including higher productivity and healthier occupants.[36]

If we cannot successfully mitigate climate change globally we will have to adapt to its impacts locally. We can reduce our exposure to sea-level rise threatening coastal areas such as New Brighton, Sumner and the Avon and Heathcote rivers through higher floor levels, relocatable buildings, and developing areas that will not require expensive flood protection.[37] With the severity of flooding predicted to increase, 'if communities cannot achieve a managed retreat, then the risk is likely to increase until a forced retreat is unavoidable.'[38]

Conclusion

Taking action in the Christchurch recovery to reduce and prepare for the impacts of climate change is economically and socially beneficial today and leaves a much less expensive legacy for future generations. Christchurch is especially vulnerable to the effects of climate change, and is not doing its share in reducing its effects. Our emissions were increasing before the earthquakes and continue to grow. Recovery plans for the central city are a chance to align well with good climate outcomes, but the wider regional land use and transport plans need to address the critical challenge of reversing current trends in emissions and energy use.

Recovery agencies have a responsibility to ensure efficient land-use; provide attractive public transport, walking and cycling options; and build sustainable, energy efficient homes and workplaces. The IPCC report emphasises that the benefits of mitigation include a stronger, resilient 'green economy', thus creating skilled jobs; building a healthy, accessible city; and attracting global talent to our doorstep. These are all aspects that are integral to the future success of Christchurch – rebuilding the city as it was will not be enough.[39]

Christchurch has been named as one of the Rockefeller Foundation's global network of one hundred Resilient Cities – a chance to lead by example in adaptation to climate change and resilience measures that lower risk and substantially reduce disaster costs in the long term.[40] Not only can we be an exemplar for other post-disaster scenarios, but through mitigation become a leading international carbon-zero city.

Demolition waste

CERA has estimated that around 4.25 million tonnes of waste material will be removed from the demolition of buildings in Christchurch after the earthquakes. This amount is the equivalent of twenty years of normal waste disposal in Christchurch – roughly 100,000 truckloads of waste, or more than 200 truckloads every day for a year. A lot of the waste has been used to reclaim land for the port in Lyttelton; around a quarter will go to the Burwood Resource Recovery Park; and much of the clean waste such as concrete and bricks will be recycled.

[1–2]

[3–6]

Why the big pile of rubble in the forest?: The question of demolition waste in post-quake Canterbury

Juliet Arnott

Juliet is the founder of Rekindle, an artist and occupational therapist. She works to reduce disposal of wood to landfill in New Zealand via waste-based design and making. Juliet sees both prophylactic and remedial therapeutic benefit in working creatively with waste, and is inspired by this degree of resourcefulness being fundamental to healthy resilient communities. She remains dedicated to enabling the transformation that occurs when recovered resources are made useful.

The 2010 and 2011 Canterbury earthquakes have resulted in the demolition of a minimum of 12,000 homes and 1500 commercial buildings culminating in an estimated 4.25 million tonnes of demolition material. This equates to approximately twenty years of the usual Canterbury municipal solid waste volume. Demolition is most commonly achieved by use of diggers and other machines that crush and remove the building quickly. The material result of this demolition is evident at the Transwaste Burwood Resource Recovery Park (BRRP) in Burwood forest, where an estimated 500,000 tonnes of earthquake-related mixed rubble is being disposed of, along with additional tonnage at other disposal sites across the region. Some recovery of reusable materials is occurring but the possibility of successful recovery of the majority of this material is as yet undetermined.

The large pile of crushed rubble at BRRP is one of the most tangible outcomes of the post-quake demolition process. The BRRP was established in March 2011 and in early 2012 stated on their website that they face 'a major challenge at the Burwood site to manage the receipt of the [building demolition] material in a safe and efficient manner'. Given the degree of challenge and cost involved in making good such a monstrosity, it is natural to question what forces are at play in creating this crushed mish-mash of materials heaped 25 metres high.

When the earthquakes themselves caused such a degree of loss, why would a course of action that creates further disempowerment and loss be consciously chosen within the city's *recovery* process itself? Upon witnessing the scale of loved homes, valued possessions, reusable resources and irreplaceable heritage being crushed and discarded by digger, questions such as 'Why so fast?', 'Why so much waste?' and 'Isn't there a better way?' understandably follow. These questions and others like them seem impossible to answer categorically due to the many-sided concerns involved and potentially conflicting priorities at play (as acknowledged in CERA's debris management goals),[1] some of which are explored in this piece.

Whilst considering the situation here, it is impossible not to inadvertently engage with some of the major underlying challenges involved in managing usual volumes of waste in New Zealand. To strive for diversion of reusable resources from landfill is not an unfamiliar concept. For over ten years Christchurch City Council (CCC) has been aspiring towards Zero Waste, which Zero Waste International Alliance defines as 'designing and managing products and processes to systematically avoid and eliminate the volume and toxicity of waste and materials, conserve and recover all resources and not burn or bury them'.[2]

This is indeed *thinking big* as far as waste management goes – it requires multi-layered change and the commitment of whole communities, from consumers through to government. The CCC's 2003 Solid and Hazardous Waste Management Plan aspired to 'avoid irreversible damage to the physical environment; minimise the adverse effects of solid waste generally; and use waste as a resource' with a goal of 'zero residual disposal of solid waste'.[3] Zero Waste is no longer just an ideal; it has become an international movement comprising ten tangible steps. Cities such as Auckland and San Francisco have taken significant steps towards reducing landfill and increasing waste diversion.[4]

What we have seen unfold post-quake with the crushing of reusable resources serves to illustrate some of the usual obstacles to Zero Waste and landfill reduction massively exaggerated by scale, haste and relative unpreparedness. In relation to what has happened here, this long-standing intention towards Zero Waste is a useful baseline for contrast, enabling an awareness of how different waste management could be.

Dr Charlotte Brown's timely thesis, *Disaster Waste Management*, completed in 2012 at Canterbury University, included a review of international case studies of post-disaster waste management (including the 2011 Canterbury earthquakes). She suggests twelve categories as critical to understanding post-disaster waste management, from volume of waste, degree of mixing of waste and presence of human and environmental health hazards through to community priorities, regulations and time constraints in the recovery process.[5] Dr Brown's work is a wide-ranging and comprehensive account of disaster waste management and should be referred to as a means of understanding the intricacies of this multifarious and complex topic. What is clear is that more planning for post-disaster waste management is required, as is a discussion around how demolition is undertaken and the potential for greater product stewardship to reduce hazardous materials in construction.

This essay explores waste management after the state of emergency had passed, through the lens of residential demolition waste. Four broader groupings based on Dr Brown's categories will be discussed as a means of exploring some of the pressing demolition-waste-related concerns encountered by the author whilst actively involved in resource recovery activities in Canterbury post-quake: community participation, the nature of waste, financial realities and legislation.

Community participation

When concerns about demolition waste management are considered in the wider context of community priorities at the time of a natural disaster, they are going to be prioritised lower than more acute issues. Similarly, psychological disempowerment within the demolition process may seem like one intangible concern amongst many more concrete issues. However, as insurance processes unfurled, the nature of demolition-waste management insidiously began to impact on each building owner or resident, one condemned property at a time.

When one considers the likely psychological impact of loss (after earthquakes) compounded by further loss (within demolition and the decision-making regarding this process), combined with other financial and interpersonal stressors and bureaucratic complexities surrounding compensation payments and repairs, it is reasonable to suppose that depression and other mental health concerns follow. The 2012 Canterbury Earthquake Recovery Authority (CERA) Wellbeing Survey found that 65 per cent of people surveyed reported 'dealing with EQC/insurance issues in relation to personal property or house' had an impact on their lives and over a third (37 per cent) reported that this had a moderate or major negative impact on their everyday life. A third (29 per cent) of people surveyed also reported that making decisions about house damage, repairs and relocation had a moderate or major negative impact on their everyday life.[6]

Success stories of homeowners who fought to save and relocate their homes were rare, and gaining consent from authorities appeared challenging. At the time of writing in mid-2014, over half of the residential red zone has been demolished, so for many homeowners the opportunity to find an alternative to machine-based demolition and off-site disposal has passed. Regardless of its desire for responsible waste management, the ability of the Canterbury community to influence change within demolition and disposal practices was limited. Relatively small-scale resource recovery initiatives were driven by some NGOs, like CanCERN, Student Volunteer Army and Rekindle. While some companies were salvaging, deconstructing and relocating homes, this was unfortunately not the predominant behaviour and many homeowners found insurers and demolition companies unsympathetic to their desire to see something useful come from the demolition of their homes.

So given the results of the CERA Wellbeing campaign and homeowners' experiences of disempowerment, what is the true cost of not involving the community proactively in the process of resource recovery? It would be useful to evaluate and quantify the actual cost of this psychological impact against the costs 'saved' in hurried residential demolition, and the later costs of intensive resource recovery off-site.

Dr Brown recommends that there is an opportunity to support recovery within the community via a reuse-based approach to resource recovery within demolition. It would seem that the community would regain a greater sense of internal control through seeing or being involved in measures taken to separate out reusable resources from thousands of homes through salvage or relocation.

There is an opportunity for post-disaster management plans of the future to include a socially supportive mechanism within the deconstruction or demolition process, so that this acts as part of a community's recovery. Research has identified a common influence on community resilience, namely 'community participation in disaster response and recovery'.[7]

The nature of this mechanism for community involvement warrants further research, but as a starter there was a small study that engaged people in deconstruction activities in New Orleans and showed that:

> Participants reported a sudden psychological shift from despair to enthusiasm as they regained control of their property and then discovered value out of the ruined buildings . . . Perhaps the single most important finding in this is the realization that the destroyed remains of a home are far more than industrial garbage for a landfill. But likewise they are more than just a pile of deconstructed materials for resale. The unfastening pieces of a home, whether blighted or damaged, barely standing or fully collapsed, hold meaning. They embody the lives, history, and culture of individuals and their surrounding community.[8]

Although deconstruction, recycling and resource recovery are viewed as relatively laborious methods of waste management, there is significant social opportunity for this to offer training and work to those who need it. The 2013 Census showed over 11,000 people were unemployed in Christchurch, and 10.8 per cent of young people aged between 15-24 were not in employment, education or training.[9] Architects at Victoria University Wellington reported that:

> Deconstruction also has significant social benefits. Deconstruction provides training for the construction industry and also has the potential to create more jobs in both the demolition and the associated recovered materials industry. It is estimated that there are 20 per cent more jobs in the recycling industry than in landfilling in NZ.[10]

The nature of waste

With post-quake waste at twenty times the usual amount dealt with day-to-day in Canterbury, it is easy to explain the pile at BRRP by the degree of general unpreparedness for such scale of demolition waste. The demolition material seen at the BRRP encompasses a majority of timber, crushed together with metals, hard fill, textiles and more. The degree to which this material can fairly be called 'waste' as opposed to 'resources yet to be recovered' remains to be seen in the level of resources *actually* recovered at the BRRP. But some of those materials have been 'wasted' in that their primary value was lost when crushed, as with structural native timbers.

The nature of the waste occurring relates to the way demolition has been approached. Following the September 2010 earthquake, Dr Brown describes that demolition was viewed as sluggish as a result of the degree of on-site separation of materials occurring. Immediately following the February 2011 earthquake Dr Brown was invited to work with Civil Defence, initially on the demolition programme and then as part of a waste management team. She recalls that at this time 'There was a lot of feeling about doing it (the demolition) quickly and having minimum on-site salvage, and that was driven by the time element, and safety as well.' This resulted in what is described by Luke Austin (CERA Debris and Waste Manager) as 'drop and haul' style demolition. He depicts the subsequent demolition behaviour change as follows:

> As was discovered in Canterbury, decisions made during the emergency, while correct at the time, can have unintended consequences when a community moves into the recovery phase, requiring changes which in turn may affect other decisions. This was demonstrated with the change from "drop and haul" though "quick pick and go" to "salvage and full separation on site", as Canterbury moved from emergency to recovery.[11]

However if it was accurate that the predominant demolition behaviour had become 'salvage and full separation on site' we would not have continued growth of the tonnage of mixed-crushed materials being piled at BRRP each day. This indicates the variance in perceptions around the level of hasty off-site disposal actually occurring. This also represents the debate between the benefits of on-site and off-site separation of materials – a fundamental issue when the result of off-site separation is the degree of crushed material apparent at BRRP. This debate involves weighing up the benefit of the quicker demolition that occurs when materials are crushed to fit in the back of a truck and transported off-site to be sorted, versus the slower separation of building materials on-site whilst the deconstruction of the building occurs.

Dealing with the scale of demolition waste involved, responsibly, requires the instigation of an appropriate mechanism to harness reusable resources. This involves deciding whether the building can remain intact and be relocated; be partially or fully deconstructed and salvaged (manually taken apart and resources recovered on-site); or undergo full machine demolition without deconstruction. The latter approach was essential when particularly high-rise and structurally-at-risk buildings were involved.

Off-site resource recovery involves finding space and facilities adequate to respond to the sudden influx of material post-disaster. Off-site separation allows a speedier demolition process in the first instance, but defers the costs of sorting resources and in doing so reduces the volume and quality of material likely to be recovered. The volume of waste in Canterbury appears to have resulted in a decision to favour off-site sorting, as seen in the BBRP's great tonnage of mixed-crushed material.

One of the biggest issues with the outcome of the BRRP and the other collections of crushed timber, is whether a viable safe solution can be found for treated timber, which contains chemicals that have led to its landfilling being banned in a number of countries, including Germany.[12] The potential degree of waste here is compounded by difficulties discriminating between treated and untreated timber. Fraser Scott's *Treated Timber Waste Minimisation Project* for Environment Canterbury (ECan) reported:

Transpacific's Gareth James has confirmed that Transwaste plans to landfill all treated and untreated timber until a productive use for it can be found. It is highly likely that the economics of individually sorting each piece of timber will be prohibitive, and thus the entire stockpile must be handled as if it is all treated.[13]

The Treated Timber Waste Minimisation Project has resulted in one or two possible processes that could provide an alternative to landfill for the treated and untreated timber recovered, however when last updated in February 2014, the application of this technology was still in the early stages of feasibility testing.

Canterbury requires a mixed model of resource recovery, one that is primarily responsive to the nature of the building. We have seen this logic being applied by a few salvage and demolition companies where they choose the approach that maximises resource recovery. To generalise this across the industry, a standardised decision-making tool could be developed based on the logic of the most resourceful salvage company, and this tool could be applied by the authorities to all buildings prior to awarding the demolition contract. In the first instance, this logic would simply discriminate between the buildings requiring demolition for structural reasons, and those for which the land itself was deemed no longer fit for use. The type of the construction involved in the building, its age and likely material content would be considered in determining which type of approach achieves the best degree of resource recovery.

The work of Garry Moore's Your Home Ltd and related home relocation initiatives has demonstrated structural and financial feasibility in the relocation of homes. This has significant potential as a constructive response with capacity for scale, especially given the dearth of homes available to those in need in Canterbury post-quake.

The ultimate challenge is to be able to consistently support the decision-making process about the future of a condemned home, with the financial realities required to fund the range of options involved.

Financial realities

Decision-making about demolition and the degree of resource recovery achieved via on-site or off-site sorting is driven by the financial viability of each demolition job. This is founded on laws of supply and demand within the market for recovered materials, and also the market for demolition services. Naturally the cost of demolition at the scale seen in Canterbury weighs heavily on those directly paying for it; it has been their choice of demolition contractor that ultimately decides the level of resource recovery. A lower price for residential demolition here seems to have indicated one of four possible things.

Firstly, the demolition contractor is effective in their salvage and on-site separation of resources by covering some labour costs with on-sale of reusable materials. This may involve partial or near to full deconstruction and salvage or full relocation of homes, and consequently lower disposal fees. The major cost-saving devices include salvage and on-sale of reusable materials, plus reduced time and cost on disposal.

Secondly, the demolition contractor is time efficient with a tightly coordinated schedule to minimise costly downtime in machinery use. They will undertake minimal on-site separation – aimed at reducing the weight and cost of disposal (e.g. concrete roof tiles) – but mainly they demolish as quickly as possible and cart crushed materials in trucks for disposal. The major cost-saving device here is the minimisation of labour costs through swift machine demolition.

Thirdly, larger demolition contractors are able to benefit from economies of scale including the coordinated use of resources across the bulk of contracts they win. This tends to relate closely to the previous approach. Swift demolition at scale is appealing to insurers as there are simpler pathways for communication via a sole firm. Here the major cost-saving device is the effective spreading of resources and overheads across a pool of jobs.

Finally, there is the contractor's desperation for survival. With increased competition in the market for demolition services, the need to manage persistent machine and labour-related overheads becomes acute. Lower bids are made just to break even or cover some costs. Here the compromise in profit margin is the major cost-saving device.

It is the demolition contract procurement process that influences the occurrence of these cost-reducing behaviours. Put simply, the nature of contract procurement for demolition services relates to the degree of control and risk the funder wishes to sustain, or is willing to relinquish to the contractor to reduce the price paid for the work. This involves two types of contracts that have been seen in Christchurch: cost reimbursement contracts and lump sum contracts.

Cost reimbursement contracts allow the funder to retain control around the time frames and outcomes of the demolition, but this involves them holding the risk and impetus to minimise costs. Lump sum contracts generally allow more contractor autonomy in terms of demolition outcomes and therefore hand the incentive to minimise costs to the contractor; the funder pays less for the job but has less influence over how it is run. This in turn tends to result in competitive pricing of jobs between contractors as they rival each other's profit-making cunning and desire to win the job. This rivalry and profit-driven behaviour may well result in ingenious creative methods that facilitate optimal revenue generation from recovered materials. Salvagers and on-sellers of recovered materials are often wily, resourceful and passionate people experienced in finding the necessary customers to turn resources that would otherwise be wasted into money.

Yet within lump sum contracts, the lack of controls could also result in the wastage of recoverable resources, because salvage is seen as too time-consuming and costly. Given the drop-off in availability of demolition contracts since the initial flood of work post-quakes and the subsequent increase in competitive tendering, there has been an estimated 30 per cent reduction in an average residential demolition price. This leaves little room for anything other than the most cost efficient outcome. Consequently other concerns (environmental, social, cultural) come into play only minimally, if at all.

In this regard Dr Brown describes that 'there is a need for project risks and control to be held by an entity with responsibility for meeting recovery objectives rather than solely profit'.[14] This approach is reminiscent of the nature of social enterprise, whereby business principles are applied to address social and environmental concerns. Social enterprise is an appropriate support mechanism in this context with its self-determined orientation toward profit and financial sustainability whilst undertaking activities that aim to meet recovery objectives. Social enterprise can act to derive optimal value from activities such as salvage, wood recovery and manufacturing of products from recovered resources.

Another crucial and unwieldy dynamic that greater controls in procurement may even struggle to address is the strength of the market for recovered resources when flooded with an unprecedented volume of materials. The immediate demand for such a supply of reclaimed materials is unlikely to be present in proportion to the scale of salvage involved, and thus it may take some years and future market developments to recompense the costs of the salvage. Naturally this delay in revenue generation weakens the business model for optimal on-site separation and resource recovery, and there are additional costs to stockpile and store resources. Accordingly, the development of incentives to support resource recovery via subsidies is necessitated by the *totality* of the direct and indirect costs involved (financial, social and environmental) in not recovering these resources.

Given the potential for the anomalies described above, Dr Brown suggests 'that disaster waste management (in particular detritus removal and demolition) should be publicly funded and directly facilitated'.[15] Planning for post-disaster recovery would ideally involve development of a business case for a mixed model of on-site sorting combined with the receipt of materials off-site at a recovery park like the BRRP. While maximal on-site separation is supported as the primary option, off-site disposal remains available when appropriate.

Legislation

The nature of procurement contracts, as described above, appears to sit at the heart of the outcome of post-disaster waste management in terms of the degree of reusable resource recovery. The potential to apply controls within the award of demolition contracts via a cost reimbursement approach appears to be the window of opportunity for the authorities to direct demolition behaviour towards its preferred outcomes. To move toward Zero Waste, the procurement process would need to set optimal resource recovery as a requirement. *This* appears to be the point at which the authorities have the power to intervene and take charge of the true cost of hurried demolition and disposal of reusable resources.

Additionally, given what unfolded in Canterbury, research is needed to assist policy development and enable future regulations that both support holistic recovery and make real the stated intention of Zero Waste. Policy development needs to take place around:

- the evaluation of the relationship of higher disposal fees combined with greater controls on alternative points of disposal, and economic incentives for recycling and resource recovery
- the feasibility of on-site separation of resources (then modelled to scale), as well as full deconstruction and relocations (then modelled to scale)
- the design and feasibility of community partnership with NGOs and social enterprises to build community engagement in waste minimisation activities
- raising a cost profile of social disempowerment often inherent in the demolition process, and research solutions to counter this
- the design and feasibility of a programme of inclusive training opportunities to boost available workforce for salvage and resource recovery
- establishing recycling outcomes for the current array of building materials (especially treated timber), which address the true cost of hazardous material disposal
- researching alternative markets for reclaimed buildings materials, and the potential for their growth
- making product stewardship in industrial product design and architecture mandatory to address the production of hazardous waste and reuse of building materials in the future.

Moving forward

With greater reflection on the demolition and waste management processes post-quake in Canterbury, it is easy to wonder what future generations will make of the scale of disposal of homes, history and irreplaceable materials. When we look back on the approach to the waste management within the demolition process one can only hope we will feel that we did our best. Certainly more thorough planning for post-disaster waste management is suggested, and much could be learned from what occurred here. As New Zealand moves towards Zero Waste, serious governmental commitment to product stewardship within the architecture and construction industries could result in a reduction of cost associated with disposal of hazardous materials, and ultimately an increase in our ability to recover and reuse resources from buildings requiring demolition.

After a demolition has been deemed necessary, there appears to be but one remaining opportunity to partially negate some of the impact of loss, this being the choice of how the demolition is undertaken. Procurement is the opportunity for governing bodies to set the priorities to be upheld within the demolition process.

Regardless of the ideas and ideals about how different the demolition waste management could have been, the reality was that Canterbury was not ready to deal with the extraordinary scale and nature of this waste by any another means, other than that which it did. It was initially difficult to perceive of alternatives, but they have very much come to exist. The alternatives seen in Canterbury include deconstruction and salvage of reusable materials (full or partial depending on quality of architecture and materials), deconstruction and 'flat-packing' of homes into containers for relocation, and full relocation of homes by truck. These alternatives have been driven by non-governmental entities, and they have often had to work counter to existing governmental priorities in order to get established. Considering that true community recovery is a holistic matter, these examples of resourcefulness in resource recovery within demolition are symptoms of fundamental wellbeing in these elements of the community.

Conversely, waste can be seen as the 'evidence that we are doing something wrong'.[16] In order to be ready to respond optimally to the problem of waste in future disasters, Dr Brown's PhD research leaves us with a succinct list of vital issues requiring attention, ranging from the development of quantity estimation techniques and flexible funding mechanisms, through to research into likely post-disaster health hazards and other issues around waste management.[17]

As Hazel Denhart so deftly reflects: 'Building removal does not have to add trauma to a neighborhood. It can act to facilitate emotional recovery through dignity, respect and empowerment. The approach to the pile on the ground makes all the difference.'[18]

Satire

Laughter and comedy can be an important escape from the sadness and difficulty of the past few years in Christchurch. It is also an important political tool. Through its insightful humour, satire encourages reflection on prominent issues in society. The results are sometimes strange, occasionally unfair and frequently hilarious. While often small in action, good satire requires big thinking, and can impact upon society and government. Caricatures come with the territory of being a public figure and so ministers (the Prime Minister and the Minister for Canterbury Earthquake Recovery), mayors (Bob Parker and Lianne Dalziel) and CEOs (Tony Marryatt, Roger Sutton and Warwick Isaacs) feature prominently.

[1]

[2–5]

We weren't laughing: Disaster capitalism and the earthquake recovery at L'Aquila

Giovanni Tiso

Giovanni Tiso is an Italian writer and translator based in Aotearoa New Zealand. In 2006 he completed a PhD at Wellington's Victoria University on the relationship between memory and technology. He's a featured writer for the Australian literary journal *Overland* and blogs at *Bat, Bean, Beam*.

In Italy, almost every generation has its own earthquake. In my childhood there were two: the one that hit Friuli in the spring of 1976, killing 989 people, and the one that shook Irpinia in the winter of 1980, killing 2914 and affecting nearly six million. I grew up therefore hearing and reading about the respective reconstructions, which might as well have happened in two different countries, if not on two different planets. The towns devastated by the earthquake in Friuli, in the far north of the country, were rebuilt inside of ten years, and on budget, whereas in the southern region of Irpinia the work continues to this day, 34 years and nearly €30 billion later, with the bill still rising.

Those two contrasting stories generated their own mythologies. The chief one was this: that the people in those northern communities did not wait for the state to provide, but rolled up their sleeves and took charge of the recovery effort themselves, while the people in the south waited passively, resignedly for help to come from above, and were thus implicated in their own misfortune. Fitting within a popular template of prejudice, this story explained the otherwise seemingly unexplainable: how could the same state respond so differently to two almost identical events within such a short span of years?

Except in Italy there have always been two states: the one that administered the modern, industrial north and the one that exploited the backward south. The first state responded to the disaster in Friuli by conforming to the expectations of citizens who were used to experiencing functioning services and a good administration. The second state saw the tragedy in Irpinia as an opportunity to broaden its network of corruption and collusion with the mafia. The outcome was like another calamity or, as journalist Antonello Caporale called it in 2000, a 'never-ending earthquake'.

The national media, thus the polity at large outside of the affected region, largely forgot about Irpinia over time, save for periodic reports from one or another of the squalid shantytowns that housed the people made homeless by the earthquake, some for over a decade. These reports may have been intended as indictments of the state bureaucracy, if not the society that allowed these indignities to occur, but one of their most immediate effects was to shame the people who lived there. They were the *terremotati*, a word literally meaning 'earthquaked people' but really connoting a class of citizens who had allowed themselves to become victims: voiceless, idle, always waiting for decisions and provisions to be made on their behalf.

The earth shook in L'Aquila at 3:32 in the morning of 6 April 2009. There had been other quakes in the preceding weeks, but the populace had been reassured that they would not lead to a significant earthquake following a special meeting of the High Risks Commission, a body charged with forecasting and preventing major risks. The commission includes the Chairperson of the National Research Council, the Chairperson of the National Institute of Geophysics and Volcanology and various other technical experts, alongside members of the state bureaucracy. This is the meeting that later led to claims in the international press that some Italian scientists had been jailed for failing to predict an earthquake, when in fact what they did was predict that there would not be one. As a consequence, some *Aquilani* who were thinking of leaving town for a few days or weeks did not, and – just as importantly – the civil defence apparatus was not put on alert, which left the city to face the disaster with a desperately small contingent of firefighters.

The High Risks Commission answers to the National Civil Defence Department. This is a body that did not exist at the time of the Friuli and Irpinia earthquakes. When it was eventually established, in 1992, the scrambling response to the disaster in Irpinia was cited as one of the rationales for transferring the responsibility from local civil and police authorities – which may themselves be affected in the event of a calamity – to a centrally coordinated national service capable of ensuring rapid and efficient interventions.

Before the biggest shock, at 3:32 a.m., there was another one that night that woke up many residents. In nearby Onna, journalist Giustino Parisse told his two children to go back to bed and not worry. The way he saw it, science had told him they need not worry. Meanwhile, in the hostel known as the *Casa dello studente* – for L'Aquila is a university town – some students joined the ones who had decided to spend the night outside, in the square, but most went back to bed. They, too, had been successfully reassured.

No one at the time blamed Civil Defence or its commission for the fact that both of Giustino Parisse's children died, nor for the catastrophic collapse of the *Casa dello studente*, which entombed eight young men and women. After all, as a matter of common sense, you cannot 'forecast and prevent' disasters of that magnitude, just respond to them. And for that response the department was unanimously praised in the days and weeks following the earthquake, when chief Guido Bertolaso was a constant presence in the evening news, projecting a reassuring image of competence and concern. The powers he was granted were extraordinary, but this is what is expected in an emergency of that magnitude. The army was called in to assist with the relief effort and guarantee the safety of the survivors, who were housed in tent villages. The mayor and the local administration had most of their powers suspended. All as you might expect, given the circumstances. Yet what would happen, in the months and years to come, is the most exemplary case yet of how management of an emergency can become institutionalised and normalised, gradually supplanting democratic institutions in the name not of a concrete, material crisis, but of an ideology.

—————————

In the years following its institution, the National Civil Defence Department became a government within the government. The system of the injunctions, introduced by the first Berlusconi government in 1994, had created a legislative instrument to bypass democratic controls and the constitutional oversight of the highest courts in the event not just of emergencies, but of so-called 'great events' as well. Over time, the definition of 'great event' became whatever the government of the day or Civil Defence decided to call a great event. The sharpest turning point may have occurred in 1999 when – under a centre-left national government and with the cooperation of then Mayor of Rome Walter Veltroni, former secretary of the *Partito Democratico* – Civil Defence and Guido Bertolaso were put in charge of the Roman Catholic Church's Great Jubilee. This would inaugurate a tradition whereby every papal visit within the Italian territory is considered a great event, allowing mayors and other civil institutions, or the department itself, to make executive decisions and allocate public funds without consulting with any elected bodies. It also normalised the idea that a department over which only the executive has oversight should be responsible not just for the prevention or response to unpredictable disasters, but also for the organisation and administration of long-planned events such as the Jubilee, or the World Aquatic Championships of 2009, or the G8 meeting at La Maddalena (then moved to L'Aquila) of the same year. At the same time, the definition of emergency was broadened to include things like the failure of the city of Naples to manage its municipal and industrial waste. In this, as in any other 'emergency', the executive is able to call in the army or declare public assemblies and protests illegal.

In simple terms, injunctions allow the central administration to ignore or circumvent existing laws and build, say, a pool complex without public consultation, the customary expenditure oversight or the obligation to adhere to the building codes. Injunctions also allow them to restructure civic life: it was under the purvey of a Civil Defence injunction following the L'Aquila earthquake that the military authority not only regulated the calling of public meetings, but even prohibited the distribution of flyers in the camps that housed the *terremotati*.

Put all of these extraordinary powers together, multiply them by the colossal amount of public money administered without accountability, and you might get a sense of the empire that grew over a decade under the leadership of Guido Bertolaso: a machine that effectively turned every 'great event' into another reconstruction of Irpinia, with every public project ballooning five to ten times over budget to better feed a dense, complicit network of building companies and supposedly independent inspectors, and the politicians who ensured that the machine kept running. As investigative journalist Manuele Bonaccorsi documented in his 2009 book *Potere Assoluto: La Protezione Civile al Tempo di Bertolaso* (*Absolute Power: Civil Defence at the Time of Bertolaso*), this empire issued over 500 injunctions and administered over €10 billion in public funds since the Jubilee.

At the very end of that year, on 30 December 2009, months into what the media lauded as the department's crowning achievement – the successful management of post-quake L'Aquila – the Berlusconi government, by means of a legislative decree, granted Civil Defence its greatest gift yet: the permission to go ahead and become a private company.

A little over seven months after the earthquake, things were going well for Guido Bertolaso and Silvio Berlusconi. Bertolaso had been the subject of countless television reports that showed him not just coordinating but also physically participating in the relief effort. He was a popular hero, almost the stuff of folklore. Berlusconi, for his part, had just fulfilled one of his most boastful and improbable pledges. Days after the disaster, he had declared to the Mayor of L'Aquila in front of live television cameras that he would personally oversee the construction of 'new towns' – he used the English phrase – consisting of modern, earthquake-proof apartment buildings on the outskirts of old L'Aquila. Always the consummate showman, he added that in each furnished apartment the newly transferred dwellers would find a bottle of champagne in the fridge. He also guaranteed that the first apartments would be ready by Christmas. And they were.

Berlusconi had some considerable personal experience in this area. His business empire began in the 1970s with the construction of a satellite town, Milano 2, on the outskirts of Milan. I had a friend who lived there, so I visited it occasionally. It was a planned suburb of a kind alien to traditional Italian urban growth, made of identical condominiums and townhouses spread amidst trees and artificial lakes. It was a dormitory town with no amenities, tailor-made for the malls that were just beginning to be built in those days. It was a place seemingly designed to breed consumers as opposed to citizens, the perfect audience for the very first local commercial television station, which Berlusconi also pioneered. It was, in other words, a project of social reform.

Now it was to be L'Aquila's turn, but with a twist: this time the project was run by Civil Defence making full use of its powers, including the powers not to consult with any elected body, to award contracts at its own discretion and to be immune from any check or balance. As a result, the cost of the housing development was an astronomical €2800 per square metre, versus the industry average of €1000 per square metre. The base isolators underneath each building could account for a mere fraction of that difference. The rest was the cost of doing business when business is left to operate on its own – set the price, do the work, check on the quality of the work – all in the name of efficiency.

What was yet to emerge at that point, is that, yes, the new towns were being built quickly, but that the staggering and mounting price tag was sucking all resources away from the reconstruction of the old towns, including the historical centre of L'Aquila. But for now the new apartments were a masterful public relations coup that allowed Berlusconi and Bertolaso to accrue the political capital necessary for that audacious move of transforming Civil Defence into a private company and achieve the ultimate alignment of business interests with the interests of the state and its citizens.

It may have been a single phone call that put an end to that.

It turned out that public prosecutors had been investigating corruption within the department since before the earthquake, and in early February they leaked to a journalist the recording of a call made in the morning of the earthquake by Francesco Maria De Vito Piscicelli, one of Civil Defence's preferred contractors, to his brother-in-law and business associate Piergiorgio Gagliardi. It was a giddy conversation in which the pair agreed that a major earthquake 'does not come along every day' and would surely turn into a major opportunity for profit so long as they moved quickly. The recording included the following, candid confession by Piscicelli: 'I was laughing this morning at three thirty in my bed.'

Five days later, 300 protesters forced the military cordon outside of L'Aquila's red zone and staged a demonstration to reclaim the heart of their city, and with it an idea of civic life based on democratic values. Some of them wore t-shirts with the slogan 'We weren't laughing'. It was a turning point in the sanitised public image of the reconstruction. In the following weeks, the magistrates' investigations stopped the privatisation of the National Civil Defence Department in its tracks. The following year, overcome by the scandals surrounding its leader, the Berlusconi government fell. In 2012, Civil Defence saw its powers severely curtailed by legislative reform. It relinquished to the Ministry of the Interior the power to declare a state of emergency; its purvey was limited again to natural disasters, and for a duration of no more than 180 days. Finally, it was mandated to consult with local authorities and elected bodies during its interventions. The Bertolaso experiment, one of the world's most literal examples of disaster capitalism at work, was finally over.

As for L'Aquila, however, very little has changed. Five years on, the city is still hollowed out, its people – the ones who did not leave or were forcibly relocated – confined to dormitory suburbs, without places in which to congregate and be a community again, inside homes that never felt like they were theirs and will never be theirs, for Berlusconi's model apartments were assigned under gratuitous loan for use only and have to be returned 'as is', including the furniture. But what was meant to be temporary becomes permanent when reconstruction never takes off. When journalist Attilio Bolzoni visited the city, in January of this year, 29 shops in the red zone had reopened out of 900: a cheese shop, an optician and a jeweller sharing the same premises, a gift shop and 25 cafes. 'This is what became of the town that propaganda rebuilt,' wrote Bolzoni, 'its historical centre has been reduced to dust.'

Twenty-eight years: this is how long Bertolaso thought the reconstruction of the city would take, as we learned from another phone call recorded in the days after the earthquake. He just never bothered to tell the *Aquilani*.

Auditor-General's map of earthquake responsibilities

In October 2012 the Auditor-General of New Zealand Lyn Provost presented a report to Parliament that identified the various risks involved in the recovery and highlighted some of the dangers in this process. The report drew on international research in post-disaster recovery and suggested that clear lines of communication and responsibility were necessary to assure quality control and accountability for the thirteen or more billion dollars that the government is contributing. The report featured the diagram below, which maps the various agencies involved and their relationships to each other.

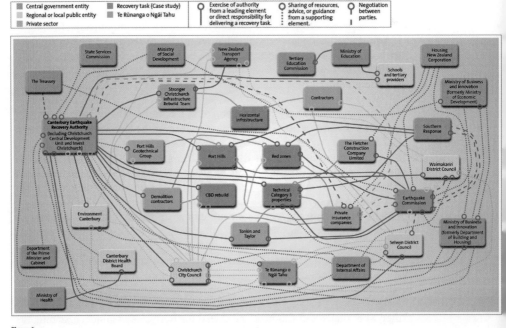

Figure 1
Relationships between public sector entities, private companies, Ngāi Tahu, and Canterbury earthquake recovery tasks

[1]

Anchornomics in Christchurch: An economist's view

Shamubeel Eaqub

Shamubeel Eaqub is a macroeconomist, who grew up and studied in Lincoln. He has worked as an economist since 2001 in various private sector organisations and is currently at NZIER, a private economic consultancy. The views in this chapter are his own and not affiliated to his place of work.

The major earthquakes that hit Christchurch in late 2010 and early 2011 dramatically changed its economic course. It went from an important second city and the economic capital of the South Island to a disaster recovery centre facing disruptions in many aspects of its economy. The recovery period has been dominated by clean-up and reconstruction, as well as languishing activity in tourism and related sectors. It has also been dominated by the Government's Christchurch Central Recovery Plan (CCRP), which is based around a number of large anchor projects, designed to kick-start the post-quake recovery. Does it make sense? Typical of an economist, my answer is: it depends.

Christchurch's economic landscape – before and after

The Canterbury region is New Zealand's third largest economy, although second by population size. Pre-quake, its economic output was around $25 billion in 2011, while Auckland and Wellington produced $69 billion and $27 billion respectively. Canterbury has a large urban core that provides a large number of services to its residents, as well as to a more sparse population across the South Island. Its central location within the island further serves its economic importance through its dominance not just in services but also logistics.

The Canterbury economy was doing pretty well before the earthquake, specialising in a broad range of sectors. Its economy was growing at the same pace as the national total. Its incomes were rising and population growth was running at just over 1.5 per cent a year, close to the national average. Strong in agriculture, it had seen dairy in particular grow rapidly in recent years. It also benefitted from two universities (University of Canterbury and Lincoln University), a polytechnic and a vibrant international student sector. A large international airport meant that Canterbury was also a gateway for tourism into New Zealand.

After the quakes, economic activity stalled for a period. But it recovered rapidly. It was helped by business interruption insurance, government assistance to businesses and social welfare. Economic growth accelerated and the GDP was boosted by a number of factors, including the size of the rebuild. The demolitions and clean-ups were counted towards GDP, but the loss of economic capital and potential in buildings, people and places were not counted against it.

The headline figures mask some important nuances. Population growth has slowed in Christchurch, but it is surging in neighbouring districts like Selwyn, Ashburton and Waimakariri. Economic growth has accelerated, but only in construction and related sectors. Between the 2006 and 2013 censuses, employment in the construction and utilities sectors surged by around 50 per cent. Total employment in Canterbury grew by 4 per cent, four times more than the national average of 1 per cent. Excluding construction and utilities, which directly benefit from the rebuild, employment has shrunk by around 0.2 per cent. Hospitality, ICT, manufacturing and rental and property services have been hit the hardest.

The earthquake also led to significant living cost increases. A suddenly reduced stock of homes lifted house prices and rents. Both have risen by over 10 per cent a year for the past three years. This has made housing unaffordable for many. Those not in the construction or utilities sectors have not received large wage increases and the higher cost of living is creating significant financial pressure.

The earthquakes have created massive economic disruptions. In the immediate aftermath some people left for other places. According to tax address changes, it was mainly to Auckland, Wellington and Nelson. But the exodus was short lived – most chose to stay or could not leave. In more recent times workers essential to the rebuild have been flocking to Canterbury from overseas, thus creating additional pressures on a limited housing stock.

The most important aspect of the recovery has been a shift in Christchurch's economic structure. Much of the region's economic recovery is now dominated by the construction sector. Most of the work is in repairs and rebuild of homes; infrastructure work is also playing a large part. Commercial buildings are also being rebuilt, but mostly on the fringes of the city rather than in the central city. Then there are many aspects of the economy that are yet to fully recover. Tourism is one example – despite the international airport. Before the quakes there were nearly 2.5 million international guest nights in Canterbury. This fell to 1.6 million in 2012. It has since risen to 1.8 million in 2013, but the sector is still in dire straits.

The tentative and hopeful assessment is that much of the 'capital' functions will be reinstated over time. The worst-case scenario is that some of the interim post-quake losses of jobs and functions from Canterbury are lost forever. Which scenario eventuates depends on how quickly the region can heal. The longer the delays, the greater the chance short-term interruptions become permanent.

The plan

In response to Christchurch's situation, the Government has created the CCRP – its main strategy for kick-starting the city centre's economy.

In this chapter I will take you through how I think about the CCRP and anchor projects, and try to make some assessments. But it is far too early to make a definitive judgment. We need a decade or more after the completion of these projects to assess their worth with certainty.

My preliminary conclusion is that many of these anchor projects would have been created anyway – even without an earthquake. The stadium, convention centre, and buildings to house civic functions like justice, health and education are necessary infrastructure for a modern and relatively large city like Christchurch. I have little disagreement with them – although some are far more grandiose than can be justified on current financial constraints.

But I disagree with two aspects of the CCRP: the central planning approach and the time it has taken to get things going.

Overly planned

The centrally planned approach is to create clusters. Government-mandated clusters rarely – if ever – work. This is because the beauty of cities is that the close proximity of different people, skills and ideas gives rise to new ways of doing things – it is the lifeblood of innovation.

Creating strict precincts based on one vision of how an economy or community is organised is misguided. In a rapidly changing economic environment, even in a post-disaster location like Canterbury where this change is accelerated, it is not possible to anticipate the needs of the future. It is not possible to plan for a paper mill that turns into a phone maker (Nokia) and then faces existential threat when the smartphone comes along.

The intent of the plan is noble. It envisages a city repopulated, as a result of government-led anchor projects. However, outcomes can be binary. An example of an aborted cluster is the planned city of Judgeford in Wellington, which never really got going. It was meant to be a model city. But then the economics didn't stack up and on top of that there was the economic crisis in the 1980s. There are now a few stranded buildings out there. A few organisations cling to the place because they have invested so much into it, but it is a hollow kernel of a city that never really started.

Docklands in Melbourne, Australia is a more encouraging example. It was slow to take off, and in the early period was blighted by vacant apartments, offices and a lack of decent coffee shops. Eventually a few anchor projects, such as the Docklands stadium, were joined by a mix of businesses and people. It is now a relatively vibrant part of Melbourne and the project will complete in 2020. It has taken much longer than anticipated for businesses to set up and generate the critical mass of residents and jobs needed before a self-sustaining economy took off. The anchor projects helped but these were not enough on their own.

A good plan in the way of action

I may seem very anti-planning. But here my position is linked to my second point: the time it has taken to get the rebuild fully under way. In contrast, post-quake Napier was a city that was mostly planned, at least in broad parameters, but built relatively quickly (partly because it was a much smaller job compared to Christchurch).

There are some lessons from the rebuild of Napier in the 1930s. The earthquake and ensuing fire caused economic damage similar to the Canterbury earthquakes. Two Royal Commissioners set broad criteria for reconstruction. General precincts and minimum standards were the main parameters. Rather than recreate the old city, Napier chose to rebuild in the art deco style, which is now celebrated. A bold decision to significantly invest in the port of Napier is paying dividends to this day. In the two decades before the 1931 quake, there was fierce disagreement over two potential locations for a deep-water port. The acrimony was only settled after the earthquakes through a rate-payer poll in 1934.

The lesson here is that the government needs to set some minimum requirements and broad settings, but if you let people get on with the rebuild, it will get done. Some projects, which can deliver many years of benefits, do need a push from government. But they also need to have a robust economic case.

Too long

It has taken too long to get a plan together and implement it. After three years, the central city is still in ruins and a significant amount of the construction work has taken place outside of the planned city. The CCRP notes that the experience of other cities after a natural disaster shows that substantial redevelopment must start within three years if recovery is to be successful.[1]

I don't want to be too harsh in my judgment on the timing of the rebuild to date. Many factors have played a part. Prolonged aftershocks and liquefaction made work impossible for some time. Issues with insurance payments and labour shortages slowed the pace of work. But the time it took for central and local government to create a credible, flexible and comprehensive plan for the city also contributed to the delay. This overly planned approach means that the city has missed the opportunity to get the redevelopment going within the three years – something that the plan's proponents recognised as critical.

The importance of timing should not be underestimated. The longer it is between disaster and recovery, the higher the chance that displaced businesses and activities atrophy and never come back. Louisiana is an extreme example. It was already in decline, but the floods of 2008 were devastating. The clean-up and rebuild have been slow and many residents and businesses have simply not returned.

If the rebuild and repair take too long, businesses and residents pop up elsewhere and do not return to the city, where they used to be. The longer a grand plan takes to formulate and implement, the bigger the costs from the wait.

Yet there are reasons to be optimistic. The economy does not stop because there is a government plan that isn't quite working. If there is demand, supply tends to spring up somewhere. This has happened in Christchurch. While the central city has been cleared of rubble and the CCRP put together, there have been huge amounts of construction outside of the central city. I was surprised to see the transformation around Show Place, Lincoln Road and Burnside. But these new spaces have popped up in spite of, not because of, the plan.

Restoration of the old or formation of the new?

It is helpful to define what any plan is trying to do and what economic success may look like. I am leaving aside social and other factors, which are very important, but not my area of expertise.

From a purely practical perspective, success is multi-staged. The first is the physical reconstruction, followed by rehabilitation and betterment of the economy and community. In Canterbury, we are still in the early stages of the physical reconstruction.

As far as an aim goes, recovery efforts can be understood to restore old patterns or to institute new ones. Yet the plan seems to be trying to accomplish both by hanging on to the past, and also trying to institute new patterns of economic and community structure. Doing both is difficult because there are so many things to optimise.

The plan tries to reimagine the city. A smaller and more compact city is no bad thing, as many would say that the previous city was too big and underutilised. Christchurch was always pretty, but some of its aspects were not well used. For example, only around two-thirds of commercial buildings were full, compared to over 90 per cent in Auckland or Wellington.

Making better use of the pretty Avon River that winds through the city is intuitively appealing. Offering high amenity value through green space and other communal spaces is good urban design. But it is not clear if the trade-offs have been considered. If firm boundaries and clusters are put in place, it will stifle development and serendipitous outcomes.

There must be a compelling case for wanting to implement new ways of planning the city and restoring what was lost. Enrico Moretti, Professor of Economics at UC Berkeley, in his book *The New Geography of Jobs* notes that:

> . . . governments must build on their existing capabilities by leveraging local strengths and expertise. The use of public funds to create jobs must be reserved for cases where there are important market failures and a community has a credible chance of building a self-sustaining cluster.[2]

While Moretti was talking about government investment to create jobs, the same principles should apply for investments in general: governments should be involved when others cannot be, but only when those investments can become self-sustaining or are required for civic and community functions.

Robust business plans for each project

This is not a critique of each project and its business plan. In fact, some of these are still pending, as the business cases for the projects were not presented in the CCRP. Each project must be assessed on its own merits and the business plans need to be robust and transparent.

The case for a convention centre for example would look at the pre-earthquake experience, requirements for related services (e.g. hotel capacity), the financial viability of the project and total community benefit. We should not build a convention centre because everyone else is, rather it should be built because it serves some greater need for the community that would not otherwise be met.

I must confess scepticism when it comes to convention centres. They are hyped up by various lobbyists, but it surprises me that if they are such a good investment they are not commercially viable on their own.

The Stadium is another project to be wary of. Stadiums are rarely a financial success. They serve an important role in sporting and cultural aspects of a community. But because a stadium is not usually financially independent, it is important to make sure they are not overly expensive to build and maintain. The financial debacle with the Dunedin stadium is an important reminder that these projects can go wrong – and they can be a financial burden for many generations.

The Dunedin stadium was built with much fanfare. It was expected to cost $188 million, but costs blew out to $224 million, as large construction projects have a tendency to. It was expected to make profits from its operations, but these fell well short of expectations. Now the residents of Dunedin are stuck with a very nice stadium but also with a large debt that is causing large increases in their local authority fees. The additional debt also means that Dunedin will have to forego other projects that might have benefited its residents.

The government, be it local or central, should not be in the business of making big investments because they are sexy. They need a hard-nosed approach to investing. There is always a long list of deserving investment projects. Budget constraints mean only the best projects should go ahead.

When money is borrowed to fund projects, they will ultimately come out of future taxes. The plan for Christchurch is grandiose in some aspects. With so many competing demands for funds, a covered 34,000 seating capacity stadium should not be a high priority. A dollar spent here is a dollar that cannot be spent somewhere else.

Balanced growth

The CCRP needs to address the idea of a growing city. One specific aspect of the plan is troublesome. The plan restricts the boundary of the city and the height of buildings. The experience of growing cities like London and Mumbai is that if you have these restrictions when faced with a growing population, it serves to drive prices higher and drive demand elsewhere. By imposing height and green-belt restrictions, the plan has to be careful to make sure Christchurch remains affordable.

Chicago is a good example of a city that was faced with a declining population in the 1970s and 1980s. Chicago has grown since 1990 by offering a dense city core, while still remaining affordable and pleasant, according to Edward Glaeser in his book *Triumph of the City*.

While Chicago had to work hard at being a good place to live, Christchurch already offers this in many respects, despite the earthquake damage. I am biased because I grew up in Lincoln, a twenty-minute drive from Christchurch, and spent much of my youth in the city with friends and family. I enjoyed the prettiness of the city, the ability to meet and gather and also to access a great choice of outdoor environments within a short driving distance.

Chicago also worked to become affordable by encouraging construction of new buildings to provide a compelling alternative to Manhattan. Christchurch will not offer a viable alternative if it cannot offer affordable accommodation costs. Rents in commercial buildings are approaching Auckland levels, but businesses cannot match Auckland profitability. House prices and rents have soared. Temporary spikes are understandable, but if accommodation for business and residents is unaffordable, it delays the economic recovery.

While Chicago allows private developers to take the risk on price, so that they can cover their costs, it is not clear the same will be true for the anchor projects planned for the city. The recovery needs to be set in such a way that constructing a building and letting it out is a viable business. There are no numbers in the CCRP on whether this will be the case, but as far as economic assessments go, it would be a killer test.

Chicago has reimagined itself into a city that can be a destination for innovative and dynamic businesses and people. Having such a proposition for the economic capital of the South Island and a viable second commercial centre of New Zealand (after Auckland) would be a good thing. It would boost New Zealand's resilience, as Auckland did following the Christchurch earthquakes.

What does success look like?

The economic view is often in the aggregate. But the reality is the plan for the city and the region has many layers. I think of the success of the plan and the region through three lenses. Firstly, there are the *stages* of recovery: reconstruction, rehabilitation and betterment. The plan is built around this. Secondly, there are the *perspectives* of recovery: individuals, local community and national community. The plan has done a credible job of stakeholder engagement, but it sidesteps inevitable competition for jobs and business locations from other regions. Finally, there are the ripple effects or echoes of the plan – perhaps through changes in regulatory settings or the make-up of the city. The changes to the District Plan to enable the CCRP have some good elements, particularly around flexibility to meet the city's needs. But there are also elements of restrictive building and urban design practices that are unwelcome.

A good enough plan – get on with it, if the business case works

The plan is a brave attempt to think ahead to a better community. It has the right intent in creating a liveable city with a dense urban core. But it has become too planned and seems oblivious to competition from Auckland and Wellington. Unless Christchurch, as a city, can offer a credible alternative, which is not only liveable with a good concentration of skilled workers but also affordable, it will not have a sustainable recovery.

Overly restrictive policies on height, density and urban limits need to be reconsidered. A knee-jerk reaction in policy making, particularly towards overly risk-averse and restrictive urban design, would be a mistake

Each project must be assessed carefully. Business plans need to be fulsome and transparent, as a dollar spent on one project will starve another. Any borrowing should be done with exceptional care and only for cases where the economic and community imperative cannot be denied.

The plan has enough good elements to get the tick, but it is taking too long to implement. The longer we wait, the higher the chances of permanent damage to Christchurch's economic future as the South Island's economic capital.

Inconvenience Store

Gap Filler's Inconvenience Store ran as a week-by-week residency. Anyone could operate the shop for a week to interrogate our convenience-based society. Over the seven-week project, there were stores where the only currency was time; where you had to craft something yourself, or wait while someone did it on the spot; where you discovered the origins of commodities (and of your own cash); where you were sent to complete tasks around the city; and more. Most ideas tapped into the new self-sufficiency movement in Christchurch and explored how Christchurch might embrace inconvenience and become distinctive from the prevalent suburban mall culture.

[1–3]

[4–8]

When vision meets reality

Raf Manji

Raf is a member of the Christchurch City Council. He is heading the Council's difficult post-quake finances and is a social entrepreneur with a background in finance, community and enterprise.

On 1 November 1755, a magnitude 9 earthquake hit off the coast of Portugal. The earthquake and the tsunami that followed devastated the capital city of Lisbon. In the following years, it became characterised as the first 'modern' disaster. Estimates were that some 40-50,000 people were killed, 13,000 houses destroyed with 10,000 seriously damaged. Two-thirds of the city was destroyed. The King, fortunately out of town that day, ordered the remaining buildings in the city to be razed and a new city to be built. Now, it's a lovely place to visit. The economic impact was estimated at some 32-48 per cent of GDP.

Strong centralised government control using funds from both the private sector and public institutions enabled the swift reconstruction of the city centre. As part of this funding, there was a 4 per cent donation to the rebuild from all local merchants. All commercial and industrial activities were supervised by the newly formed Junta de Comercio, which worked together with government in setting up economic policies for the commercial and industrial sectors.

The principle of the reconstruction was that the common good should precede everything else. Everyone needed to work together and, parallel to this, a centralised delivery mechanism emerged as the best structure for managing big public projects.

This importance of a joined-up approach was also seen after the 1871 Great Chicago Fire. The management of relief was assigned to a private organisation, the Chicago Relief and Aid Society – thereby providing both clear leadership and a structure for the government partnership with both the private sector and the military.

In modern times we have examples of how this approach hasn't been used. Post-Katrina New Orleans may well be remembered as a classic case of infighting among all levels of government – city, parish, state and federal – that has yielded a destructive inability to cohere around a single plan for recovery.

Many of the most celebrated instances of disaster recovery – such as the rebuilding of Lisbon – have depended on a level of centralised political and economic control that simply would not be tolerated in a modern-day democracy. In democratic regimes – especially those with a federal system of nested and overlapping jurisdictions – the task of directing disaster recovery in a manner that respects local wishes and priorities is simply much more difficult. However, if we look at some less-than-democratic regimes, we can see that this unilateral approach to city-building also has its pitfalls.

Masdar City, a planned development near Abu Dhabi in the United Arab Emirates, is a great example of what you can do when you have a single authority and an open chequebook. You can take a patch of sand and turn it into an amazingly smart city – albeit one with hardly anyone living there. Masdar's initial completion date was 2016, but this had been delayed for up to ten years by the flow-on effects from the Global Financial Crisis (GFC). Single authority projects can founder when that authority finds itself in an unexpected situation.

Masdar is an example of supply-side planning, where some authority decides something needs to happen and has the power and the money – most of the time – to make it happen. This approach removes obstacles and barriers to development and construction, and allows for grand projects to be developed. However, demand from tenants is not pre-tested; this type of planning employs a 'build it and they will come' philosophy. Another city built out of the sand dunes – Dubai – is planning a new 2000-seat opera house. Again, money is no object and planning is not a problem. Business cases are also optional. Whether these projects are financially and environmentally sustainable is another matter.

Dreamed up for an island near Shanghai, Dongtan was planned as the world's first great eco-city – and it's still a plan. It was, like Masdar, a supply side initiative, but with a business case that didn't quite pan out, as funding dried up in the risk-averse, post-GFC world. It was meant to accommodate 10,000 people in 2010, with grand aspirations of 500,000 people by 2050. As of the time of writing, work is yet to begin, and no one lives there.

Masdar, Dongtan and even the new Dubai Opera House are examples where centralised political and economic control, and an initially robust capital source, has enabled quick action on the development front. However this single source approach has also proved problematic once market forces take effect. Supply must be matched by demand and, in the case of new, planned cities, this is by no means certain.

In the case of disasters, work has to be done and often the ability to create a single point agent for delivery is very helpful. As demonstrated in the Lisbon response, bringing government and business together allows for a good mix of authority, finance and commercial input. Initial supply-side approaches may be useful, but with funding generally limited, attention to demand is needed.

So what does all of this mean for Christchurch? I see that we have some challenges. We need clarity: Who is making the decisions? Central or local government? Where is the commercial and community sector? There are lots of strategic partners, but still confusion over the right one to talk to. The rebuild lacks oversight: who is keeping an eye on things? Again, multiple agencies are involved – but rigour and transparency are light. Do we have a 'Team Christchurch' approach, or are people pulling in different directions? Is the Christchurch proposition clear? What exactly can anyone invest in?

I think there are ways, from a commercial point of view, to ensure that the Christchurch rebuild is a success. Firstly, we need a single point of authority and control. This can have multiple partners involved, but must speak with one voice. This allows for greater scale, competitive procurement, timeline management and ultimately lower costs. We also need to ensure that we have a single point of entry for investors. Time is money and investors like to have clearly defined and owned propositions to invest in. Any confusion just adds risk to any proposal. Once the regulatory environment has been created, the rebuild is just a commercial project, so you need a commercial board to drive the process.

We need to have a clearer position on incentivisation of development. We tell people not to build outside the central city, and then tell them to get lost if they ask for incentives. We are sending mixed messages – either we want it to happen or we are happy for it not to. We need to see robust business cases for key projects. This is the demand-side issue. We don't have an open chequebook and so we cannot just magic up a new eco-city or top-of-the-range opera house. We need to know that the costs of any project can be serviced, even after including the public good component. Part of this is ensuring that there is proper oversight for large-scale projects. Funders need to be able to make sure they are getting value for money, whether they are from central or local government. The private sector does this as a matter of course, and there is no reason that the public sector should accept lower standards.

I believe we should be investigating whether the government can step up to provide alternative funding mechanisms. We should be looking at all options to fund public infrastructure, even cheap government funding. They did it in 1936, with the provision of low-cost loans through the State Advances Corporation, and they could do it again. If we can create that structure, then I think we can raise confidence in the process and give greater certainty about the outcome of the rebuild. Ultimately, the market will decide on the outcome. Unless you have a bottomless pit of money, reality will bite at some point and normal rules of engagement will re-emerge. The mashing up of vision and reality is the key to making the rebuild a success. That means developing structures where all players are at the table and all voices are heard. Christchurch is now entering that phase.

Chapter 6   Acting Small

Tahia tōu marae

New Zealand's do-it-yourself 'Number 8 wire mentality' is almost a founding myth. We've always been a long way away from the rest of the world, isolated from the latest inventions and innovations. But we've found a way to make the best of the situation.

In many cases, the biggest ideas are wrapped up inside the smallest projects. Small ventures entail risking less – and if they do go wrong, not as much is lost. As we see here in an essay about Newcastle, Australia, failure is a key requirement for a truly flourishing ecosystem of ideas. Another author contrasts this with the heavy regulation of central and local government; the risk threshold is so high as to prevent participation by anyone but the richest developers. One emergent theme is that thinking local and acting in small gestures (as suggested in the *All Right?* campaign) doesn't require money to be successful.

In many cases, community groups don't worry about the risk of doing something, but rather the cost of not acting. The earthquakes shook up community structures, and local people were the best placed to respond. In some cases, the community stepped in to renew, recreate and redefine the way people interacted with each other. While internet and cellphone networks were down, person-to-person networks filled the gaps that the government couldn't reach – or didn't even know existed. Small gestures and local actions meant more than any of the policies that came from the top.

The acting small mindset, forged out of necessity in the days after the disaster, can still be found in parts of the rebuilding city. There is a strong drive to learn from the successes – and proud failures – of many of the schemes and enterprises that emerged, and to demonstrate that the collective effect of many small gestures can be substantial. We also can't ignore the sense of empowerment that individuals and communities can experience by having control over things that affect them – even when they are small.

The failure strategy

Marcus Westbury

Marcus Westbury is a broadcaster, writer, media maker and festival director who has been responsible for some of Australia's more innovative, unconventional and successful cultural projects and events. He has also worked across a range of media as a writer, producer, director and presenter covering fields as diverse as culture, art, media, urban planning, sport and politics. In 2008 Marcus founded Renew Newcastle with his own funds and energy.

For most of my adult life, I watched my home town of Newcastle, Australia – a city roughly the same size as Christchurch – lurch from crisis to crisis and from disaster to disaster. There were the physical shocks. Australia's largest earthquake (at the time the most expensive natural disaster in Australia) in 1989 broke the city and catalysed the permanent move of retail and commercial business from the city to the suburbs. There were the economic shocks. The BHP steelworks and associated industries closed and shed 20,000 jobs in two decades. The shipyards closed and thousands of other manufacturing jobs went with them. Less visible were slow burning structural problems that rendered the city centre less and less fit for purpose. I woke up one day in 2008 and found myself walking down the two main streets and casually counting 150 empty buildings – shops and offices with 'For Lease' signs, and derelict sites.

That experience led to the establishment of Renew Newcastle. It's a not-for-profit company that 'borrows' empty buildings on a rolling short term basis and lends them to creative projects – art galleries, studios, community groups, co-working spaces, jewellers, craftspeople, film-makers, design studios, fashion labels and the like – looking for a toehold, a cheap place to start and a low-risk way of trying an often high-risk idea. Five years later, Renew Newcastle has done – at last count – 140 projects in 60 empty buildings. Dozens of successful business and initiatives have been given a start. Two have gone on to buy buildings in a city that has since changed around them. Once regarded as Sydney's rough, tough working-class cousin, Newcastle increasingly appears on lists of the world's 'hippest' and 'most bohemian' cities and Australia's 'coolest' neighbourhoods.

Figures 1 & 2: Before (left) and after (right) in Hunters Mall. Through Renew Newcastle, otherwise empty spaces are transformed with pop up ventures.

There are various ways you can think about what we have done through Renew Newcastle. Renew is an art project, an economic development project and an empty space project. But to understand the deeper logic of it, it helps to think of it as a *failure* project. It's about creating a city, a system and a dynamic that allows people to try unlikely things. The idea is not to ensure that things fail – but it begins by letting go of the assumption that everything will succeed. It creates a space for the emergence of things that might not. It allows failure by lowering the price and risk of it. Renew allows people to try things with uncertain or unknown outcomes. Through the seeding of unpredictable ideas and experiments, interesting and unanticipated possibilities begin to emerge.

Cities are experiments. The most successful cities are the accumulated remains of hundreds, thousands or even millions of failed experiments. They are layer upon layer of business ideas, community groups, social movements, supportive or divided communities, entrepreneurialism, innovations and other forms of possibilities translated into actions. Those actions build up over time. Even in a city that hasn't experienced the abrupt disruption of Newcastle, or the devastation of Christchurch, most of the things that have ever made any city aren't actually there anymore. Yet their legacies live on in the DNA of people's inspiration and lived experiences, in the built environment, in the serendipitous chains of events where someone's first job becomes the precursor to founding a multi-million dollar company or enduring community project two decades later.

Natural and economic disasters abruptly break this chain of continuous experiments. Part of the problem with Newcastle in 2008 was that the city had become so beaten up that no one was trying anything much anymore. It had become so fixated with grand plans it had forgotten to address the small ones. Those with capital were holding back waiting for big developments and infrastructure plays – many of which have never happened and never will. Others still remain two, five or ten years away as they pretty much always have been. In order for Newcastle to succeed in the short term it needed people to try new things. It needed people to fail fast, fail cheap and fail often – to use a well-worn Silicon Valley cliché.

In times of crisis there is too often a tendency to seek certainty in fixed plans and big schemes. But cities are dynamic and endlessly changing labs of possibilities. They are not predictable. Masterplanning can only get you so far. There are no 'right' answers a lot of the time. In my experience no solution ever arrives fully formed. No plan – no matter how well conceived and perfectly implemented (and rarely do both of those conditions apply) – actually solves every problem. Once you admit that limitation, it becomes instantly obvious that the best way to find out what works is to do lots of things.

Christchurch, as Newcastle did, needs *innovation*. Not in the sexy high tech sense where a billion dollar company might develop their app or their widget there, but in the grounded sense, where lots of people are incrementally toying with ideas, communities and business models that weren't there before. In a perverse way, Christchurch is uniquely positioned to seed experimentation and imagination now. A lot of actual innovation is really perseverance, trial, error, good ideas and good luck. While good ideas and good luck are hard to mandate, the trial and error bit is something you can plan for – and Kiwi resilience and resourcefulness is begrudgingly acknowledged and admired, even from across the Tasman.

Newcastle needed then, and Christchurch needs now, to find better ways to experiment, innovate and fail. Yet it is tricky to make that a policy imperative and, under the traditional rules of the game, it is a huge burden to place the cost of each failed venture upon individuals, artists, small companies and others. Then there is the reality that many of those who contemplate trying something will do so elsewhere – somewhere less run down and despairing – where the equation of potential payoff makes a lot more sense.

Five years ago, Renew Newcastle began to create ways to reduce the scale and risk of individual failure down to one that could be distributed cheaply among the community. We created a space – physically, legally and psychologically – where it was cheap to fail and easy to experiment. No one individual needed to lose their house, break up their family, over-capitalise, sign a five-year lease or take a hundred thousand dollar loan. No government department needed to write a cheque with six or seven zeroes on the end and then try and justify the smoking ruins left behind as a valuable learning experience.

Figures 3 & 4: Another before (left) and after (right) of a transformed space.

By lowering the cost, you change the equation of risk and reward. You diversify who can experiment. The people with the money don't always have the ideas. In most cities and towns it is usually a relatively small subset of the population who are sufficiently entrepreneurial and sufficiently resourced to open new shops, pet projects, new spaces and new businesses. They aren't always the most imaginative or innovative. Add the problems of broken infrastructure, poverty or other structural issues found in many communities and there are very few people who have the capacity to risk the kind of experimentation that struggling places desperately need.

Rarely do policymakers view the processes of initiative and experimentation on the small scale as something they can catalyse and control. To a community that has lost thousands of jobs, buildings and businesses, the idea of building up many marginal initiatives as an economic development strategy is counterintuitive. It is often politically difficult to sell and explain when there are headlines to be grabbed with a metaphorical monorail. They fail to simply ask: what can people do here and how do we allow them to do it?

What experimentation should a city like Christchurch encourage? It needs pioneers to develop new ways of building, using and adapting spaces. It needs creativity, community and imagination. It needs innovative building techniques, lateral solutions and low-cost problem solving. It needs improvisation and innovation. It needs ingenuity as much as it needs engineering.

Artists and creative communities are a vital part of the picture and in this context they are pragmatically ideal. They bring new layers of life, economy and activity to communities. They are willing to take initiative and engage in a process of experimentation precisely because they aren't primarily concerned with commercial returns.

Christchurch is already building a reputation – unwanted but not unwarranted – as one of the great urban laboratories of the early twenty-first century. It is attracting leaders and thinkers from across the region and around the world. It should never lose sight of its own ingenuity, and it should never cease to bring out the best from the bedrooms, spare rooms and garages by encouraging the initiatives and ideas that already exist. It cannot fall into the trap of betting big on a single thing, a single demographic or a single idea where all succeeds or all fails. It cannot risk the danger of waiting five, ten or twenty years for big changes at the expense of accumulating the smaller ones.

Christchurch is in a unique position. It is faced with a potentially stark choice. On one path there is the danger that it will become a twenty-first century anywhere. There is the risk of becoming a perfect international amalgam of best practice planning and efficient, appropriate but uninspiring architecture. But just as with Newcastle in 2008, or Berlin in 1989, Christchurch has been given an opportunity to create something that can only happen there – a generational challenge and a historic opportunity. It is not something to squander. It is these things, and not the generic plans of ideal cities, that will ultimately define what the city will become. It would be a tragedy if Christchurch were to fail for failing to fail enough.

Bars and cafes

A study by researchers at the University of Canterbury in mid-2014 stated that the city's nightlife – its bars, restaurants and cafes – was back to 95 per cent of pre-quake levels. 907 of these businesses are operating in the city – an increase of around 11 per cent from 2013. There is a mix of establishments that survived the quakes, ones that closed and have now re-opened (in the same or other locations), and others that are new. The pictures below depict a range of these.

[1]

[2–7]

[8–12]

[13–16]

The plan against the rebuild

Eric Crampton

From 2003 until July 2014, Dr Eric Crampton served as Lecturer and Senior Lecturer in Economics at the University of Canterbury, where he lectured on economic policy, including the economics of the city and the economics of political decision-making. In July 2014, he left the University to serve as Head of Research with the New Zealand Initiative in Wellington. He blogs at *Offsetting Behaviour*.

There is a great deal of ruin in a city, to paraphrase Adam Smith's calm reply to those heralding the doom of Britain after the battle of Saratoga. In other words, it takes a lot to really wreck either a city or a nation. An earthquake alone cannot do it, or at least not one the size of ours. But, an earthquake, combined with paralysing land-use regulatory structures, a confused intersection of building codes and insurance rules, and an army of bureaucrats each equipped with an all-powerful 'No', can come much closer than we'd really like.

After February's earthquake, we had some hope that the city's planners were starting to recognise the importance of the bottom-up, decentralised response that lets each of us see how best to adapt to the new realities. Coffee shops that were relocating to garages and sheds in Lyttelton were being allowed to operate regardless of zoning regulations – eminently sensible. People were finding ways to help themselves, and each other.

The first sign that this light-handed approach was not to last was the bureaucracy's attempt to block the University of Canterbury's student volunteer army. Sam Johnson's team of volunteers, coordinated by Facebook and responding to a grassroots-level need for help, were hindered by bureaucrats who wanted to micromanage. This, writ large, explains rather well why, in June 2014, so much of downtown remains a shambles. Christchurch's glacial post-quake recovery really can be traced to these three main factors.

The first, highly restrictive land-use regulations, existed well prior to the either the February 2011 or the September 2010 earthquakes, and are mirrored by similarly stultifying strictures in every major city in New Zealand. This part of the post-quake disaster is a chronicle of a failure long foretold, and easily avoided.

The paralysis generated by the sequence of earthquakes and New Zealand's particular public-private insurance market, and the problems caused when Christchurch City Council (CCC) changed the building code subsequent to the insured event, were only partially foretold. The Earthquake Commission (EQC) warned the incoming National Party coalition government in November 2008 that EQC had no capacity to carry out home inspections after a disaster, that the cap on EQC's coverage per home was too low, and that EQC needed better capitalisation. Governments have a difficult time dealing with things that are important but not urgent; setting EQC on sounder footing never seems important until it's really very important and too late. But, many of the larger problems were not well anticipated and constitute hard-taught lessons; we would do well to learn from these and fix regulation accordingly before any substantial Wellington event.

Finally, the confusopoly of CCC, EQC, the Canterbury Earthquake Recovery Authority (CERA) and the Christchurch Central Development Unit (CCDU) was entirely unanticipated, or at least I had never expected that this could happen in New Zealand.

I had always held New Zealand governance in the highest of esteem, reckoning it to be the world's best. And perhaps New Zealand's overall governance really is as good as it gets and other countries are only able to deal with these kinds of events by virtue of greater size and wealth. But no level, branch or agency of government covered itself in glory in the months and years following the initial disaster phase. If this be the best of all possible governments, as international surveys of such things often tell us, what hells be all the others?

While CERA and the CCDU were surely established with the best of intentions, the result was the creation of far too many people who could veto new developments or changes in land use. Economists are well familiar with the Tragedy of the Commons that results when nobody can exercise veto rights over the use of property: the Commons are then over-grazed. But fewer are familiar with the Tragedy of the Anticommons that results when too many people are allowed to say no. Traditionally applied in analysis of intellectual property, the Tragedy of the Anticommons applied with vehemence in post-quake Christchurch. When any one of many bureaucrats can delay or ban you from rebuilding, either by explicitly saying 'no' or by failing to get around to providing a needed 'yes', it's hard to get anything done. Christchurch has too many veto players.

While the failures are separate, they share a common root: an utter failure of the government, both CCC and central government, simply to allow property owners to get on with the job at hand and to make those changes necessary to allow them to do it.

My colleague, economist Seamus Hogan, reminds us of the analogy in $M^*A^*S^*H$ that, sometimes, meatball surgery is needed. In the Korean War's mobile army surgical hospitals near the front lines, an extra hour spent providing perfect treatment to one patient doomed others consequently left untreated. In Christchurch, the three-year-long quest for the perfect central city plan stopped anyone downtown from proceeding with any work at all for far too long, bleeding downtown's prospective recovery as businesses fled for the suburbs, or left town entirely.

In my view, too many city planners spent far too much of their youths playing *SimCity*, a city planning videogame popular in the mid-1990s, in which you can always press the pause button while you think about your next move and where nobody much objects if you bulldoze their houses or businesses to put up a new park or stadium. Real cities are not like that.

The city would have fared far better had neither CCC nor central government embarked on adventures in planning and instead concentrated on core city functions: ensuring that land-use planning did not stand in the way of expanding the supply of housing after the earthquakes, focusing on core infrastructure rather than masterplanned precincts and buildings, avoiding regulatory and planning uncertainty so that property owners knew where they stood, and quickly sorting out the legal and regulatory morasses that we were too late to avoid entirely after the earthquakes.

The failure long foretold: Rigid land-use planning before and after the Christchurch earthquakes

Restrictive zoning practices are hardly unique to Christchurch, or to New Zealand. The effects everywhere are similar: housing has become extraordinarily expensive. While more sensible parts of the Right and Left recognise that we simply have not been building enough new dwellings for some time, they disagree on solutions: the Right lauds new subdivisions while blocking others' plans to increase density; the Left cheers intensification while blocking others' moves to increase land supply on the city's fringes. Meanwhile, councils recognise that home-owning voters reward them for the ever-increasing housing prices that come from restricted supply. Consequently, as Matthew Yglesias put it in his recent Kindle Single, 'The Rent Is Too Damned High'.

Christchurch was certainly no worse than many places in New Zealand prior to the earthquakes, and was certainly in better shape than Auckland. But the regulatory constraints that served only to mildly increase the cost of housing in Christchurch before the earthquakes became very important after the earthquakes.

Prior to the earthquakes, expansion outwards from Christchurch was fairly constrained, as was any substantial densification outside of specific zoned areas. Solutions found in cities like Vancouver, in which many homeowners built self-contained flats within their existing homes, were prohibited in Christchurch by rules preventing a permitted dwelling from having more than one kitchen.

Surprisingly, neither the September 2010 nor the February 2011 earthquakes resulted in any expedient substantive relaxation of either zoned density regulations or the number of permissible sections on Christchurch's fringes. Over 12,000 homes were destroyed in the earthquakes, about 7 per cent of the housing stock, with 8000 of those homes located within the residential red zone where rebuilding was prohibited. New subdivisions, increased density, or both were necessary to accommodate the homeless, the families whose homes were being repaired and the influx of construction workers.

CCC did little to ease the resulting pressure on housing. In the short term, new construction would have been very difficult even without council impediment as the ongoing aftershocks made insurance on any new building project unobtainable. But even on those margins where CCC could have helped, they seemed instead more concerned with upholding the existing pre-earthquake rules and protecting amenities for homeowners in the wealthier suburbs.

The worst exemplar here was Council's steadfast refusal to allow homeowners to build secondary rental flats within their existing homes or on their properties. While insurance on a new building was unobtainable, owners of existing homes with ongoing insurance policies could maintain their existing insurance while undertaking either earthquake repairs or home renovations. This would have provided an opportunity for owners to build self-contained flats. While it is unlikely that thousands of such units would have been built, even a few hundred would have been helpful where people otherwise lived in uninsulated garages, sheds, caravans and broken homes over a couple of winters. These aren't just apocryphal or inventions of *Campbell Live*: people were living in our neighbour's garden shed for rather some time after the earthquakes.

The usual objections to densification manifestly failed to apply in the case of secondary suites. Unlike an apartment block, they provide no concentrated burden that must be accommodated by trunk infrastructure like water, sewerage or roading. They impose no shading or other real, substantive, demonstrable impediment on neighbours. But, the only cases in which they were allowed were for family units where the owner could guarantee that a family member would live in the flat. Under later CERA regulations, secondary flats were permitted where the owner could guarantee, prior to construction, that the dwelling would be used by someone displaced by the earthquakes rather than by an incoming construction worker; the flat also needed to be removed by no later than 2016.

The only sense I can make of Council's intransigence on secondary flats is a combination of bureaucratic inertia and fear that homeowners near the University of Canterbury would object if their neighbours used the regulatory provision to accommodate students. It seems a pretty thin basis on which to block what could have been a helpful and expeditious way of getting new affordable accommodation onto the market after the earthquakes.

The regulations that were, pre-quake, relatively innocuous, became highly constraining after the earthquakes. These were rules that had nothing to do with building safety or standards but rather aesthetic considerations around minimum lot sizes, mandatory parking minimums, maximum allowed density, and the pace at which new greenfield properties could be developed. While these may have arguable benefits in normal times, surely after a destructive earthquake the balance should have been tipped in favour of increasing housing supply. Council utterly failed to relax the pre-quake zoning rules or to quickly release land to enable new construction.

And this was a chronicle of a housing failure long foretold. Shortly after the September earthquakes, developer Hugh Pavletich argued for the release of more land on the more stable western city fringes. Nothing happened. And, amazingly, neither did anything happen after the February earthquakes.

The failure partially foretold: The consequences of planning rigidities, new building codes and insurance

Council failed to move with sufficient alacrity to allow new housing to come to market. Sorting out the regulatory mess blocking the construction of new dwellings was not going to be easy. Council's consenting office was overwhelmed, though they could potentially have coped under a streamlined and simplified set of rules. Heritage preservation regulations worked at cross-purposes to earthquake-strengthening regulations after the September 2010 earthquakes. Density regulations and restrictions on 'granny flats' prevented densification on brownfield sites where the land was sound on the west side of town. Council changed the building regulations after the February insured event, but before insurance-funded rebuilding, thus guaranteeing legal uncertainty as to the extent of insurers' liability where meeting the new code would constitute betterment but where building to less than the new standard was forbidden. Finally, the slow trickle of land released for new development had important and easily foreseeable implications, though ones that apparently were not foreseen by the planners.

It is worth briefly walking through how the slow release of land at the edges of town can have pervasive negative effects regardless of whether the released land would be sufficient for some number of years' supply. When only a small amount of land can be released for development every year on a known path, it is relatively easy for developers to buy up the newly zoned land and to release it even more slowly, keeping land prices very high. When land prices are very high, and where those prices are high due to zoning rather than due to the inherent nature of the land, developers face particular incentives to provide larger and more expensive homes on zoned sections: why put a $100,000 house on a $300,000 section? The top-end of the market, with higher margins for developers, gets served first. That part of the market puts fairly high value on restrictive building covenants preventing their neighbours from putting up houses that might reduce their own property values.

Consequently, much of the new development on the edges of Christchurch provided higher priced homes bound up by covenants. Homeowners in the residential red zone, then, were largely precluded from moving their homes onto new land in new developments. While it's easy to blame developers for those covenants' restrictions, they're fundamentally a consequence of a severely limited supply of zoned land. In the absence of those restrictions, a farmer on one of the thousands of hectares adjoining Christchurch could have turned a paddock into a subdivision for houses from the red zone. Instead, Christchurch was *exporting* red zone houses in 2012 to places as far away as Gore.[1] In the midst of a terrible housing shortage, we were sending houses away because our regulations made it too hard to let people live in them.

It consequently has been extraordinarily frustrating to hear the Christchurch rebuild described as exemplar of the failures of leaving things to the market. Really, we have been in the worst of all possible worlds here. A well-run government rebuild would have been better than what we've had. An unhampered market approach led by developers and property owners would have been far better than what we've had. Instead, we've had developers and property owners trying to provide new housing as and where they could under the somewhat important government constraint that building wasn't really allowed.

Blame cannot lie solely with CCC though. Shortly after the September 2010 earthquakes, the central government, in an all-party consensus, passed the Canterbury Earthquake Response and Recovery Bill enabling central government to do, effectively, anything it wanted in Christchurch. CERA was established a month after the February earthquakes to coordinate the recovery. Such an agency could have been helpful in finding the problems in regulation, or in insurance markets, that were stymying the rebuild. It manifestly failed to do so.

When CERA was established, I was hopeful. In June 2011, CERA CEO Roger Sutton said, 'I have quite extraordinary powers to actually bypass these planning laws, but my preference would be for the normal legal process to work.'[2] He noted the lack of lower priced sections on Christchurch's fringes and the potential for cutting the costs involved with planning and resource consents.

But nothing happened. Where CERA was supposed to cut through the regulatory morass so that the rebuild could happen, they seemed oblivious to the severity of the regulatory problem. Roger Sutton's appearance on TVNZ's *CloseUp* in May 2012 provided ample demonstration of CERA's problems. The Christchurch *Press*, and the #eqnz Twitter hashtag, had been filled with stories of the problems involved in trying to get red zone houses relocated to new developments. One Christchurch couple, the Haywoods, were particularly active in documenting and publicising through social media the exact regulatory difficulties they had been encountering in trying to move their house from the residential red zone. But when Sutton appeared on *CloseUp* and was presented with the story, he said 'The first I heard of this and the difficulties was today.' The agency that was supposed to have sorted a way through the regulations to allow the rebuild simply didn't know what was going on. How could we hope that they might fix the regulatory mess if they were seemingly clueless as to its effects?

I attended one meeting of CERA's Canterbury Economic Indicators External Review Panel in 2013 at which many of us asked very pointed questions about what was being planned to allow for the accommodation of an expected inflow of 15,000 construction workers in 2014, with nobody in CERA, and none of the representatives of the other agencies, knowing where they might possibly live given the constraints against housing construction. I was left with the impression of an agency that wanted to do good but that really didn't know what it could do for fear of judicial review, despite its broad enabling legislation. What a waste.

Instead of moving nimbly to shed the most restrictive regulations and consequently to allow rapid densification on good land and expansion out into the suburbs, CCC's planners instead hunkered down and stuck with what they knew best: an overly zealous approach to regulatory compliance, an obsession with masterplanning that makes the best the enemy of the good, and a refusal to consider that maybe, just maybe, getting people out of garages and sheds in the east might be worth regulatory changes that might upset people in Gerry Brownlee's constituency. The fix in housing would have been relatively simple. In any future earthquake event, we should have a regulatory switch that simply flips automatically enacting the following:

- A four-year window in which all density restrictions are removed. So long as a building meets building code, it can go up. We do not need extensive planning and handwringing over the essential characteristics of particular neighbourhoods and whether they're consistent with intensification: people stuck living in uninsulated garages count for more than that. Let developers and insurers decide which bits of land can stand taller buildings and let them go up. If Council moves to return to the ex ante land use restrictions after that window closes, any buildings already consented during that window are grandfathered in.
- A similar window in which all green belt or Metropolitan Urban Limit restrictions are removed, barring those that exist to avoid substantial and demonstrable environmental harm. The window here can be shorter because greenfield development is faster than brownfield.
- All restrictions against building secondary units within a dwelling or on-site at existing properties are removed.

Had Christchurch taken this approach, a lot of houses would quickly have gone into construction to the southwest of Christchurch while other subdivisions would have opened up where red zoned houses could have been placed. During the early period, homeowners would have added flats within existing homes or granny flats on existing properties to let out to accommodate the spike in demand caused by the combination of incoming construction workers, displaced families, and ongoing student accommodation demand. We would not have had families living in uninsulated sheds for two or three winters. All government needed to do was to get out of the way.

Downtown confusopoly: The unexpected failure

Commercial redevelopment in Christchurch has been no less shambolic. In the immediate post-quake period, business owners, even those with their own privately hired search and rescue technicians, were not allowed to access their companies' files and records within the downtown cordon. But if you were a young bride needing to get her wedding gown out of a cordoned dressmaker's shop, you could get through. While this was only one example, it demonstrates the arbitrariness of the cordon's restrictions.

After the initial crisis phase, we found the commercial confusopoly. Because CCC changed the building code after the insured event, restoring a building to 'as new' status (the terms of at least some insurance contracts) was insufficient; upgrading it to the new code would constitute a betterment. The government should have sought a declaratory judgment over a few standard insurance contracts to resolve uncertainty and allow construction to proceed, and similar declaratory judgments over insurance cases where the insurer wished to rebuild on-site but where the government deemed the land unfit; uncertainty instead prevailed for years.

The bigger problem, though, was the regime uncertainty brought about by the Government's refusal to commit to a central city plan. Economists use the term 'regime uncertainty' to describe a state of affairs in which nobody really knows what the rules are or what they will be over the next few years. In the first six months after the February earthquake, downtown property owners really could not do much while they waited for Council to decide on its central city plan. By April 2012, the Government had thrown out the proposed CCC plan and established the Christchurch Central Development Unit to come up with a new city plan. The eventual plan that was released was long on visions of precincts, but a bit short on respect for the property rights of existing owners.

Outside of the central city and away from Brownlee's thumb, business owners were simply getting on with things. Cassels and Sons opened a new brewpub in Woolston only one week after the July 2011 earthquake, then expanded to a full new retail development. But, downtown, nobody could tell you whether your proposed development was consistent with the grand plan. You'd have to wait to find out. Would there be a new convention centre? If there would be, and you'd owned a hotel, you'd want to rebuild your hotel near it. If there weren't, then you needed to make other plans.

And, if your hotel happened to be in the newly designated Performing Arts Precinct, whether you'd be allowed to rebuild on your current site would depend on some yet-to-be-made decision as to whether hotels were consistent land use within an arts precinct.[3] At Day 757 after the February earthquakes, the owners of the Copthorne Hotel simply did not know whether they were allowed to rebuild, despite an urgent shortage of hotel spaces in the city. Their insurer had settled and the hotel was keen to rebuild. But they risked expropriation if they did, because nobody yet knew whether it would be decided that hotels weren't meant for arts precincts. As CCDU official Greg Wilson said in the *Press*, 'The test is whether the proposed use would prevent or hinder the public work – in this case the development of the Performing Arts Precinct.'[4] The Copthorne couldn't do anything until Earthquake Recovery Minister Gerry Brownlee provided consent, and his office was not known for expeditious decisions about anything. In *SimCity*, you can pause while you figure out precincts. Christchurch's pause button was rather more costly.

I had never expected that a purportedly market-oriented National Party government would preside over a dirigiste take-over of city planning. Rather than forcing CCC to get on with things, they instead put their own planners in place for the downtown, with exactly the same predilection for making the best the enemy of the good-enough. As I write this, in June 2014, we still do not know whether the National Party government will force an expensive stadium on Christchurch, who will run a new convention centre, or what will be happening with rather too many of the Government's anchor projects. On some of these, simply getting *any* decision two years ago would have been better than the dithering. Businesses can at least get on with the rebuild within a less-than-ideal plan. It's harder to do that under continued regime uncertainty.

Some of the goals of the CCDU seemed laudable. They wanted a vibrant, sustainable downtown of more compact form than that which we had prior to the earthquakes. But they made an utter hash of the job. They established a Green Frame within downtown to reduce the area of land potentially available for downtown development, claiming it a virtue that land prices would thereby stay high. But in a functioning market, land prices are imputed from potential rent. Tenants willing to pay prices consistent with those valuations were few. Consequently, many moved quickly to the suburbs. If, instead of pursuing the grand precinct visions, the CCDU had simply let existing property owners make what best use of their land that they could, we would have had less flight to the suburbs.

Again, government would have done better by simply getting out of the way. But there were important and constructive things that the government could have facilitated for downtown redevelopment. Insurance test cases would have been extraordinarily helpful.

Much of downtown was under pretty fragmented ownership in small lots, and it is entirely plausible that redevelopment would have been better pursued with more concentrated ownership. But rather than look either to compulsory purchase or to mandatory joint-ventures in the downtown retail area, they could simply have maintained a database of ready contact details for existing owners and encouraged the use of dominant assurance contracts for land assembly. Or, they could have moved quickly to set up the anchor projects, committed to the locations and to the funding, and simply then let precincts emerge from the distributed decisions of Christchurch's downtown property owners given certainty around the public projects.

If we learn anything from the intersection of the work of Jane Jacobs and of Ed Glaeser, it's that cities are *organic*. The best parts of cities emerge from the distributed decisions of thousands of property owners, building near each other to take advantage of complementarities in location that they could foresee and that the planners couldn't envision. *SimCity* takes no account of the wishes and dreams of the Sims. All of the small actions of distributed individuals can add up to something wonderful, if only Council and the bureaucrats would get out of the way and let it happen. Instead, we had the worst of all possible worlds: the insistence that a perfect central plan supercede these decentralised decisions, but absolutely no bureaucratic capacity to set or follow through with a plan.

It has taken me far longer than this book's editors would have liked to write this chapter. I'm an economist who works best when considering issues dispassionately. I cannot maintain any reasonable mental state when reflecting on what the planners, both from CCC and those imposed on us from elsewhere, have done to Christchurch. I have had to keep looking away from this Dementor's gaze. But if *we* keep looking away, worse will happen to Wellington when its earthquake comes. There are substantial regulatory problems that need addressing ahead of any future earthquakes. Let's not have another tragedy well-foreseen. We should know better by now.

Simple things that bring joy: The *All Right?* campaign

Lucy D'Aeth

Dr Lucy D'Aeth works as a Public Health Specialist for Community and Public Health, Canterbury District Health Board, where part of her role focuses on the *All Right?* campaign. She has a PhD in Theology from the University of Birmingham, UK. She has worked in community development and health promotion in the UK and Switzerland but she feels most at home in Canterbury.

All Right? is the question that starts a conversation about wellbeing. Since March 2013, the *All Right?* campaign has been producing social-marketing messages on posters, billboards, buses, in the media and online with the aim of supporting Canterbury communities as they recover from the earthquakes and the subsequent stressors. By sharing simple messages, it emphasises that people need to be at the centre of the recovery process.

Through local research, the campaign aims to understand the population's emotional state and recognise people's experiences and the challenges they face. This process identifies what the public sees as important. For example, the criticism that Canterbury's recovery is focused on buildings more than people is supported by noting that 76 per cent of respondents believed that authorities are focused on the wrong priorities and that they should be fixing homes, not building new stadiums.[1]

Since its earliest phases, the campaign has received large amounts of unsolicited positive feedback, indicating that it has 'captured hearts and minds' through an 'ability to articulate the collective psychology of the city'.[2] *All Right?* is also a collective effort – it is a Healthy Christchurch collaboration, led by the Canterbury District Health Board and the Mental Health Foundation, in partnership with NZ Red Cross, SKIP,[3] Christchurch City Council and Waimakariri District Council. The initiative is funded through the Ministry of Health and the Ministry of Social Development.

In 2011, in a briefing paper on the psychosocial impacts of disaster, Sir Peter Gluckman, the Prime Minister's Chief Science Advisor, wrote: 'A comprehensive and effective psychosocial strategy needs to support the majority of the population who need some psychosocial support within the community . . . to allow their innate psychological resilience and coping mechanisms to come to the fore.'[4]

The *All Right?* campaign aims to resource Cantabrians with simple messages about the importance of prioritising mental wellbeing and tips on how to do this. It aims to reassure Canterbury populations that much of what they are currently feeling, whether it be 'pretty stoked' or 'over it right now', is a typical response to the experience of living through a major disaster and the secondary stressors that accompany the recovery process.

A population-focused campaign is valuable in raising awareness of wellbeing issues but relies on a range of services being available to those who require more individual support. *All Right?* works closely with the interagency Greater Christchurch Psychosocial Committee that oversees various initiatives operating to support Cantabrians through the recovery, including the 0800 Canterbury Support Line, the Earthquake Support Coordination Service and counselling through Relationships Aotearoa.

The campaign is committed to incorporating robust evidence on mental health promotion. The five ways to wellbeing, identified by the New Economics Foundation for the 2008 UK Foresight project on Mental Capital and Wellbeing,[5] form an important basis for messaging, since there is strong evidence that giving, connecting, taking notice, being active and learning are simple, accessible actions that promote wellbeing. While mental health promotion campaigns based on the five ways exist elsewhere, *All Right?* appears to be the world's first example of a public health social media campaign to address wellbeing in a disaster-affected area.

All Right? undertakes regular, in-depth local research into how the local populations feel and the hurdles they face. This has been an iterative process of key informant interviews, focus groups and telephone interviews to quantify findings to assure their statistical accuracy for populations across Christchurch, Selwyn and Waimakariri. Research informs every development of the campaign messages, ensuring that they resonate well with local populations. Evaluation of the reach and impact of the campaign, through telephone surveys, indicates that this local flavour is likely a key factor in the campaign's success.

All Right? works with local creative agency Make Collective to ensure that the campaign's creative material is attractive and eye-catching. While the first phases of the campaign focused on street posters and adshels, there has been a progression to using buses and billboards. The most successful phase has been the 'free compliments' posters, which enable passers-by to choose and tear off a specific compliment to give.

Figure 1: The first stages of the campaign focused on street posters and adshels.

Figure 2: The most popular part of the campaign has been the tear-off 'free compliments'.

In its first year, *All Right?* has succeeded in creating an emphasis on the need to place the wellbeing of individuals and their families at the centre of the recovery process. The campaign recognises that it cannot be a universal panacea and that its messages may not be effective with those who are experiencing the most severe hardship or trauma in their recovery. There is plenty that is simply not all right.

Figure 3: The campaign now also employs billboards to spread its simple messages.

Highlighting some of the issues identified in the research is one way that the campaign can contribute to long-term solutions to some of the more intractable recovery issues. For example, research with the Māori and Pacific communities locally has identified that pre-existing challenges facing these communities have been exacerbated and compounded over the past three years as damaged houses, increasing rents and school closures take their toll. This research both enables the campaign to tailor its messages more effectively to particular communities and supports these groups to articulate their recovery experience and needs to authorities and service providers. Similarly, research with parents has identified that the pressures of managing recovery and repairs on top of already busy lives is sometimes distracting parents from prioritising family leisure time. In conjunction with SKIP, *All Right?* has produced a 'Pack of Tiny Adventures' – cards outlining ideas for simple, fun and cheap activities. These have proved extremely popular and are being distributed through Child, Youth and Family; Plunket; early childhood centres and schools.[6]

The response to *All Right?* and the emergence of willing partners indicate the relevance of the campaign to the current Canterbury environment. The earthquakes and the recovery process present Cantabrians with a unique opportunity to reflect on our priorities, individual and collective. If appropriately engaged with, this is a chance for Christchurch to become one of the most resilient and emotionally literate cities on earth. The campaign vision is 'A Canterbury that's more than just all right' and while this is deliberately understated it recognises that people's wellbeing needs to be at the heart of Canterbury's recovery.

Volunteering

From the moment the systems of the city started to fail in the immediate aftermath of the quake, to the ongoing rebuild of the city, volunteers and the act of volunteering have been a powerful and positive force. Each phase of the recovery – as the city has cleaned up, knocked down, moved around and started to rebuild – has facilitated different types of volunteering. Hundreds of groups and tens of thousands of people have contributed many hours in response to different needs. The groups include Student Volunteer Army, Farmy Army, Addington Action, various transitional groups, Volunteering Canterbury, Red Cross, schools, corporates and many others.

[1–2]

[3–4]

Riot clean up

Dan Thompson

Dan is an artist, writer, explorer and photographer who initiated the #riotcleanup campaign after the London riots in 2011.

There really are no jobs that are too big to be done. Whether you're building a garden shed or a tower block, the principle is the same: break it down into small actions. The handyman's to-do list is just a quantity surveyor's spreadsheet, but at a human scale.

Christchurch's post-quake recovery has, when seen from here on the south coast of England, worked at both those scales. Gap Filler's interventions, and its work as an intermediary between landowners and people with ideas, is human-scaled and driven by a genuine belief in 'people, people, people'. Visit the Canterbury Earthquake Recovery Authority's website and there are land zones, strategies, cordons and mentions of buzzwords like health, wellbeing and community – but there is precious little about people. It's a central authority working on a scale that's unimaginable in a country like the UK where the ground stays solid.

It's unsurprising that I'm drawn more to Gap Filler's agile, creative approach. It's under very different circumstances, but matches the approach I've been leading in the UK's failing town centres, where around 15 per cent of shops are empty and large plots of land were cleared for developments that stalled when the country's economy crashed in 2008. We made our disaster ourselves, trusting in a finance system as solid as the Emperor's new clothes. I've animated spaces across the UK, as pop-up shops and temporary workspaces, as shared community spaces and as training spaces for young people. And that work, under the Empty Shops Network banner, has been open source, allowing a movement to grow around shared knowledge and experience.

I have some experience of leading recovery efforts as well, although on a much smaller scale and again, for a problem we made for ourselves. In August 2011, sparked by a police shooting but quickly escalating to people unaffected by that incident, riots broke out in England. This isn't unusual – despite our reputation for a stiff upper lip, queues and good manners, we have rioted often throughout history, and done it well. Queen Boudicca burnt down Roman cities; the Diggers occupied common land; and the Luddites smashed machinery. August 2011's riots were different though; while the past targets of political elites, landowners and evil capitalists are perhaps fair game, these riots destroyed small, independent shops and the homes of working people.

So after four days of rioting, with BBC rolling news showing more buildings burning and my Twitter feed filling with people barricading the doors or fleeing London entirely, I felt the need to help people. My work bringing creative projects to struggling town centres had taught me that those small shops being destroyed weren't run by a rich elite, but by hard-working people struggling to hold on and make enough to feed their family. So using Twitter, I asked people to help them – to get up the next morning, take a broom and a black sack, and offer to help a local shop clean up and start trading. Once we could start those small conversations that happen while buying a pint of milk and a newspaper, we could start the bigger conversations about inequality, poor policing and the price of housing.

With a few thousand followers on Twitter, I thought I could mobilise perhaps 50 people to help. That target was smashed in the next 24 hours. United by the hashtag #riotcleanup, around 12,000 people, mobilised and managed through Twitter, cleaned up at a dozen locations across London. With over 70,000 Twitter followers in a day and media across the world watching, the story turned from riots to a very British resilience and recovery. The energy behind the clean-up day itself was channelled over the next few weeks, first into relief efforts that delivered supplies to hundreds who'd lost their homes, then into rebuilding small shops so they could be open again within weeks, and finally into local attempts to understand what had happened and bring neighbourhoods back together – a process that continues today.

At the heart of it all #riotcleanup was non-hierarchical, belonging to everybody and controlled by nobody. While I started it and was very much in the middle on that first day, it relied on people locally standing up, gathering the minimum of resources they needed, and making decisions as they found circumstances changing on the ground. It was, in the truest sense, anarchy.

That makes it unusual, politically. Singer Billy Bragg said of it:

> The people who spontaneously came out to help tidy up, that's anarchy. Anarchy's not smashing windows and taking tellies, anarchy's not setting light to branches of McDonalds. That don't change nothing. Anarchy is people organising themselves for the common good in some way, without anyone coming round and giving them orders.

But our right-wing Prime Minister also liked it. David Cameron said 'Dan Thompson showed the best of Britain by helping organise the clean-up operation after last summer's riots. He also demonstrated the power of the Internet as a force for good: bringing people together to make a difference in their community.'

And 12,000 people across London also liked it, because it was theirs. They were making the most important decisions, deciding where their resources were best deployed, carrying out impromptu risk assessments and liaising with police and fire services on the street. That couldn't have been done with a central control system, certainly not in the accelerated time scale we were working with. This was the 'organising without organisations' that Clay Shirky had predicted in his book *Here Comes Everybody*, delivering real results.

So what is the role of the individual in a scenario like this?

Even in the middle of a flat, open, uncopyrighted movement one person is still useful. Mobilising this many people as part of a recovery needs somebody to drive, push and encourage. I started calling for people on Monday evening – I didn't stop working until Tuesday evening. That was a solid 24 hours of work, without proper sleep.

And while #riotcleanup was open, most people still wanted somebody to say 'yes' to them: 'yes' you can start a local action; 'yes' you can go and help; 'yes' it's safe. I spent a day delegating an authority that was only earned by the actions of the people I delegated it to.

You still need somebody who can make the connections, too. I had cultivated and crafted networks through my work with town centres that meant that, when needed, I could reach and influence people. You simply couldn't start something like #riotcleanup from scratch; other people had sent 'we should help clean up' tweets earlier than mine, but without strong networks, they were tweeting to themselves.

#riotcleanup was a very trivial undertaking compared to the work of Gap Filler, but it does show that ad hoc and agile responses to disasters and emergencies can be useful. It started a trend for using social media to respond, which continued recently when England flooded. Most importantly, it reminded people that they have power, that they can make a difference, and that loose collaboration has a power and magic that committees, local councils and central control can't take away from us.

Temporary projects, permanent impact

Brie Sherow

Brie Sherow is experienced in urban planning, spatial analysis and international community development. She has been involved in the Christchurch earthquake rebuild in both a technical and strategic capacity, as a Spatial Analyst at Stronger Christchurch Infrastructure Rebuild Team (SCIRT) and as Projects Manager of Life in Vacant Spaces Charitable Trust.

Over 1300 buildings have been demolished in Christchurch's central city since the February 2011 quake. The loss of physical infrastructure leaves an unavoidable visual impact as the city is now full of demolition sites and vacant lots. The loss of social infrastructure is just as pervasive. Responder organisations such as Gap Filler emerged post-quake to fill vacant lots with events and installations, actively taking part in recreating their city. They realised that a significant amount of the work occurred before a project appeared on site, as landowner negotiations and legal paperwork started to dominate actual project plans. Gap Filler worked with Christchurch City Council (CCC) to create a separate trust to broker access to unused spaces and provide support to participants during project planning stages. Life in Vacant Spaces (LIVS) was the result – it was initiated in September 2012 to unlock permissions and provide a framework for groups to use available space.

LIVS is a small team of two, a director and a projects manager, supported by CCC and Canterbury Community Trust. Our work includes negotiations with local and national government, private developers and local landowners, community groups and neighbouring businesses. We cover practical considerations like legal agreements, insurances, site preparations and connections to utilities and services where possible. As LIVS evolves it has taken a leading role in strategy discussions, advocating for policies friendly towards transitional use of space. LIVS primarily works in the central city but liaises with neighbourhood groups carrying out similar work in the suburbs, such as Renew Brighton and Project Lyttelton.

After a year and a half in existence LIVS has received hundreds of enquiries and project proposals; close to 75 have been activated through LIVS in the central city. The projects have ranged in scale. Some have been static installations or involved slight landscaping of the site. Others have called for massive transformations involving built structures and hundreds of volunteers, and have attracted thousands of visitors. Whether the project 'works' or not has less to do with the scale and more to do with the commitment and capability of the team managing the project.

Varieties of projects

Transitional projects fall into five main categories: events, installations, landscaping, social enterprises and small businesses. Events range from outdoor concerts organised by experienced production companies, such as Fledge, to plays coordinated by youth theatre company Two Productions. Installations have included replica artworks placed on walls by Christchurch Art Gallery and the large-scale built artwork Temple for Christchurch. Installations have also explored innovative buildings such as micro-architecture in the case of Gap Filler's office and Agropolis Urban Farm's earthen shed.

Landscaping is undertaken by experienced gardening groups such as Canterbury Horticultural Society, guerrilla gardeners such as Plant Gang and urban agriculture advocates such as Garden City 2.0. Social entrepreneurs coordinate projects such as a 3-D printing fabrication lab at the Makercrate and a community bike workshop at Gap Filler's RAD Bikes. Small businesses include new local fashion designers Blackeyepeach and old businesses that have been displaced since the quakes such as Arts Central. Then there are projects that don't fit easily into any category, such as a relocatable international artist residency set in a live-in caravan on a vacant site, managed by arts collective The Social.

Figure 1: LIVS on New Regent Street includes Canterbury Horticultural Society's Alhambra Gardens, Jed Joyce's Rollickin' Gelato Caravan and Christchurch Art Gallery's Rita Angus replica.

Experience and flexibility

Experienced groups and start-ups alike have had difficulties. While established groups may benefit from years of experience, they must learn to function in a new context. Projects that attempt to begin with the 'finished, polished plan', or that respond to the status quo, often fall flat at their initiation. New groups are often advantaged because they can adapt rapidly. In either case, the most successful groups are the ones that are flexible and learn by doing.

Successful groups explore synergies with other organisations rather than adhering to a decisive plan that places their project in a vacuum. They reconcile their plans within the wider context of the city and the specific context of a vacant site rather than developing a project merely to place on a site. It takes time and many different inputs to create something worthwhile. A project starts out slow and DIY, testing different designs and materials. Project coordinators may work with many different volunteers and people as they seek specific skill sets. The projects and the spaces evolve over time together, eventually reaching a point where they gain a critical mass that often includes attention from the wider community, media and sponsors.

Private property versus public space

Activating a private property site takes more work than coordinating events in a public space. The demolished lots in Christchurch are not granted to project participants in a comfortable state: they are full of ungraded rubble, rebar and pieces of foundation, and lack access to basic utilities and services. LIVS participants have found themselves in the position of not only managing their project, but also preparing their site and providing power and water. While local government maintains public spaces such as city parks, the general upkeep and security of private property sites are best managed by ensuring the site is well-used through regular hours of activities or frequent events.

Importance of collaboration

The most well-used sites have been the result of multi-team efforts. One team adds landscaping, another adds additional amenities such as structures, another organises events, and yet another looks after the site by opening their business at regular hours. The successful spaces become microcosms of city life and are used in different ways at different times by different people, just the way that a city street or a neighbourhood is.

Project initiators that have a willingness to align agendas, share information, and are motivated to learn and improve along the way create successful sites. Success may stem from creating educational opportunities, enhancing infrastructure or encouraging innovation. Many sites benefit from a core project (e.g. the Pallet Pavilion at The Commons or the RAD Bikes workshop on High Street) that has a high level of influence on the site's design and can initiate further development such as markets or food caravans. The core projects are quick-response site anchors, testing ideas rather than providing solutions. However, when an idea is tested and it works, this creates a solution.

Figure 2: The Commons

Outsourcing design

LIVS is able to remain organisationally light as it outsources the design work to the public. When groups propose a project, LIVS may be involved during the planning stages, but once the project is on site the daily management is the responsibility of the participants. The group then has direct control and responsibility over the outcomes. LIVS is able to avoid lengthy consultation phases with the assumption that the project proposal itself is evidence that there is a community that supports the plan. These projects can be enacted cheaply – often groups gain support from social or professional networks and are able to recruit designers, builders and project managers as volunteers. Top-heavy organisations would be paying a premium for these services. The downside is that when the expected support doesn't come through, projects end up poorly maintained or with a rough look.

Complexities of land ownership

Vacant lots may appear to be a single open space but the reality is that they are comprised of many land parcels with different landowners. Landowners are faced with uncertainties about development time frames, insurance pay-outs and potential land sales. Locally based small-scale landowners are often amenable to making their property available because they have firsthand experience with the results. If land is owned by overseas development trusts it can be difficult to reach a decision maker. Decision makers are likely managing many properties and may be unfamiliar with the local context, so specific sites in Christchurch are not a high priority for them. The CCC property team was among the first to make land available to LIVS, and Council also provides small grants for transitional activities.

Relationship with CERA

Initially LIVS had expected to work closely with the Canterbury Earthquake Recovery Authority (CERA) since the Crown is the single largest landowner in the central city and many of their anchor projects will take years to realise. LIVS was included in the CERA recovery plan but the relationship has been difficult. While many individuals within CERA are supportive of transitional-use projects, the hierarchical structure of the organisation means that it can be very difficult to reach decision makers. Projects occurring on land designated for Government anchor projects require twenty-one signatures before they are approved, even for minimal impact projects such as a zen garden that simply involved rearranging materials on a site. Even after projects had official approval there were instances of internal communication issues at CERA that caused licenses not to be honoured.

Communication improved in spring 2013 when CERA approached LIVS to coordinate transitional use of a section in the East Frame. The land was granted to LIVS 'immediately', and six months later the proposal had received twenty of the twenty-one signatures required for sign-off. CCDU Director Warwick Isaacs' signature was the last needed for approval, but after months of further consideration he rejected the proposal. CERA has previously expressed concern regarding the unpolished manner in which many of these projects start, but the East Frame proposal included significant sponsorship and well-known delivery partners. Isaacs' concern in this instance was that the people of Christchurch might become too attached to the temporary work.

This situation demonstrates the skewed priorities of those in power, who would prefer that nothing happen rather than something popular happen that they themselves didn't initiate. LIVS has backed away from its relationship with CERA; it's difficult to be agile and community-focused when requiring individual project approvals from a government ministry. Ultimately the success of the recovery will depend on top-level coordination with grassroots initiatives, and as momentum and international focus grows in the transitional movement it's becoming clear that slow beginnings can yield impressive results. Transitional projects may be on site only temporarily, but the ideas and experiences are becoming a permanent part of the city.

Supporting startups

With so much work to do within such a dynamic environment, there are extraordinary opportunities for new businesses, social enterprises and startups to emerge in Christchurch at the moment. Several organisations have been started (or adapted) to provide the support, capital and collaborative work environments that allow these emergent businesses to succeed (or fail and try again). Prominent amongst these are the Enterprise Precinct and Innovation Campus (EPIC), the Ministry of Awesome, Life in Vacant Spaces and the Canterbury Community Trust's new Social Enterprise Fund.

[1]

[2–3]

Acting Small

A cause for CanCERN

James Macbeth Dann

James Macbeth Dann has lived in the heart of the central city for most of the last decade – which proved to be a bit of a challenge after the 2010 and 2011 quakes. He is studying for a doctorate at the University of Otago, Christchurch. James has been active in the water rights protest movement in Canterbury and the struggle to save heritage buildings, and is an outspoken critic of the National government's recovery strategy.

Of the few 'silver linings' that came out following the quakes, the reawakening of a sense of community is perhaps the one that was most remarkable, but least remarked upon. Individuals found a need and bound together to make the best they could of less than ideal circumstances. These nascent community networks were the glue that kept families, houses, streets and suburbs from falling apart completely. It was a much needed – if fleeting – reminder that when faced with a crisis situation, humans are at their best: a kind, friendly, helpful and giving species.

The rise of the community-led localised recovery was a significant event that hasn't been fully acknowledged. It didn't happen overnight, and it didn't happen without reason. All across the city, but especially in the most damaged areas, neighbourhood groups were formed, reformed, repurposed and reactivated. They filled a vacuum, an empty space where the official response wouldn't be, shouldn't be or simply wasn't able to be.

My experiences of the group I was involved with are informative, if not typical. At the time of the September quake, I was living in Cashel Street, right in the heart of the central business district (CBD). On the morning following the quake, I packed a bag of things and went to stay with family, not knowing how long it would be before we were allowed in again. As the Civil Defence (CD) operation swung into action, a cordon was placed around the CBD, preventing access to businesses and residences in the area. Initially, this was a novelty, but it fast became an inconvenience. As building inspectors and media descended on the area, it was clear that there was no mechanism for residents to gain access to their homes (this was due to there being a very small number of people living in the core of the CBD). As I had friends and acquaintances that lived in the area, I formed the Inner City Residents Association (ICRA). We met once or twice, but mainly communicated via Facebook. After ten days, most of the cordon was down and we were able to re-enter our properties.

As the immediate need dwindled, so did interest in the group. However, the need for such a network resurfaced after the 22 February quake. Once again, the city centre went into lock down – this time for months and years, rather than weeks. The group found that residents – most of whom were tenants, rather than owners – were the last people Civil Defence looked out for. Clearly, this was a disaster situation, and a coordinated response was difficult, if not impossible. We found that there was no way to identify who lived at a particular address, so we worked with the authorities to provide the names and contacts of the people in our group.

ICRA was ineffective on its own. As a representative for the group, I started attending CanCERN meetings. CanCERN (Canterbury Communities' Earthquake Recovery Network) is a 'network of Residents Association and Community Group representatives from the earthquake-affected neighbourhoods of Canterbury'. It formed after September, but really took off after February, when representatives from across the city could meet and share their challenges and successes. The strength of the community connection was reasonably quickly recognised by those at Civil Defence, and CanCERN was given regular access to the CD controller and his staff. For the inner city residents, this was a chance to ask for access to our own flats; for those in the broken east of the city, it was an opportunity to tell CD where the greatest need for portaloos or fresh drinking water was. CD could see that harnessing these networks, which were strongest in the areas with the most acute demands, was an efficient way of gauging the needs of the community. Top-down control met bottom-up demand.

The success of CanCERN was in part due to the organisational ability of those involved, and their connections to the communities that they represented. But it was also due to the gap in local representation that had been created by a generation of changes in local government. Christchurch had seen major changes in the way local decisions and representation were managed. In 1989, the Christchurch City Council was formed from the amalgamation of five local councils. Initially a model council, in 1993 Christchurch shared the Carl Bertelsmann Prize[1] for 'Democracy and efficiency in local government' with Phoenix, Arizona. It recognised the city 'for their administrative agencies, which are effective, employee-centered and responsive to the public's needs'. A decade later, the number of councillors was halved from twenty-four to twelve. When the disaster struck, the councillors and community boards found themselves largely unable to respond in the way in which the community groups were able to. Less than two decades from being named the best governed small city in the world, the Christchurch City Council had descended to bickering and dysfunction, with a hugely unpopular Chief Executive and the Council being stripped of its ability to issue building consents. With the legitimacy and competence of the local council in serious question, small community groups, with their local focus and genuine connections, became critical to many suburbs.

These organisations thrived because they were frameworks through which information could be shared. Though the New Zealand media went into 24-hour coverage mode, much of this was done from out of town, and was focused on the camera-friendly destruction in the centre of town. There was also the problem that many houses, especially in the east, didn't have access to power, so weren't able to see the images on TV. Community hubs provided spaces where notes could be placed, information from the authorities could be disseminated, and there was often free power for people to charge cellphones and check the internet. Information was key, but the most important was the most localised information.

As the recovery moved from the immediate disaster response phase and into the short- to medium-term recovery phase, the authorities were unsure of how to deal with the community groups. Clearly, they needed to have community input – if not for logistical reasons then at least for political expediency. A community-led forum was proposed early in the discussions about the structure of the recovery authority. With such a complex task at hand, and much of the decision-making to be done behind closed doors, having the input of community representatives was vital. It was also key in legitimising the remit of the Canterbury Earthquake Recovery Authority (CERA) itself.

In initial proposals, the community forum was one of only three stakeholder groups to have direct access to the Minister for Canterbury Earthquake Recovery. In April 2011, applications were solicited for members for the community forum. There was much speculation about who might be on it.[2] In the end, 31 people from various backgrounds were chosen. And that was pretty much the last thing that was heard from the community forum.

The forum itself still meets, about every month. By looking through the attendance records as part of the minutes of the forum, it is clear that the relevant ministers are not supporting it with the same enthusiasm that formed the forum. The Minister, associate Minister, and CERA chief executive send their apologies more often than not;[3] subsequently, the attendance of the community members has also tapered off. The voice of the community was mandated, legislated, coordinated – and then never heard from again.

The successes of the various community groups in the city, immediately following the quakes, were something that brought a sense of pride and communal spirit back to the city. As we moved further from the day of the disaster, that spirit and unity became harder to rekindle. Our leaders tried to capture it, to keep the fire burning, but largely failed. This isn't to say the fault lies with either the community groups or the government; localised groups are strongest when they form in response to an immediate crisis, but if they are formed in response to a single factor, they lack a common purpose once the crisis has subsided, and subsequently struggle to find a unifying reason to continue. Without a sole purpose, the movement and the energy dissipate, and the members move on.

Successful community groups are high on credibility, but low on cash. They have genuine, earned relationships with the people they represent, which are based on repeated, localised interactions and the transmission of useful information. This is the sort of credibility and trust that all sorts of organisations would kill to have. Luckily for the government, they don't need to kill; they just need to spend. For a relatively small sum, they can get quite a lot. Firstly, they get the legitimacy of community engagement. This is crucial for political viability. It gives the ability to enact policy that might be unpopular, but then when criticised, to be able to turn around as say 'well, we have the community on our side'. Secondly, that community may feel less able to speak out in opposition to decisions made by the body that helps fund them. This can result in the silencing of the most authentic local voices, a boon for any authority that is acutely aware of any criticisms about their legitimacy to lead.

Any recovery after disaster is always going to have a blunt top-down response meeting a small but important community action. The measure of success for a response will be in how the interface between the two is managed. Initially in Christchurch, it looked like there was a new way of doing business, that communities and government were going to forge an understanding that would last beyond the crisis situation. As weeks turned to months, that hope dissipated, until we returned to a situation that was effectively the same as that before the quakes. With the most recent council elections, a number of candidates who ran on a ticket of better relationships with the community were elected to office; it will be interesting to see whether they can deliver on that promise during this term.

The initial success of small-scale community responses to the quake strongly contrasts with the lead-footed attempts of the authorities. The desire of the latter to integrate the former into recovery plans shows how crucial it is for council and government to have genuine community buy-in to their vision. As my own experiences with inner city residents showed, an initial enthusiasm can be hard to sustain beyond the immediate event; for people with busy lives, any time for the community is time they can little spare to give. The challenge for those at the top is to enable a system that empowers communities without patronising or exploiting them.

Community networks are often made up of friends and family; like friends and family, they can be relied upon when times get tough. But these relationships also need to be nurtured in the good times, to ensure that when a crisis emerges, they have the capacity to respond to the challenge. The lesson from Christchurch is that though acting small, these networks should not be overlooked.

Co-working spaces

The combination of creative energy in the rebuild and the lack of affordable office space – the lack of *any* office space – in the city has resulted in the establishment of many collective workspaces. In these spaces a variety of disciplines and professions share facilities and employ both temporary and permanent arrangements, often with atypical organisational and physical infrastructure. In the urgency to replace much of the lost amenity of the city, people cleverly or unwittingly have sown the seeds for longer-term change.

[1–2]

[3–4]

Acting Small

First of all, we are citizens

Alejandro Haiek Coll

Alejandro is an architect, artist and core member of the laboratory of experimental art and applied science, LabProFab. He has won several international awards and has served as a guest professor across the globe, from South and Central America through to Japan, New Zealand and the USA. Alejandro's works explore the renewal and resuscitation of inactive landscapes of postindustrial cities, and survival tactics for enhancing community urban scenarios. He is an Artist in Residence at Elam School of Fine Arts (2014). (This piece was translated from the Spanish by Kaila Colbin.)

In one of his most interesting works, *Anarchitecture*, Lebbeus Woods describes architecture as a political act, not so much because of its capacity for reconciliation, consensus or diplomacy, but rather because it is so often a manifestation of dominant social forces. He writes about the difficult relationship that architecture has with forces of domination and resistance:

> The world is so filled with injustices and oppressions, with absurdities made up to look like self-evident truths, with bad ideas that will so clearly lead to disaster but are institutionalized as good policies, with aggressions against human dignity, and insults to common sense, that, as one school of thought would have it, human existence is nothing but a sustained form resistance to all that would overwhelm it.[1]

In the majority of cases architecture is oppressive, totalitarian and even militaristic, but Woods makes clear the power of architecture to resist these forces and to transform into dynamics and protocols of collective adaptation. This political architecture is capable of reactivating, renovating or reprogramming complex contexts and situations such as those during and after disaster. The protocols and practices that define this transformation are as varied as the communities, collectives and cooperatives that create them, but they have in common a resistance to the dominant forces in their respective societies. These small acts of citizenry, whether in Christchurch or Caracas, Venezuela, can have profound effects upon the urban fabric and encourage the transformative power of urban design.

Many Latin American cities show characteristics of depredation, degeneration, decadence and uncertainty caused by inept practices of state bureaucracy such as corruption, short-term thinking and the regular movement of resources to meet political goals. Enduring this phenomenon are many social movements and collectives that are transforming this state of crisis into opportunities for participatory democracy. In this essay I will explore the transformational potential of community-led architecture.

Figure 1: Favela in
Caracas, Venezula

Cultural micro-economies and cultural capital

Understanding diversity is one of the keys to acquiring, producing and transferring new knowledge. It is through diverse societies, ecologies and manifestations that contemporary culture finds its greatest splendour. New lines of exploration and experimentation in citizen practice can mature if, and only if, they are derived in open, flexible, adaptable and upgradable systems. The production of diverse new knowledge and values that counteract the shortcomings of the dominant systems of capital is the principle tactic for emergent practices, such as small design firms, community-led projects and other configurations that are engaging in urban activation and regeneration.

Many of these practices have developed financial models based on horizontal micro-economies, which are capable of treating participants equally, and of operating with a system of exchange based on common benefits. They can be evaluated by considering a developmental balance rather than models that emphasise excessive enrichment. This doesn't mean they oppose the forces of capital, but rather that these diverse practices reorganise protocols to favour collective demands, which tend to prioritise infrastructural and operational needs.

It is through the street, the building and urban fabric that these new economic modes can progressively transform into scaffolding for collective learning. At best these new models don't operate as objects and systems of economic value, but as a cooperative construction that reveals its processes like an open book – ready to be consulted and to instigate new relational experiences. From this perspective, architecture, urbanism and design can serve purely and simply as a foundation for a collective and participatory democracy in a city in constant consultation and permanent evolution. This type of democracy and urbanism integrates continuous and sustained transitional processes, and leaves behind the perfection that motivates the type of masterplanning predominant in Caracas and in Christchurch, which favours elements of domination and the silence of citizens.

Below I offer three cases that establish horizontal lines between the new financial modes described above with the political dimensions of architecture and urbanism practices. They illustrate the pragmatism of contemporary life,

Acting Small

and allow the imagining of possible futures through real cases of community empowerment, citizenship, collective legislation, self-government and self-management. They are examples of the intersection between cultural micro-economies and transformative architecture.

Social multisport complex

This multisport complex project (figs 2-4) was spearheaded and managed by the local community council, alongside cultural and sporting associations and the active participation of the local and national governments. Proposals from the community were identified and developed cooperatively, with the inclusion of private companies that provided training for local workers. The project led to the establishment of a new model of hybrid management.

The complex is located in the Sucre Parish, which has approximately 400,000 people, in an urbanised area in Caracas. The Lomas de Urdaneta (Urdaneta Hills) favela (slum) constitutes a belt that has been marginalised for more than half a century. This informal growth developed in the west of the valley in a complex topographical zone and, in reality, its inhabitants have achieved important improvements in terms of accessibility, service infrastructure and social betterment. The community has organised itself into geopolitical cells called community councils. This local organisational structure allows them to map, discuss, evaluate and prioritise their local problems, needs and demands with a high level of participation, thanks to its flexible and horizontal nature. These cells are promoted by the government, which facilitates the actions undertaken by the collective organisation in an emergent but legal framework.

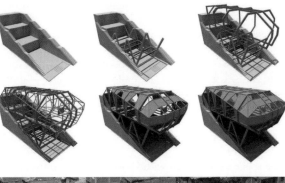

Figure 2: Renders of sports complex illustrating integration with steps and built landscape

Figure 3: Aerial view of unfinished steel structure

Figure 4: Concrete
formwork and interior
under construction

Even though the legal scaffolding is fragile, the state apparatus is forced to
channel public resources into projects such as this because they are supported
by the community councils through public discussion and open voting.

Interstitial Park

This project (figs 5-7) emerges from within a complex urban story. The area
has been badly affected by slow infrastructure development and suffers from
low-quality social housing interventions by the state in the 70s. The area is
dominated by a sophisticated modernist road network and an overwhelming
slum, the inhabitants of which are skilled at integrating their local knowledge
with new waves of culture. Add to this a strong military presence (Fuerte Tiuna
military base) and all of this combines to create an intricate geomorphology.

In the middle of this complex structure, Tiuna El Fuerte Cultural Park was
developed. Promoted by local artists and a significant number of urban
activists, the park managed to occupy an old and abandoned parking lot
thanks to a legal loophole that allows for the use of unused lands under a
bailment structure (that is, without transfer of ownership) for twenty years.
Out of this first community action sprang a whole chain of cultural ones,
which progressively transformed the inactive ground into a sophisticated
support system for the collective dynamics of the community.

The space experiments with various administrative, organisational,
operational and political formats (foundations, companies, social
enterprises, NGOs, collectives, groups and investigation labs), employing
as a participation methodology an internal weekly assembly during which
basic items of maintenance, entrepreneurship, and project formulation and
revision are discussed, as well as other issues such as systems for the exchange
of values and information, alternative pedagogy, and a productive and
autonomous society. The space and its infrastructure (workshops, classrooms,
radio station, recording studio, video and communications rooms, library,
auditoria and a small cafeteria) are open to the public and only require that
participants develop educational and formative programmes in line with this
ethos. This has resulted in a model of self-governance being converted into an
alternative cooperative for social, environmental and cultural movements.

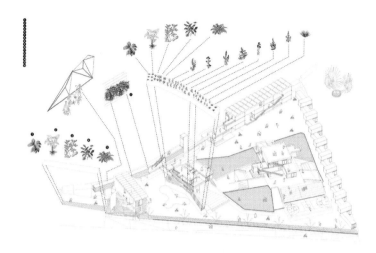

Figure 5: This drawing illustrates the types of vegetation found in the park.

Figure 6: Cantilevered containers and colourful artworks give the space a powerful aesthetic quality.

Figure 7: The horizontal balustrades and circular windows add to the character of the project.

Botanic Plaza

El Valle and Coche, located in Caracas, and their slums, El Setenta and El Loro among others, are known for their musical vigour and for their cultural and political profundity. It is and has been a territory of social thought and action, finding itself at the centre of socio-cultural and political protests of great importance at the local and national level. For this reason, it's worth noting that these movements of community liberation and equality have in the past suffered repression at the hands of state security forces at various historic moments.

The Plaza Bolivar in El Valle is perhaps one of the most important examples of community management and participatory urbanism in Caracas, since it has managed to reprogramme approximately one hectare of interstitial terrain that suffered from high levels of dereliction, drainage problems and poor public health (figs 8-10). The initiative was born from popular demand and from the desires of the inhabitants to reconstruct the historical memory and cultural and environmental heritage of the place. It is from this platform that they managed to establish four levels of management:

- Technological: they identified systems of local manufacturing and constructed new urban technologies with teachers in the community.
- Environmental: out of this systematisation of knowledge, a capillary irrigation system was configured with a circuit for the re-collection

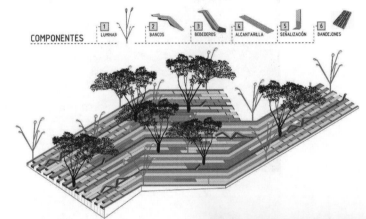

Figure 8: Six design elements in the park are shown in this drawing.

Figure 9: (left) Other design elements with human interface are shown here.

Figure 10: (right) Aerial view of the park after it was completed.

and canalisation of water, allowing in this case hundred-year-old trees to be saved.
- Cultural: community actors were linked, thus establishing a cartography of talents that began to use the plaza as an open theatre and as a surface for expression.
- Social: the project was placed in the public consciousness using the distinct instances of local, regional and national participation established by state politics but also by introducing new mechanisms for mass participation and community empowerment.

Only partial conclusions

Regardless of whether one is in Caracas or Christchurch it is clear to me that the democratic default position is debate and confrontation. Architecture and urbanism are practices that have accompanied power – during long and recurring historical periods – and have rarely developed mechanisms to enable resistance. Despite global advancement in constitution design and the creation of new laws, these developments are, generally speaking, still foreign to disciplinary practices of urbanism and architecture.

Therefore in the first instance we must substitute the role of expert for that of the citizen. By doing so we add ourselves to networks of mobilisation and convocation that are in reality already distancing themselves from traditional protest movements. Yet it is important to remember that those contemporaries who have begun to distribute themselves through a complex web of creative citizenship will only constitute a greater force than that of the state if they are capable of replicating experiences and promoting multiple forms of participation and integrative collaboration.

The challenge in the future will be to take on legislation and develop new modes of collective action, as well as urban spaces for citizenry. Each building and each space, can in and of itself constitute a model of citizenship that understands the variables of the system as laboratory tests, which can be substituted, re-examined and relocated. A new space that allows for the generation of opportunities will be crucial for the democratisation of the urban setting. This would allow for the rethinking of the city so that cultural investment and the formation of new political individuals capable of contributing to the city's transformation are valued as much as economic investment.

As new forms of participatory democracy continue to emerge and develop around the world, it is clear that they cannot be easily separated from new forms of participatory design. Charles de Gaulle once said that 'Politics is too serious a matter to be left to the politicians'[2] and the shift in focus from experts to citizens can be summarised by the notion that architecture is far too important to be left to architects.

Chapter 7

Meeting in the Middle

Aroha atu, aroha mai

The success or failure of high-level institutional or community-led responses can be spun by either side to show that their way is the best way. Generally, it's at the interface between the two – the mess in the middle – where things really happen. People need money; money needs ideas; ideas need champions to become reality.

Nowhere is this more striking than in the arts community. Perpetually short of cash, Christchurch's artists found themselves after the quakes in need of the things we often take for granted: galleries, practice spaces, concert venues and a market to sell to. And Christchurch found itself in need of the arts – and of the creativity and adaptability of artists – as never before. These key components of our city's cultural life reshaped their practice to fit the changed, and still changing, terrain. Temporary and permanent-temporary spaces emerged.

It's true in the high-tech sector and tertiary education as well: this interface between the top and the bottom – the power and the ideas, the capital and the creativity – is what's really driving the rebuild. Getting outcomes is the fun part, but getting to the point where multiple parties with a grab-bag of priorities can work together is hard. In this chapter, we look at a range of examples where this has worked – and some where it hasn't.

Far away in both distance and scale, the recovery in New Orleans has some similarities to the situation in Christchurch. There, a range of competing government bodies had to find a middle ground on which to meet; perhaps in that, there is a lesson for our own leaders. When power becomes as concentrated as it has been in post-quake Christchurch, the desire to dictate often trumps the compulsion to compromise. Ultimately, the longest lasting projects and plans should be the ones that are built upon the strongest consensus. That consensus can only be reached when the parties involved are able to find common ground to work together in the wider interests of the city.

A new city through the arts?

George Parker

Dr George Parker is a member of Free Theatre Christchurch, New Zealand's longest running producer of experimental theatre.

Arts Voice Christchurch is an arts advocacy group that emerged in the early days following the 22 February earthquake. It grew out of a series of meetings initiated by the country's primary funding body for the arts, Creative New Zealand (CNZ). Asking how Christchurch might retain artists post-quake and provide an effective voice for the arts community in the highly politicised post-quake environment, CNZ proposed that volunteers put their names forward to be part of a yet-to-be-defined response to the current environment. At a subsequent meeting, those forty or so individuals that had volunteered decided that a 'steering group' of seven would act as an advocacy group for the arts community in conversations with local and national government. Nominations were made from those present, votes were cast, and a group was elected that represented some of the major arts organisations and institutions in the city.

As one of the original seven, I have experienced the changing fortunes of Arts Voice, which reflect the political process that has taken place in Christchurch post-quakes. Specifically, it is possible to identify two distinct periods before and after the imposition of the government process, which led to the Christchurch Central Recovery Plan. To understand the effects of the restrictive government process, it is important to consider what came before. The contrast between the two shows how the initial explosion of ideas, enthusiasm and collaboration that was seen as revolutionising the arts community in Christchurch – namely how Christchurch thought about the arts and how we thought about Christchurch through art – has been smothered by a process that has reverted to a top-down, conservative notion of urban design, where art is utilised largely for beautification purposes.

This official view sees art as an agent for covering up the cracks rather than as a means for exploring the divides and gaps that make up our contemporary political, social and physical reality. To simply dismiss art as a rarefied activity practiced by precious beings 'expressing themselves' on 'empty' walls and in 'vacant' lots is to miss art's potential potency as an efficacious act in engaging the community with their new city becoming. This misunderstanding of what art is, or can be, kills off exactly what we need from it.

Following the quakes and before the government took control of the process, Arts Voice operated in the extraordinary, community-active environment of a post-disaster zone, typified by the Share an Idea campaign. Arts Voice members attended community forums and meetings, unprecedented in number, and held a number of their own in order to gauge how artists might play a role in the new city emerging. The aim was to canvass not just the views of the arts community but also those of the wider public. What came through loud and clear was that, rather than being a 'nice to have' luxury considered after all else was built, the arts needed to be an integral feature in effecting a new contemporary city. There was also a desire to move beyond the silo mentality of pre-quake Christchurch, where the arts were segregated to a part of the city for a middle class, middle-aged arty crowd, and where arts organisations all worked in isolation. An overwhelming number of people saw this as an opportunity to change.

And the culture had already changed. The earthquakes had forced a more communal, collaborative approach between organisations. This approach saw the emergence of unusual new venues, a rethink of festivals, and new initiatives that have been credited with bringing life and hope to the city. The arts community became an example within the wider city of a sector working together to find new ways to operate – a new culture emerging from the ground up – through the cracks, so to speak. And indeed this new verve did reflect a historical situation where Christchurch has played a strong role in producing a distinct national identity through literature, music, visual arts, performance and film, as local artists pushed up against the conservatism of the place. One might say that with the earthquakes, this spirit moved from the periphery of the city's culture to the centre, as a place once well-known and settled began to question itself like never before.

It was this spirit that infused the outcomes of the initial phase for Arts Voice, which included formal written submissions before and after the release of the Christchurch City Council's Draft Central City Plan (CCP). The submission preceding the release of the plan identified key themes alongside that of 'integration' that recurred during the many community forums: collaboration, collocation, diversity, innovation, sustainability and engagement. Arts Voice proposed an overarching idea, the River of Arts, which might encapsulate these themes and see a way for the diverse voices of the arts community to contribute to the emergence of the new city. Given that a re-engagement with the central Ōtākaro-Avon River had been recognised by the city council as a primary goal of the community, reflecting a desire to embrace the new ecologically conscious values of the twenty-first century, the river seemed an apt metaphor through which the arts community might find relevance as the city actively questioned its identity.

While the River of Arts concept worked with the plan that was emerging, it also looked to offer an intervention. Early indications of the CCP suggested a preoccupation with buildings that addressed pre-earthquake needs, which also suggested it would be inflexible and non-responsive to the changes that were sure to take place as the new city emerged. What Arts Voice proposed instead, through the River of Arts concept, was an approach that would encourage an adaptable urban design, including the integration of arts-based projects through the city, connected via wayfinding, interactive attractions, public art and events that were ever-adaptive. In other words, Arts Voice proposed that the city be considered from an artistic point of view. Not only might artists play a leading role in engaging the community in the creation of the city emerging, but they should also offer planners ideas for the city's development, informed by the creative process with which artists have a great deal of experience.

Central to these aims was the phase marked as 'transitional' in the CCP. It became a key feature of Arts Voice advocacy, as it most readily provoked an artistic response to the city. More than simply a phase through which artists could cheer everyone up with quirky and colourful distractions, from an artistic point of view it was perhaps the most important phase in the creation of the city – it allowed for experiments that would affect the new city becoming and, as an active, inclusive process, reverse the urban decline and lack of social engagement that dogged the city pre-earthquakes. In other words, the transitional emphasised process over product-oriented thinking and thus allowed for a more active response to the inevitable changes that would take place and allow for the unimagined to occur through collective, creative thinking.

Arts Voice advocated for a number of transitional projects and proposed a new, larger project called Arts Circus. Inspired by the Tollwood Festival in Munich, the Arts Circus was designed as a collection of smaller temporary venues that collocated a range of arts (from the conventional to the experimental), entertainment, hospitality and education around a central market. As a wellspring for the River of Arts, this project could connect with others that were also arts-based but, more importantly, integrate with other post-quake transitional initiatives, such as Re:START and EPIC, which represented a creative, collaborative meeting in the middle between the bottom-up and the top-down. It also tied in with proposed projects such as the New Zealand Centre for Urban Resilience (NZCUR), which was proposed as a collaboration between the major Christchurch tertiary education institutions, involving students in the rethinking of the city – a pragmatic and inspired idea.

Figure 1: The proposed Arts Circus venue at the Arts Centre

In concert, these projects had the potential to provide creative, open-ended responses that would engage the wider community and avoid a passive return to the status quo ante. However, these larger transitional projects came to be viewed from above as static, unrelated gap fillers, and so the opportunity to maximise their extraordinary potential to work the creative middle ground between the community and local and national government has not been achieved. While the potential of NZCUR, for example, appears to have been shelved because of inter-university politics, community-inclusive projects like Re:START have not built on the original community excitement for a unique and distinct transitional city. Re:START could have introduced new components that drew a wider audience into the city centre; imagine what might have happened for instance if a project like Arts Circus had partnered with the container mall to integrate a range of arts and hospitality offerings into the retail mix. With inspired local people involved, such a creative response would have matched anything a suburban mall could offer and gone far beyond to provide a unique meeting place in the middle.

Unfortunately, we have been left with a chasm between the small but symbolically powerful community projects of Gap Filler and company, and the very large, generic behemoths proposed in the Blueprint. The creative middle has been neglected. For example, the Arts Circus was thrown into limbo with the introduction of the Blueprint process, which involved a team of experts moving in and sidelining the project as their attention turned to a newly proposed arts project that better aligned with its precinct concept: the Performing Arts Precinct. Furthermore, the River of Arts concept appears to have been relegated to an 'Art Trail' for the Ōtākaro-Avon Precinct – hopefully this will not simply be an exercise in expensive place-faking, where a series of sculptures are lined up along the river's edge in a static, business-park style arrangement.

Ultimately, there's still time to change the road you're on. And as cities are continuously evolving, there is still hope that Christchurch might learn from the recent past and find a path that allows the various city communities – artists, businesses, architects, planners, builders and so on – to work together with local and national government. The aim should be to create a place where everyone feels a sense of kaitiaki (guardianship) because it has been created *with* and not *for* the community. This means taking more time than the product-oriented approach that seems exacerbated by the party-political process, where the scale of thinking is restricted to three-year cycles that are peppered with photo ops and catchy sound bites. But it also means the arts community (artists, organisers, managers and patrons) must make the most of this time and break its own ingrained mindset that frames art as a 'luxury' for the middle classes; rather, now is the time to seek out the radical, emancipatory potential that seriously engaged art can play in shaping the form and content of an engaging twenty-first century city that we all feel excited about living in.

CCC Transitional City Projects Fund

To encourage and enable a community-led recovery, Christchurch City Council supports transitional projects by offering advice, facilitation, interim use of land and two funds established in 2012. Both funds focus on developing partnerships, building community capacity and supporting the retention of creative and innovative talent.

The Transitional City Projects Fund broadens opportunities for people to lead vacant space projects, building on support provided to Gap Filler and Greening the Rubble since late 2010, and to Life in Vacant Spaces since 2012. Projects explore Christchurch's identity, improve people's connection with the recovery and improve amenity in vacant spaces within commercial areas. Grant cycles run at least every eight weeks, which enables projects to develop in a short time frame. Longer-term arts development is supported by the Creative Industries Support Fund.

[1–4]

[5–7]

[8–10]

[11–14]

Developing the arts ecology of Christchurch

Melanie Oliver

Melanie Oliver is a writer and curator, and is currently the director of The Physics Room, a contemporary art space in Christchurch.

According to central government's Christchurch Central Recovery Plan (CCRP), 'fostering the arts and creative industries is crucial to building a 21st century international city'.[1] Cultural revitalisation is highlighted as critical for both community wellbeing and the prosperity of the city. In order to achieve this vibrant arts culture, four major arts institutions are proposed for the central city: two new, Te Puna Ahurea Cultural Centre and the Performing Arts Precinct; and two extant, the Christchurch Art Gallery and the Arts Centre of Christchurch. Yet it is hard to see how these large institutions alone will develop a thriving, diverse arts culture.

The plan includes few incentives to support artists, smaller arts organisations or the creative initiatives that have proven to be so vital over the past three years, and there has been little attempt to incorporate dynamic models or responsive processes into the bigger picture. Large institutions provide stability and other aspects fundamental to healthy arts infrastructure, but the lack of consideration for how a range of different arts organisations may operate more collaboratively into the future misses the opportunity to create a more innovative and effective arts ecology for the city. From small dealer spaces to grassroots initiatives, there are a variety of experimental arts practices that could inform the arts' and the city's recovery.

The planned response for regenerating the arts

Although it is over three years since the major quakes and eighteen months since the Blueprint was launched, there is still a lack of strategic vision or detailed information regarding the four key arts institutions outlined in the CCRP. This makes it difficult to draw any substantial conclusions, but it seems the new venues will follow traditional models. Te Puna Ahurea Cultural Centre is intended to showcase and celebrate Ngāi Tahu, Māori and Polynesian arts and culture, and this reflects positively on the effectiveness of the Christchurch City Council (CCC) consultation process. Despite this valuable recognition of Ngāi Tahu through a dedicated space, there has been a lack of ongoing public discussion around its development. With a focus on providing an experience for international visitors, it could become a cultural heritage tourist venture, unlikely to support contemporary arts and performance practices.

The Performing Arts Precinct is similarly vague and appears to be designed for profitable, traditional forms of performance rather than acknowledging the possibility for contemporary, collaborative or interdisciplinary practices.

The plan states that this precinct will offer facilities for theatre, music, dance and other expressive forms. By maintaining a discipline focus and proposing to house three existing arts organisations – the Court Theatre, Christchurch Symphony Orchestra and Music Centre of Christchurch – an opportunity to integrate a broader vision of how different artists and organisations might utilise such a resource is missed.

There are flexible, multi-purpose models that could be followed (such as Carriageworks in Sydney or the Court Theatre's current home, The Shed), yet, without consulting a range of stakeholders to create a more ambitious strategic vision, the precinct will be a large-scale venue for facilitating conventional performing arts. Furthermore, the funding for the precinct is to be reallocated from the insurance claim for the damaged Christchurch Town Hall. With most of the funds needed to restore this important heritage building, there is not a large amount left with which to develop a major building project.[2] Instead of attempting to generate a thriving arts culture through only large-scale venues (with limited funding), taking a more pragmatic and lateral approach could generate an exciting, dynamic space for performing arts that allows for organic growth into the future.

The two existing institutions included in the recovery plan reflect this lateral vision: both have become more responsive as a result of the earthquakes. The Christchurch Art Gallery had to adopt a more ephemeral, project-based approach, since the gallery building remains inaccessible to the public while major repair work is completed. The gallery initiated 'Outer Spaces', a series of events and exhibitions in unconventional sites or temporary venues throughout the city. While this is not particularly radical or unusual for a gallery forced to operate off-site, the team managed to generate an interesting programme under challenging new conditions, and it is likely they will incorporate aspects of their experience when they return to the gallery.

The other large existing organisation included in the CCRP, the Arts Centre of Christchurch, has signalled a refreshing shift in focus. According to Chief Executive André Lovatt, the emphasis will be less on tourism and international visitors than it was prior to the earthquakes, and the aim is to create a place for arts, crafts, hospitality and entertainment that local residents will frequent. As a collection of heritage buildings that can house many different organisations and initiatives, this has the potential to become an active cultural hub. In comparison to the old-fashioned approach of the Performing Arts Precinct and Te Puna Ahurea Cultural Centre, the Arts Centre has signalled that adaptability will remain a key value into the future.

The need for collaboration in a healthy arts ecology

Aside from these four key initiatives, none of the smaller existing arts organisations in Christchurch, like the Jonathan Smart Gallery or The Physics Room, were mentioned in the plan. Large institutions are obviously important to consider since they involve significant financial investment, but there seems to be a lack of understanding around the arts ecology of a city, and how artists and smaller arts organisations also play a critical role in a healthy arts infrastructure. Discussion around how diverse arts organisations inform this vision is crucial, for without a more holistic overview of the art scene, it is difficult to generate a coherent plan, share information or work in a complementary way.

A narrow audit of the arts in Christchurch was apparently undertaken for internal use by CERA (the Canterbury Earthquake Authority), but this should have been comprehensive, public and conducted as a tool to identify common needs and developments that could then inform the CCRP. In such an unusual and dynamic environment, communication among arts organisations and institutional bodies has been challenging. The national funding body Creative New Zealand (CNZ) and the CCC have offered significant support through special grants for the arts and practical assistance to help get a range of organisations up and running. However, the problems facing organisations were unfamiliar (with the ramifications of insurance policies and building compliance), so assessing and supporting current activity seems more important than ever.

At the prompting of CNZ, a selection of representative arts professionals formed the advocacy group Arts Voice. The elected group has called for greater integration, collaboration, collocation, sustainability, engagement, diversity and innovation. Although Arts Voice offers a narrow perspective given the small sample of members, they have provided an articulate manifesto. Unfortunately, even this collective voice seems to have been overlooked in the plan.

Using what we have

There is no acknowledgment in the plan of what has survived or been initiated since the earthquakes, and no attempt to connect independent initiatives. That these existing relationships and collaborations have been ignored reflects the plan's lack of detailed consideration for interrelationships of the precincts and sectors, particularly in relation to the arts. The majority of the smaller existing arts projects are located on the southern side of the central city, with a cluster focused around a couple of blocks in the proposed Innovation Precinct, encompassing the NG building (tagged to be morphed into the giant new sports stadium), the Old Post Office Building, St Asaph Street and up to Moorhouse Avenue. The National Contemporary Jewellery Gallery and The Physics Room contemporary art space have been joined by Christchurch Art Gallery temporary exhibition spaces, new ventures such as Artbox, the artist-run space Room Four and the Chambers 241 studio and gallery complex. Other initiatives established themselves on the outskirts of the city: artist-run ABC Gallery in Addington and Dog Park Project Space in Waltham, and commercial dealer Jonathan Smart Gallery in Sydenham. These boutique venues generate stimulating programmes of contemporary visual arts and, while they are not major public institutions, they collectively contribute to the richness of arts and culture that remains and is burgeoning in Christchurch. These spaces are attempting to sustain the growth and development of the arts, despite many young artists leaving due to a lack of accessible studio spaces.

Simultaneously, the Innovation Precinct described in the Blueprint fails to mention the social entrepreneurial ventures that creative initiatives have founded, or the links that currently exist between industry and the arts. An example is the mutually beneficial relationship between the Enterprise Precinct and Innovation Campus (EPIC) companies and Ministry of Awesome, an organisation focused on helping people to realise a diverse range of creative projects.

The Commons is another hub for creativity within the central city and demonstrates the importance of interrelationships, collocation and collaboration for a healthy arts sector. Creative urban regeneration leaders coexist on this site in a series of small buildings that house the offices for Gap Filler, public space brokers Life in Vacant Spaces and other such initiatives. The architectural Arcades Project was also erected on this site and for the past couple of years Gap Filler's bright blue Pallet Pavilion provided public visibility and a gathering or performance venue. Consolidating the creative energy of these grassroots initiatives, this site is the heart of the dynamic transitional movement that has garnered Christchurch attention internationally.

The need to incorporate dynamic new responses

Over the last few years, grassroots initiatives have provided innovative cultural responses crucial to Christchurch's cultural wellbeing. Since immediately after the earthquakes, creative individuals and groups have generated small temporary interventions throughout the city, including a library in an old fridge, gardens planted in the rubble, a minigolf course and the Dance-O-Mat that plays music on a coin-operated system. These simple yet inspirational projects harnessed community spirit and collective action in the wake of the quakes, and continue to contribute to the vibrancy of the central city. Both the creative thinking inherent to their responses and the utilisation of the arts as a way to enliven the city, providing hope and critique, were exceptional, exciting and popular.

A new annual festival has also been instigated subsequent to the earthquakes. The Festival of Transitional Architecture (FESTA) integrates architecture, performance, visual arts, theatre, music and dance into a multidisciplinary celebration of the transitional city ethos. The two festivals staged so far have provided an interesting platform through which to consider issues of urbanism and alternative ideas for how the rebuild can progress. While based around a central project each year, LUXCITY and then Canterbury Tales, the open call for proposals allows for a broad range and scale of projects that bring the city to life in different ways.

Despite enthusiastic community participation and extensive local, national and international media coverage of these creative responses over the past three years, the significance of temporary, self-organised arts projects and their potential for long-term impact have been largely overlooked in the recovery plan. The social entrepreneurship and creativity displayed by FESTA, artists such as Mike Hewson and Liv Worsnop, art collective The Social, urban regenerators Gap Filler, Greening the Rubble, Life in Vacant Spaces, Rekindle and so on, have been widely celebrated and recognised for reenergising the central city both socially and economically. Politicians have happily claimed the cultural capital that the transitional movement has generated, but the transitional city voice and their innovative, responsive models are not considered in the CCRP.

Artist-led responses to challenging situations

Social engagement and collaborative processes are increasingly important in terms of public art. Internationally, artists and commissioning organisations have shifted away from large, permanent sculptural works towards a greater focus on ephemeral, social and participatory projects. While permanent sculpture is still included in urban planning, many artists are interested in developing site-specific and interdisciplinary works that are appropriate to an area and its community. There are plans in the CCRP for an Arts Trail to run alongside the river, but again this follows a limited concept of public art rather than providing the facility for artistic collaborations within the wider city or open-ended commissions. Sculpture can activate a space and create meaning for its public, but the process for inviting artists in this case seems to prescribe where, how and what will eventuate.

The Christchurch environment has been exceptionally challenging for the usual public art commissioning organisations. The 6th and 7th SCAPE Biennials of Art in Public Space, for example, were disrupted significantly by each of the major earthquakes and, when the events were finally presented, the artists involved struggled to compete for attention against the visually stimulating backdrop of the ravaged city. This is a unique environment for public art that demands an unusual response.

While artists and arts organisations are still grappling with how to work within this situation, these are the very individuals most skilled at exploring the unknown. Artists are constantly challenging the given conditions and experimenting with new ideas, processes and materials. A fundamental aim for art is to question, suggest alternatives and bring together concepts in unpredictable ways – to propose different potential futures. There was no inclusion of artists in the early stages of the planning and design of the city, when even small cases of consultation with artists could generate some truly innovative and unconventional ideas for enhancing the liveability of the city.

Missed opportunity for a mixed model

This is a missed opportunity to reconsider how the arts infrastructure could be developed with different values in mind – as an interrelated ecological system that encourages and supports institutions to trial new ways of working by reaching out to different communities and forging a variety of collaborations. A strong arts ecology has larger institutional spaces – those that can present and commission major new work – as well as the ability to take chances. Smaller initiatives are more nimble in this sense and, if encouraged to focus on facilitating experimental spaces for art, can make ambitious projects happen too. Grassroots transitional organisations offer an example of adaptability, and as smart, responsive projects they retain the spontaneity and action-focused attitude that is required in Christchurch currently, with provision for iteration and succession. If the diversity of the arts is valued and institutions are encouraged to interact, collaborate and learn from each other, then our arts infrastructure will consistently be robust, dynamic and relevant.

There is no single appropriate way for artists or the arts to operate in any time or place, but diversity is especially needed in this instance. The situation in Christchurch is ideal for testing new structures, allowing experimental, transitional and established institutions to coexist and intermingle in a unique way. The idea of a government-issued plan for the arts, not merely one that overlooks the majority of current activity, is problematic. Yet what if the creative approach afforded by artists and the arts were embedded within the recovery plan as an integral component, not just for cultural capital, tourism or social benefits, but in order to generate debate and challenge culture? This moment demands responsive, dynamic processes to not only foster the arts and creative industries, but also enable a more creative approach to the rebuild.

Transitional Cathedral Square

For more than two years, Cathedral Square, in the central city, was cordoned off to the public. Since the cordon was removed on 30 June 2013, many locals and tourists have returned to the Square to view the damaged Cathedral and neighbouring demolitions. The Christchurch City Council temporary ornamentation has provided information signs, public toilets, seating, planting and viewing areas to make the public experience more informative and enjoyable. The project contains transitional artworks by Chris Heaphy and Sarah Hughes, including a modern interpretation of stained glass windows using Māori motifs, a planted 'green' whare (house), and a flag wall celebrating possible futures for the city.

[1–5]

Leadership models in disaster recovery: The Louisiana experience post-Katrina

Amanda Guma, David Bowman & Robin Keegan

Amanda was the Health and Human Services Policy Director at Louisiana Recovery Authority, later the Office of Community Development. David currently serves as the Director of Strategic Initiatives and Performance Management at the Office of Community Development's Disaster Recovery Unit in the State of Louisiana. Robin has over eighteen years of experience in housing, economic development, community planning and housing programme design. She is currently leading a team of subject matter experts supporting New York State's recovery efforts from Superstorm Sandy.

This paper examines the model of coordination among various levels of leadership implemented after hurricanes Katrina and Rita hit the entire Gulf Coast of the United States in 2005. The model from one of those states, the Louisiana Recovery Authority (LRA), may offer relevant lessons in future disasters that address the challenge of centrally coordinating a range of resources to meet a variety of needs, while enabling communities to develop appropriate strategies to address their local rebuilding priorities.

Context of disaster

Louisiana has always experienced hurricanes. These major wind events are part and parcel of being a coastal state. However, in the late summer of 2005, two back-to-back storms – hurricanes Katrina and Rita – struck the Gulf Coast of the United States with unprecedented force. The storms, which made landfall within three weeks of one another on 29 August and 24 September respectively, caused damage from the eastern edge of Texas to the western coast of Florida. The entire southern half of Louisiana was devastated. In the New Orleans metropolitan area, storm surge from Katrina breached the city's levee protection system, leaving 80 per cent of the city underwater and thousands stranded. An estimated 1836 people died as a result of Hurricane Katrina, and 1.2 million people were displaced. Hurricane Katrina remains the most expensive natural disaster in the history of the United States, with a total damage estimate of $108 billion.

In times of major disaster, such as Hurricane Katrina, the tension between executing the administrative steps to access necessary funds and allowing sufficient opportunity for a robust community planning process can be particularly difficult. There is constant tension between the need to get resources out quickly and the need to rebuild in a planned and coordinated way that improves lives and fosters resilience to future disasters. The obstacles outlined below exacerbate an already cumbersome process for individuals and local governments applying for and accessing resources from the federal government. In the best of circumstances, with knowledgeable staff on the local level and a supportive administration on the federal level, the process for releasing funds often does not happen in a timely enough fashion to meet urgent recovery needs.

The US government provides disaster recovery assistance to individuals and communities through three primary agencies: the Federal Emergency Management Agency, the Small Business Administration and the Department of Housing and Urban Development. Following a disaster event, the State Governor will seek assistance from the President of the US for a federal disaster declaration, which is the formal catalyst for releasing federal support for local disaster recovery efforts. In general, funding from these agencies supports the following recovery needs:

- Federal Emergency Management Agency (FEMA): debris removal, restoration of damaged infrastructure, hazard mitigation, individual assistance for temporary rental and living expenses
- Small Business Administration: low interest loans for impacted businesses and homeowners
- Department of Housing and Urban Development (HUD): housing, community development, economic development, additional infrastructure needs and planning.

The delivery of disaster funding depends on the scale of the storm. In catastrophic disasters, the federal government may direct certain emergency operations and rebuilding from a central federal office. However, in most cases, state governments are given oversight of the funding to implement rebuilding programmes. Localities within the states rely either on direct programme implementation by the state or on a separate allocation of funding from the state to implement their own local recovery programmes. Most often it is a combination of centrally run state programmes and local allocations.

Following Katrina and Rita, the federal partners directed their funding through the states. Louisiana chose both to administer programmes at the state level and to make direct allocations to communities. Within this funding continuum, the tension of coordination amongst the various levels of government and the prioritisation of local choice becomes the central challenge.

Common recovery obstacles

During disaster recovery, the ultimate challenge to address is: how to ensure that communities and citizens have the ability to identify and address recovery priorities utilising best practices for long-term resiliency? This is particularly challenging given the centralised nature of recovery resources and the associated inherent obstacles. These obstacles can be categorised into four major areas:

- lack of expertise at the federal, state and local levels to respond and recover
- lack of capacity at the local level (especially in heavily impacted areas that are still in response mode or where key actors may still be displaced from their homes)
- competing priorities of federal, state and local entities
- political relationships that are not conducive to ensuring progress.

Lack of expertise

The lack of know-how is a reality for the federal government, as well as state and local implementing bodies. At the federal level, the rules that regulate the resources and programmes for small-scale disasters were misplaced in the aftermath of a catastrophic disaster. No single entity at the federal, state or local levels had sufficient expertise to respond to the scale of the 2005 disaster, resulting in delays in getting resources on the ground.

Following hurricanes Katrina and Rita, there was no playbook, or comparable experience from which to draw guidance for officials across the levels of government. For local governments, in particular, it is generally not practical or economically feasible to maintain disaster expertise in preparation for catastrophic disasters that only occur every century. While state and local governments looked to their federal partners for assistance, the federal partners waited for the local and state governments to tell them what they needed. At the time of Hurricane Katrina, however, there was no 'menu' of assistance to choose from, making it virtually impossible for local and state governments to even know what options were available to them.

Lack of capacity

Although planning is generally done at the local level, local capacity varies widely. Local organisations are typically knee-deep in disaster response while they are being asked to determine their long-term recovery needs. Staff that have the capacity to understand federal requirements may not be available immediately following a disaster, due to displacement or other immediate response duties. Depending on the tax base and size of the community, they may even lack the capacity during non-disaster periods for adequate long-term planning. Permit and land use offices can be quickly overwhelmed by disaster needs, and records and systems may have been destroyed. In these cases, additional assistance from state and federal sources is critical to assist local agencies in accessing resources.

Competing priorities

Federal, state and local agencies often have different priorities that can hamper recovery. Federal agents are often most concerned that recovery resources will be spent within 'programme guidelines'. They can tend to be risk-averse and want to make sure that they are not responsible for any public dollars being 'misspent'. This can cause significant delays in the time that money comes available to local governments to impact recovery. On the other hand, states and localities tend to be very concerned about how the disaster will impact budgets – and will want to move quickly to put resources in place to fill urgent needs. For example, local governments tend to be responsible for infrastructure such as roads, drainage, sewer lines etc., while housing repair and replacement is typically the responsibility of individual homeowners or property managers. Therefore, following a disaster local governments tend to prioritise allocating resources and developing programmes for infrastructure rebuilding over housing repair.

An example of the tension between federal and local recovery priorities encountered in Louisiana was the Alternative Housing Pilot Program. As a result of Hurricane Katrina, the size and scope of housing destruction demanded multiple strategies and solutions that required a centralised execution. When the primary temporary housing option offered by the federal government (commonly referred to as 'FEMA trailers') presented unexpected health and safety concerns, the LRA worked quickly to design and implement an alternative housing programme, which sought to create safer, more durable housing structures for displaced residents. This programme faced significant delays in launching, primarily because the federal agency involved could not easily adapt to a creative model.

Political relationships

While generally disasters tend to remind us of our common humanity, politics can come into play, especially when election cycles are involved. Poor political relationships, particularly where there is a lack of trust, can have a negative influence on expediting relief and recovery. Tension between parties or politicians can lead to decisions based on who will look successful (or not successful) and how that will affect political perceptions. The challenge of any recovery authority is to mediate the politics and ensure that all involved are focused on impacted communities and citizens.

The Louisiana model

Given the unique nature of recovery, different mechanisms are needed for different scales of disaster. Following Hurricane Katrina, each of the states along the Gulf Coast implemented its own structure for the rebuilding process. While some states centralised the response within the governor's office and had little in the way of public participation, others, like Louisiana, set up authorities to govern the policies and implementation of the federal recovery funding.

Leadership and structure

In Louisiana, the governor at the time, Kathleen Babineaux Blanco, established the Louisiana Recovery Authority to oversee the many facets of recovery. Modelled after a similar authority created in New York City after 11 September, the LRA was established to provide a non-partisan, non-political response to the recovery and rebuilding process. The overarching purpose of the LRA was to oversee the recovery, advocate to the federal government to secure the needed resources and to cut through bureaucratic red tape, and develop recovery and rebuilding policies and strategies. The structure included civic leaders who represented communities throughout the impacted regions and across the state, which allowed the LRA to break down some of the political obstacles that may have further impeded recovery. It also provided a venue for public input to the recovery process. In order to manage the scope of the rebuilding effort, the LRA established committees to focus on key recovery areas, including infrastructure, housing, economic development, transportation, environment and human services. A small staff (which included the authors) with specialised expertise was hired to support the decision-making of the board and to provide daily facilitation between the various levels of government.

Coordination and prioritisation of resources

The LRA's mission was to rebuild safer, stronger and smarter – while remaining a responsible steward of public resources. The LRA developed priorities based on best practices and input from national experts, local communities and residents. The agency was positioned to assess damages and needs across the state so that resources could be prioritised for an equitable distribution across the state. Because there would never be enough recovery funding to accomplish everything, the LRA, in concert with local leaders, had to make difficult decisions regarding priorities.

Using political clout, the LRA was able to bring federal partners together and engage leadership at the national level in order to break down some of the inherent bureaucracies and marry existing programmes with local needs. Uniquely, the LRA acted as a conduit between local governments and federal government to give voice to the needs of local communities. And importantly, in the planning process, the state participated as a facilitator of the process and a partner in implementation, but locally developed priorities were the key to its success.

Facilitation of local planning and public participation
In addition to coordination with the federal government, the LRA focused heavily on efforts to build local capacity and ensure local input and participation. Recognising gaps in local planning and project management capacity, the LRA had the ability to provide a framework for planning and implementation that included critical elements of community input and long-term resiliency. The authority identified and prioritised resources to provide that capacity. Individuals and communities needed to have a say in their own recovery. With a true commitment to public input, the LRA established a regional planning process – called Louisiana Speaks – that allowed for public input into the establishment of rebuilding priorities. While some immediate and short-term recovery priorities were better served at a macro state-led level (i.e. housing recovery, small business grants and loans), others required local decision-making. The LRA also supported local planning efforts within the twenty-six most-impacted parishes (akin to counties in the rest of the United States). In fact, each parish was required to conduct local planning in order to receive recovery funding. The authority then developed a programme, called the Long Term Community Recovery Program, which put $700 million in recovery funds directly into the hands of communities upon completion of their locally based planning efforts. These funds allowed local governments to implement the vision of their planning process and were used for a variety of purposes including the reconstruction of health facilities, land acquisition, drainage improvements and even the reimagining of streetscapes to make more walkable communities. The LRA then offered assistance as a partner to provide resources, technical assistance and grants management to the parishes in the implementation of their local plans and rebuilding projects.

The LRA also undertook one of the largest land acquisitions in the country acquiring 10,000 properties from homeowners that wanted to release their hurricane-damaged property to the state. Many of these homeowners had relocated to other areas of their parishes, or within the state, and had no interest in retaining a property that had undergone such extensive damage. The authority left the planning effort of how to return these properties to commerce within communities to the local leaders, but established the Louisiana Land Trust to then work with communities to return those properties through a careful disposition strategy that would not undermine property values within communities.

Lessons for recovery

This model may not work in every circumstance, but there are lessons that can be drawn from the work of this agency that may be helpful to other communities in the midst of recovery and rebuilding.

Communities were built back safer, smarter and stronger due to decision-making

As the third anniversary of the 2005 storms was being memorialised, Louisiana was hit by another set of powerful storms. In the first week of September 2008, hurricanes Gustav and Ike roared across the coastal areas of the state within a ten-day period. The storms hit local areas that were still in the midst of rebuilding from Katrina and Rita, and caused significant damage to central and northern Louisiana as well. In all, Hurricane Gustav impacted 43 parishes, and Hurricane Ike impacted fourteen. Together, these storms caused 51 deaths and over $1 billion in public infrastructure damage. Housing damages included over $1.7 billion in uninsured losses, with over 12,000 homes flooded and over 150,000 homes damaged. The total estimated economic losses for the 2008 storms were $5 billion.

Because of the LRA's promotion of International Building Codes, which required elevation and storm-proofing for rebuilt homes, the damage from these new storms was limited in buildings that had been rebuilt to adhere to these codes. For homeowners and other property owners who had not taken the same precautions, the picture of damage was like déjà vu to the residents of Louisiana and the Gulf Coast – homes moved off their bases, mobile homes flung into trees and fishing boats found far away from the coast.

Out of crisis comes opportunity

The scale of the disaster, the crisis of leadership at the local level and the engagement of the community in a planning process allowed for opportunity and innovation in rebuilding in New Orleans. Throughout the city, major systems had to be rebuilt, including the already fractured school system, the healthcare infrastructure and the criminal justice system, as well as large infrastructure systems, such as the investment in a $15 billion storm-protection system. These large-scale overhauls required coordinated input from the public to ensure that the new systems were rebuilt in a vision of what the city could be, not only what it was before the disaster. The decision-making was not easy and not all decisions were popular, but through these efforts New Orleans has become a leader in innovation and continues to push boundaries to be the best city it can be. The input and commitment of the public to participate in the multiple planning processes was essential to the success of the city's rebirth.

Improvement of the federal-state partnership

The LRA, through both its use of concrete data and political influence, was able to rectify the incongruous allocation of resources that initially followed

Hurricane Katrina. Through successive storms in 2008 and 2012, federal and state partnerships have improved considerably. With the more recent disaster allocations associated with Superstorm Sandy, instead of responding to political lobbying, HUD allocated resources based on very specific formulas the LRA had promoted. FEMA and HUD have begun to develop a stronger coordination around recovery programme implementation and to share information with the states in a much timelier manner. For Louisiana, the value of this enhanced level of cooperation became evident with state and local partners following the response to the British Petroleum oil spill off the coast of Louisiana in April 2010. Although the LRA did not play an official role in that recovery, it used its relationships with local governments and non-profit organisations to help them come together and structure the immediate response. At the federal government, the work to foster coordination and partnership in recovery continues. Following Hurricane Katrina, the federal government developed a National Disaster Recovery Framework (NDRF), which mandates interagency cooperation and a framework for long-term recovery planning involving agencies at the federal, state and local levels. Following recent disasters such as Superstorm Sandy, these partnerships have been put to the test for communities in the northeastern United States that are in the rebuilding process. The lessons from Katrina at the federal, state and local levels are being shared throughout this region to foster increased partnerships and speed the recovery efforts.

Conclusion

Louisiana's recovery from hurricanes Katrina and Rita is ongoing and was by no means a perfect process. However, it does offer a good model in large-scale disasters that require hard decisions based on local input. The Louisiana Recovery Authority was able to serve as catalyst, mediator and enabler of local recovery priorities. Its success was predicated by the structure of the LRA, which was non-partisan, locally and nationally connected, and well respected by the public. It provided a transparent forum for decision-making and actively engaged the impacted citizenry through a participative community planning process. In the end, the recovery was neither top-down nor bottom-up, but rather a facilitated recovery that considered both the overall needs of the region as a whole and the desire for citizens and local governments to have a say in the future of their communities.

Pallet Pavilion

Gap Filler's Pallet Pavilion (December 2012–April 2014) was a temporary community venue constructed by volunteers from 3000 CHEP pallets. It responded to a pressing need for city venues and showcased the possibilities of temporary architecture. The project hosted more than 200 events ranging from markets to live music, outdoor cinema, lectures and more. It also supported a range of food caravans and a small bar. Volunteers deconstructed the project in May and June 2014, with the pallets, crates, plants and other components being returned to previous uses or repurposed. The site is now called The Commons and is being developed for future experimental community use.

[1]

[2–6]

An EPIC view of innovation

Colin Andersen and Wil McLellan

Wil has over fifteen years of experience in the technology industry. He has co-founded several gaming studios where he created partnerships with global entertainment brands and worked with New Zealand government trade agencies. Post-quake, these relationships helped Wil create the Enterprise Precinct and Innovation Campus (EPIC) with co-founder Colin Andersen. Colin is co-founder and Executive Director of Effectus Ltd, a national IT and consulting business. Prior to Effectus, Colin was founding CEO of SQL services, growing this into an international database services organisation before completing the successful sale of the company.

What is EPIC Christchurch and why did we do it?

EPIC Christchurch (Enterprise Precinct and Innovation Campus) was created to establish a collaborative home for displaced technology companies following the Christchurch earthquakes of February 2011. After working with partners such as Google and Weta to develop the innovation hub from concept to reality, we successfully opened EPIC in November 2012. The EPIC Sanctuary building was one of the first new developments constructed in the central city red zone within the heart of Christchurch. It now houses twenty innovation-focused companies in a campus-style building with shared space environments. The campus promotes shared services for business efficiency and inter-company collaboration for new opportunity development – it provides a platform for sharing knowledge and interconnectivity.

Despite the challenging circumstances of the post-quake central city, there is no doubt that EPIC has been a success; in addition to having twenty happy tenant companies and over 250 staff housed within the campus, EPIC has become a focus for both national and international companies working on ICT and high growth tech activity within New Zealand. Economic Development Minister Steven Joyce stated in parliament in April 2012 that EPIC '. . . is a positive example of a public-private partnership that is not just about recovery; it is about encouraging new economic growth'.

In an effort to stimulate innovation, EPIC held nearly 200 public events in the first eighteen months since its opening. These have included international speakers from Google, global venture capital organisations, social networking organisations, business start-up courses and events, and engagements with education for hundreds of people.

Anyone in New Zealand can join in on EPIC events (not just the tenants), and it is this open and collaborative environment that has helped the campus really thrive. We are happy to say that we have had numerous organisations visit EPIC, from the US Embassy and the UK Prime Minister's office to the Head of Innovation for the World Bank. All of these organisations have one thing in common: they want to better understand how we can work together to build the bridges of innovation to stimulate economic growth between our countries.

How EPIC relates to the Christchurch Central Recovery Plan

Our engagements with the New Zealand government regarding the construction of EPIC were very positive. The EPIC directors focused upon asking for what was easy for both local government and central government to provide – based upon their resources and objectives. EPIC had already successfully secured tenant interest, bank support, professional advisors and underwriting required for the project. It was this progress that gave the Government the confidence to support our initiative. As such we received the use of vacant land from the Christchurch City Council (CCC) for five years, and grants totalling $1.8million from the Ministry of Science and Innovation and New Zealand Trade and Enterprise. This backing was given as EPIC met the objectives of CCC by getting displaced companies back into the city – in a safe and collaborative environment – and met the central government objectives of supporting companies focused on a mix of technology, exports and new product development – it was a win, win, win situation.

As EPIC progressed rapidly from concept to reality, we worked closely with CCC, Canterbury Earthquake Recovery Authority (CERA) and Christchurch Central Development Unit (CCDU) as we built one of the first buildings in the devastated central city. It was clear that we all had the same objective of supporting business in Christchurch and of building a brighter future for New Zealand.

It was with great anticipation that EPIC viewed the proposed Blueprint when it was first released, and we supported its concept of precincts – specifically the Innovation Precinct, which aligned strongly with our own vision. Our support was based on the premise that precincts act as focal points or hubs for people to gather, share ideas and ultimately collaborate. This is not to say that 'innovation' will not occur outside of an innovation precinct – it will occur wherever people are working to develop new products and services – but it is *facilitated* through collocation.

Our support of precincts was also based upon observations of theme parks, science and innovation parks and discussions with Google. The simple facts we focused upon are that people like experiences to be enjoyable and effortless; the access to information and services they require should be convenient. As such, in theme parks there are many zoned areas where people can access certain types of attractions – young children's areas or more adventurous rides for older children and adults and so forth. EPIC's work with Google and their property team also reinforced the value of focal points within a city and focal points within buildings. Ultimately, all of our research culminated on the value of centralising core services and drawing people to key areas where they can attend relevant events and meet likeminded individuals.

It is important to add that the use of precincts creates the risk of 'silos' of activity – where people feel isolated or excluded if they are not part of the precinct, or it's too remote. Again our research across the globe validated that innovation and science parks require strong interconnectivity both for the physical movement of people through convenient transport and routes, but also regarding awareness, lines of communication and social connectivity.

To be clear EPIC is not proposing Christchurch should be built like a theme park. The point to emphasise is that we focus on the fact that people like to know what to expect at a destination, and they like it to be convenient – the explosion in the growth of out-of-town shopping malls and the subsequent death of many central cities stands as testament to this fact.

One great example of the EPIC hub's benefits has been the support that the directors have received from nearby bars and cafes. These businesses have shown strong support for the campus – not just because of the business our 250 tenant employees bring, but the added business from people who meet with EPIC's tenants and the hundreds of people who use the venue for meetings and events. This is a complementary relationship because one of the main reasons we wanted the campus in the city was to provide food and entertainment choice to tenants and event attendees, and in doing so, contribute to the creation a vibrant central city.

Due to the success of EPIC Sanctuary (Stage 1) we experienced a rapid influx of tenant requests for a subsequent development. As such we began to explore the potential to develop a larger scale EPIC Sigma (Stage 2) within the Innovation Precinct. Yet this was to prove a challenge. Despite the zoning of precincts in the Blueprint, there was little impetus to support the development of the Innovation Precinct. Furthermore, land was still privately owned in a market where land prices were distorted and property development compromised. Some owners had raised land prices 200-300 per cent above starting values; some were waiting for an offer from the Government. As EPIC was founded on the principle of providing shared space for small to medium sized businesses focused on innovation, these land prices made any further development in the Innovation Precinct a real challenge from an economic perspective.

In short the cost of land was generating an office rental proposition that very few organisations could have justified. Our specific challenge is that innovation-focused companies need to invest in people and product and service development – not in high rent. As such innovation hubs are usually out of town or in cheap rent areas, whereas here we were attempting to find a way to build on expensive land – the maths just didn't add up. As a result many prospective tenants were forced to sign long-term lease deals outside the core city zone.

This was a very disappointing outcome for all involved, especially considering that we believe everyone involved – both those in Government and locally – was trying to do the right thing. The Government saw the value of precincts and the value of having an Innovation Precinct, which was reflected in the Blueprint, and landowners simply wanted the best price for their land.

Lessons learned

Our experience of working with both central and local government initiatives immediately after the earthquakes was very positive. Discussion and advisory groups were formed, and we engaged with city planning and industry advisory boards that felt well represented and well consulted. Importantly, these early groups and government facilitators showed strong, tangible support for business, demonstrated great enthusiasm and a positive 'can do' attitude, valued consultation, and perhaps most importantly of all demonstrated tangible action. This phase of activity leaned heavily on a major pro-bono effort of volunteers who were motivated to make a difference and be part of the recovery process.

As time progressed after the release of the Blueprint, it felt like the process for change and innovation decelerated into cycles of design, planning and administration. We appreciated that EPIC Stage 1 moved quickly because it was a short-term solution and therefore relatively easy to action. EPIC Stage 2 slowed considerably because we were looking to do something permanent – something that would influence the future face of the city.

Whilst it is accepted that rebuilding a city is no small feat, and will take many years, it appears some decision-making became entrenched in formal process, inter-departmental consultation and risk analysis. The compulsory acquisition of land and backing of key projects seems to have slowed, and the focus on precincts seems to have de-motivated rather than motivated people.

One suggestion in response to how the recovery plan's processes to date could be improved is that rather than have specific rules about what can and cannot happen within precincts, thus restricting what can be attempted, an alternative approach could be to incentivise people to work on certain developments within a precinct. Establishing overall precinct principles that guide and assist the entrepreneurs, property developers and creative locals as they evolve and create a new environment could be very powerful indeed.

The magic that EPIC has created exceeded our expectations. The campus environment and developing ecosystem is powerful: people working together and attracting new groups (both national and international) into the Canterbury and New Zealand business networks – it's heady stuff. We have proved the value of what we have created; the challenge now is to work together to make this a long-term economic driver for New Zealand, which can then be expanded and connected to other hubs of innovation across New Zealand and the globe.

There is still a long road ahead for Christchurch. The wonderful resilient, creative energy that has flourished post-earthquake must be allowed to flow if we are to build the city of tomorrow that Christchurch promises to be. EPIC is about people. People define Christchurch and New Zealand. We know from recent experience that if we work together there is nothing we cannot achieve.

Nature Play Park /
Papatākaro Ao Tūroa

Nature Play Park – a little slice of Canterbury complete with braided river – was created in a partnership between the Department of Conservation and Greening the Rubble Trust. The park was designed to encourage families to discover – through free play – what is special about Canterbury plants and wildlife, and how they can make conservation part of their urban lives as they recover from the devastating earthquakes. Interactive and exploratory, it allows for unstructured play in a 'reconstructed wilderness', a safe place for a possible first river splash, rock hop or log leap. The project challenged both organisations. It was the largest project for the Greening the Rubble Trust with excavation and construction works, and the first 'urban park' for DOC.

[1–4]

Studio Christchurch: Meeting of minds

Camia Young and Uwe Rieger

Camia Young taught the 'Future Christchurch' course (2011-2013), and conceived of Studio Christchurch in collaboration with Associate Professor Uwe Rieger. In her capacity she partnered studios and students with local projects. Uwe Rieger is the Chair of the newly formed Studio Christchurch Management Group and led the urban installation event LUXCITY.

Studio Christchurch, a collaborative research and design platform for architecture and related disciplines formed by six New Zealand tertiary institutes, emerged as a response to the earthquakes.[1] With the rebuild being New Zealand's largest construction effort in history, it became an obvious place to test a collaborative cross-institutional design programme. It was also obvious that a multi-disciplinary platform was necessary – one where a range of experts could actively engage in the rebuild by providing design propositions that contend with the relevant and challenging issues facing the city today. Studio Christchurch not only connects students' design projects with real-world outcomes, thus creating a rich educational experience that prepares young students for practice, but it also creates a collective body of knowledge from the students' projects that professionals can draw on to make informed decisions.

Figure 1: Studio Christchurch's Green Frame exhibition

A specific advantage of doing this in Christchurch is the shared agenda for an exemplary rebuild, which allows for both cross-disciplinary collaboration as well as collaboration between institutions, officials and the public. Studio Christchurch has made alliances with the profession, as well as government bodies, with the intention to support those who are making challenging design decisions by offering a platform to discuss ideas that shape the urban fabric.

Studio Christchurch work focuses on three areas: testing solutions through design, the communication of ideas through public urban events and the collection of background data. The projects produced by Studio Christchurch are different from conventional design studios, in that the work is outcome focused and has a long-term perspective. These are also the result of cross-disciplinary processes, where the individual student contributions are embedded in a way of learning and creating that builds upon one another's ideas. This means the students' projects move away from the individual and one-off outputs and become part of a collective body of knowledge that is shared with a wider public audience. The aim is to influence a collective consciousness and raise the literacy of architecture and urban design.

Figure 2: The nineteen large-scale student installations at LUXCITY attracted 20,000 visitors.

LUXCITY in October 2012, a collaboration between Studio Christchurch and the Festival of Transitional Architecture (FESTA), introduced a highly effective and engaging form of architectural communication where local bars, restaurants and clubs worked in collaboration with the design studios to create temporary sculptural venues on demolished building sites. This one-night event aimed at generating a public desire for architectural design and a returning urbanity. A total of 350 students from CPIT, Unitec, Victoria University, AUT and the University of Auckland, organised into sixteen design courses, worked for one semester on large-scale installations. The design studios utilised light and ephemeral materials in combination with large demolition machinery to present ideas for the future of the city. The City of Light brought over 20,000 people back into the vacant city centre of Christchurch. LUXCITY was selected 'Event of the Year 2012' by the Christchurch *Press*[2] and is highly regarded as an exemplary project in Christchurch's transitional period.[3] LUXCITY was both a proposal for the future and an instant realisation of urbanity, which the public shared in.

Since 2011 the School of Architecture and Planning at the University of Auckland has been running design studios at undergraduate and postgraduate levels under the title of 'Future Christchurch'. These have become an essential part of the Studio Christchurch project in that they bring with them substantial background knowledge through their research-driven approach. Future Christchurch has published seven volumes that range in focus: *V1 Research and Design*, *V2 Materials and Resources*, *V3 Economies*, *V4 Emerging Identities*, *V5 Architecture & Structure*, *V6 Questioning the Blueprint* and *V7 The Polycentric City*. The 2012 Future Christchurch Masters Thesis team of students was awarded highly commended for their research and innovative team approach at the prestigious New Zealand Institute of Architects National Student Design Awards.[4] The outcomes of the Future Christchurch Group have been presented in form of public talks and summarised in the Future Christchurch book series.[5] These generate a wide range of interest – the Canterbury Earthquake Recovery Authority (CERA), Christchurch City Council (CCC) and members of the profession and the industry have purchased these books.

Within its first year, Studio Christchurch demonstrated the effectiveness and the demand for an exchange platform within the Christchurch context. Students and tutors, as participants of this platform, actively assemble, edit and produce knowledge that moves beyond pure architectural education and towards purpose-driven, collective outcomes.

Studio Christchurch offers three unique opportunities for architecture schools and related disciplines to connect studio work with real-world issues. Firstly, it produces practice-oriented outcomes on a clear subject area that allows for transdisciplinary collaboration with a focused common goal. Because of its local engagement, Studio Christchurch attracts collaboration and knowledge sharing. Secondly, as an independent centre, Studio Christchurch has the time and people power to collect information and develop a broad range of solutions. This 'time to think' is a scarce resource amongst the professionals who are working on day-to-day deadlines. In this way the students' projects bridge the educational and professional realms and provide studies on which to make informed decisions. Finally, Studio Christchurch can effectively support students to feel confident with complex thinking and to emerge as graduates who can solve real problems through knowledge sharing and collaboration.

Christchurch today has a range of political voices contributing to the rebuild, with conflicting opinions and differing levels of power. By providing an open platform to discuss the students' ideas, Studio Christchurch removes political barriers and brings together professionals (who are otherwise bound by confidentiality agreements) to consider and critique designs for the future of the city. The students' projects are disarming in that they allow for creative conversations where professionals can share knowledge, as they do not need to refer to their own confidential projects in order to discuss design in concrete terms. As a neutral platform, Studio Christchurch can investigate different alternatives without being biased by a financial interest, a government mandate or corporate strategy – students and experts are free to explore other influences outside these confines. With a large number of partners involved, the diverse theoretical and practical starting points foster a variety of outcomes. While areas and aims of the investigations are clearly framed, the problems behind them are inherently complex. This is why the work requires the consideration of multiple perspectives, and relies on a multidisciplinary and collaborative approach.

It is important to recognise that Christchurch is in a pivotal time in its history and decisions made now of what to build where and when will come to define the city. Resources for reconstruction are limited, so it is critical to think strategically about what types of construction could attract further investment, and what projects are more likely to act as catalysts for growth than others. Studio Christchurch addresses these issues through investigations and aims to provide a knowledge base on which professionals can make informed decisions.

Temple for Christchurch

The Temple for Christchurch drew its inspiration from the annual Burning Man arts festival held in the Black Rock Desert of Nevada, USA, where a temple has been built and burned each of the last thirteen years. A number of people who had been to Burning Man and its New Zealand counterpart Kiwiburn felt strongly that the cathartic process of the temple experience would be of benefit to the local community after the traumatic earthquakes. The design was the brainchild of Hippathy Valentine who took seismic data from the main 22 February aftershock and interpreted it to form a three-dimensional representation of the quake.

[1–6]

Shock of the view

Rebecca Macfie

Rebecca is a senior writer for the *Listener*. Since starting out in journalism in 1988 she has written for the *Christchurch Star*, *Press*, *National Business Review*, *Independent Business Weekly*, *North&South*, *Unlimited magazine* and *NZ Herald*. She lives in Christchurch. In 2013 she wrote *Tragedy at Pike River Mine: How and Why 29 Men Died*, about the 2010 mine explosion on New Zealand's West Coast. An abbreviated version of this article was first published in the *Listener* in April 2014.

Owen Dippie's ballerina took shape like a giant orb of blue light in the dying days of a soggy Christchurch autumn.

Week by week the Tauranga artist worked in sweeps of his spray can to shape her slender arms and hands, form the curve of her collar bones and shoulder muscles, bring detail to her ruffled headdress, and fill her tutu with movement.

Pushing on towards her completion through a bleak southerly, he pulled his hoodie up over his mop of curls and kept working on his vast concrete canvas from high on his cherry picker.

Enormous – at 25 metres in diameter she covers almost the entire back wall of the Isaac Theatre Royal – yet delicate, the ballerina's finished form towers over an archetypal Christchurch foreground of portacoms, builders' utes, hazard boards, security fences and broken concrete.

She is visible in bright glimpses from blocks away through a thicket of traffic cones, road closure signs and an endless haze of hurricane wire fences.

In a shaken city where art has taken to the streets and where the surprising and fleeting have become the norm, her soaring beauty amid the rubble is at once completely startling and utterly ordinary.

Directly across the road, the former PriceWaterhouse building – once the city's premier high-rise – has been reduced to a large hole in the ground where the underground car park used to be. A couple of decoy ducks bob in its pool of fetid water, apparently anchored to the spot by someone determined to bring a dash of humour to the cavernous site. Traffic cones submerged just beneath the water's surface look at first glance like giant goldfish.

The stumps of the building's concrete columns sprout rusting reinforcing steel like unkempt whiskers. In the reflected beauty of the ballerina, it's possible to see the broken remnants of what was once a closed shop of commercial endeavour as a daring public sculpture.

A temporary pocket garden on a vacant block of land at the end of New Regent Street offers a more serene perspective of the ballerina. Here, the Canterbury Horticultural Society teamed up with landscape architect Robert Watson and Life in Vacant Spaces – a post-quake brokerage service that matches desolate sites and empty buildings with community projects and start-up businesses – to form Alhambra Gardens, a quiet outdoor room of simple wooden seating, potted maples and olives, and flowering annuals.

On the bare wall behind, decades-old cursive script – exposed by the demolition of the building that once stood here – advertises the business of Petersen's Limited Jewellers. Further down the wall, Rita Angus's 'Portrait of O'Donnell Moffett' casts an innocent young gaze across the flattened city. The photographic replica is part of the Christchurch Art Gallery's 'Faces from the Collection' project, undertaken as part of its post-quake effort to populate the city with art that would otherwise be locked away in the still-closed city gallery.

All this might all be gone next week, next month or next year. The seating, plants and art are designed to be taken away, swapped for something else, reassembled elsewhere in a different form – although Dippie's ballerina will hopefully remain visible for years to come. Neil Cox, chief executive of the Isaac Theatre Royal, which commissioned the painting as part of the three-month RISE street art festival, says a car park is destined for the empty plot in front (now owned by the Government as part of a proposed Performing Arts Precinct), and he hopes it will be a low-rise structure that won't blot out the painting.

Just as Dippie was putting the last touches on his work, a couple of blocks away on the former site of the expansive Crowne Plaza hotel dozens of orange-vested volunteers were in the throes of dismantling the most ambitious temporary installation yet seen in post-quake Christchurch. The hugely successful Pallet Pavilion – an open-air performance and meeting space built entirely by volunteers from 3000 blue pallets, and landscaped with hundreds of potted natives – was coming down.

This plot of Christchurch City Council-owned land, where once stood the landmark Warren and Mahoney-designed hotel, has been renamed The Commons by those who use it: Gap Filler, the urban activist group that has been involved in 35 different projects in the last year, including the Pallet Pavilion; eateries and cafes operating out of caravans; a 3-D prototyping outfit named Makercrate that works from a container; a Gap Filler-designed mini-golf course.

Marching across the site are the Arcades, a temporary structure comprised of six-metre-high laminated timber arches, created last year as part of the annual post-quake Festival of Transitional Architecture (FESTA). They lend shape to the site, create a pedestrian linkage between Victoria Park at one end and Victoria Street at the other, and are designed to be reconfigured, uplifted and set down somewhere else at a later date.

The Pallet Pavilion was bid farewell with a final concert on a wet Saturday night in April with a rowdy and rhythmic percussion performance by the Deconstruction Orchestra (temporarily put together for the night), featuring tin drums, glockenspiel, angle grinders and empty water containers. Gap Filler's Coralie Winn urged the sold-out crowd of 200 not to grieve the end of the pavilion. Thanks to a crowdfunding effort that raised $82,000 to help cover the site's 24-hour security requirements (the fire service was terrified the place would go up like a stack of kindling), it had already stayed for a year longer than originally intended.

For eighteen months, the ordinary stuff of everyday life – storage pallets, vegetable crates, recycled concrete foundation slabs, electrical conduit – had been stored as temporary architecture and served as a venue for 250 entertainment and community events. Now, said Winn, it was time to take it apart and despatch the constituent parts to other users – the pallets and crates will go back to the multinational logistics company CHEP where they have many more years of functional life ahead of them, the concrete slabs will go to farmers who need them to get cows across creeks, the plants will go to community groups or be returned to the nurseries that loaned them.

The site will be landscaped and another project will be hatched for next summer. 'Gap Filler was never set up to run venues long term,' says the indefatigable Winn, an Australian who has made Christchurch home. 'Our mission is to be the tester of new ideas.'

Across what was once Christchurch's central business district – a zone of apocalyptic destruction where 80 per cent of buildings have been demolished – hotspots of creativity and experimentation are bringing life and colour where otherwise there would be none. The Re:START shopping centre, built from artfully-arranged and painted shipping containers, is on the move to a new site, having demonstrated by prototype the kind of urban form that suits the Christchurch climate. It's doubtful that, after Re:START, anyone will ever again build the shaded wind-tunnels of old; instead, there will be compact, sunny and sheltered nooks where people can eat, talk and linger.

The temporary cardboard Cathedral, designed by renowned Japanese architect Shigeru Ban and located opposite the site of the CTV Building that killed 115 people, draws a steady stream of grave-faced tourists. Meanwhile the decaying corpse of the badly-damaged Christ Church Cathedral in the Square is screened off by elaborately detailed hoardings, and can be viewed from the inside of a plant-covered whare created by artist Chris Heaphy. An enormous wall of 648 coloured flags, created by artist Sara Hughes, flutters over the Square. Hughes says her installation is intended to 'blow optimism and good will into the site'.

A stone's throw away, on the otherwise barren corner of Colombo and Gloucester Streets, artist Julia Morison has created Tree Houses for Swamp Dwellers, a SCAPE Public Art project. The timber structures can be sat on, played under and walked through. A fusion of art and architecture, it stands as a thing of grace and survival against the broken brick building on the neighbouring site. Modular and relocatable, it is destined to be moved at intervals to other spots in need of regeneration.

The re-engineered washing machine and dance floor that has served as Gap Filler's moveable Dance-O-Mat for three years is on the adjacent site. Opposite is another temporary parklet, furnished with gigantic street furniture installed by the city council, a garden created by Greening the Rubble and musical instruments hewn by artists from old fire extinguishers, steel tubes and various bits of wood and wire.

Down in High Street, much of which still looks as if it has been the target of sustained aerial bombing, a relocatable shed is home to RAD (Recycle a Dunger) Bikes, where volunteers help all-comers build bikes from the discarded parts of old ones. Further along, a tiny community garden dubbed Agropolis is taking shape where once stood the city's trendiest laneways, on vacant land designated under the Government's central city Blueprint as part of a proposed Innovation Precinct. On an exposed brick wall across the street there's a giant replica of Tony Fomison's painting, *No!*, placed there by the Christchurch Art Gallery. Almost as soon as the piece went up (admittedly over part of a tagger's signature), the tagger returned with a competing message: 'Keep your shit art 4 the galleries xx.' There was some discussion about whether the tagger's work should be removed, but it was decided that it ought to be left. 'I quite liked the engagement,' says the gallery's Jenny Harper. 'And we didn't think Tony Fomison would have minded.'

It would be tempting to categorise all this creative energy as the work of a few enthusiasts to pretty up the rubble and keep the tourists amused – although it does serve that function too. The emergence of temporary installations and vibrant street art has won the endorsement of Lonely Planet, and put Christchurch at Number 2 on the *New York Times'* list of 'Places to Go in 2014'. If not for the likes of Gap Filler, Greening the Rubble, Re:START, the cardboard cathedral, FESTA (which has drawn tens of thousands of people into the centre of Christchurch with its annual extravaganzas of experimental architecture and performance) and the efforts of the Christchurch Art Gallery to continue bringing art to the community despite the closure of the gallery, there would be nothing but a dusty grey desert for the tourists to see.

It would be tempting, too, to write it all off as a short term diversion to keep the locals distracted while the government attends to the serious stuff – in particular, the central city Blueprint which remains, in large measure, a glossy wishlist of mega-facilities with neither clear budgets nor proven public support.

But there is much more to it than that. Often defiant, sometimes anarchic, often beautiful and frequently garish, temporary architecture and street art is providing one of the few substantive ways to influence how the city recovers from the disaster. Just as the tagger contested the art gallery's positioning of Fomison's *No!*, the flourishing community of urban activists and creatives is contesting the unilateral power of the government to impose a central city rebuild plan dominated by a massive convention centre, costly covered rugby stadium and neatly-ordered business 'precincts'.

Architectural historian and FESTA director Jessica Halliday:

> It's about defiance against the situation and context. The reality is that Christchurch is still a hard place to live. Yet these projects give you energy, and an outlet for your hopes and dreams. And right now it is one of the few ways that quite ordinary citizens can feel part of the remaking of the city. Because a lot of the time we feel we haven't been invited in and consulted and we haven't been part of the process. So this is our way of saying, actually, we are part of the remaking of the city whether you officially ask us or not.

Graphic designer and artist Holly Ross did just that, launching an audacious street art project late last year. Twenty-nine-year-old Ross joined with a couple of friends to form From The Ground Up, which orchestrated a short, sharp flurry of activity in which 30 street artists from Christchurch and around the country created twenty huge public wall paintings in a week. Her goal was simple: 'There were a lot of blank walls around that needed to be brightened up.'

No one was paid – the project relied entirely on sponsorship, the goodwill of building owners and hard work. Ross believes such a project simply wouldn't have happened pre-quake, and nor would the public reception have been so positive.

Some works might vanish when the buildings they are on are demolished; others will become hidden behind new buildings. No matter, says Ross – street art is meant to be temporary. Inspired by the favela-painting movement that aims to strengthen communities in the ghettos of Rio de Janiero, she hopes to lead another project this year in a community still struggling in the aftermath of the quakes.

To George Shaw's eyes, something remarkable is happening in Christchurch. He perceives that the place has been tipped upside down by the quakes not just physically, but socially. His view is that of an outsider – he and his partner Shannon Webster moved from the UK to Nelson with their large personal collection of Banksy street art four and a half years ago. In collaboration with Christchurch urban development group the Ministry of Awesome, they brought their RISE street art festival to the city over the summer. Owen Dippie's ballerina was the last in a series of 'big wall' works to be produced by visiting and local artists as part of the festival.

The exhibition of Banksy and other international street artists was hosted at the Canterbury Museum and drew record crowds – almost a quarter of a million people visited over three months. 'That's staggering, unbelievable,' says Shaw. Proportional to the population, he says, that's a bigger turnout than when Banksy staged a high-profile 100-work show in his home town of Bristol in 2009.

'There is an energy in Christchurch that we love,' says Shaw. 'All the artists that came to the city loved it as well, and felt that energy hugely.'

So taken with this strange, broken yet energetic place that he and his family plan to come and live, and will install their Banksy collection as a permanent Christchurch exhibition and develop RISE as an even larger event.

While the context for all this is peculiar to Christchurch's post-quake upheaval, Halliday stresses it also reflects a well-established movement. Tactical urbanism, adaptive urbanism, transitional architecture, placemaking – it goes by a variety of loose-fitting names. Broadly, it is about experimental projects that bring life to decrepit spaces and trial new patterns of pedestrian, cycle and vehicle movement, and the use of art and architecture to engage communities in the development of their own shared spaces.

So, for example, Times Square in New York was experimentally closed to traffic against a howl of disbelief; since then, the decision has been made to permanently pedestrianise it. A global movement involving the positioning of painted pianos in public places, called 'Play me, I'm yours', has spread across 43 cities, with 1300 pianos installed in bus shelters, parks, markets and train stations. Anyone may sit and play them. In Manchester, artists have been encouraged to take up residence in cheap buildings in the rundown Northern Quarter, in a bid to stimulate economic renewal.

'Other fully functioning cities actually have the transitional as a component of what they do, because transitional is cheap and flexible and you can involve the community,' says the Christchurch City Council's Urban Design and Regeneration unit manager, Carolyn Ingles. It's a concept that the council has embraced since the earthquakes. It has allocated funding to support Gap Filler, Greening the Rubble and Life in Vacant Spaces; supported the establishment of temporary exhibition spaces including ArtBox, a system of modular, relocatable steel-framed boxes; and commissioned a swathe of temporary installations to enliven the battered streetscape.

'We recognise that artists are early movers,' says Ingles. 'In places like Manchester and Berlin they've had cheap buildings to work with. We have to think differently in Christchurch because the buildings aren't there, and so it's about the use of space.'

While the powerful Canterbury Earthquake Recovery Authority and the CCDU have done little to facilitate such transitional projects – putting an installation or running a project on the immense acreage of central city land acquired by the government for the big Blueprint projects is a bureaucratic nightmare – there are tiny signs the community of urban activists has begun to have some influence.

Halliday says Agropolis – 'such a modest yet important project' – was set up to spur a conversation about the role of edibles in the city as it rebuilds. Now, all of a sudden, the CCDU is talking about including community gardens as part of a planned zone of inner city residential housing in the East Frame.

The Arcades project, intended to stay for only a year or two on the former Crowne Plaza site, has since taken the fancy of the CCDU, which wants it kept there for several more years while its big-ticket Avon River Precinct – a park-like promenade along a 3.2 kilometre stretch of the river – is gradually developed.

But there is a danger that all of this will be seen as an alibi for the 'real' rebuild, rather than a genuine chance for people to shape and influence the way their city develops – 'to build a community from the inside out' - as George Parker, a trustee of FESTA and long-time member of Christchurch's Free Theatre, puts it.

Mike Reynolds shares a similar fear. Reynolds, whose family lost their home and jobs in the central city after the quakes, worries that the social entrepreneurship and innovation led by the likes of Gap Filler is pigeon-holed as transitional, and that 'at some point in the future . . . someone will decide that the transitional period has finished. Does that spell the end of this amazing outburst of creativity and community engagement, or is there a way that we can start to incorporate these things in a more permanent sense within our city?'

To the plethora of urban activist movements born since the quakes, Reynolds has recently added another. He and his wife Rose launched Brave New City at the end of March, aiming to build a foundation of supporters to 'put the human experience back at the centre of the conversation about how the city is rebuilt'.

Instead of a rebuild dictated by a government blueprint whipped up in secret in 100 days, Reynolds aims to provoke public conversations through urban design experiments and community-centred events that will influence the way the city is reconstructed. 'We need to make CERA and the city council's job easier by helping to demonstrate what the public wants, and what is feasible.

'I'm a passionate Christchurch citizen and I'm not willing to sit back and let this city be the place that missed its chance. We have the opportunity to create an amazing place to live, but I feel every day that opportunity is slipping through our fingers. It's not all about the buildings. We're talking about the stuff in between – how we live in the city, how people emotionally connect with the city, how we relate to each other, how we move around the city – those have got to be the priorities in building a new city.'

Chapter 8

———

Building Back Better

———

Me whakapai ake, ka tika

The chapter title Building Back Better might seem self-explanatory, but does it come with an exclamation or a question mark? Will new necessarily entail better? Are the processes by which we are putting the city back together also being improved? If we invest cleverly now, will we save ourselves – and the cash-strapped council – money in the long run?

The rebuild is an opportunity not just to reshape a city, but also – and perhaps more importantly – to reassess the frameworks in which we allow commerce and communities to grow. The definition of 'better' is contested, and hard to reach consensus on. For a commercial tenant, better may mean a new build that exceeds the required code, has lower energy costs and is closer to clients; for a community group, it may mean a simple build in the right location that is readily accessible for a wide range of users. For a couple with a young family, better might be a well-insulated house that costs less to heat, is close to a bus route and is walking distance from the local school. A city might become better not only by its built environment, but by the community and cultural amenities – yet these social factors seem to get much less attention than do the concrete aspects of the city.

Post-quake Christchurch has been described as a once in a lifetime situation, but this opportunity comes with opportunity cost and the duty to continually assess the (lost potential) value of all the paths not taken. The term 'betterment' is one that has joined the post-quake lexicon. Depending on the details of the policy, many insurance companies will pay for like-for-like replacement, but not for betterment. It would be much cheaper to add cycling infrastructure when resealing the roads, for instance. But a policy might require the roads to be returned to pre-2011 condition – after which Council will have to pay more to dig them up again if they want to add new cycle lanes. Being better isn't always easy. It certainly isn't cheap. In this chapter, we look at the challenges encountered in the face of improvement, and the smart ways that people are looking to overcome them.

Shaping cities, shaping health

Skye Duncan

Skye is an international urban design consultant and teaches at Columbia University's Graduate School of Architecture, Planning and Preservation, where she studied as a Fulbright Scholar. She is currently Senior Urban Designer at the NYC Department of City Planning, Office of the Chief Urban Designer, where she has worked on a number of large-scale site specific projects that look to improve the health, sustainability and resiliency of New York's built fabric.

How can Christchurch's recovery shape our health through a great footpath experience?

As we consider shaping urban environments for future generations, it becomes difficult to ignore the fact that today the children entering this world, for the first time in centuries, are being projected to have a shorter life expectancy than their parents.[1] Accounting for over 60 per cent of deaths globally each year,[2] chronic diseases – such as heart disease, stroke, cancer, chronic respiratory diseases, obesity and diabetes – present some of the most common, costly and preventable health problems we are faced with. These are often called diseases of energy, relating to the imbalance of our energy intake (through unhealthy diets) and our energy output (physical inactivity), and along with other factors such as tobacco and harmful use of alcohol, these four leading risk factors account for 80 per cent of the deaths related to chronic diseases.[3]

Energy in:
FOOD

Energy out:
PHYSICAL ACTIVITY

Figure 1: Chronic diseases account for over 60 per cent of global deaths, and often relate to the imbalance of our energy intake and our energy output.

According to the UN-Habitat, 70 per cent of the global population is expected to be living in cities by the year 2050, meaning the decisions we make with regards to the policies and designs that shape these urban environments will have a significant impact on the quality of life offered by each place. How we shape the buildings, streets, infrastructure, footpaths and public realm in places like Christchurch will determine how enjoyable the city is to live in and how healthy the lifestyles offered are. Where each city chooses to invest its money and what it prioritises will inform (among other things) how easily people can access affordable housing, healthy food, parks and nature; which modes of transport are most efficient and enticing to use; and of course how enjoyable and easy it is to walk. How we shape our cities in terms of such considerations can contribute to how physically active a city's population is, and in turn the overall health of our future communities.

As Christchurch works to recover from the devastating events of 2011, it presents a rare and exciting chance to develop a comprehensive vision for the future of the city. With this unbelievable opportunity, however, comes a responsibility to learn from past mistakes, to rebuild the good, and to fix the bad. To save reinventing the wheel, cities should borrow and adapt ideas and best practices from each other, morphing relevant applications to the local conditions and context. At some point the decisions need to be made as to whether to build back exactly what was lost, to build back *better* and *stronger* in a way that meets known best practices, or to try to build back in a manner that goes *above and beyond*, setting new global precedents and lifting the bar in the world competition of the greatest, most liveable and walkable city.

Each city around the world is unique but, regardless of context, or of how visionary a future vision is, a comprehensive and safe network of walking infrastructure – the footpaths – should provide the fundamental bones to any city. These are a city's most democratic spaces, the places that can be most equitably inhabited within the built fabric, and they provide the lifeblood that connects neighbourhoods together. Like our cities at large, footpaths are fundamentally places for *people*. It is from this perspective – of the person inhabiting the city footpath – that people experience their everyday city, that a neighbourhood's identity will be read, that the citizens' pride will be shaped and that the long-term future success of any rebuilding processes will ultimately be judged. It is also from the footpaths that the health and wellbeing of the many billions of people within our ever-increasing urbanised areas can be shaped.

Walking is one of the most fundamental, affordable and equitable forms of physical activity, and a great form of sustainable non-carbon emitting transportation. Most people like to walk, and they want to walk, but if it is not an accessible and easy option, they are less likely to do so. With large portions of the population not reaching the minimum daily recommended physical activity levels, opportunities for incorporating even small ten-minute bouts of physical activity spread throughout the day can work toward reaching the suggested 150 minutes of moderate-intensity activity per week.[4] Within urban environments, it is generally the comprehensive network of constructed footpaths that provides the primary form of infrastructure facilitating our impetus to actually *choose* to walk as part of our daily routines.

While a global movement between the design of the urban environment and the health of its inhabitants is growing and awareness increasing, this relationship is not at all new. In the late 1800s many overcrowded urban conditions, combined with inadequate systems for water, sanitation and sewerage, led to major epidemics of infectious diseases such as tuberculosis, cholera and yellow fever. The response to these health challenges of the time was in fact through policy and design moves that shaped physical cities. In New York City (NYC), for example, new water aqueducts, Central Park, the subway and a new sanitation department helped to provide relief from the density, offering a cleaner, safer environment. Building and zoning codes simultaneously ensured light and air could access the streets and buildings, while segregating toxic land uses. The results were that infectious disease rates dropped from 57.1 per cent in 1880 to 11.3 per cent in 1940, noting that this drop of over 45 percentage points was before the widespread use of antibiotics – and since then, infectious disease rates have only dropped minimally to 9 per cent today.[5]

With advances in technology and shifting trends in neighbourhood and city planning, the following century brought with it many additional changes to the design of our physical urban environments. Among other factors, increased highway construction, easier access to personal automobiles and abundant cheap fuel fostered a shift of population from central cities (perceived as being infected and diseased) towards the growing suburbs with their promises of vast green lawns and bright blue skies. There have been many great innovations that have been undoubtedly beneficial to society, but with these drastic changes to the built environment has also come a dramatic change in individual behaviour patterns, shifting populations towards largely sedentary lifestyles. Elevators now dominate over stairs, driving cars has become easier and safer than walking or biking even short distances, and computers and the internet allow societies to complete work and social networking without leaving their seats. For decades now, physical activity has been slowly designed out of our daily routines, but these hidden dangers of constant inactivity are contributing to the shift from infectious diseases to the chronic diseases the world is faced with today.

In recent political and policy debates, the costs of providing treatment-focused healthcare are often cast in direct competition with the allocation of public and private resources that could otherwise provide for education, housing, mobility (physical and economic) and a host of other things that contribute to the quality of life and environment in our cities. In 2008, the United States estimated the annual obesity related costs were $147 billion, and if current trends continue, these costs are projected to reach over $900 billion per year by 2030.[6]

With an identified sense of urgency of the importance of the relationship between health and the built environment, a collaboration was born in New York City between health professionals, designers, policy makers and community groups. In 2006, multiple city agencies joined with other local partners to discuss the chronic disease epidemics facing today's global societies at the first of what was to become a series of annual conferences called Fit City. The health professionals could clearly identify and provide evidence of the climbing rates of chronic diseases, but they realised that there needed to be a shift from focusing on only treating the diseases, to looking at prevention strategies through encouraging healthy and active lifestyles. How could they help to positively impact people's health before they even needed to step into the doctor's office? A commitment at one of the early Fit City conferences was made to produce a collaborative set of guidelines that could help those who shaped the built environment to consider positive health outcomes early in their processes before budgets and schedules were set. These were called the *Active Design Guidelines* (2010).[7] Covering both urban and building scales, the guidelines called for a vast range of strategies to promote opportunities for physical activity, involving land use and density decisions, streetscape design, active transportation support, public transit, healthy fresh food access, staircase design, building design and motivational signage.

The award winning guidelines quickly became a great tool to mentor other cities and guide new urban developments, and evolved to include additional supplemental documents.

A subsequent grant from the US Center of Disease Control and Prevention through the NYC Department of Health and Mental Hygiene created an opportunity for the Office of the Chief Urban Designer at the NYC Department of City Planning to produce a nationally applicable study and publication titled *Shaping the Sidewalk Experience* (2013),[8] focusing on one of the most fundamental forms of urban infrastructure, the sidewalk (or footpath).

Typically considered in two-dimensional plan and section drawings, the footpath is examined through a more dynamic and spatial lens in this document, which presents the conceptual framework of a sidewalk room as the space where people truly experience their cities. Shaped by four planes – the ground plane, the roadside plane, the roof plane and the building wall plane – the authors embarked on the study from the perspective of those who inhabit the sidewalk room, the pedestrian. Structured around three overarching themes, the publication focuses on the human experience, how this experience is shaped in large part by the physical space surrounding the pedestrian and finally how this physical space is in turn regulated by a series of policies and regulations.

ure 2: Shaped by the
ound, the roadside,
roof plane and
building wall,
'sidewalk room'
sents cities from the
destrian's perspective.

By promoting a more spatial and dynamic lens to look at our fundamental urban walking infrastructure, the hope was to broaden the list of players that are responsible for shaping the sidewalk room. Each urban experience is highly individual and influenced by a number of uncontrollable factors, but understanding what those who do shape the physical environment can control is critical to providing an enjoyable and enticing sidewalk experience, and in turn promoting walkability. By complementing the efforts of innovative transportation agencies (under whose jurisdiction the ground plane typically falls) and asking policy makers, designers, architects, owners and advocates to identify where their role lies in shaping a great pedestrian experience, more stakeholders could be working toward healthier and more walkable future cities.

Six key contributing factors were identified that impact upon the pedestrian experience. They consider all human senses; the varying speeds people might be moving at; and the diverse footpath contexts that are critical to shaping the identity and character of neighbourhood.

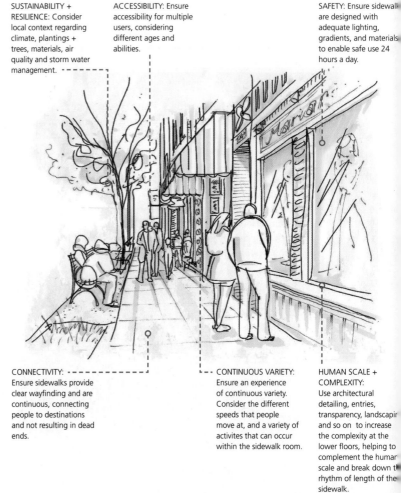

SUSTAINABILITY + RESILIENCE: Consider local context regarding climate, plantings + trees, materials, air quality and storm water management.

ACCESSIBILITY: Ensure accessibility for multiple users, considering different ages and abilities.

SAFETY: Ensure sidewalk are designed with adequate lighting, gradients, and materials to enable safe use 24 hours a day.

CONNECTIVITY: Ensure sidewalks provide clear wayfinding and are continuous, connecting people to destinations and not resulting in dead ends.

CONTINUOUS VARIETY: Ensure an experience of continuous variety. Consider the different speeds that people move at, and a variety of activites that can occur within the sidewalk room.

HUMAN SCALE + COMPLEXITY: Use architectural detailing, entries, transparency, landscapir and so on to increase the complexity at the lower floors, helping to complement the human scale and break down the rhythm of length of the sidewalk.

Figure 3: These six key contributing factors will shape how enjoyable and enticing it is for someone to walk in the city.

When considering the various scales of the physical space of the sidewalk, the neighbourhood fabric will be shaped by land use mix and density decisions, determining where destinations such as schools, transit stops, parks and shops are located in relationship to where people live and work, and how well connected and walkable they are. At the scale of the street, a drastic rebalance of how we distribute our limited roadbeds is needed, but we should not strive to demonise the car; instead we should equitably share the real estate to provide safe and reliable choices for people utilising multiple mode of transportation including public transit, bicycling and walking. The scales and heights of buildings on each side of the street will inform the sense of enclosure and human scale of the space. How each façade is designed to carefully touch the footpath, or sit back from the property line, will drastically impact the pedestrian experience.

Within the sidewalk room itself, a series of physical characteristics and elements collectively shape each individual plane. While the ground plane is the most fundamental (given without it the sidewalk does not exist), one of the key defining characteristics of a footpath experience is where a building sits in relationship to the footpath edge. When buildings sit strongly on the property line, their architectural details, frequent and active entrances, appropriate transparency levels, small shifts in plane and outdoor uses such as sidewalk cafes will add visual interest and variety, engaging the walker and making travel distances seem shorter. When buildings are set back, the landscaping, fencing and what sits in the setback area become the defining characteristics for this plane.

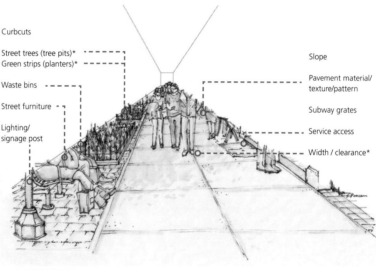

Curbcuts

Street trees (tree pits)*
Green strips (planters)*

Slope

Waste bins

Pavement material/ texture/pattern

Street furniture

Subway grates

Lighting/ signage post

Service access

Width / clearance*

Figure 4: a) The ground plane is the most fundamental; without it, the sidewalk does not exist at all.

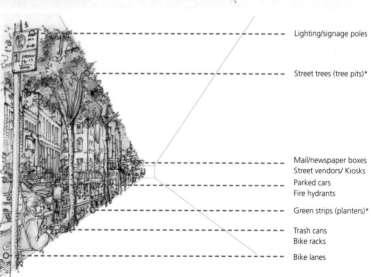

Lighting/signage poles

Street trees (tree pits)*

Mail/newspaper boxes
Street vendors/ Kiosks
Parked cars
Fire hydrants

Green strips (planters)*

b) The roadside plane is strongly defined by the rhythm and spacing of street trees, vertical light posts and signs, peppered with pedestrian amenities.

Trash cans
Bike racks

Bike lanes

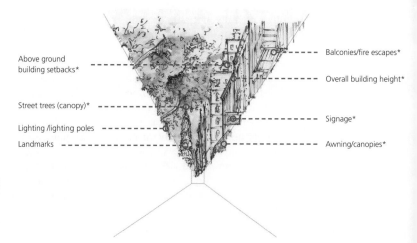

Above ground building setbacks*

Street trees (canopy)*

Lighting /lighting poles

Landmarks

Balconies/fire escapes*

Overall building height*

Signage*

Awning/canopies*

c) Above the pedestrian's head, the cornice lines of buildings and canopies of trees shape the roof plane and determine the amount of visible sky.

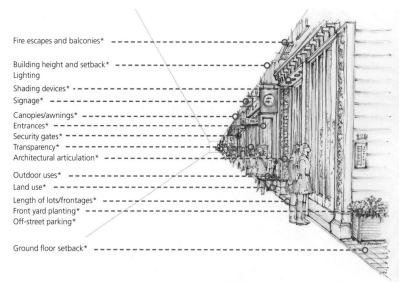

Fire escapes and balconies*

Building height and setback*
Lighting
Shading devices*
Signage*
Canopies/awnings*
Entrances*
Security gates*
Transparency*
Architectural articulation*
Outdoor uses*
Land use*
Length of lots/frontages*
Front yard planting*
Off-street parking*

Ground floor setback*

d) Buildings on the property line add architectural interest and activity to the building-wall plane. When buildings are set back, landscaping and fencing become the defining characteristics.

While the list of elements is vast, this process of breaking down the sidewalk room into the four planes, and subsequently into the series of physical elements that form them, allows some of the specific policies and stakeholders that shape them to become more apparent. Understanding who the different players are, and where their responsibilities lie, can help to ensure a comprehensive approach to shaping walkable neighbourhoods.

Most architects and designers would not realise that each time they are designing a building, they are in fact designing the sidewalk experience right next to it. How they detail each building to touch the ground will impact how most people experience their building. Many policy makers might not be cognisant that whether they are mandating, allowing, incentivising, guiding or removing impediments to certain practices, they are often shaping the future sidewalk rooms, impacting the walkability and influencing the public

1. ─────
2. ─────
3. ─────
4. ─────
5. ─────
6. ─────
7. ─────
8. ─────
9. ─────
10. ─────
11. ─────

1. Departments of planning are often responsible for the overall allowable building heights, setback dimensions, ground-floor uses, curb cut locations, entrances, levels of transparency, and outdoor uses.

2. Departments of building often regulate what can project beyond a building or private property line into the public right-of-way.

3. Designers and architects are responsible for how interesting and engaging the building wall plane is to walk past

4. Landmark agencies identify and designate city landmarks

5. Departments of transportation regulate sidewalk widths and clear paths in conjunction with the overall distribution of the right-of-way.

6. Departments of consumer affairs regulate sidewalk cafes by issuing licenses and enforcing compliance.

7. Transit authorities might require transportation infrastructure within the sidewalk room.

8. Departments of sanitation organize trash collection and recycling, impacting the overall cleanliness of the sidewalk room.

9. Departments of environmental protection manage the storm water that runs onto sidewalks through curbside drains.

10. Departments of people with disabilities work to ensure safe and accessible sidewalks for people with diminished abilities.

11. Private property owners and tenants are responsible for front yards, entrance spaces, and are also frequently required to build and maintain the sidewalk in front of their property.

Figure 5: The various players who shape the sidewalk room

health of a neighbourhood. Considering how these strategic tools might relate to subjects such as ground floor uses, establishment sizes, entrances, setbacks, transparency levels, curb cuts, front yard planting requirements, sidewalk cafes, fresh food access, signage and so on, presents an opportunity to be proactive in shaping enticing sidewalk experiences in Christchurch. It is important to remain aware of the original intent of any specific policy, of the danger of over-regulating and of any potential unintended consequences that may result from a specific policy. Our cities are not static, and so there is a need to ensure the policies that shape them remain current and appropriate in terms of the environments we strive to shape.

Ensuring the critical infrastructure of a city's footpaths is coordinated and provided at the outset of a rebuilding process can allow the fundamental bones of a great city to be put in place, ensuring baseline quality, overall accessibility and general maintenance is met. But maintaining a level of flexibility and adaptability is key to allowing some of the more unique and thrilling parts of cities to occur. Active and vibrant spaces, artwork and unexpected moments of delight and surprise can contribute to the individual character and identity of each neighbourhood and will be critical in fostering a larger walkable network. Considering how these physical spaces can be shaped into urban places that people want to use is important in ensuring Christchurch presents a place that has soul, that's distinctly unique. A place that invites a variety of experiences and one that offers a multitude of choices.

This article explores a particular aspect of public health in relationship to shaping future cities and attempts to shift from the perspective of considering health treatment facilities within the built environment, to how healthy lifestyles and chronic disease prevention for urban citizens can be shaped by healthy cities. The hope is to broaden the collective list of those who should take shared responsibility in shaping great footpath experiences, asking each person to be aware and conscious of the impact of their decisions as they shape the built environment. Identify where your responsibilities lie, whether in writing policies, designing landscapes, shaping buildings, laying out urban infrastructure, planning programmes, or advocating for future conditions.

How can you shape the best possible sidewalk experiences in your city and what can you do to help shape the health of generations to come?

Stronger Christchurch Infrastructure Rebuild Team

SCIRT formed in 2011 to repair Christchurch's earthquake-damaged horizontal infrastructure: publicly owned water, wastewater, storm water and road networks, bridges and retaining walls. SCIRT is a partnership between government (CERA, Christchurch City Council and the New Zealand Transport Agency) and five construction companies (City Care, Downer, Fletcher, Fulton Hogan and McConnell Dowell). With around 750 kilometres of damaged pipes and 1.3 million square metres of damaged roads to repair within five years, SCIRT has over 600 construction projects to complete and manages up to 150 of these projects at any one time. SCIRT's programme of work is the biggest civil engineering challenge in New Zealand's history.

[1–5]

[6–9]

Transport: Post-quake impacts and new beginnings

Glen Koorey

Glen is a Senior Lecturer in Transportation Engineering in the Department of Civil and Natural Resources Engineering at the University of Canterbury, with a focus in the areas of safety and sustainable transport. Prior to joining the University in 2004, he worked for ten years with Opus International Consultants as a transportation engineer and researcher.

Transport is not an end in itself; it exists to allow people to access various activities and services. Hence, transport involves a complicated relationship between the various land uses present (residential, employment, recreation, education, commercial) and the different transport networks and services provided (roads, paths, bus services, railways, and more). These interact to form the 'flow pattern' that we experience: the heavy transport routes, how many people use the bus, what times of the day and week are busiest and so on. Typically these patterns in a city only change gradually over time, as land uses and population patterns alter and new transport facilities are developed or changed.

All that changed dramatically in Christchurch following the 2010 and 2011 earthquakes. In a very short time, the city experienced rapid changes in the shape of both the transport network and the surrounding land uses. While that created significant problems for the provision of adequate transport options, it has also allowed the opportunity to radically rethink the nature of how we get around the city in the future.

Immediate post-quake effects

The September 2010 earthquake had the distinct immediate 'advantage' that most people were still at home when it occurred in the early morning. This limited the amount of traffic that was on the streets at the time. By contrast, the February 2011 quake and many of the other significant aftershocks occurred during the daytime when many people were at work, school or out shopping. As a result, there was significant traffic congestion immediately following these quakes, as major buildings were typically evacuated and people were sent home. Damage to parts of the road network and traffic signals also contributed to the ensuing gridlock in many parts of the city.

Interestingly, a very resilient travel choice in those immediate post-quake times was cycling. People who were cycling home were generally able to ride past queued traffic and also get around many obstacles on the street that were too big to allow motor vehicles through. The importance of a travel mode like the bicycle in times of emergency should not be underestimated;

indeed, in Portland, Oregon, they hold annual 'disaster relief trials' using a variety of cargo-carrying cycles to navigate an obstacle course and to 'deliver' emergency supplies.[1]

The major quakes in Christchurch resulted in many instances of flooding due to ground liquefaction and burst pipes. Many roads were very uneven due to ground movements, and in some cases damaged by major slips or sinkholes. Many services in the ground (e.g. manholes and sumps) also rose relative to the road surface, creating additional solid obstacles to negotiate. Similarly, bridges often ended up at a different level to the adjacent roads, making it difficult or impossible to use them, and most bridges and tunnels also had to be closed following each major shake to be checked for structural damage.

Good transport connections are important for maintaining normal freight supplies; following a disaster like this they also become a lifeline for other essential needs. For example, much of Christchurch was without clean drinking water following the major quakes. Therefore, plans were organised to bring in supplies from out of town by rail and then distribute them via local community tankers.

Fuel supplies into Christchurch were generally well managed following the major earthquakes, with normal port deliveries able to be carried out. Despite this, rumours abounded about potential fuel shortages, resulting in long queues at service stations while everyone filled up their tanks 'just in case'.

Land use changes

Many people's homes were seriously damaged, thus requiring them to find new accommodation. Typically, these new abodes were in outer suburbs that had suffered less damage, including parts of the adjacent Waimakariri and Selwyn districts. Quite quickly, new subdivisions have also sprung up on the periphery of the city to cater for the demand. The net effect has been to increase the average travel distances for people to get to work, school and other common destinations.

With many business premises out of action following the quakes, employers were also forced to improvise. Relocated workplaces (whether temporary or permanent) sprung up rapidly, typically outside of the central business district (CBD) that had been hit the hardest (and it was cordoned off for as much as two years). As a result, employees had to learn new travel patterns to their new workplaces.

Alternatively, some businesses shifted to more staff working at home; Telecom call centre staff were given the necessary systems to do their work from home.[2] The University of Canterbury made greater use of its online learning system when staff and students were restricted from being on campus. It may be that some of the resulting trip reductions become permanent as these 'tele-commuting' techniques gain wider acceptance.

Schools also had to change their habits. A number of schools temporarily shared sites to assist those schools with serious damage.[3] School timetables were adjusted to fit two compressed teaching blocks into each day, with one school using the site in the morning and one in the afternoon. To minimise the potential traffic impacts, the 'visitor' school pupils were transported to their host site every day via a fleet of buses.

These land use changes led to some significant changes to transport patterns. The shift in trip origins and destinations saw some dramatic swings in traffic flows, with eastern parts of the city and the CBD typically seeing less traffic, and western parts of the city and the outskirts seeing greater flows (fig. 1). In many cases, the busier roads were not well equipped to handle the 'overnight' increases in traffic. Travellers' previously developed habits were disrupted by having to journey to and from new places. If they previously took a bus, this option may have been less obvious or available now (especially with so many bus routes historically travelling to the now-empty CBD). If they biked, a suitably safe route on their new trip may also not have been evident. The longer average journeys also meant that those used to walking and cycling often made a switch to driving.

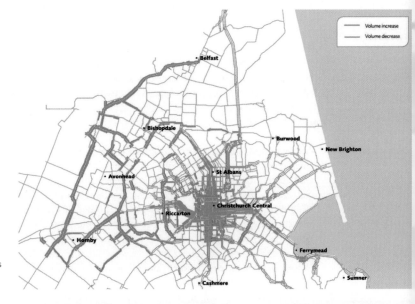

Figure 1: Map of changes to traffic flows around Christchurch, April 2011

Another interesting phenomenon with the ongoing aftershocks was many people's desire to keep their cars close by, in case they had to get to family following another major shake. This undoubtedly had an impact on travel by other modes, especially buses. Ironically, the reasoning was probably somewhat misplaced, given that many cars were trapped in carpark buildings following the major quakes and the ensuing congestion heading home invariably made it quicker to get around the city by biking or even walking.

Short-term transport treatments

While bus services were suspended immediately following the major earthquakes, limited services typically resumed within days, although some routes were redirected to avoid road closures. The previous CBD Bus

Exchange was severely damaged, and two temporary interchanges were set up on the outskirts of the CBD, each servicing half the city with a free link bus connecting them. A trip across the city on the same bus might now take three buses; not surprisingly this sub-optimal system resulted in approximately 50 per cent of previous patronage levels. The situation was finally resolved in October 2011 when an interim central station in the CBD was able to take on the role of the previous Exchange until more permanent facilities were constructed later.

Another series of controversial short-term operational changes in April 2011 were the removal of some parking lanes and cycle lanes near congested intersections to enable additional traffic lanes to be extended.[4] These were pushed through very quickly under emergency powers, but drew widespread criticism from cycling circles. Ostensibly these moves were to 'reduce congestion'; yet making it harder to ride safely on Christchurch's streets obviously discouraged this travel choice. It is notable that no emergency powers were used to remove parking and implement any bus or cycle lanes that may have improved alternative transport options.

Opportunities for change

With the immediate transport issues resolved, thoughts turned to how to reconfigure the transport system while rebuilding the city. The Christchurch City Council's Share an Idea campaign elicited considerable public feedback on this topic. Some of the most common transport suggestions included:
  shifting to a more 'people-friendly' central city, with a much better
- environment for walking
  reviving Christchurch's historic high use of cycling (reputedly the highest
- per capita in the world in the 1950s)[5] by providing suitable cycleways
  developing a rail-based public transport system, using both the existing
- main trunk lines and new light rail routes
  abolishing the CBD's one-way streets, which were cited as a blight on
- urban streetscapes
  removing requirements for CBD developments to have a minimum number of car parks, allowing developers to determine their own needs and to encourage more use of other transport modes.

It is notable that, just prior to the earthquakes, the Council had commissioned prominent international urban space experts Gehl Architects to investigate options for revitalising the central city. Gehl's recommendations included virtually all of the above ideas, yet the Council's response to it at the time was decidedly muted.[6] Only the circuit-breaker of the devastating earthquakes allowed the Council to reconsider some of the 'radical' ideas suggested by Gehl.

CERA (the Canterbury Earthquake Recovery Authority) took the Council's resulting Draft Central City Plan, which was submitted to central government in December 2011, and then announced the development of its own Christchurch Central Recovery Plan (CCRP), loosely based on these concepts. While the CCRP was developed in a whirlwind 100-day period and released in July 2012, the transport component was held back to allow for the detailed modelling of potential options. It wasn't until November 2012 that the draft transport chapter of the CCRP, An Accessible City, was released for consultation. After submissions closed in February 2013, CERA's final transport plan was released in October 2013,[7] with notably little change from the original draft and nearly two years after the Council had submitted its own transport plan.

The initial Council plan had quite a strong push for rail-based public transport, including the development of new light rail routes (fig. 2). The first proposed route, from town to the University of Canterbury via Riccarton (and ultimately to the airport) was costed at around $400 million. Further connections out to other suburbs would ultimately take the price tag to $1.5 billion. However, by the time CERA's plan emerged, the word 'rail' wasn't even mentioned, with enhanced bus corridors being the preferred public transport option. Meanwhile, although the one-way streets received a lot of condemnation, CERA's plan will convert only one of the existing four pairs back to two-way. However, the 'look and feel' of these routes will be considerably changed, and efforts will be made to encourage cross-city traffic onto the wider 'four avenues' that ring the CBD.

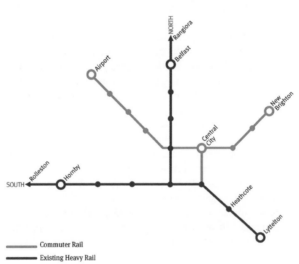

Figure 2: Proposed Christchurch Passenger Rail Network

—————— Commuter Rail
—————— Existing Heavy Rail

An Accessible City also proposes a more people-friendly CBD 'core' where active travel modes (especially walking) will receive priority and safety. This core will include various traffic-free areas as well as a comprehensive 30 km/h zone for much of the central city. Cycling will also receive a boost via a combination of separated cycleways and various quiet streets and 'greenway' connections throughout the CBD.

In parallel with CERA developing its plan, the Council had continued to work on developing its Christchurch Transport Strategic Plan,[8] a 30-year blueprint for the whole city, which had been well in development prior to the quakes. This contains a similar shift in focus towards more sustainable transport options, while recognising the Government's desire to roll out Roads of National Significance around the city's periphery. Unlike CERA's plan, the Transport Strategic Plan still mentions the potential for rail-based public transport, but typically couches it as a sufficiently future possibility.

An Accessible City also recognised that the rebuilt city would have to better accommodate those people for whom accessibility is an issue, such as wheelchair users and vision-impaired pedestrians. In the immediate aftermath of the quakes, many of the temporary walking routes around the city were virtually impassable by people with such impediments, with a lack of recognisable cues, kerb ramps and the like. Over time this improved during the rebuild, with some contractors arranging for 'walkability audits' of their work sites. The finished city should better incorporate such accessibility features to truly provide for all users.

Cycling came in for increased attention, and Council's Transport Strategic Plan aimed to develop a series of high quality 'major cycleway' routes connected by other local cycleways to form a comprehensive city-wide network. Initially it looked like this would be a slow-burning development across the ensuing decades. However, in July 2013, the Council allocated $69 million over five years for a programme of thirteen major cycleway routes across the city. This was informed by the development that year of the Christchurch Cycle Design Guidelines,[9] which painted a vision of how many of the new routes would incorporate features commonplace in more cycle-friendly parts of the world but quite new to New Zealand. About the same time, a short length of separated cycleway was developed near the University of Canterbury in Ilam, which enabled some trialling of design and process issues for the rollout of the cycleways en masse.

The notion of a new people-friendly city was celebrated in September 2013 by means of a 'ciclovia' or 'Open Streets Festival'.[10] In a first for a New Zealand city, the streets throughout the central city were closed off to motor traffic for a day allowing people on foot or bike free rein of the central city.

It wasn't just public organisations that saw the opportunities for new transport networks in the rebuild. Two particular grassroots community organisations arose that resonated strongly with the general public and ultimately the politicians. The Christchurch Coastal Pathway group proposed a new walking and cycling route along the foreshore from Ferrymead out to Sumner (about 8 km) for both transport and recreation; by 2013 the Council had committed to $9 million of its expected $19 million pricetag. And the Avon-Ōtākaro Network proposed new pathways along the largely red-zoned Avon River from the CBD out to New Brighton; a petition to Parliament in 2012 gathered more than 18,000 signatures.

Managing the transport rebuild

Notwithstanding the dramatic changes prescribed for much of the city's transport network, a more immediate issue was the need to repair a large proportion of the city's roading stock and underlying pipe infrastructure. Virtually all of the streets on the eastern side would require reconstruction and many on the western side too.

Traditional client-contractor arrangements were seen as too cumbersome for the sheer scale of works required. Therefore a radical new arrangement was needed to efficiently implement the $2.5 billion of basic 'horizontal infrastructure' works. A new alliance of three clients (CCC, CERA and NZTA – the New Zealand Transport Agency) and five contractors came together to form SCIRT – the Stronger Christchurch Infrastructure Rebuild Team. Staff from these organisations and some engineering consultancies were seconded to SCIRT to help plan and design the rebuild works and progressively roll them out across the city over about six years.

SCIRT is a highly efficient arrangement for the reconstruction of 'like for like' facilities, with the costs being covered by insurance. However the sheer pace of work undertaken meant that opportunities were often missed to reconfigure a street for modern-day design philosophies (e.g. speed management of local streets) or to add extra value at the same time (e.g. new cycleways). Only as some of the city's other strategic plans are being finalised is there now the chance to consider how to take advantage of the ongoing rebuild programme to build back better at the same time.

The increasingly busy traffic patterns around the city also resulted in better coordination between the Council (responsible for local roads), Environment Canterbury (responsible for bus services), and NZTA (responsible for state highways). A 'Christchurch Traffic Operations Centre' was set up to oversee the combined road networks (for example, developing real-time travel time information), and a new website 'Transport for Christchurch' promoted the many different transport options available to people and described current road-works closures.

Lessons learned

The Canterbury earthquakes have identified a number of valuable lessons for other areas faced with similar disasters. Firstly, the road network may be significantly affected by the utilities infrastructure that is *under* it when an earthquake strikes. For example, changes in density between 'soft' underlying ground and adjacent 'hard' structures (bridges, sumps etc.) can produce a network that is very uneven and hard to navigate by motor vehicle. Secondly, many innovative and workable solutions can be found following a disaster to accommodate damage to housing, workplaces, schools and so on. It is vital, however, to consider the transport implications of such changes, especially when they involve longer travel distances than before and potential reductions in use of sustainable transport modes.

Lastly, the 'blank canvas' afforded in many cases following the quakes has allowed the city to plan for a future transport network that will be radically quite different in direction to previous plans; for example, more immediate implementation of sustainable transport initiatives. The transitional nature of many parts of the transport network (and adjacent land uses) post-disaster has allowed an element of 'experimentation' to be undertaken that politically may have been difficult to achieve otherwise. While certainly not a desirable way to reach this state, it does provide a rare opportunity to reinvent the transport mix in the city for ultimately a better outcome.

New cycleways

Since the earthquakes there has been a resurgence of interest in cycling in Christchurch. As part of creating a cycle friendly city the Christchurch City Council will build thirteen major cycleways by 2018. The new cycleways will provide safe and attractive routes around Christchurch with separated cycle paths and priority for cyclists at traffic signals. The technical standards for the new cycleways have been developed with assistance from the Netherlands. The cycling programme is targeted at supporting people who are 'interested in cycling but concerned to do so', and includes cycle education for schools and regulatory requirements to provide cycle facilities in new commercial buildings.

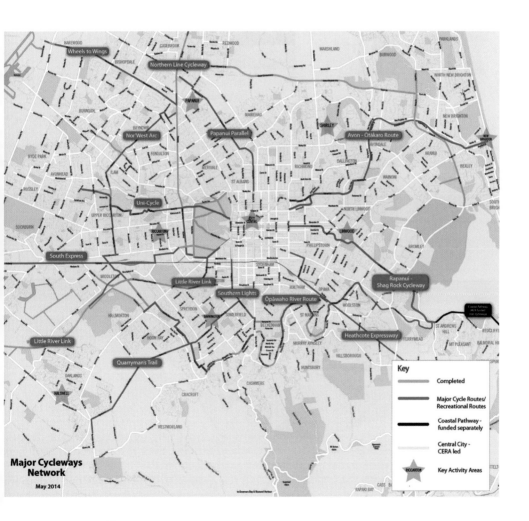

[1]

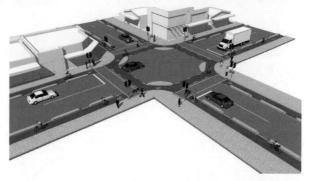
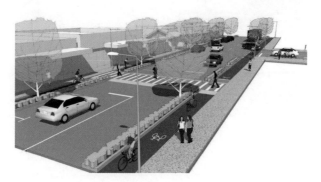

[2–5]

How Christchurch can build light rail – and create the centres it needs in the process

Peter Newman

Professor Peter Newman (born 1945) is Professor of Sustainability at Curtin University and since 2008 a board member of Infrastructure Australia. Peter is best known internationally for popularising the term 'automobile dependence' in the second half of the 1980s. He is author of numerous publications on sustainable cities and a lead author for Transport on the IPCC (Intergovernmental Panel on Climate Change). He was an Erskine Fellow at University of Canterbury in 2013.

I have been coming to Christchurch and talking about light rail since the 1980s – not long after we began to win the same battle in my hometown. Christchurch obviously wanted light rail but couldn't quite pull it off financially. Now we have a new opportunity as Christchurch recreates itself following the earthquake. I also now know a lot more about how it can be financed using land value capture.

Global trends

The challenge for urban transport and sustainable development is to radically reduce resource consumption and a centre's ecological footprint whilst improving the liveability of cities. This seems rather daunting but the data from most developed cities suggests that the transition has begun. The peaking of car use, the rapid growth in public transport, bicycling and walking, and the regeneration of central areas all suggest that a major transformation to reduce car dependence is underway.[1]

Jeff Kenworthy and I first coined the term 'automobile dependence' in 1989 in our book *Cities and Automobile Dependence*, which investigated 32 global cities. We have expanded this survey to all parts of the world including Christchurch. Twenty-five years later, the parameters are all showing that automobile dependence has begun to decline and perhaps we are witnessing its demise.[2] The one hundred year growth in the use of the automobile in cities appears to have plateaued and then declined across the world's developed cities.[3] The same patterns can be seen in New Zealand cities as shown in figure 1.

Demonstrations of how automobile cities are being restructured with rail transit are now being seen everywhere. This trend back to rail-based transit is perhaps to be expected in the relatively dense cities and countries in Europe, the Middle East and Asia. However, perhaps the more surprising trends have been in the traditional, car dependent cities of the US, Canada and Australia that once only considered bus transit suitable for their suburbs. They are now seeing a future based around rail. Perhaps this list could now include Christchurch.

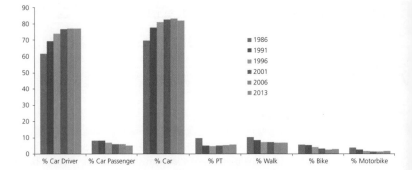

Figure 1: Peak car use in New Zealand

The need for a modern rail system is not just due to its transport system benefits but also its transformative force in reshaping urban centres. This has been recognised globally[4] with indications that public transport is a key element in ensuring a competitive city.[5]

Light rail attracts denser, mixed-use urban development that has less need for parking. It can therefore enable development in the city centre and along its route in sub-centres, including places like the University of Canterbury in Ilam. These denser centres are where real innovation in sustainability can be focused. It is where people-oriented urban design at street level begins to be meaningful.[6] Car-based suburbs and shopping centres are never going to be the basis of a sustainable and resilient city but with a vibrant city centre and an adjacent set of centres with a quality light rail linking them, then the suburbs and city centre can have a new life.

There is one fundamental that I believe about the city centre: it is going to need all the help it can get to revive. Investment does not come just because you plan the right zoning and say the words 'please come, we are ready'. The redevelopment of the city centre is unlikely to have the market force it needs for establishing dense residential and commercial activity unless it is linked to a new light rail project. There is now a lot of global experience in city centres damaged not by earthquakes but by too much highway and suburban shopping centre development.[7] Most cities in the US and Australia have turned to rail projects that are magnets for urban development. The Gold Coast, Sydney, Canberra and Perth are all in various stages of developing new light rail lines that are closely linked to new urban developments. Melbourne of course has the world's largest tram system and all new central area developments have trams built into them.

Can Christchurch do this? Probably not – unless we can find a new funding mechanism. In recent years our research team at CUSP (Curtin University Sustainability Policy Institute) has been working on the new mechanism of land value capture. This mechanism ensures dense redevelopment is part of the integrated transport land-use financing package. The mechanism is now being adopted in the UK following many US cities and new data on how it can work in Perth suggests it is highly viable. A step-by-step approach will suggest how this can be achieved.

Why rail in Christchurch?

Rail is not just about transport; it is a city shaping mechanism, as outlined above. If a city wants to build up its central area and any sub-centres then it links them together along a new light rail line. This has been a proven formula for many years in small towns throughout Europe and now towns of all sizes in the US and Australia. In my own town of Perth rail has been transformative; it has gone from carrying 7 million passengers a year to 70 million and is seen as something of a model for how to get people out of cars in an automobile dependent city.[8] At the same time there has been a complete turn around in the fortunes of the Perth city centre. Once called Dullsville, it is now a thriving centre day and night.

Christchurch has a huge problem in attracting central area development and in creating real sub-centres that are not just shopping centres. Could a light rail help with this – not only providing a fast and comfortable transport service but at the same time enabling the city centre and sub-centres to attract mixed-use development?

Light rail

There are 545 cities with light rail, 118 of which have populations under 150,000.[9] This appears to suggest that a changing appreciation of the value of light rail in small cities has occurred. The change is probably associated with the shift in value associated with the trends in peak car use, fuel prices, urban traffic speed trends and urban economic and cultural changes as outlined in Newman et al. (2013).[10]

Perhaps the most significant trend in recent years in Australia (and America) has been the emergence of light rail as an issue in small car-dependent cities. Lobby groups in Australia have been actively pushing the political case for light rail in Canberra, Hobart, Bendigo, Darwin, Newcastle, Cairns, the Sunshine Coast and Parramatta (although embedded within Sydney, it is like a small town, as it would need to be an independent and isolated system servicing a local population, not unlike the other smaller cities). These cities are mostly well under 300,000 people, Canberra being the largest at a little over 300,000. Similar trends have been observed in the US.[11]

The question needs to be asked whether light rail is likely to be a viable option for these small cities, since the traditional approach would suggest it was not. Buses have long been considered the only viable public transport option for small cities. However, the above dramatic turnaround in the fortunes of light rail may be indicating that a new era of desirability and viability for light rail in small cities is emerging. The case for these cities to be considered suitable for light rail is based on an understanding of what is likely to be causing the trends outlined above in traditionally car-dominated cities, as well as some new options for assessing and funding light rail in such cities.

Figure 2: Light rail in Canberra (a smaller city than Christchurch) is about to happen after twenty years of discussion; it is based on a value capture funding scheme.

New approaches to funding rail through value capture

Rail infrastructure increases land value due to its accessibility benefits. This increase in financial value can be captured and used to help fund the infrastructure. A four-step process can work in the following way:

1) *Accessibility benefits analysis.* This will demonstrate the land area where owners will benefit most from the new infrastructure.
2) *Land value data collection of the difference between those areas varying in accessibility.* This can be around 20-25 per cent for residential land values and over 50 per cent for commercial land values. Along Perth's Southern Rail line the value of land went up 42 per cent over the first five years after the announcement and then building of the railway.[12]
3) *Assessment of the various potential financing mechanisms available in the city through public and private value capture.* There is likely to be government land that could be contributed to the package being delivered to raise funds. This active fund raising is done in cities like Hong Kong and Tokyo. American cities, and recently London and Manchester, use a way of tapping into private land adjacent to train stations whereby the increased land value from the train translates into increased land-based rates and taxes; these are then 'ring fenced' into a special Transit Fund. In the Perth case study we found that 80 per cent of the cost of building the Southern Rail could have been raised using the value capture mechanism.[13]
4) *Delivery through a planning mechanism, probably in a PPP (public-private partnership).* The opportunity is there to use such Transit Funds as a way of bringing in private sector interests who have experience building new technology light rail in combination with land development. The local government could even consider seeking Expressions of Interest from consortia who could build, own and operate the system as well as design the value capture system that could help pay for the capital and operating costs. This intriguing possibility is being considered by a number of cities.

If rail is going to continue to grow and car use to decline then a range of sophisticated value capture mechanisms can be developed for each city to make the most of this opportunity for funding. Rail is getting off the welfare system that kept it alive for decades and is becoming a serious market in cities across the globe. In Manchester the next thirty years will see three new rail lines funded through this means. Christchurch needs to do a detailed assessment of its possibility.

Conclusions

Christchurch has some amazing grassroots innovations occurring that are deeply impressive and suggest a great future for the city (see my film Christchurch: Resilient City).[14] But the basic structure of the city will remain car dependent and dominated by suburban centres unless a light rail can be brought to the city. There are many examples of small cities like Christchurch developing light rail and trends would suggest a future with many more cities doing this. The big question is how to fund it. Land value capture may be the way as it will help lock in the redevelopment of the city centre and some sub-centres along its corridor. Quality transit services attract people and hence urban development, thus opening up a mechanism for involving the private sector in creating the rail project. Can Christchurch take this new opportunity? Can it afford not to?

Margaret Mahy Family Playground

Expanding on the Christchurch City Council idea to put a large playground in the central city, this CCDU-led project was developed with considerable input from both primary and secondary school children. A design competition enabled more than 6000 Christchurch kids to feed their ideas and visions for the park to the designers. The park will combine stories from Ngāi Tahu, Margaret Mahy and Elsie Locke. The park is part of the East Frame, placed alongside the southern edge of the Avon River. It will cost between $20 and $30 million.

[1–4]

[5–6]

Breathe: A case study in the difficulties of breaking convention

Jon King

Jon is the founder of Design King Company Architects that is based in Sydney. An entry from Design King Company was shortlisted in the international competition run by CCC, CERA and CCDU. The practice's work has been widely published, featuring in *Elle Decoration* in the UK, *Architectural Design* in Italy, *Monument, Belle, House and Garden*, and in books such as *Tropical Minimal, Beach Houses of Australia, 100 Top Houses from Down Under* and Adam Mornement's recent and superbly illustrated *Boathouses*.

Christchurch is blessed with an extraordinary context, a simple city grid and generous network of public parks and spaces. And with its rich cultural, architectural and landscape heritage and a determined people recovering from the devastating quakes of 2010-11, I believed that here it would be possible to redefine the way modern cities are conceived of and built. It was after submitting a proposal for a Housing New Zealand social housing development in Christchurch that the Residential Development Project – the Breathe competition – came to my attention. The brief was a compelling document that sprang from the energetic masterplan prepared in the aftermath of the quakes to provide a vision and a framework for the rebuild.

Although quickly prepared, the Christchurch Central Recovery Plan (CCRP) was informed by sound strategic advice from institutional and professional bodies and was a clear well-ordered concept for the future shape of the city. The Breathe briefing document imagined a central city that would be repopulated, highly livable and sustainable. The new housing envisaged by the brief would be mixed-use, architecturally distinctive, of higher density and better connected than the largely split business/suburban Christchurch of before the earthquakes. The brief reinforced that this was a once-in-a-lifetime opportunity to build an exemplary twenty-first century city. The one-hectare site proposed for the competition would provide the people of Christchurch with an innovative example that would lead the way for the development of new housing in the revitalised central city.

The written and supporting material implied that government at all levels was focused and intent on delivering an innovative solution, and the carefully selected competition jury, which included high-profile designer Kevin McCloud with architect Stuart Gardyne as chair, had enough diversity in interests and backgrounds to ensure that the selection processes would be serious and astutely handled. All architectural entries needed a development partner to put feasibility and build-ability right at the forefront. While this was challenging for a small architectural practice it signaled to me that a successful entry would need to be more than just a good piece of design work, but would require creative thinking in the broadest possible sense.

On the ground Christchurch had already given rise to the commercial Re:START container mall and Gap Filler and others were actively engaged with the production of a new landscape of creative interventions. The rebuilding of inner-city residential precincts would and should have continued along these lines and encouraged creative, innovative and participatory engagement with the task of the rebuild. In this context, mainstream and risk-averse development models would not work, nor be the right approach. I concluded that the nature of the competition, the determination of government at all levels and the need for Christchurch to quickly rebuild and reestablish its central city would ensure something altogether more radical, more cosmopolitan and more exciting than conventional development would occur.

As I flew across the Tasman, over the Southern Alps and onto the Canterbury Plains I felt a sense of genuine determination to be involved in the rebuild in any way I could. It was the right time and place to test my ideas about the modern city and the perfect time and place to tackle the dominant suburban ideologies of Australia and New Zealand.

The beginnings: Creating a sense of place

During 2012 I had been involved with a Master of Architecture program at UTS (the University of Technology Sydney) with Professor Steve Harfield, where with graduate students we were exploring issues related to community and placemaking and the role architectural structure and space might play in this process. So with a team of select graduate students working with my office, we began the Breathe project in earnest in late 2012. It was no simple task and it would engage the resources of my small office in Sydney for almost a year. From the beginning we believed that the restoration of a 'sense of place' was essential to the recovery and revitalisation of post-quake Christchurch. The re-population and activation of the central city, we believed, would be underpinned by the provision of affordable, quickly realised mixed-use housing, with a high quality public realm that was adaptable enough to respond to the dynamic of the rebuild. In short, it had to be an incremental model that would help in the creative transformation of the city from a place of trauma and disaster into something more progressive, energetic and optimistic.

We imagined a central Christchurch of finer grain and scale, better connected by public transport, by foot and by bicycle. We considered how the city could encourage and facilitate opportunities for young, clever and ambitious people to engage with the public realm and reinvent the city in a form suitable and attractive to a younger generation. We imagined innovative systems of governance that empowered and encouraged individuals and communities to make adaptations to the environment as it evolved over the course of the rebuild. Ultimately we hoped through this project to encourage people to play a part in the physical act of placemaking and, at the same time, help facilitate the building of vibrant communities with well-conceived and intelligent architectural and public infrastructure.

A solution emerges

Motivated by the opportunity to be part of something so significant, our thinking quickly moved beyond the competition site as we analysed the capacity of the CCRP to deliver a central city of the type imagined by the Breathe brief. We considered how 10,000 new households in the central city (in line with government targets) could be delivered within a 25-year time frame. We aimed at a solution where the focus was not just ascribed to the buildings, but also to the spaces between the buildings – making it possible to create a finer network of public spaces within the existing street grid. In these smaller spaces people would feel encouraged to engage, interact and enact activities that would form and nurture a 'life on the street' culture.

Figure 1: Stage 1 aerial view

We proposed a series of laneways and small public spaces that would be permeable and interconnected to other similar sites, initially made of simple vertically composed modular buildings of a scale and form that could suppor the density and provide the framework for a rich and vibrant ground-floor city. I drew by hand and felt a fundamental passion and connection to these imagined lives, spaces and potential futures.

The housing depicted was aimed at a younger and diverse demographic who we viewed as the future of Christchurch – and a group more likely to have the creative energy and ambition to deal with the transitional nature of the central city during the rebuild. We were skeptical of conventional high-quality, high-cost architectural solutions aimed at investors and downsizing baby boomers. Instead we envisaged a somewhat chaotically assembled environment devoid of formal perfection that aimed to create opportunities t fill the spaces between. Building costs would be rationalised and affordability managed through prefabrication, clever construction techniques and a sense of partial completion. With an open and permeable framework we thought we might be able to deliver the sought after transformative economic opportunity that a previous generation had enjoyed in cities like Sydney and Melbourne 30-40 years ago. These home-owning opportunities are now sadly out of reach for the younger generations in most cities. I felt it was the right approach to encourage a city to rebuild for a new epoch and for Christchurch to position itself as a place of economic and creative opportunity.

The finalists announced

In March 2013 our submission partners Ganellen were asked if they were prepared to submit a Stage 2 entry based on our scheme. The undertaking was a prerequisite for being shortlisted as a finalist. While pleased to be associated with the entry, Ganellen were far from convinced about the commercial viability of the venture and Stage 2 would require real financial risk. The Stage 1 financial modeling did not stack up and the all-important land value was far from clear. In fact Ganellen went as far as suggesting that unless the land was thrown in at zero cost by the Government they would not be interested.

Nevertheless, our submission was selected as one of the four finalists. At the official announcement, Building and Construction Minister Maurice Williamson described our submission as presenting 'edgy urban living' and reaching for the 'Holy Grail' of affordability. One could have been forgiven for thinking that there was real intent on the part of the Government to take on the unsustainable suburban planning models of mainstream politics and planning, and to rebuild Christchurch in a new and innovative form.

The four finalists were a mixture of architectural approaches, styles and development models and it was hard to read what the jury saw as the future character of the central city. At the high end was the highly detailed Jasmax/Viva scheme (funded by a community organisation), and the more conventional and architecturally resolved Ansclmi Cresco Holloway scheme. And while representing looser and more organic forms of urbanism, the Walker Architecture submission and our own scheme delivered entirely different densities, scales and construction methodologies. The jury seemed to be searching for alternatives rather than predicting or delivering a preferred solution.

Stage 2: The hard work begins

From the beginning of Breathe Stage 2, it was clear that all concerned were feeling their way. While the feedback on the individual schemes was well organised and the jury delivered good solid and reasoned critique, little could be understood about the availability or the actual cost of the land being provided as the competition site, nor the context into which it would be placed. Even when and how the promised $20,000 in prize money would be delivered to the four finalists remained unclear. Most importantly, questions were raised as to how and on what basis the commercial component of the individual team bids would be compared and reviewed. This was an issue that remained in limbo until the very end of the competition. As information trickled through from the organisers it appeared that the due diligence, risk assessment costs and process were largely to be driven and provided by the entrants. Martin Udale, the jury's development specialist, was clearly unimpressed as he recognised the commercial difficulties faced by the finalists. I think it is fair to say he remained sceptical about the commercial reality through to the end. The competition process and its advisory group seemed oddly removed from the commercial and financial realities imposed by the competition. On the surface this still appeared to be a design-based competition not a serious development proposition.

Ganellen, as the developer in the partnership, now became more involved as they assessed the risks and potential opportunities of building and financing what was essentially a concept design. Ganellen are successful builders with genuine experience in the delivery of medium density housing in Australia and experienced in bids for high-profile public projects in New South Wales. They were also very much on the ground in Christchurch, having built the Press Building in central Christchurch and bidding for, and winning, much of the redevelopment work in and around central Christchurch. They had good operational knowledge of the Christchurch market and were also naturally positioned for tendering on some of the big anchor projects envisaged by Government in the central city. They were rightly very cautious about development of any kind in the central city. But they were enthusiastic about our scheme, about the future opportunities in Christchurch and about positioning themselves in the centre of the rebuild. So the architectural team, at this point still very much unfunded and largely unsupported, pushed on with the concept in order to clarify our position and respond to feedback from the jury.

By the mid-term presentation in Christchurch one could detect a good deal of frustration from all the finalists with the unknowns and indeterminate nature of the development opportunity. Ganellen threatened to pull out of the competition unless more complete geotechnical information was given to the teams and an extension of the deadline by an additional month approved. At this point lawyers for the Government also delivered a draft development contract and stated for the first time that Government intended to support the chosen developer by helping to fund the eventual winner with a favourable agreement for the purchase of the land, now valued at $5.95 million. Until this point it had been assumed that each of the entrants would make an offer for the land based on the feasibility of their schemes. It was now made very clear that the development agreement needed to be based on the so called 'commercial land value' of the site so it would serve to demonstrate feasibility and encourage the private sector to follow in the competition's wake. Testing the feasibility of our model required the now extensive building and consultant team to produce outline documentation for realistic cost planning and programming. Once again this work was unfunded and a huge burden on a small architectural practice and student team. It also meant a rationalisation of many of the more interesting aspects proposed for the prefabrication and incremental construction of the building elements as certainty over the feasibility demanded that Ganellen could guarantee the cost of building the 136 apartments and associated infrastructure. As the concept architects for the project we were really now captive to the commercial modelling and the appetite for risk of a commercial builder. The nature of the competition also put the commercial model front and centre, notwithstanding the jury's primary concerns for liveability, sustainability and connectivity.

Figure 3: (left) Stage 2 montage of inner public square. This shows in contrast with Stage 1 (see Figure 2) how the 'true' public space changed with the realities, such private gardens etc., which were imposed on us.

Figure 4: (right) perspective from the corner of Madras and Gloucester streets in Stage 2

However with building costs now better understood, Ganellen began to explore ways to fund the project. They enlisted MacroPlan Dimasi to explore the underlying economics and metrics of the proposal. These well-regarded financial analysts had been involved in the development of a number of public-private partnerships in Australasia and were also doing extensive consulting work for the Government in post-quake Christchurch. Their commercial modeling of our project reinforced the fact that a conventional development model was not going to deliver the much-needed population in the central city quickly enough or without government risk and intervention. In their words, 'The Breathe competition forms a critical component in the rebuild of the Christchurch CBD [central business district]. Inner-city residential density will be a fundamental driver of activity within the CBD, providing accommodation for inner-city workers, temporary workers and young/mobile residents and will support day and night businesses in the CBD.'

The proposed model could be built immediately and the proposed population accommodated within two years of construction beginning. It was a practical, realistic and deliverable development model in their view and relied on sourcing tenants from a rental market that would be bursting at the seams by 2015 when the construction workforce was projected to peak in Christchurch. Ganellen described it as a 'Build, Operate, Transfer' model where a government-secured loan would finance the construction and delivery of the $45 million project. Ganellen would only take out the $45 million on delivery of the project. Ganellen would then guarantee complete asset management for a 20-year period where the government had no operational responsibility or risk but was guaranteed a sizeable annual return plus 80 per cent of the profits. After the 20-year period expired, the asset would be transported to government ownership.

Figure 5: (left) Stage 2 montage of night-time laneway activation

Figure 6: (right) Typical apartment interior view in Stage 2

It was sound, conservative and even created alignments between the design aims and financial model. As such there was a palpable passion for what we had collectively delivered as architects, builders, economists and social theorists, and the opportunities this presented for further thinking and refinement. It would require up to five Breathe sites to be developed simultaneously every year for the next 25 years to achieve the Government's goal of 20,000 people living in the city by 2028, and this was a model that could kick start the process.

The presentation

A great deal of energy went into the production of our final material. We presented three booklets containing detailed and developed architectural plans; models and illustrations; extensive consultant material and capability statements; a fully elaborated elemental Bill of Quantities; and a very detailed financial and economic analysis of the proposal. We presented as a team from our various perspectives but the core and impassioned backbone of the presentation was the architectural component, where we outlined our ambition to provide an affordable and timely solution for the rebuilding of an activated and re-populated urban core.

The jury, and representatives of Christchurch City Council and central government, seemed unanimously impressed by the proposal and overwhelmed by the fact that we were presenting a scheme with a guaranteed construction cost and with the metrics and financial modelling ready for detailed negotiations with government.

While our proposal sought to deliver up to 4000 dwellings as the development model was rolled out, the bid was based on the single competition site. We felt that we had delivered a complete and very attractive opportunity to the jury and their advisors. By this time, unbeknownst to us, the Jasmax/Viva team had withdrawn. The Anselmi Cresco Holloway and Walker Architecture teams were putting conventional development models on the table and the architectural schemes remained pretty much as illustrated in their stage one submissions.

The final decision

The success of our proposal was underpinned by good and collaborative critical thinking. We saw the overall recovery of the central city as dependent on the provision of affordable and mixed-use housing, but we also wanted to develop a solution that was replicable and scalable as a piece of thinking, not just a singular piece of architectural design. While we recognised that any solution must bring some stylistic integrity, fundamentally we saw the act of architecture as a process of providing a spatial and tectonic framework that could absorb and react to the real social, commercial and technical challenges confronting the rebuild.

As developers of the project, Ganellen were invited back to the table to negotiate with government. It was hinted that our scheme was the preferred solution by the jury; however, Ganellen were being asked to modify their bid into a more conventional form. They ultimately refused the opportunity, believing that their proposed development model was the right one. They also believed the model might still be taken up for housing in the East Frame if they failed to win Breathe and this was still very much in their sights. As architects we were not privy to this process, and I might retrospectively ask whether Ganellen should have compromised their approach a little just to get things moving. As the announcement of a winner approached I found out (eventually and fairly indirectly) that we were not going to have the opportunity to refine our ideas and develop our thinking. It was a big disappointment and a blow to the team who believed so much in the work we had presented. At this point I had no idea who the winner might be.

The disappointment

It is always difficult to attend competition and award announcements as a runner up, but I felt I owed it to the design team and myself to attend, experience the process and achieve some sort of closure. Ganellen were also keen to push the merits of the model to government advisors and the Minister for Earthquake Recovery. On the way to the presentation I met the jury chairman Stuart Gardyne, who lamented that the competition was coupled to a development model. They hadn't envisaged that it would end up driving jury decisions or the process.

The Cardboard (Transitional) Cathedral was full of the fanfare and excitement that accompany these events, but it remained an event somewhat remote from the challenges of actually doing the work and putting the scheme together. With the arrival in town of Kevin McCloud, Minister Maurice Williamson and a new mayor for Christchurch, there was much to commend the night. But apart from Kevin McCloud indicating that Christchurch needed to get on with it, there was very little discussion or debate about the real issues facing Christchurch and what this competition actually brought to that debate. In reality a very complex and deliberate twelve-month process had seemingly delivered only one viable scheme. While a commendable architectural scheme, the winning Anselmi Cresco and Holloway consortium delivered a development that will have significant feasibility challenges and offers little to invite a review of the status quo. In my view it will at best deliver high-cost apartments for the usual suspects and one suspects that Government may still have a part to play in financing the construction as the process unfolds. While there is nothing inherently wrong with this approach the brief for Breathe reached and aimed for something tangibly different that would be a 'game-changer'. The lasting memory of the night for me remains trying to track down how to get the $20,000 in prize money promised all those months ago to offset some of the cost.

It is hard to put a full stop on this process given the Government has recently announced it is looking to partner with developers and release land in the East Frame earmarked for housing and mixed use of the type we proposed. However there is certainly cause to reflect upon the competition process and what it achieved. It was clear from the number and quality of the entries to the Breathe competition that the architectural community embraced it as a great platform to investigate and explore ideas about the making of contemporary cities. This remains its lasting legacy in my view, with the Stage 1 entries displaying a level of resolution and diversity that reflected well on the profession.

However, the competition brief and the values and commitments embodied in it were never going to translate into effective and alternative housing solutions if left entirely to the market. Not unless the Government stood behind the vision and the words of the brief, and significantly helped in the shaping of the new city, would the competition translate into anything other than an ideas generator. By divesting itself of any role in openly and consciously supporting the delivery of these ambitions, Government ultimately compromised the key driver for delivering a sustainable and activated central city in post earthquake Christchurch: affordable and innovative housing.

Christchurch deserves the very best of what constitutes a liveable twenty-first century city. They have had good advice and publicly make the right sort of noises. But if the rebuild is to deliver an exemplary public infrastructure supported by truly innovative housing and mixed-use development, the Government must take the initiative and do more than just pay lip service to notions of liveability and sustainability.

Te Papa Ōtākaro / Avon River Precinct

The $100 million redevelopment of the Avon River surroundings has had strong support since the quakes. Ōtākaro holds great significance for Ngāi Tahu and Te Ngāi Tūāhuriri Rūnanga: the river was their commercial vein, transport route and the place by which they lived and traded. Restoring the mahinga kai is a crucial objective. The visual contrast between the curving river and the linear grid of the streets is a key element of the city's urban form. The park zone will be about 30 metres wide on either side of the water and include many walks and cycle paths. Cafes and bars will re-emerge; new buildings, including hotels, will enjoy river views.

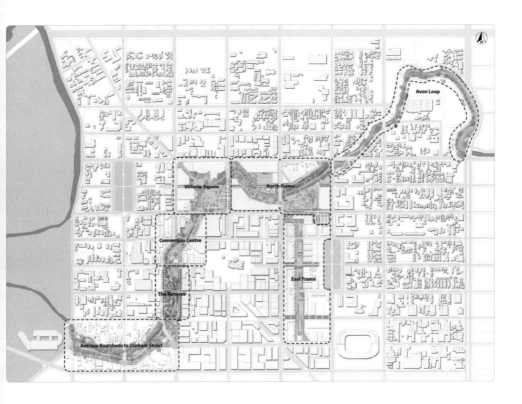

[1]

[2–7]

Our River: Public realm design brief at its best – are we doing our best with it?

Jessica Staples

Jessica Staples is a registered landscape architect who recently returned to Christchurch after practising in Hong Kong for over seven years. During this time she led high profile landscape and urban design portfolios throughout Asia and the Middle East. Jessica is well versed in the processes and issues associated with public realm and urban design having led the design of Abu Dhabi's internationally significant Saadiyat Island Cultural District Public Realm project.

Among the eight precincts created by the Canterbury Earthquake Recovery Authority (CERA) under the Christchurch Central Recovery Plan (CCRP), the Te Papa Ōtākaro / Avon River Precinct should be the most accessible and exciting. This is *the* major open public space development in the rebuild – a space that should be highly frequented by all members of the community. Taking a broader look, one will find that the Avon River Precinct is the largest public realm project being carried out in New Zealand at present, both in terms of budget and physical size, and yet it's being rolled out faster than any of the other anchor projects. Given its importance, both as a public space and financially, we should all be taking note of what is happening down at this particular riverside. How did this project come into being? How was the project awarded and how is our 'world-class amenity' shaping up?[1]

Stretching from Rolleston Avenue in the west to Fitzgerald Avenue in the east, the Te Papa Ōtākaro site passes through and around the central city for a length of 3.2 kilometres, spanning approximately 30 metres either side of the Avon River. The contract area also includes Victoria Square, and open spaces in the northern and eastern Frame. The project involves a budget of just under $100 million for a high profile site in a developed nation with resources and means. It has significant cultural and ecological values to draw from and the post-earthquake setting offers a sense of design freedom – a chance to reimagine Christchurch. It is a fantastic brief. Capture this within an open, international design competition and you expose the world to this excitement.

The primary merits of holding Te Papa Ōtākaro as a public design competition are twofold: firstly it is a democratic process – anyone can put forward an idea; secondly these ideas are displayed in public. Initially, it would have cost more and extended the timeline, but for a project of such importance the primary focus should be on gathering the best ideas possible. This is not to say that the public would have had a hand in selecting the winning design, but it would have exposed the public to the possibilities that this space holds. It would be a true shame to end up with a substandard or even standard design simply because the public didn't know and therefore demand any better.

But this is not how this project has played out. In fact none of the precinct work or monumental public buildings has been opened up to design competitions, aside from two: Breathe (the Residential Demonstration urban village competition) and the Margaret Mahy Family Playground. Both of these demonstrated the benefits of competition-led design.

The Breathe competition allowed teams from around the world to generate ideas for Christchurch to draw from, and time to develop them. The four finalist teams had six months to refine their designs before presenting them to the judges and public. One can still easily access these presentations, complete with a level of detail and design-reasoning comparable with, if not more thorough, than what is publically available on the Te Papa Ōtākaro proposal. Breathe also appears to have a much greater presence in the international design community, within industry publications and websites, compared with the other precinct work – a testament to the international attention design competitions bring to a project.

The Margaret Mahy Family Playground was open to children throughout the Canterbury region. As a result this space is likely to produce the most creative design out of all the precinct work. It may even stand up to its sales pitch of being 'the world's best playground'. Watch Christchurch Central Development Unit's promotional video online and the overwhelming message from the competing children is that it gave them a chance to truly participate and comment on the design of the city, something that has been missing from the rebuild process since the unveiling of the Blueprint in 2012.

So if Te Papa Ōtākaro wasn't run as a competition how was the current design team appointed? Initially developed by the Christchurch City Council (CCC), CERA recognised its importance and captured the Avon River Park within its collection of precincts. In 2012 CERA drew up a brief and opened Te Papa Ōtākaro up to expressions of interest (EOI) via the New Zealand Government Electronic Tenders Service (GETS), the first hurdle to open design opportunity. This system requires registration for a company to receive notifications of relevant projects and EOIs. It is open internationally, but who beyond our shores would know of it and therefore think to register?

The second hurdle comes at the preparation of the EOI itself. Requirements of EOIs are often very tedious – the resulting proposal can run into volumes in order to cover the required technical and financial information. This is all before anyone even thinks of putting pencil to paper to generate actual design ideas. The EOI process can be a great tool for filtering out the serious contenders and resource stable companies, but it can also exclude smaller firms and independents from participating at all.

But the EOI procedure was the path taken and over twenty EOIs were received. In mid-2012 CERA refined these to a shortlist of six teams whom they invited to tender for the $100 million project. In December 2012 the contract was awarded to a design team led by Opus and UK-based BDP. Given that the judging criteria and their respective weightings are unknown to the public, the awarding of this project remains opaque. What we do know is that when asked why the Opus consortium won the project, CERA's

CEO Roger Sutton said it was 'the quality of the people and the quality of experience they can actually point to'.[2] This is interesting given it is now evident that new urban design and landscape architectural offices, most of which were part of teams that lost out on the original bid, have been brought on board to supplement the Opus-BDP collective. Whilst we can take heart that the CCDU is reacting and adapting to strengthen the design team when it recognises the need, what was wrong with the original team when according to Christchurch Central Project Delivery General Manager, Greg Wilson, 'we've employed the best to do the job'?[3] And where exactly in the budget are these new consultant fees being drawn from?

So how are the plans progressing for, as Mr Sutton put it, this 'gutsy park that really adds to the city'?[4] This brings us to 'Watermark', the first stage of the Avon River Precinct and the first anchor project of the entire rebuild to be implemented and open to public use. The resulting space (the stretch of riverbed and true left riverbank between the Antigua Boatsheds and Montreal Street) is rather underwhelming for a place that, according to Opus, 'provides the public with a snapshot of the precinct's entire design concept plan'.[5]

Had this been run as a competition there would have been a clear design vision established from the outset. A strong design proposal would have underscored why the team won the project in the first place. Instead the design of this major public space is being conducted out of the public eye, with snippets being released once it is relatively finalised. Though Watermark has been open for public comment since its official opening in August 2013, it is the only part of the design to date that CCDU has invited public feedback on. According to CCDU's Anchor Projects Overview document, the design phase for the remaining stages finished in the second quarter of 2014.[6] Where in this design process have allowances been made for public review and assessment of the design *before* it is implemented? It appears we won't really know what we are getting until it's already set in concrete, literally.

The river development is constantly promoted as a 'world-class waterfront'. This means that the space should stand up against comparison with the most creative, inspiring and socially engaging designs from around the world. It is here that people may start dropping names such as Pier 42 in New York, Singapore's Marina Bay, the South Bank along the Thames River in London and Melbourne's own Southbank. Why not start a little closer to home? New Zealanders don't have to travel beyond our shores to find examples of what is considered worthy of international benchmarking. Wellington has Kumutoto and Auckland has its Wynyard Quarter, both of which continue to prove themselves as successful, publicly driven, waterfront spaces.

The point here is not only to celebrate that New Zealand is more than capable of delivering designs of international standing, but also consider that Christchurch has tough competition from places to live and visit both beyond and within New Zealand. In marketing the Avon redevelopment as one of international standard, we must ask: Is the construction so far and proposed design equal to, or ideally better than what we have elsewhere? Will it win international design competitions? Does it match with the public's vision? This a particularly pertinent question for this particular precinct as it involves public realm design – this space is highly frequented and experienced on a daily basis by the full cross-section of the community. Public opinion on the design of Te Papa Ōtākaro should be strong and loud, and it should be heard.

Yet something is missing from the design so far. There is a tangible lack of artistic integration, innovative lighting, wayfinding and furnishing detail present, all of which contribute to the memorability of a space. To understand why this lack of detail exists, we need to talk about the Art Trail.

The Art Trail is the public art scheme for the river project area. Though it is greatly encouraging to know that the Art Trail exists as a project, it is difficult to see the value in designing and administering it independently from the Avon River Precinct work. International best practice shows that richer, more innovative design results from an integrated, collaborative approach. This separation of contracts has a strong likelihood of resulting in a weakened art strategy that will be placed 'on top' of the Avon River Precinct design, rather than sitting 'within' it. Furthermore it is difficult to see how these two projects will work together when they are following different time frames. While the Art Trail is still working on its funding strategy, the Avon River Precinct has already delivered one section of its design and is planning on delivering its final stage in mid-2015. Is the Avon team expecting to leave 'gaps' in the design to be filled, hopefully, once the Art Trail commences?

Best practice shows that art inclusion strategies are now more commonly written into the core public realm design brief. This means that opportunities for artists to collaborate with the lead design team can be identified at the concept stage and developed side by side as the project progresses. The end result is that the art sits within the overall design instead of following the traditional view of art as a separate object placed in an open space.

A collaborative approach can also result in the production of elements that are part of the core brief, so that the cost of their design, implementation and maintenance can be captured to some degree as part of the core contract implementation cost. If the art and design contracts were combined we create a more efficient platform for reducing overall costs. All design is guided to some degree by costs and one of the main obstacles the Art Trail has is that it first must come up with a strategy to fund its projected $12 million budget. Is the Art Trail destined to fail before it even starts?

Budget issues aside, we haven't yet considered what is bound to be a political headache for each of the teams as they decide where the artwork will go, what the scope of art design is and even what the physical boundaries of the artworks will be. Though it is understood that the Opus-BDP team will outline these basic parameters, it is inevitable that there will be key areas along the banks of Te Papa Ōtākaro that both teams are going to want to claim. If they were working as a joint team this wouldn't be an issue; instead, they would be working together in a truly multi-disciplinary studio environment.

So here we are, midway through 2014 and midway through CCDU's indicative project delivery schedule for Te Papa Ōtākaro.[7] Have we made the most of this amazing opportunity yet? I think not. Is there still a chance we can do this? Yes, but it would take a change in timelines and process to achieve. At a minimum we should make the design more open to the public. Unveil the plans for the rest of Te Papa Ōtākaro so that we can appreciate the entire plan in its detail, Art Trail included. Perhaps it will reveal that the 'wow' factor is there, yet to come. Then give us a moment to pause and to provide some feedback before sending the diggers on further downstream. We need to reimagine the design process to date so that that we can respond with more than simple recovery, but with a nationally and internationally celebrated resource, by and for all.

Chapter 9

Reimagining Recovery

He aha ia te whakahaumanu

Festival of Transitional Architecture (FESTA)

Valley section: A new instrument for the Garden City
Chris Moller

WikiHouseNZ

Does the Blueprint support the creation of a healthy ecological
urban environment?
Di Lucas

I Like Your Form

What has Ōtautahi revealed? Māori urban planning in post-
quake Christchurch
Craig Pauling, Shaun Awatere & Shadrach Rolleston

Shop Eight Food & Wine

Digging where we stand
Bailey Peryman, Oliver Peryman & Michelle Marquet

Rekindle

More than buildings: Growing biodiversity and happiness in
communities
Kevin McCloud

We can't tell you what the future will bring, but a number of the authors in this chapter suggest it should be a future that doesn't forget its past. When the grid pattern for the city was laid out in 1850, it paved over many of the original streams and waterways that were in the area; this knowledge was written out of the maps and out of Christchurch's history. With the acknowledgment that many of the buildings located near these historic waterways performed worse than others, there is also an acknowledgment that as we press forward, we cannot afford to forget again.

Future Christchurch. A Brighter Future. Progress Central. It's Never Been More Vibrant. For those of us living in Christchurch, there has been a massive gap between the everyday reality in which we live and the breathless predictions of a better tomorrow. The promise that the city will be back, and will be better, has helped so many of us keep going when everything else seemed unendingly bleak. But what is the future of Christchurch, and will it be appreciably different from the past?

The authors in this section look at the opportunity to reimagine the city, exploring ambitious – but plausible – aspirations that come from taking stock of our context. There are calls for us to design more in keeping with the natural environment here, to reconsider the relationship between the city and the countryside and to embrace that we are a Pacific nation with an indigenous population possessing its own rich design culture and history.

Even our food production is looking backwards to push us forward. Small, community-led schemes such as Agropolis, fruit and vege cooperatives and the Local Food Project may not yet be causing the big supermarkets any sleepless nights. But by entering a market disrupted by the earthquakes, they have shown that there is an alternative to the consumer-capitalist system that has become so entrenched, at least in the Developed World. Any challenge to the many socially constructed things that we take as normal is a step towards helping people imagine other possibilities.

FESTA

Christchurch's annual Festival of Transitional Architecture (FESTA) presents the public with a free programme of multidisciplinary creative projects, events and community-based activities in the fragmented urban setting of the central city. The inaugural FESTA burst onto the scene in 2012 and is now held every Labour Weekend. FESTA celebrates and expands the local culture of transitional urbanism via a gathering of experimental art, architecture and performance that draws in national and international participants to create an event of urban scale and density. The festival aims to build and strengthen the passion and involvement of local communities in the regeneration of the central city and contribute to the creation of a unique, diverse and exciting Christchurch. (Page 427 contains images of Free Theatre's Cantrbury Tales at FESTA 2013; page 428's images are from Studio Christchurch's LUXCITY at FESTA 2012.)

[1–5]

[6–10]

[11–15]

Reimagining Recovery

Valley section: A new instrument for the Garden City

Chris Moller

Chris founded architecture and urbanism studio CMA+U in Wellington following twenty years in Europe, where he worked as Senior Urbanist for the City of Groningen, taught at the London Architecture Association and founded S333 Architecture + Urbanism. Currently he teaches at Victoria University. He has been advising Melbourne on urban strategy for Fishermans Bend, and is working on the Urban Development Strategy for Thames and the new Mt Pleasant Community Centre Building in Christchurch.

The attempt to understand a city and how it works is often approached from a view that assumes the city is complete and fully functional. Tourist marketing, for example, tends to focus on the city image such as Christchurch as garden city, while academic research or urban policy often views a city in terms of its social, economic or spatial qualities and capabilities. To be useful these views require the city to be intact as a complete entity so that it conveys a coherent picture. While these perspectives are valuable, they often miss dimensions that can help inform unrealised potentials of the city, deeper clues that could help re-shape its future personality and identity.

Given Christchurch's currently suspended condition following the huge natural disasters of earthquakes and floods, there is a critical opportunity to see its qualities through a different lens. This lens needs to be robust enough to transcend the immediate messy processes of redevelopment and to help see new and often fragile interrelationships or opportunities between its broken pieces. In particular it needs to respond to the potentials and capabilities inherent in the underlying landscape that sustains and supports the city. To achieve such a perspective it is necessary to consider the various dimensions of the urban fabric. These dimensions can be described as the hardware (physical structure), software (activities or qualities that can inhabit and inform the hardware) and orgware (organisational structure and culture and their means to control both hardware and software). The valley section is a way to understand and combine these three dimensions and examine the city through an interconnected spatial vision.

Hardware: City plan or valley section?

The original 1850 Christchurch plan set out by surveyor Captain Joseph Thomas (fig. 1) was based on a standard rectangular grid of colonial settlement adopted for ease of survey and to facilitate land sales.[1] This grid pattern surrounded a central city square, similar to those in Philadelphia, Savannah and Adelaide. Christchurch followed these precedents and set out ambitions for a garden city. The original city plan also had a series of eccentricities that broke with the grid such as the course of the Avon River, green squares (Latimer and Cranmer), Hagley Park and the diagonal streets of High Street and Victoria Street.[2] It is this original plan that has also informed the garden city image and the ideas underpinning the Christchurch Central Recovery Plan (CCRP), which utilises the concept of a green frame to redefine or re-frame the original Garden City and a series of new public projects to stimulate investment and redevelopment in the almost entirely demolished historic city centre.

Figure 1: Christchurch
1850 Black Map

Yet neither the original 1850 Christchurch plan nor the new CCRP responds to the surrounding and underlying landscape that sustain and support the city – instead they employ a grid. It appears that while eccentricities have been embraced (such as the Avon River, now reinterpreted within the Green Frame), it is their interesting romantic qualities that help inform the Garden City rather than a deeper connection with the previous natural ecosystem, wider context or underlying character of the place. The fact that the area was essentially a swamp, with an uneven topography that shaped the flow of the Avon and a multitude of small river courses that flowed into it as part of a larger braided river system, seems to have been overlooked. It was this underlying structure that became evident in the earthquakes of 2010 and 2011 with many ground fissures and damaged buildings lying directly on the same lines of the underlying streams and river levies. This suggests that there is a deeper plan consisting of this braided river landscape, which has not been carefully listened to or utilised to help inform a suitable pattern for sustainable long-term urban settlement.

The use of the grid in colonial town planning has a long history dating back to Roman times. It offered order and regularity, clear orientation, simplicity and ease of navigation, speed of layout, and adaptability to local conditions.[3] However, there have been counter theories for how urban settlement could be shaped. For example, Patrick Geddes (1854-1932) – biologist, sociologist, geographer and pioneering town planner – believed the grid geometry used in colonial town design often failed to tackle the critical problems of urban blight that it purported to solve. Geddes' analysis showed that use of grid plans didn't consider the importance of existing homes or community life in its layout, often resulting in the expulsion of large populations, who would then end up in congested areas elsewhere.[4] To deal with these shortcomings Geddes developed what he called the 'valley section', which he used to help clarify the complex interrelationships between humans and their environment to encourage better-informed planning models. The valley section was based on careful and thorough diagnosis or civic survey of the geology, geography, climate, economic and social conditions in order to understand more deeply the underlying qualities and structures of a town or region.

To help inform the city plan, a deeper understanding of the value of Geddes' valley section could be explored and developed within the context of Christchurch. This would place Christchurch within its broader region (between mountains and sea), and in the context of recent earthquake movements and exposure to flooding. Such a valley section could help immensely to redefine the structure of Christchurch for future development, by indicating where to tread sensitively, where to intensify and how. A fully developed survey would be required to achieve appropriate results. Nevertheless, it is interesting to speculate how a survey focused on Christchurch's valley section might inform the traditional focus on plans.

So how might the valley section be translated and put to use in Christchurch? By starting with a sectional understanding (imagine a layer cake) of the underlying landscape patterns, we could see different kinds of urban settlement patterns appropriate to Christchurch's context. The recently changed elevation of the city following the earthquakes, combined with rising sea levels from global warming suggests that there is an urgent need to deal with swamp conditions and regularly recurring floods.

A sectional understanding would begin with sub-layers of geology (shingles, silts, sands, peat and clays); river and swamp-land typography and hydrology; layers of native fauna and flora. The question is how these then might inform appropriate responses for urban activities, infrastructures and building typologies. Architecture is best informed directly by the qualities of the surrounding natural environments. By working backwards from the extreme edges of the estuary, waterways and swamp habitats, one could define when to tread lightly – where to build sensitively with minimal infrastructures, jetties, boardwalks and swales. This approach would also indicate where more intensive development could be robustly optimised in high-density, mixed-use urban villages, filled with productive plants and useful habitat like a good medieval hill town.

By adjusting the nature of the valley section to each elevation and acknowledging the appropriate palette of species, human activities and building typologies that could be best suited to these conditions or able to adapt to the constant shifts of New Zealand's dynamic landscape, one can achieve an appropriate response to the surrounding landscape. This approach could be utilised to combine (rather than separate) uses by articulating varieties of mixed uses, and seeing potential for more complex inter-relationships of activities or 'software'.

Software

The software of a city can be understood as the activities or qualities that inhabit or inform the hardware of the city. Generally in planning terms, the activities or uses of a city are defined by separate zones. These formal zones are generic definitions, such as housing or industry, that miss the subtleties of everyday life and its many unexpected or spontaneous dimensions. Other forms of software, such as informal activities, defy zoning categories and can spring up anywhere through the initiatives of motivated individuals, action groups or communities. These informal activities often stimulate creative, innovative and experimental behaviours that bring vitality to an area.

The challenge for Christchurch is that the cumulative software of both formal and informal activity in the urban core was wiped out after the earthquakes and the social energy of the city disappeared or moved to the periphery. With the demolition of most buildings within the city centre, there was nowhere for the software to go. Institutions like the Christchurch Art Gallery had to reinvent themselves and find other ways to operate – through digital social media, websites and temporary facilities. But perhaps more interesting was that art had to redefine itself to address this situation, and to find new kinds of spaces to inhabit in order to reach its public. Other forms of informal software in response to this strange situation have been invented from scratch such as the Gap Filler projects and the Festival of Transitional Architecture, which are seeding new ideas about what can be possible in public space. These activities are beginning to catalyse a different kind of public life and fill the void in the empty centre.

Currently there is a big disconnect between the CCRP ambitions (which are largely focused on the development of large scale, long-term hardware infrastructures and projects for the inner city with little understanding of how to create a subtle, vital and diverse software) and the informal initiatives and festivals that have yet to find a link to the long-term formal structures of the city. However with the right mind-set it could be possible for the formal structures of local government to stimulate or support the informal and often spontaneous activities of artists, action groups and other cultural initiatives. Christchurch City Council has been trying this out through its support of initiatives such as Gap Filler, but there is a deeper question of how these positive new beginnings can become more robustly embedded into the emerging personality of the post-earthquake city rather than just a temporary sideshow. More importantly, how can these kinds of vital software activities be utilised to inform and even shape the quality of long-term ambitions of the city's hardware?

What kind of hardware would be more appropriate, more sensitive and more useful to these new forms of software that are emerging? How could public spaces and public institutions be reconsidered and redefined to embrace these qualities that have sprung up? Is there room for these new beginnings to be appreciated, let alone have the chance to establish links with the deeper sustaining nature of a valley section for Christchurch?

Lessons can be learnt from other cities that invest in the value of a vibrant creative culture that explores and tests a range of approaches to urban transformation. This requires risk-taking together with cohesive reflection on what has been learnt from each new wave of projects. Cities as diverse as Barcelona, Amsterdam, Oldham, Curitiba and Groningen are good examples of this. Groningen in the Netherlands is a particularly interesting example; its vibrant economy is built on a strong creative engagement between large-scale economic drivers, the sustainable management of ecological resources, and an experimental and creative design culture that embraces risk-taking as an essential way to solve challenges and renew itself.

The transformation of the CiBoGa terrain (Groningen) has been one such project: an inner city mixed-use revitalisation of an old industrial brownfield area directly adjacent to the regional academic hospital on one side, and a city park on the other. A high-density medium-rise (maximum of eight levels) with differentiated uses and densities across the site mixes living, working, shopping and recreational activities through a clever use of sectional thinking. Recreational space is woven into the very fabric of each urban block using building rooftops, green walls and courtyard spaces as an extension and reinforcement of the diverse habitats present in the neighbouring urban park. Water run-off is absorbed and released slowly or harvested for reuse in gardens and toilets. Energy and heat are utilised from the unused capacity of the adjacent hospital power plant. All of these things form part of an interconnected sectional thinking that carefully links the unused potential of various resources (fig. 2).

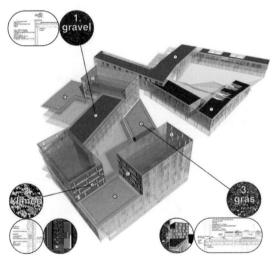

Figure 2: CiBoGa Terrain, Groningen, the Netherlands.

Closer to home, valley section joined-up thinking has been used in a recent urban development strategy for the township of Thames in Coromandel. The creative involvement of numerous large- and small-scale stakeholders has helped inform a new spatial vision, a kind of Thamesopoly urban design strategy that seeks to catalyse the transformation of the local economy, which is focused on new forms of urban living that promote a sustainable, mixed-use townscape sensitive to its rich architectural heritage. The strategy prioritises walking and cycling to create diverse urban neighbourhoods, and good connections to its regional recreational resources, edible landscapes, native habitat and water edge. It connects the regional landscapes from the mountains and river to the estuary with the town forming an important integral link spatially, economically and ecologically to the whole system (fig. 3).

THAMES+
URBAN DEVELOPMENT STRATEGY
Volume One - Vision/Urban Design Framework

CMA+U

CRANLEIGH
JUNE 2013

Figure 3: Thames Urban Development Strategy and Design Framework.

To achieve this kind of approach Christchurch needs to use joined-up, sectional thinking to increase density and mix up activities and uses, so that the same expensive infrastructure can be used many times by different activities at different times of the day or week. For example in Thames the main street will enable different activities at different times: farmers market one day, Anzac parade ground the next, a car park or cycle touring event space.

Secondly, to achieve a critical mass of urban dwellers that live and work in the heart of town, their city needs to be used as a place of production – to grow food, make things, fix things and exchange things. The goal is to do more with less, by putting new developments or investments in direct adjacency to one another so that synergetic combinations are catalysed. A good example of this new hybrid of public facilities is Thames's proposed civic hub, which combines the old Civic Centre together with Waikato Institute of Technology facilities, the library, new business hub and commercial support facilities.

Thirdly, key deliverables need to be identified as catalysts that are strategically spread through the urban fabric and intentionally linked to creative public events, manifestations and festivals to kick start the process of urban transformation – especially in the short to medium term, with the ability to inform long-term goals. Each of these catalysts will play a significant role, like acupuncture in specific spots across the whole town centre.

Finally, the valley section approach requires a more generalist take on whole systems thinking. This involves embracing the important cyclical feedback loops such as how water systems work and their implications for the environment as a whole.

Orgware

To understand how these issues could be addressed it is important to understand the organisational structures and their means to control both hardware and software. Following the earthquakes in Christchurch new organisational structures were required in addition to the Christchurch City Council to deal with the huge challenges of recovery. The critical importance of the city to the surrounding Canterbury region, the South Island, and the New Zealand economy meant that a special new organisation needed to be set up by government to provide the necessary resources to achieve a rapid and comprehensive recovery. The Canterbury Earthquake Recovery Authority (CERA) was formed and was given wide-ranging powers and the ability to suspend laws and regulations for the purpose of earthquake recovery. In April 2012 the Christchurch Central Development Unit (CCDU) was established as a unit within CERA to focus on rebuilding the central business district of Christchurch.

Currently these new authorities are primarily focused on the serious stuff of quickly realising a new generation of hardware. However, as mentioned above, without the right kinds of tools and understandings it is difficult to bring the potentials and opportunities of appropriate software into a synergetic and beneficial interrelationship with the hardware structures, let alone a strong interrelationship with the underlying landscape that sustains and supports the city. For hardware and software to respond more appropriately and become more useful, the organisational authorities that make decisions for Christchurch must become aware of these hardware and software conflicts – in other words, between long-term and short-term goals. They also need to be aware of the emerging but often fragile potentials of projects like Gap Filler, which offer clues for a different way forward and are critically important to the quality of life for those that will inhabit the future city.

Currently there is a lack of strong creative engagement between the formal large scale orgware structures such as CERA or CCDU and the smaller informal or community-based structures that have a much better bottom-up understanding of local needs, potentials, values and cultural complexities. These things are crucial to enable meaningful and usable investments in the rebuild. Without this engagement there is a huge danger of creating a series of white elephants that are not useful, appropriate or well-connected to the local economy and local geography that underpin the long-term capability and wellbeing of the area.

Once a deeper understanding of ecological and informal cultural systems is embraced by citizens, communities, action groups and government authorities as a critical sustaining layer for urban development, then the value of combining the hardware and software tools of the valley section and city plan could be utilised in synergetic combinations to enable a more enlightened and long term sustainable mixed-use development. The Christchurch grid could be further enriched and more informed, perhaps even intentionally erased where appropriate, through a series of important improvements to unlock its fuller potentials and link it more deeply to its underlying and sustaining valley section.

WikiHouseNZ

WikiHouse is a global open-source construction set allowing anyone to design, adapt, share and manufacture high-performance buildings that can be assembled with minimal formal skills or training. The WikiHouseNZ lab was founded in 2011 to address the chronic lack of affordable quality housing solutions in Canterbury. It was quickly recognised globally as leading the collaborative development of this manufactured kitset system. Space Craft Systems, the social enterprise founded to develop WikiHouse in New Zealand, is built upon core values of using adaptable design that empowers people to create their own protective environments. WikiHouseNZ is currently working towards a relocatable, self-reliant micro-house.

[1–4]

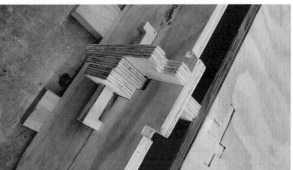

[5–8]

Does the Blueprint support the creation of a healthy ecological urban environment?

Di Lucas

Di Lucas is qualified in natural science and landscape architecture. Her landscape practice has been based in central Christchurch since 1987 and involves landscape planning, community-based placemaking charrettes, ecosystem guidance and heritage analysis around Aotearoa New Zealand. Di has held government advisory roles for more than 30 years, is a certified RMA consents commissioner, a Christchurch Urban Design Panel member and is instigator of the post-quake Peterborough Village *pita kāik*.

The nature of the place

I wander up river, through the poplar-lined river corridor, Barker Avenue. I ponder the Christchurch Beautifying Association planting thousands of native plants along here from 1897. The meanders provide myriad spaces in our city. The wonder of the grid design, enabling the viewshafts to mountains and Port Hills; the grid allowing a sense of orientation across the convolutions of the Ōtākaro-Avon River. I lean on the Colombo Bridge. In the clear, nor-west air, the North Colombo vista frames Tekoa, the Hurunui mountain far away. I ponder the Canterbury Settlement surveyor exactly 150 years ago aligning his design for junction of formal grid and meandering river, orienting it to this perfect cone. The river waters and life, and the grid viewshafts: enduring city signatures.
– spring 2010

The natural character of the city's core: deep soils of the central city land; stream, spring and rain waters passing through; the sun enjoyed and winds buffeting; the trees and other vegetation, plus the birds and fishes. The management of the city's natural character has changed little in more than a century. Post-quake, management of its nuances provides opportunity for a healthier ecological urban environment. The nature of the city provides substantial opportunity to contribute to eco-recovery and to making central Christchurch a twenty-first century garden city. But is it happening?

The land

The flat lands of Christchurch were deposited by mountain-sourced rivers, winds and coastal processes, resulting in an intricate diversity of ecosystems in ever-changing patterns. For millions of years the mountain source of greywacke rock shattered, eroded and tumbled out with the sprawling braided Waimakariri River to form broad and deep greywacke gravel plains. Large greywacke boulders are abandoned by the river on the inland high plains, with smaller gravels transported further seaward, though these infrequently reach the coast.

Coastal fringe, including coastal
wetlands, estuaries & lagoons

Naturally poor drained plains (tends to
be lower plains)

Naturally well drained plains (tends to
be upper plains) & inland basins (e.g.,
Culverden, Hakataramea)

Recent floodplains (both
alpine-sourced braided
rivers and foothill rivers)

Figure 1: Landforms of
the Canterbury Plains

Behind coastal dunes, lying close to sea level (hence with groundwater close to
the surface and bountiful springs), wetland ecosystems built up peat deposits
which were intermittently buried by flood-borne alluvium. The layers and
pockets of land deposited by river, wind, forest or sea result in differing and
variously dynamic substrates on which to place urban form, harvest and drain
water, insert infrastructure, grow food, respond to earthquakes, regenerate
ecosystems and create amenity. The complex land patterning of the city's flats
is variously vulnerable to wind erosion, liquefaction, lateral spread, subsidence,
burial, artesian waters, flooding and wave action. Natural processes formed
and continue to shape these fringe coastal plains' lands (fig. 1).

Historically, after emerging from the inland mountains, valleys and basins,
the Waimakariri pivoted north and south, depositing alluvial greywacke gravel
plains out to and around the volcanic 'island' of Banks Peninsula. Greywacke
outwash plains thus met the volcanic hill country of the Port Hills – their
rocks, soils and waterways differ dramatically: they are contrasting terrestrial
ecosystems.

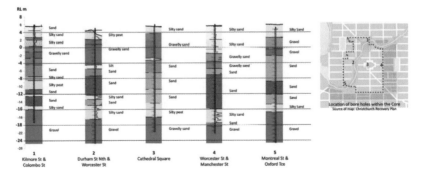

Figure 2: Drill cores into
central city land

Gravels deposited hundreds of metres deep by the great Waimakariri braided
river system underlie the central city. Deep, pure aquifers flow seawards
through these. The thick gravel wedge is overlaid by interfingering silt, sand,
peat and gravels with unconfined groundwaters to a depth of roughly 20
metres (fig. 2). A former breakout channel of the Waimakariri through the
city now accommodates the gentle spring-fed Ōtākaro-Avon (fig. 3).

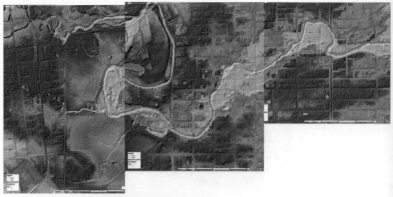

Figure 3: LiDAR of Christchurch from a distance

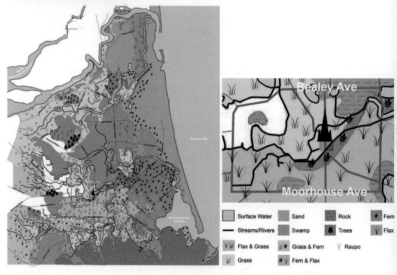

Figure 4: 1850 landcover of Christchurch

When the site for the Canterbury settlement core was selected on the plains land in 1849, its identified advantages included the dry and level land, a handy forest and the navigable river with water 'clearer than crystal' running through the adjoining site (fig. 4). Although durable Totara stumps are regularly encountered during site excavations and deep piling throughout the central city exposing former forest cover (figs 5a & 5b), these lush forests had all gone through fires and floods before the settlers' arrival.[1] The 1849 surveyors' camp was placed in Tautahi's kāinga (settlement). Their blueprint was placed on the centuries-old settlement of Puari, on the Ōtākaro. This blueprint for the settlement centre involved a band of reserve land enclosing a core area of dry land – a gravel lobe clothed in grass, fern and tutu – with wetlands to north, east and south largely confined within this band: a green frame, an intended Town Reserve.[2] Expansion was to be beyond this frame, to north, south and west, with no east expansion intended.

Waimakariri River floodwaters have periodically flowed into and down the Ōtākaro-Avon, but gravels do not extend beyond the Avon headwaters. Our 1995 mapping of Christchurch ecosystems showed the lobe of dry plains through the city centre, surrounded by naturally wet plains.[3] Drill data shows

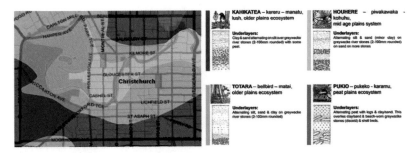

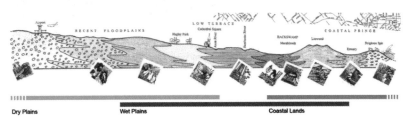

the 2012 Blueprint's city Core is well founded on gravels at depth. As shown in the more recent quakes, Waimakariri stopbank defences are somewhat vulnerable and recognition of the floodpath through the central city requires consideration.

The surface soils, waters and vegetation of the city have been mapped through the past 160 years, and numerous well and drill data recorded. There is no known mapping to show the layering of varying deposits through time for the Ōtākaro-Avon, though the elevation patterning legible on LiDAR images indicate previous flow paths.

The mapping by the city's 1850 designers recorded the presence of the natural patterning then evident within this coastal plains ecosystem – particularly the river, banks, minor streams and wetlands, dunes and vegetative cover (see fig. 4). The meandering Ōtākaro-Avon, which forks and collects spring-fed tributaries along its length, and changes course in response to floods, was by 1850 confined to flow through a fixed corridor within a formal grid delineating streets, parks and lots. This grid layout continues as the central city today. It is assumed and neither analysed nor challenged in the post-quake Blueprint for the central city.

As was clearly demonstrated by the earthquakes, lands deposited by high energy environments, such as the sand dunes formed by coastal processes, do not suffer from liquefaction. In contrast, materials deposited in low energy environments, such as those formed by the estuary and wetlands, typically suffered substantial liquefaction. The liquefaction mapping shows that, except alongside stream margins, there was scant liquefaction on the dry plains land. The natural levees ruptured dramatically along both existing and previous natural waterways (fig. 6). The memory of stream pathways embedded within the land calls for the recognition of these former stream corridors – either explicitly or at least implicitly by leaving them as unbuilt green ways (fig. 7). In addition to the liquefaction (of which many thousands of tonnes have

Manchester Street

Figures 6 and 7: Fracture lines run along former waterways in Christchurch streets.

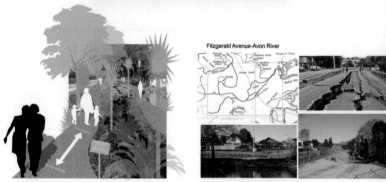

Fitzgerald Avenue-Avon River

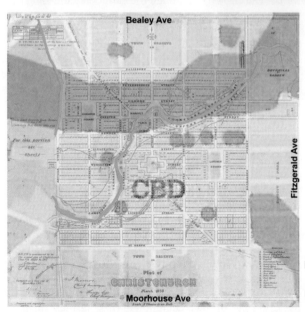

Bealey Ave

CBD

Fitzgerald Ave

Moorhouse Ave

■ Moderate to severe liquefaction

□ Moderate to low liquefaction

Figure 8: Liquefaction spread across the grid.

Figure 9: Land surfaces that have subsided or been raised by earthquakes.

been removed), lateral spread, slumping and subsidence have occurred across substantial areas of the city.

Mapping of liquefaction (fig. 8), levee rupture causing lateral spread, subsidence (fig. 9) and resultant increased flood proneness shows there were comparatively minor effects within the core of the central city, except for along the Avon corridor. With land subsidence raising relative water levels, plus lateral spread narrowing the river corridor, saltwater now migrates kilometres further upstream than it did prior to the quakes. Lateral spread and the decreased flow capacity of floodways is recognised in the Blueprint with the allowance for a 30 metre park zone either side of the river. No mention is made of restoration of the natural ecosystem, but an attractive river corridor is sought. Subsequent communications purport river 'restoration' in the city precinct. However volcanic rock, faster waters and concrete walling is not 'restoration' of a naturally gentle, soft mud and sand bedded waterway (fig. 11).

Figures 10 & 11: The Avon as it currently exists (left) and its proposed iteration in the CCRP (right).

In past millennia, particularly during ice ages, vast quantities of sediment poured down rivers from the Southern Alps and built up the Canterbury Plains. Just 18,000 years ago, the Canterbury coast was considerably further offshore.[4] The country sank and sea level rose so that 6000 years ago the beach was through what became Hagley Park – dunes remain evident (fig. 12). The coastal edge migrated across the central city, inland and seaward, for several thousand years. It has been located in its current position at Brighton for a thousand years, but some migration inland again is anticipated over coming decades and centuries. Official predictions of a 1 metre sea level rise, accompanied by several metres' high storm surges, will result in substantial inundation across the east of Christchurch by 2115. The city core lands are not considered vulnerable.

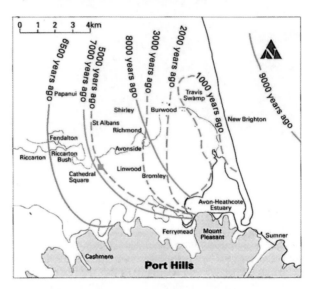

Figure 12: Former coastlines of the Christchurch area

It makes sense that the underlying stratigraphy of Ōtautahi Christchurch should command respect: located on the Pacific Rim, this earthquake-affected city lies on soft spring-fed ground close to rising sea level. Following prompts from others, the historic nature is cursorily recognised in the Chirstchurch Central Recovery Plan (CCRP) but not conceptually progressed from the 1850 Black Map (fig. 13).

Figure 13: The 1850 Black Map with the 1850 Town Reserve shown in green.

The 1850 plan's green frame or Town Reserve involved a therapeutic recreational space to achieve the 'Greatest Health for the Greatest Number'. Providing breathing places through public parks and environmental reform was central to the Benthamite designers' approach. However that frame was replaced by development by 1862. Thus areas of the central city have less access to green space than originally intended. The Blueprint provides little analysis of this in terms of actually providing adequately accessible green space for those who are to live, work and play in the city centre.

I endorse the Blueprint intent for residential density within the central city. But that should be supported by protection of the food-producing land around the city and confinement of the city from greenfield sprawl. Neither is happening. Instead government is supporting greenfield sprawl over some of New Zealand's more productive land (fig. 14).

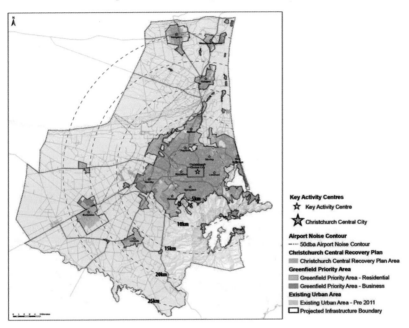

Figure 14: The greenfield priority areas of the Land Use Recovery Plan

The waters

Coming close to the plains' land surface as the groundwater nears the coast, springs are an important natural characteristic of the city lowlands. The Avon is a spring-fed waterway, and its spring-fed tributaries were largely piped last century.

As referenced in Neil Dawson's sculpture *Chalice* (2000), artesian waters are typical of these spring-fed coastal plain lands. Springs previously flowed into city basements where the pure waters were appreciated and utilised. Each home and business was typically supplied by a shallow artesian well. A hole dug in Cathedral Square reportedly resulted in water spurting up almost 2 metres above ground level. With land contamination and risks, unconfined artesian sources are now typically capped. However the quakes moved and freed many water sources to flow again. Most have subsequently been capped and many sites dewatered.

The Christchurch Art Gallery proudly proclaims its location on a spring – Te Puna o Waiwhetu (puna means spring of water). Sadly those spring waters are not evident, but piped away. Yet springs, streams and wetlands are not only useful in terms of water supply, but are also the tantalising natural assets of modern, environmentally-sensitive cities.[5] In progressive cities elsewhere, riparian buffers, rain gardens, swales and daylighted streams are increasingly core features of city redevelopment and provide cleansed rainwater to urban streams.

Central city Christchurch had an abundance of natural springs and streams that were previously blocked and piped. Dry land was pretended. In 2000, the Christchurch City Council (CCC) approved a strategy to 'Recognise that the numerous spring-fed tributaries of the Avon River are an essential part of the character of Christchurch', and to 'Sustain spring flows through restoration, groundwater management and monitoring'.[6] Sadly, more than a decade later the City Plan remains silent on springs, with nothing added post-quake. Whilst around fifteen years ago CCC undertook a wonderful programme of wetland and waterway restoration, this work had largely ceased pre-quake.[7] Whilst downtown Wellington and Auckland waterfronts proudly revealed their waters, Christchurch has lagged in its programme. To merely place the names of buried waters onto new places is not enough.

With an almost total rebuild of so much of central Christchurch now intended, there is an opportunity to reveal and nurture natural groundwaters as well as treat rainwater more naturally. The CCRP states this intent and we hope to see it as reality on public and private land. But there is no encouragement, not even guidance for the waterways – as they emerge in the rebuild, magnificent flows are again being blocked up or diverted into stormwater pipes. In public projects, streets are being rebuilt to again shed contaminated stormwater to the river and only token rain gardens are proposed to cleanse runoff – disappointingly these were not specified for even the 9 metre widened Manchester Boulevard.

The CCRP seeks to protect and enhance springs and waterways but implementation or encouragement is not evident. A confined city core in this naturally spring-fed land with a high water table has opportunity for a modern garden city with tantalising lakes, wetlands, pools and streams. Perhaps the proposed Margaret Mahy Family Playground will demonstrate this character. Furthermore, it is important that the Te Papa o Ōtākaro / Avon River Precinct not be treated merely as a cultural heritage and amenity feature, nor as an opportunity to create a different type of waterway. For that corridor and the associated catchment would more appropriately be addressed as a spring-fed natural system. Sadly the current purported 'restoration' denies this.

The CCRP's objectives 'to improve water quality and to treat and manage stormwater'[8] are also little evident. This is not occurring in the private developments which cover a substantial area of the central city. New central city developments are entirely impervious. Once more, the land beneath is ignored: there is no rainwater soakage to the ground; groundwater is pumped out and barricaded off. With sea level rise, groundwater will also rise. Public developments also demonstrate this attitude. The Hagley Oval Anchor Project is now under development. Whilst the Blueprint states the intent to improve the quality and health of waters in the central city, the vigorous spring-fed Addington Stream, an Avon tributary running through the Hagley Oval site, is the most contaminated waterway in Canterbury, with exceptional arsenic levels. Whilst there is space in the vicinity, disappointingly the Hagley Oval development plans (a Blueprint denoted Anchor Project) included no water treatment measures to address the existing degraded situation.

Whilst as a basic principle it is ecologically and culturally appropriate to separate groundwater from contaminated stormwater, only lip service is being paid.

The winds

Despite the temperate and relatively dry climate of the city, with rain falling on fewer days than in New Zealand's other major cities, persistent cool easterly winds – the notorious Barbeque Blast – reduce amenity value. Whilst the wind pattern would likely not have been so well known by the designers in 1850, surprisingly the Blueprint does not address microclimate management. The east-west street corridors of the central city grid exacerbate the effects of the cool easterly. The Blueprint enabled an opportunity to address micro-climate management in the central city at the broader scale. Although the government has purchased land to be redeveloped differently (including some green space), East Frame concepts have not as yet taken up the opportunity to 'stuff the grid' with vegetation in street corridors to provide shelter from the easterly. With a disaster likely to be the only time in our city's history that enables the urban form to be re-shaped, the opportunity to twist the grid across the path of the cold winds has unfortunately not been taken up (fig. 15).

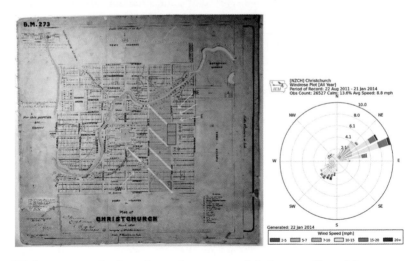

Figure 15: Twisting the grid on account of prevailing winds

Whilst aspect and orientation, solar access and shelter are all crucial aspects for people's enjoyment of the Christchurch environment and for energy management, there is unfortunately no encouragement to constructively manage microclimates – to provide sheltered spaces and routes – in the design of projects for the central city rebuild.

The vegetation

Beginning in 1897, the Christchurch Beautifying Association sought to make Christchurch a garden city as much through the use and celebration of native flora as through the use of garden plants imported from around the world. Some of these plantings survive, such as on Poplar Crescent (Barker Avenue) and the scatter of native trees and shrubs nearby. A century later this city became a world leader in the research and provision of information as to what biota belonged naturally in each area and micro-site, and this information guided restoration. Whilst the tree-lined river corridor is perhaps the most intact heritage in the city centre, and funds are tight, almost $100 million is being spent on the river corridor makeover for the River Precinct anchor project.

Yet the CCRP measures do little to encourage vegetation within developments. The measures are typically visual only – such as for screening. For the River Precinct, the CCRP proposes to increase natural cover only on the river's true left, and sadly there is no direction to reference or to restore any dimensions of the underlying natural ecosystems. The public sought green spaces, sheltered spaces, recreated native ecosystems, green roofs and walls through Share an Idea and Ngāi Tūāhuriri have also sought greening.

Whilst vegetation is known to be important for contributing to managing water quality, air quality, micro-climates, energy demand, wildlife and the many experiential dimensions of the city, there is a dearth of encouragement for enhancement of the city environment with vegetation. The basics are ignored, such as on-site water management and green roofs. Whilst green roofs are widespread in some international cities (such as Toronto, Berlin and Stuttgart)[9] they are not occurring in the Christchurch rebuild, nor facilitated through guidance, inducement or regulation. Other than in an old-fashioned amenity style, the central city planning measures largely ignore the potential for multi-dimensional urban enhancement through the use of vegetation.

Conclusion

The aspiration quoted in the Christchurch Central Recovery Plan is 'A greener, more attractive central Christchurch, which includes measures against climate change'.[10] The Blueprint for the central city, where the 'work, live and play' core for the city is again planned, delineates the purchase of lands for the Frame – a bold move in redefining the central city morphology. The rebuild in the city involves adequately robust lands. Considering the elevation, the centrality to the overall urban form takes into consideration anticipated coastal retreat, the flood patterns, the lands vulnerable to liquefaction and subsidence, I agree that the lands chosen as the focus for the Blueprint and for the city's recovery centre are appropriate. However their diversity – their fine-grained patterning – has not been explored or responded to in the Blueprint. While the desire has been expressed to better reference and maximise the natural underlayers and dynamic systems that belong here, in line with a modern eco-friendly city, there is scant indication that the opportunities will be adequately explored or maximised. Eco-recovery opportunities should instead be encouraged when there is such an opportunity to reimagine our city.

I Like Your Form

Lonnie Hutchinson's *I Like Your Form* transforms the Arcades Project and acknowledges the historic – and future – importance of this location to Ngāi Tahu. Both works, produced by FESTA, intermingle elements of the past with a proposition for our new city and identity. As temporary works of differing duration, their dialogue is both with the surrounding area and with each other. *I Like Your Form* acknowledges the Ōtākaro-Avon River as an important mahinga kai (traditional resources) site and breeding ground for tuna (eel) and inaka (whitebait) and prefigures the re-emerging context of the area as one steeped in cultural expression and art.

[1]

[2–3]

What has Ōtautahi revealed?: Māori urban planning in post-earthquake Christchurch

Craig Pauling, Shaun Awatere & Shadrach Rolleston

Craig Pauling (Ngāi Tahu, Kāti Mamoe, Waitaha, Ngāti Mutunga) has worked across iwi, councils, government and industry to strengthen the role of mātauranga Māori in the landscape. He works at Boffa Miskell and is the co-chair of Ngā Aho – the national network of Māori design and planning professionals. Shaun Awatere (Ngāti Porou) holds a PhD in economics and works as a resource economist for Manaaki Whenua Landcare Research, focusing on improving the incorporation of mātauranga Māori into resource management. Shadrach Rolleston (Ngāi Te Rangi, Ngāti Ranginui, Ngāti Haua) has worked as an adviser and planner for government, the private sector and his iwi/hapū. He currently works for BECA.

Kupu Whakataki – Introduction

The challenge for most organisations is how to apply a set of principles in practice. In New Zealand, this challenge has been played out over the past two decades through attempts to incorporate Māori values and principles in resource management planning and decision-making. In the wake of these attempts, post-earthquake Christchurch has provided a fertile field of opportunities for applying the values of the community, and in particular those of tangata whenua[1] through the city's rebuild and recovery. Importantly, this has seen Te Rūnanga o Ngāi Tahu, Te Ngāi Tūāhuriri Rūnanga and the other Papatipu Rūnanga[2] in the greater Christchurch area working with the Christchurch City Council (CCC) and the Canterbury Earthquake Recovery Authority (CERA), to take steps towards applying and implementing Ngāi Tahu values and principles through the Christchurch Central Recovery Plan (CCRP).

The CCRP and its resulting Blueprint have attempted to integrate cultural, social, ecological and economic goals, and perhaps most importantly, reflect and celebrate the unique bi-cultural heritage of Ōtautahi-Christchurch. Innovatively, the CCRP has led to the engagement of mana whenua[3] as a co-designer to the city redevelopment with the aim of integrating mātauranga Māori (Māori knowledge) into city planning, decision-making and urban design. The ongoing challenge will be in continuing to build and strengthen these relationships and applying the shared values and principles arising from these positive responses to what was a major natural disaster.

Tāhuhu Kōrero – Background

Since 2004, Manaaki Whenua Landcare Research has been working alongside iwi (tribes) and hapū (sub-tribes), including Ngāi Tahu, to both understand and develop processes for the incorporation of mātauranga Māori into urban design and planning. The research has focused on identifying and addressing strengths, weaknesses and knowledge gaps in New Zealand's urban planning environment by examining a range of case studies that involve iwi and hapū from throughout country.

Of significance to the Christchurch rebuild, the research programme also supported a two-day symposium, called Ōtautahi Revealed, that brought together approximately 100 design and planning professionals to discuss historical and emerging issues and lessons garnered from Māori-inspired design, planning and development initiatives across New Zealand. It also served as a forum to discuss how the Christchurch Central Recovery Plan could deliver on its vision of embracing Ngāi Tahu values through the rebuild. The symposium was a celebration of a research area that is still in its infancy and an exploration of the interface between mātauranga Māori and a Western planning tradition.[4]

Integration of mātauranga Māori into mainstream planning

While post-earthquake Christchurch may have taken some steps towards incorporating mātauranga Māori through its recovery planning, Māori participation and engagement in the planning process varies throughout New Zealand. The degree of participation has increased as Māori have become more politically, economically, socially and technically involved in resource management issues. The integration of Māori knowledge systems into mainstream planning has been progressive, and is ongoing. The notion of self-determination continues to shape Māori perceptions of reality and efforts for change, and collectively Māori also continue to push the political boundaries to effect positive change.

Formal urban planning law was first introduced in 1926 with the enactment of the Town and Country Planning Act (TCPA), which determined zones for commercial, retail, industrial, residential and rural activities. The process of zoning had a significant detrimental effect on Māori land by affecting rights to manage it and through subsequent land alienation. During this period, local authorities failed to adequately recognise and provide for Māori needs and perspectives. This was largely the result of poor relationships between iwi/hapū and the Crown (including councils), poor consultation processes, and the marginalisation of Māori from most planning and policy activity.[5]

In and around Christchurch, for example, the zoning of Māori reservations under the TCPA (and continued under the Resource Management Act 1991 or RMA) had detrimental consequences for both Māori communities and land owners. The reservations, including Māori Reserve 873 around Tuahiwi, were set aside and envisioned as urban centres as part of the original Crown land purchases from Ngāi Tahu in the nineteenth century. However, because the reserve lands were located in 'rural' areas beyond the city limits, they were subsequently zoned as rural land, rather than as living zones. Rural zoning resulted in owners being unable to build intensively, which in turn contributed to urbanisation in Christchurch city. With limited input into, or ability to contest zoning rules, as well as a lack of provision of council infrastructure and services, and no option to build houses for their growing families on their own land, many moved into Christchurch suburbs to find housing. Many families moved to the eastern suburbs that were adversely affected by the earthquakes.[6]

Throughout the 1960s, the New Zealand Māori Council (NZMC) challenged the prevailing orthodoxy and promoted a more active response to address Māori planning needs via the bilingual quarterly publication *Tè Ao Hou – The New World*. The key issues promoted by the NZMC included removing restrictions and limitations placed on the development of Māori land, raising the standard of poor quality rural housing, the protection of urupā (burial grounds) and the conservation of kaimoana (seafood).[7] Māori voices, however, were virtually non-existent in local authority planning. In the following decade, a groundswell of change was about to occur. The battle lines had been declared and at the vanguard of the Māori Renaissance were the Māori protest movements in the late 1960s and early 1970s. This movement culminated in the introduction of the Waitangi Tribunal in 1975 and the launching of a number of environmental and cultural claims.[8]

It was not until a legislative review of the TCPA in 1977 that Māori values were finally given formal recognition within planning statutes. In this revised version of the Act, section 3(1)(g) declares: 'the relationship of Māori and their culture and traditions with their ancestral land is a matter of national importance to be recognised and provided for in the preparation, implementation and administration of regional, district and maritime schemes'. This clause contributed to the development of a number of planning responses, including the Māori Planning Kit, which the Auckland Māori Planning Committee developed in 1981 to provide guidance to planners regarding Māori land.[9] In 1983 the Town and Country Planning Division of the Ministry of Works and Development also promoted the need for urban planning schemes to recognise and provide for Māori living in urban areas.[10] The latter report is one of the earliest calls for greater recognition of Māori voices within an urban setting. While section 3(1)(g) of the Act was a significant step towards recognising Māori values in planning, its initial implementation was found to be quite limited due to the absence of case law.

In 1987, a second consecutive term Labour Government initiated a comprehensive reform of resource management in New Zealand, which was led by the then Environment Minister, Geoffrey Palmer. The intention was to bring together several disparate acts of environmental legislation under one umbrella. Following major free market reform in NZ, the fourth Labour Government set about merging two seemingly incompatible philosophies: neo-classical economic ideology and sustainable resource management. Out of the reforms emerged the Resource Management Act, a major piece of legislation that underpins all urban planning and policy. The landmark change under the RMA was that it included provisions to recognise and take into account iwi and hapū environmental interests under sections 6(e), 7(a) and 8. However Māori perspectives of the RMA, particularly from iwi/hapū, have commonly differed with interpretations used in local authorities. This is highlighted by T. Tutua-Nathan who stated that before these sections could be effectively implemented, 'tikanga Māori has to be understood by local and central authorities, the courts, and the general public'.[11] Hirini Matunga also notes that while the RMA acknowledges a Māori planning tradition, it lacks the desire to effectively incorporate and/or integrate a Māori planning approach in any meaningful way.[12]

Māori values and principles for urban planning

Since the commencement of the RMA, Māori participation in resource management and urban planning has slowly developed, as have the relationships between local and central government and iwi and hapū, albeit with different outcomes in different locations.[13] Over the past decade in particular, a range of initiatives and projects have investigated how mātauranga Māori values and principles can be utilised to inform the distinct and emerging discipline of urban planning, and have identified key Māori values and principles that are critical in doing so. This section provides an overview of three of these initiatives (which the authors have been involved in) that outline some of these values and principles. These examples are provided to give a context for understanding how the Christchurch Central Recovery Plan has attempted to recognise and provide for mātauranga Māori values and principles.

Tū Whare Ora: Māori driven design in sustainable settlement development

The Tū Whare Ora research project began in 2004 as an initiative flowing from the Low Impact Urban Design and Development (LIUDD) research programme led by Manaaki Whenua Landcare Research. The project, funded by Ngā Pae o Te Māramatanga (a Māori Centre of Research and Excellence), reviewed the history of Māori built environments, from the traditional design and development of pā (fortified village), kāinga (settlement/village), whare (house) and marae (communal facility) to the contemporary values expressed through papakāinga development and urban planning. The project also identified processes for both the design and planning of papakāinga, as well as discussing ways to assess papakāinga developments.

The project identified nine key Māori principles drawn from the literature as well as the examination of two Māori settlement case studies, one with Ngāti Whatua o Ōrakei in Auckland and the other with Ngāti Ranginui at Oikimoke, near Tauranga. The principles highlight a uniquely Māori approach to urban design and planning that aims to effectively incorporate cultural aspirations, needs and character into urban environments. The nine principles are provided in figure 1, along with a brief description, purpose and an outline of potential applications and responses for urban planning and design.[14]

Te Aranga Māori Cultural Landscape Strategy

The Te Aranga Māori Cultural Landscape Strategy is significant in the development of Māori involvement and action in relation to urban design and planning in New Zealand. It instigated a considered and collective response to the lack of a Māori perspective contained in a national Urban Design Protocol developed by the Ministry for the Environment in 2005. Importantly, the development of the strategy also led to the subsequent establishment of Ngā Aho – a national network of Māori design and planning professionals. Through its members, Ngā Aho has refined the Te Aranga strategy, gained support from iwi and hapū, and developed and promoted a set of key principles underlying the strategy through numerous projects throughout the country, and has also become involved in urban planning processes in Auckland and Christchurch.

Principle	Description	Purpose	Response
Kotahitanga *Cohesion and Collaboration*	Collective cooperative and effective partnerships and collaboration with community	To encourage community unity and identity	Community centre, amphitheatre, community facilities, parks, reserves, walkways, good access links between spaces
Wairuatanga *Embedded Emotion / Spirit*	Emotional connection with the environment that links people	To maintain and preserve the essence of Tangata Whenua	Site orientation to important landmarks important to Tangata Whenua, sight lines, environmental restoration projects
Manaakitanga *Hospitality and Security*	Acceptance and hospitality given toward visitors, and protection and security of community	To embrace and welcome all peoples especially visitors and to provide a safe and secure community environment	Restore and access traditional medicinal and food resources, communal gardens, design community using CPTED principles – Crime Prevention Through Urban Design
Whanaungatanga *Participation and Membership*	Participation and membership in the community and social setting	To encourage community participation and pride through building and emphasising community identity	Communal facilities, community centre, communal Laundromat, open reserves, parks, communal gardens, common and civic spaces reflecting local identity
Kaitiakitanga *Guardianship and Stewardship*	Protection of significant landscape features important to the local community	To support the protection of important environmental and cultural features through community ownership and collective responsibility	On-site mitigation for three waters, recognition and protection of spiritual guardians, restoration of waterways and natural areas, cluster buildings to maximise communal reserves and the natural environments
Rangatiratanga *Leadership, Identity and Self-Determination*	Community can lead and take responsibility for creating and determining their own future	To promote self-determination and independence	Live and work from home, mix use high density living environments, clustering of dwellings, heritage markers (pou)
Mauritanga *Essence / Life-force*	Life-force or essence of a natural environment	To identify and promote the maintenance or restoration of mauri	Community monitoring of natural environment, swale systems for stormwater, rain-tank collection systems, grey-water recycling systems, passive solar design
Orangatanga	Maintain health and wellbeing of the community	To promote environmental protection and a safe community	Restoration projects, maintain community access to resources (flax, eels, waterways etc), indigenous flora on public and encouraged on private space, encourage walking and cycling by linking spaces, traffic calming measures, CPTED principles, public transport available
Mātauranga	Understanding of community history, identities, character	To encourage community understanding and pride through shared knowledge	Education promotions, interpretation boards, heritage markers (pou), heritage trails

Figure 1: Māori Urban design principles

Ngā Mātāpono / Principles	Ngā Hua / Outcome	Ahuatanga / Attributes	He Tauira / Application
Mana Rangatiratanga, Authority	The status of iwi and hapū as mana whenua is recognised and respected	Recognises Te Tiriti o Waitangi / The Treaty of Waitangi and the Wai 262 Ko Aotearoa Tēnei framework for Treaty Partnerships in 21st Century Aotearoa New Zealand as the basis for all relationships pertaining development Provides a platform for working relationships where manawhenua values, world views, tikanga, cultural narratives and visual identity can be appropriately expressed in the design environment High quality Treaty based relationships are fundamental to the application of the other Te Aranga principles	The development of high level Treaty based relationships with mana whenua is essential prior to finalising design approaches and will maximise the opportunities for design outcomes. Important to identify any primary mana whenua groups as well as wider mana whenua interests in any given development.
Whakapapa Names & Naming	Māori names are celebrated	Recognises and celebrates the significance of mana whenua ancestral names Recognises ancestral names as entry points for exploring and honouring t puna, historical narratives and customary practises associated with development sites and their ability to enhance sense of place connections	Mana whenua consultation and research on the use of correct ancestral names, including macrons Recognition of traditional place names through signage and wayfinding Use of appropriate names to inform design processes
Tohu The wider cultural landscape	Mana whenua significant sites and cultural landmarks are acknowledged	Acknowledges a Māori world view of the wider significance of tohu / landmarks and their ability to inform the design of specific development sites Supports a process whereby significant sites can be identified, managed, protected and enhanced Celebrates local and wider unique cultural heritage and community characteristics that reinforce sense of place and identity	Recognition of tohu, including wāhi tapu, maunga, awa, puna, mahinga kai and ancestral kainga Allows visual connection to significant sites to be created, preserved and enhanced Wider cultural landmarks and associated narratives able to inform building / spatial orientation and general design responses Heritage trails, markers and interpretation boards
Taiao The natural environment	The natural environment is protected, restored and / or enhanced	Sustains and enhances the natural environment Local flora and fauna which are familiar and significant to mana whenua are key natural landscape elements within urban and / or modified areas Natural environments are protected, restored or enhanced to levels where sustainable mana whenua harvesting is possible	Re-establishment of local biodiversity Creating and connecting ecological corridors Planting of appropriate indigenous flora in public places, strategies to encourage native planting in private spaces Selection of plant and tree species as seasonal markers and attractors of native bird life Establishment and management of traditional food and cultural resource areas allowing for active kaitiakitanga
Mauri Tū Environmental Health	Environmental health is protected, maintained and / or enhanced	The wider development area and all elements and developments within the site are considered on the basis of protecting, maintaining or enhancing mauri The quality of wai, whenua, ngāhere and air are actively monitored Water, energy and material resources are conserved Community wellbeing is enhanced	Daylighting, restoration and planting of waterways Contaminated areas of soil are remediated Rainwater collection systems, grey-water recycling systems and passive solar design opportunities are explored in the design process Hard landscape and building materials which are locally sourced and of high cultural value to mana whenua are explored in the design process
Mahi Toi Creative Expression	Iwi/hapū narratives are captured and expressed creatively and appropriately	Ancestral names, local tohu and iwi narratives are creatively reinscribed into the design environment including: landscape; architecture; interior design and public art Iwi / hapū mandated design professionals and artists are appropriately engaged in such processes	Mana whenua assist in establishing design consortia which are equipped to translate iwi/hapū cultural narratives into the design environment Civic / shared landscapes are created to reflect local iwi/hapū identity and contribute to sense of place Iwi/hapū narratives are reinscribed in the environment through public art and design
Ahi Kā The Living Presence	Iwi/hapū have a living and enduring presence and are secure and valued within their rohe	Mana whenua live, work and play within their own rohe Acknowledges the post Treaty of Waitangi settlement environment where iwi living presences can include customary, cultural and commercial dimensions Living iwi/hapū presences and associated kaitiaki roles are resumed within urban areas	Access to natural resources (weaving species, mahinga kai, waterways, etc) facilitates, maintains and /or enhances mana whenua ahi kā and kaitiakitanga Civic/iwi joint venture developments ensure ahi kā and sense of place relationships are enhanced Iwi/private sector joint venture developments enhance employment and ahi kā relationships

Figure 2: Te Aranga Māori design principles

What has Ōtautahi revealed?

The seven Te Aranga Māori Design Principles, shown in figure 2, were developed in conjunction with iwi in Auckland, as part of the new Auckland City Council planning process. Importantly, these design principles are focused on providing practical guidance for the incorporation of Māori values in urban design and highlight the critical importance of working with Māori, under a co-design arrangement, for authentic results in urban design.[15]

Kaitiakitanga of Urban Settlements

The Kaitiakitanga of Urban Settlements research programme was funded by the Ministry of Science and Innovation from 2009 to 2012 and was led by Manaaki Whenua Landcare Research. The programme used an extensive literature review, workshops and comprehensive case-study research in both Christchurch and Auckland to highlight key barriers and solutions for the incorporation of Māori values into urban design and planning.

The programme also developed tools, methods and processes to help planners, iwi and hapū groups actively apply mātauranga Māori values and principles within urban planning and design. The nine case studies examined local council planning processes, private sub-division development and iwi-led urban developments to determine the important factors for success as well as the barriers to uptake of mātauranga Māori.

The research identified five key features that were important across the case studies, which include having positive relationships between iwi/hapū, property developers and local and central government; utilising appropriate frameworks (including Māori based evaluation processes), methods, and tools for guiding engagement, communication and integration; developing and valuing iwi/hapū capability as professional advice; ensuring timely and open access to quality information; and seeking innovation and adaptability in solutions.

As part of the research an evaluation method was proposed that can be used to inform urban planning and design, guide decision-making and assess outcomes. The tool is based on criteria drawn from the research case studies, including a cultural assessment undertaken in relation to a proposed Ngāi Tahu tribal office building in central Christchurch. Using a Likert-type scale (0 negative effect – 5 positive effect), a proposal can be evaluated against the criteria to determine which elements of the proposal are seen positively or negatively from an iwi/hapū perspective. Additional qualitative comments can provide observations on how proposals could be improved. This information can be used to demonstrate support, changes or opposition to the proposal. The evaluation tool, including criteria and scoring examples, is shown in figure 3.[16]

Te Mahere 'Maraka Ōtautahi' – the Christchurch Central Recovery Plan

This section provides examples of how Māori principles, such as those identified above, have been integrated into the Christchurch Central Recovery Plan. In doing this we review four key principles identified by Ngāi Tahu within the recovery plan including rangatiratanga (leadership and authority); kaitiakitanga (stewardship); tohungatanga (knowledge and wise consideration of decisions); manaakitanga (love and respect for people).

Criteria		Scores
Mana Whenua *(tribal prestige and authority):*	Does the proposal acknowledge, recognise and provide for tangata whenua involvement?	5: Working relationship with mana whenua, mana whenua are involved in the design and implementation and their participation is adequately compensated. 0: No-working relationship with mana whenua
Ngā Wai Tipuna *(waterways):*	Does the proposal protect and/ or enhance natural waterways, and consider the appropriate use/ reuse, treatment and disposal of water?	5: Protects and enhances natural waterways, i.e. sustainable water use and there is no discharge into waterways 0: Waterways are befouled and/or unsustainable water use
Ngā Otaota Maori *(indigenous flora and fauna):*	Does the proposal protect and/or enhance native flora, fauna, habitats, ecosystems, and biodiversity (particularly waterways and wetlands)?	5: Ecosystems are protected and enhanced, biodiversity is enhanced, landscaping and riparian zones use native plants 0: Ecosystems are destroyed, biodiversity loss occurs, landscaping and riparian zone use non-native plants
Wāhi Tapu/Taonga *(culturally significant sites):*	Does the proposal acknowledge, protect, enhance and/or appropriately interpret culturally significant sites?	5: Wāhi tapu/taonga are identified, protected, and enhanced 0: Wāhi tapu/taonga are not identified and are destroyed
Kaitiakitanga *(sustainable resource management):*	Does the proposal consider the reduction of waste and pollution (to air, land, water and coastal environments) as well as minimise the reliance on and/or improve existing infrastructure (e.g. sewage, storm-water and energy systems)?	5: Low impact urban design solutions are used, sustainable transport options are utilised, and kaitiaki have access to mahinga kai 0: Urban design is unsustainable and access to mahinga kai is prohibited
Tohungatanga *(expertise / knowledge):*	Does the proposal consider investment in technology, knowledge, products, and systems that are energy, water and resource efficient, and involve ongoing monitoring and reporting?	5: Most buildings have a greenstar rating of 5 or a homestar rating of 10, recycled timber is used, renewable energy is utilised, and raw materials are sourced locally 0: The majority of buildings have poor, if any, greenstar or homestar ratings, non-renewable energy is utilised, and raw materials are sourced externally
Whakapapa *(cultural identity):*	Does the proposal provide a connection to, and/or protect and enhance the local landscape and iwi/hapū identity and integrity?	5: Recognises and provides for mana whenua tikanga, history, and identity through artwork, pouwhenua, appropriate street names, reserves for wāhi tapu, whare taonga, whare karakia, and involvement in ceremonies 0: Does not recognise and provide for mana whenua tikanga, history, and identity
Whanaungatanga/ Manaakitanga *(community development):*	Does the proposal provide environments and practices that are uniquely Māori, and places where iwi/hapū and manuhiri alike are welcome, encouraged, and proud to be involved?	5: Utilises the local labour force, local businesses are preferred retailers and suppliers, provides for recreational areas and community centres 0: Does not utilise the local labour force, local businesses are not the preferred retailers and suppliers, no recreational areas or community centres are provided for
Rangatiratanga *(empowered communities):*	Does the proposal implement management systems that encourage clients, employees and suppliers to identify, and act upon opportunities to protect biodiversity, prevent pollution, and continually improve environmental performance?	5: Clients, employees and suppliers are to empowered to protect biodiversity, prevent pollution, and continually improve environmental performance 0: Clients, employees and suppliers are not empowered to protect biodiversity, prevent pollution, and continually improve environmental performance

Figure 3: Mātauranga Māori based evaluation tool

Before reviewing the CCRP, it is important to note that it was developed in two distinct stages, which involved differing levels of involvement and outcomes for mana whenua and the wider community. The first stage, led by the Christchurch City Council (CCC) during 2011, involved the extensive Share an Idea campaign and public submission process that resulted in the Draft Central City Plan (CCP) submitted to the Minister for Canterbury Earthquake Recovery in December 2011. The second stage was led by the Canterbury Earthquake Recovery Authority during the first half of 2012. It involved a further round of public submissions as well as the secondment of a team of urban planners and designers from across the public and private sector, including from Te Rūnanga o Ngāi Tahu and the CCC, to develop the final Christchurch Central Recovery Plan (CCRP) and its associated Blueprint of anchor projects. The following review provides examples from both processes and highlights differences where relevant.

Rangatiratanga

In a planning context, the principle of rangatiratanga most closely aligns with the concepts of leadership and authority, and is focused on the appropriate engagement and involvement of iwi and hapū in the planning process. The concept of 'co-planning', where Crown agencies and local authorities work in partnership with local iwi and hapū, is a useful strategy to empower Māori to participate effectively in urban planning and policy development and give effect to the principles of the Treaty of Waitangi, which is required by the majority of New Zealand's resource management law.

The planning process for the city's recovery involved both iwi and hapū from an early stage. This included staff from both the tribal authority, Te Rūnanga o Ngāi Tahu, and Mahaanui Kura Taiao Ltd (the resource management consultancy of the six Ngāi Tahu Papatipu Rūnanga representing local sub-tribes with traditional interests in the greater Christchurch area, including Banks Peninsula) working alongside the Christchurch City Council during the development of the Draft Central City Plan. These staff in turn reported to a sub-committee established by Te Rūnanga o Ngāi Tahu to deal with earthquake recovery matters called Te Awheawhe Rūwhenua, which provided a further layer of representation of mana whenua in the process.

During the second phase of plan development, a staff member and a team of advisors mandated by Te Awheawhe Rūwhenua worked alongside CERA and CCC to complete the final plan. Following the completion of the plan, Ngāi Tahu, CERA and CCC have continued to develop and evolve a working relationship, which has resulted in the more direct involvement of Te Ngāi Tūāhuriri Rūnanga through its own earthquake recovery committee called Matapopore. Matapopore is the key Ngāi Tahu entity involved in the implementation of the CCRP and is playing a major role in design and planning processes for all of the anchor projects. A further initiative resulting from the plan is the development of the Joint Management Board, which is a partnership between Ngāi Tahu, CERA and CCC that considers new planning decisions within the central core area identified in the CCRP.

All of the engagement surrounding the CCRP can be seen as positive, and even *better* than best practice, because real and meaningful efforts were made to involve Ngāi Tahu as a key partner in the process, at both the tribal and, most importantly, the sub-tribal level. A key factor in facilitating this process was the inclusion of Te Rūnanga o Ngāi Tahu as a statutory partner in the Canterbury Earthquake Recovery Act 2011, alongside central and local government. This status gave appropriate weight and meaning to the involvement of Ngāi Tahu and allowed all parties to get on with the job rather than debate the merits of why iwi and hapū should be around the table, as has happened previously. However, it must also be acknowledged that the experience and development of Ngāi Tahu, particularly since its 1998 Treaty of Waitangi settlement and the active participation and resourcing of Ngāi Tahu representation within the planning process over the past two decades, was critical. Significant steps have been taken by all sides, which have resulted in unique partnership processes and structures that are still evolving, and that have the potential to leave a distinctive mark on Ōtautahi-Christchurch.

Kaitiakitanga

The principle of kaitiakitanga is similar to the concept of sustainable resource management but it also recognises the special relationship tangata whenua have with their local ecology and environment. Both the draft CCP and the final CCRP recognise the role iwi/hapū have in maintaining long-standing relationships with important places and species, as well as protecting and enhancing the health of the natural environment, particularly in relation to critical mahinga kai values.[17] Both plans include a specific tangata whenua spatial layer identifying sites of contemporary and historical significance to Ngāi Tahu within the plan area, as well as associated explanations of key values and tribal history. This information has helped ensure that the history and relationship of Ngāi Tahu is reflected and celebrated and that future development minimises impacts on and/or appropriately enhances these significant sites and values.

Both versions of the plan also provide for the 'green city' theme, championed by Christchurch residents through the Share an Idea campaign, and projects that support the enhancement of the natural environment, such as the Te Papa Ōtākaro / Avon River Precinct. These projects specifically recognise cultural values, the important role of Ngāi Tahu and the importance of enhancing indigenous biodiversity. In relation to biodiversity the aim is to ensure an adequate balance of indigenous and exotic plantings – in terms of size, scale and species numbers – throughout the city, thus improving overall environmental health. Key references to cultural values should ensure that Ngāi Tahu are afforded opportunities to engage in kaitiakitanga-based activities going forward, such as increasing the future potential of mahinga kai. A significant feature of the final plan that reflects the value of kaitiakitanga, which was not included in the CCC draft, is the Frame. This was envisioned by both Ngāi Tahu and CERA as a key green space framing the central city, balancing Hagley Park and providing a gateway and connections to key cultural and historical sites, including the traditional kāinga of Tautahi, a significant Ngāi Tahu ancestor who had a settlement near the fire station on Kilmore Street (from which the modern Māori name for Christchurch takes its name).

Tohungatanga

Accessing and utilising expert knowledge to assist decision-making is another essential ingredient for the effective incorporation of mātauranga Māori values and principles into urban planning. Co-planning arrangements that utilise skilled individuals with both planning and mātauranga Māori expertise are more likely to achieve good outcomes for both iwi/hapū and the wider community. While the earthquakes provided a catalyst for a closer working relationship between Ngāi Tahu and local and central government in the area of urban planning, the active development and involvement of Ngāi Tahu in resource management matters were also important. Ngāi Tahu were also heavily involved in earthquake response and recovery; many Ngāi Tahu marae, including Tuahiwi, were set up as civil defence centres to look after affected residents (Māori and non-Māori). A Māori response network was established and Te Rūnanga o Ngāi Tahu also set up and resourced its earthquake recovery committee – Te Awheawhe Rūwhenua.

The planning process also provided an opportunity for both CCC and CERA to second and work alongside staff from Te Rūnanga o Ngāi Tahu, in order to utilise appropriate knowledge and skills to develop a more informed plan. This involvement helped ensure the inclusion of key references and statements within both plans that are important for the overall effect, as well as plan implementation. In particular, this included the use of bilingual headings; whakatauki (proverbial sayings) and cultural values and principles throughout the document, and specifically within the plan's vision; the inclusion of a Ngāi Tahu mihi (greeting); a foreword alongside the other partners; and the recognition of the role of Ngāi Tahu in the implementation of the plan and key anchor projects. A significant feature of the final plan, not included in the CCC draft, is the inclusion of the Te Puna Ahurea Cultural Centre as an anchor project.

Manaakitanga

Developing strong communities can lead to better long-term solutions in urban design and planning through encouraging active programmes and environments that engage with and reflect the identities of people. Manaakitanga revolves around the provision of hospitality and care to manuhiri (visitors) and is also closely aligned with the value of whanaungatanga or building and maintaining relationships. This principle is hard to assess in relation to the plan, and in planning generally, as it is something that is more obvious through plan implementation and the development of the built environments flowing from plans. In saying this, a reflection of manaakitanga is more prevalent in the draft CCC plan than the final CCRP.

The Draft Central City Plan was more community focused and provided specific provision for Māori design influences in the development of the Metro Sports Facility, Performing Arts Precinct, public art network and the Central City Playground (now called the Margaret Mahy Family Playground). It also made specific reference to incorporating and celebrating Ngāi Tahu culture and identity in bringing back tourists and commercial development into the city through the re-development of the Convention Centre, Visitors Centre, markets and other buildings. The draft plan also provided for specific cultural and natural heritage targets and recognition in

'Distinctive City' projects, precincts and neighbourhoods as well as within the monitoring measures of the plan. These provisions were either not included or are less prevalent in the final CCRP, although the CCRP does include the provision for the Te Puna Ahurea Cultural Centre as highlighted previously.

In the end, it will be through the implementation of the plan that the value of manaakitanga may or may not be realised. This will depend on how the relationships between Ngāi Tahu, CERA, CCC and the wider community are maintained and enhanced. Early signs are promising, however, as the development of the direct and meaningful relationship between Ngāi Tūāhuriri and CERA is showing. Moreover, Ngāi Tūāhuriri have been forthright in promoting the value of manaakitanga for the rebuild and have gone further in promoting the concept of 'Atawhai ki te iwi – Care for the people' through the implementation of the plan and their work on the anchor projects. This concept is attributed to Pita Te Hori, the first Upoko Rūnanga of Ngāi Tūāhuriri, who in 1861 reassured the Christchurch community of their support for law and peace during a time of wars in the North Island.[18] This is a clear example that authentic attempts are being made to both incorporate and reflect values and principles in the rebuild of Christchurch. Time, as always, will provide the true test of how well we will do.

He whakamutunga – Conclusion

While the authentic inclusion of mātauranga Māori within urban planning and design is evolving and has an interesting recent history in New Zealand, there are generic features, including key methods and processes that, if adhered to, can lead to more effective values-based urban design and planning. The following key features are therefore important to highlight, particularly in relation to the positive aspects of the Christchurch Central Recovery Plan, so that further progress can be made in developing a truly bicultural planning paradigm, which will result in both built and natural environments that reflect the shared values and heritage of modern Aotearoa New Zealand.

Firstly, developing, building and maintaining relationships between iwi, hapū, private developers and local and central government is essential for ensuring the meaningful recognition and provision for mātauranga Māori in contemporary urban planning, design and development. Relationships need to be based on mutual respect and the importance of the partnership and principles enshrined in the Treaty of Waitangi.

Secondly, developing and utilising appropriate tools and processes that can be clearly understood, communicated and applied are crucial to the uptake of mātauranga Māori based values and principles. Models such as the Te Aranga principles developed for the Auckland Plan shown in figure 2 and the evaluation process shown in figure 3 can help provide context, structure and robustness that supports informed decision-making.

Thirdly, recognising and valuing the critical role of expert cultural advice that can facilitate the development of high-quality, and otherwise often undiscoverable, information in the planning, design and development process, will improve overall outcomes and help ensure these have the support of iwi and hapū. All parties need quality information to make informed and robust decisions. Therefore, open two-way 'co-planning/ co-design' processes involving knowledge and information from a range of disciplines are critical in influencing outcomes. Processes that allow for mutual understanding provide beneficial outcomes for all.

We believe that the CCRP and its processes and outcomes have attempted to utilise these features and in doing so have made an important contribution to the development of a more bicultural planning paradigm. The plan and, most importantly, its early implementation have attempted to integrate key Māori values and principles and has led to the direct engagement of local hapū, Ngāi Tūāhuriri, as a co-designer of the city redevelopment. This is something that was missed during the development of Christchurch in the nineteenth century, but that we now all have the chance to resolve. We believe this bodes well for a result that can lead to outcomes that celebrate the unique and shared bicultural heritage of Ōtautahi-Christchurch and leave a significant and positive mark on the city, mō tātou, ā, mō uri a muri ake nei – for us, and our children after us.

Shop Eight Food & Wine

The team at Shop Eight are committed to using almost exclusively (95 per cent) local produce and have developed strong working relationships with regional farmers, growers and artisans. Cressy Farm raises healthy pigs and kills them ethically, in partnership with their butcher at Euro Deli Meats. As sustainable fishing is not practised off the shores of Canterbury, together with Roots Restaurant in Lyttelton, Shop Eight gets a regular delivery of fish from Lee Fisheries Northland. They are working to create a viable market for sustainably caught fish in the South Island. Logan of Spring Fed Ltd grows fantastic vegetables, some of which are not grown on a commercial scale, and are unrecognisable and exciting!

[1–2]

We value and practice
resourcefulness, localism and
creativity. The kitchen, café and
studio are b_____ materials
that would _____
_____

____
ensu
mission.

[3–7]

Reimagining Recovery

Digging where we stand: Visions of urbundance and the role of food production in Christchurch

Bailey Peryman, Oliver Peryman & Michelle Marquet

The authors make up the team that owns, directs and manages Garden City 2.0, a company designed to grow resilience in our local food system by working with Christchurch communities. Their expertise involves community development, permacultural design and development, and qualitative research at post-graduate level on topics including Environmental Management, Social Sustainability and Education. Each enjoys the pursuit of health in all spheres of being.

Amidst the chaos and the sadness during the immediate aftermath of the earthquakes, we observed our communities 'digging where they stood' in an upsurge of solidarity and togetherness. In these times, we realised some of our most simple needs for living: food, water, shelter and community. The Share an Idea process gave rise to strong themes of sustainability and green living – a 'city in a garden'. This included specific projects like community gardens and neighbourhood-scale initiatives to continue fostering the collective benefits that cooperation between individuals and groups produced. The Council's Draft Central City Plan appeared to respond to this new found role for 'social capital', yet so far the recovery process has failed to link its value with the potential for generating environmental benefits. So much has been said for the rise in socially innovative projects in Christchurch, yet so few of these or the plans being prepared for the city are addressing the biggest social issues of our time, which are profoundly environmental crises. Flooding, poor water quality in our rivers, soil contamination and housing built on vulnerable land – these examples demonstrate how little the collective action being taken is doing to improve the (dis)harmony we have with the landscape that supports us.

At Garden City 2.0 we are continuing to dig where we stand in order to build on our hopes for urban living in a healthy habitat: a place that is nourishing to live, work and play in. In order to create this environment, we focus on growing resilience in our local food system through building community around the production and distribution of high quality foods that are seasonal, organic and locally grown. Improving resilience is an important response to the shortcomings in our current food system, the insecurities of which were highlighted post-quake. Sometimes, we refer to a vision of 'urbundance' – an abundant and resilient urban fabric that promotes a lively, healthy habitat. These visions for regenerating health are also being articulated by a wide range of people and organisations, and it is this variety that we feel is a precursor to the richness that characterises a healthy habitat. There is a growing body of academic research that considers these expressions in terms of 'urban ecology' and resilience in socio-ecological systems.[1]

Habitat wellbeing: The connections between food, land and us

We feel the planning processes that are defining and have already defined so much of our 'recovery' are failing to dig deep enough to genuinely reveal the true strengths of our local environment, and therefore encourage a healthy urban ecology. In his influential book *One Straw Revolution* Masanobu Fukuoka says 'Sickness comes when people draw apart from nature. The severity of the disease is directly proportional to the degree of separation.'[2] The environment is, after all, our basis for habitation, the source of so much ongoing disruption in our lives now in Christchurch, and that which ultimately impacts on our health and wellbeing.

One way of reducing the degree of separation is by promoting the immediately tangible relationship we could have with our habitat through food. The quality of this relationship depends on the integrity of our ecosystems and the services they gift to us: water, soil and sources of energy. Environmental quality and resilient socio-ecological systems are therefore related to the wellbeing of people, directly through our sources of food (and water).

At the moment, however, this separation from our habitat is highlighted through the loss of significant connection to the foods we eat – something that has occurred in the space of little more than one or two generations. In particular, we have become distant from the knowledge of how we grow and eat certain foods that our ancestors knew were health-giving on many levels. In our increasingly urban lives, backyard gardens and small-scale family agriculture have mostly been replaced by imported foods trucked into our supermarkets from unknown origins. Our health statistics are revealing the ill effects of our modern industrialised food system[3] that also contributes significantly to compounding environmental crises around the world.[4]

This disconnection with the land, and subsequently with our food production, goes back to the founding of Christchurch. The garden city concept was born out of concern for people's living conditions during the industrial revolution, particularly in urban quarters. As a blueprint for urban development, this concept was re-appropriated for Christchurch – a grid pattern of city streets was imposed upon, and in stark contrast to, the natural flow of the landscape (see page 30). This approach failed to incorporate the environment containing the food baskets (mahinga kai) for Ōtautahi, Puari and Ōtākaro,[5] which have long since been lost to urbanisation.

The Central City Recovery Plan and Land Use Recovery Plan are merely reinforcing this same incongruence. The natural characteristics of the landscape have been suppressed and modified to suit the extraction and consumption of goods and displacement of our waste. Sprawling, car-centric subdivisions built on prime productive soils (e.g. Prestons-Marshlands, Wigram-Halswell) are clear examples of this. Current recovery planning fails to support the types of participation and ongoing relationships we see as necessary for in-depth dicussion about the health of our people and the urban ecology of Christchurch.

Opportunities for re-establishing food resilience

The fragility of our food system was highlighted after the earthquakes. Our reliance on broken roads, closed or distant supermarkets that stock processed foods, the levels of pollution in our rivers, heavily contaminated soils and the obesity epidemic[6] – all of these things point to systemic failure of our urban ecology. Ultimately, we live in a food insecure region where we cannot see the fields that sustain us.[7]

Yet the earthquakes also brought with them the opportunity to change and cultivate food resilience. In the aftermath of February 2011, people were content to work with each other to help make our places liveable, at least temporarily. We saw immense bonds between people and place where previously there had been considerable distance. With encouraging and enabling recovery structures, people might have begun to sow large gardens with the use of tools and seeds from community gardens, knowing that supermarkets would be closed in certain areas for some years to come. From this a culture of transition towards urban ecological resilience could emerge.

Garden City 2.0 responded to this opportunity and now works to encourage this resilience through community food production. It also seeks to uncover and promote the knowledge involved in this work. Its primary operation is a commercial organic food distribution service and retail outlet, sourcing seasonal fruit and vegetables from local growers. The company works alongside Soil and Health Canterbury to strengthen the community food sector through various collaborative arrangements, such as the Agropolis Urban Farm initiative. This emerging sector spans household, school and community garden education and small-scale local food production, and is connected to the wider organic agricultural sector. Garden City 2.0 also participates in the emerging 'Food Resilience Network' that is organising itself around urbundance visions for greater Christchurch.

Creating community through digging where we stand

In our view, foods and their associated environments can be great platforms for developing respectful relationships and therefore promoting the health of the socio-ecological system. Using our local food distribution service as an example, we seek growers working 'organically' with their farmland (fig. 1). When working with these growers, we make decisions through relationships that favour cooperation instead of competition; we allow the growers to set fair prices and in return we gather invaluable knowledge and experience of how food is grown and distributed sustainably in Christchurch. These are urbundance visions coming to life; the physical changes to our habitat and the failures of the food system have created space and opportunities to begin realising an urban ecology that supports local communities to work collectively to meet their health needs.

Figure 1: (left) A Garden City 2.0 staff member checking out a lettuce crop in Halswell. The relationship with our suppliers goes beyond financial transactions.

Figure 2 & 3: (right) Agropolis urban farm

This philosophy of local food, organics and transitional cities is something that was active in Christchurch long before the earthquakes, just as the Blueprint is a collection of pre-existing ideas.[8] The concept of 'recovery' is somewhat of a misnomer in that it seems to miss the point. None of the anchor projects prioritises improving the quality of relationships between people and their habitat, not least through connections made using food. For example, the Avon-Ōtākaro River Precinct might state these aims through an emphasis on mahinga kai values, but the poor quality of its surrounding environment and ongoing storm- and waste-water overflows mean we are still far from regenerating the kind of abundance it is revered for historically.

While opportunities for dialogue have been present, many decisions are still being made outside of the general reach of the public. For example, Agropolis Urban Farm is a project designed to provide people a chance to participate in regenerating the inner-city environment through urban farming. It is technically illegal as it is yet to be signed off by the Minister for Canterbury Earthquake Recovery as a legitimate use of land designated for the Innovation Precinct. As a result, the people working voluntarily to restore community in the inner-city, by developing a community garden, are shrouded in uncertainty and illegitimacy.

The visions we experience in working to regenerate healthy water, healthy soil, healthy food and healthy people in Christchurch are taking Garden City 2.0 deeper into conversations about how we relate to the natural world. We call this approach 'digging where we stand'.[9] Creating an environment that is free from domination requires a different seed of thought and a system of people-interactions that is genuinely liberating. As an organisation that values biological diversity and deep historical observations of place, we expect also for there to be a diversity and plurality of planning voices supported by similar principles. Start imagining a city restored to health: this is a seed for urbundance in the garden city of the twenty-first century.

Rekindle

Rekindle is a social enterprise that enables the rerouting of reusable resources from waste via creativity and craftsmanship. Seeing waste as a resource full of latent creative opportunity fuels the work. Rekindle initially focused on diverting timber from waste within residential demolition in Christchurch, turning this into high quality saleable products including furniture, interiors, sculpture and jewellery. Rekindle wants to grow its capacity to support communities to utilise their waste fully and, in so doing, maximise the wider benefits of being engaged in purposeful work. As a social enterprise the majority of profits are dedicated to furthering development of this work.

[1–4]

[5–6]

[7–9]

Rekindle 473

More than buildings: Growing biodiversity and happiness in communities

Kevin McCloud

Kevin has visited Christchurch twice since the earthquakes and helped instigate and judge the Breathe (Residential Demonstration Project) competition to design one of the city blocks. Here he writes about the contribution that imagination brings to placemaking and how his experiences in growing his own development company have led him to believe that Christchurch should take a radical step and regrow as a ground-up collaboration between community and designers.

In 2007 I started a housing business, Happiness Architecture and Beauty (HAB). HAB was founded in a fervour of interest in how our built environment can alter our wellbeing, a fervour that grew in the twenty-first century following a welter of studies by modern sociologists[1] and in the wake of the New Urbanist movement in America.

HAB remains a group of dedicated and innovative thinkers. Early on we found succour in works like *Building Happiness,* a collection of essays edited by Jane Wernick,[2] and in Alain de Botton's *Architecture of Happiness.* We found inspiration in Bioregional's groundbreaking BedZED One Planet Living housing scheme; we looked back to the empowering self-build projects of Walter Segal and pioneering housing schemes of the twentieth century.

But we are not philosophers or teachers. We are developers, enablers and placemakers. Seven years on we are growing the business to construct 1000 homes a year according to a set of principles that we have matured across our early housing schemes in the UK. Those principles include working to context, social inclusion, community engagement, the importance of self-build and custom-build in the housing mix, blind tenure (where it's not possible to distinguish between homes in ownership and those in rent), social sustainability and biodiversity. All are civilised means of building by any standard but they are often overlooked or paid lip-service in the brutal world of construction and development.

So we build and we improve the biodiversity of sites as we build.[3] Our architecture (in collaboration with fine, dynamic practices) delivers a positive experience that lifts the spirits, and helps our residents to flourish; our homes look like they belong where they are and they are built in a contemporary language that reflects the spirit of a place. In this we have been much influenced by the idea of local distinctiveness, championed by the charity Common Ground.

To achieve this, we deliberately create design teams around places, choosing to work with one particular architectural practice in just one town in order to develop a stylistic language for that one community. Another town will merit collaboration with another practice. On large sites we work with more than one practice to bring diversity. And we ask our architects to explore the narrative of a place and make a contribution to that through their building. We look for, and reinforce at every opportunity, stories and links that will give our developments character and resonance. From the choices of construction materials and the colours of render and paintwork to the naming of streets and the imaginative design of public spaces and allotments, we construct new narratives that add a chapter to the history of a place. This is meticulous work and it requires the involvement of existing communities and much research. But it pays off, every time.

I foster a quiet hope that as Christchurch is rebuilt, its new narratives are carefully woven. I hope it is not constructed as a clone city or rebuilt to the same blunt model, around a central business district, as every other international city has for the last one hundred years. It could instead be a community city, designed around the vitality that people bring to a place when they are allowed and encouraged to flourish. Melbourne demonstrates what happens when you relax planning laws and allow people to repopulate a city centre: it springs alive. Christchurch can go much further. It has the opportunity to reinvent itself: as a series of villages or new neighbourhoods that could be self-sufficient in food and energy; as a super-sustainable and resilient city prototype perhaps; as a place that takes biodiversity, landscape and Māori design principles to its very heart. It might look and feel different to every other city on the planet.

The architecture of Christchurch could be different to anywhere else. It should be. The planning of the city could and should break down some of the rigid grid forms of the old ground plan. Communities should be encouraged and facilitated to rebuild, self-build and reinhabit the city centre (it is, after all, the job of civil servants, designers and planners to facilitate community). And there is an important, less defined contribution to be made from another quarter. We should also place great store by the design of spaces in between buildings. Jeremy Till has written that 'buildings do not produce "aesthetic" space but are settings for social space . . . Architecture's offering lies here exactly – in its contribution to the formation of social relations.'[4] At HAB, we share with our collaborator, the great landscape architect Luke Engleback (who writes elsewhere in this book), the belief that without a properly designed public realm, a housing scheme is meaningless. You can create beautiful buildings but the results will turn to ugliness if you don't provide people with the means to interact and form relationships with each other, inside and outside; you can build the highest spec eco-homes but they will not function properly until residents of a scheme learn to become interdependent and to help each other. This is social sustainability: the creation of a durable, resilient community – the mark of which is the magic social glue that is formed between people.

This glue can never be manufactured by architects or builders but we can light the fire and lay out the ingredients for it in the way we set out the infrastructure and public realm design for a scheme: in visibly expressed water courses from roofs and gutters in which children can play; in the underground crating of water that can be hand-pumped to water gardens and wash cars; in the provision of electric bike and car clubs to reduce car ownership (and save residents money for that matter); in the way that fallen tree trunks, a hedge or a dry stone wall can be at once a play facility, an amenity, a boundary and a haven of biodiversity. Overlapping, ambiguity and the evolution of ideas are crucial to this, in order that residents can imprint their own imaginative narratives on places and features. So, a small rectangle of tarmac and some chalk (for hopscotch or any number of games) become as important as a tightly designed and highly functional recycling facility.

True social sustainability cannot occur unless you encourage people to collectively reduce their environmental footprint by sharing. And through all our work, that basic principle runs like a golden thread. We like to see food grown and shared so we put in Luke's edible hedgerows and fruity streets. The ambiguous car park is also an orchard. The allotments are shared. The boundaries to private gardens (these boundaries are themselves fruiting bushes which residents are encouraged to negotiate over) lead to a shared garden where a shared trampoline, sandpit and shed sit. And a community land trust might run it all. In the UK we are building schemes of 50, 100 and 200 homes that embody these ideas and move towards the One Planet Living ideals of low-carbon, low-resource but high-happiness living. Wouldn't it be extraordinary to see Christchurch grow into the template of what the twenty-first century city should be? Super-sustainable, diverse, contextual, shared and unique?

I've seen what might be possible. Our work is just properly starting in the UK. The results are nevertheless promising, sometimes loosely defined, often fuzzy and certainly creative. The places we've built are forays into a new way of making places and already they pulse with a loose and shifting vitality. But it is not the unison hymn of architectural order and planning control we can hear. It is the quiet humming of a community growing: the Song of the Magic Glue

Conclusion: The Song of the Magic Glue

'There's a crack in everything. That's how the light gets in.'
– Leonard Cohen, *Anthem*

While the city has been shaken to its core, it's worth remembering that most of what was here pre-quake goes on, albeit in a cracked, compromised way. In post-quake Christchurch, there *is* a crack in everything. There are cracks in the physical world: the roads, pavements and foundations of people's houses. And there are cracks in our society: in the ways people interact with one another and their environment, and in the functioning of organisations, businesses and governments. But cracks let the light in. They allow us to glimpse the complex networks and structures at play, and to better understand what makes our society work. They also enable us – perhaps – to better understand what we hold important and why: what makes *us* work.

The earthquakes have been great revealers, bringing into public life a thousand previously hidden and quiet aspects of our society, our laws, our ways of being, our relationship with the environment and the ways we relate to each other. We now see – and continue to be aware – that there are vast networks of typically invisible associations between insurance, planning laws, history, nature, governments, the public and every little aspect of the city. Things have been made visible here, and this is both exhilarating and exhausting. We now see the possibility – and feel the responsibility – to fashion a city that offers new and different ways of being.

Things have been made visible, but this does not make them easier to understand. Perspective is difficult, and success hard to define. As editors, we identified some recurrent themes at the beginning of the book, and hope that readers have discovered other motifs that we haven't noticed or been able to articulate.

In calling for and commissioning the essays that comprise this book, we were not prescriptive; we didn't have a clear outcome in mind. Through the process of editing *Once in a Lifetime*, there have been many turns along the way; the book you are holding today is not the book we thought we would produce when we started this process in August of 2013. Most contributors came back with work that has surprised us, and we've adapted to accommodate. We'd like to think there are some similarities between the way we have edited the book, and the way in which the recovery could be approached: as an iterative, adaptable and open process that allows for a broad range of perspectives to be included. Perhaps the most repeated message that has come from the contributors is that inclusive and sometimes open-ended processes are critical to the long-term health and success of the city.

Cities are always in a process of unfolding; they are never finished. *Once in a Lifetime* could have offered a number of cohesive, attractive-looking proposals and propositions, beautiful drawings and design projects as alternatives to the Blueprint plan – and there may have been some value in this. But to do this would have reinforced the idea that there is an already-known and preferable outcome rather than a multitude of possibilities to explore. It would have also risked obscuring the rich networks rendered visible in the past few years. Presenting fixed schemes and proposals would merely plaster over the cracks that have recently been laid bare: recovery by means of re-covering.

Kevin McCloud writes of the 'loosely defined', 'fuzzy' and 'shifting vitality' that comprises what he terms the Song of the Magic Glue – the indescribable and hard-to-identify tune of a community that simply 'works' – where the countless disparate elements of the city are somehow held together. This indefinable something feels tantalisingly and paradoxically close to revealing itself in the singularity of post-disaster Christchurch – as if the component parts of some unknown rhythm are beginning to be heard over and through the cacophony.

In the next thirty to one hundred years, every city in the world is going to have to retrofit and redesign itself to adapt to new technologies, new environmental demands, population shifts and changed climate conditions. The ongoing urbanisation of humanity will continue into the twenty-first century and be led by cities the size of Christchurch that are reworking themselves into large metropolitan areas.

This book does not aim to offer tidy solutions and takeaway designs. By expanding on the issues that confront this city, and giving space for people to articulate the nature of complex problems, this book aims to help all of us, in time, to gather a broader and richer understanding of the issues at stake in city-building.

Chapter 1: Making Plans

Resisting erasure
Sally Blundell

[1] Sue Bennett, "Twenty Reasons to Visit Christchurch," *Sydney Morning Herald*, November 10, 2013.

[2] Nicola McDougall, "Rebuilding Christchurch," *REIQ Journal* (June 2013): 21.

[3] Canterbury Earthquake Recovery Authority, "Canterbury Earthquakes Recovery Processes," in *New Zealand Official Yearbook 2012*, ed. Statistics NZ (Wellington: NZ Government, 2013), accessed April 25, 2014, http://www.stats.govt.nz/browse_for_stats/snapshots-of-nz/yearbook/people/region/cera.

[4] McDougall, "What Would it Take to Rebuild a City from Scratch? The Christchurch Experience," *Property Observer*, July 2, 2013, accessed April 23, 2014, http://www.propertyobserver.com.au/ /finding/residential-investment/24162-wednesday-july-3-what-would-it-take-to-rebuild-a-city-from-scratch-the-christchurch-example-nicola-mcdougall.html.

[5] P. D. Smith, *City: A Guidebook for the Urban Age* (London: Bloomsbury, 2012), 44.

[6] Quoted in John Cookson and Graeme Dunstall, eds, *Southern Capital: Christchurch – Towards a City Biography 1850-2000* (Christchurch: Canterbury UP, 2000), 63.

[7] Ibid., 30-31.

[8] Diane Brand and Hugh Nicholson, "Learning from Lisbon: Contemporary Cities in the Aftermath of Natural Disasters," in *Approaches to Disaster Management – Examining the Implications of Hazards, Emergencies and Disasters,* ed. John Tiefenbacher (Intech, 2013), chapter 8.

[9] Simon Schama, *Landscape and Memory* (London: HarperCollins, 1995), 6.

[10] James Dann, "Those Left Standing," March 10, 2014, comment on *Rebuilding Christchurch*, accessed March 18, 2014, http://rebuildingchristchurch.wordpress.com/2014/03/10/those-left-standing/.

[11] Rebecca Macfie, *Report from Christchurch* (Wellington: Bridget Williams Books, 2013), 36, ebook.

[12] Laurie Duggan, "A Sort of Mythical Thing: Canberra as an Imaginary Capital," *Journal of Australian Studies* 57 (1998): 83-92, accessed May 2, 2014, http://www.apinetwork.com/main/pdf/scholars/jas57_duggan.pdf.

[13] Benjamin Schwarz, "Oscar Niemeyer: A Vision in Concrete," *The Atlantic*, December 6, 2012, accessed April 30, 2014, http://www.theatlantic.com/international/archive/2012/12/oscar-niemeyer-a-vision-in-concrete/265969/.

[14] Quoted in Duggan, "A Sort of Mythical Thing."

[15] Ibid.

[16] Ibid.

[17] Smith, *City*, 44.

[18] Ian Lochhead, "Reactions to the Christchurch Central Recovery Plan," *Cross Section*, September 2012, accessed April 1, 2014. http://www.crosssection.net.nz/Current-Issue-1103.htm.

[19] Edwin Heathcote, "Urban Outfitters," *Financial Times*, June 29, 2007.

[20] Deyan Sudjic, "Cities on the Edge of Chaos," *Observer*, March 9, 2008.

[21] Heathcote, "Urban Outfitters."

[22] Lochhead, "Reactions."

[23] Canterbury Earthquake Recovery Authority, *Christchurch Central Recovery Plan* (Christchurch: Canterbury Earthquake Recovery Authority, 2012), 1.

[24] Sudjic, "Cities."

[25] Ibid.

On the origin of precincts
Gary Franklin

[1] "Trouble in Utopia," episode of *The Shock of the New* (BBC and Time-Life Films,1980; New York, NY: Ambrose Video Publishing, 2001 dvd).

[2] "The Smallest House of Amsterdam Oude Hoogstraat 22: History," accessed May 28, 2014, http://www.thesmallesthouseofamsterdam.com/english/home.html.

[3] Robert Hughes, *The Shock of the New* (London: Thames and Hudson, 1991).

A history of planning through the broken lens of disaster
Dr Suzanne Vallance

[1] H Carter, *An Introduction to Urban Historical Geography* (London: Edward Arnold, 1983).

[2] W Ramroth, *Planning for Disaster: How Natural and Manmade Disasters Shape the Built Environment* (New York: Kaplan, 2007).

[3] Ramroth, *Planning for Disaster*, 32.

[4] Ramroth, *Planning for Disaster*, 33.

[5] M Laurence, "Visioning cities," in *Explorations in Human Geography: Encountering Place*, eds R. Le Heron, L. Murphy, P. Forer and M. Goldstone (Auckland: Oxford University Press, 1999), 296.

[6] In P Hall, *Cities of Tomorrow: An Intellectual History of Urban Planning and Design in the Twentieth Century* (Oxford, Blackwell Publishers, 2002), 13.

[7] Ramroth, *Planning for Disaster*, 73.

[8] R Fischler, "Planning for Social Betterment: From Standard of Living to Quality of Life," in *Urban Planning in a Changing World*, ed. R. Freestone (New York: Spon Press, 2000), 142.

[9] M Van Rooijen, "Open Space, Urban Planning and the Evolution of the Green City," in *Urban Planning in a Changing World*, ed. R. Freestone (New York: Spon Press, 2000), 221.

[10] M Scott, *Seeing Like a State: How Certain Schemes to Improve the Human Condition Have Failed* (Hartford: Yale University Press, 1998), 4.

[11] Ramroth, *Planning for Disaster*, 163.

[12] E Blum, *Love Canal Revisited; Race, Class and Gender in Environmental Activism* (Kansas: University Press of Kansas, 2008).

[13] U Beck, *Risk Society: Towards a New Modernity* (London: Sage Publications, 1992).

[14] M Gunder and C Mouat, "Symbolic Violence and Victimization in Planning Processes: A Reconnoitre of the New Zealand Resource Management Act," *Planning*

Theory 1 (2002): 124 -145.

[15] B Flyvbjerg, *Rationality and Power: Democracy in Practice* (Chicago: University of Chicago Press, 1998).

[16] Ramroth, *Planning for Disaster*, 207.

[17] Olshansky and L Johnson, *Clear as Mud: Planning for the Rebuilding of New Orleans* (New Orleans, APA Planners Press, 2010), 10-11.

[18] Olshansky and Johnson, *Clear as Mud*, 12.

[19] See, for example, the CERD Shadow Report *Hurricane Katrina: Racial Discrimination and Ethnic Cleansing in the United States in the Aftermath of Hurricane Katrina*, 2008. http://www.ushrnetwork.org/resources-media/hurricane-katrina-racial-discrimination-ethnic-cleansing-united-states-aftermath#sthash.M1CCvvgf.dpuf.

[20] Olshansky and Johnson, *Clear as Mud*, 50.

[21] Ibid., 218.

[22] S Vallance, "Early Disaster Recovery: A Citizens' Guide," *Australasian Journal of Disaster and Trauma Studies* (2011-2): 19-25.

[23] Canterbury Earthquake Recovery Authority (2012), *The Greater Christchurch Recovery Strategy*, available on http://cera.govt.nz/sites/cera.govt.nz/files/common/recovery-strategy-for-greater-christchurch.pdf, accessed Dec 2013, 20.

[24] S Owens, "Engaging the Public: Information and Deliberation in Environmental Policy," *Environment and Planning A* 32 (2000): 1141–1148.

[25] P Allmendinger, "Towards a Post-positivist Typology of Planning Theory," *Planning Theory* 1 (2002): 77-99.

[26] J Agyeman and A Briony, "The Role of Civic Environmentalism in the Pursuit of Sustainable Communities," *Journal of Environmental Planning and Management* 46 (2003): 345-363.

[27] P Wilson, "Deliberative Planning for Disaster Recovery: Re-membering New Orleans," *Journal of Public Deliberation* 5 (2009): 1-25.

[28] Olshansky and Johnson, *Clear as Mud*, 239.

[29] J Bergman, "52 places to go in 2014," *New York Times*, Jan 10, 2014, accessed February 10, 2014, http://www.nytimes.com/interactive/2014/01/10/travel/2014-places-to-go.html?_r=2.

[30] S McClennen, "Neoliberalism as Terrorism; or State of Disaster Exceptionalism," in *Terror, Theory and the Humanities*, eds J. Di Leo and U. Mehan (Ann Arbor: Open Humanities Press, University of Michigan Library), 2012.

Why Christchurch should not plan for the future
Dr Stuart Candy

[1] Horst W. J. Rittel and Melvin M. Webber, "Dilemmas in a General Theory of Planning," *Policy Sciences* 4 (1973): 155-169; James Gleick, *Faster: The Acceleration of Just About Everything* (London: Little, Brown, 1999).

[2] The original observation that this modern business-school quote distils was Helmuth Von Moltke in the mid-nineteenth century: "No plan of operations survives the first collision with the main body of the enemy." See Foreword in *Moltke on the Art of War: Selected Writings*, ed. Daniel J. Hughes (Novato, CA: Presidio Press, 1993).

[3] This article has not been written as a specific commentary on the Christchurch Central Recovery Plan; more grounded and locally informed responses are elsewhere throughout this collection. It is instead a set of general observations from an observer abroad (an Australian futurist living in Canada) on the conceptual context in which the Christchurch conversation is taking place.

[4] Perhaps the most comprehensive overview of foresight as a field, though it is not easy to obtain: Richard A. Slaughter, ed., *The Knowledge Base of Futures Studies* (5 vols, Professional edition, CDROM) (Indooroopilly, Queensland: Foresight International, 2005).

[5] A powerful statement of this perspective appears in Ashis Nandy, "Bearing Witness to the Future," *Futures* 28 (1996): 636-639.

[6] Consider Dator's first law of the future: '"The future" cannot be "predicted" zbecause "the future" does not exist.' Jim Dator, "What Futures Studies Is, and Is Not" (Honolulu: Hawaii Research Center for Futures Studies, 1995), http://futures.hawaii.edu/publications/futures-studies/WhatFSis1995.pdf.

[7] James A. Dator, "The Futures of Culture or Cultures of the Future," in *Perspectives on Cross-Cultural Psychology*, eds Anthony J. Marsella, Roland G. Tharp and Thomas J. Ciboroski (New York: Academic Press, 1979), 369-388; see also: Jim Dator, "Alternative Futures at the Manoa School", *Journal of Futures Studies* 14, no. 2 (2009): 1-18, http://www.jfs.tku.edu.tw/14-2/A01.pdf.

[8] For a comparative examination of scenario generation approaches see for instance: Andrew Curry and Wendy Schultz, "Roads Less Travelled: Different Methods, Different Futures," *Journal of Futures Studies* 13, no. 4 (2009): 35-60. http://www.jfs.tku.edu.tw/13-4/AE03.pdf.

[9] See for example: Paul J. H. Schoemaker, "Scenario Planning: A Tool for Strategic Thinking," *MIT Sloan Management Review*, Winter (1995), http://sloanreview.mit.edu/article/scenario-planning-a-tool-for-strategic-thinking/ and Charles Roxburgh, "The Use and Abuse of Scenarios," *McKinsey Quarterly*, November (2009), http://www.mckinsey.com/insights/strategy/the_use_and_abuse_of_scenarios.

[10] Kurt Vonnegut, *Slapstick: or, Lonesome no more!* (New York: Delacorte Press / Seymour Lawrence, 1976), 226.

[11] This trio is usually (mis)attributed to the article which popularised it: Roy Amara, "The Futures Field: Searching for Definitions and Boundaries," *The Futurist* 15(1) (1981): 25-29. However these terms appeared over a decade earlier in Toffler's bestselling *Future Shock*: 'Every society faces not merely a Succession of *Probable* Futures, but an Array of *Possible* Futures, and a Conflict over *Preferable* Futures,' Alvin Toffler, ed., *Future Shock* (New York: Random House, 1970), 460. Earlier still, the introduction to de Jouvenel's seminal *The Art of Conjecture* offers a similar – if less memorably alliterative – typology. See Bertrand de Jouvenel, *The Art of Conjecture* (trans. Nikita Lary) (London: Weidenfeld and Nicholson, 1967), 3-21.

[12] For a marvellously process-minded way of looking at a place, see this talk by former festival organiser and broadcaster Marcus Westbury, who initiated a project called 'Renew Newcastle' that has been credited with turning around the fortunes of the downtown core in that Australian city: Marcus Westbury, "The City as a Process" (presentation delivered at Arup Melbourne, Foresight and Innovation Talks series, February 3, 2012), http://vimeo.com/38546750.

13 In the phrase of Elise Boulding, from her Translator's Preface to the abridged single-volume edition of Polak's work: Fred Polak, *The Image of the Future*, trans. and abridged by Elise Boulding (San Francisco: Jossey-Bass, 1973), viii.

14 Fred L. Polak, *The Image of the Future: Enlightening the Past, Orientating the Present, Forecasting the Future*, 2 vols, trans. Elise Boulding, (Leyden: A. W. Sythoff, 1961).

15 Polak 1973, *The Image of the Future*, 19.

16 See for instance the story of 'Hawaii 2000', a public foresight process of unparalleled scale and ambition which ran in the islands in 1970-71, and yet which failed to be carried forward by political institutions and processes, and so did not catalyse its hoped-for outcomes by the turn of the century. Jim Dator et al., *Hawaii 2000: Past, Present and Future* (report prepared for the Office of Planning, Department of Business, Economic Development and Tourism, Honolulu, Hawaii 1999), http://hawaii2050. org/images/uploads/HI2KDBEDTReport_1299.pdf.

17 Government of Singapore, *A Lively and Liveable Singapore: Strategies for Sustainable Growth* (Ministry of the Environment and Water Resources and Ministry of National Development, Singapore 2009), http://app.mewr.gov.sg/data/imgcont/1292/sustainbleblueprint_forweb.pdf.

18 Winston Churchill, 28 October 1943, (speech to Britain's House of Commons), quoted in Berry, Leonard L. et al., 'The Business Case for Better Buildings,' Frontiers of Health Services Management 21(1), 5, http://faculty.arch. tamu.edu/khamilton/HamiltonPDFs/Publications/Berry_etal_TheBusinessCaseForBetterBuildings.PDF.

19 A. Kuskis, 2013, "We Shape our Tools and Thereafter our Tools Shape Us," *McLuhan Galaxy*, 1 April, http://mcluhangalaxy.wordpress.com/2013/04/01/we-shape-our-tools-and-thereafter-our-tools-shape-us/. This formula was adopted by futurist Jim Dator as his 'Third law of the future'.

20 Eric Raymond, *The Cathedral and the Bazaar: Musings on Linux and Open Source by an Accidental Revolutionary*, revised edition (Sebastopol, CA: O'Reilly, 2001).

21 Gap Filler website, http://www.gapfiller.org.nz; FESTA website, http://festa.org.nz; see also: Barnaby Bennett, Eugenio Boidi and Irene Boles, eds, *Christchurch: The Transitional City, Pt. IV* (rev. ed.) (Christchurch: Freerange Press, 2012).

22 Charley Mann, "Festival Brings Light Back to Inner City," *The Press*, October 21, 2012, http://www.stuff.co.nz/the-press/news/7844726/Festival-brings-light-back-to-inner-city.

23 "Faculty: Natalie Jeremijenko," New York University, accessed June 14, 2014, http://steinhardt.nyu.edu/faculty_bios/view/Natalie_Jeremijenko; see also: Tim O'Reilly, "The Architecture of Participation," O'Reilly website, June 2004, http://oreilly.com/pub/a/oreilly/tim/articles/architecture_of_participation.html.

24 "Wikipedia," Wikipedia, accessed June 14, 2014, http://en.wikipedia.org/wiki/Wikipedia.

25 Burning Man website, http://www.burningman.com/.

26 Melbourne's Digital City Unconference Overview: CoMConnect, 2012, http://vimeo.com/52357281.

27 We were working with a (non-proprietary) meeting format called Open Space, which has been used thousands of times around the world over the past three decades. See for example: Harrison Owen, *Open Space Technology: A User's Guide,* 3rd edition (San Francisco: Berrett-Koehler, 2008). Others have used the same process to redesign an Olympic pavilion in three days; to redesign aircraft doors; to downsize and restructure part of a large organisation, and so on. For a range of (early) case studies see: Harrison Owen, *Tales from Open Space* (Cabin John, MD: Abbott Publishing, 1995), http://www.openspaceworld.com/tales.pdf.

28 IAP2 (International Association for Public Participation), 2007, "IAP2 Spectrum of Public Participation," IAP2 website, http://www.iap2.org/resource/resmgr/imported/IAP2%20Spectrum_vertical.pdf. In an increasingly networked polity, systemic pressures seem to be pushing public expectations swiftly and steadily to the right of this continuum; that is, towards more frequent, direct and deep involvement in matters where public sector representatives used to have more discretion; on the application of OST for foresight purposes, see: Stuart Candy, "Open Space for Futures: A Brief Introduction," *Journal of Futures Studies* 10, no. 1 (2005): 109-114, http://www.jfs.tku.edu.tw/10.1.109.pdf, and Stuart Candy, "Open Space for Analog Crowdsourcing" (presentation given at Crowdsourcing Week, Singapore, June 5, 2013), https://www.youtube.com/watch?v=1fAO_RhtHq8.

29 Greg Van Alstyne and Robert K. Logan, "Designing for Emergence and Innovation: Redesigning Design," *Artifact* 1, no. 2 (2007), https://scholarworks.iu.edu/journals/index.php/artifact/article/view/1360.

30 Richard A. Slaughter, "Futures Studies: From Individual to Social Capacity,"*Futures*, 28, no. 8 (1996): 751-762.

31 Stuart Candy, *The Futures of Everyday Life* (doctoral dissertation, Department of Political Science, University of Hawaii at Manoa, 2010), http://www.scribd.com/doc/68901075/Candy-2010-The-Futures-of-Everyday-Life; also: The Sceptical Futuryst website, http://futuryst.blogspot.com.

32 Candy, 2010, Chapter 7, 287-317.

33 See Stuart Candy, "Dreaming Together: Experiential Futures as a Platform for Public Imagination," in ed. Tim Durfee and Mimi Zeiger, *Made Up: Design's Fictions* (Zurich: Art Center Graduate Press / JRP Ringier, forthcoming).

34 "City Vision," *The Press*, Mainlander section, February 22, 2014, C1-C4, http://www.scribd.com/doc/214017769/The-Press-22-February-2014-Christchurch-in-2031.

Chapter 2: Selling the Plan

Design and democracy
Barnaby Bennett

1 Noortje Marres, "Issues Spark a Public into Being: A Key but Often Forgotten Point of the Lippmann-Dewey Debate," in *Making Things Public*, ed. Bruno Latour (Cambridge, MA: MIT Press, 2005).

2 Dorothy Day, *The Long Loneliness: The Autobiography of the Legendary Catholic Social Activist* (New York: HarperCollins, 2009).

3 Prof. Sir Peter Gluckman, "The Psychosocial Consequences of the Canterbury Earthquakes" (letter from the Office

of the Prime Minister's Chief Scientific Advisor, May 10, 2011), www.pmcsa.org.nz/wp-content/uploads/Christchurch-Earthquake-Briefing-Psychosocial-Effects-10May11.pdf.

[4] Local Government Act 2002, New Zealand Legislation, last modified April 1, 2014, www.legislation.govt.nz/act/public/2002/0084/latest/DLM172327.html.

[5] "The RMA Quality Planning Resource," Quality Planning, accessed May 23, 2014, www.qualityplanning.org.nz/index.php/plan-development-components/consultation/understanding-the-different-stages.

[6] "New Unit for the Christchurch Rebuild," Canterbury Earthquake Authority, last modified 18 April, 2012, http://cera.govt.nz/news/2012/new-unit-for-the-rebuild-of-central-christchurch-18-april-2012.

The Enervation Precinct
Stephen Judd

[1] Tess McClure, "EPIC Pulls Out Over Innovation Precinct Saga," *The Press,* May 3, 2014, accessed May 31, 2014, http://www.stuff.co.nz/the-press/business/the-rebuild/10003855/EPIC-pulls-out-over-innovation-precinct-saga.

[2] Eric S. Raymond, "Release Early, Release Often," Eric S. Raymond's Home Page, accessed June 1, 2014, http://www.catb.org/~esr/writings/cathedral-bazaar/cathedral-bazaar/ar01s04.html.

[3] Richard P. Gabriel, "The Rise of Worse is Better," Dreamsongs, accessed June 1, 2014, http://dreamsongs.com/RiseOfWorseIsBetter.html.

[4] C. Northcote Parkinson, *Parkinson's Law* (London: John Murray, 1958), 84-85.

Valuing everyday life
Claes Caldenby

[1] Virserum Art Museum is a very active institution that was founded in 1998 in a small and shrinking factory town, once based on the furniture industry. It is situated in woodland in south-eastern Sweden. In 2009 Virserum Art Museum took the initiative of launching an appeal for an Architecture of Necessity, which has received international acclaim. In 2010 the museum held the first of a planned series of triennials on sustainable architecture, Wood 2010. In connection with the second triennial, Wood 2013, an invitation for entries was sent out globally. One hundred forty contributions from across the globe were received. For further information see http://architectureofnecessity.blogspot.se.

A message and a messenger
Matthew Galloway

[1] Metahaven and Marina Vishmidt, *Uncorporate identity* (Baden: Lars Müller, 2010), 451.

[2] Mayor Bob Parker speaking at the launch of the Share an Idea campaign, May 5, 2011, accessed May 5, 2011, http://www.stuff.co.nz/the-press/news/christchurch-earthquake-2011/4972131/Share-your-ideas-for-city-redevelopment.

[3] David Singh Grewal, *Network Power: The Social Dynamics of Globalization* (New Haven: Yale University Press, 2008), 4.

[4] Canterbury Earthquake Recovery Act 2011, New Zealand Legislation, last modified July 1, 2013, http://www.legislation.co.nz/act/public/2011/0012/26.0/whole.html?search=qs_act_social%2C+economic%2C+environmental+and+cultural+well-being+of+communities_resel&p=1.

[5] Grewal, *Network Power*, 4.

Telling our own tales
Gerard Smyth

[1] Sam Anderson and Zita Joyce, "What do Christchurch Viewers See of Themselves and Their Region on New Zealand Television" (unpublished research, University of Canterbury, Christchurch, 2012).

[2] Environment Canterbury, *Preliminary Draft Land Use Recovery Plan, Fact Sheet 2: Housing* (Canterbury, 2013), accessed May 15, 2013, http://www.developingchoices.org.nz/docs/housing-factsheet.pdf.

[3] Ministry of Business, Innovation & Employment, *Housing Pressures in Christchurch: A Summary of the Evidence 2013* (Wellington, 2013), accessed May 15, 2013, http://www.dbh.govt.nz/UserFiles/File/Publications/Sector/pdf/christchurch-housing-report.pdf.

[4] Alan Wood, "February Quake 'Third Most Expensive'," *The Press,* March 3, 2012.

Open conversations
Nick Sargent

[1] John McCrone, "Plan Will Change the Face of Christchurch," *The Press,* August 4, 2012, accessed June 1, 2014, http://www.stuff.co.nz/the-press/news/7413466/Plan-will-change-the-face-of-Christchurch.

[2] Canterbury Earthquake Recovery Authority, *Seize the Opportunity to Invest in New Zealand's Second Largest City* (Christchurch: Canterbury Earthquake Recovery Authority, 2013), 2.

[3] Adam Kahane, "Changing the World by Changing How We Talk and Listen," in *Leader to Leader* 26 (2002): 34-40, http://www.c2d2.ca/sites/default/files/Kahane%20on%20talking%20and%20listening.pdf.

[4] Ibid.

[5] Ibid.

[6] Ibid.

[7] "Playing Favourites with Peter Marshall," *Saturday Morning*, Radio New Zealand National (New Zealand: Radio NZ, February 22, 2014).

[8] Peter Robb, "Total Rebuild," *Sydney Morning Herald*, March 22, 2014, accessed June 1, 2014, http://www.smh.com.au/world/total-rebuild-20140317-34way.html.

Chapter 3: Rewriting the Rules

Adopting and implementing a legislative framework for recovery
Gerard Cleary

[1] Minister for Canterbury Earthquake Recovery, "Foreword from the Minister for Canterbury Earthquake Recovery,"

in Canterbury Earthquake Recovery Authority's *Statement of Intent* (Christchurch: CERA, 2011).

2 Canterbury Earthquake Recovery Act 2011 Section 27(1).

3 The RMA is New Zealand's key piece of environmental legislation. Its purpose is to promote the sustainable management of natural and physical resources, including land, air and water.

4 Sections 29-32

5 Section 38

6 Section 52

7 Section 53

8 Section 68(1)

9 Section 69(1)(a)

10 Section 83

11 Section 18(1)

12 Section 14(2)

13 Section 17(4)

14 Canterbury Earthquake Recovery Authority, *Christchurch Central Recovery Plan* (Christchurch: Canterbury Earthquake Recovery Authority, 2012); Appendix 1 to *Christchurch Central Recovery Plan*, Rule 2.2.2, 7.

15 Canterbury Earthquake Recovery Authority, *Christchurch Central Recovery Plan*.

Christchurch – a state of emergency
Jane Smith

1 Clinton Rossiter as quoted in Giorgio Agamben, *State of Exception* (Chicago: University of Chicago Press, 2005), 8.

2 Agamben, *State of Exception*, 4-5.

3 Ibid., 9-10.

4 Section 27, Canterbury Earthquake Recovery Act 2011 (CER Act 2011), reprint as at 20 May 2014.

5 Section 11, CER Act 2011.

6 Section 11, CER Act 2011.

7 Sections 48 and 49, CER Act 2011.

8 Section 50, CER Act 2011.

9 Section 28, CER Act 2011.

10 Sections 54 and 64, CER Act 2011.

11 Sections 35 and 36, CER Act 2011.

12 Sections 29 and 51, CER Act 2011.

13 Sections 33 and 34, CER Act 2011

14 Sections 38 and 39, CER Act 2011.

15 Sections 45 and 46, CER Act 2011.

16 Section 44, CER Act 2011.

17 Section 46, CER Act 2011.

18 Section 71, CER Act 2011.

19 Sections 42, 47 and 77, CER Act 2011.

20 Sections 68, 69, 70, 79 and 80, CER Act 2011.

21 Steven Colatrella, "Nothing Exceptional: Against Agamben," *Journal for Critical Education Policy Studies*, vol. 9, no. 1 (2011).

22 David Bromwich, "Secrecy, Surveillance, and Public Safety," *Huffington Post*, May 16, 2013, accessed May 1, 2014, http://www.huffingtonpost.com/david-bromwich/obama-holder-secrecy-surveillance_b_3288581.html.

23 Agamben, *State of Exception*, 24-5.

24 Christchurch Housing Accord 2014, New Zealand Government and Christchurch City Council.

25 Canterbury Earthquake (Resource Management Act Port of Lyttleton Recovery) Order 2011 (SR2011/48).

26 Eva Horn, "Logics of Political Secrecy," *Theory, Culture &*

Society, vol. 28, no. 7 (2011):103-122.

27 Mark Pelling and Kathleen Dill, *Natural Disasters as Catalysts of Political Action*, ISP/NSC Briefing Paper 06/01 (London: Chatham House, 2006), 4-6.

28 Pelling and Dill, *Natural Disasters*, 5.

29 Carl Friedreich as quoted in Agamben, *State of Exception*, 8.

The Quake Outcasts and the third source of government power
Natalie Jones

1 *Ngan v R* [2007] NZSC 105.

2 *Ngan v R* [2007] NZCS 105 at [97].

3 Compare *R v Somerset County Council ex p Fewings* [1995] 1 All ER 513; *Malone v Metropolitan Police Commissioner* [1979] 2 Ch 344; *R (on application of Hooper) v Secretary of State for Work and Pensions* [2005] 1 WLR 1681. Also see the famous statement of Lord Camden in *Entick v Carrington* (1765) 95 ER 807.

4 Canterbury Earthquake Recovery Authority, "Purchase Offer Supporting Information for Residential Red Zone," March 2013, accessed June 2, 2014, http://cera.govt.nz/sites/cera.govt.nz/files/common/residential-red-zone-purchase-offer-supporting-information-booklet-20130327.pdf.

5 *Fowler Developments Limited v The Chief Executive of the Canterbury Earthquake Recovery Authority* [2013] NZHC 2173.

6 Canterbury Earthquake Recovery Act 2011, sections 11, 27, 30, 53.

7 Canterbury Earthquake Recovery Act 2011, section 10.

8 Canterbury Earthquake Recovery Act 2011, section 10; *Canterbury Regional Council v Independent Fisheries* [2012] NZCA 601.

9 Canterbury Earthquake Recovery Act 2011, section 13.

10 International Covenant on Civil and Political Rights (opened for signature 16 December 1966, entered into force 23 March 1976), Article 17.

11 *The Minister for Canterbury Earthquake Recovery v Fowler Developments Limited* [2013] NZCA 588.

12 Marc Greenhill, "Residents Find New Land Values Perplexing," *The Press*, March 13, 2014, accessed June 2, 2014, http://www.stuff.co.nz/the-press/business/your-property/9821626/Residents-find-new-land-values-perplexing.

13 Marc Greenhill, "No More Mail for Red-Zone Homes," *The Press*, July 4, 2013, accessed June 2, 2014, http://www.stuff.co.nz/the-press/news/8878477/No-more-mail-for-red-zone-homes.

14 Georgina Stylianou and Lois Cairns, "Public to Have Say on Red-Zone Future," *The Press*, January 31, 2014, accessed June 2, 2014, http://www.stuff.co.nz/the-press/news/christchurch-earthquake-2011/9669348/Public-to-have-say-on-red-zone-future.

15 Bruce Harris, "The 'Third Source' of Authority for Government Action," *Law Quarterly Review* 108 (1992): 626-651.

16 Mai Chen, "Mai Chen: Quakes a True Test of Government," *The New Zealand Herald*, June 23, 2011, accessed June 2, 2014, http://www.nzherald.co.nz/opinion/news/article.cfm?c_id=466&objectid=10733869.

17 *Canterbury Regional Council v Independent Fisheries Ltd* [2012] NZCA 601, [2013] 2 NZLR 57.

18 John Hopkins, "Fowler Developments Ltd v Minister for Canterbury Earthquake Recovery," *New Zealand Law Journal* (2013): 337.

19 Marc Greenhill and Michael Fox, "Prime Minister Sorry for Threat that Angered Outcasts," *The Press*, August 28, 2013, accessed June 2, 2014, http://www.stuff.co.nz/the-press/news/christchurch-earthquake-2011/9094360/Prime-Minister-sorry-for-threat-that-angered-Outcasts.

20 Blair Ensor and Ashleigh Stewart "Brownlee Takes Swipe at Judge," *The Press*, November 18, 2013, accessed June 2, 2014, http://www.stuff.co.nz/national/politics/9410640/Brownlee-takes-swipe-at-judge.

21 Andrew Geddis, "Next year's Public Law Exam Question is Here Somewhere . . . ," *Pundit*, December 3 2013, accessed June 2, 2014, http://pundit.co.nz/content/next-years-public-law-exam-question-is-here-somewhere.

Desire for the gap
Ryan Reynolds

1 Georg Simmel, "The Metropolis and Mental Life (1903)," in *On Individuality and Social Forms* (Chicago: University of Chicago Press, 1972), 338.

2 Georg Simmel, "Sociability (1910)," in *On Individuality and Social Forms* (Chicago: University of Chicago Press, 1972), 136.

3 Georg Simmel, *The Conflict in Modern Culture, and Other Essays*, 25.

4 *Ibid.*, 12.

Reimagining and rebuilding local democracy
Bronwyn Hayward

1 I am grateful to Professor Graham Smith of Westminster University, UK and fellow trustee on the Foundation for Democracy and Sustainable Development, London, for an opportunity to review an early manuscript reflection on the principles and culture of democracy.

2 M. Warren, "Citizen Participation and Democratic Deficits: Considerations from the Perspective of Democratic Theory," in *Activating the Citizen*, eds Joan DeBardeleben and Jon Pammett (London: Palgrave MacMillan, 2009), 17-40.

3 K. Abbas, I. Christie, F. Demassieux, B. Hayward, T. Jackson and F. Pierre, "Sustainable Consumption and Lifestyles? Children and Youth in Cities," in *ISSC/UNESCO, World Science Report 2013: Changing Global Environments* (Paris: OECD Publishing and UNESCO Publishing, 2009), 357-364.

4 B. Honig, *Emergency Politics: Paradox, Law, Democracy* (Princeton: Princeton University Press, 2009).

5 B. Hayward, *Children, Citizenship and Environment: Nurturing a Democratic Imagination in a Changing World* (London: Earthscan / Routledge, 2012).

6 B. Hayward, H. Donald and E. Okeroa, "Flourishing: Young Lives Well Lived in New Zealand," in *Visions for Change: Country Papers* (Paris: United Nations Environment Programme, 2011), 45-56.

7 S. Russell, B. Frame and J. Lennox, *Old Problems: New Solutions* (Lincoln: Landcare Research, 2011); Waitangi Tribunal, *The Ngai Tahu Report*, 3 vols (Wellington: Brooker and Friend Ltd, 1991).

8 Detailed findings from the Auditor-General's inquiry into the decision by the Christchurch City Council in July 2008 to purchase five central city properties; letter from the Chief Ombudsman to the Chief Executive of the Christchurch City Council, January 12, 2009, accessed June 2, 2014, http://www.oag.govt.nz/2009/christchurch/docs/oag-christchurch-letter.pdf .

9 "Black Day for Democracy in Canterbury and the Nation," *The Press*, September 8, 2012, accessed June 1, 2014, http://www.stuff.co.nz/the-press/opinion/editorials/7636520/Black-day-for-democracy-in-Canterbury-and-the-nation; B Hayward, "Canterbury's Political Quake," *The Press*, March 3, 2012, accessed April 10, 2014, http://www.stuff.co.nz/the-press/opinion/perspective/6664104/Canterburys-political-quake.

10 F. Farrell, "Free Market Quakes Turn Citizens into Assets," *The Press*, July 27, 2011, accessed April 11, 2014, http://www.stuff.co.nz/the-press/opinion/perspective/5351237/Free-market-quake-turns-citizens-into-assets.

11 L. Gibbs et al., "Core Principles for a Community-based Approach to Supporting Child Disaster Recovery," *Australian Journal of Emergency Management* 29 (2014), accessed April 10, 2014, http://www.em.gov.au/Publications/Australianjournalofemergencymanagement/Pastissue/Pages/AJEM29ONECoreprinciplesforacommunitybasedapproachtosupportingchilddisasterrecovery.aspx.

12 B. Barber, *If Mayors Ruled the World: Dysfunctional Nations, Rising Cities* (Connecticut: Yale Press, 2013).

13 J. Jacobs, *The Life and Death of Great American Cities* (New York: Random House, 1961).

14 L. Cooke et al., *Super City State of Auckland* (Auckland: AUT Social Sciences and Public Policy, 2013), accessed May 1, 2014, http://www.supercityproject.aut.ac.nz/__data/assets/pdf_file/0020/401483/Report_final.pdf.

15 S. Vallance, "Early Disaster Recovery: A Guide for Communities," *Australian Journal of Disaster Recovery & Trauma Studies* 20, no. 11-12 (2011): 19-25.

16 J. Hayward, "Citizens Assemblies and Policy Reform," *Policy Quarterly* 9, no. 2 (May 2013).

17 M. Wagner and E. Zeglovits, "The Austrian Experience Shows that There is Little Risk and Much to Gain from Giving 16-year-olds the Vote," *Constitutional Blog*, London School of Economics, January 31, 2014, accessed April 10, 2014, http://blogs.lse.ac.uk/politicsandpolicy/archives/39195?utm_content=buffera9289&utm_medium=social&utm_source=twitter.com&utm_campaign=buffer.

18 O. Carville, "Poverty Strikes at Home, Children First Victims," *The Press*, February 15, 2013, accessed April 12, 2014, http://www.stuff.co.nz/national/health/8306750/Poverty-strikes-at-home-children-first-victims.

Chapter 4: Considering the Common Good

The inverse care law
Philippa Howden-Chapman et al.

1 P. Zhao, R. Chapman, E. Randal, and P. Howden-Chapman, "Understanding Resilient Urban Futures: A Systemic Modelling Approach," *Sustainability* 5 (2013): 3202-23.

2 A. Sen, *The Idea of Justice* (London: Penguin Books, 2009).

3 A. Kaiser, C. Holden, J. Beavan, D. Beetham, R. Benites, A. Celentano et al., "The Mw 6.2 Christchurch Earthquake of February 2011: Preliminary Report," *New Zealand Journal of Geology and Geophysics* 55 (2012): 67-90.

4 Human Rights Commission, *Monitoring Human Rights in the Canterbury Earthquake Recovery* (Wellington: The Human Rights Commission, 2013).

5 T. Kunioka and G.M. Waller, "In (a) Democracy We Trust: Social and Economic Determinants of Support for Democratic Procedures in Central and Eastern Europe," *The Journal of Socio-Economics* 28 (1999): 577-96.

6 "Proceedings of the Rhise Group Symposium," *New Zealand Medical Journal* 1386 (2013).

7 Canterbury Earthquake Recovery Authority (CERA), "Wellbeing Survey" (Christchurch: CERA, 2013).

8 New Zealand House of Representatives Finance and Expenditure Committee on Environmental Health, *Report of the Finance and Expenditure Committee on Environmental Health: 2012/13 Estimates for Vote Canterbury Earthquake Recovery* (Wellington: New Zealand House of Representatives, 2012), accessed May 5, 2014, http://www.parliament.nz/NR/rdonlyres/29D77B6A-F138-46D5-A0FC-972029664AE4/241405/DBSCH_SCR_5578_201213EstimatesforVoteCanterburyEar.pdf.

9 Treasury, *Financial Statements of the Government of New Zealand-B11* (Wellington: New Zealand Treasury, 2013).

10 "Canterbury Earthquake Research Strategy," Natural Hazards Research Platform, http://www.gns.cri.nz/index.php/gns/NHRP/Publications/Establishment-Strategy/Canterbury-Earthquake-Research-Strategy/Background.

11 Human Rights Commission, *Monitoring Human Rights in the Canterbury Earthquake Recovery.*

12 Dan Martin, Personal communication, 2014.

13 C. Gates, "Red-zone Demolition Behind Schedule," *The Press*, March 25, 2013.

14 "2013 Census QuickStats About Greater Christchurch: Dwellings," Statistics New Zealand, accessed March 11, 2014, http://www.stats.govt.nz/Census/2013-census/profile-and-summary-reports/quickstats-about-greater-chch/dwellings.aspx.

15 "2013 Census QuickStats about Greater Christchurch: Dwellings," Statistics New Zealand.

16 T. H. Holmes and R. H. Rahe, "The Social Readjustment Rating Scale," *Journal of Psychosomatic Research* 11 (1967): 213-18.

17 "2013 Census QuickStats About Greater Christchurch: Population Change," Statistics New Zealand, accessed March12, 2014, http://www.stats.govt.nz/Census/2013-census/profile-and-summary-reports/quickstats-about-greater-chch/population-change.aspx.

18 Ministry of Business and Innovation, *Housing Pressures in Christchurch: A Summary of the Evidence 2013* (Wellington: MBIE, 2013).

19 Ibid.

20 Tenants Protection Association Christchurch, *Rental Survey 2013: A Study of Increasing Rents and Housing Conditions in the Greater Christchurch Area* (TPA: 2013), accessed March 5, 2014, http://tpa.org.nz/sites/default/files/TPARentalSurveyReport2013_00.pdf.

21 Tenants Protection Association Christchurch, *Rental Survey 2013.*

22 Finance and Expenditure Committee on Environmental Health, *2012/13 Estimates for Vote Canterbury Earthquake Recovery.*

23 "EQC Scorecard: Home Repairs," Earthquake Commission, accessed March 6, 2014, http://www.eqc.govt.nz/canterbury-earthquakes/progress-updates/scorecard.

24 N. Smith, "Housing Accords Work Expanded to Christchurch, Wellington and Tauranga," accessed March 6, 2014, http://www.beehive.govt.nz/release/housing-accords-work-expanded-christchurch-wellington-and-tauranga.

25 "Christchurch Housing Accord," New Zealand Government and Christchurch City Council, April 16, 2014, accessed May 5, 2014, http://www.beehive.govt.nz/sites/all/files/Christchurch_Housing_Accord.pdf.

26 Lois Cairns, Marc Greenhill and Rachel Young, "City Council in Consent Crisis Talks," *The Press,* June 18, 2013, accessed 10 April 2014, http://www.stuff.co.nz/the-press/business/the-rebuild/8806933/Brownlee-sends-in-consent-troops-to-CCC.

27 Finance and Expenditure Committee, *2012/13 Estimates for Vote Canterbury.*

28 Lois Cairns, "Council May Offer Affordable Rental Homes," *The Press,* February 12, 2014, accessed May 5, 2014, http://www.stuff.co.nz/the-press/news/9710535/Council-may-offer-affordable-rental-homes.

29 Tudor Hart, "The Inverse Care Law," *The Lancet* 287-7696 (1971): 405-12.

30 Ministry of Business and Innovation, *Housing Pressures in Christchurch: A Summary of the Evidence 2013.*

31 G. Brownlee, "Social Housing is Council's Shame," March 14, 2013, accessed March 4, 2014, now available at: http://www.stuff.co.nz/the-press/business/the-rebuild/8806933/Brownlee-sends-in-consent-troops-to-CCC.

32 N. Smith, "Question for Oral Answer," November 19, 2013, accessed March 4, 2014, http://www.parliament.nz/en-nz/pb/business/qoa/50HansQ_20131121_00000009/9-christchurch-recovery%E2%80%94state-and-social-housing.

33 N. Smith, "Letter of Expectation 2012" (Wellington: Parliament, 2012).

34 "Housing New Zealand Announced New Development for Inner City," Housing New Zealand, accessed March 4, 2014, http://www.hnzc.co.nz/news/september-2013/housing-new-zealand-announces-new-development-for-inner-city.

35 O. Carville, "Christchurch People in Dire Need of Homes," *The Press*, December 12, 2013.

36 Ministry of Business and Innovation, "Housing Pressures in Christchurch."

37 Statistics New Zealand, *New Zealand Definition of Homelessness* (Wellington: Statistics New Zealand, 2009).

38 "2013 Census QuickStats About Greater Christchurch: Families and Households," Statistics New Zealand, accessed April 4, 2014, http://www.stats.govt.nz/Census/2013-census/profile-and-summary-reports/quickstats-about-greater-chch/families-households.aspx.

39 M. Baker, L. Telfar Barnard, A. Kvalsvig, A. Verrall, J. Zhang, M. Keall et al., "Increasing Incidence of Serious Infectious Diseases and Inequalities in New Zealand: A National Epidemiological Study," *The Lancet* 379 (2012): 1112-19.

[40] P. J. Ross, "Place in Time: Abridged Interview from the Avonside Project," *Griffith Review* 43 (2014): 254-8.

[41] Peter Townsend, "Small Business: Peter Townsend on Business Insurance," *The New Zealand Herald*, February 4, 2013, accessed May 10, 2014, http://www.nzherald.co.nz/business/news/article.cfm?c_id=3&objectid=10863292.

[42] "EQC Scorecard, Home Repairs," Earthquake Commission.

[43] "Build Back Smarter," Future Christchurch, accessed May 5, 2014, http://www.futurechristchurch.co.nz/smart-building/build-back-smarter.

[44] World Health Organization, *Health in the Green Economy: Health Co-benefits of Climate Change Mitigation – housing Sector* (Geneva: World Health Organization, 2011).

[45] M. J. V. White, A. Grieve, "Human Rights and Dignity: Lessons from the Canterbury Rebuild and Recovery Effort," ed. S. Butt et al., *Asia-Pacific Disaster Management* (Heidelberg: Springer-Verlag, 2014).

[46] P. Howden-Chapman, H. Viggers, R. Chapman, K. O'Sullivan, L. Telfar Barnard, B. Lloyd, "Tackling Cold Housing and Fuel Poverty in New Zealand: A Review of Policies, Research, and Health Impacts," *Energy Policy* 49 (2012):134–42.

[47] A. L. Pearson, L. Telfar-Barnard, J. Pearce, S. Kingham, P. Howden-Chapman, "Housing Quality and Resilience in New Zealand," *Building Research & Information* 42-2 (2014): 182-90.

[48] M. D. Keall, P. Howden-Chapman, M. G. Baker et al., "Formulating a Programme of Repairs to Structural Home Injury Hazards in New Zealand," *Accident Analysis & Prevention* 57 (2013):124-30, doi, http://dx.doi.org/10.1016/j.aap.2013.04.011.

[49] I. Kawachi, S. V. Subramanian, "Neighbourhood influences on health," *Journal of Epidemiology and Community Health* 61 (2007): 3-4.

[50] WHO, "Health in the Green Economy."

[51] Sarah Bierre, Philippa Howden-Chapman and Lisa Early, *Homes People Can Afford* (Wellington: Steele Roberts, 2013).

[52] S. Murray, N. Bertram, L. Khor, D. Rowe, B. Meyer, P. Newton et al., "Design Innovations Delivered Under the Nation Building Economic Stimulus Plan-Social Housing Initiative" (Melbourne: Australian Housing and Urban Research Institute, 2013).

[53] Productivity Commission, "Housing Affordability," April 2012, accessed May 5, 2014. http://www.productivity.govt.nz/inquiry-content/1509?stage=4.

[54] Sarah Bierre, Philippa Howden-Chapman and Lisa Early, *Homes People Can Afford*.

The structures that support bad transport decisions
Simon Kingham

[1] Adrian Humphris, "Public Transport – Public Transport Funding," *Te Ara – Encyclopdeia of New Zealand*, updated July 13, 2012, www.TeAra.govt.nz/en/piblic-transport/page-7.

[2] Exposure here refers to the quality of the air in the vicinity of the traveller, and does not account for respiration rates.

[3] Simon Kingham, Ian Longley, Jennifer Salmond, Woodroe Pattinson and Kreepa Shrestha, "Variations in Exposure to Traffic Pollution While Travelling by Different Modes in a Low Density, Less Congested City," *Environmental Pollution* 181 (2013): 211-218.

[4] John Pucher, Ralph Buehler, David Bassett and Andrew Dannenberg, "Walking and Cycling to Health. A Comparative Analysis of City, State, and International Data," *American Journal of Public Health* 100 (2010): 1986–1992.

[5] Karen Villanueva, Billie Giles-Corti and Gavin McCormack, "Achieving 10,000 steps: A comparison of Public Transport Users and Drivers in a University Setting," *Preventive Medicine* 47 (2008): 338-341; Ugon Lachapelle and Laurence Frank, "Transit and Health: Mode of Transport, Employer-Sponsored Public Transit Pass Programs, and Physical Activity," *Journal of Public Health Policy* 30 (2009): S73–S94; Lilah Besser and Andrew Dannenberg, "Walking to Public Transit. Steps to Help Meet Physical Activity Recommendations," *American Journal of Preventive Medicine* 29 (2005): 273-280.

[6] Richard Wener and Gary Evans, "A Morning Stroll. Levels of Physical Activity in Car and Mass Transit Commuting," *Environment and Behavior* 39 (2007): 62-74; John MacDonald, Robert Stokes, Deborah Cohen, Aaron Kofner and Greg Ridgeway, "The Effect of Light Rail Transit on Body Mass Index and Physical Activity," *American Journal of Preventive Medicine* 39 (2010): 105–112; Barbara Brown and Carol Werner, "Before and After a New Light Rail Stop: Resident Attitudes, Travel Behavior, and Obesity,' *Journal of the American Planning Association*, 75 (2008): 5-12.

[7] Karen Lucas, ed., *Transport & Social Exclusion. A Survey of the Group of Seven Nations*, (report produced for the FIA Foundation for the Automobile and Society, 2004).

[8] Organisation for Economic Co-operation and Development, *Environmentally Sustainable Transport. Futures, strategies and Best practices. Synthesis Report of the OECD project on Environmentally Sustainable Transport (EST)*, (Prepared on behalf of the Austrian Federal Ministry for Agriculture, Forestry, Environment and Water Management in co-operation with the OECD, 2000).

[9] Todd Litman, "Evaluating Transportation Land Use Impacts. Considering the Impacts, Benefits and Costs of Different Land Use Development Patterns," Victoria Transport Policy Institute, updated April 24, 2014, www.vtpi.org/landuse.pdf.

[10] Ministry of Transport, "Surface Transport Costs and Charges: Main Report" (prepared for the Ministry of Transport by Booz Allen Hamilton with Institute for Transport Studies, University of Leeds and associated consultants, 2005).

[11] Susan Bidwell, *Review of Studies that have Quantified the Economic Benefits of Interventions to Increase Walking and Cycling for Transport* (report prepared by Crown Public Health, part of the Canterbury District Health Board), updated December 5, 2012, www.cph.co.nz/Files/QuantEconBenefitPhysicalActive.pdf.

[12] Ministry of Transport, "Government Policy Statement on Land Transport Funding 2009/10–2018/19," May 2009, amended November 2010, www.transport.govt.nz/assets/Import/Documents/Amended-GPS-November-2010.pdf.

[13] For bus services, farebox recovery is intended to cover 50 per cent of the costs of running the bus service; the

remainder covered equally by local ECan rates and central government funds through the National Land Transport Fund. Since the earthquakes, as bus use has dropped, farebox recovery has dropped below 50 per cent. There are virtually no bus services where farebox recovery attempts to cover the full costs.

14 Opposition from businesses to bus lanes and a bus interchange on Riccarton Road have proved insurmountable for those ideas in the past.

15 New Zealand Transport Agency, *Economic evaluation manual*, 2013, www.nzta.govt.nz/resources/economic-evaluation-manual/economic-evaluation-manual/docs/eem-manual.pdf.

16 Christchurch City Council, *Draft Central City Plan* (Christchurch: 2011), no longer available, http://resources.ccc.govt.nz/files/CentralCityDecember2011/FinalDraftPlan/FinaldraftCentralCityPlan.pdf.

17 Canterbury Earthquake Recovery Authority, *Christchurch Central Recovery Plan* (Christchurch: 2012), http://ccdu.govt.nz/sites/ccdu.govt.nz/files/documents/christchurch-central-recovery-plan.pdf.

18 Canterbury Earthquake Recovery Authority, "An Accessible City," in *Christchurch Central Recovery Plan* (Christchurch: 2013), http://ccdu.govt.nz/the-plan/an-accessible-city.

19 Christchurch City Council, *Christchurch Transport Strategic Plan 2012–2042* (Christchurch: 2012), http://resources.ccc.govt.nz/files/TheCouncil/policiesreportsstrategies/transportplan/ ChristchurchStrategyTransportPlan2012.

20 "Cycleways in Christchurch," Christchurch City Council, accessed March 2014, www.ccc.govt.nz/cityleisure/projectstoimprovechristchurch/transport/cycleways/index.aspx.

21 Jason Krupp, "Otaki Strays from Economic Rigour," *New Zealand Business Review* August 2013, accessed March 2014, www.nbr.co.nz/article/otaki-expressway-strays-economic-rigor-wr.

22 "Transport Funding Cancellation of Otaki to Levin Expressway," New Zealand Parliament, accessed March 2014, http://www.parliament.nz/en-nz/pb/business/qoa/50HansQ_20120717_00000006/6-transport-funding—cancellation-of-Otaki-to-levin-expressway.

Losing our collective memory: The importance of preserving heritage architecture
Jessica Halliday

1 These include: the International Council on Monuments and Sites (ICOMOS), the United Nations Educational, Scientific and Cultural Organization (UNESCO), Blue Shield, The Hague Convention for the Protection of Cultural Property in the Event of Armed Conflict, the World Heritage Convention and the World Heritage Committee.

2 "Reshuffle Frees Brownlee to Focus on Tragedy," *The Press*, February 25, 2011, A10.

3 "500 Unsafe Buildings in Centre," *The Press*, February 28, 2011, A3.

4 Kate Chapman, "Lives before Christchurch Earthquake Damaged Buildings," March 1, 2011, accessed March 14, 2014, http://www.stuff.co.nz/national/christchurch-earthquake/4715003/Lives-before-Christchurch-earthquake-damaged-historic-buildings.

5 Ann Brower, "What's the Price of Pain," *NZ Herald*, February 16, 2013, accessed March 16 ,2014, http://www.nzherald.co.nz/nz/news/article.cfm?c_id=1&objectid=10865687.

6 Those strengthened to less than 33% did not perform significantly better than those that had not been strengthened at all. Rebecca Macfie, "Earthquake-prone Buildings: How to Reduce the Risk: A Short Summary of the EQ Commission's Key Points," *NZ Listener*, December 7, 2012, accessed March 15, 2014, http://www.listener.co.nz/commentary/letter-from-christchurch/earthquake-prone-buildings-how-to-reduce-the-risk/.

7 For example the International Covenant on Economic, Social and Cultural Rights (adopted by the UN in 1966, signed by New Zealand in 1968 and ratified in 1978) recognises the right to participate in cultural life.

8 Berma Klein Goldewiji, Georg Frerks and Els van der Plas, Introduction to *Cultural Emergency in Conflict and Disaster*, ed Goldewiji, Frerks and van der Plas (Rotterdam: NAI Publishers, 2011), 10.

9 The experience of Christchurch post-earthquake suggests that to some there is no acknowledgment of the value of the past or even the connection between the past, the present and the future. The desperate call to 'move on', to focus on the future not the past, is a determined coping mechanism in the face of such upheaval (see Georg Frerks, "Positioning Culture in Humanitarian Emergency Relief," *Cultural Emergency in Conflict and Disaster*, ed Goldewiji, Frerks and van der Plas (Rotterdam: NAI Publishers, 2011), 377. Many in government and amongst the citizenry in Christchurch create a false dichotomy between the past and the future, as if the earthquake entirely severed the longer, wider processes of time.

10 Paul Connerton, *How Societies Remember* (Cambridge: Cambridge University Press, 1989).

11 Erica Avrami, Randall Mason and Marta de la Toree, *Values and Heritage Conservation*, research report (Los Angeles: The Getty Conservation Institute, 2000), 4.

12 Donovan D. Rypkema, "The Multiple Contributions of Heritage Conservation" (transcript of lecture given to New Zealand Heritage Places Trust, November, 2010).

13 "The Greenest building: Quantifying the Environmental Value of Building Reuse," Preservation Green Lab of the National Trust for Historic Preservation, 2011, accessed March 20, 2014, http://www.preservationnation.org/information-center/sustainable-communities/green-lab/lca/The_Greenest_Building_lowres.pdf; see also: Lloyd Alter, "Proof that the Greenest Building *is* the One Already Standing Released in New Report from Preservation Green Lab," *Treehugger*, January 24, 2012, accessed March 20, 2014, http://www.treehugger.com/green-architecture/proof-greenest-building-one-already-standing-released-new-report-preservation-green-lab.html.

14 See the CER Act 2011 and James Marriner, "CERA Declines Demolition Notice for Christchurch Public Trust Building," *Russell McVeagh Resource Management News*, March 2014, accessed March 19, 2014, https://www.russellmcveagh.com/Publications/ViewPublication/tabid/176/Title/resource-management-news-march-2014/pid/281/Default.aspx.

15 As of 14 March 2014 there are 235 listed and/or registered

demolished heritage buildings listed in the archive of the website *Canterbury Heritage Demolition*, http://canterburyearthquakedemolist.weebly.com/. Naturally this figure excludes any buildings that had not yet been considered for listing, in particular notable works of architecture from the post-war period, such as Trengrove, Trengrove and Marshall's Reserve Bank (1965) or Warren and Mahoney's SIMU building (1966).

[16] Dean Knight, "CERA Mark II: my submission," *Elephants and the Law*, April 12, 2011, accessed March 18, 2014, http://www.laws179.co.nz/2011/04/cera-mark-ii-my-submission.html.

[17] The fate of several other heritage buildings in the South Frame remains uncertain: St James (Odeon) Theatre (1883); the Lawrie and Wilson building (1910); the Longden and Le Cren store (Pegasus Arms) (1852-1869); and the Duncan's Buildings (1905).

[18] Canterbury Earthquake Recovery Authority, *Recovery Strategy for Greater Christchurch Mahere Haumanutanga o Waitaha* (Christchurch: Canterbury Earthquake Recovery Authority, 2012).

[19] ICONIC submission on the Heritage Buildings and Places Recovery Programme, March 14, 2014. Unpublished.

[20] Nurhan Abujidi, "Urbicide in Nablus: Social Resilience and the Remaking of Space in the Post-disaster Environment," *Cultural Emergency*, ed Goldewiji, Frerks and van der Plas (Rotterdam: NAI Publishers, 2011), 328. Abujidi restricts the use of urbicide only to instances caused by war; I suggest the experience of Christchurch illustrates the worth of extending urbicide to instances of urban destruction during and after other kinds of disasters which also result in the 'radical devastation and transformation of urbanity through an exceptional event' (329).

[21] Aldo Rossi, *The Architecture of the City* (Cambridge, Massachusetts: MIT Press) 1982, 34.

[22] An undated statement from Dr Stefano Pampanin MIPENZ (President, New Zealand Society for Earthquake Engineering Inc.) and John Hare MIPENZ (President, Structural Engineering Society New Zealand Inc.), accessed March 20, 2014, http://iconicchristchurch.weebly.com/uploads/9/7/7/2/9772594/ipenz_sesoc_seismic_assessment_of_heritage_buildings.pdf.

[23] HRH Prince Constantijn of the Netherlands, "Cultural Emergency Response," *Cultural Emergency in Conflict and Disaster*, ed Goldewiji, Frerks and van der Plas (Rotterdam: NAI Publishers, 2011), 4. Specialist assistance is available from at least two sources: the Committee of the Blue Shield (ICBS), composed of the non-governmental organisations ICOM (International Council of Museums), ICOMOS (International Council on Monuments and Sites), ICA (International Council on Archives), IFLA (International Federation of Library Associations) and CCAAA (Coordinating Council of Audiovisual Archives Associations); and also from the Cultural Emergency Response programme of the Prince Claus Fund in the Netherlands.

[24] As cited in Sally Blundell's "What Will Become of Christchurch's Fallen Glory?," *New Zealand Geographic*, May-June (2013), 71.

[25] Marta de la Torre and Randall Mason, Introduction to *Assessing the Values of Cultural Heritage*, ed. Marta de la Torre, research report, (Los Angeles: The Getty Conservation Institute, 2002), 3.

[26] Ibid., 4.

Placemaking and post-quake identity – creating a unique Ōtautahi identity
Dr Rebecca Kiddle and Amiria Kiddle

[1] Canterbury Earthquake Recovery Authority, *Christchurch Central Recovery Plan (CCRP)* (Christchurch: Canterbury Earthquake Recovery Authority, 2013), 17, accessed February 10, 2014, http://ccdu.govt.nz/the-plan.

[2] Ibid., 39.

[3] Canterbury Earthquake Recovery Authority, *Christchurch Central Recovery Plan (CCRP)*,23; Ngāi Tahu (n.d.) *Whakaoratia Otautahi: Aspirations for Christchurch Recovery and Rebuild*, accessed February 15, 2014, http://ngaitahu.iwi.nz/wp-content/uploads/2013/06/Whakaoratia-Otautahi.pdf.

[4] Canterbury Earthquake Recovery Authority, *Christchurch Central Recovery Plan (CCRP)*, 23.

[5] Ibid., 39.

[6] F. Duffy, "Measuring Building Performance," *Facilities* 8, no.5 (1990): 17–20; S. Brand, *How Buildings Learn: What Happens After They're Built* (New York; London: Viking, 1994).

[7] S. Brand, *How Buildings Learn*, 17.

[8] G. Butina Watson and I. Bentley, *Identity By Design* (Oxford: Elsevier, 2007).

[9] M. Carmona et al. note in *Public Spaces-Urban Places*, that 'Butina Watson and Bentley (2007:13-4) highlight the complex and divergent range of local cultural landscapes found across the world, and the need for careful study of both historic precedent and of contemporary case study examples that have been able to capture important cultural references while avoiding pastiche.' (Oxford: Architectural Press, 2011).

[10] See I. Bentley et al.'s book *Responsive Environments*, (Oxford: Elsevier, 1985) for a comprehensive discussion on the importance of choice.

[11] Canterbury Earthquake Recovery Authority, *Christchurch Central Recovery Plan (CCRP)*, 55.

[12] Ibid.

[13] Ibid.

[14] Ngāi Tahu (n.d.), *Whakaoratia Otautahi: Aspirations for Christchurch Recovery and Rebuild.*

[15] Canterbury Earthquake Recovery Authority, *Christchurch Central Recovery Plan (CCRP)*, 60.

[16] See L. Smith, *Decolonizing Methodologies: Research and Indigenous Peoples* (Dunedin: University of Otago Press, 1999); F. Cram and K. Pipi, *Maori/Iwi Provider Success: Report on the Pilot Project* (Tamaki-Makaurau; IRI, 2000).

[17] J. Jacobs, *The Death and Life of Great American cities* (New York: Random House LLC, 1961), 73.

[18] Canterbury Earthquake Recovery Authority, *Christchurch Central Recovery Plan (CCRP)*, 41.

[19] Ibid., 83.

[20] Ibid., 50.

[21] Public Health Association Press Release, "Marae Lead the Way for Christchurch Earthquake Recovery," *The Press*, 17 September 17, 2013, accessed March 5, 2014, http://www.scoop.co.nz/stories/AK1309/S00571/marae-lead-the-way-for-christchurch-earthquake-recovery.htm.

Territorial visions in post-quake Aquila: Creating community and identity
Claudia Mattogno

[1] A. Clementi and E. Piroddi, *Le città nella storia d'Italia: L'Aquila* (Bari: Laterza, 1986).

[2] L. M. Calandra, ed., *Territorio e democrazia: Un laboratorio di geografia sociale nel doposisma aquilano* (L'Aquila: Edizioni L'Una, 2012).

[3] J. F. Cabestan, "L'Aquila, ville reconstruite mais abandonée," *AMC Le Moniteur Architecture* 217 (2012): 18-21.

[4] G. J. Frisch, ed., *L'Aquila Non si uccide così anche una città?* (Napoli: Clean, 2009).

[5] F. Erbani, *Il disastro: L'Aquila dopo il terremoto: le scelte e le colpe* (Bari: Laterza, 2010).

[6] E. Pulcini, *La cura del mondo: Paura e responsabilità nell'età globale* (Torino: Bollati Boringhieri, 2009).

[7] C. Mattogno, "Territori fragili. La cura come pratica di progetto," *Tafterjournal: Esperienze e strumenti per cultura e territory*, 50 (2012).

[8] C. Mattogno, "Non più centro e non più territorio: L'Aquila dopo il 6 aprile," *AR bimestrale dell'Ordine degli Architetti di Roma e Provincia*, 86 (2009): 48-51.

[9] C. Mattogno, "L'Aquila: Riannodare I legami: Centro storico_periferia_territorio_paesaggio," *DoCoMoMo Italia Giornale* 25 (2009): 4.

[10] V. Shiva, *Making Peace with the Earth: Beyond Resource, Land and Food Wars* (Cambridge: South End Press, 2012).

[11] A. K. Jha, ed., *Safer Homes, Stronger Communities: A Handbook for Reconstructing after Natural Disasters* (Washington DC: The World Bank, 2010).

Chapter 5: Thinking Big

What should a garden city of the twenty-first century aim to be like?
Luke Engleback

[1] According to *Eco2 Cities*, an additional 400,000 sqkm of new urban built-up area is projected to be built by 2030, which is equal to the entire world's urban area as of 2000. H. Suzuki, A. Dastur, S. Moffatt, H. Maruyama, *Eco2 Cities* (World Bank, 2010): 1.

[2] Ebenezer Howard (1850-1928) published *Tomorrow: A Peaceful Path to Real Reform* in 1898 and went on to re-publish this as *Tomorrow: A Peaceful Path to Real Reform* as *Garden Cities of To-Morrow* in 1902.

[3] United Nations Population Division global population growth forecast.

[4] Intergovernmental Panel on Climate Change (IPCC), *Fifth Assessment Report* (New York: Cambridge University Press, March 2014).

[5] D. Hansford, "Liquidation," *New Zealand Geographic* 125 Jan/Feb 2014, 49.

[6] Indicative number based on median of average dairy cow belching 250-500 litres of methane per day according to K. A. Johnson and D. E. Johnson in "Methane Emissions from Cows," *Journal of Animal Science* 73 (1995), and producing 28 litres of milk a day.

[7] National architectural styles can be seen in the use of window shutters throughout France; Germany's steep roofs and half-timbered vernacular; and the village-inspired brick and hung tile of Voysey.

[8] Cardinal Richelieu (1585-1642) was Secretary of State in France from 1616. His model town, which is 700 metres by 500 metres, was built on Renaissance principles and named after him.

[9] The British Reform Movement followed on from the Enlightenment's ideas. The greatest success of the Reformers was the Reform Act 1832, which changed social policy on health, voting rights and living conditions.

[10] Titus Salt (1803-1876) was a textile manufacturer who consolidated his manufacturing at Shipley and built a workers village commencing 1851.

[11] Industrial philanthropists took models from an earlier era where villages and cottages had been tied to the farms of landed gentry. With this came the risk of losing the home if the breadwinner died or there were other problems.

[12] A turning point was the writing and campaigning of Rachel Carson in the late 1950s and publication of her magnum opus, which is still in print today: *Silent Spring* (Penguin Modern Classics, 1962).

[13] WWF was founded in November 1961 to promote conservation of wildlife and habitats. Friends of the Earth was founded 1969 initially as an anti-nuclear group. Greenpeace also started life in 1969 as an anti-nuclear pressure group.

[14] The call for two new garden cities earlier in 2014 was followed by UK Chancellor George Osbourne's investment of £200 million in a brownfield site garden city at Ebbsfleet in northeast Kent.

[15] The UK Town and Country Planning Association has continued to promote garden cities but largely on the traditional model, as seen in their 2012 report *Creating Garden Cities and Suburbs Today: Policies, Practices, Partnerships and Model Approaches*.

[16] R. Rogers et al., *The Urban Taskforce Report* (The Office of the Deputy Prime Minister, 1999).

[17] T. Malthus, *An Essay on the Principle of Population* (London: J. Johnson in St Paul's churchyard,1794).

[18] Donella Meadows, Jorgen Randers and Dennis Meadows, *The Limits to Growth* (New York: Signet, 1972).

[19] E. F. Schumacher, *Small is Beautiful: Economics as if People Mattered* (New York: Harper & Row, 1973), 61.

[20] M. Wackernagel et al., *Tracking the Ecological Overshoot of the Human Economy*, ed. Edward O. Wilson (Cambridge, MA: Harvard University, 2002).

[21] P. Hawkens, A. Lovins and L. H. Lovins, *Natural Capitalism: Creating the Next Industrial Revolution* (New York: Little, Brown & Company, 1999).

[22] Ecology, the scientific study of the relation of living organisms to each other and their surroundings, was a term first coined by Ernst Haeckel in the 1880s. The ecosystem approach is now considered one of the most important principles in sustainable environmental management, as a linear approach is insufficient in dealing with biological systems (this reductionist approach led to Ludwig Von Bertalanffy developing the General Systems Theory in the 30s).

[23] The United Nations Convention on Biological Diversity was presented for signature at the Rio Earth Summit in 1992 and entered into force at the end of 1993.

24 E. Maltby, "The Ecosystem Approach: From Principle to Practice" (Ecosystem Service and Sustainable Watershed Management in North China International Conference, Beijing, P. R. China, August 23-25, 2000.)

25 I first came across this term in a book by an architect colleague Miguel Ruano titled *Ecourbanismo* (Barcelona, 1999).

26 "Our Common Future" (UN World Commission on Environment and Development, 1987), chaired by Gro Harlem Bruntland.

27 "NZ's Eco Footprint Sixth Largest," last modified October 29, 2008, www.stuff.co.nz/environment/694713/NZs-eco-footprint-sixth-largest ; Statistics NZ reported an average waste per household of 1.255 tonnes per year, compared to the average UK household of 1 tonne per year.

28 D. Hansford, "Liquidation," 53.

29 As seen in the November 2012 report *Green Growth: Opportunities for New Zealand* by Pure Advantage, which set out advantages such as investment in sustainable agriculture, smart grid and biofuels.

30 The Ottawa Charter (1986) of the World Health Organisation (WHO) established the idea that human health and wellbeing is created within the settings of everyday life.

31 BREEAM (Building Research Establishment Environmental Assessment Methodology) is the world's longest established and most widely used method of assessing, rating and certifying the sustainability of buildings. The measures used represent a broad range of categories and criteria from energy to ecology. They include aspects related to energy and water use, the internal environment (health and wellbeing), pollution, transport, materials, waste, ecology and management processes. LEED (Leadership in Energy and Environmental Design) was developed by the United States Green Building Council and launched in 2000 and is currently the second most widely used environment assessment method.

32 The ecological accounting aspect of building codes has improved, but there is still an inconsistency; the Ecohomes standard, for example, looked at increasing the number of plant species per square metre, but this tends to favour micro or small species over shrubs that may provide habitat and food for birds, and of course there was no accounting of the fauna. So this aspect is still crude compared to the buildings accounting.

33 J. Lovelock, *The Revenge of Gaia: Why the Earth is Fighting Back and How We Can Still Save Humanity* (Penguin Books, 2006), 7 & 149.

34 Phosphates are essential for plant growth and their application drives enhanced arable yields; but at current rates of use, we have an estimated 30 years remaining of reserves, 70% of which are located in one place – Morocco.

35 Three very hot years have already reduced yields by 26%, which along with similar poor harvests in Australia, China, India and Russia have led to a doubling in the price of grain.

36 In *New Zealand Geographic's* "Liquidation" Hansford notes that agriculture comprises 70% of NZ exports, and that Canterbury uses 60% of all water drawn in New Zealand.

37 "IPCC Report Paints Bleak Picture of War, Famine and Pestilence," *The Independent*, March 31, 2014, 5.

38 In *The Water Footprint of Modern Consumer Society* (Routledge, 2013) Hoekstra shows that imports of water-intensive products can highly benefit water-scarce countries, but that this also creates a dependency on foreign water resources. For example, it is calculated that it takes 15,000 litres of water to produce 1 kg of beef.

39 UK National Ecological Assessment, *The UK National Ecological Assessment: A Synthesis of Key Findings* (Cambridge: UNEP, 2011).

40 David J. C. MacKay, *Sustainable Energy – Without the Hot Air* (UIT Cambridge, 2009), 5.

41 *Energy in New Zealand 2013*, Ministry of Business Innovation and Employment.

42 Low Impact Development is a technique that started in the USA primarily to address storm water runoff – calling for a network of small storm retention installations that include planted swales, green roofs, rain gardens, permeable paving and tree planting.

43 A. Viljoen, ed, *Continuous Productive Urban Landscapes* (Oxford: Architectural Press, 2005).

44 R. Constanza, B. G. Norton and B. D. Haskell, eds, *Ecosystem Health – New Goals for Environmental Management* (Washington DC: Island Press, 1992).

45 J. Jacobs, *The Death and Life of Great American Cities* (New York: Random House,1961). This book introduced Sociology concepts such as 'eyes on the street' and 'social capital'; S. Woodcraft et al., *Design for Social Sustainability – A Framework for Creating Thriving New Communities* 2 (The Young Foundation, 2011).

46 Nesta is an innovation charity in the UK with a mission to help people and organisations bring great ideas to life.

47 "Green Infrastructure Toolkit," Horticultural Trade Association, October, 2011, https://www.the-hta.org.uk.

48 *The Freiburg Charter for Sustainable Urbansim* (Freiburg: Im Breisgau & the Academy of Urbanism, 2012).

49 Changed storm patterns, rising sea levels and tidal surges are of concern to coastal cities like Christchurch. Average sea levels vary particularly in the southern hemisphere, which is 80% ocean and affected by El Nino and La Nina cycles that will be exacerbated by sea level rises, due to thermal expansion and melting ice caps. See the Christchurch City Council and Tonkin & Taylor Ltd *Effects of Sea Level Rise for Christchurch City* (2013); and NZ Climate Change Office (Ministry for the Environment) by Harris Consulting in conjunction with Christchurch City Council (2001).

Next generation infrastructure
Peter Cockrem and Clayton Prest

1 Ministry for the Environment, *New Zealand's Sixth National Communication to the United Nations Framework Convention on Climate Change* (Wellington: MFE, 2013), 2.

2 '97% of published climate papers with a position on global warming agree global warming is happening and we are the cause.' "The Consensus Project," accessed March 31, 2014, http://theconsensusproject.com/.

3 AAAS Climate Science Panel, *What We Know: The Reality, Risks and Response to Climate Change* (American Association for the Advancement of Science), accessed April 14, 2014, http://whatweknow.aaas.org/wp-content/uploads/2014/03/AAAS-What-We-Know.pdf.

4 The IPCC report builds on previous research published in 1990, 1995, 2001,and 2007; IPCC, *Climate Change 2014: Mitigation of Climate Change* (Contribution of Working Group III to the Fifth Assessment Report of the Intergovernmental Panel on Climate Change (AR5), 2014).

5 IPCC, *Climate Change 2014: The Physical Science Basis*; "According to economists' estimates climate-related damage is already costing us more than 1.2 trillion dollars worldwide in global GDP," from Fiona Harvey's "Climate Change is Already Damaging the Economy," *The Guardian*, 26 September 2012, accessed May 2, 2014, http://www.theguardian.com/environment/2012/sep/26/climate-change-damaging-global-economy.

6 MFE, *New Zealand's Sixth National Communication*, 149; "Global Warming Warning after ChCh floods," 3News, accessed May 12, 2014, http://www.3news.co.nz/Global-warming-warning-after-ChCh-floods/tabid/423/articleID/334865/Default.aspx.

7 Jan Burck et al., *Climate Change Performance Index* (Germanwatch, 2013), 18-19.

8 "Climate Change Minister Welcomes IPCC Report," New Zealand Government, accessed May 3, 2014, http://www.beehive.govt.nz/release/climate-change-minister-welcomes-ipcc-report; "Greenhouse gas emissions and removals," Ministry for the Environment, accessed April 23, 2014, http://www.mfe.govt.nz/environmental-reporting/atmosphere/greenhouse-gases/emissions.html.

9 73 per cent in 2012, according to MFE in *Sixth National Communication on Climate Change*; "ChCh Energy Use," Christchurch Agency for Energy, accessed May 11, 2014, http://www.cafe.gen.nz/database.

10 MFE acknowledges that New Zealand is committed to playing its part in a global response and sets conditional reduction targets of 10-20% in its *Sixth National Communication on Climate Change*.

11 New Zealand's emissions of greenhouse gases are accelerating from 2.2% in 2012, from 1.4% in 2011. MFE, *Sixth National Communication on Climate Change*, 49.

12 "The effects will fall capriciously and unevenly, and local bodies cannot be expected to meet them," from "Climate Change Everyone's Issue," *The Dominion Post*, accessed May 9, 2014, http://i.stuff.co.nz/dominion-post/comment/9897674/Editorial-Climate-change-everyones-issue.

13 Christchurch City Council, *Climate Smart Strategy 2010-2025*, (Christchurch: CCC, 2010).

14 MFE, *Sixth National Communication on Climate Change*, 11.

15 CCC, *Climate Smart Strategy 2010-2025*.

16 Total energy use in Christchurch has increased 66 percent since 1990; Ibid.

17 CCC also established a 'Target Sustainability' initiative, in *Climate Smart Strategy 2010-2025*.

18 Copenhagen Clean Tech, *Copenhagen 2025 Climate Plan* (Copenhagen Clean Tech, 2012).

19 Christchurch City Council, *Sustainable Energy Strategy for Christchurch 2008 - 2018* (Christchurch: CCC, 2008), 11.

20 Between the 2006 and 2013 census population growth by 32.6% in Selwyn and 16.7% in Waimakariri while Christchurch City decreased by 2%. "Quick stats about Greater Christchurch," Statistics New Zealand, accessed May 4, 2014, http://www.stats.govt.nz/Census/2013-census/profile-and-summary-reports/quickstats-about-greater-chch/population-change.aspx; public transport use dropped 44% from 2010 to 2012 with the loss of 50,000 jobs in the central city and the central bus exchange, Energy Efficiency and Conservation Authority, *Powering Public Transport in New Zealand* (EECA, 2012), accessed May 3, 2014, http://www.eeca.govt.nz/sites/all/files/powering-public-transport-in-new-zealand-oct-2012.pdf.

21 Energy use has risen predominantly due to a 26% rise in diesel use from heavy demolition vehicles, "Christchurch Agency for Energy," CAfE, accessed May 2, 2014, http://www.cafe.gen.nz/database.

22 Canterbury Earthquake Recovery Authority (CERA), *Christchurch Central Recovery Plan* (Christchurch: CERA, 2012), 23.

23 Christchurch City Council, *Christchurch District Plan Review: Draft Transport Chapter* (Christchurch City Council, 2014).

24 CERA, *Christchurch Central Recovery Plan*; Green Star assessments are currently used by 50% of all new commercial buildings in NZ.

25 IPCC, AR5 SPM WG-III, 21; "Building codes . . . if well designed and implemented, have been among the most environmentally and cost-effective instruments for emissions reduction," in IPCC AR5 SPM WG-III, 26.

26 "BASE: A Green Building Assessment Tool for Christchurch," NZGBC, accessed May 2, 2014, http://www.nzgbc.org.nz/images/stories/BASE_Factsheet_V11.pdf.

27 The Christchurch Agency for Energy has established a $1.8 million fund in a bid to reduce carbon emissions by encouraging sustainable energy initiatives in the city rebuild. "New Energy Grant's for the Christchurch Rebuild," CCC, accessed May 1, 2014, http://www.ccc.govt.nz/thecouncil/newsmedia/mediareleases/2013/201308142.aspx; "Energy performance improvements should be included in the 'standard' repair of earthquake damaged homes," from "What is the Build Back Smarter Project," Beacon Pathway, accessed May 4, 2014, http://www.beaconpathway.co.nz/existing-homes/article/what_is_the_build_back_smarter_project.

28 IPCC, AR5 SPM WG-III, 28.

29 Brent Toderian,"Density Done Well, and Not Just Downtown," Planetizen, accessed April 28, 2014, http://www.planetizen.com/node/61643; "Christchurch Sustainable Urban Villages," The Viva Project, accessed March 21, 2014, http://thevivaproject.org.nz/.

30 Richard Florida, "What Cities Really Need to Attract Entrepreneurs, According to Entrepreneurs," The Atlantic CityLab, February 11, 2014, accessed April 17, 2014, http://www.theatlanticcities.com/jobs-and-economy/2014/02/what-cities-really-need-attract-entrepreneurs-according-entrepreneurs/8349/.

31 IPCC, AR5 SPM WG-III, 25; Ibid., 24.

32 MRCagney Ltd, *Powering Public Transport in New Zealand* (Auckland: EECA, 2012), accessed May 3, 2014, http://www.eeca.govt.nz/sites/all/files/powering-public-transport-in-new-zealand-oct-2012.pdf.

33 David Killick, "Commuter Rail Needed for Rebuilt City," *The Press*, October 16, 2013, accessed May 6, 2014, http://www.stuff.co.nz/the-press/news/transport/9287697/Commuter-rail-needed-for-rebuilt-city.

[34] IPCC, AR5 SPM WG-III, 26.

[35] 0.45 tonnes/square metre; John, Stephen et al., *The Carbon Footprint of Multi-storey Buildings Using Different Construction Materials* (Christchurch: University of Canterbury, 2010), accessed May 5, 2014, http://www.branz.co.nz/cms_show_download.php?id=e6343b12939a4f34e-8083bc0c8699502c5b5766f.

[36] IPCC, AR5 SPM WG-III, 26.

[37] Tonkin & Taylor, *Effects of Sea Level Rise for Christchurch City* (Christchurch: Christchurch City Council, 2013), 63.

[38] Tonkin & Taylor, *Effects of Sea Level Rise*.

[39] Georgina Stylianou, "Can Christchurch be Saved?" *The Press*, May 4, 2014, accessed May 5, 2014, http://www.stuff.co.nz/the-press/10002634/Can-Christchurch-be-saved.

[40] CCC, accessed May 3, 2014, http://www.ccc.govt.nz/thecouncil/newsmedia/mediareleases/2013/201312041.aspx.

Why the big pile of rubble in the forest?: The question of demolition waste in post-quake Canterbury
Juliet Arnott

[1] The Canterbury Earthquake Recovery Authority's (CERA) Debris Management Policy demonstrates potentially conflicting elements in the priorities at play, and these appear challenging to reconcile. These include: protecting public and worker health and safety; enabling the rapid and affordable recovery of Christchurch; avoiding or mitigating harmful effects of waste; maximising the efficient use of resources; sensitivity in the handling of buildings and vehicles where fatalities have occurred; identifying and protecting heritage items; and establishing transparent and equitable processes. "Debris Disposal," Canterbury Earthquake Authority, accessed June 10, 2104, http://cera.govt.nz/demolitions/debris-disposal.

[2] "ZW Definition," Zero Waste International Alliance, last modified 2009, http://zwia.org/standards/zw-definition/.

[3] Water and Waste Unit Solid Waste Team, *Solid Waste Education and Communication Strategy* (Christchurch: Christchurch City Council, 2004), 3, http://resources.ccc.govt.nz/files/solidwasteeducationandcommunicationstrategy-docs.pdf.

[4] Auckland's new Waste Management and Minimisation Plan in 2012 aims to reduce the 1.2 million tonnes of waste currently sent to landfill each year and to be at Zero Waste by 2040. Auckland Council *Waste Management and Minimisation Plan*, accessed June 10, 2014, http://wasteplan.aucklandcouncil.govt.nz/; San Francisco has progressively increased diversion of waste to 80% by 2012, as seen in P. H. Connett's *The Zero Waste Solution: Untrashing the Planet One Community at a Time* (Vermont: Chelsea Green Publishing, 2013), 93.

[5] Other categories include real extent of the waste, community priorities, funding mechanism, (peace-time) regulations, costs, resource availability and appropriate management approaches. C. Brown, *Disaster Waste Management: A Systems Approach* (doctorial thesis, University of Canterbury, 2012).

[6] CERA, Canterbury Wellbeing Index: Mental wellbeing (Christchurch: CERA, 2012), http://cera.govt.nz/sites/default/files/common/2013-06-26-canterbury-wellbeing-index-07-mental-wellbeing.pdf.

[7] L. Thornley, J. Ball, L. Signal, K. Lawson-Te Aho and E. Rawson, *Building Community Resilience: Learning from the Canterbury Earthquakes* (final report to Health Research Council and Canterbury Medical Research Foundation, 2013), 2, http://www.communityresearch.org.nz/wp-content/uploads/formidable/Building-Community-Resilience-report-March-2013.pdf.

[8] H. Denhart, "Deconstructing Disaster: Psycho-social Impact of Building Deconstruction in Post-Katrina New Orleans," *Cities*, 26, no.4 (2009):195, 200.

[9] "2013 Census QuickStats about Greater Christchurch: Work," Statistics New Zealand, last modified 2013, http://www.stats.govt.nz/Census/2013-census/profile-and-summary-reports/quickstats-about-greater-chch/work.aspx.

[10] J. Storey, M. Gjerde, A. Charleson and M. Pedersen, *State of Deconstruction in New Zealand – Synopsis* (Wellington: Centre for Building Performance Research, Victoria University, 2003), 2, http://www.zerowaste.co.nz/assets/Councilssolutions/TheStateofDeconstructioninNZSynopsis.pdf.

[11] L. Austin, *Christchurch Demolitions – Perspective from a Debris & Waste Manager* (Christchurch: Canterbury Earthquake Recovery Authority, 2012), 8, http://www.wasteminz.org.nz/wp-content/uploads/Christchurch-demolitions-perspective-from-a-debris-and-waste-manager-paper.pdf.

[12] True North Consulting, *Treated Timber Waste Minimisation Project: Milestone 1 – Industry Overview* (report prepared for Environment Canterbury, May 2013), 35.

[13] Ibid., 14.

[14] C. Brown, *Disaster Waste Management: A Systems Approach* (doctoral thesis, University of Canterbury, 2012), 165.

[15] Ibid., vii-viii.

[16] P. H. Connett, *The Zero Waste Solution: Untrashing the Planet One Community at a Time* (Vermont: Chelsea Green Publishing, 2013)

[17] For Dr Brown's full list of issues requiring attention in disaster waste management, please see pages 262-67 of her doctoral thesis, https://static.squarespace.com/static/5006875e24ac21f35d8de8d2/t/51623d8ce4b080e51177f84b/1365392780423/Disaster%20Waste%20Management%20-%20A%20Systems%20Approach.pdf.

[18] H. Denhart, "Deconstructing Disaster," 200.

Anchornomics in Christchurch: An economist's view
Shamubeel Eaqub

[1] Canterbury Earthquake Recovery Authority, *Christchurch Central Recovery Plan* (Christchurch: CERA, 2012), 3.

[2] Enrico Moretti, *The New Geography of Jobs* (Boston: Houghton Mifflin Harcourt, 2012), 214.

Chapter 6: Acting Small

The plan against the rebuild
Eric Crampton

[1] I discussed the export of Christchurch houses, and the link to our zoning regulations, in posts at *Offsetting Behaviour*

in April and June of 2012. See http://offsettingbehaviour. blogspot.co.nz/2012/04/connect-dots.html and http:// offsettingbehaviour.blogspot.co.nz/2012/06/oh-christchurch.html.

[2] Marc Greenhill, "Land Price Issue of 'Real Concern'," stuff. co.nz, last modified June 28, 2011, http://www.stuff. co.nz/national/christchurch-earthquake/5199320/Land-price-issue-of-real-concern.

[3] I discussed this case at *Offsetting Behaviour*, March 20, 2013, http://offsettingbehaviour.blogspot.co.nz/2013/03/day-757-continued-regime-uncertainty.html.

[4] Alan Wood, "Precinct Plan Puts Hotel Hopes in Limbo," *The Press*, last modified May 20, 2013, http://www.stuff.co.nz/business/rebuilding-christchurch/8449598/Precinct-plan-puts-hotel-hopes-in-limbo.

Simple things that bring joy: The *All Right?* campaign
Lucy D'Aeth

[1] Opinions Market Research Ltd, *Taking the Pulse 2014: Quantitative Research among Greater Christchurch Residents* (CDHB and Mental Health Foundation, April 2014).

[2] K. Calder, *Evaluation of the All Right? Campaign* (Community and Public Health / Canterbury District Health Board, 2014).

[3] SKIP is a campaign led by the Ministry of Social Development. "Strategies with Kids, Information for Parents," http://www.skip.org.nz/.

[4] P. Gluckman, *The Psychosocial Consequences of the Canterbury Earthquakes: A Briefing Paper* (Office of the Prime Minister's Science Advisory Committee, 2011), 2.

[5] Sam Thompson, Jody Aked, Nic Marks and Corina Cordon, *Five Ways to Wellbeing* (New Economics Foundation, 2008), http://b.3cdn.net/nefoundation/8984c5089d5c2285ee_t4m6bhqq5.pdf.

[6] All Right? resources are available free to Cantabrians via http://www.cph.co.nz/Resources/default.asp.

A cause for CanCERN
James Dann

[1] "Carl Bertelsmann Prize for 'Democracy and efficiency in local government,'" Bertelsmann Stiftung Foundation, accessed July 18, 2014, http://www.bertelsmann-stiftung. de/cps/rde/xchg/SID-1A80F3D6-200314BF/bst_engl/hs.xsl/2088_9626.html.

[2] The author was one of the 230 people who applied to be on the forum. His application was unsuccessful.

[3] James Dann, "Putting the Munt back into Community," *Rebuilding Christchurch*, April 14, 2014, https://rebuildingchristchurch.wordpress.com/2014/04/14/putting-the-munt-back-into-community/.

First of all, we are citizens
Alejandro Haiek Coll

[1] Lebbeus Woods, "Thoughts on Architecture of Resistance," accessed June 10, 2014, 5, http://www.lebbeuswoods.net/LW-ResistanceText2.pdf.

[2] This is commonly attributed to Charles de Gaulle however the date or circumstance in which it was said is difficult

to find. T. S. Eliot also wrote a very similar sentence in "A Commentary," *The Criterion* VI, 4 (November 1927), 387: "Politics has become too serious a matter to be left to politicians."

Chapter 7: Meeting in the Middle

Developing the arts ecology of Christchurch
Melanie Oliver

[1] "Performing Arts Precinct," Christchurch Central Development Unit, last accessed June 15, 2014, https://ccdu.govt.nz/projects-and-precincts/performing-arts-precinct.

[2] "Lost Opportunities in the Precinct," *The Press*, last modified April 26, 2014, http://www.stuff.co.nz/the-press/opinion/editorials/9980008/Editorial-Lost-opportunities-in-precinct.

Studio Christchurch: Meeting of minds
Camia Young and Associate Professor Uwe Rieger

[1] Members of the Studio Christchurch Committee are the University of Canterbury, Department for Civil and Natural Resources Engineering; University of Canterbury Geography Department; Lincoln University, School of Landscape Architecture; CPIT, Architectural Studies; Unitec, Architecture Department; Victoria University, School of Architecture; and the University of Auckland, School of Architecture and Planning.

[2] "The Best of the New Christchurch," *The Press*, February 22, 2013.

[3] ". . . The opening event LUXCITY, was stunning and brought thousands of Christchurch residents and visitors back to the central city at night. The experience was highly symbolic in its celebration of the creative opportunities in Christchurch's rebuild . . . I would especially like to thank the undergraduate architecture students who, with the support of their supervisors, designed the spectacular large-scale fabrications and flew to our city from across the country to work alongside the construction industry to install them onsite. The many hours they contributed on a voluntary basis I hope provided them with valuable experience as well as creating fantastic event for our community. . . Thank you for giving the people of Christchurch this opportunity to experience this interesting and thought-provoking approach to Christchurch, the Transitional City. I wish you every success should you hold this festival again in the future." Bob Parker, Mayor of Christchurch, letter to the organisers of the Festival of Transitional Architecture and the heads of school at UoA, AUT, Victoria University, CPIT and Unitec, December 3, 2012.

[4] NZIA Jury justified their awarding of the Graphisoft Award in 2012: "This is an exceptionally professional treatment of a challenging situation – the reconstruction of post-earthquake Christchurch – presented in an exemplary manner. Indeed, the presentation would be the envy of many professional bodies or agencies. The rigour of the research is evident, as is the concerted effort to make sense of the findings. The whole exercise demonstrates the virtue

of collaboration; the project could not have been realised to this level if it had not been a collective effort. Therefore, besides being admirable in itself, it shows the way forward for the architectural profession by highlighting the skills architects bring to complex urban problems."

5 Future Christchurch publications: Derek Kawiti and Camia Young, *Future Christchurch: V1 Research and Design* (Blurb, 2011); Camia Young, *Future Christchurch V3.0 Prototype City* (Blurb, 2013); Alex Haryowiseno, *Future Christchurch V3.1: Innovation Economy* (Blurb, 2012); Che Wei Lee, *Future Christchurch V3.2: Towards an Efficient Economy* (Blurb, 2012); Zhi Wong, *Future Christchurch V3.3: A Green Economy* (Blurb 2012); Praveen Karunsinghe, *Future Christchurch V3.4: Creating Creative Christchurch* (Blurb, 2012); Biran He, *Future Christchurch V3.5: An Adaptable Housing Solution* (Blurb, 2012); Erica Austin, *Future Christchurch V3.6: The Experience Economy* (Blurb, 2012); Camia Young, *Future Christchurch V6.0: The Blueprint* (Blurb, 2014).

Chapter 8: Building Back Better

Shaping cities, shaping health
Skye Duncan

1 American Heart Association, "Getting Healthy," *Overweight in Children*, accessed March 17, 2014, https://www.heart.org/HEARTORG/GettingHealthy/HealthierKids/ChildhoodObesity/Overweight-in-Children_UCM_304054_Article.jsp.

2 United States Centers for Disease Control and Prevention, "Chronic Disease and Health Promotion," *Chronic Diseases: The Leading Cause of Death and Disability in the United States,* accessed May 22, 2014, http://www.cdc.gov/chronicdisease/overview/index.htm#1.

3 "Media Centre – Noncommunicable Diseases Key Facts," World Health Organization, accessed 1 June, 2014, http://www.who.int/mediacentre/factsheets/fs355/en/.

4 The United States Department of Health and Human Services, *2008 Physical Activity Guidelines for Americans* (Washington, DC: 2008), vii. Note: For substantial health benefits, adults should do at least 150 minutes (2 hours and 30 minutes) a week of moderate-intensity, or 75 minutes (1 hour and 15 minutes) a week of vigorous-intensity aerobic physical activity, or an equivalent combination of moderate- and vigorous-intensity aerobic activity.

5 City of New York, *Active Design Guidelines, Promoting Physical Activity and Health in Design* (City of New York: 2010), 13.

6 "Overweight and Obesity – Adult Obesity Facts," United States Centers for Disease Control and Prevention, accessed May 22, 2014, http://www.cdc.gov/obesity/data/adult.html.

7 City of New York, *Active Design Guidelines, Promoting Physical Activity and Health in Design* (City of New York: 2010), http://a856-citystore.nyc.gov/2/Municipal-Publications/12/Surveys-Reports/90/Active-Design-Guidelines. The Active Design Guidelines resulted from a collaborative, multidisciplinary effort among twelve New

York City agencies; New York's health, planning, design and architecture communities; and academic institutions from across the United States. Those who led the effort included NYC Departments' of Health and Mental Hygiene, Design and Construction, City Planning and Transportation and the local American Institute of Architects.

8 City of New York, *Active Design: Shaping the Sidewalk Experience* (City of New York: 2013), http://www.nyc.gov/html/dcp/html/sidewalk_experience/index.shtml.

Transport: Post-quake impacts and new beginnings
Glen Koorey

1 "DRT 2013 Essentials," TRANSPORT/LAND, June 25, 2013, http://transportland.org/2013/06/drt-2013-essentials/.

2 Marta Steeman, "Christchurch Telecom Call Centre Homely," *Stuff.co.nz*, April 15, 2011, accessed June 15, 2014, http://www.stuff.co.nz/business/industries/telecoms-it-media/4890274/Christchurch-Telecom-call-centre-homely.

3 Vince Ham et al., *Evaluative Study of Co-located Schools Established following the Christchurch Earthquake* (New Zealand: Ministry of Education, December 2012), http://www.educationcounts.govt.nz/publications/schooling/115174.

4 Canterbury Emergency Management Group, "Temporary Removal of Cycle Lanes to Reduce Traffic Congestion," Canterbury Earthquake, April 14, 2011, accessed June 19, 2014, http://canterburyearthquake.org.nz/2011/04/14/7435/.

5 Christchurch City Council, *Contextual Historical Overview for Christchurch City* (Christchurch: CCC, June 2005), http://www.ccc.govt.nz/cityleisure/artsculture/christchurchheritage/publications/.

6 Christchurch City Council, *A City for People – Action Plan* (Christchurch: CCC, February 2010), http://www.ccc.govt.nz/cityleisure/projectstoimprovechristchurch/projectcentralcity/acityforpeople.aspx.

7 Christchurch Central Development Unit, *Christchurch Central Recovery Plan Replacement Transport Chapter: An Accessible City* (Christchurch: Canterbury Earthquake Recovery Authority, October 2013), http://ccdu.govt.nz/the-plan/an-accessible-city.

8 Christchurch City Council, *Christchurch Transport Strategic Plan 2012–2042* (Christchurch: CCC, November 2012), http://www.ccc.govt.nz/thecouncil/policiesreportsstrategies/transportplan/.

9 Christchurch City Council, *Christchurch Cycle Design Guidelines* (Christchurch: CCC, April 2013), http://www.ccc.govt.nz/cityleisure/projectstoimprovechristchurch/transport/cycleways/.

10 Glen Koorey, "It's Back – Open Streets Ciclovía, Sun Sept 29," *Cycling in Christchurch*, September 15, 2013, http://cyclingchristchurch.co.nz/2013/09/15/its-back-open-streets-ciclovia-sun-sept-29th/.

How Christchurch can build light rail – and create the centres it needs in the process
Peter Newman

1 Peter Newman, Jeffrey Kenworthy and Gary Glazebrook, "Peak Car Use and the Rise of Global Rail: Why This

Is Happening and What It Means for Large and Small Cities," *Journal of Transporation Technologies* 3 (2013): 272-287.

[2] Newman et al, "Peak Car Use," 272-287.

[3] Benjamin Davis, Tony Dutzik and Phineas Baxandall, *Transportation and the New Generation: Why Young People Are Driving Less and What It Means for Transportation Policy* (Washington D.C.: Frontier Group & U.S. PIRG Education Fund, 2012); Brookings Institution Metropolitan Program, "The Road . . . Less Traveled: An Analysis of Vehicle Miles Traveled Trends in the U.S.," *Metropolitan Infrastructure Initiative Series* (Washington D.C.: Brookings Institution, 2008); Steve Melia, "A Future Beyond the Car: Editorial Introduction," *World Transport Policy and Practice* 17, no.4 (2011): 3-6; David Gargett, "Traffic Growth: Modelling a Global Phenomenon," *World Transport Policy and Practice* 18.4 (2012): 27-45; Peter Newman and Jeffrey Kenworthy, "'Peak Car Use': Understanding the Demise of Automobile Dependence," *World Transport Policy and Practice* 17, no.3 (2011): 31-42.

[4] Tim Beatley and Peter Newman, *Green Urbanism Down Under: Learning from Sustainable Communities in Australia* (Washington D.C.: Island Press, 2009); Peter Newman and Jeffrey Kenworthy, *Sustainability and Cities: Overcoming Automobile Dependence* (Washington D.C.: Island Press, 1999).

[5] Peter Newman and Jeffrey Kenworthy, "'Peak Car Use," 31-42.

[6] Jan Gehl, *Cities for People* (Washington D.C.: Island Press, 2010).

[7] Peter Newman and Jeffrey Kenworthy, *Sustainability and Cities: Overcoming Automobile Dependence*.

[8] James McIntosh, Peter Newman and Gary Glazebrook, "Why Fast Trains Work: An Assessment of a Fast Regional Rail System in Perth, Australia," *Journal of Transportation Technologies* 3 (2013): 37-47.

[9] Peter Newman, Jeffrey Kenworthy and Gary Glazebrook, "Peak Car Use and the Rise of Global Rail," 272-287.

[10] Ibid.

[11] Glen D. Bottoms, "Continuing Developments in Light Rail Transit in Western Europe: United Kingdom, France, Spain, Portugal and Italy," *9th National Light Rail Conference* (Portland: Transportation Research Board and APTA, 2003).

[12] James McIntosh, Peter Newman, Roman Trubka and Jeffrey Kenworthy (forthcoming), "Framework for Land Value Capture From the Investment in Transit in Car Dependent Cities," *Journal Of Land Use and Transport*.

[13] McIntosh et al., "Framework for Land Value Capture," forthcoming.

[14] Tim Beatley, Linda Blagg and Peter Newman, *Christchurch: Resilient City*, video, 49 minutes, 2014, https://vimeo.com/90474333.

Our River: Public realm design brief at its best – are we doing our best with it?
Jessica Staples

[1] Christchurch Central Development Unit – CCDU, *Anchor Projects Overview, as at 02/2014* (Christchurch: Canterbury Earthquake Recovery Authority, 2014), accessed May 21, 2014, https://ccdu.govt.nz/sites/default/files/documents/anchor-projects-overview-february-2014.pdf.

[2] "Te Papa Ōtākaro – Avon River Precinct announcement – 20 December 2012," YouTube video, 13:43, posted by Christchurch Central Development Unit, November 20, 2013, https://www.youtube.com/watch?v=0wp2Hu3I1mw.

[3] Christchurch Central Development Unit, "Local and International Experts to Lead Design of Te Papa Otakaro/Avon River Precinct," *Invest Christchurch* 4 (2013).

[4] "Te Papa Ōtākaro – Avon River Precinct announcement," YouTube video.

[5] OPUS, "OPUS Celebrates Opening of First Stage of Te Papa Ōtākaro/Avon River Precinct," *Newsflash* (September 2013).

[6] Christchurch Central Development Unit – CCDU, *Anchor Projects Overview, as at 02/2014* (Christchurch: Canterbury Earthquake Recovery Authority, 2014), accessed May 21, 2014, https://ccdu.govt.nz/sites/default/files/documents/anchor-projects-overview-february-2014.pdf.

[7] Christchurch Central Development Unit – CCDU, *Indicative Anchor Project Delivery Schedule* (Christchurch: Canterbury Earthquake Recovery Authority, 2014), accessed 21 May, 2014, https://ccdu.govt.nz/sites/default/files/indicative-anchor-project-delivery-schedule-2013-10-11.pdf.

Chapter 9: Reimagining Recovery

Valley section: A new instrument for the Garden City
Chris Moller

[1] John Wilson, "Contextual Historical Overview for Christchurch City" (contextual study for Christchurch City Council, 2005), 11, accessed June 25, 2014, http://resources.ccc.govt.nz/files/ChristchurchCityContextualHistoryOverviewFull-docs.pdf.

[2] Ibid., 11-12.

[3] Patrick Geddes, "Report on the Towns in the Madras Presidency, 1915 Tangore," in Jacqueline Tyrwhill, *Patrick Geddes in India* (London: Lund Humphries, 1947), 17.

[4] Ibid.

Does the Blueprint support the creation of a healthy ecological urban environment?
Di Lucas

[1] Christchurch City Council, Christchurch Naturally : Discovering the City's Wild Side (Christchurch: CCC, 2000), 22-23.

[2] Ibid., 25-29.

[3] Lucas Associates, *Indigenous Ecosystems of Otautahi Christchurch: The Coastal Plains of Hagley-Ferrymead & Burwood-Pegasus* (Christchurch-Otautahi Agenda 21 Forum and the Community Boards, 1996).

[4] J. A. Kenny, and B. W. Hayward, *On the Edge: Celebrating the Diversity of New Zealand's Coastal Landforms* (Geoscience Society of New Zealand, 2013), 25.

[5] Lucas Associates, *Surface Water Strategy: Landscape Values' Assessment for Christchurch and Banks Peninsula* (Report to Christchurch City Council, 2008).

[6] Christchurch City Council, "Waterways and Wetlands Natural Asset Management Strategy" (Christchurch, 2000).

[7] Lucas Associates, Colin Meurk and Christchurch City Council, *What to plant and how to maintain native plants along freshwater streams in Christchurch* (Leaflet,1997).

[8] Canterbury Earthquake Recovery Authority, *Christchurch Central Recovery Plan* (Christchurch: CERA, 2013), 53.

[9] Kirsten Curry and Anna Larsson, 2014. *Green Roofs in the Christchurch Rebuild: Barriers and Motivations Influencing Implementation* (Christchurch: 2014, University of Canterbury), 17.

[10] Canterbury Earthquake Recovery Authority, *Christchurch Central Recovery Plan*, 23.

What has Ōtautahi revealed? Māori urban planning in post-quake Christchurch

Craig Pauling, Shaun Awatere and Shadrach Rolleston

[1] Māori tribal group of a particular locality.

[2] Marae or sub-tribal based councils.

[3] A Māori tribal group with customary authority over a particular locality. In the case of central Christchurch the mana whenua is the Ngāi Tahu hapū, Ngāi Tūāhuriri, based at their marae in Tuahiwi, to the north of the city.

[4] See "Ōtautahi Revelead," Ngā Aho, http://www.ngaaho.maori.nz/page.php?m=177.

[5] C. Marr, *Public Works Takings of Māori Land 1840-1981*, Rangahaua Whanui Series (Wellington: Waitangi Tribunal Division, 1997).

[6] R. T. M. Tau, "Ngai Tahu: Forced Urban Settlement Migration" (presentation to Ōtautahi Revealed, Christchurch, November 1, 2012); R. T. M. Tau, "Rebuilding Christchurch After the Earthquake: Incorporating Māori Values in New Zealand's Most English City," in *Stanford Woods Environmental Forum* (California, USA: Stanford University, 2012).

[7] J. Booth, "The N.Z. Māori Council Begins Its Work," *Te Ao Hou – The New World* 43, June (1963): 1; "The N.Z. Māori Council Some Important Issues," *Te Ao Hou – The New World* 44, September (1963): 51.

[8] Waitangi Tribunal, *Report of the Waitangi Tribunal on the Kaituna River Claim (Wai 4)*, 1st ed. (Wellington: The Waitangi Tribunal, 1992); *Report of the Waitangi Tribunal on the Mangonui Sewerage Claim (Wai 17)*, 2nd ed. (Wellington: The Waitangi Tribunal, 1988); *Report of the Waitangi Tribunal on the Manukau Claim (Wai 8)*, 2nd ed. (Wellington: The Waitangi Tribunal, 1989); *Report of the Waitangi Tribunal on the Motonui – Waitara Claim (Wai 6)*, 2nd ed. (Wellington: The Waitangi Tribunal, 1989).

[9] P. Kingi and G. Asher, *Māori Planning Kit* (Auckland: Auckland Māori Planning Committee, 1981).

[10] R. Anderson, *Planning for Māori Needs* (Auckland: Town & Country Planning Division, Ministry of Works and Development, 1983).

[11] T. Tutua-Nathan, "Kaitiakitanga: A Commentary on the Resource Management Act 1991," in *Local Government and the Treaty of Waitangi*, ed. J. Hayward (Auckland: Oxford University Press, 2003), 39-42.

[12] H. Matunga, "Decolonising Planning: The Treaty of Waitangi, the Environment and Dual Planning Tradition," in *Environmental Planning and Management in New Zealand*, eds. P. A. Memon and H. C. Perkins (Palmerston North: Dunmore Press, 2000), 36-47.

[13] For more information see D. Crengle, *Taking into Account the Principles of the Treaty of Waitangi: Ideas for the Implementation of Section 8, Resource Management Act 1991* (Wellington: Ministry for the Environment, 1993); M. Kawharu, "Kaitiakitanga: A Māori Anthropological Perspective of the Māori Socio-Environmental Ethic of Resource Management," *Journal of the Polynesian Society* 109, no. 4 (2000): 349-70; M. Love, "Resource Management, Local Government, and the Treaty of Waitangi," in *Local Government and the Treaty of Waitangi*, 21-37; Ministry for the Environment, *Case Law on Tangata Whenua Consultation* (Wellington: Ministry for the Environment, 1999); *He Tohu Whakamārama: A Report on the Interactions Between Local Government and Māori Organisations in Resource Management Act Processes* (Wellington: Ministry for the Environment, 1998).

[14] S. Awatere, C. Pauling, S. Rolleston, R. Hoskins and K. Wixon, *Tu Whare Ora – Building Capacity for Māori Driven Design in Sustainable Settlement Development* (report to Ngā Pae o Te Maramatanga, 2008); S. Rolleston and S. Awatere, "Ngā Hua Papakāinga: Habitation Design Principles," *MAI Review* 2 (2009): 1-13.

[15] See: R. Hoskins and J. Kake, "Auckland as a unique place – Te Aranga Māori Design Principles," *Auckland Design Manual* (NZ: Ngā Aho Incorporated, 2014), http://aucklanddesignmanual.co.nz; *Te Aranga – Māori Cultural Landscape Strategy* (2007), www.tearanga.maori.nz.

[16] S. Awatere, G. Harmsworth, S. Rolleston, C. Pauling, T. K. Morgan and R. Hoskins, *Kaitiakitanga o Ngā Ngahere Pohatu: Kaitiakitanga of Urban Settlements* (Report to the Ministry of Science and Innovation, 2011).

[17] Mahinga kai refers to the gathering, production and procurement of food and the associated places, species and practices involved.

[18] "Positive partnership behind city rebuild," *Te Pānui Rūnaka* (May 2014), 13, http://www.tepanui.co.nz/tpr/2014-2/may-2014/.

Digging where we stand

Bailey Peryman, Oliver Peryman & Michelle Marquet

[1] Carl Folke, "Resilience: The emergence of a perspective for social-ecological systems," *Global Environmental Change* 16 (2006): 253-267.

[2] Masanobu Fukuoka, *The One-Straw Revolution: An Introduction to Natural Farming* (Emmaus:Rodale Press, 1978).

[3] Canterbury District Health Board, Community and Public Health, "Christchurch City Health Profile: Obesity," last modified March, 2013, http://www.healthychristchurch.org.nz/media/11938/obesity.pdf.

[4] Ben Lilliston, "New UN Report Calls for Transformation in Agriculture," Institute for Agriculture and Trade Policy, September 20, 2014, http://www.iatp.org/blog/201309/new-un-report-calls-for-transformation-in-agriculture.

[5] Te Marie Tau, *The Values and History of the Ōtākaro and*

North and East Frames (Ngāi Tahu Research Centre, 2014).

[6] Canterbury District Health Board, "Christchurch City Health Profile: Obesity."

[7] Food security is often defined in terms of access and affordability, and primarily reported on as a health and social justice issue. Localising food systems and empowering organic community food initiatives are common solutions applied globally. The affordability of fresh food is improved by shortening the supply chain by connecting growers direct with consumers, and more accessible due to its proximity – especially true of home gardens and urban farms. Nutritional value is greater through the food being unprocessed, fresh and organic.

[8] John McCrone, "Christchurch Rebuild: A City Stalled," *The Press*, March 8, 2014, http://www.stuff.co.nz/the-press/business/the-rebuild/9805314/Christchurch-rebuild-A-city-stalled.

[9] Alistair McIntosh, *Soil and Soul: People Versus Corporate Power* (London: Aurum Press, 2001).

More than buildings: Growing biodiversity and happiness in communities
Kevin McCloud

[1] Such as Zygmunt Bauman in *Society Under Siege* (Cambridge: Polity Press, 2002).

[2] J. Wernick, ed., *Building Happiness* (London: Black Dog Press / RIBA Building Futures, 2008).

[3] See Dirk Maxeiner and Michael Miersch's "The Urban Jungle" in J. Normand's *Living for the City* (London: Policy Exchange, 2006).

[4] Jeremy Till, "A Happy Age (before the days of architects)," in *Building Happiness* (London: Black Dog Press / RIBA Building Futures, 2008); For further reference see also Fritz Haeg, *Edible Estates: Attack on the Front Lawn* (Metropolis, 2008); www.habhousing.co.uk; www.bioregional.co.uk; and www.commonground.org.uk.

IMAGE CREDITS

Please read Images in the visual essays in a clockwise direction, starting at the top left-hand side of each page.

Pages 36-39
All images of central Christchurch 2014 by Barnaby Bennett

Chapter 1: Making Plans

Broken buildings

Page 42
Images 1-6: Central city, various. April 2011. Courtesy of Sabin Holloway and Jason Mill.

Page 43
Images 7-15: Central city, various. April 2011. Courtesy of Sabin Holloway and Jason Mill.

Page 44
Images 16-23: Central city, various. 2012-2014. Courtesy of Barnaby Bennett.

Share an Idea

Page 59
Image 1: Share an Idea Expo, CBS Arena. 14-15 May 2011. Courtesy of Christchurch City Council.
Image 2: Share an Idea graphic showing key themes. June 2011. Courtesy of Christchurch City Council.
Image 3: David Sim, Gehl Architects, speaking at Share an Idea Expo, CBS Arena. 14-15 May 2011. Courtesy of Simon Goddard, Gehl Architects.
Image 4: Members of public recording ideas on wall, Share an Idea Expo. 14-15 May 2011. Courtesy of Simon Goddard, Gehl Architects.
Image 5: Christchurch City Council deliberations on Share an Idea and the draft Central city Plan. 26 October 2011. Courtesy of Hugh Nicholson.

New buildings

Page 67
Image 1: St Elmo Courts, Cnr Hereford and Montreal Streets. 2014. Courtesy of Chris Keen from the collection www.facebook.com/AvenuesFour.
Image 2: 53 Victoria Street. 2014. Courtesy of Chris Keen from the collection www.facebook.com/AvenuesFour.
Image 3: 337 St Asaph Street. 2014. Courtesy of Chris Keen from the collection www.facebook.com/AvenuesFour.

Image 4: Westende House, Manchester Street. 2014. Courtesy of Chris Keen from the collection www. facebook.com/AvenuesFour.
Image 5: 819 Colombo Street. 2014. Courtesy of Chris Keen from the collection www.facebook.com/ AvenuesFour.
Image 6: Anderson Lloyd House, 70-72 Gloucester Street. 2014. Courtesy of Chris Keen from the collection www. facebook.com/AvenuesFour.

Page 68
Images 7, 8, 9, 10 and 13: Victoria Street. 2013-2014. Courtesy of Barnaby Bennett
Image 11: Botanical Gardens Information Centre. 2014. Courtesy of Chris Keen from the collection www. facebook.com/AvenuesFour.
Image 12: Forte Health, Kilmore Street. 2014. Courtesy of Barnaby Bennett.

Page 69
Image 14: Standish & Preece, Tuam Street. 2014. Courtesy of Barnaby Bennett.
Image 15: Strangers Building, High Street. 2014. Courtesy of Barnaby Bennett.
Image 16: 163 Montreal Street. 2014. Courtesy of Scott McKenzie.
Image 17: Victoria Street. 2014. Courtesy of Scott McKenzie.
Image 18: TVNZ. 2014. Courtesy of Chris Keen from the collection www.facebook.com/AvenuesFour.
Image 19: Victoria Street. 2014. Courtesy of Scott McKenzie.
Image 20: Cnr Moorhouse Avenue and Durham Street. 2014. Courtesy of Scott McKenzie.

Chapter 2: Selling the Plan

Planning documents

Page 100
Image 1: Document cover: "Christchurch City Council Annual Plan 2012-13". 2012. Copyright: Christchurch City Council.
Image 2: Document cover: "Christchurch Central Recovery Plan." 2012. Copyright: CCDU and CERA.
Image 3: Document cover: "Central city Plan: Draft Central city Recovery Plan for Ministerial Approval." December 2011. Copyright: Christchurch City Council.
Image 4: Document cover: "Central city Plan Business Overview." Date: 2011. Copyright: Christchurch City Council.
Image 5: Document cover: "Seize the opportunity to invest in New Zealand's second largest city." 2014. Copyright: CERA.
Image 6: Document cover: "An Accessible City." December 2014. Copyright: CERA.

Anchor project billboards

Page 109
Images 1-6: Central city, Various. 2014. Courtesy of Barnaby Bennett.

A message and a messenger (Matthew Galloway)

Figure 1: Visuals from Share an Idea campaign by Christchurch City Council, licensed under CC BY 3.0
Figure 2: Christchurch City Council logo by Christchurch City Council, licensed under CC BY 3.0
Figure 3: Draft Central city Plan by Christchurch City Council, licensed under CC BY 3.0
Figure 4: Christchurch Central Recovery Plan (CCRP) by Christchurch Central Development Unit, licensed under CC BY 3.0
Figure 5: CCRP launch video screen shots by Christchurch Central Development Unit, licensed under CC BY 3.0

Newspaper headlines

Page 117
Image 1: Document: Front cover of the *Press*. 31 July 2012. Copyright: Fairfax Media New Zealand / the *Press*.

Blueprint launch

Page 122
Image 1-8: Stills from video of launch of the CCDU Blueprint. 30 July 2012. Courtesy of Gerard Smyth.

Blueprint launch video

Pages 129-130
Images 1-18: Stills from video of CCDU Blueprint launch video. 30 July 2012. Copyright: Canterbury Earthquake Recovery Authority. Creative Commons Attribution 3.0 New Zealand License.

Chapter 3: Rewriting the Rules

Central city red zone

Page 150
Images 1-6: Location: Central city, various. April 2011. With Permission from: Sabin Holloway and Jason Mill.

Page 151
Images 7-12: Location: Central city, various. April 2011. With Permission from: Sabin Holloway and Jason Mill.

Cargo containers

Page 158
Images 1-6. Various locations. 2011-2014. Courtesy of Barnaby Bennett.

Page 159
Images 7-11. Various locations. 2011-2014. Courtesy of Barnaby Bennett.

Street art

Page 164
Image 1: Artist: Jeremy Sauzier. Madras Street. 2011-2014. Courtesy of Barnaby Bennett

Image 2: Artist: BC Crew. Cashel Street. 15 April 2014.
Courtesy of Reuben Woods.
Image 3: Artist: JFK Crew. Wainoni Road, Wainoni. 27
February 2014. Courtesy of Reuben Woods.
Image 4: Colombo and Gloucester Streets. 24 December
2013. Courtesy of Reuben Woods.
Image 5: Manchester Street. 4 January 2014. Courtesy of
Reuben Woods.
Image 6: Cashel Street. 15 April 2014. Courtesy of Reuben
Woods.

Page 165

Image 7: Artist: Berst. Painted as part of From The Ground
Up festival. 2013. Photography by Luke Shirlaw.
Image 8: Artist: Wongi. Painted as part of From The
Ground Up festival. 2013. Photography by Luke Shirlaw.
Image 9: Artist: Askew. Painted as part of From The
Ground Up festival. 2013. Photography by Luke Shirlaw.
Image 10: Artist: Drypnz. Painted as part of From The
Ground Up festival.2013. Photography by Luke Shirlaw.
Image 11: Artist: Misery. Painted as part of From The
Ground Up festival. 2013. Photography by Luke Shirlaw.
Image 12: Artists: Olivia and Holly. Painted as part of From
The Ground Up festival.
2013. Photography by Luke Shirlaw.
Image 13: Artist: Berst. Painted as part of From The
Ground Up festival. 2013. Photography by Luke Shirlaw.

Page 166

Image 14: Artists: Beastman and Vans The Omega.
Painted as part of Oi YOU! presents RISE festival. 2013.
Photography by Luke Shirlaw.
Image 15: Artist: Vans the Omega. Painted as part of Oi
YOU! presents RISE festival.
2013. Photography by Luke Shirlaw.
Image 16: Artist: Askew. Painted as part of Oi YOU!
presents RISE festival. 2013.
Photography by Luke Shirlaw.
Image 17: Artist: Sofles. Painted as part of Oi YOU!
presents RISE festival. 2013. Photography by Luke Shirlaw.
Image 18: Artist: BMD. Painted as part of Oi YOU!
presents RISE festival. 2013. Photography by Luke Shirlaw.
Image 19: Artist: Deak Williams. Painted as part of Oi
YOU! presents RISE festival. 2013.
Photography by Luke Shirlaw.
Image 20: Artist: Owen Dippie. Painted as part of Oi YOU!
presents RISE festival. 2014.
Photography by Luke Shirlaw.

Desire for the gap (Ryan Reynolds)

All figures courtesy of and by Gap Filler except
Figure 3: Courtesy of Ross Becker, 2011
Figure 8: Courtesy of Barnaby Bennett, 2013

Protest signs

Page 177

Images 1-3: Various locations, central city. 2012-2014.
Courtesy of Barnaby Bennett.
Image 4: Artist: Cubey. 4 January 2013. Courtesy of
Reuben Woods.

Page 178

Image 5: High Street. 28 February 2014. Courtesy of
Reuben Woods.
Images 6-8: Various locations, central city. 2012-2014.
Courtesy of Barnaby Bennett.
Image 9: Unknown artist: Wake Up. Gloucester and
Colombo Street. 15 April 2014. Image by Reuben Woods.
Image 10: Customs Stickers (I Hate It Here). Colombo
Street. 15 April 2014. Courtesy of Reuben Woods.

Chapter 4: Considering the Common Good

The inverse care law (Philippa Howden-Chapman et al.)

Figures 1 & 2: Cartography by Amber L. Pearson, 2014;
data sourced from Statistics New Zealand.

Plant Gang

Page 199

Image 1: The Zen Garden. Corner Manchester and Cashel
Street. 2013. Courtesy of Liv Worsnop.

Page 200

Images 2-3: Cotters Lane Guerrilla Garden. 2014.
Courtesy of Barnaby Bennett.
Images 4-6: Site Clean, Guerrilla Sage Fields. 2013-2014.
Courtesy of Liv Worsnop.

Page 201

Images 7-13: Volunteers, Succulent Guerrilla Gardens, The
Zen Garden. 2013-2014. Courtesy of Liv Worsnop.

The structures that support bad transport decisions
(Simon Kingham)

Figure 1 Reproduced by permission from Victoria
Transport Policy Trust.
Figure 2 Reproduced by permission from Cycling
Promotion Fund, 2012.
Figure 3 Share an Idea campaign by Christchurch City
Council, licensed under CC BY 3.0, sourced from www.
shareanidea.org.nz/move.

RAD Bikes

Page 208

Image 1: High Street, central city. 2014. Courtesy of
Richard Sewell.

Page 209

Images 2-4: High Street, central city. 2014. Courtesy of
Richard Sewell.

Lost heritage

Page 217

Image 1: Peter Beaven (1925-2012). Lyttelton Road
Tunnel Authority Administration Building 1962-63, Tunnel
Road, Christchurch. Courtesy Art History Visual Resources

Collection, University of Canterbury.

Image 2: Benjamin W. Mountfort (1825-98). Holy Trinity Church, Stanmore Road, Avonside, Christchurch 1874. Courtesy of Art History Visual Resources Collection, University of Canterbury.

Image 3: B. W. Mountfort. Church of the Good Shepherd, 42 Phillips Street, Phillipstown, Christchurch 1884-1929. Courtesy of Art History Visual Resources Collection, University of Canterbury.

Image 4: Sydney Luttrell (1872-1932) and Alfred Luttrell (1865-1924). Regent Theatre, Cathedral Square, Christchurch 1908. Courtesy of Art History Visual Resources Collection, University of Canterbury.

Image 5: Collins & Harman. Press Building, Cathedral Square, Chirstchurch, 1908-09 2014. Courtesy of Art History Visual Resources Collection, University of Canterbury

Page 218

Image 6: William B. Armson (1834-1883). Christchurch Girls High School, 46 Armagh Street, Christchurch, 1880. Courtesy of Art History Visual Resources Collection, University of Canterbury.

Image 7: W. B. Armson. Fisher's Building, 134 Hereford and 280 High Street corner, Christchurch 1880. Courtesy of Ian Lochhead.

Image 8: Samuel Hurst Seager (1854-1933), Cecil Wood (1878-1948), JF Munnings (1879-1937). Sisters of the Mission's Convent Chapel, 140 Barbadoes St, Christchurch 1907.Courtesy of Art History Visual Resources Collection, University of Canterbury.

Image 9: Francis W. Petre (1847-1918). Convent of the Sisters of the Mission, 140 Barbadoes Street, Christchurch 1881: Courtesy of Art History Visual Resources Collection, University of Canterbury.

Image 10: Samuel Farr (1825-1914). St Paul's Presbyterian Church, later St Paul's Pacific Trinity Church, 236 Cashel Street, Christchurch, 1877. Courtesy of Art History Visual Resources Collection, University of Canterbury.

Image 11: Ben J. Ager (nd). McKenzie & Willis Building, 120 Hereford Street, Christchurch 1928. Courtesy of Art History Visual Resources Collection, University of Canterbury.

Image 12: W. B. Armson, Canterbury Public Library, 109 Cambridge Terrace, Christchurch 1875. Courtesy of Department of Art History, University of Canterbury.

Page 219

Image 13: Luck's Building, 751 Colombo Street, c. 1880 (left); Commercial Buildings, 753-759 Colombo Street c.1905 (right), Christchurch. 2007. Courtesy of Robert Cutts, "An Old Building in Colombo St, Christchurch, NZ," https://www.flickr.com/photos/21678559@N06/4279226137, CC BY 2.0

Image 14: George Hart (1879-1961). Miller's Building (later Christchurch City Council Offices), 163 Tuam Street, Christchurch 1938: Courtesy of Art History Visual Resources Collection, University of Canterbury.

Image 15: V Hean (nd). MED (Municipal Electricity Department) Building, 218 Manchester Street, Christchurch (corner Armagh Street), 1937-39. Courtesy of Art History Visual Resources Collection, University of Canterbury.

Image 16: A. W. Fielder (nd). Horse Bazaar (later The Bedford), 141 Lichfield Street, Christchurch, 1903. 2 January 2010. Courtesy of Iain Ferguson, "Formerly the Canterbury Horse Bazaar, now the Bedford," https://www.flickr.com/photos/76728666@N00/4235832823, CC CY-SA 2.0

Image 17: S. & A. Luttrell. Jockey Club, 128 Oxford Terrace, Christchurch, 1910 Courtesy of Art History Visual Resources Collection, University of Canterbury.

Image 18: S. Farr and Thomas Cane (1830-1905), Christchurch Normal School, Montreal Street, Christchurch; left: Cane's additions 1879; far right: Farr's original building, 1873-75. Image date: 20 Feb 2010. Courtesy of Ian Lochhead.

Image 19: B. W. Mountfort. Canterbury Society of Arts Gallery (later Environment Court), 286 Durham Street, Christchurch, 1890. Courtesy of Ian Lochhead.

Image 20: Collins & Harman. Canterbury Society of Arts Gallery additions, 282 Durham Street, Christchurch, 1894. Courtesy of Ian Lochhead.

Page 220

Image 21: A. W. Simpson. A. J. Whites Building, 236 Tuam Street, Christchurch 1978-79. Courtesy of Ian Lochhead.

Image 22: W. B. Armson. NZ Loan and Mercantile Woolstore, 116 Durham Street South, Christchurch, 1881. Courtesy of Art History Visual Resources Collection, University of Canterbury.

Image 23: Location: WB Armson. Anderson's building, Cashel Street, Christchurch 1881 (later Bell's Arcade). Courtesy of Art History Visual Resources Collection, University of Canterbury

Image 24: S. & A. Luttrell. Lyttelton Times (Star) Building, 56 Cathedral Square, Christchurch, 1902-3. Courtesy of Ian Lochhead.

Image 25: S. & A. Luttrell. NZ Express Co Building (later MLC), 158-160 Manchester Street, Christchurch, 1908. September 2010. Courtesy of Ian Lochhead.

Placemaking and post-quake identity – creating a unique Ōtautahi identity (Dr Rebecca Kiddle and Amiria Kiddle)

All figures by Amiria Kiddle except:
3: Adapted from Christchurch City Council Black Maps and Christchurch Central Recovery Plan by CCDU, licensed under CC BY 3.0.

The Commons

Page 228

Image 1: The Commons aerial photo. 2013. Courtesy of Paul Willyams, www.pwillyams.co.nz.

Page 229

Image 2: A gathering at The Commons making use of the earthen pizza oven built by CPIT in 2012. Summer, 2013. Courtesy of Gap Filler.

Image 3: Gap Filler HQ. 2012. Courtesy of Gap Filler.

Image 4: The Arcades Project being used for a market. March 2014. Courtesy of Gap Filler.

Territorial visions in post-quake Aquila: Creating community and identity (Claudia Mattogno)

Tables 1 & 2: Claudia Mattogno, adapted from official data by the Municipality of L'Aquila 2009
Figures 1 & 2: Claudia Mattogno, 2014
Figure 3: Aldo Benedetti, 2009
Figure 4: Claudia Mattogno, 2013
Figure 5: Aldo Benedetti, 2009

Chapter 5: Thinking Big

What should a garden city of the twenty-first century aim to be like?
(Luke Engleback)

All figures by Studio Engleback, sources as noted:
Figure 2: Sourced from: An urban approach to climate change by M. Rohinton Emmanuel
Figure 3: Sourced from: World Wildlife Planet Report 2010
Figure 4: Adapted from: Carley & Christies, 1992
Figure 5: Adapted from: Wohlymeyer's Unconcious Driving Forces of Landscape Perception, 1998; OECD Environmental indicators for agriculture: Methods and results

New motorway

Page 250
Image 1: Map of Christchurch. 2013. Courtesy of NZ Transport Agency.
Images 2-4: Various locations. 2013. Photos by UpHigh Photos, courtesy of NZ Transport Agency.

Next generation infrastructure (Peter Cockrem and Clayton Prest)

Figure: Niko Elsen, 2013

Demolition Waste

Page 257
Image 1: Te Awaparahi Bay. 24 June 2014. Courtesy of Lyttelton Port Company Ltd.
Image 2: Photos looking west from Colombo over bridge. 2 October 2012. Courtesy of Barnaby Bennett.

Page 258
Image 3-5: Burwood Resource Recovery Park. October 2012. Image by Ash Robinson.
Image 6: Burwood Resource Recovery Park. 11 July 2014. Courtesy of Ben Cannon.

Satire

Page 269
Image 1: 2013. Creative Commons Attribution-ShareAlike 3.0 New Zealand License, courtesy of Joe Wylie (www.porcupinefarm.blogspot.co.nz).

Page 279
Image 2: 2013. Creative Commons Attribution-ShareAlike 3.0 New Zealand License, courtesy of Joe Wylie (www.porcupinefarm.blogspot.co.nz).
Image 3: Three Wise Men by Cubey. 2012. Photo courtesy of Barnaby Bennett.
Image 4: Gerry Brownlee as King Henry the VIII. 2011. Courtesy of Lyndon Hood.
Image 5: 2012. Creative Commons Attribution-ShareAlike 3.0 New Zealand License, courtesy of Joe Wylie (www.porcupinefarm.blogspot.co.nz).

Auditor-General's map of earthquake responsibilities

Page 276
Image 1: Image from Chapter 2 of the report Roles, Responsibilities, and Funding of Public Entities after the Canterbury Earthquakes by Lyn Provost, Controller and Auditor General
8 October 2012. Image use: Crown Copyright with permission from the Office of the Auditor General

Inconvenience Store

Page 285
Image 1: Cathedral Junction, Masha's Impossible Products. 4 March 2014. Courtesy of Ryan Reynolds.
Image 2: Cathedral Junction, Masha's Impossible Products. 4 March 2014. Courtesy of Ryan Reynolds.
Image 3: Cathedral Junction, Anita's Fine Fare. 20 March 2014. Courtesy of Ryan Reynolds.

Page 286
Image 4: Cathedral Junction, Rosalee's Contrary Cornucopia. 1 April 2014. Courtesy of Rosalee Jenkin.
Image 5: Cathedral Junction, Rosalee's Contrary Cornucopia. 1 April 2014. Courtesy of Rosalee Jenkin.
Image 6: Cathedral Junction, Anita's Fine Fare. 20 March 2014. Courtesy of Ryan Reynolds.
Image 7: Cathedral Junction, Bridget's Two-Hour Shop. 11 March 2014. Courtesy of Ryan Reynolds.
Image 8: Cathedral Junction, Bridget's Two-Hour Shop. 12 March 2014. Courtesy of Centuri Chan.

Chapter 6: Acting Small

The failure strategy (Marcus Westbury)

All figures reproduced courtesy of Renew Newcastle

Bars and cafes

Page 296
Images 1: Black Betty. 27 March 2014. Courtesy of Marcia Butterfield from Neat Places website.

Page 297
Image 2: Underground. 14 January 2014. Courtesy of Marcia Butterfield from Neat Places website.
Image 3: C4. 8 May 2014. Courtesy of Marcia Butterfield

from Neat Places website.
Image 4: Caffeine Lab. 18 February 2014. Courtesy of Marcia Butterfield from Neat Places website.
Image 5: Dukes of Sandwich. 18 February 2014. Courtesy of Marcia Butterfield from Neat Places website.
Image 6: Pure Café. 2014. Courtesy of Marcia Butterfield from Neat Places website.
Image 7: The Last Word. 18 February 2014. Courtesy of Marcia Butterfield from Neat Places website.

Page 298
Image 8: Tommy Taco. 22 April 2014. Courtesy of Marcia Butterfield from Neat Places website.
Image 9: The Tannery. 16 December 2013. Courtesy of Marcia Butterfield from Neat Places website.
Image 10: Astro Lounge. 19 May 2014. Courtesy of Marcia Butterfield from Neat Places website.
Image 11: Backyard Bar. 19 May 2014. Courtesy of Marcia Butterfield from Neat Places website.
Image 12: Port Hole. 19 May 2014. Courtesy of Marcia Butterfield from Neat Places website.

Page 299
Image 13: Rekindle and Auricle. 16 January 2014. Courtesy of Marcia Butterfield from Neat Places website.
Image 14: Smash Palace. 2012. Courtesy of Irene Boles.
Images 15: Dark Room. Courtesy of Marcia Butterfield from Neat Places website.
Images 16: Pegasus Arms. Courtesy of Marcia Butterfield from Neat Places website.

Simple things that bring joy (Lucy D'Aeth)

Figures 1 & 2: reproduced courtesy of *All Right?* campaign
Figure 3: by Aaron Campbell Photography

Volunteering

Page 312
Image 1: Location: Infogap Project with UTS students. Corner of Peterborough and Colombo Streets. Date: 20th April 2012. Image by Barnaby Bennett.
Image 2: Location: Gap Filler office construction. 20th January 2012. Image by Barnaby Bennett.

Page 313.
Image 3: Team members from the Student Volunteer Army. Feb 2012. Courtesy of Sam Johnson and UC Photography.
Image 4: Courtesy of Addington Action.

Temporary projects, permanent impact (Brie Sherow)

Figure 1: Tania Smith, 2013
Figure 2: Jonny Knopp, Peanut Productions

Supporting startups

Page 321
Image 1: Enterprise Precinct and Innovation Campus. 21st October 2012. Courtesy of Barnaby Bennett.

Page 322
Image 2: Location: Coffee and Jam at EPIC organized by Ministry of Awesome. 21st October 2012. Courtesy of Erica Austin – Peanut Productions.
Image 3: Life in Vacant Spaces office. Labour weekend 2013. Courtesy of Barnaby Bennett.

Co-working spaces

Page 327
Image 1: Location: Kirkwood Pods, University of Canterbury. mid-July 2011. Courtesy of Eric Crampton.
Image 2: Co-working space at McCarthy Design in the NG Building. July 2014. Courtesy of Barnaby Bennett.

Page 328
Image 3: Location: Awesome HQ co-working space. 4th June 2014. Courtesy of Erica Austin – Peanut Productions.
Images 4: Rekindle co-working space. Date: 2013. Courtesy of Liz Phelan

Chapter 7: Meeting in the Middle

A new city through the arts? (George Parker)

Figure by George Parker, Jason Mill and Sam Martin. Reproduced courtesy of Pivnice Architecture.

CCC Transitional City Projects Fund

Page 342
Image 1: Songs for Christchurch Launch, 79 Cashel St. 21st February 2013. Courtesy of Barnaby Bennett.
Images 2: 'Frieeze' by Jeremy Sauzier, artist and shadow catcher. 23 New Regent St.
Date: 2014. Courtesy of Jeremy Sauzier, myshadowcatcher.com
Image 3: 'Giraffing Around' by Tess Sheerin. 8 Liverpool St. 2013. Courtesy of Ross French.
Image 4: 'Alhambra Gardens' by Canterbury Horticultural Society. 2013-14. Courtesy of Tony Kunowski.

Page 343
Image 5: 'Prop Hide (Prop) ' by Mike Hewson. 2014. Courtesy of Mike Hewson.
Image 6: New Zealand Geographic Photographer of the Year 2013 Exhibition. 9 August-8 September 2013. Courtesy of New Zealand Geographic.
Image 7: 'Palimpsest: The Things Which I Have Seen I Now Can See No More' by Kate Belton. 2013-14. Courtesy of Kate Belton.

Page 344
Image 8: The Arcades Project designed by Andrew Just. 2013-14. Courtesy of Ed Lust.
Image 9: Project: 'Picture House' by Tessa Peach and Heather Hayward. Labour weekend 2013. Courtesy of Tessa Peach and Heather Hayward,
Image 10: 'The Orange Tree' by Peter and Joyce Majendie. 2013-14. Courtesy of Joyce Majendie.

Page 345

Image 11: 'The Powerful Event' by Two Productions Ltd at 132 Manchester St. 2013. Courtesy of Two Productions.

Image 12: 'Faux Arcadia' by Michaela Cox. Near St Asaph Street Kitchen. 2013-14. Courtesy of Michaela Cox.

Image 13: Sound installation for Audacious Festival of Sonic Arts by sound artist Adam Willetts. 2014. Courtesy of Paul Willets.

Image 14: Project: 'The Offcut Series 4' Rekindle Inner City Sculptural Installation Project. Work by Kara Burrowes. 2013. Courtesy of Emma Byrne.

Developing the arts ecology of Christchurch
(Melanie Oliver)

Figure 1: Reproduced by courtesy of Melanie Oliver

Figure 2: By Stacey Weaver, 2012

Transitional Cathedral Square

Page 352

Image 1: Three dimensional Image of Transitional Cathedral Square project. April 2013. With Permission from: Christchurch City Council.

Image 2: Hoarding artwork by Chris Heaphy, Cathedral Square. July 2013. With Permission from: Christchurch City Council

Image 3: Visitors experiencing the Transitional Cathedral Square project. Date: July 2013. With Permission from: Christchurch City Council

Image 4: Flag wall by Sarah Hughes, Cathedral Square. July 2014. Courtesy of John Collie and Christchurch City Council.

Image 5: Planted 'green' whare by Chris Heaphy, Cathedral Square. July 2014. Courtesy of John Collie and Christchurch City Council.

Pallet Pavilion

Page 360

Image 1: Pallet Pavilion, former site of the Crown Plaza Hotel. December 2012. Courtesy of Maja Moritz.

Page 361

Image 2: Pallet Pavilion. February 2013. Courtesy of Glen Jansen.

Image 3: Pallet Pavilion. December 2012. Courtesy of Guy Frederick.

Image 4: Wall detail of the Pallet Pavilion. December 2012. Courtesy of Guy Frederick.

Image 5: Pallet Pavilion by night. February 2013. Courtesy of Barnaby Bennett.

Image 6: Pallet Pavilion by night. December 2012. Courtesy of Maja Moritz.

Nature Play Park / Papatakaro Ao Turoa

Page 366

Image 1-3: Nature Play Park / Papatakaro Ao Turoa, corner Hereford and Latimer Square. launched 2013. Courtesy of Greening the Rubble (www.

greeningtherubble.org.nz).

Image 4: Location: Nature Play Park / Papatakaro Ao Turoa, corner Hereford and Latimer Square. Labour weekend during FESTA. Courtesy of Ed Lust.

Studio Christchurch: Meeting of minds
(Camia Young and Uwe Rieger)

Figure 1: Erica Austin, 2013

Figure 2: Mark Gore, 2012

Temple for Christchurch

Page 370

Images 1, 4-6: Location: Temple for Christchurch on the former Convention Centre site on Kilmore St. 2013. Courtesy of Kyle Kastner.

Image 2-3: Temple for Christchurch. 13th September 2013. Courtesy of Barnaby Bennett.

Chapter 8: Building Back Better

Shaping cites, shaping health

All figures by and reproduced courtesy of Skye Duncan, NYC Department of City Planning

Stronger Christchurch Infrastructure Rebuild Team

Page 389

Image 1: Centaurus Road, May 2012. Courtesy of SCIRT and Neil Macbeth.

Image 2: Location: River Road. November 2011. Courtesy of SCIRT and Neil Macbeth.

Image 3: Coppell Place. May 2013. Courtesy of SCIRT and Neil Macbeth.

Image 4: Centaurus Road. October 2013. Courtesy of SCIRT and Nicola Hunt.

Image 5: Netley Place. November 2011. Courtesy of SCIRT and Neil Macbeth.

Page 390

Image 6: Shirley. October 2013. Courtesy of SCIRT and Neil Macbeth.

Image 7: Buckleys Road. November 2012. Courtesy of SCIRT and Neil Macbeth.

Image 8: Aranui. May 2014. Courtesy of SCIRT and Neil Macbeth.

Image 9: Canterbury Street. November 2012. Courtesy of SCIRT and Neil Macbeth.

Page 391

Image 10: North Avon Road. May 2012. Courtesy of SCIRT and Neil Macbeth.

Image 11: Armagh Street Bridge. April 2014. Courtesy of SCIRT and Neil Macbeth.

Image 12: Chester Street West. November 2013. Courtesy of SCIRT and Neil Macbeth.

Image 13: Rangatira Terrace. September 2012. Courtesy of SCIRT and Neil Macbeth.

Transport: Post-quake impacts and new beginnings
(Glen Koorey)

Figure 1: *Connecting New Zealand: A Summary of the Government's Policy Direction for Transport* by Ministry of Transport, September 2011; licensed under CC by 3.0
Figure 2: Proposed Christchurch Passenger Rail Network in *Draft Central city Recovery Plan* by Christchurch City Council, 2011; licenced under CC by 3.0

New cycleways

Page 399
Image 1: Map of proposed cycle lanes. May 2014. With Permission from: Christchurch City Council.

Page 400
Images 2-3: Various photos of bicycle users. April 2013. With Permission from: Christchurch City Council.
Images 4-5: Various proposed cycle lane designs. March 2013. With Permission from: Christchurch City Council.

How Christchurch can build light rail and create the centres it needs in the process (Peter Newman)

Figure by Peter Newman, data sourced from Census New Zealand

Margaret Mahy Family Playground

Page 406
Image 1: Amazing Place Playground Competition Year 6 second place from Mount Somers Springburn School. 2013. Usage: Crown Copyright. Used under Creative Commons Attribution 3.0 New Zealand Licence.
Image 2: Amazing Place Playground Competition Competition workshop. 2013. Crown Copyright. Used under Creative Commons Attribution 3.0 New Zealand Licence.
Image 3: Amazing Place Playground Competition Pricegiving. 2013. Crown Copyright. Used under Creative Commons Attribution 3.0 New Zealand Licence.
Image 4: Amazing Place Playground Competition Year 6 first place Selywin House
2013. Crown Copyright. Used under Creative Commons Attribution 3.0 New Zealand Licence.

Page 407
Image 5: Margaret Mahy Playground concept design. 2014. Crown Copyright. Used under Creative Commons Attribution 3.0 New Zealand Licence.
Image 6: Margaret Mahy Playground concept design. 2014. Crown Copyright. Used under Creative Commons Attribution 3.0 New Zealand Licence.

Breathe: A case study in the difficulties of breaking convention (Jon King)

All figures by and reproduced courtesy of Design King Company.

Te Papa Ōtākaro / Avon River Precinct

Page 417
Image 1: Map of Avon River. 2012. Crown Copyright. Used under Creative Commons Attribution 3.0 New Zealand Licence.

Page 418
Images 2-7: Various renders and photographs of Avon River Precinct. 2012-14. Crown Copyright. Used under Creative Commons Attribution 3.0 New Zealand Licence.

Chapter 9: Reimagining Recovery

FESTA

Page 426
Image 1: 'Intersection Point' by Amiria Kiddle and Helen Trappitt. October 2013 (on-going until the building is demolished). Courtesy of FESTA and Ed Lust.
Image 2: 'Supernova City' led by Byron Kinnaird. October 27th 2013. Courtesy of FESTA and Erica Austin.
Image 3: 'Sound Garden' by Gap Filler. October 26th 2013. Courtesy of FESTA and Erica Austin.
Image 4: 'Nature Play Park' by Department of Conservation and Greening the Rubble.
Date: October 26th 2013. Courtesy of FESTA and Ed Lust.
Image 5: 'Nomadic Sauna' by Fabricio Fernandes. Labour Weekend, 2013. Courtesy of FESTA and Ed Lust

Page 427
Image 6: 'The Knight' and 'The Friar' from *Canterbury Tales* by Free Theatre Christchurch
Date: Labour Weekend, 2013. Courtesy of Bridgit Anderson.
Image 7: 'The Friar' from *Canterbury Tales* by Free Theatre Christchurch. Labour Weekend, 2013. Courtesy of Jonny Knopp.
Image 8: *Canterbury Tales* by Free Theatre Christchurch. Labour Weekend, 2013. Courtesy of Jonny Knopp.
Image 9: 'The Knight' from *Canterbury Tales* by Free Theatre Christchurch. Labour Weekend, 2013. Courtesy of Jonny Knopp.
Image 10: *Canterbury Tales* by Free Theatre Christchurch. Labour Weekend, 2013. Courtesy of Bridgit Anderson

Page 428
Image 11: Halo at 'LUXCITY' by students from Auckland University of Technology. 20 October 2012. Courtesy of FESTA and Mark Gore.
Image 12: Etch-a-sketch at 'LUXCITY' by students from The University of Auckland. 20 October 2012. Courtesy of FESTA and Douglas Horrell.
Image 13: Murmer at 'LUXCITY' by students from The University of Auckland. 20 October 2012. Courtesy of FESTA and Bridgit Anderson.
Images 14-15: In Your Face at 'LUXCITY' by students from The University of Auckland
Date: 20 October 2012. Courtesy of FESTA and Bridgit Anderson.

Valley section: A new instrument for the Garden City
(Chris Moller)

Figure 1: Christchurch Black May 1850 by Edward Jollie, sourced from Wikipedia http://commons.wikimedia.org/wiki/File:Black_Map_Christchurch_1850.jpg
Figures 3 & 4: by and reproduced courtesy of CMA+U Architecture and Urbanism

WikiHouseNZ

Page 436
Image 1-4: Various images of Wikihouse. Courtesy of Space Craft Systems.

Page 437
Image 5: 2014. Courtesy of Erica Austin I Peanut Productions.
Images 6-8: Courtesy of Space Craft Systems.

Does the Blueprint support the creation of a healthy ecological urban environment? (Di Lucas)

All figures by and reproduced courtesy of Di Lucas Associates except as listed below.

Figure 9: Adapted from Earthquake Related Elevation Change (pre September 2010 to post June/December 2011), by EQC, sourced at http://www.canterburymaps.govt.nz/Portal.
Figure 11: Avon River Precinct, Christhchurch Central Development Unit, 2014. Licensed under CC by 3.0
Figure 12: Former coastlines adapted from Brown & Weeber (1992)
Figure 13: Adapted from 1850 Christchurch Black Map by Edward Jollie
Figure 14: Adapted from Greenfield Priority Areas, Land Use Recovery Plan by Christchurch Earthquake Recovery Authority, October 2013, http://www.canterburymaps.govt.nz/Portall.

I Like Your Form

Page 450
Image 1: Lonnie Hutchinson, 'I Like Your Form' for FESTA. July 28, 2014. Courtesy of Jo Mair

Page 451
Images 2-4: Lonnie Hutchinson, 'I Like Your Form' for FESTA. July 28, 2014. Courtesy of Jo Mair

What has Ōtautahi revealed? Māori urban planning in post-quake Christchurch
(Craig Pauling, Shaun Awatere and Shadrach Rolleston)

Figure 1: By S. Rolleston and S. Awatere, sourced from "Ngā Hua Papak inga: Habitation Design Principles,"*MAI Review* 2 (2009): 1-13
Figure 2: By S.Awatere, G. Harmsworth,S.Rolleston,C. Pauling, T.K Morgan, and R. Hoskins, and sourced from *Kaitiakitanga o Ngā Ngahere P hatu: Kaitiakitanga of Urban Settlements* (Report to the Ministry of Science and Innovation, 2011).
Figure 3: Adapted from "Auckland as a unique place-Te Aranga Māori Design Principles" by R. Hoskins, R. & J., Kake Auckland Design Manual, http://aucklanddesignmanual.co.nz, 2014.

Shop Eight Food & Wine

Page 465
Images 1-2: Shop Eight. 30 June 2014. Photo courtesy of Kate McCaskill – Kaleidoscope Photography.

Page 466
Images 3-7: Shop 8 and markets. 2013-2014. Photo courtesy of Liz Phelan.
Image 6: Shop Eight. July 2014. Photo courtesy of Naomi Haussmann – Gone Sailing Photography

Digging where we stand: Visions of urbundance and the role of food production in Christchurch
(Bailey Peryman, Oliver Peryman and Michelle Marquet)

Figure 1: By and reproduced courtesy of Garden City 2.0
Figure 2: Agropolis 2014, Courtesy of Barnaby Bennett

Rekindle

Page 471
Image 1: Emma Byrne, Corner Springfield Rd and Bealey Ave Chch. 20th October 2012. Juliet Arnott.
Image 2: Avonside Drive, Christchurch. 25th August 2012. Courtesy of Juliet Arnott.
Image 3: 210 Avonside Drive, Christchurch. 25th August 2012. Courtesy of Juliet Arnott.
Image 4: 73 Patten Street, Christchurch. 27th March 2013. Courtesy of Juliet Arnott.

Page 472
Image 5: Studio of Jeremy Leeming. 28th May 2013. Courtesy of Laura Forest.
Image 6: Mt Pleasant-Heathcote – Ferrymead Presbyterian Church, Christchurch (now deconsecrated). 12th March 2013. Courtesy of Juliet Arnott.

Page 473
Image 7: Private home. 28th May 2013. Courtesy of Laura Forest.
Image 8: Rekindle Studio, New Regent Street, Christchurch. 28th May 2013. Courtesy of Laura Forest.
Image 9: Rekindle Studio, New Regent Street, Christchurch. 28th May 2013. Courtesy of Laura Forest.

INDEX

transport post-quake, 397
valley section, 429-435

potential for innovation
climate change, 244-49, 251-256
community city, 133, 475
designing with the land, 431, 446
eco-recovery, 449
in the arts, 351
in housing, 196-200, 416
mixed-scale urban design, 435
mixed-use urban design, 434
through the arts, 340-41

precincts
concept, 66-69
critique of, 51, 279, 363-64
in Christchurch, 51
support for, 363
See also anchor projects

priorities
city and housing, 53
competing interests post-quake, 104
health resources, 382

private-public partnerships
EPIC, 363
SCIRT (see separate entry)
Studio Christchurch, 367-69

property development
as process, 168
citizen-led, 167
incentives-based, 71, 289
private (definition), 168
public (definition), 168
small scale, 294

public consultation
legal requirements of, 95
in Avon River Precinct, 96, 419-20

public participation
benefits of, 81, 422, 359
citizen-led initiatives, 87, 323-326
lack of in Christchurch, 66, 180
in London riot clean up, 315
in Louisiana recovery efforts, 357
in urbanism, 133, 329-35
perception of, 115
structures of, 87, 170
See also Share an Idea campaign

public wellbeing
All Right? campaign, 309-11
community empowerment, 232-33, 261, 335
cultural diversity, 221, 452
cultural revitalisation, 346
health 76, 246-47
negative impacts on, 190
public engagement, 94, 97, 262

public space, 230-31, 235, 381-88, 409, 475
social sustainability, 190-198, 475-76

rebuild opportunities
building back better, 54, *see also* chapter 8
collaborative research and design, 367
eco-recovery, 449

recovery obstacles
confusion over stakeholders' roles, 292, 355
lack of expertise, 106, 355
political relationships/competing priorities, 103, 288, 355-56
regulations, 104, 365, 302-306, 320

red zone
in Aquila, 231
residential, 153
city, 150-51, 323

regulations
building code, 60
economic impact of, 279
problems arising from a lack of, 76
See also recovery obstacles.

relationships
citizen networks, 315-16, 323-26
collaboration, 319, 350, 367-69
interface between top-down and bottom-up, 326, *see also* chapter 7
iwi and hapū, 460-61,463-64
leadership post-Katrina, 353, 358-59
local and national government, 182-83
need for clarity in, 292, 301, 306-07
public-private, 363, 365
transitional and government, 320, 350
urban design and public health, 246-47, 381

resilience
environmental considerations, 244
food, 246, 469
health considerations, 311
how to promote, 234
importance of, 190, 239
opportunities to be, 198, 249
ways to achieve, 249, 469-70

Share an Idea campaign
participation, 59, 82
public response to, 94, 131
scope, 19, 47, 469
time frames, 19, 61
transport, 205-06
used in Blueprint, 47, 54-55

Stronger Christchurch Infrastructure Rebuild Team,
389-91
managing transport rebuild, 397-98
private-public partnership, 398

transitional, 371-377
architecture, 368